A Companion to F

First published 2012 by Camden House
Transferred to digital printing 2013
Reprinted in paperback 2015

Camden House is an imprint of Boydell & Brewer Inc.
668 Mt. Hope Avenue, Rochester, NY 14620, USA
www.camden-house.com
and of Boydell & Brewer Limited
PO Box 9, Woodbridge, Suffolk IP12 3DF, UK
www.boydellandbrewer.com

Paperback ISBN-13: 978-1-57113-930-6
Paperback ISBN-10: 1-57113-930-3
Hardcover ISBN-13: 978-1-57113-327-4
Hardcover ISBN-10: 1-57113-327-5

Library of Congress Cataloging-in-Publication Data

A companion to Friedrich Nietzsche : life and works / edited by Paul Bishop.
    p. cm. — (Studies in German literature, linguistics, and culture)
Includes bibliographical references and index.
ISBN 978-1-57113-327-4 (hardcover : alk. paper) —
ISBN 1-57113-327-5 (hardcover : alk. paper)
    1. Nietzsche, Friedrich Wilhelm, 1844–1900. 2. Philosophers—
Germany—Biography.   I. Bishop, Paul, 1967– II. Title.

B3316.C645 2012
193—dc23
[B]   2012001488

This publication is printed on acid-free paper.
Printed in the United States of America.

Ein neues Mittelalter nun grade befürchte ich nicht [. . .] aber eine immer ödere, immer frechere "Jetztzeit" [. . .] in entsetzlichster Steigerung: Zweckmäßigkeit überall und ein völliges Abdorren aller tiefsten Kräfte, aller künstlerischen, schaffenden Fähigkeit.

[I do not fear a new Middle Ages, but an ever drearier, ever more impertinent "Today," forever surpassing itself in awfulness: rank utilitarianism everywhere, and a complete withering away of all the most profound powers, of every artistic, creative capacity.]

— Erwin Rohde to Nietzsche,
11 December 1870; KGB II.2, 280

Es ist ein ganz radikales Wahrheitswesen hier [auf der Universität] nicht möglich. Insbesondre wird etwas wahrhaft Umwälzendes von hier auch nicht seinen Ausgang nehmen können.

[To lead a life dedicated radically to truth is here [at the university] simply not possible. In particular, nothing truly revolutionary will be able to find a starting-point here.]

— Nietzsche to Rohde,
15 December 1870; KSB 3, 165

Jetzt, wo ich [dies kleine Buch] kennen lerne — denn bei seiner Entstehung fehlt mir dazu die Zeit, und inzwischen war ich krank — erschüttert es mich durch und durch und ich bin nach jeder Seite in Thränen.

[Now that I am getting to know this small book — while it was being written I didn't have the time, and then I was ill — I am completely shaken by it, and after every page I am in tears.]

— Nietzsche to Karl Hillebrand on *Ecce Homo*,
24 May 1883; KSB 6, 380

Contents

Acknowledgments

M Y CHIEF DEBT IS TO THE CONTRIBUTORS TO THIS VOLUME, with whom it has been a pleasure to work. Some of them I knew before this project began, others I have only learnt to know through correspondence with them, and I am very grateful to them all. In particular, I am especially indebted to Keith Ansell-Pearson and Daniel Conway for supporting and joining this project at a critical juncture.

I also owe an immense debt of thanks to Jim Walker of Camden House for his enthusiasm and encouragement from the initial proposal stage through to completion.

Following longstanding complaints to his family and friends about the cold, at the instigation of his mother (*KGB* III.6, 10–11), albeit after initial reluctance (*KSB* 8, 10), but following positive experiences in Nice (*KSB* 8, 201–2 and 216–17) and negotiations about costs with the manufacturer (*KSB* 8, 455 and 459–60), in the winter of 1888 Nietzsche ordered a small, portable, domestic stove from a company in Dresden called Nieske. The stove burned special logs, made of carbon-nitron, which ensured a smokeless source of heat (*KSB* 8, 461 and 469). Nietzsche was concerned with safety issues (*KSB* 8, 489) but set a good deal of store by the stove's reputation (*KSB* 8, 523); in the end, however, its arrival coincided with the run-up to his mental collapse. Did Nietzsche ever get to use his stove? According to various sources, he gave it to the Finos, his landlord and landlady in Turin; and thereafter, in the psychiatric clinics in Basel and Jena, and then under the care of his mother, then his sister, in Naumburg, then Weimar, Nietzsche had other problems — or none at all. Thanks to my work on installing a stove as part of renovations on our home during work on this Companion, I first noticed this motif in Nietzsche's correspondence, and it prompts me to dedicate this volume to my partner, Helen — a true source of warmth in this (sometimes, cold) world.

A Note on Editions and Abbreviations

Editions

FOR CONVENIENCE'S SAKE, the following editions of Nietzsche's works and letters have been used:

KSA   Friedrich Nietzsche, *Sämtliche Werke: Kritische Studienausgabe*, ed. Giorgio Colli and Mazzino Montinari, 15 vols. Berlin and New York/Munich: Walter de Gruyter/Deutscher Taschenbuch Verlag, 1967–1977 and 1988.

KSB   Friedrich Nietzsche, *Sämtliche Briefe: Kritische Studienausgabe*, ed. Giorgio Colli and Mazzino Montinari, 8 vols. Berlin and New York/Munich: Walter de Gruyter/Deutscher Taschenbuch Verlag, 1975–1984.

Wherever texts are not available in these editions, however, the following are also used:

BAW   Friedrich Nietzsche, *Frühe Schriften, 1854–1869*, ed. Hans Joachim Mette, Karl Schlechta, and Carl Koch, 5 vols. [1933–1940]. Munich: Beck, 1994.

KGB   Friedrich Nietzsche, *Briefwechsel: Kritische Gesamtausgabe*, ed. Giorgio Colli and Mazzino Montinari. Berlin and New York: Walter de Gruyter, 1975–.

KGW   Friedrich Nietzsche, *Werke: Kritische Gesamtausgabe*, ed. Giorgio Colli and Mazzino Montinari, then Volker Gerhardt, Norbert Miller, Wolfgang Müller-Lauter, Karl Pestalozzi, and the Berlin-Brandenburgische Akademie der Wissenschaften, 40 vols. in 9 sections. Berlin and New York: Walter de Gruyter, 1967–.

W   Friedrich Nietzsche, *Werke in drei Bänden*, ed. Karl Schlechta, 3 vols. plus bibliography. Munich: Hanser, 1966.

Individual Works

To refer to individual works by Nietzsche, the following abbreviations are used:

AC   *The Anti-Christ* (*Der Anti-Christ*)

BGE   *Beyond Good and Evil* (*Jenseits von Gut und Böse*)

BT   *The Birth of Tragedy* (*Die Geburt der Tragödie*)

CW   *The Case of Wagner* (*Der Fall Wagner*)

D   *Daybreak* (*Morgenröthe*)

EH   *Ecce Homo* (*Ecce Homo*)

GM   *On the Genealogy of Morals* (*Zur Genealogie der Moral*)

GS   *The Gay Science* (*Die fröhliche Wissenschaft*)

HA   *Human, All Too Human* (*Menschliches, Allzumenschliches*)

NCW   *Nietzsche contra Wagner*

TI   *Twilight of the Idols* (*Götzen-Dämmerung*)

UM   *Untimely Meditations* (*Unzeitgemässe Betrachtungen*)

UW   *Die Unschuld des Werdens* [extracts from *Nachlass*, untranslated]

WP   *The Will to Power* (*Der Wille zur Macht*)

Z   *Thus Spoke Zarathustra* (*Also sprach Zarathustra*)

Nietzsche is cited according to works and sections, using the abbreviations above, followed by a reference to the *KSA* or *Sämtliche Werke: Kritische Studienausgabe*, consisting of volume number and page reference (or, in the case of material from the *Nachlass*, volume number, section reference, and page reference). In the case of *Zarathustra* and *Ecce Homo*, subchapter references and chapters using titles as chapter headings are also included.

So a quotation from section 276 of *The Gay Science* is cited thus: (*GS* §276; *KSA* 3, 521); a passage from section 7 of the chapter entitled "Of Old and New Law-Tables" in Part Three of *Zarathustra* is cited thus: (*Z* III 12 §7; *KSA* 4, 251); and a text, such as the following — "One must feel about the 'cross' as Goethe did" ("Man muß das 'Kreuz' empfinden wie Goethe") — is cited thus: (*KSA* 12, 10[181], 565). Where a text is not available in the *KSA*, it is cited from the *Werke: Kritische Gesamtausgabe* (*KGW*), using the following reference style: "My philosophy, inverted Platonism —: the further away from what truly is, the purer, the more beautiful, the better it is. Life in semblance is the goal" ("Meine Philosophie umgedrehter Platonismus —: je weiter ab vom wahrhaft Seienden, um so reiner schöner besser ist es. Das Leben im Scheine ist das Ziel"; *KGW* III.5/1, 120). Finally, letters by Nietzsche are referred to by name of correspondent and date, for instance: Nietzsche's letter to Erwin Rohde of 25 October 1872, but a reference to the *Sämtliche Briefe: Kritische Studienausgabe* is also included, thus: (*KSB* 4, 70–71).

Introduction

Paul Bishop

FRIEDRICH NIETZSCHE (1844–1900) IS A FIGURE from the mid-nine-teenth century whose influence reached well into the twentieth century and extends beyond, into our own time. Both his professional (and professorial) beginnings and his tragic personal end condition our perception of his philosophical achievement: his appointment, at the extremely young age of twenty-four, to a chair of classical philology, and his final decade of insanity, following his mental collapse in 1889. From a body of writings that went virtually unnoticed when they were first published has arisen a tradition of commentary and analysis that sometimes threatens almost to obscure Nietzsche's philosophical achievement, so extensive has the secondary literature become.

Indeed, Nietzsche has in some ways become so much part of our mental furniture that it would be easy to underestimate the impact of his thought. But according to the German Modernist poet Gottfried Benn (1886–1956), everything that his generation "had discussed, had thought out inside itself, one might say: suffered, one might also say: done to death — all that had already been expressed and exhausted in Nietzsche, had found definitive formulation; all the rest was mere exegesis" (Eigentlich hat alles, was meine Generation diskutierte, innerlich sich auseinanderdachte, man kann sagen: erlitt, man kann auch sagen: breittrat — alles das hatte sich bereits bei Nietzsche ausgesprochen und erschöpft, definitive Formulierung gefunden).[1] To the members of Benn's Nietzsche-influenced generation one might reckon many figures. In the field of music, one thinks of Gustav Mahler (1860–1911), whose Third Symphony (1893–96) includes as its fourth movement a setting of the "Midnight Song" ("Mitternachtslied") from *Zarathustra*; of Richard Strauss (1864–1949), whose tone-poem *Also sprach Zarathustra* (1896) offers a musical synthesis of Nietzsche's central work; or of Frederick Delius (1862–1934), whose *A Mass of Life* (1904–5) is based on a sequence of passages from *Zarathustra*.[2] One thinks of such *Jugendstil* artists as Max Klinger (1857–1920) or Henry van de Velde (1863–1957), or of such Expressionist artists as Max Beckmann (1884–1950), Franz Marc (1880–1916), or Otto Dix (1891–1969), in whose works Nietzschean themes, both implicit and explicit, can be found.[3] One thinks of the vast philosophical reception of Nietzsche, beginning with Wilhelm Dilthey (1833–1911), for whom Nietzsche's apparent lack of systematicity placed him in the tradition of such thinkers as Marcus Aurelius, Montaigne, Carlyle, Emerson, Ruskin, Tolstoy, and Maeterlinck,[4] or Georg Simmel (1858–1918), for whom Nietzsche's thought offered nothing less than a new vision of life itself:

> Nietzsche's attempt is to remove the meaning-giving goal of life from its illusory position outside of life and to put that goal back into life itself. There is no more radical way to do this than through a vision of life in which self-directed augmentation is but the realization of what life provides as potential, including means and values. Every stage of human existence now finds its meaning not in something absolute and definite, but in something higher that succeeds it in which everything antecedent, having been only potential and germinal, wakes up to greater efficiency and expansion. Life as such has become fuller and richer: there is an increase in life.

> [Es handelt sich für Nietzsche darum, den sinngebenden Zweck des Lebens, der an seinem Ort außerhalb des Lebens illusionär geworden war, wie durch eine Rückwärtsdrehung in das Leben selbst zu verlegen. Dies konnte nicht radikaler geschehen, als durch ein Bild des Lebens, in dem seine in ihm selbst indizierte Erhöhung, die bloße Verwirklichung dessen, was das Leben rein als solches an Steigerungsmöglichkeiten enthält, alle Zwecke und Werte des Lebens in sich schließt. Jedes Stadium des menschheitlichen Daseins findet jetzt seinen Zweck nicht in einem Absoluten und Definitiven, sondern in dem nächsthöheren, in dem alles in dem früher nur Angelegte zu größerer Weite und Wirkung erwacht ist, in dem also das Leben voller und reicher geworden ist, in dem mehr Leben ist.][5]

Later, his philosophical reception included the large monograph by Karl Jaspers (1883–1969),[6] and the seminars given by Martin Heidegger (1889–1976) between 1936 and 1946.[7] One should also note Nietzsche's remarkable importance, both acknowledged and unacknowledged, for psychoanalysis: disavowed in suspiciously explicit terms by Sigmund Freud (1856–1939),[8] but significant as a source for the analysis of the inferiority complex proposed by Alfred Adler (1870–1937),[9] and as a major starting point for the analytical psychology developed by Carl Gustav Jung (1875–1961).[10] At the same time, Nietzsche was an important figure for Rudolf Steiner (1861–1925), the founder of anthroposophy, who for a short time was part of the editorial team chosen by Elisabeth Förster-Nietzsche to work on her brother's *Nachlass*.[11]

The role played by Nietzsche in the intellectual life of the highly influential circle around Stefan George (1868–1933) was no less immense,[12] one fruit of which was the major study by Ernst Bertram (1884–1957) published in 1918.[13] In a lecture given to the PEN Club in Stockholm in 1947, Thomas Mann (1875–1955) drew attention to the continuity between, on the one hand, Schiller's *On Naïve and Sentimental Poetry* (*Über naive und sentimentalische Dichtung*, 1795) and the fragments of Novalis, and, on the other, *The Birth of Tragedy* (*Die Geburt der Tragödie*, 1872) and Nietzsche's critique of morality.[14] Mann proclaimed his admiration for Nietzsche as a writer and thinker — as "an experience of immense fullness and complexity encompassing the whole of European culture, which absorbed much of the past and recalled or repeated it with greater or less conscious imitation and emulation, making it actual again in a mythic way" (eine Erscheinung von ungeheuerer, das Europäische resumierender, kultureller Fülle und Komplexität, welche vieles Vergangene in sich aufgenommen hatte, das sie in mehr oder weniger bewußter Nachahmung und Nachfolge erinnerte, wiederholte, auf mythische Art wieder gegenwärtig machte).[15]

And this was just Nietzsche's reception in the German-speaking world.[16] As well as his influence on the literature and culture of America,[17] Russia,[18] and Spain,[19] there was — and is — a huge amount of work undertaken on Nietzsche in France.[20] His reception there began with the six-volume biography, *Nietzsche, sa vie et sa pensée* (1920–31), by Charles Andler (1866–1933),[21] and Nietzsche proved to be a fascinating figure to Paul Valéry (1871–1945),[22] Albert Camus (1913–60), who refers extensively to Nietzsche in his *Carnets*,[23] and Jean-Paul Sartre (1905–80), who sketched plans for (but never completed) a novel about Nietzsche and the Wagners at Tribschen.[24] This reception continued with exponents of a style of Nietzsche interpretation dubbed "French" or "New Nietzsche,"[25] notably Michel Foucault (1926–84) and Jacques Derrida (1930–2004),[26] as well as Georges Bataille (1897–1962),[27] Maurice Blanchot (1907–2003),[28] Jean Baudrillard (1929–2007),[29] Eric Blondel (b. 1942),[30] Jean Granier (b. 1933),[31] Sarah Kofman (1934–94),[32] Pierre Klossowski (1905–2001),[33] and Gilles Deleuze (1925–95).[34] In fact, the extent of Nietzsche's reception in France has been so large that a series of French thinkers chose to demarcate themselves by describing themselves as being — unlike, it is implied, their philosophical compatriots — *not* Nietzscheans.[35] This has not precluded one of their number, Luc Ferry, subsequently releasing a CD of lectures on Nietzsche,[36] joining other recordings of discussions of Nietzsche by, for example, Philippe Sollers,[37] while the entire series of lectures given by Michel Onfray at the Université populaire in Caen in 2008–9 was broadcast in the summer of 2009 on France Culture.[38]

At the same time, in addition to this philosophical reception *sur le continent*, there is a substantial body of commentary on Nietzsche's thought by American philosophers and commentators, who work to varying degrees in the analytical and continental traditions, including Alexander

Nehemas, Maudemarie Clark, Richard Schacht, and Brian Leiter.[39] Given the extent of Nietzsche's reach, it will, I hope, not seem too parochial or particularist to mention his influence in Scotland. In his *Diaries of a Dying Man* (published posthumously in 1954), the Scottish poet William Soutar (1898–1943) recorded his own attachment to Nietzsche:

> Nietzsche is one of the very few philosophers who remain poets in the midst of their philosophising; perhaps he is the only one. His words are often as near to actual living as it is possible for words to be — they are very nearly made flesh. Often, when reading Nietzsche, one feels as if one were on a high hill in a bright windy day; we are always aware of action, space and an atmosphere which is best rendered by the word "caller." We may call Nietzsche's philosophy pantomimic — every word is bold gesture, a moment in a noble dance.[40]

Behind Soutar's comments lies an unexpectedly intense reception of Nietzsche north of Hadrian's Wall. In Glasgow, Alexander Tille (1866–1912), a lecturer in the Department of German at the university, developed an interest in Nietzsche from a Social Darwinist perspective, reflected in his *Von Darwin bis Nietzsche* (1895).[41] He made the first translation into English of *Zarathustra*, which in 1896 was included in the *Collected Works* of Nietzsche he edited.[42] On the other side of Scotland, as it happens, another translation of *Zarathustra* was prepared by Thomas Common, who lived in Costorphine (near and now part of Edinburgh), and this version was included in *The Works of Friedrich Nietzsche* (1909–13), edited by Oscar Levy.[43] And another Scotsman, John Davidson (1857–1909), born in East Renfrewshire, and active as a journalist in London, helped popularize Nietzsche, publishing an article based on a discussion of Nietzsche by the Polish-born critic Téodor de Wyzewa (1863–1917)[44] in *The Speaker* (28 November 1891) and the *Glasgow Herald* (18 March 1893).[45] Together with Anthony Ludovici (1882–1971), the author of a series of studies on Nietzsche,[46] Levy and Tille helped situate Nietzsche politically on the Right in the eyes of the Anglo-American public, and this explains why Bertrand Russell, writing in 1946, brings the chapter on Nietzsche in *A History of Western Philosophy* to a close with the acerbic remark: "Nietzsche despises universal love: I feel it the motive power to all I desire as regards the world. His followers may have had their innings, but we may hope that it is coming rapidly to an end."[47] Already in 1942, however, a more differentiated approach had been taken by Frederick Copleston, SJ (1907–94),[48] followed in 1948 by G. Wilson Knight (1897–1985),[49] before the "revolution" of Walter Kaufmann's *Nietzsche: Philosopher, Psychologist, Antichrist* in 1950.[50] Nevertheless, commentators appear to remain divided on whether we should assign Nietzsche to the right,[51] or to the left,[52] wing of the political spectrum. It has even been suggested that Nietzsche is an essentially right-wing thinker who succeeded in infiltrating the left.[53]

* * * * *

This volume offers itself as a companion to the life and works of Friedrich Nietzsche, taking as its starting point a principle adopted by Nietzsche and enunciated in his letter of 16 September 1882 to Lou von Salomé (1861–1937) — herself one of Nietzsche's earliest, and most gifted, commentators:[54]

> Your idea of reducing philosophical systems to the personal deeds of their originators is truly an idea from a "kindred mind": I myself in Basel related the history of ancient philosophy in *this* way and I used to like to tell my audience: "This system is refuted and dead — but the *person* behind it is irrefutable, the person always remains immortal" — for instance, Plato.

> [Ihr Gedanke einer Reduktion der philosophischen Systeme auf Personal-Acten ihrer Urheber ist recht ein Gedanke aus dem "Geschwistergehirn": ich selber habe in Basel in *diesem* Sinne Geschichte der alten Philosophie erzählt und sagte gern meinen Zuhörern: "dies System ist widerlegt und todt — aber die *Person* dahinter ist unwiderlegbar, die Person ist gar nicht todt zu machen" — zum Beispiel Plato. (*KSB* 6, 259)]

But it was not only in front of his former pupils of classical philology in Basel, nor only in correspondence and conversation with Lou von Salomé, but throughout his own writings and indeed to the whole of philosophy — this was how far Nietzsche sought to extend this principle, as he suggested in *Beyond Good and Evil* (*Jenseits von Gut und Böse*, 1886):

> Gradually I have understood what every great philosophy until now has been: namely, the personal confession of its originator, and a kind of involuntary and unnoticed memoir; equally, that the moral (and immoral) intentions in every philosophy constitute the real germ-seed from which the entire plant has sprung.

> [Allmählich hat sich mir herausgestellt, was jede grosse Philosophie bisher war: nämlich das Selbstbekenntnis ihres Urhebers und eine Art ungewollter und unvermerkter mémoires: insgleichen, dass die moralischen (oder unmoralischen) Absichten in jeder Philosophie den eigentlichen Lebenskeim ausmachen, aus dem jedesmal die ganze Pflanze gewachsen ist. (*BGE* §6; *KSA* 5, 19–20)]

And as his 1887 preface to *The Gay Science* (*Die fröhliche Wissenschaft*, 1882) makes clear, this "germ-seed" of every philosophy is essentially physiological: "Often enough I have asked myself whether, on the whole, philosophy up until now has been nothing more than an interpretation of the body and a *misunderstanding of the body*" (Oft genug habe ich mich gefragt, ob nicht, im Grossen gerechnet, Philosophie bisher überhaupt nur eine Auslegung des Leibes und ein *Missverständniss des Leibes* gewesen ist; *GS* preface §2; *KSA* 3, 348).

In this sense, then, philosophy becomes something personal for Nietzsche: not simply in the sense that, as Fichte suggested, "the kind of philosophy one chooses thus depends [. . .] upon the kind of person one is. For a philosophical system is not a lifeless household item one can put aside or pick up as one wishes; instead, it is animated by the very soul of the person who adopts it" (Was für eine Philosophie man wähle, hänge [. . .] davon ab, was man für ein Mensch ist: denn ein philosophisches System ist nicht ein toter Hausrat, den man ablegen oder annehmen könnte, wie es uns beliebte, sondern es ist beseelt durch die Seele des Menschen, der es hat).[55] Rather, also in the sense that, as Nietzsche put it, "one has, assuming that one is a person, necessarily the philosophy of one's own person" (man hat nämlich, vorausgesetzt, dass man eine Person ist, nothwendig auch die Philosophie seiner Person; *GS* preface §2; *KSA* 3, 347). We find this idea expressed in a more psycho-biological, more vitalist way in Nietzsche's letter to Lou von Salomé of 24 November 1882: "Spirit? What does spirit matter to me! What does knowledge matter to me! I value nothing other than *drives*" (Geist? Was ist mir Geist! Was ist mir Erkenntniß! Ich schätze nichts als *Antriebe*; *KSB* 6, 282). In other words, knowledge itself is subordinated to the goal of life, and for this reason Nietzsche is acknowledged as one of the foremost exponents of *Lebensphilosophie*, or vitalism.[56]

In recognition of Nietzsche's fundamental conviction about the reciprocity of biography and creativity, this Companion was conceived as a guide to the life *and* works of Nietzsche. Accordingly, each contributor was invited to submit a chapter on an individual work (or, in the case of the extensive *Nachlass* material, a collection of texts), focusing on the biographical background to the composition of the text(s), the relationship between preceding works and the text(s) in question, a discussion of the chief intellectual innovations (in relation to Nietzsche's thought and in relation to philosophy in general) and stylistic features of the text(s), and the relation between the text(s) and Nietzsche's next work. Short biographical summaries link these chapters, with a view to highlighting the personal circumstances in which Nietzsche's texts were written, thus relating the stages of Nietzsche's thought to the stages of his life as well.

This Companion is addressed to the usual dual readership of such Camden House volumes, namely, to those approaching Nietzsche for the first time, as well as to his more seasoned readers: it seeks to offer something to beginners and connoisseurs alike. But it also seeks a dual audience in another respect, being written for Germanists and non-Germanists alike (especially philosophers, historians of ideas, scholars of comparative literature, etc.). For this reason quotations are given in English, *then* in the original German, with the aim of encouraging those who read Nietzsche in translation to consider reading him in the original. Above all, it is addressed to those who would like to find (in the words that Nietzsche used to describe his final, and never-completed, project) "a book for thinking, nothing more" (ein Buch zum Denken, nichts weiter) that will accompany them on their journey to become "those for whom thinking is a pleasure, nothing more . . ." (Denen, welchen Denken *Vergnügen* macht, nichts weiter . . .; *KSA* 12, 9[188], 450).

Notes

[1] Gottfried Benn, "Nietzsche — nach fünfzig Jahren" (1950), in *Gesammelte Werke*, ed. Dieter Wellershoff (Wiesbaden: Limes, 1968), 4:1046–57; here: 1046.

[2] Perhaps significantly, these composers focused on Nietzsche's literary, rather than musical, output for their inspiration; for reasons of space, Nietzsche's compositions are not considered in this volume, but the existence of his musical output should nevertheless be signaled. Several recordings of his compositions exist, including the following: *Friedrich Nietzsche — Piano Music*, featuring John Bell Young with Constance Keene, Newport Classic Premier, NPD 85513, 1992; *Lieder — Piano Works — Melodrama*, featuring Dietrich Fischer-Dieskau (baritone), Aribert Reimann (piano), and Elmar Budde (piano), Philips 426 863-2, 1995 (two disks of digital recordings with the celebrated interpreter of German *Lieder*); *The Music of / La Musique de Friedrich Nietzsche*, featuring Valerie Kinslow (soprano), Erik Oland (baritone), The Orpheus Singers, Sven Meier (violin), Lauretta Altman (piano), and Wolfgang Bottenberg (piano), ATMA Classique, ACD 2 2148/49, 1998 (two disks produced as an interdisciplinary project at Concordia University, Montreal, Canada); and *"Ohne Heimat": Lieder und Texte des jungen Nietzsche*, featuring Tjark Baumann (tenor), Holger Kuhmann (piano and organ), and Mathis Schrader (voice), HörZeichen 37-1, 2006.

[3] See Ivo Frenzel, "Prophet, Pioneer, Seducer: Friedrich Nietzsche's Influence on Art, Literature and Philosophy in Germany," in *German Art in the 20th Century: Painting and Sculpture 1905–1985*, ed. Christos M. Joachimides, Norman Rosenthal, and Wieland Schmied (London and Munich: Royal Academy of Arts; Prestel-Verlag, 1985), 75–81. For further expression, see *Zur Wirkung Nietzsches: Der deutsche Expressionismus*, ed. Hans Ester and Meindert Evers (Würzburg: Königshausen & Neumann, 2001).

[4] Wilhelm Dilthey, *Das Wesen der Philosophie* (1907), ed. Manfred Riedel (Stuttgart: Reclam, 1984), trans. Stephen A. and William T. Emery as *The Essence of Philosophy* (Chapel Hill, NC: U of North Carolina P, 1954), 31 and 72.

[5] Georg Simmel, *Schopenhauer und Nietzsche: Ein Vortragszyklus* (Leipzig: Duncker & Humblot, 1907), 6; trans. Helmut Loiskandl, Deena Weinstein, and

Michael Weinstein as *Schopenhauer and Nietzsche* (Urbana and Chicago: U of Illinois P, 1991), 6–7.

[6] Karl Jaspers, *Nietzsche: Einführung in das Verständnis seines Philosophierens* (Berlin and Leipzig: Walter de Gruyter, 1936); in English as *Nietzsche: An Introduction to the Understanding of His Philosophical Activity*, trans. Charles F. Wallraff and Frederick J. Schmitz (Tucson: U of Arizona P, 1965).

[7] Martin Heidegger, *Nietzsche*, 2 vols. (Pfullingen: Neske, 1961); Martin Heidegger, *Nietzsche*, ed. David Farrell Krell, trans. David Farrell Krell et al., 4 vols. (San Francisco: Harper and Row, 1979–87). For further discussion, see Louis P. Blond, *Heidegger and Nietzsche: Overcoming Metaphysics* (London and New York: Continuum, 2010).

[8] For further discussion, see Paul-Lauren Assoun, *Freud et Nietzsche* (Paris: PUF, 1980), trans. Richard L. Collier Jr. as *Freud and Nietzsche* (London: Athlone P, 2000); Ronald Lehrer, *Nietzsche's Presence in Freud's Life and Thought: On the Origins of a Psychology of Dynamic Unconscious Mental Functioning* (Albany, NY: SUNY P, 1995); Michel Henry, *Généalogie de la psychanalyse: Le commencement perdu* (Paris: PUF, 1985), trans. Douglas Brick as *The Genealogy of Psychoanalysis*, trans. Douglas Brick (Stanford: Stanford UP, 1993); Reinhard Gasser, *Nietzsche und Freud* (Berlin and New York: Walter de Gruyter, 1997); and É. Vartzbed, *La troisième oreille: Essai sur un précurseur de Freud* (Paris: Éditions L'Harmattan, 2003).

[9] Alfred Adler, *Über den nervösen Charakter* (1912) (Frankfurt: Fischer, 1972).

[10] See C. G. Jung, Nietzsche's *"Zarathustra": Notes of the Seminars given in 1934–1939*, ed. James L. Jarrett, 2 vols. (Princeton: Princeton UP, 1988); for further discussion, see Paul Bishop, *The Dionysian Self: C. G. Jung's Reception of Friedrich Nietzsche* (Berlin and New York: Walter de Gruyter, 1995); Gerhard Schmitt, *Zyklus und Kompensation: Zur Denkfigur bei Nietzsche und Jung* (Frankfurt am Main, Berlin, Bern: Lang, 1998); Patricia Dixon, *Nietzsche and Jung: Sailing a Deeper Night* (New York: Peter Lang, 1999); and Lucy Huskinson, *Nietzsche and Jung: The Whole Self in the Union of Opposites* (Hove and New York: Brunner-Routledge, 2004); as well as a series of articles by Martin Liebscher, including "Jungs Abkehr von Freud im Lichte seiner Nietzsche-Rezeption," in *Zeitenwende — Wertewende: Internationaler Kongreß der Nietzsche-Gesellschaft zum 100. Todestag Friedrich Nietzsches vom 24.–27. August 2000 in Naumburg*, ed. Renate Reschke (Berlin: Akademie-Verlag, 2001), 255–60; "'Wotan' und 'Puer Aeternus': Die zeithistorische Verstrickung von C. G. Jungs Zarathustrainterpretation," *Nietzsche-Studien: Internationales Jahrbuch für die Nietzsche-Forschung* 30 (2001): 329–50; "Zarathustra — Der Archetypus des 'Alten Weisen,'" *Nietzscheforschung* 9 (2002): 233–45; "Die unheimliche Ähnlichkeit: Nietzsches Hermeneutik der Macht und analytische Interpretation bei Carl Gustav Jung," in *Ecce Opus: Nietzsche-Revisionen im 20. Jahrhundert*, ed. Rüdiger Görner and Duncan Large (Göttingen: Vandenhoeck & Ruprecht, 2003), 37–50; and "C. G. Jung — Die gedanklichen Werkzeuge des Unbewussten," in *Macht und Dynamik des Unbewussten: Auseinandersetzungen in Philosophie, Medizin und Psychanalyse*, ed. Michael B. Buchholz and Günter Gödde (Gießen: Psychosozial Verlag, 2005), 383–96.

[11] See Rudolf Steiner, *Friedrich Nietzsche: Ein Kämpfer gegen seine Zeit* (Dornach: Rudolf Steiner Verlag, 1983); trans. Margaret Ingram deRis as *Friedrich Nietzsche: Fighter for Freedom*, 2nd ed. (Blauvelt, NY: Spiritual Science Library, 1985).

[12] See Heinz Raschel, *Das Nietzsche-Bild im George-Kreis: Ein Beitrag zur Geschichte der deutschen Mythologeme* (Berlin and New York: Walter de Gruyter, 1984).

[13] Ernst Bertram, *Nietzsche: Versuch einer Mythologie* (Bonn: Bouvier, 1918; 10th ed., 1989); *Nietzsche: Attempt at a Mythology*, trans. Robert E. Norton (Urbana and Chicago: U of Illinois P, 2009).

[14] Thomas Mann, "Nietzsche's Philosophie in Lichte unserer Erfahrung," in *Gesammelte Werke in dreizehn Bänden* (Frankfurt am Main: Fischer, 1974), 9:675–712. On Novalis, see 13:693 and 700; cf. Novalis, *Schriften*, 6 vols. in 9 (Stuttgart: Kohlhammer, 1960–), 2:556 and 576. For further discussion, see Paul Bishop, "The Intellectual World of Thomas Mann," in *The Cambridge Companion to Thomas Mann*, ed. Ritchie Robertson (Cambridge: Cambridge UP, 2002), 22–42.

[15] Mann, *Werke*, 13:675.

[16] See Steven E. Aschheim, *The Nietzsche Legacy in Germany 1890–1990* (Berkeley: U of California P, 1994).

[17] See Manfred Pütz, ed., *Nietzsche in American Literature and Thought* (Columbia, SC: Camden House, 1995).

[18] See Bernice Glatzer Rosenthal, ed., *Nietzsche in Russia* (Princeton, NJ: Princeton UP, 1986).

[19] Paul Ilie, "Nietzsche in Spain: 1890–1910," *Publications of the Modern Language Association* 79/1 (March 1964): 80–96.

[20] For a discussion of early French Nietzsche reception, see Christopher E. Forth, *Zarathustra in Paris: The Nietzsche Vogue in France 1891–1918* (Dekalb, IL: Northern Illinois UP, 2001).

[21] Charles Andler, *Nietzsche, sa vie et sa pensée* (Paris: Bossard, 1920–31), consisting of vol. 1, *Les précurseurs de Nietzsche* (1920); vol. 2, *Le jeunesse de Nietzsche jusqu'à la rupture avec Bayreuth* (1921); vol. 3, *Le pessimisme esthétique de Nietzsche, sa philosophie à l'époque wagnérienne* (1921); vol. 4, *La maturité de Nietzsche jusqu'à sa mort* (1928); vol. 5, *Nietzsche et le transformisme intellectualiste* (1922); vol. 6, *La dernière philosophie de Nietzsche* (1931).

[22] See Valéry's "Lettres et Notes sur Nietzsche," in *Valéry, pour quoi? Précédé de Paul Valéry, Lettres et Notes sur Nietzsche* (Paris: Les Impressions Nouvelles, 1987), 7–52.

[23] See the various references to Nietzsche in Camus's *Carnets*, 1935–48, in Albert Camus, *Œuvres complètes*, 4 vols. (Paris: Gallimard, 2006–8), 2:793–1125. For further discussion, see F. C. St Aubyn, "A Note on Nietzsche and Camus," *Comparative Literature* 20/2 (Spring 1968): 110–15; and George F. Sefler, "The Existential vs. the Absurd: The Aesthetics of Nietzsche and Camus," *The Journal of Aesthetics and Art Criticism* 32/3 (Spring 1974): 415–21.

[24] See Jean-Paul Sartre, *Une défaite* (1926–27), published in Sartre, *Écrits de jeunesse*, ed. Michel Contat and Michel Rybalka (Paris: Gallimard, 1990), 266–86. For further discussion, see Jean-François Louette, *Sartre* contra *Nietzsche (Les Mouches, Huis Clos, Les Mots)* (Grenoble: Presses universitaires de Grenoble, 1996); and Christine Daigle, *Le nihilisme est-il un humanisme? Étude sur Nietzsche et Sartre* (Quebec: Les Presses de l'Université Laval, 2005).

[25] For an anthology of these commentators, see David B. Allison, ed., *The New Nietzsche: Contemporary Styles of Interpretation* (Cambridge, MA and London: MIT P, 1985); and Keith Ansell-Pearson and Howard Caygill, eds., *The Fate of the New Nietzsche* (Aldershot: Ashgate, 1993).

[26] Michel Foucault, "Nietzsche, la généalogie, l'histoire," in *Dits et Écrits II* (Paris: Gallimard, 2001), 136–56; "Nietzsche, Genealogy, History" (1971), trans. Donald F. Bouchard and Sherry Simon, in *Essential Works of Foucault 1954–1984*, vol. 2, *Aesthetics, Methodology, and Epistemology*, ed. James D. Faubion (New York: New P, 1998), 369–91; and Jacques Derrida, *Spurs: Nietzsche's Styles; Éperons: Les styles de Nietzsche*, (facing-page translation), trans. Barbara Harlow (Chicago: U of Chicago P, 1978).

[27] Georges Bataille, *Sur Nietzsche* (Paris: Gallimard, 1945), trans. Bruce Boone as *On Nietzsche* (London: Athlone, 1992).

[28] Maurice Blanchot, *L'Entretien infini* (Paris: Gallimard, 1969), trans. Susan Hanson as *The Infinite Conversation* (Minneapolis: U of Minnesota P, 1994); and *Le Pas au-delà* (Paris: Gallimard, 1973), trans. Lycette Nelson as *The Step Not Beyond* (Albany, NY: SUNY P, 1992).

[29] Jean Baudrillard, *Simulacres et simulation* (Paris: Galilée, 1981), trans. Sheila Faria Glaser as *Simulacra and Simulation* (Ann Arbor: U of Michigan P, 1994).

[30] Eric Blondel, *Nietzsche, le corps et la culture: La philosophie comme généalogie philologique* (Paris: PUF, 1986); trans. Seán Hand as *Nietzsche: The Body and Culture: Philosophy as a Philological Genealogy* (London: Athlone, 1991).

[31] Jean Granier, *Le Problème de la vérité dans la philosophie de Nietzsche* (Paris: Seuil, 1966) and *Nietzsche* (Paris: PUF, 1982).

[32] Sarah Kofman, *Nietzsche et la métaphore* (Paris: Payot, 1972), trans. Duncan Large as *Nietzsche and Metaphor* (London: Athlone, 1993); and *Nietzsche et la scène philosophique* (Paris: Union générale d'éditions, 1979).

[33] Pierre Klossowski, *Nietzsche et le cercle vicieux* (Paris: Mercure de France, 1969), trans. Daniel W. Smith as *Nietzsche and the Vicious Circle* (London: Athlone, 1997).

[34] Gilles Deleuze, *Nietzsche et la philosophie* (Paris: PUF, 1962), trans. Hugh Tomlinson as *Nietzsche* (London: Athlone, 1983); and *Nietzsche* (Paris: PUF, 1965).

[35] See Alain Boyer, André Comte-Sponville, Vincent Descombes, Luc Ferry, Robert Legros, Philippe Raynaud, Alain Renaut, and Pierre-André Taguieff, *Pourquoi nous ne sommes pas nietzschéens* (Paris: Grasset, 1991), trans. Robert de Loaiza as *Why We Are Not Nietzscheans* (Chicago: U of Chicago P, 1997).

[36] Luc Ferry, *Nietzsche: L'œuvre philosophique expliquée: Un cours particulier* (Vincennes: Frémeaux et Associés, FA 5233, 2008).

[37] Philippe Sollers, *Écoute de Nietzsche: Leçon philosophique* [recordings made in 2002 and 2003] (Vincennes: Frémeaux et Associés, FA 5198, 2008).

[38] Michel Onfray, *Nietzsche* [*Contre-histoire de la philosophie*, vol. 14; seminars held at the Université populaire de Caen, 2008–9, broadcast on France Culture 2009] (Vincennes: Frémeaux et Associés, 2010, FA 5154). Michel Onfray is also the author of a dramatic biography, *L'innocence du devenir: la vie de Frédéric Nietzsche* (Paris: Galilée, 2007), subsequently turned into a *bande dessinée*, illustrated by Maximilien Le Roy, entitled *Nietzsche: Se créer liberté* (Brussells: Le Lombard, 2010), and he has also written *La sagesse tragique: Du bon usage de Nietzsche* (Paris: Librairie générale française, 2006).

[39] For the work of these and other contemporary commentators, see John Richardson and Brian Leiter, *Nietzsche* (Oxford: Oxford UP, 2001).

[40] William Soutar, *Diaries of a Dying Man* (1954) (Edinburgh: Canongate, 1968), 26.

[41] Alexander Tille, *Von Darwin bis Nietzsche: Ein Buch Entwicklungsethik* (Leipzig: Naumann, 1895). For information about Tille, I am indebted to the following: Stefan Manz, "Translating Nietzsche, Mediating Literature: Alexander Tille and the Limits of Anglo-German Intercultural Transfer," *Neophilologus* 91 (2007): 117–34.

[42] *The Works of Friedrich Nietzsche*, ed. Alexander Tille, 11 vols. (London and Leipzig: Unwin, 1896–1909).

[43] For further discussion, see Dan Stone, *Breeding Superman: Nietzsche, Race and Eugenics in Edwardian and Interwar Britain* (Liverpool: Liverpool UP, 2002), esp. chap. 1, "Oscar Levy: A Nietzschean Vision," 12–38.

[44] Téodor de Wyzewa, "Frédéric Nietzsche, le dernier métaphysicien," *Revue bleue*, vol. 48 (7 November 1891), 586–92.

[45] See John A. Lester, Jr., "Friedrich Nietzsche and John Davidson: A Study in Influence," *Journal of the History of Ideas* 18/3 (June 1957): 411–29. Davidson's articles appeared in *The Speaker*, vol. 4 (28 November 1891): 641–42, under the title "The New Sophist," and in the *Glasgow Herald*, Saturday, March 18, 1893, issue 66, page 4, under title "Frederick Nietsche" [*sic*].

[46] Anthony M. Ludovici, *Who Is to Be Master of the World? An Introduction to the Philosophy of Friedrich Nietzsche* (Edinburgh: T. N. Foulis, 1909); *Nietzsche: His Life and Works* (London: Constable, 1910); and *Nietzsche and Art* (London: Boston; New York: Constable, J. W. Luce; Haskell House, 1911).

[47] Bertrand Russell, *A History of Western Philosophy* (London: George Allen and Unwin, 1946; 1979), 739.

[48] Frederick Copleston, *Friedrich Nietzsche: Philosopher of Culture* (London: Burns Oates and Washbourne, 1942).

[49] G. Wilson Knight, *Christ and Nietzsche: An Essay in Poetic Wisdom* (London and New York: Staples P, 1948).

[50] Walter Kaufmann, *Nietzsche: Philosopher, Psychologist, Antichrist* (Princeton, NJ: Princeton UP, 1974). Although Kaufmann has fallen out of favor in recent years, this study, along with the study entitled *Nietzsche, Heidegger, and Buber* (1980),

the second volume of his three-part account *Discovering the Mind* (New Brunswick, NJ and London: Transaction, 1991–92) — the other volumes are entitled *Goethe, Kant, and Hegel* (1980) and *Freud, Adler, and Jung* (1980) — are by no means without their value as introductory guides.

[51] See Georg Lukács, *The Destruction of Reason* (1962), trans. Peter Palmer (Atlantic Highlands, NJ: Humanities Press, 1981); and Aymeric Monville, *Misère du "nietzschéisme de gauche" de Georges Bataille et Michel Onfray* (Brussels: Éditions Aden, 2007).

[52] Seth Taylor, *Left-Wing Nietzscheans: The Politics of German Expressionism 1910–1920* (Berlin: Walter de Gruyter, 1990).

[53] Geoff Waite, *Nietzsche's Corps/e: Aesthetics, Politics, Prophecy, or, The Spectacular Technoculture of Everyday Life* (Durham, NC and London: Duke UP, 1996).

[54] See Lou Andreas-Salomé, *Nietzsche in seinen Werken* [1894], ed. Ernst Pfeiffer (Frankfurt am Main: Insel, 1983); *Nietzsche*, ed. and trans. Siegfried Mandel (Champaign, IL: U of Illinois P, 2001).

[55] Johann Gottlieb Fichte, "Erste Einleitung in die Wissenschaftslehre," §5, in Fichte, *Introductions to the Wissenschaftslehre and Other Writings (1797–1800)*, ed. and trans. Daniel Breazeale (Indianapolis: Hackett, 1994), 20; "Versuch einer neuen Darstellung der Wissenschaftslehre" (1797/1798), "Einleitung," in Fichte, *Gesamtausgabe der Bayerischen Akademie der Wissenschaften*, ed. Reinhard Lauth and Hans Gliwitzsky (Stuttgart-Bad Cannstatt: Frommann-Holzboog, 1962–), I.4:183–281 (intro. 186–208) [here: 195]).

[56] For further discussion of Nietzsche in the context of *Lebensphilosophie*, see Herbert Schnädelbach, *Philosophie in Deutschland 1831–1933* (Frankfurt am Main: Suhrkamp, 1991), chap. 5, "Leben," 174–96; trans. Eric Matthews as *Philosophy in Germany 1831–1933* (Cambridge: Cambridge UP, 1984), chap. 5; Josef M. Werle, *Nietzsches Projekt "Philosoph des Lebens"* (Würzburg: Konigshausen & Neumann, 2003) and Robert Josef Kozljanič, *Lebensphilosophie: Eine Einführung* (Stuttgart: Kohlhammer, 2004), chap. 5, "Friedrich Nietzsche: Leben als dionysische Ekstase, Denken als sokratische Kritik, Wollen als Machvermehrung," 85–104, which includes further suggestions for reading Nietzsche in a vitalist perspective.

Link to Nietzsche's Early Writings

At ten o'clock in the morning on Tuesday, 15 October 1844, a child was born to Franziska Nietzsche, née Oehler, and Karl Ludwig Nietzsche, the pastor of the village of Röcken, near Lützen in the eastern part of Germany.[1] On 24 October, the boy was christened Friedrich Wilhelm; his father, on the anniversary of whose own baptism the service had taken place, gave his son the following *Taufspruch* or baptismal motto: "What manner of child shall this be? And the hand of the Lord was with him" (Luke 1:66).

As Nietzsche was well aware, he was the descendant of a whole line of Christian ministers,[2] and in an early autobiographical sketch he wrote: "As a plant I was born close to the churchyard, and as a human being in a vicarage" (Ich bin als Pflanze nahe dem Gottesacker, als Mensch in einem Pfarrhause geboren).[3] In fact, long before he wrote *Ecce Homo*, Nietzsche was an insatiable writer of autobiographical sketches, quickly becoming aware of how, "if the basic characteristics of every individual are, as it were, innate, time and circumstance develop these simple seeds and leave their specific marks on them, which then over time become firm and ineradicable" (wenn auch die Grundzüge des Charakters jedem Menschen gleichsam angeboren sind, so bilden doch erst die Zeit und die Umstände diese rohen Keime aus und prägen ihnen bestimmte Formen auf, die dann durch die Dauer fest und unverlöschlich werden).[4]

One such circumstance, the impact of which Nietzsche himself must have pondered, was his father's illness, which began in the revolutionary year of 1848, leading to his death a year later in 1849, when Nietzsche was five years old. "My father had to endure terrible pain" (Ungeheure Schmerzen mußte mein geliebter Vater ertragen); "finally he lost his eyesight and had to endure the remainder of his sufferings in eternal darkness" (endlich erlosch sogar sein Augenlicht und im ewigen Dunkel mußte er noch den Rest seiner Leiden erdulden); his last words were addressed to his son: "Fränzchen, Fränzchen." Nietzsche recalled: "The thought of being separated for ever from my beloved father took hold of me, and I cried bitterly" (der Gedanke, mich immer von dem geliebten Vater getrennt zu sehn, ergriff mich und ich weinte bitterlich).[5]

Less than a year later, Nietzsche's younger brother, Ludwig Joseph, died shortly before his second birthday. In his memoirs, Nietzsche recalls a premonition of this event in a dream that also reveals a sense of anxiety following their father's death:

In the church I could hear the organ playing, as if there was a funeral. Then [. . .] a grave suddenly opened and my father, dressed in a shroud, climbs out of it. He hurries into the church and soon returns with a small child in his arms. The grave opens again, he steps in, and the stone covers up the opening. Immediately the roar of the organ falls silent, and I wake up.

[Ich hörte in der Kirche Orgelton wie beim Begräbnis. Da [. . .] erhob sich plötzlich ein Grab und mein Vater im Sterbekleid entsteigt demselben. Er eilt in die Kirche und kommt in kurzem mit einem kleinen Kinde im Arm wieder. Der Grabhügel öffnet sich, er steigt hinein und die Decke sinkt wieder auf die Öffnung. Sogleich schweigt der rauschende Orgelschall und ich erwache.][6]

His father's death, followed by his brother's, left Nietzsche in a household dominated by women: his younger sister (Elisabeth Alexandra); his mother, his grandmother, two unmarried aunts, and the family maid. Looking back, Nietzsche wondered whether it was "a bad thing that henceforth my entire development did not have a man's eye looking after it" (ein Übelstand, daß meine ganze Entwicklung von da an von keinem männlichen Auge beaufsichtigt wurde).[7]

In 1850, the Nietzsche household moved to Naumburg, where Nietzsche attended the local primary school, then a private institute run by Karl Moritz Weber, before attending the grammar school (*Gymnasium*) attached to the cathedral. As a six-year-old, Nietzsche's ability to cite biblical passages and sing hymns earned him the reputation of being *der kleine Pastor* ("the little pastor").[8] In this context his sister Elisabeth recalled how once, after school when it was pouring heavily with rain, all the other boys ran home, whereas Fritzchen walked calmly home, with his cap under his slate-board, covered with his handkerchief. When Franziska scolded him for getting completely soaked, he reminded her that, according to the school rules, pupils were forbidden to run home.[9]

At least in the eyes of his family, Nietzsche was destined to be a church minister, and when he was fourteen he was sent to Schulpforta, the famous school that, among others, Klopstock and Fichte had attended. His diary entries from 1859 record the pattern of a typical school day, which began with the unlocking of the dormitories at four o'clock, the pupils washed and dressed by five, then prayer, then study alternating with instruction throughout the day. At twelve, after a prayer, lunch, then play; in the afternoon, more instruction; then a *Vesper* (a kind of high tea) at four; then more study; then, after supper, playtime, before evening prayers and everyone in bed by nine o'clock. The older students were permitted to read for a further hour, until ten.[10] Whether Nietzsche underwent the initiation rites for new students is not known, although presumably he did; on these occasions, the new pupil was shouted at, a mixture of ink, vinegar, beer, and mustard poured in his mouth, and he was beaten with hazel switches. Another student at Schulpforta recalled: "The whole thing was a brutal procedure [. . .] but it didn't do us any harm" (Das Ganze war ein roher Vorgang [. . .] Aber geschadet hat es uns nichts).[11] Schulpforta itself enforced a strict code of discipline; but Nietzsche appears to have been a model pupil. In an autobiographical sketch from 1868/1869, Nietzsche regretted that, since his father's death, he had been deprived of "the strict and superior guidance of a masculine intellect" (die strenge und überlegne Leitung eines männlichen Intellekts), and suggested that in Schulpforta he had found "a surrogate of paternal upbringing" (ein Surrogat der väterlichen Erziehung); "this almost military compulsion" (dieser fast militärische Zwang) in "the uniformed discipline of a well-ordered school" (die uniformierende Disziplin einer geordneten Schule) had ultimately, he believed, "led me back to myself again" (führte mich wieder auf mich selbst zurück).[12]

At Schulpforta Nietzsche developed his love of classics, demonstrating remarkable proficiency in Greek and Latin. His passion for knowledge and learning was entirely genuine; and with fellow pupils Wilhelm Pinder (1844–1928) and Gustav Krug (1844–1902), he founded a literary society called *Germania*. The ideals of *Germania* adumbrate his later thinking about the relevance of antiquity for modern life. "Every day we are becoming *more and more Greek*" (Wir werden von Tag zu Tag *griechischer*), he would write in 1885, "to begin with, as is proper, in our concepts and in our value judgments [. . .]: but at some stage, one hopes, also with our *body!* Here lies (and here has always lain) my hope for the Germans!" (zuerst, wie billig, in Begriffen und Werthschätzungen, gleichsam als gräcisirende Gespenster: aber dereinst, hoffentlich auch mit unserem *Leibe!* Hierin liegt (und lag von jeher) meine Hoffnung für das deutsche Wesen! *KSA* 11, 41[4], 679).

As well as for the ancients, he began to develop his love for classical German literature and the German Romantics: for Goethe, one of whose aphorisms he carefully explicated (*BAW* 2:183–86) and for Schiller, whose play *The Robbers* (*Die Räuber*) he admired (*BAW* 1:137) and the centenary celebrations for whom he found stirring (*W* 3:75–77; *BAW* 1:186–88); for Novalis, whose works he read in his uncle's library (*W* 3:69), for Jean Paul, his favorite writer (*BAW* 1:141) and for Hölderlin, his favorite poet (*KGW* I.2, 338–41). An anecdote told by his sister Elisabeth captures the existential earnestness of Nietzsche's passion for classical literature. One day he heard some younger pupils talking about Gaius Mucius Scaevola, a legendary Roman who, according to Livy's history of Rome (book 2, chapter 12), was taken prisoner and to show his indifference to death, thrust his hand into a fire. Surely, one of them said, no one could have really done that. Why do you say that?, Nietzsche asked, calmly setting fire to some sticks of wood, and placing the burning twigs on his outstretched left hand — to the amazement of his fellow pupils, and to the horror of one of the prefects.[13] For Nietzsche, it seems, the past was not just alive — *it could still be lived (out)*.

Hence his early efforts in literary creation: poems, in German and Latin; historical sketches, such as his interest in Ermanarich, king of the Goths (*BAW* 1:290–99); commentaries (on the *Nibelungenlied* and the *Hildebrandslied*, for example) and essays, such as his reflective piece on "Moods" ("Über Stimmungen"; *W* 3:113–16); and musical compositions. Another anecdote shows a surprisingly physical side to a pupil who, the rest of the time, was prone to being ill. A diary entry for 1859 records a swimming marathon, held with characteristically Schulpfortean military precision: the students marched in ranks down to the Saale, and, still in their groups, were ordered into the river. Once they had swum up the river, the students climbed out, their clothes — taken along in a boat — were returned to them, and the students marched back to the school. Nietzsche found the experience "really wonderfully beautiful" (wirklich wunderhübsch; *BAW* 1:130).

On his family's side, the plan was still for Nietzsche to become a minister, so after Schulpforta he went to university in Bonn to study theology. But his school-leaving dissertation, "Theognis as a Poet" ("Theognis als Dichter"), served as a reminder of what was now his real passion: classical philology. And there is evidence that religious doubts were creeping into Nietzsche's late teenage mind. Already a sketch, dated 18 September 1863, indicates the sense of doubt — and a concomitant sense of liberation — in the nineteen-year-old Nietzsche: "And so the human being grows out of everything that used to embrace him; he does not need to break his shackles, for unexpectedly, when a god bids it, they fall away; and where is the ring that in the end still encircles him? Is it the world? Is it God? —" (Und so entwächst der Mensch allem, was ihn einst umschlang; er braucht nicht die fesseln zu sprengen, sondern unvermutet, wenn ein Gott es gebeut, fallen sie ab; und wo ist der Ring, der ihn endlich noch umfaßt? Ist es die Welt? Ist es Gott? —; *W* 3:110). According to his sister Elisabeth differences of opinion in matters of religion led, not surprisingly, to increasing tensions between him and Franziska, his mother.[14] In a remarkably frank letter to his sister, written on 11 June 1865, he asked: "Do we, in our enquiries, seek rest, peace, happiness? No, only truth, however abhorrent and ugly it may be" (Suchen wir denn bei unserem Forschen Ruhe, Friede, Glück? Nein, nur die Wahrheit, und wäre sie höchst abschreckend und häßlich; *KSB* 2, 61). And he diagnosed for her the moment of caesura he was facing, in the following dramatic phrase: "Here the ways of men part: if you want to strive for peace of mind and happiness, then believe; but if you want to be a disciple of truth, then enquire" (Hier scheiden sich nun die Wege der Menschen; willst Du Seelenruhe und Glück erstreben, nun so glaube, willst Du ein Jünger der Wahrheit sein, so forsche; *KSB* 2, 61).

Thus his change from theology to philology, undertaken in 1865, formalized in curricular terms a switch of focus that had already taken place. What was Nietzsche like as a student in Bonn? He joined a *Burschenschaft* or student fraternity, called Frankonia, but soon tired of the traditional student predilection for alcohol or what he called their *Biermaterialismus* (letter to Carl von Gersdorff, 25 May 1865; *KSB* 2, 55). Although he initially joined in and received his own drinking name — "Gluck" or, presumably, *glug* (letter to Franziska Nietzsche, 7–9 December 1864; *KSB* 2, 22) — he gained a reputation, as he was aware, for being not just an authority on all matters musical, but also for being — well, a bit of an odd fellow ("sonderbarer Kauz"); he could, as he himself admitted, be a bit of a pain ("ein wenig Quälgeist") for himself as for others (letter to Franziska and Elisabeth Nietzsche, 18 February 1865; *KSB* 2, 43). What about other traditional nineteenth-century pursuits? In German universities at this time, it was common practice to engage in dueling. But Nietzsche's approach was typically idiosyncratic. One story relates how Nietzsche got to know a fellow student and discussed with him matters of art and literature, at the end of which Nietzsche asked the other whether he would fight a duel with him. The next day, the two met and crossed swords: at the end of the short exchange, Nietzsche's nose had been wounded, and he left bleeding. Although he had been struck, he seems that it was Nietzsche who was, in a more profound sense, "satisfied"; and the resultant scar was judged to suit him well.[15] And what about women? Nietzsche's friend, Paul Deussen (1845–1919) — who is the source for the anecdote about the duel — is responsible for creating one of the great Nietzsche legends: his visit to a brothel in Cologne. On Deussen's account, Nietzsche visited the city to admire its architecture, and asked his guide to take him to a restaurant. Instead, he was taken to "a house of ill-repute" (ein übel berüchtigtes Haus). As Nietzsche reportedly told Deussen, he suddenly found himself surrounded by "half a dozen figures in jewelry and veils" (ein halbes Dutzend Erscheinungen in Flitter und Gaze), looking at him expectantly. Speechless, Nietzsche stood there, until he noticed a piano, "the only thing with any soul among them" (das einzige seelenhafte Wesen in der Gesellschaft), toward which he "instinctively" moved and played a few chords. Released from his paralysis, Nietzsche escaped.[16] Now, whatever the truth of this story, it was treated seriously by H. W. Brann,[17] turned into a central episode of Thomas Mann's novel, *Doktor Faustus* (1947), and continues to inform the popular image of Nietzsche (to the extent that there is one). While Nietzsche's (alleged) consternation in front of these scantily clad women is easily derided (and is so frequently), his attraction to a musical instrument, rather than a human being, as being *seelenhaft* or "full of soul" is itself an eloquent symbol of Nietzsche's deeply aesthetic sensibilities.

When his favorite lecturer, the great classical scholar Friedrich Ritschl (1806–76), moved from Bonn to Leipzig, Nietzsche decided to switch universities as well; as he told his sister and mother, he would also be closer to his friends in Naumburg and to them, and he looked forward to the cultural life of Leipzig (letter of 29 May 1865; *KSB* 2, 58).[18] An autobiographical sketch entitled "Retrospective View of my Two Years in Leipzig" ("Rückblick auf meine zwei Leipziger Jahre") records Nietzsche's sense of enchantment on arriving in Leipzig, accompanied by his friend Hermann Mushacke (1845–1906) (*BAW* 3, 293–96). Ritschl's exclamation, "Look! Nietzsche is here, too!" (Ei da ist ja auch Herr Nietzsche!), when he spotted his student among the audience at his inaugural lecture, entitled "On the Value and Use of Philology" ("Über den Wert und Nutzen der Philologie"), captures his sense of excitement at the intellectual world in Leipzig, shared by Nietzsche until he gradually began to question precisely the value and use of philology.

Nietzsche's matriculation at the university in Leipzig took place on the same date that, a hundred years earlier, Goethe had become a student there: in his "Retrospective View," Nietzsche records the fact with great satisfaction: "I cannot say what a refreshing effect this coincidence had on me" (Ich kann nicht sagen, wie erfrischend dieses zufällige Ereigniß auf mich wirkte; *BAW* 3:295). In later years, Nietzsche even claimed to be a descendant of Goethe: in one of his drafts for the third section of "Why I Am So Wise" ("Warum ich so weise bin") in *Ecce Homo*, he wrote that his paternal grandmother, Erdmuthe Dorothea Nietzsche, née Krause (1778–1856), had belonged to the circle around Goethe in Weimar, and he identified her with the figure of Muthgen, mentioned in Goethe's diary (*KSA* 14, 472).[19] Nietzsche knew, from his own investigation at the Goethe-Archive in Weimar, that this lineage could not be taken seriously, and Julian Young has suggested that "since Goethe was his greatest hero, his paradigm of mental health, a personal connection — perhaps he even entertained the possibility of Goethe's blood flowing in his own veins — would have been," for Nietzsche, "a great joy."[20] But maybe we should read the notion of a relation to Goethe not in a biological but in an intellectual or cultural sense: after all, Goethean themes persist in Nietzsche's writing throughout his life. After all, a remark made by Goethe (in a letter to Charlotte von Stein of 3 March 1785, and noted by Nietzsche in the winter of 1872–73) that "the *causa finalis* of global and human action is dramatic poetry" (die causa finalis der Welt- und Menschenhändel ist die dramatische Dichtkunst) anticipates the central argument of *The Birth of Tragedy* (*Die Geburt der Tragödie*) that the world can only be justified aesthetically.[21]

"To fashion for myself a life of my own that suits me was all that concerned me from dawn to dusk" (Mir ein eignes anpassendes Leben zu zimmern war mein Bestreben von früh bis abend; *BAW* 3:297), Nietzsche wrote in this brief memoir, and two thinkers radically changed how he conceived his own life and the function of philology. The first was Arthur Schopenhauer (1788–1860), the post-Kantian Idealist and proto-*Lebensphilosoph*; in late October 1865 Nietzsche brought a copy of *Die Welt als Wille und Vorstellung* (1819; [2]1844; [3]1859; *The World as Will and Representation*) from a secondhand bookshop, and was overwhelmed by Schopenhauer's worldview (*BAW* 3:298). The second was the neo-Kantian philosopher and sociologist Friedrich Albert Lange (1828–75), whose account of materialism, *Geschichte des Materialismus und Kritik seiner Bedeutung in der Gegenwart* (1866), he began reading in August 1866.

During his two years in Leipzig, Nietzsche was entirely committed to the ideals of philology: together with fellow students Heinrich Wilhelm Wisser (1843–1935), Wilhelm Heinrich Roscher (1845–1923), and Richard Arnold (1845–1910), he founded a philological society, the Philologischer Verein; worked on Theognis and Diogenes Laertius; and met regularly with friends in the Café Kintschy to discuss philology and philosophy. (As Roscher wryly remarked, Nietzsche abstained from drinking, smoking, and sex; but not coffee and cake.)[22] Through another philological society, the Ritschlsche Sozietät, Nietzsche met fellow student Erwin Rohde (1845–98), with whom a close friendship developed; writing to Wisser on 29 November 1867, Rohde described his relationship to Nietzsche as "something utterly undeserved and almost inexplicable to me" (etwas rein Unverdientes und mir fast Unerklärliches).[23] Once the two friends went riding, and appeared to those around them "like two young gods" (wie zwei junge Götter);[24] Rohde's account of a visit they made to the Bavarian Forest in August 1867 records the intensity of their intellectual exchanges.

Thus it was Rohde to whom Nietzsche confided his enthusiasm for the great contemporary composer, Richard Wagner (1813–83); on Sunday, 8 November 1868 Nietzsche met Wagner in person in the house of the Orientalist Hermann Brockhaus (1806–77), whose wife, Ottilie, was Wagner's sister; and so began the remarkably intense friendship between Nietzsche and Wagner, which eventually exploded into extraordinarily bitter enmity, a tale which Nietzsche later told, from his point of view, in *The Case of Wagner* (*Der Fall Wagner*, 1888) and *Nietzsche contra Wagner* (1889).[25] In a letter of 8 October 1868, he told Rohde: "What appeals to me in Wagner is what appeals to me in Schopenhauer, the ethical atmosphere, the Faustian odor, cross, death, and crypt" (Mir behagt an Wagner, was mir an Schopenhauer behagt, die ethische Luft, der faustische Duft, Kreuz, Tod und Gruft usw.; *KSB* 2, 322); or as Nietzsche wrote to Wagner on 22 May 1869, what he found in the composer and the philosopher alike was "the Germanic seriousness toward life [. . .], a profound meditation on our so puzzling and disturbing existence" (dem germanischen Lebensernst, [. . .] einer vertieften Betrachtung dieses so räthselvollen und bedenklichen Daseins; *KSB* 3, 9).

As this letter suggests, the disappearance of earlier, inherited religious convictions was accompanied by an increasingly strong intuition of the uncanniness of the world, as reflected in this sketch from 1868/1869:

> What I am afraid of is not the terrible shape behind my chair, but its voice: nor its words, but the dreadfully unarticulated and inhuman tone of that shape's voice. If only it were to talk as human beings talk!

> [Was ich fürchte, ist nicht die schreckliche Gestalt hinter meinem Stuhle, sondern ihre Stimme: auch nicht die Worte, sondern der schauderhaft unartikulierte und unmenschliche Ton jener Gestalt. Ja, wenn sie noch redete, wie Menschen reden! (*W* 3:148)]

On the strength of the philological excellence of his publications in the academic journal the *Rheinisches Museum für Philologie*, Ritschl — one of its co-editors — urged his colleagues in Basel to appoint Nietzsche to their Chair for Greek language and literature. Ritschl wrote to his colleague Adolf Kießling in December 1868 that, of all the "young talent" (junge Kräfte) he had seen in the last thirty-nine years, he had never come across someone who had been "so mature, while so early and so young" (so früh und so jung schon so reif) as Nietzsche, and he hailed him as "the idol and (without wishing to be) the leader of the world of young philologists here in Leipzig" (der Abgott und (ohne es zu wollen) Führer der ganzen jungen Philologenwelt hier in Leipzig).[26]

And so, despite his enthusiasm for his military service in the mounted artillery that began in October 1867, from which he was released a year later because of ill health, and despite his subsequent plan to abandon philology and study chemistry (see his letter to Rohde of 16 January 1869; *KSB* 2, 359–60), Nietzsche became a classics professor. To be precise, in April 1869 he was appointed Extraordinary Professor of Classical Philology at the University of Basel, at the age of twenty-four. The remarkable speed and extent of Nietzsche's promotion should not be underestimated; nor should his eventual and scathing disillusionment with the profession in which he had been so swiftly advanced, leading him to write (in a letter of 6 January 1889, addressed to his former colleague Jacob Burckhardt [1818–97]) the bitingly satirical sentence: "In the end I would much rather have been a professor at Basel than God" (Zuletzt wäre ich sehr viel lieber Basler Professor als Gott; *KSB* 8, 577).

In Basel Nietzsche set about his professorial duties with typical commitment and energy, holding his inaugural lecture on 28 May 1869, later published as "Homer and Classical Philology ("Homer und die klassische Philologie").[27] But a few days earlier, on 17 May (or Whit-Monday), he had paid his first visit to Wagner in Tribschen, just outside Lucerne — that is, to Wagner and his wife, Cosima. Nietzsche's career in Basel can be read as an attempt to accommodate two different kinds of intellectual activity, or two different aspects of Nietzsche's own personality, and in the end his life as a scholar proved unable to combine both of them. On one hand, there was his activity as a philologist, reflected in his lectures (on, among other subjects, Aeschylus, Plato, the pre-Socratics, Aristotle, and ancient Greek religion) to groups of five or six students (his smallest group was two, his largest nineteen) and in his publications (on the Florentine treatise on Homer and Hesiod, on Socrates and Greek tragedy, and on the future of education). On the other hand, there was his discipleship of Wagner and its concomitant sense of cultural mission. It is in light of this commitment that such texts as "The Dionysian World-View" ("Die dionysische Weltanschauung"), the explicitly political overtone to some of his remarks about the Jews, and even his brief participation as a medical orderly in the Franco-Prussian War (before diphtheria intervened and he had to leave the front) should be seen. His texts from this period, which focus around the central concept of *tragedy*, anticipate his later writings, but constitute fascinating documents in their own right; they are discussed in the following contribution by Thomas Brobjer.

Notes

[1] These brief biographical notes linking the individual contributions to this Companion draw on the following sources: Ivo Frenzel, *Nietzsche mit Selbstzeugnissen und Bilddokumenten dargestellt* (Reinbek bei Hamburg: Rowohlt, 1966); "Zeit- und Lebenstafel," in *Werke in drei Bänden*, ed. Karl Schlechta, 3 vols. (Munich: Hanser, 1966), 1359–82; Curt Paul Janz, *Friedrich Nietzsche: Eine Biographie*, 3 vols. (Munich and Vienna: Hanser, 1978); Raymond J. Benders and Stephan Oettermann, *Friedrich Nietzsche: Chronik in Bildern und Texten* (Munich and Vienna: Hanser, 2000); Rüdiger Safranksi, *Nietzsche: Biographie seines Denkens* (Munich and Vienna: Hanser, 2000); Curtis Cate, *Friedrich Nietzsche* (London: Hutchinson, 2002); William H. Schaberg, *Nietzsches Werke: Eine Publikationsgeschichte und kommentierte Bibliographie*, trans. Michael Leuenberger (Basel: Schwabe, 2002); Peter Zudeick, *Nietzsche für Eilige* (Berlin: Aufbau, 2005); Julian Young, *Friedrich Nietzsche: A Philosophical Biography* (Cambridge: Cambridge UP, 2010); Dorian Astor, *Nietzsche* (Paris: Gallimard, 2011); and Michel Onfray, *La construction du surhomme: Jean-Marie Guyau, Friedrich Nietzsche [Contre-histoire de la philosophie*, vol. 7] (Paris: Grasset, 2012).

[2] Nietzsche, letter to Heinrich Köselitz of 21 July 1881; *KSB* 6:109.

[3] "Aus meinem Leben" (1863), in *W* 3:107.

[4] "Mein Lebenslauf" (1861), in *W* 3:90.

[5] "Aus meinem Leben," in *BAW* 1:4–5; *W* 3:16.

[6] "Aus meinem Leben," in *BAW* 1:6; *W* 3:17; cf. "Mein Lebenslauf," in *BAW* 1:282; *W* 3:93.

[7] "Mein Leben" (1864), in *W* 3:117. For further discussion of the impact of women on Nietzsche's life, see Mario Leis, *Frauen um Nietzsche* (Reinbek bei Hamburg: Rowohlt, 2000).

[8] Elisabeth Förster-Nietzsche, *Das Leben Friedrich Nietzsche's*, 3 vols. (Leipzig: Naumann, 1895–1904), 1:30.

[9] Förster-Nietzsche, *Das Leben Friedrich Nietzsche's*, 1:31.

[10] *BAW* 1:119–31; *W* 3:44–55.

[11] Heinrich Niemöller, *Aus goldener Jugendzeit* (Elberfeld: Buchhandlung der Evangelischen Gesellschaft für Deutschland, 1936), 36–37.

[12] ["Aus den Jahren 1868/89]," in *W* 3:151.

[13] Förster-Nietzsche, *Das Leben Friedrich Nietzsche's*, 1:105–6.

[14] Förster-Nietzsche, *Das Leben Friedrich Nietzsche's*, 1:208–9; Elisabeth Förster-Nietzsche, *Der junge Nietzsche* (Leipzig: Kröner, 1912), 154–55.

[15] Paul Deussen, *Erinnerungen an Friedrich Nietzsche* (Leipzig: Brockhaus, 1901), 22–23.

[16] Deussen, *Erinnerungen an Friedrich Nietzsche*, 24.

[17] See Henry Walter Brann, *Nietzsche und die Frauen* (1931) (Bonn: Bouvier, 1978).

[18] For discussion of Nietzsche's time in Leipzig, see Ulf Heise, *"Ei da ist ja auch Herr Nietzsche": Leipziger Werdejahre eines Philosophen* (Beucha: Sax-Verlag, 2000).

[19] For further discussion, see Janz, *Friedrich Nietzsche*, 2:538 and 589. For the reference to Muthgen in Goethe's diary entry of 25 March 1777, see Goethe, *Werke: Weimarer Ausgabe*, edited Johann Ludwig Gustav von Loeper, Erich Schmidt, Paul Raabe, im Auftrage der Großherzogin Sophie von Sachsen; 4 parts, 133 vols. in 143 (Weimar: Hermann Böhlau, 1887–1919), III.1:120.

[20] Young, *Friedrich Nietzsche*, 455.

[21] *KSA* 7, 24[8], 563; cf. Goethe, *Briefe*, ed. Kurt Robert Mandelkow, 4 vols. (Hamburg: Wegner, 1962–67), 1:473; cited in Young, *Friedrich Nietzsche*, 179. For further discussion of Nietzsche in relation to Goethe, see Aldo Venturelli, "Das Klassische als Vollendung des Sentimentalischen: Der junge Nietzsche als Leser des Briefwechsels zwischen Schiller und Goethe," *Nietzsche-Studien* 18 (1989): 182–202; Paul Bishop and R. H. Stephenson, *Friedrich Nietzsche and Weimar Classicism* (Rochester, NY: Camden House, 2005); and Pierre Hadot, *N'oublie pas de vivre: Goethe et la tradition des exercices spirituels* (Paris: Albin Michel, 2008), 256–67.

[22] Elisabeth Förster-Nietzsche, "Nietzsches Krankheit", *Der Tag*, 14 January 1910; cited in *Nietzsche-Chronik*, p. 145. Compare Deussen's willingness to apply to Nietzsche the expression *mulierum nunquam attigit* (*Erinnerungen*, p. 24).

[23] Friedrich Nietzsche, *Briefe: Historisch-kritische Gesamtausgabe*, 4 vols. (Munich: Beck, 1934–40), 2:392.

[24] Förster-Nietzsche, *Der junge Nietzsche*, 190–91.

[25] For fuller documentation, see Dieter Borchmeyer and Jörg Salaquarda, eds., *Nietzsche und Wagner: Stationen einer epochalen Begegnung*, 2 vols. (Frankfurt am Main and Leipzig: Insel, 1994).

[26] Cited in Johannes Stroux, *Nietzsches Professur in Basel* (Jena: Frommann, 1925), 32.

[27] Following this inaugural lecture, Nietzsche delivered a series of addresses, including (in 1870) "The Greek Music Drama" ("Das griechische Musikdrama"), "Socrates and Tragedy" ("Socrates und die Tragoedie"), "The Dionysian World-View" ("Die dionysische Weltanschauung") and (in 1871) "Socrates and Greek Tragedy" ("Sokrates und die griechische Tragoedie"). For further discussion, see T. Moody Campbell, "Nietzsche-Wagner, to January, 1872," *Publications of the Modern Language Association* 56/2 (June, 1941): 544–77.

1: Nietzsche's Early Writings

Thomas H. Brobjer

THERE IS MUCH EXTANT MATERIAL from and about the young and early Nietzsche, including large numbers of early poems, school essays, school records, general notes, etc. In fact, Nietzsche seems, of all the great philosophers and of all important nineteenth-century intellectuals, to be the one about whom we have the most early extant material.[1] The German critical edition of Nietzsche's writings covering the period after he became professor in Basel in 1869, the *Kritische Studienausgabe* (*KSA*), consists of thirteen volumes (as well as two volumes of philological commentary and chronology), of which six contain his published texts (along with a few unpublished works), and seven larger volumes of notes from his "literary remains" or *Nachlass*. Nietzsche's writings for the period before he became a professor in 1869 (including his philological publications and lecture notes) consist of some further ten volumes, contained in the *Kritische Gesamtausgabe* (*KGW*) of Nietzsche's works. All of this material, including some of the unpublished material from *KSA*, volume 1, will be the subject of this chapter. In the space available here, I can only give an overview of the most important material, point to some of the most relevant texts, and briefly discuss a few selected works. I cannot aim here for completeness; instead, I will focus on those texts that are of greater general interest (such as autobiographical texts), philosophically oriented, or relevant for his later thinking and published books.

Nietzsche's early writings can be classified and categorized according to several different principles, but for our purpose, it is perhaps best to divide them into three categories: (1) early general writings (pre-1869); (2) philological writings in a more narrow sense, covering the period 1867 to 1873: (3) post-1869 texts not published by Nietzsche himself, but which are more or less finished products (and which were subsequently published in *KSA*, volume 1).[2] It should be noted that these categories overlap, especially when it comes to texts that involve the subject of antiquity.

Early General Writings (pre-1869)

Nietzsche's very early general writings can be further subdivided into poetry and other literary texts (including drafts for several short plays), school work and early scholarly work (much of the more interesting work was done for the small cultural society *Germania*), early autobiographical writing, and other work. About Nietzsche's school days in the Domgymnasium and at Schulpforta, during the period 1855 to 1864, we have a lot of detailed information, including most of his school essays, schedules, school reports, etc. From Nietzsche's years at university (including his military service and his half-year of convalescence after a riding accident), from 1864 to 1869, there are fewer completed or nearly completed texts, and most of his notes and works are philological in nature.

During his first year at university in Bonn, from 1864 to 1865, Nietzsche studied a fairly wide variety of subjects (and, after the second semester, stopped studying theology, thus finally ending his mother's hope that he would follow in his father's footsteps). The courses he attended included art, literature, and politics, and three of which had an explicitly philosophical relevance: lectures on "Plato's *Symposion*," given by the classicist Otto Jahn, and two courses given by the philosopher Karl Schaarschmidt, "Plato's Life and Teaching" and "An Introduction to the History of Philosophy." During the following years at university in Leipzig, Nietzsche's studies were much more oriented toward more focused courses on classical philology. Few completed texts exist from this period (except philological ones, see below). The philosophically most relevant work Nietzsche did was on Democritus (consisting of many notes, but it was never even brought close to completion), his philological work on the oldest extant history of philosophy (that of Diogenes Laertius), and his plans for a brief period to write his doctoral dissertation on philosophy (as did some of his acquaintances) rather than in the field of philology.

Three of Nietzsche's earliest works are remarkably mature, and also relevant for understanding his later development: his earliest autobiographical writings, his school essay on Hölderlin, and his essay "Fate and History" (together with its companion "Freedom of the Will and Fate"). After a brief discussion of these, I will move on to Nietzsche's relation to tragedy, to Plato and Theognis, and then turn to his plans for a doctoral dissertation in philosophy in 1868.

For Nietzsche, more than for most other philosophers, there is a close connection between his life and his writings. Knowing about and understanding his life aids our understanding of his philosophy, but it also goes beyond this, inasmuch as, throughout his life, Nietzsche emphasized this close connection as a method. Already in the preface to "Philosophy in the Tragic Age of the Greeks" ("Die Philosophie im tragischen Zeitalter der Griechen"), he expresses the belief in the close connection between a man and his writings and his interest in the character behind the work:

> On the other hand, whoever rejoices in great human beings will also rejoice in philosophical systems, even if completely erroneous. They always have one wholly incontrovertible point: personal mood, color. [. . .] The task is to bring to light what we *must ever love and honor* and what no subsequent enlightenment can take away: great individual human beings. [. . .] But I have selected those doctrines in which resound most clearly the personality of the individual philosopher.

> [Wer dagegen an großen Menschen überhaupt seine Freude hat, hat auch seine Freude an solchen Systemen, seien sie auch ganz irrthümlich: sie haben doch einen Punkt an sich, der ganz unwiderleglich ist, eine persönliche Stimmung, Farbe [. . .] die Aufgabe ist das an's Licht zu bringen, was wir *immer lieben* und *verehren* müssen und was uns durch keine spätere Erkenntniß geraubt werden kann: der große Mensch. [. . .] Es sind aber die Lehren ausgewählt worden, in denen das Persönliche eines Philosophen am stärksten nachklingt. (*KSA* 1, 801–3)][3]

This continues to be Nietzsche's method for the rest of his life. In *Beyond Good and Evil* (*Jenseits von Gut und Böse*), he expresses this method as follows: "It has gradually become clear to me what every great philosophy has hitherto been: a confession on the part of its author and a kind of involuntary and unconscious memoir" (Allmählich hat sich mir herausgestellt, was jede grosse Philosophie bisher war: nämlich das Selbstbekenntnis ihres Urhebers und eine Art ungewollter und unvermerkter mémoires; *BGE* §6; *KSA* 5, 19). Similar statements can be found throughout Nietzsche's writings.

If we return to Nietzsche's early writings, we can observe that he was immensely fond of — and gifted at — discussing and analyzing his own thoughts and life from a very early age. In fact, the very earliest "mature" writing by him is his detailed autobiography "From My Life" ("Aus meinem Leben"), written in the autumn of 1858 when he was thirteen, which runs to some thirty-one printed pages.[4] Comparing it with other texts from this time, one may conclude that Nietzsche showed exceptional aptitude for autobiographical writing. The text contains a remarkably mature discussion of his life and writings (especially his poetry) that is of the utmost importance for anyone interested in the young Nietzsche. It ends with a strongly religious sentiment: "In everything God has safely guided me [. . .] I have firmly determined to dedicate myself to his service forever" (in allen hat mich Gott sicher geleitet [. . .] Ich habe es fest in mir beschlossen, mich seinem Dienste auf immer zu widmen; *KGW* I.1, 310 = *BAW* 1, 31).

Nietzsche continued to write autobiographical notes, texts, and diaries (and his correspondence also had strong autobiographical elements), and although there is no document of a similar length or with such a broad scope until *Ecce Homo* in 1888, one can find over ten further autobiographies or partial autobiographies among his early writings, many of them written for specific purposes (such as school assignments, university graduation, a presentation of himself for Basel, a self-presentation for a philosophical journal), as well as others that were written more for his own sake.

Nietzsche's education at Schulpforta (from 1858 to 1864) laid the foundation for much of his future development and activities. It was here that he came to know and value antiquity profoundly and to learn Latin and Greek as well as the method of historical criticism and of textual interpretation in general. These major influences are visible in many concrete instances. His favorite author at this time, Friedrich Hölderlin, with his contempt for German philistines and love of Greek culture, was probably a stimulus for Nietzsche's own self-development and view of himself; Nietzsche was also very fond of Byron and Shakespeare.

In October 1861, at the beginning of his fourth year at Schulpforta, Nietzsche wrote a school essay entitled "Letter to My Friend, in which I Recommend that He Read My Favorite Poet" ("Brief an meinen Freund, in dem ich ihm meinen Lieblingsdichter zum Lesen empfehle"), in which he commends and praises Hölderlin.[5] This school essay is, among all the texts he wrote before he became professor in Basel in 1869, the one that has received the most attention, and it has been used to illustrate Nietzsche's maturity. Many of the comments regarding this essay have, however, been based on a misunderstanding, for it was not a "free" essay by Nietzsche, much less a genuine letter, but was composed on a set theme, and Nietzsche excerpted almost all of his literary judgments directly from a work by William Neumann, his *Moderne Klassiker: Deutsche Literaturgeschichte der neueren Zeit in Biographien, Kritiken und Proben: Friedrich Hölderlin* (Cassel, 1853; 1859). If there is any originality in the essay, it is in the choice of poet and in the skillful scholarly comments. What we see in the essay is thus not primarily Nietzsche's "profound critical ability," but an early example of his habit of evaluating and criticizing with little personal experience. Compare, for example, the adult Nietzsche's extensive discussions and critique of Kant, Rousseau, Spinoza, Descartes, and others — whom he seems to have known almost solely at second hand.

Nietzsche's earliest philosophical writings are two essays from March or April 1862 with the titles "Fate and History" ("Fatum und Geschichte") and "Freedom of the Will and Fate" ("Willensfreiheit und Fatum"), covering some six and three printed pages respectively, both of which are deeply influenced by Emerson.[6] One or maybe both of them

were presented as "lectures" at the Germania, to his two friends Wilhelm
Pinder and Gustav Krug. Both essays are of great interest and contain
much that foreshadows Nietzsche's future philosophy, including his break
with Christianity:

> An endless confusion of thought in the people is the bleak result.
> There will be great revolutions once the masses finally realize that
> the totality of Christianity is grounded in presuppositions; the exis-
> tence of God, immortality, Biblical authority, inspiration and other
> doctrines will always remain problems. I have attempted to deny
> everything: Oh, pulling down is easy; but rebuilding! [. . .] the ques-
> tion whether mankind hasn't been deceived for two thousand years
> by a phantom.

> [Eine unendliche Gedankenverwirrung im Volke ist das trostlose
> Resultat; es stehen noch große Umwälzungen bevor, wenn die Menge
> erst begriffen hat, daß das ganze Christenthum sich auf Annahmen
> gründet; die Existenz Gottes, Unsterblichkeit, Bibelautorität, Inspira-
> tion u. anderes werden immer Probleme bleiben. Ich habe alles zu
> leugnen versucht: o, niederreißen ist leicht, aber aufbauen! [. . .] der
> Zweifel, ob nicht zweitausend Jahre schon die Menschheit durch ein
> Trugbild irre geleitet. (*KGW* I.2, 13[6], 433)][7]

The essays are also relevant as an expression of Nietzsche's early view of
nature and history, and as a demonstration of his interest in the natural
sciences.

> How often has the longing for natural science and history crept over
> me in the course of my fruitless speculations! History and natural
> science, the wonderful legacies of our past, the harbingers of our
> future: They alone are the secure foundation upon which we can
> build the tower of our speculation.

> [Geschichte u. Naturwissenschaft, die wundervollen Vermächtnisse
> unsrer ganzen Vergangenheit, die Verkünderinnen unsrer Zukunft,
> sie allein sind die sichern Grundlagen, auf denen wir den Thurm
> unsrer Spekulation bauen können. (*KGW* I.2, 13[6], 432)][8]

In this text Nietzsche also expresses evolutionary ideas: "Is man not perhaps the development of stone through the medium of plant or animal?
[. . .] Has this eternal becoming no end?" (Ist nicht vielleicht der Mensch
nur die Entwicklung des Steines durch das Medium Pflanze, Tier? [. . .]
Hat dies ewige Werden nie ein Ende?; *KGW* I.2, 13[6], 434). This strong
emphasis on natural science is not found in any of Nietzsche's other contemporary notes, but it resurfaces in his planned dissertation and in his
discussion of the pre-Platonic philosophers.

In his introduction to Nietzsche (1936), Karl Jaspers quotes and briefly discusses these essays, and is amazed at the degree to which Nietzsche, "even as a boy," expressed, "impulses and thoughts belonging to his later philosophy," and he mentions several specific themes and beliefs that are characteristic of the mature Nietzsche but are already visible here, including the critique of Christianity, the concept of man who becomes more than man, and the ideas of eternal recurrence and *amor fati*.[9] Curt Paul Janz, in his standard biography of Nietzsche, quotes and discusses these essays in detail. He claims that "almost all of his more important themes" are here "already visible," and says that he quotes extensively from Nietzsche's early works "because they already show all the impulses of Nietzsche's thinking and because they already circumscribe all the crucial problems," so that "whoever reads them attentively will here find everything exhibited."[10] Janz exemplifies these strong claims by listing nineteen significant themes that are foreshadowed here, including atheism, the revaluation of all values, the relativity of morality, the philosophy of becoming, the innocence of becoming, the insight that Man is something to be overcome (including the thought of the *Übermensch*, the eternal recurrence, the philosopher as prophet and lawgiver, *amor fati*, and the "positivistic ideas" of the middle Nietzsche), and so on. Janz goes so far as to contend that these essays are "like a program for his whole life and thinking," and while such claims seem excessive, they nevertheless contain a good deal of truth. If we take Janz's statements as being largely true, but relativize them by combining them with a knowledge of the essays' profound debt to Emerson, they can be seen to illustrate the immense importance, not always sufficiently appreciated, of Emerson, not simply for the young Nietzsche, but also for his later philosophy.

Already, while at Schulpforta, Nietzsche's interest was oriented toward early, pre-classical Greek culture (in particular, the early poets Anacreon and Theognis of Megara, Homer and tragedy), later to be supplemented by his interest in the pre-Socratics. At this stage, then, he discerned a dichotomy between an ancient (Greek, tragic) and a modern *Weltanschauung* or "worldview." Tragedy — and a tragic *Weltanschauung* — would remain a constant contrast to modernity for Nietzsche. For example, in *Ecce Homo*, Nietzsche says that, if his attack on two millennia and his revaluation of all values succeeds, he promises "a *tragic* age: the highest art of saying 'yes' to life, tragedy, will be reborn" (ein *tragisches* Zeitalter: die höchste Kunst im Jasagen zum Leben, die Tragödie, wird wiedergeboren werden; *EH BT* §4; *KSA* 6, 313).

Nietzsche's view of tragedy can be traced back to his commentary on the first choir song of Sophocles's *King Oedipus*, entitled "Primum Oedipodis regis carmen choricum," written as a school essay at Schulpforta in Latin, Greek, and German during the spring of 1864.[11] Here

Nietzsche discusses, among other things, the origins of Greek drama. He emphasizes the difference between German and Greek drama and the importance of the choir and music in ancient times; indeed, he argues that Greek drama had its *origin* in lyric and music. He even foreshadows his great debt to Wagner: "The sublime Greeks avoided the idiocy on which our opera until this day rests — with the exception of the brilliant plans of reform and deeds of R. Wagner — the horrific misunderstanding of the relation between music and text, between tone and feeling" (wir müßten denn annehmen, daß die feinfühligen Griechen zu dem Unsinn herabgekommen wären, in dem sich unsre Oper bis auf diese Tage — die genialen Reformpläne und Thaten R. Wagners abgerechnet — befindet, zu dem ungeheuerlichen Mißverhältniß zwischen Musik und Text, zwischen Ton und Empfindung; *KGW* I.3, 17[1], 341 = *BAW* 2, 376). Although Nietzsche had not yet began to use the dichotomy between the Apollonian and the Dionysian (based as it is on a Kantian and Schopenhauerian philosophical two-world view, which he had not yet encountered), he discusses both deities and associates them with vision and music respectively. We thus see already here many of the fundamental themes of Nietzsche's first book, *The Birth of Tragedy out of the Spirit of Music* (*Die Geburt der Tragödie aus dem Geiste der Musik*, 1872).

Philosophy was not a school subject at Schulpforta, and there is little discussion of philosophy by Nietzsche while he was there. The most obvious philosophical subject and interest, apart from the fate essays, is his relation to Plato. In August 1864 Nietzsche wrote a school essay entitled "About the Relation of Alcibiades's Speech to the Other Speeches in the Platonic *Symposium*" ("Ueber das Verhältniß der Rede des Alcibiades zu den übrigen Reden des platonischen Symposions"),[12] and in a short autobiography entitled "My Life" ("Mein Leben"), which he wrote at this time on the occasion of leaving Schulpforta after six years, he stated: "I remember with the greatest pleasure the first impressions of Sophocles, Aeschylus, Plato, especially in my favorite piece, the Symposion, and then the Greek lyricists" (Ich gedenke mit der angenehmsten Erinnerung der ersten Eindrücke des Sophokles, des Aeschylos, des Plato vornehmlich in meiner Lieblingsdichtung, dem Symposion, dann der griechischen Lyriker; *KGW* I.3, 18[2], 419 = *BAW* 3:68). However, with the exception of this school essay, Nietzsche hardly ever mentioned Plato, either in letters, notes, or other school essays, before or during his time at Schulpforta. Thus it seems likely that his interest in Plato only began during his last few months there.

At university in Bonn in 1865, Nietzsche attended two courses on Plato, but these lectures — to the extent that he actually went to them — do not seem to have left any mark on his writings of the time. More generally, during his years as a university student, from 1864 to 1869, he made a large number of references to Plato, but almost all of them were scholarly and oriented toward questions of classical philology, and not directed at Plato himself or his thinking. Instead, Nietzsche used Plato and his writings at this time to discuss other topics (especially Theognis and Democritus). It is only after he became a professor at Basel in 1869 that we find evidence of a more serious consideration of Plato, Platonic philosophy, and Platonic questions in their own right and for their own sake — or, perhaps more accurately, for the sake of teaching them. He began to teach Plato at the Pädagogium during his first term in Basel, in the summer of 1869, and at the university during the winter term of 1871/1872. The other stimulus for thinking about Plato at this time was his work on *The Birth of Tragedy*. Nietzsche's independent views about Plato were beginning to emerge — both positive and negative ones, although the negative seem to have prevailed. In 1869 and 1870 he referred to Plato's ethical optimism, associating him with Socrates and Euripides as a theoretical man (*KSA* 7, 3[93]-3[94], 85), a view that he later restated in *The Birth of Tragedy*. He also referred to Plato's hostility to art at this time, a statement that he repeated a number of times in the following years. In early 1871 he again blamed Socrates, Euripides, and Plato for the separation of the Apollonian and the Dionysian, that is, for the disintegration of Greek culture (*KSA* 7, 7[70], 154), and he then made his most spectacular statement in regard to Platonism, in which he defines himself in relation to — or rather against — Plato: "My philosophy, *inverted Platonism*: the further away from true being, the more pure, beautiful, better it is. The life of appearance as goal" (Meine Philosophie *umgedrehter Platonismus*: je weiter ab vom wahrhaft Seienden, um so reiner schöner besser ist es. Das Leben im Schein als Ziel; *KSA* 7, 7[156], 199).

However, Nietzsche's references to Plato after this statement were not significantly more critical than his earlier statements. His attitude seems to have remained ambivalent, although some of the positive statements he made may merely have been efforts to engage the interest of his students (compare with the discussion below of Nietzsche's lecture notes on Plato).

Nietzsche decided to write his ambitious "Valediktionsarbeit" during his last semester at Schulpforta on the early Greek poet Theognis,[13] thereby foreshadowing or possibly initiating his later interest in, and sympathy for, the early pre-Socratic and aristocratic culture, values, and morality of the Greeks. During the first two years at university, Nietzsche revised this final school essay on Theognis and turned it into a lecture at the philological society (of which Nietzsche was a founding member and chairman for a year). He thereafter showed it to Friedrich Ritschl, who was so impressed that he recommended Nietzsche rewrite it for publication in the journal *Rheinisches Museum für Philologie*, of which Ritschl was editor. By August 1866 Nietzsche had given Ritschl the finished manuscript for what was to become his first publication.

At this time, in late 1865, Nietzsche discovered Schopenhauer's *The World as Will and Representation* (*Die Welt als Wille und Vorstellung*) in a bookshop and immediately became a Schopenhauerian. He would remain one for the next ten years, and Schopenhauerian philosophy, including pessimism, would color almost everything he wrote during this period, although he rarely wrote explicitly on these themes. During the following two years Nietzsche did his military service and was for a period seriously ill. Philologically he worked on a larger essay on Democritus, and another essay on Homer and Hesiod, continued his work on Diogenes Laertius, and (partly with the help of his sister) compiled an index for twenty-four volumes of the *Rheinisches Museum*. During his last year in Leipzig, in 1868, he began to have grave doubts about philology and considered philosophy as a better alternative.[14] In this spirit it seems that, for a short while during the spring of 1868, Nietzsche intended to write his dissertation in the field of philosophy instead of in philology, considering two closely related topics and titles: "The Concept of the Organic after Kant" and "Teleology after Kant."[15] This work was inspired by his reading of Schopenhauer and F. A. Lange, who both dealt with these questions in some detail, and by a dissertation entitled *I. Kant's Ansicht von der Willensfreiheit* (1868), written by an acquaintance, Otto Kohl, which contained an extensive critique of Schopenhauer. In several ways, these plans also connect with Nietzsche's earlier essays on fate, as well as with his thinking in his middle, more positivistic period (from 1876 to 1882).

In the notes Nietzsche wrote down in preparation for this work, which consisted of an examination and denial of the philosophical arguments for a belief in teleology (or purpose), he denies several times that the existence of life is a proof of the existence of purpose (or a divine purpose). Closely related to this are his references to Empedocles's discussion of how something apparently teleological (purposive) can come from many occurrences of something without purpose. He frequently refers to this point in the notes. Nietzsche seems to deny both teleology and that there is any fundamental difference between organic and inorganic matter. These fairly extensive notes, with a continual emphasis on eternal becoming, on *das ewig Werdende*, were often based on excerpts from Lange's *History of Materialism* (*Geschichte des Materialismus*), on Kuno Fischer's massive study of Kant's philosophy, on Kant's *Critique of Judgment* (*Kritik der Urteilskraft*), and on Schopenhauer's writings, to which Nietzsche added his own reflections and arguments. We can here see that he had by now already rejected teleology, and he seems to have, to a large extent, adopted evolutionism and naturalism.

Nietzsche had planned to have a "free" year of study in Paris in 1869 or 1870 after he had finished his dissertation. In January 1869, however, he was — on account of his articles in the *Rheinisches Museum* and strong recommendations by Ritschl — given an offer he could not refuse:

a professorship in classical philology in Basel. At the end of 1868 he had also met Richard Wagner, who rekindled and stimulated his thinking in a more idealistic and metaphysical orientation and stimulated his interests in the direction of culture in general and music in particular.

Philological Writings, 1867–73

It would be almost impossible to overestimate the importance of antiquity for Nietzsche's thinking. His *Weltanschauung*, his philosophy, and his critique of modernity (including Christianity) all have their roots in his conception of, and involvement with, antiquity. Homer, whom he encountered even before he began at Schulpforta, was probably the most important early influence. As a scholar, Nietzsche worked especially on the writings of Theognis, Simonides of Ceos, the Suda, Diogenes Laertius, and Democritus. Of these, the last two, together with Plato, were important for his philosophical development, while the first two were possibly responsible for reinforcing his aristocratic values.

Already in July 1862 Nietzsche wrote in his notebook a sentence that could stand as a motto for his whole philosophical and cultural endeavor: "I prefer the past to the present; but I believe in a better future" (Die Vergangenheit ist mir lieber als die Gegenwart; aber ich glaube an eine bessere Zukunft; *KGW* I.1, 13[10], 444 = *BAW* 2, 68). By "the past," Nietzsche, even at this early stage, meant especially Greek antiquity. In 1875 he expressed essentially the same thought, only a little differently, when he wrote: "My aim is: to create complete hostility between our modern 'culture' and the ancient world. Whosoever wants to serve the former must *hate* the latter" (Mein Ziel ist: volle Feindschaft zwischen unserer jetzigen "Cultur" und dem Alterthum zu erzeugen. Wer der ersten dienen will, muss das letztere *hassen*; *KSA* 8, 3[68], 33).[16]

Nietzsche was educated as a classical scholar, and hence was more familiar with historical methods than philosophical analysis. The method of historical criticism that Nietzsche learned at Schulpforta was one of the most important causes for his first revaluation of all his own values — his conversion from Christianity to atheism (and a corresponding deepening attachment to antiquity) in the period from 1861 to 1865. From this time on, Homer and antiquity in general took the place of the Bible in Nietzsche's *Weltanschauung*. This (relatively early) replacement of a Christian *Weltanschauung* with an ancient Greek one had a major effect on Nietzsche's overall philosophy. For a major theme of Nietzsche's early thinking, in the period from 1869 to 1875, was an attempt at the resurrection of a Greek spirit and *Weltanschauung*. Equally, however, ancient values continued to constitute an important point of reference for Nietzsche's later thinking, including his project of a revaluation of all values.

As we have seen, during the time period in question Nietzsche published a number of specialist classical philological articles and did much
other philological work that is too specialized to be discussed in detail
here. In the rest of this section we will discuss three principal areas of
Nietzsche's production from this time period that have implications
beyond classical philology: his work on an index, his inaugural lecture
on Homer's personality, and some of his extensive lecture notes from his
time as professor. (Other themes could also have been chosen.)

In the second half of 1866 Nietzsche began working on a dictionary
to Aeschylus, which soon become a less ambitious index to Aeschylus, and
in the end came to nothing; but not due to Nietzsche's fault. His teacher,
Ritschl, who edited the prestigious classical philological journal *Rheinisches Museum für Philologie*, then suggested that he could make an index
to the first twenty-four volumes of the journal. This was no small task,
and it came to occupy Nietzsche for extended periods of time the following several years until it was published at the end of 1871 or early in 1872
(at the same time as Nietzsche's *The Birth of Tragedy*). The index, which
was published as a separate booklet — without mention of Nietzsche's
name although he had done all the work himself, with a little help from
his sister — consists of 176 pages that index approximately 24,000 pages
(the volumes from 1842–69). It is probable that this booklet, which contains nothing creative by Nietzsche and is not even generally regarded as
part of the Nietzsche corpus, cost him more work and time than any of
his other twenty or so books.[17] However, it reflects his wide and detailed
philological reading and knowledge, and the work on it constitutes an
important background and source of information, and perhaps of ideas,
for his work on *The Birth of Tragedy* and for his thinking generally.

Besides Socrates and Plato, Homer is the figure from antiquity to
whom Nietzsche refers most frequently in all his published writings, and
here we have a chance to connect Nietzsche's early thought with his later,
better-known works. Of special interest are those references that reflect
Nietzsche's response to Homer's *Weltanschauung*, ethics, and values.
For Nietzsche claims that Homer's art reflects a happy soul, and he views
him as a creator of gods and as an artist of apotheosis. Like Thucydides,
Homer is regarded as a realist, and as such Nietzsche sees him as someone
who, in contrast to Socrates and Plato, denies generality and abstraction,
as he would later write in *Human, All Too Human* (*HA* "Wanderer and
His Shadow" §6; *KSA* 2, 542–43). Equally important is the way in which
Homer represents and expresses aristocratic values, based on the fundamental value-dichotomy of noble versus contemptible, rather than good
versus evil. At the same time Nietzsche sees in Homer a reflection of his
own views on ethics, his *Weltanschauung* and beliefs as an "immoralist."
In *Human, All Too Human*, the belief that the evil (or the bad) should
not be denied or attempted to be reformed away (*HA* "Assorted Opinions

and Maxims" §220; *KSA* 2, 474), and that good and evil (or good and bad) belong together (*HA* "Assorted Opinions and Maxims" §212; *KSA* 2, 469), implies greatness requires both good and evil. Homer also represents immoralism, in the sense that great men will always be skeptics, possessing the right to deny or throw off any system or set of values (*KSA* 12, 9[157], 428). Furthermore, in *On the Genealogy of Morals*, Nietzsche affirms the Homeric view that the misdeeds of mortals are "foolishness, *not* sin!" (Thorheit, *nicht* Sünde! *GM* II §23; *KSA* 5, 334). This illustrates well the contrast between, on the one hand, Homer and Nietzsche, and, on the other, Christianity and modern morality. Finally, as if summarizing his view of Homer's realism, his affirmation of life and his healthy character, Nietzsche writes: "Plato *versus* Homer: that is the complete, the genuine antagonism — there the sincerest advocate of the 'beyond,' the great slanderer of life; here the instinctive deifier, the *golden* nature" (Plato *gegen* Homer: das ist der ganze, der ächte Antagonismus — dort der "Jenseitige" besten Willens, der grosse Verleumder des Lebens, hier dessen unfreiwilliger Vergöttlicher, die *goldene* Natur; *GM* III §25; *KSA* 5, 402–3).

Nietzsche chose to talk about Homer, and how Homer has been regarded in classical philology, in his inaugural lecture, entitled "On Homer's Personality" (Über die Persönlichkeit Homers), subsequently printed privately by Nietzsche under the title *Homer and Classical Philology* (*Homer und die klassische Philologie*), which he delivered in Basel in May 1869.[18] This is Nietzsche's earliest and also most extensive discussion of Homer. Much of the lecture deals with the methods and goals of classical philology, and how this relates to our understanding of Homer today. A prominent theme is Nietzsche's discussion of the dualism between art and scholarship, between an aesthetic and a historic understanding of antiquity and of Homer. Like Friedrich August Wolf (a classical scholar who influenced Barthold Georg Niebuhr and Leopold von Ranke and, together with them, was the father of the new historical approach and methods), to whom he approvingly refers, Nietzsche affirms *both* the ideal and *Bildung* associated with art *and* the newly discovered truths and methods of scholarship. At the end of the lecture he attempts, somewhat provocatively, a sort of synthesis between them (while giving priority to *Bildung*), citing as his Latin motto "philosophia facta est quae philologia fuit," which means: "that which has been philology has become philosophy." In other words, the details of philological scholarship need be placed into a philosophical *Weltanschauung*, which alone can give sense to them. This realization of the importance of history and scholarship, as well as his tendency to regard them as less important than good philosophy, would characterize almost all of Nietzsche's later thinking.

Nietzsche's lecture notes from his time as professor in Basel constitute nearly two thousand pages (see *KGW*, section II, volumes 2–5).

These notes form the basis for the various series of lectures Nietzsche gave during this period, and several of these series of notes (or parts of them) are interesting and relevant for various questions and themes, not all of them connected to philology. Of especial philosophical interest are the two lecture series, "Introduction to the Study of the Platonic Dialogues" ("Einführung in das Studium der platonischen Dialoge") and "The Pre-Platonic Philosophers" ("Die vorplatonischen Philosophen"), of around 180 and 155 printed pages, respectively, and we will restrict our discussion to those texts.

At the University of Basel, Nietzsche lectured on Plato during the winter terms of 1871/1872 and 1873/1874, the summer term of 1876, and finally during the winter term of 1878/1879.[19] Anyone who expects the notes for these lectures to contain an account of Nietzsche's interpretation of Plato and his philosophy is likely to find them disappointing. The purpose of the lectures was, after all, to introduce students to Plato, and therefore they do not so much contain Nietzsche's own interpretation as offer general summaries of Plato's writings and philosophy, based mainly on secondary literature and on reformulations of Plato's texts. So in these lecture notes it is Nietzsche the conscientious teacher, rather than Nietzsche the iconoclastic philosopher who is speaking. Furthermore, it should be remembered that the courses were given to students of classical philology rather than to students of philosophy, and hence much of the discussion concerns philological questions. It is therefore sometimes difficult to know which parts of the notes are in Nietzsche's own voice, which derive from secondary literature (which he used when writing his lectures), and which are simply paraphrase of issues under discussion.

The lectures themselves consist of two parts. The notes begin with a brief introduction of about two pages, which is of considerable interest. In it Nietzsche emphasizes his interest in the man Plato, rather than in his philosophy: "Examinations of this kind have their eye on either the philosophy or the philosopher; we want the latter: we only use the system. The man is still more remarkable than his books" (Bei Untersuchungen der Art ist es entweder auf die Philosophie oder auf den Philosophen abgesehen; wir wollen das letztere: wir benutzen das System nur. Der Mensch noch merkwürdiger als seine Bücher; KGW II.4, 7). The early Nietzsche (of around 1869 to 1876) was sympathetic to metaphysics, or at least to a sort of metaphysics of aesthetics, and he agreed with Kant's attempt to find the limits of reason (in order to find room for other, artistic and subconscious, aspects of life). Already on the first page of the notes he approves of, criticizes, and goes beyond Plato, all at once:

> The theory of ideas is something fantastic, an invaluable preparation for Kantian idealism. Here is taught, with every means, including that of myths, the correct opposition between Ding-an-sich and

appearance: with which every more profound philosophy begins: while here always the usual opposition between body and intellect needs to be overcome.

[Die Ideenlehre ist etwas sehr Erstaunliches, eine unschätzbare Vorbereitung für den Kantischen Idealismus. Hier wird mit allen Mitteln, auch dem des Mythus, der richtige Gegensatz von Ding an sich und Erscheinung gelehrt: womit jede tiefere Philosophie beginnt: während hier immer erst der übliche Gegensatz von Körper und Geist zu überwinden ist. (*KGW* II.4, 7–8)][20]

Early in this introduction Nietzsche emphasizes that Plato's writings also constitute a substitute for the great writings of the pre-Platonic philosophers, whose writings have largely been lost.

In the introduction, and further on in the lectures, Nietzsche highlights how Plato, although an artist, was primarily motivated by ethical and political objectives. "We should not regard him as a systematic thinker [. . .], but as a political agitator" ("Wir dürfen ihn nicht als Systematiker [. . .] betrachten, sondern als agitatorischen Politiker"), he says (*KGW* II.4, 9). In this spirit he also claims that "the *Republic* is much more of a fundamental text than the *Gorgias* or the *Symposion*, but is nonetheless of much lower aesthetic level" (Die Republik ist vielmehr eine Hauptschrift als der Gorgias oder das Symposion u. doch aesthetisch viel geringer; *KGW* II.4, 14). The early Nietzsche frequently discussed the *Republic*, but from around the middle of the 1870s it seems that he lost interest in this text. The interpretation of Plato as primarily an ethical and political thinker is part of Nietzsche's own opposition to Plato, for Nietzsche himself emphasized the importance of aesthetic perspectives, at least in *The Birth of Tragedy*. This is largely what Nietzsche meant when, in the passage cited above, he referred to his own philosophy as "*inverted Platonism*"; "the life of appearance" refers to life in (and for) art. The actual lectures begin with an extensive discussion of the secondary literature (around twenty pages) followed by a second section (around thirty pages), where Plato's life is discussed in considerable philological detail. Thereafter, in the longest section (around 100 pages), the individual dialogues are summarized and sometimes briefly discussed. Most dialogues are summarized within two to three pages, but the section opens with a thirteen-page summary and discussion of the *Republic*.

Philosophically, the most interesting part of the lecture notes is the second part, entitled "Plato's Philosophy as Witness to the Man Plato" ("Platons Philosophie als Hauptzeugniß für den Menschen Plato"), of around forty pages in length. This begins with the words, written even above the title: "In the first chapter we have made the problems generally known, reference to *my* thesis. To be able to correctly understand the *life* we need to have an overall *psychological* picture as a point of reference"

(Im ersten Capitel mit den Probl. allgemein bekannt gemacht, auf *meine* These hingewiesen. Um das *Leben* recht zu verstehen, müssen wir ein *psycholog.* Gesammtbild als Regulativ haben; *KGW* II.4, 148). He summarizes Plato's position in the following words:

> Picture the perfect philosopher. He lives completely among pure abstractions, sees and hears nothing any longer, values no longer what other humans value, hates the real world and attempts to spread his contempt. [. . .] [Plato] fights for life and death against all existing political organizations and was a revolutionary of the most radical sort [. . .] very soon a tyrannic streak can be seen.

> [Bild des vollkommenen Philosophen. Er lebt ganz in den reinsten Abstractionen, sieht u. hört nicht mehr, schätzt nicht mehr, was die Menschen schätzen, haßt die wirkliche Welt u. sucht seine Verachtung zu verbreiten. [. . .] Das heißt, er kämpfte auf Leben und Tod gegen alle bestehenden Staatsverhältnisse an und war ein Revolutionär der radikalsten Art. [. . .] sehr bald zeigt sie eine tyrannische Ader. (*KGW* II.4, 154–55)]

In several sections he discusses the importance for Plato of the "Ideenlehre" (or the doctrine of Platonic Ideas) and of the immortality of the soul, and holds that life is determined by a metaphysical assumption (as shown, for example, in the myths of the *Republic*, the *Phaedo*, and the *Gorgias*). We can thus see that Nietzsche treats and interprets Plato in a relatively conventional manner as a metaphysical philosopher, which is also how he uses Plato in his published books.

Nietzsche had a special interest in (and affinity with) the pre-Socratic, or pre-Platonic, philosophers in general. This interest almost certainly evolved from his earlier interest in tragedy and in the pre-classical Greek *Weltanschauung* and literature, especially his work on Theognis, and from his interest in Homer, Aeschylus, Sophocles, and several of the early Greek poets, such as Pindar and Anacreon. The first of the pre-Socratics to whom he studied, philologically and philosophically, was Democritus (most intensively during 1867 and 1868), but he never finished the planned philological article on Democritus on which he was working at that time. After he became a professor in 1869, he developed a specific enthusiasm that focused primarily on Heraclitus and, to a lesser extent, on Empedocles.

Nietzsche's interest in the pre-Socratics is shown and most extensively expressed in his notes to his lectures on "The Pre-Platonic Philosophers," which he delivered three times between 1872 and 1876;[21] in his never-completed companion volume to *The Birth of Tragedy*, to be entitled "Philosophy in the Tragic Age of the Greeks," but also in much of his *Nachlass* from the first half of the 1870s.

After a longer introduction, Nietzsche turns in his lectures on the pre-Platonic philosophers to the most well-known of the pre-Socratics: namely, Thales, Anaximander, Anaximenes, Pythagoras, Heraclitus, Parmenides (and Xenophanes), Zeno of Elea, Anaxagoras, Empedocles, Leucippus and Democritus, the Pythagoreans, and Socrates (including some discussion of the Sophists). Although substantial parts of the lectures concern philological questions and presentations, Nietzsche's own voice can be heard throughout, and he attempts to make the seven fundamentally different *Weltanschauungen* that he finds in their thinking comprehensible to the modern listener (or reader) by including brief discussions of modern science and philosophers such as Kant, F. A. Lange, and Locke. For example, he emphasizes that in several important ways Kantian idealism stands in opposition to that of Parmenides and Zeno.[22] These lectures also constitute the material out of which, in the following year, "Philosophy in the Tragic Age of the Greeks" began to be constructed.

The Unpublished Works from 1870 to 1873

These writings can be divided into three categories: (1) texts that constitute early stages of what was to become *The Birth of Tragedy*; (2) the pedagogically-oriented text, "On the Future of Our Educational Institutions" ("Ueber die Zukunft unserer Bildungsanstalten"); and (3) other texts from the period of 1872 to 1873. It is the texts in this third category that have, rightly, attracted most attention from critics and commentators.

But let us turn, first, to those texts that represent early stages on Nietzsche's way to *The Birth of Tragedy*.[23] This work bears as its date of publication the year 1872, and the first copies of the book arrived in Nietzsche's hands in the first days of January. Some of the ideas contained in it go back, as we have seen above, at least as far as Nietzsche's Schulpforta days, but as far as most of its concrete content is concerned, the first half of the year 1870 is seminal, even though Nietzsche continued to work intensively on it during much of 1871. In early 1870, he gave two lectures: on 18 January, "The Greek Music Drama" ("Das griechische Musikdrama") and, on 1 February, "Socrates and Tragedy" ("Socrates und die Tragödie"); while in the summer of the same year he wrote the essay "The Dionysian World-View" ("Die dionysische Weltanschauung").[24] These works contain many of the fundamental ideas of *The Birth of Tragedy*; the first lecture sketches much of the general content of the book, especially as far as the origin of tragedy is concerned (cf. *BT* §5–§10) and the Wagnerian view that Greek tragedy should be seen as an all-inclusive-work-of-art, or *Gesamtkunstwerk*. The second lecture contains much of what is said in *The Birth of Tragedy* about the decline of tragedy due to Socrates (and Euripides), sometimes almost word for word (cf. *BT* §11–§15), while the essay on the Dionysian *Weltanschauung* brings together much of the text of the two lectures and adds the *leitmotif* of *The Birth of Tragedy*, the dichotomy between the Apollonian and the Dionysian (cf. *BT* §1–§4). However, these texts also contain concepts, ideas, and emphases that were eventually not included in *The Birth of Tragedy*, and are valuable to read not only as early versions of that book, but also because they show how Nietzsche sought to interpret Greek antiquity and tragedy.[25]

Nietzsche always maintained an interest in education and in *Bildung*. It is a topic that is present throughout his writings, including in his last books: for example, in the short chapter entitled "What the Germans Lack" ("Was den Deutschen abgeht") in *Twilight of the Idols* (*Götzen-Dämmerung*; *KSA* 6, 103–10). His earliest extended views in this field, which are strongly colored by Wagner's, find expression in his essay "On the Future of Our Educational Institutions."[26] The text is based on five public lectures (he seems never to have held the sixth and final lecture, although it had been planned and announced) given during the first months of 1872 (that is, just after *The Birth of Tragedy* had been published). His experiences at Schulpforta and with the small cultural society Germania, together with those gained as a teacher at Basel, determined much of its content. It seems that during the early part of 1872 Nietzsche had plans to publish the lectures, even writing two prefaces for them, but later that year he became dissatisfied with them and decided against publication. In them, however, Nietzsche criticizes, with much pathos, modern higher education and *Bildung*, largely because of their insistence that education be useful, reducing education to a narrow specialist training. In Nietzsche's eyes, modern education also falls short because it is aimed at and includes the many, rather than the few, and because it has become subordinated to the state. Against this Nietzsche sets up Greek antiquity, and more broadly philosophy as inspired by Schopenhauer and by Wagner.

Of the other projects undertaken by Nietzsche in the period 1872 to 1873, three in particular stand out: his "Five Prefaces for Five Unwritten Books" ("Fünf Vorreden zu fünf ungeschriebenen Büchern"), "On Truth and Lies in a Non-Moral Sense" ("Ueber Wahrheit und Lüge im aussermoralischen Sinne"), and "Philosophy in the Tragic Age of the Greeks." At the very end of 1872, Nietzsche wrote down five texts that he called "Five Prefaces for Five Unwritten Books" and sent them, bound in leather, as a gift to Cosima Wagner.[27] They vary in length from three to fourteen pages, and, not surprisingly, overlap with or supplement his other early writings. The titles of the five unwritten books are "On the Pathos of Truth" ("Ueber das Pathos der Wahrheit"), "Thoughts on the Future of Our Educational Institutions" ("Gedanken über die Zukunft unserer Bildungsanstalten"), "The Greek State" ("Der griechische Staat"), "The Relation between Schopenhauerian Philosophy and a German Culture" ("Das Verhältniss der Schopenhauerischen Philosophie zu einer deutschen Culture"), and "Homer's Contest" ("Homer's Wettkampf").

All the "prefaces" revolve around the themes of Greek antiquity, philosophy, history, and *Bildung*. It should be remembered that none of them was meant for publication; in letters, Nietzsche expanded the title as "Five Prefaces for Five Unwritten (and Not to Be Written) Books" ("Fünf Vorreden zu fünf ungeschriebenen und nicht zu schreibenden Büchern").[28] In the first preface Nietzsche discusses truth and knowledge and their relation to art, with frequent references to Heraclitus (and, implicitly, to Schopenhauer). These themes are also present in *The Birth of Tragedy*, which had already been published, and Nietzsche returned to them in "On Truth and Lies in a Non-Moral Sense" and in "Philosophy in the Tragic Age of the Greeks." In his letter to Erwin Rohde of 31 January 1873, he states that it is the first preface, on the "pathos of truth," that is the important one (*KSB* 4, 120). In this text Nietzsche suggests that Man is "eternally condemned to untruth" (ewig zur Unwahrheit verdammt; *KSA* 1, 760), and he ends with the conclusion that "art is more powerful than knowledge, because *it* desires life, whereas knowledge attains as its final goal only — annihilation" (die Kunst ist mächtiger als die Erkenntniß, denn *sie* will das Leben, und jene erreicht als letztes Ziel nur — die Vernichtung; *KSA* 1, 760). This statement can be compared to Nietzsche's similar arguments in the second *Untimely Meditation* (on history) and in the third essay of *On the Genealogy of Morals* (*Zur Genealogie der Moral*).

The second preface is a reworked version of the second preface to "On the Future of Our Educational Institutions," but in its content it is not limited to that work. A modern reader will be reminded of, among others, the prefaces to *Daybreak* (*Morgenröthe*) and *The Anti-Christ* (*Der Antichrist*), inasmuch as, here as there, Nietzsche discusses the sort of reader he wants: one of the few who read slowly, with an open mind and with a sense of distance, and who at the same time think while they are reading (and continue thinking after reading) and who can, moreover, read between the lines.

In the third text, as in the other prefaces, Nietzsche sets up a dichotomy between the ancient Greek world and modernity — and then criticizes the latter in the light of the former. This preface is strongly Schopenhauerian and Wagnerian in spirit, and although important aspects of the mature Nietzsche can be discerned, there is much that he was soon to leave behind. Nietzsche sets up a further dichotomy between politics and culture, arguing that slavery belongs to the essence of a culture. The value of existence is, frankly, nil, apart from the creation of art and of geniuses. But modern man has become weak, and regards the state only as a means to further his personal egotism, whereas Greek politics produced Greek society, Greek culture, and Greek geniuses.

In the fourth short text Nietzsche adopts a Schopenhauerian perspective from which to view, critically, "contemporary German culture," above all its use of (and relation to) history, rejecting it as being pedestrian and philistine, lacking in ideals and enthusiasm. This text thus adumbrates both the second and, to a lesser extent, the third of the *Untimely Meditations* (on history and on Schopenhauer, respectively).

In the final preface, "Homer's Contest," Nietzsche argues that when we speak of humaneness it can appear as if this trait in us is something separate from what is natural, but that this is not, in fact, the case — for Man is all nature. The Greeks, the most humane people in antiquity, also carried in them a streak of cruelty, but it is a streak that can be most fruitful for culture. Early Greek culture in particular placed great emphasis on the importance of strife, struggle, and contest (even if there existed two kinds of strife, good and bad), and there is nothing that more separates their world from ours. We today fear ambition, while they affirmed competition and contest, and thus transformed hatred and cruelty into stimuli to great deeds and to the creation of great human beings. Nietzsche would return to the role of cruelty in the second essay of *On the Genealogy of Morals*.

Of all the early texts written by Nietzsche, "Philosophy in the Tragic Age of the Greeks" is arguably the most important; by far the longest, it can be read in several different ways.[29] It can be read as an interesting account of early Greek thinking (about the origin of philosophy); or as offering insight into Nietzsche's relation to the pre-Socratics; or it can be read as an expression of Nietzsche's early views concerning the task and nature of philosophy. Here, there is not space for anything more than a brief paraphrase and general discussion of this text, which Nietzsche conceived of as a companion volume to *The Birth of Tragedy* (its proximity to which is visible even in its title). In the latter work, Nietzsche placed art at the center, while in this present text he attempts to give that same place to philosophy.

Nietzsche worked on this incomplete but extensive manuscript during 1872 and in early 1873, and there exist two short prefaces (quoted above at the beginning of our chapter), the second of which Nietzsche probably dictated to his mother as late as in the winter of 1875/1876. Once again working within a fundamentally Schopenhauerian perspective, Nietzsche here treats early Greek philosophers, not primarily (as is usual) as leading up to the classical philosophers, but instead as thinkers deserving even greater interest in their own right and as expressing several different versions of a tragic *Weltanschauung*, in which a fundamental insight — that existence is without meaning — is transformed into a redeeming worldview. After an introduction and having discussed Thales and Anaximander, the text reaches a crescendo in its sections (§5 to §8) about Heraclitus, which end with the resounding words: "What he saw, *the teaching of the law in becoming and of play in necessity*, must be eternally kept in sight from now on" (Das, was er schaute, *die Lehre vom Gesetz im Werden und vom Spiel in der Nothwendigkeit*, muß von jetzt ab ewig geschaut werden; *KSA* 1, 835).[30] It is possible to argue that Heraclitus, as a less metaphysical and more life-affirming thinker, helped Nietzsche to begin his transcendence of Schopenhauerian philosophy and pessimism. Nietzsche's discussion and analysis of Parmenides and the Eleatic school (in sections §9 to §13) is less sympathetic, and he describes their thinking as abstract and wholly petrified by logical rigidity. In his treatment of Heraclitus and Parmenides, one can see how Nietzsche is already separating historical from metaphysical philosophy, and affirms the former over the latter. Throughout the text, but especially in the last sections on Anaxagoras (§14 to §19), Nietzsche discusses in some detail the problems of change and movement, as well as how to think about the one and the many fundamental substances proposed by these thinkers. Nietzsche's discussions in this work of questions relating to truth and knowledge differ rather substantially from what he says in "On Truth and Lies in a Non-Moral Sense." The two works also differ, as Giorgio Colli has pointed out, in their view of time, which is seen as subjective in the one and as objective in the other (*KSA* 1, 918–19). As in *The Birth of Tragedy*, Nietzsche challenges traditional classical scholarship by being subjective, freely interpretative, and by almost completely ignoring philological methods and conventions.

By 1872, as a classical philologist dedicated to Schopenhauer's philosophy, Nietzsche had developed a philosophy of language under the influence of F. A. Lange, Eduard von Hartmann, and Kant.[31] In September 1872, Nietzsche borrowed Gustav Gerber's *Die Sprache als Kunst* (*Language as Art*) (1871), and used it extensively for the notes to his lectures "Description of Ancient Rhetoric" ("Darstellung der antiken Rhetorik"), which he gave during the winter term of 1872/1873;[32] and much of the content of Gerber's book also found its way into Nietzsche's text "On Truth and Lies in a Non-Moral Sense," which he dictated to Gersdorff during the summer of 1873 on the basis of notes he had written the previous year.[33] This interesting text has received much attention, but one would do well to remember that it was not intended for publication, and it appears that Nietzsche never even mentioned it in a single letter. In this text, Nietzsche discusses and criticizes the concept of objective truth and knowledge, arguing that, because they are based on language, they amount to no more than illusions and self-contradictions. The text opens with a beautiful, short, pessimistic fable, which aims to show how aimless and arbitrary the human intellect looks within nature. Nietzsche then asks, "What then is truth?" (Was ist also Wahrheit?), and he answers:

A movable host of metaphors, metonymies, and anthropomorphisms: in short, a sum of human relations that have been poetically and rhetorically intensified, transferred, and embellished, and that, after long usage, seem to a people to be fixed, canonical, and bind-ing. Truths are illusions which we have forgotten are illusions.

[Ein bewegliches Heer von Metaphern, Metonymien, Anthropo-morphismen kurz eine Summe von menschlichen Relationen, die, poetisch und rhetorisch gesteigert, übertragen, geschmückt wurden, und die nach langem Gebrauche einem Volke fest, canonisch und verbindlich dünken: die Wahrheiten sind Illusionen, von denen man vergessen hat, dass sie welche sind. (*KSA* 1, 880–81)]

We can only find in language, as in nature, what we ourselves already have put there. Nietzsche treats language as rhetorical: we are forced to con-tinually lie, and we are unable to escape mere appearance. On the other hand, Nietzsche emphasizes that it is precisely this fact that turns us into creators and artists. The text ends with an unresolved dichotomy between two different desires to rule over life: between the "rational" and prudent as opposed to the intuitive and artistic.

Thus in many of these early texts, we come across themes that would later appear and sometimes determine the contents of his later, published books. Especially prominent are the different aspects of Greek thought and values, and, as we have seen, the continual tension between a scien-tific, philosophical view of the world and a more artistic, aesthetic one.

Notes

In this essay, the following translations have been used: Friedrich Nietzsche, *"The Birth of Tragedy" and "The Case of Wagner,"* trans. Walter Kaufmann (New York: Random House, 1967); Friedrich Nietzsche, *Beyond Good and Evil* (New York: Random House, 1973); and Friedrich Nietzsche, *Ecce Homo*, trans. Duncan Large (Oxford: Oxford UP, 2009). The translations from the German of Nietzsche's early, unpublished material are my own.

Acknowledgement: This work has received support from the Swedish Research Council: 2009-1547.

[1] Johann Figl, "Vorwort," in *KGW* I.1, v–xiv (here: v).

[2] The German critical edition of Nietzsche's writings exists in two versions, *KSA* and *KGW* (where many volumes are still to come). The former contains his pub-lished works, volumes 1 to 6, and his notes, volumes 7 to 13, with two further volumes with philological commentary and chronology. The first volume also contains some by Nietzsche unpublished essays and lectures, those discussed in the third category in this present study. For other works, and for more detailed philological commentaries, one needs to go to *KGW*. It is divided into sections. The first one contains his non-philological writing before 1869, and consists of five volumes (to be supplemented by a philological commentary in the future). Most of this material, including a few of the lecture-notes, had earlier been pub-lished in the five volume edition called the *BAW*. The first volume of section two,

KGW II.1, contains Nietzsche's philological publications, with four further volumes which contain his lecture notes from the time as professor in Basel, from 1869 to 1879 (to be supplemented by philological commentary in the future).

[3] See Friedrich Nietzsche, *Philosophy in the Tragic Age of the Greeks*, trans. Marianne Cowan (Chicago: Gateway, 1962), 23–25.

[4] See *KGW* I.1, 281–311 = *BAW* 1, 1–32.

[5] The essay is published in *KGW* I.2, 12[1]-12[2], 338–41 = *BAW* 2, 1–5. The essay is dated 19 October 1861, and it has been translated into English by Christopher Middleton in his excellent *Selected Letters of Friedrich Nietzsche* (Indianapolis; Cambridge: Hackett, 1969), 4–6.

[6] *KGW* I.2, 13[6]-13[7], 431–37, and 437–40. See also *KGW* I.2, 12[27]-12[30], 381–83, and *KGW* I.2, 13[5], 430 (previously published in *BAW* 2, 54–59 and 60–62). These important essays have been translated and published in English, with valuable comments and discussions, in George J. Stack, "Nietzsche's Earliest Essays: Translation and Commentary on "Fate and History" and "Freedom of Will and Fate," *Philosophy Today*, vol. 37, no. 2 (Summer 1993): 153–69.

[7] Nietzsche, "Freedom of Will and Fate," trans. Stack, 154.

[8] Nietzsche, "Freedom of Will and Fate," trans. Stack, 156.

[9] Karl Jaspers, *Nietzsche: An Introduction to the Understanding of His Philosophical Activity*, trans. Charles F. Wallraff and Frederick J. Schmitz (New York and London: UP of America, 1965), 56 and 367.

[10] Curt Paul Janz, *Friedrich Nietzsche*, 3 volumes (Munich and Vienna: Hanser, 1978; second revised ed., 1993), vol. 1, 98–104 (98 and 103).

[11] See *KGW* I.3, 17[1], 329–64 = *BAW* 2, 364–99.

[12] *KGW* I.3, 17[12], 384–88 = *BAW* 2, 420–24.

[13] See "De Theognide Megarensi," in *KGW* I.3, 18[2], 420–63 = *BAW* 3, 21–64.

[14] See, for example, Nietzsche's letter to Paul Deussen of the second half of October 1868 (*KSB* 2, 327–30).

[15] See Nietzsche's letters to Erwin Rohde of 3 April 1868 (*KSB* 2, 261–65) and to Paul Deussen of the end of April/early May 1868 (*KSB* 2, 267–71). In this second letter, Nietzsche claims that his dissertation will be half-philosophical, half-natural-scientific, and that the preliminary work was already almost finished; Nietzsche's notes for this work have been published in *KGW* I.4, 62[3]-62[57], 548–78, and in *BAW* 3, 371–94.

[16] This is part of the notes to Nietzsche's planned *Untimely Meditation*, entitled "Wir Philologen" ("We Classicists"); see Friedrich Nietzsche, *Unmodern Observations*, ed. and trans. William Arrowsmith (New Haven and London: Yale UP, 1990), 341.

[17] For a longer discussion of this work, see Thomas Brobjer, "Nietzsche's Forgotten Book: The Index to the *Rheinisches Museum für Philologie*," *New Nietzsche Studies* 4 (2000): 157–61.

[18] See *KGW* II.1, 247–69.

[19] See *KGW* II.4, 1–188.

20 In "Die Philosophie im tragischen Zeitalter der Griechen" ("Philosophy in the Tragic Age of the Greeks"), section 10, Nietzsche expresses this need to overcome the opposition between body and intellect even more strongly (*KSA* 1, 839–44). A similar statement to this one is made about the relation between Plato and Kant, but in regard to morality and a moral "beyond," in a footnote (*KGW* II.4, 87). In his lectures entitled "Encyclopädie der klassischen Philologie" ("Encyclopedia of Classical Philology"), first held in the summer of 1871, Nietzsche recommended to philologists that they should study philosophy and see the grand perspectives, and for this purpose he especially recommended the unity of Plato's and Kant's thinking (*KGW* II.3, 372).

21 See *KGW* II.4, 207–362. It is not known for certain whether Nietzsche gave these lectures for the first time in the winter term of 1869/1870 (when they were first announced) or in the summer term of 1872. He thereafter gave them in the winter term of 1875/1876, and for the last time in the summer term of 1876. Considering our knowledge about when Nietzsche read the pre-Socratics, the summer semester of 1872 is the more likely alternative (that is also the conclusion of the editors in *KGW* II.7/1, 150). These lectures have been translated into English with a "reconstructive editorial strategy" in Friedrich Nietzsche, *The Pre-Platonic Philosophers*, ed. and trans. Greg Whitlock (Urbana and Chicago: U of Illinois P, 2001; 2006).

22 See *KGW* II.4, 294–95 and 301.

23 All of these texts are published in *KSA* 1, 513–640.

24 Toward the end of 1870, Nietzsche copied the text of "The Dionysian Worldview," making some minor variations and changing its title to "Die Geburt des tragischen Gedankens" ("The Birth of Tragic Thought"). He gave the work as a present to Cosima Wagner.

25 During his intensive work on *The Birth of Tragedy* in 1871, Nietzsche had an early version of the text privately printed under the title "Sokrates und die griechische Tragoedie" ("Socrates and Greek Tragedy"). These thirty-eight or so printed pages correspond to §11–§12, §8–§10, and §12–§15 of *The Birth of Tragedy*.

26 See *KSA* 1, 641–752.

27 See *KSA* 1, 753–92.

28 See Nietzsche's letters of 23 December 1872 to Carl von Gersdorff and of 4 January 1873 to Erwin Rohde (*KSB* 4, 108 and 110).

29 See *KSA* 1, 799–872; and *Philosophy in the Tragic Age of the Greeks*, trans. Cowan.

30 Nietzsche, *Philosophy in the Tragic Age of the Greeks*, trans. Cowan, 68.

31 See Claudia Crawford, *The Beginnings of Nietzsche's Theory of Language* (Berlin and New York: Walter de Gruyter, 1988).

32 Nietzsche's dependence on Gerber was first pointed out by Philippe Lacoue-Labarthe and Jean-Luc Nancy in "Friedrich Nietzsche: Rhétorique et langage," *Poétique* 5 (1971): 99–142, and has subsequently been more extensively examined by Anthonie Meijers and Martin Stingelin in "Konkordanz zu den wörtlichen Abschriften und Übernahmen von Beispielen und Zitaten aus Gustav Gerber:

Die Sprache als Kunst (Bromberg 1871) in Nietzsches Rhetorik-Vorlesung und in 'Ueber Wahrheit und Lüge im aussermoralischen Sinne,'" *Nietzsche-Studien* 17 (1988): 350–68, and by Tilman Borsche, "Natur-Sprache: Herder — Humboldt — Nietzsche," in Tilman Borsche, Frederico Gerratana, and Aldo Venturelli, eds., *"Centauren-Geburten": Wissenschaft, Kunst und Philosophie beim jungen Nietzsche* (Berlin and New York: Walter de Gruyter, 1994), 112–30 (this work contains several further interesting and informative papers on Nietzsche's relation to language). For further discussion, see the numerous references in Hans G. Hödl, *Nietzsches frühe Sprachkritik: Lektüren zu "Über Wahrheit und Lüge im aussermoralischen Sinne"* (Vienna: WUV Universitätsverlag, 1997).

33 *KSA* 1, 873–90. It has been translated into English several times, but here I am using the version offered in *Philosophy and Truth: Selections from Nietzsche's Notebooks of the Early 1870s*, ed. and trans. Daniel Breazeale (London: Humanities Press International, 1979; 1991), 84.

Link to *The Birth of Tragedy*

Following his inaugural lecture on Homer, Nietzsche settled in to his professorial duties: to his teaching, his research, and to socializing with his university colleagues, including the philologists Jacob Mähly and Hermann Usener. His lecture on Homer had made a favorable impression, or so Nietzsche initially thought (see his letters to Erwin Rohde of 29 May 1869 and to Franziska Nietzsche of mid-June 1869; *KSB* 3, 13 and 15). Writing to Rohde a few months later, however, in mid-July 1869, Nietzsche sounded more cautious: "With my 'colleagues' I am having a strange experience: I feel among them as I used to feel among students: entirely without any need to get to know them more closely, but also without any envy" (An meinen "Collegen" mache ich eine seltsame Erfahrung: ich fühle mich unter ihnen, wie ich mich ehedem unter Studenten fühlte: im Ganzen ohnes jedes Bedürfniß mich mit ihnen näher abzugeben, aber auch ohne allen Neid); and Nietzsche went so far as to admit: "In fact, to be truthful, I feel a small grain of contempt for them in me, with which very polite and obliging intercourse goes indeed quite well" (ja genau genommen, fühle ich einen kleinen Gran von Verachtung gegen sie in mir, mit dem sich ja ein sehr höflicher und gefälliger Verkehr ganz gut verträgt; *KSB* 3, 28).

One of Nietzsche's coping strategies was his status as a guest at Tribschen, where he regularly visited Richard Wagner[1] — and Cosima, too.[2] The proximity of the Wagners was, he told them, his "comfort" (Trost; *KSB* 3, 17). The friendship with the Wagners blossomed, and even survived Nietzsche's conversion to vegetarianism. And when Erwin Rohde visited Nietzsche in Basel in May and June 1870, he was impressed by Nietzsche's renditions on the piano of scenes from *Die Meistersinger von Nürnberg*.

Among his colleagues in Basel, Nietzsche developed firm friendships outside philological circles with the cultural historian Jacob Burckhardt (1818–97)[3] and the theologian Franz Overbeck (1837–1905).[4] But in terms of international relations, developments were afoot: on 15 July 1870, the French parliament declared war on Prussia, and the Franco-Prussian War began. According to Nietzsche's account in *Ecce Homo*, and to his "Attempt at a Self-Criticism" appended to the work's second edition, the genesis of *The Birth of Tragedy* (*Die Geburt der Tragödie*) goes back to the Franco-Prussian War of 1870–71 — to be precise, to the Battle of Wörth, during which Nietzsche was posted as a medical orderly in the French town of Metz (*EH BT* §1; *KSA* 6, 309–10, and *BT* "Attempt" §1; *KSA* 1, 11). (When the war broke out, Nietzsche saw it as his patriotic duty to enroll for service, and at the front he contracted diphtheria.) Although Nietzsche places the significance of his work in a military-political context, its central thrust is a cultural-political one.

On hearing of the declaration of the Franco-Prussian War, Nietzsche wrote an excited letter to Erwin Rohde on 16 July 1870, but the excitement was not about the war itself but about what would come after: "We could already be at the beginning of the end! What a laying-waste! We shall need monasteries again. And we shall be the first brothers" (Wir können bereits am Anfang von Ende sein! Welche Wüstenei! Wir werden wieder Klöster brauchen. Und wir werden die ersten fratres sein; *KSB* 3, 130–31). (Rohde would pick up on this idea of a secular monastery in his letter to Nietzsche of 11 December 1870 [*KGW* II.2, 279], and in his reply of 15 December 1870 Nietzsche suggested publishing books as a way of financing their "new *Greek* academy" (neue *griechische* Akademie), or their "monastic-artistic community" (klösterlich-künstlerische Genossenschaft) [*KSB* 3, 165–66].)[5] Amid increasing dissatisfaction with his life as a professor, reflected in that letter and elsewhere (*KSB* 3, 72 and 178), Nietzsche was developing a different sense of priorities, reflected in his failed application for a chair in philosophy, not philology, in Basel (*KSB* 3, 175–76 and 193). Those priorities are reflected in the following outburst, in a letter to Wilhelm Vischer-Bilfinger, of 27 May 1871 —

> The news of recent days has been so terrible that I can no longer get into a mood that is even bearable. What is one, as a scholar, confronted with such earthquakes of culture! How small one feels! One uses one's whole life and best powers to understand better and to explain better a period of culture; how does this job appear, when in a single miserable day the most precious documents of such a period are burned to ashes! This is the worst day of my life.
>
> [Die Nachrichten der letzten Tage waren so schrecklich, dass ich gar nicht mehr zu einer auch nur erträglichen Stimmung komme. Was ist man, solchen Erdbeben der Cultur gegenüber, als Gelehrter! Wie atomistisch fühlt man sich! Sein ganzes Leben und seine beste Kraft benutzt man, eine Periode der Cultur besser zu verstehen und besser zu erklären; wie erscheint dieser Beruf, wenn ein einziger unseliger Tag die kostbarsten Documente solcher Perioden zu Asche verbrennt! Es ist der schlimmste Tag meines Lebens. (*KSB* 3, 195)]

— occasioned by a report, which turned out to be false, that the Louvre had been set on fire. In a note written between the end of 1870 and April 1871, Nietzsche speculated *à propos* of the Franco-Prussian War: "I could imagine that on the German side the war was fought to liberate the Venus [i.e., the famous Venus of Milo] from the Louvre, as a second Helena. This would be the spiritual interpretation of this war. The beautiful ancient rigidity of existence inaugurates by means of this war — there begins the time of earnestness — we believe that it will also become the time of *art*" ((Ich könnte mir einbilden, man habe deutscher Seite den Krieg geführt, um die Venus aus dem Louvre zu befreien, als eine zweite Helena. Dies wäre die pneumatische Auslegung dieses Krieges. Die schöne antike Starrheit des Daseins durch diesen Krieg inaugurirt — es beginnt die Zeit des Ernstes — wir glauben daß es auch die der *Kunst* sein wird; *KSA* 7, 7[88], 158).

Thus Nietzsche conceived *The Birth of Tragedy* not simply as a philological exercise to account for the origin of Greek tragedy, but as a cultural-political defense of the new Aeschylus, Richard Wagner.[6] The fascination with Greek culture was, of course, not new. From Johann Joachim Winckelmann, via Goethe (who, for instance, told Eckermann "study Molière, study Shakespeare; but, above all things, the ancient Greeks, and always the Greeks" (man studiere Molière, man studiere Shakespeare, aber vor allen Dingen die alten Griechen und immer die Griechen),[7] to G. W. F. Hegel, the culture of ancient Greek had fascinated German writers, thinkers, and artists, classical and Romantic alike. To his subject Nietzsche brought the opposition between the Dionysian and the Apolloninan, an opposition from which, so he told Rohde on 4 August 1871, he believed he could derive much (*KSB* 3, 215), but before Nietzsche, others (including Friedrich Schlegel, Friedrich Creuzer, and F. W. J. Schelling) had attached significance to the god Dionysos.[8] For Nietzsche, however, Apollo and Dionysos, referred to in *The Birth of Tragedy* as gods or "art deities" (*Kunstgottheiten*), as creative human drives or *Triebe*, and as physiological states, namely *Traum* (dream) and *Rausch* (frenzy) (*BT* §1; *KSA* 1, 25–26). It is important to understand the experiential dimension of Nietzsche's argument; as Rüdiger Safranski has suggested, anyone who listens to a Walkman or iPod sitting on the underground or jogging in the park knows of Nietzsche's dualistic worldview: inasmuch as we sit or jog, we are Apollonian; but inasmuch as we listen to music, we are Dionysian.[9] (The flood of music, not just in pubs and clubs, but in shops, restaurants, even in the streets confirms our predisposition for the prelinguistic, acoustic realm of Dionysos.)

The Birth of Tragedy — its birth, as the subtitle of the first edition of 1872 emphasized, "out of the spirit of music" (aus dem Geiste der Musik) — is a complex, difficult, subtle work, whose central lines of strategic argument are explained and clarified in the following contribution by Adrian Del Caro. Yet its immediate reception showed no awareness of this subtlety and complexity. True, Wagner loved the book — "I have never read anything more beautiful than your book!" (Schöneres als Ihr Buch habe ich noch nichts gelesen! *KGW* II.2, 493) — and this delighted

Nietzsche (*KSB* 3, 272–73). (Indeed, according to Elisabeth Förster-Nietzsche, the publication of *The Birth of Tragedy* made Nietzsche — literally want to dance.)[10] But the response of his professional colleagues was silence, and then rejection. On 30 January 1872, Nietzsche wrote an indignant letter to his former mentor in Leipzig, Friedrich Ritschl, expressing his surprise at Ritschl's lack of response (*KSB* 3, 281–82); for his part, Ritschl wrote to Wilhelm Vischer-Bilfinger, the senior philologist in Basel, on 2 February 1872: "But our Nietzsche! — this is a really sad story [. . .] he is too giddyingly high-flying for me" (Aber unser Nietzsche! — ja das ist wirklich eine recht betrübtes Kapitel [. . .] er ist mir zu schwindelhaft hoch). What annoyed Ritschl most, however, was "his impiety toward his own mother, who has suckled him at her breast: philology" (seine Impietät gegen seine eigentliche Mutter, die ihm an ihren Brüsten gesäugt hat: die Philologie; *KGW* II.7.1, 622). When the young Berlin philologist Ulrich von Wilamowitz-Moellendorff (1848–1931) published an attack on *The Birth of Tragedy* entitled *The Philology of the Future* (*Zukunftsphilologie*; Berlin, 1872), Nietzsche's friend Erwin Rohde, who had already reviewed *The Birth of Tragedy* in glowing terms, responded on his behalf with a vigorous defense entitled *Afterphilologie* (Leipzig, 1872), perhaps best translated as *Philology of the Posterior*.[11] But Nietzsche now found himself, in effect, deprived of "both mission and profession."[12] Composed amid war, *The Birth of Tragedy* launched a war of words: and perhaps it marks the beginning of Nietzsche's strategic withdrawal from the sphere of philology.

Notes

[1] On Nietzsche's relationship to Wagner, see Luitpold Griesser, *Nietzsche und Wagner: Neue Beiträge zur Geschichte und Philologie ihrer Freundschaft* (Vienna and Leipzig: Hölder-Pichler-Tempsky, 1923); and Dietrich Fischer-Dieskau, *Wagner und Nietzsche: Der Mystagoge und sein Abtrünniger* (Stuttgart: Deutsche Verlags-Anstalt, 1974).

[2] For further discussion of Nietzsche's relationship to Cosima, see Joachim Köhler, *Friedrich Nietzsche und Cosima Wagner: Die Schule der Unterwerfung* (Berlin: Rowohlt, 1996); translated by Ronald Taylor as *Nietzsche and Wagner: A Lesson in Subjugation* (New Haven and London: Yale UP, 1998).

[3] For further discussion, see Lionel Gossman, *Basel in the Age of Burckhardt: A Study in Unseasonable Ideas* (Chicago and London: U of Chicago P, 2000).

[4] See Katrin Meyer and Barbara von Reibnitz, eds., *Friedrich Nietzsche, Franz und Ida Overbeck: Briefwechsel* (Stuttgart and Weimar: Metzler, 2000).

[5] On the theme of the secular monastery in Nietzsche, see Olivier Ponton, *Nietzsche, philosophe de légèreté* (Berlin and New York: Walter de Gruyter, 2007), "Le cloître pour esprits libres," 254–87.

[6] Compare Nietzsche's argument in *The Birth of Tragedy* that Euripides fought the death struggle of tragedy (*BT* §11–§13; *KSA* 1, 75–91) with Schiller's intuition that Euripides marks the point of a change in the Greeks' relation to nature (*Über naïve und sentimentalische Dichtung*, ed. William F. Mainland (Oxford: Blackwell, 1957), 18 (see Gary Brown, "Introduction" [to "Richard Wagner in Bayreuth"], in Friedrich Nietzsche, *Unmodern Observations*, ed. William Arrowsmith [New Haven and London: Yale UP, 1990], 227–52 [here: 234]).

[7] Johann Peter Eckermann, *Gespräche mit Goethe in den letzten Jahren seines Lebens*, ed. Fritz Bergemann (Frankfurt am Main: Insel, 1981), conversation of 1 April 1827, 572.

[8] See Max Baeumer, "Nietzsche and the Tradition of the Dionysian," in *Studies in Nietzsche and the Classical Tradition* (Chapel Hill, NC: U of North Carolina P. 1976), ed. James C. O'Flaherty, Timothy F. Sellner, and Robert M. Helms, 165–89; and Manfred Frank, *Der kommende Gott: Vorlesungen über die Neue Mythologie, I. Teil* (Frankfurt am Main: Suhrkamp, 1982), esp. 73–106. As James Porter rightly remarks, Nietzsche's "uses of Dionysus" are both "a product of the Dionysian tradition that runs from Herder to Friedrich Schlegel, Creuzer, Schelling, Heyne, Bachofen, and beyond" — a fact that his contemporaries could see in a way we no longer do" — and "a polemical commentary on this tradition, which is to say on the German obsession with Germanic traits, in the guise of Hellenism and Dionysianism" (James I. Porter, *Nietzsche and the Philology of the Future* (Stanford, CA: Stanford UP, 2000), 262–63).

[9] Rüdiger Safranski, *Nietzsche: Biographie seines Denkens* (Munich and Vienna: Hanser, 2000), 97.

[10] Elisabeth Förster-Nietzsche, *Wagner und Nietzsche zur Zeit ihrer Freundschaft* (Munich: Müller, 1915), 95.

[11] The documents from the debate on *The Birth of Tragedy* are available in the following edition: Karlfried Gründer, ed., *Der Streit um Nietzsches "Geburt der Tragödie": Die Schriften von E. Rohde, R. Wagner, U. von Wilamowitz-Moellendorff* (Hildesheim: Olms, 1969; 1989); and see also William Musgrave Calder III, "The Wilamowitz-Nietzsche Struggle: New Documents and a Reappraisal," *Nietzsche-Studien* 12 (1983): 214–54.

[12] Gary Brown, "Introduction" to "Richard Wagner in Bayreuth," in Friedrich Nietzsche, *Unmodern Observations*, ed. William Arrowsmith (New Haven and London: Yale UP, 1990), 227–52 (here: 238).

2: The Birth of Tragedy

Adrian Del Caro

THE DRAMATIC DIFFERENCE between the first edition of *The Birth of Tragedy* (*Die Geburt der Tragödie*), published in 1872, and the new edition — technically the third — of 1886 does not involve the content of the work itself, but is limited to the manner in which the new edition is framed.[1] The early title had been *The Birth of Tragedy from the Spirit of Music* (*Die Geburt der Tragödie aus dem Geiste der Musik*), now changed to *The Birth of Tragedy: Or, Hellenism and Pessimism* (*Die Geburt der Tragödie: Oder Griechenthum und Pessimismus*). Appended to the title of this 1886 edition were the words: "New Edition with an Attempt at a Self-Critique" (Neue Ausgabe mit dem Versuch einer Selbstkritik), while, conspicuously, the original "Preface to Richard Wagner" (Vorwort an Richard Wagner) was deleted. Thus Nietzsche's own critique of the early work functionally replaces the preface to his erstwhile mentor, and the change in title with its non-mention of music and instatement of Hellenism likewise performs the removal of Wagner and his world from the book that owed much to him. If the 1886 edition did not present a new *Birth of Tragedy*, its framing certainly presented a new Nietzsche.

In producing the brilliant hybrid *The Birth of Tragedy*, Nietzsche was able to find inspiration in the rich Romantic tradition fueled by Winckelmann and Herder, along with, in matters of tragedy, Goethe, Schiller, and the Schlegel brothers.[2] The influence of August Wilhelm Schlegel was much stronger than Nietzsche revealed, and he probably chose to mute his reliance on Schlegel in order to claim ownership of the important concept of tragedy's decline at the hands of Euripides, which features prominently in the structure of *The Birth of Tragedy* and provides much of the energy for Nietzsche's lifelong critique of Socrates, the theorist behind Euripides's dramas. Beyond these auspicious predecessors, who in the case of Goethe and Schiller were not only theorists but also outstanding playwrights, Nietzsche drew considerable philosophical inspiration from Schopenhauer, whose ideas on art, suffering, pessimism, and the principle of individuation strongly inform his argument, and of course from Wagner, who represented an amalgam of classical and Romantic traits, and whose theoretical writings and operas represented to the young Nietzsche the possibility of recalibrating the modern sensibility along the lines of tragic, Dionysian wisdom.[3]

Nietzsche became aware of Wagner's theoretical writings, beginning with *Opera and Drama* (*Oper und Drama*), in 1868, and in the same year he was introduced to Wagner, arguably the single greatest influence on his life in terms of intellectual development.[4] The highest point of Wagner's influence on Nietzsche was the period from autumn 1870 to the end of 1871,[5] coinciding with the period in which Nietzsche made notes on Greek tragedy for two lectures he gave in Basel in January and February 1870, and worked on related writings on tragedy including "The Dionysian Worldview" ("Die dionysische Weltanschauung"), "The Birth of the Tragic Idea" ("Die Geburt des tragischen Gedankens"), "Origin and Goal of Tragedy" ("Ursprung und Ziel der Tragödie"), "Socrates and Greek Tragedy" ("Sokrates und die griechische Tragödie"), "Music and Tragedy" ("Musik und Tragödie"), and finally *The Birth of Tragedy from the Spirit of Music*, which was completed in autumn 1871 and published early in 1872 by Richard Wagner's publisher.[6] It is significant that all of these writings on tragedy were completed during the period in which Nietzsche was most strongly influenced by Wagner and his wife Cosima Wagner; the essay "Origin and Goal of Tragedy," like the book that appeared in 1872, even includes a preface dedicated to Richard Wagner.[7]

The convergence of Nietzsche's thoughts on music and tragedy at the precise time of his cordial friendship with Wagner does not sufficiently explain the background and motivation for *The Birth of Tragedy*. Silk and Stern speak of three "preoccupations" of young Nietzsche, namely music, philosophy, and the Greeks, with the latter rising to special prominence because, for Nietzsche as for earlier Romantic Hellenists, there is no studying the Greeks merely as a professional concern — rather, such study transforms one's life.[8] All of these preoccupations existed before the Wagnerian experience and after it, with music receding in theoretical importance relative to the task of transforming Greek tragedy, in particular the Dionysian, into a philosophy for moderns. Wagner's influence on Nietzsche's thought prompted him to view art holistically and to project this view onto the ancient Greeks.[9] Nietzsche did this not solely on the basis of Wagner's writings and music but, more importantly, on the basis of Wagner's personality; Hollingdale describes how Nietzsche became a "psychologist" during the Wagnerian experience, with Wagner a case study in domination and will to power.[10] For young Nietzsche, still under the thrall of Wagner's powerful personality, Wagner represented a modern-day incarnation of Aeschylus, who as originator of Greek tragedy was therefore closest to its origins in music;[11] young Nietzsche was also clearly drawn to Wagner as an innovator and trailblazer, whose life was a triumph over obstacles.[12]

Before long it dawned on Nietzsche that he had seriously deceived himself about Wagner, and he had a strong inkling that becoming a Wagnerian, and devoting himself both personally and professionally to Wagnerian ideals would be a dubious step. The early letters to his friend Rohde already contained observations sharply critical of Wagner's followers, with the sarcastic phrase "the brothers *in Wagnero*" (die Brüder in Wagnero) and a reference to them as both stupid and capable only of disgusting writings on the master.[13] After the break with Wagner turned to outright enmity and feuding between the two, Nietzsche's writings began to contain attacks on Wagner as a composer and as a human being. These attacks are too frequent and too numerous to ignore or to ascribe to wounded vanity, disillusionment, envy, betrayal, or any of the usual emotions that accompany a bitter parting of ways — in fact, they constitute a deliberate, sustained *agon* or contest with Wagner, in the spirit of the ancient Greek tradition of the *agon* designed to inspire individuals to their best performance through positive competition. Here it should be noted that the *agon* was not literally engaged by Wagner and Nietzsche, but was instead carried out by Nietzsche with Wagner as the looming figure in the background, the great one against whom Nietzsche continued to measure himself. After *The Birth of Tragedy* the name of Dionysus, so prominent in that work and so fundamental to Nietzsche's thought, does not appear again in Nietzsche's published writings until 1886 in *Beyond Good and Evil* (*Jenseits von Gut und Böse*), where Nietzsche declares Dionysus a philosopher-god and himself the last disciple of this philosopher-god (*BGE* §295; *KSA* 5, 238). This is another instatement of himself, as a philosopher, in the place of Wagner the artist, with Dionysus conspicuously "promoted" from *Kunstgottheit* (art deity) to philosopher-god. The role of the *agon* meanwhile, promulgated by Nietzsche in his essay "Homer's Contest" ("Homers Wettkampf") of 1872, plays a central role in *The Birth of Tragedy*, where it illustrates the contest and interplay between Dionysus and Apollo. This duality, skillfully depicting fundamental drives and structures of the psyche, had a profound, sweeping effect on twentieth-century thinkers and artists, and it went on to animate the world of psychoanalysis.[14] A very strong case has been made by Rudolf Kreis that Nietzsche's *Thus Spoke Zarathustra* (*Also sprach Zarathustra*) was written in part as a response and counter to Wagner's opera *Parsifal* and to the mission that Wagner had assumed for himself as an ideological Christian.[15] To underestimate the importance of Wagner for Nietzsche's life and oeuvre would be a mistake, for he served as a catalyst for many of Nietzsche's most compelling formulations and criticisms, not only during the period of *The Birth of Tragedy* but right up to the mental breakdown.

Nietzsche's preceding work had consisted of scholarly articles in the classics journal *Das rheinische Museum*, edited by his mentor Friedrich Ritschl,[16] and the various lectures and essays that later on became

The Birth of Tragedy as described above. As Nietzsche's first book, it was problematic in many respects, not the least of which was the obvious tailoring of his argument to suit the needs of positioning Wagner as a tragic innovator and the modern-day portal to a revival of tragic, Dionysian culture. We should also bear in mind that he had not written a dissertation but received his appointment as professor at Basel on the strength of his early scholarly articles and Ritschl's strong recommendation and intercession. One can easily agree with Kaufmann when he disparages chapters 16–25 of the book, which contain the bulk of Nietzsche's Wagnerian panegyrics,[17] but even in these chapters there are substantive ideas and formulations that are capable of standing on their own. Generally speaking, despite the influence of Wagner, which prompted Nietzsche to rework some of his own ideas and insights, the energy, ingenuity, and appeal of *The Birth of Tragedy* are all Nietzsche, vintage Nietzsche in fact, and no one else was capable of writing this book. In what follows I will describe the major argument based on the dichotomy of the Apollonian and the Dionysian, which is then elaborated by reformulations and qualifications that Nietzsche introduced throughout.[18] In the course of presenting the argument, I will discuss seven key innovations as they have influenced modern aesthetics, intellectual history, and philosophy: the Apollonian-Dionysian opposition; the primal unity (*das Ur-Eine*); lyrical subjectivity and aesthetic existentialism; the satyr chorus; the death of myth; Socratic optimism; and the primacy of the Dionysian.

The terms "Apollonian" and "Dionysian," which Nietzsche elevates to principles and spheres of influence based on the artistic deities Apollo and Dionysus, were not conceptually developed by the Greeks, and Nietzsche issues this disclaimer on the first page of his book (*BT* §1; *KSA* 1, 25). It is therefore important to bear in mind that in using these terms, Nietzsche had no intention of providing a "straightforward, unmediated account of the 'origins' of art"; instead, in Nietzsche's "borrowing" (*entlehnen*) of these terms from the Greeks, we can infer not only a duality but a degree of duplicity in Nietzsche's founding opposition.[19] Clearly these are Nietzsche's modern extrapolations of what Apollo and Dionysus meant to the pre-Socratic Greeks; hence what we find appealing about *The Birth of Tragedy* is not so much a philological "discovery" of materials previously overlooked by scholars, but instead a philosophical "invention" of intellectual and aesthetic properties attributed to the ancients but relevant to moderns.

According to Nietzsche, Apollo and Dionysus engage in agonistic opposition, inspiring one another to new and stronger births until they produce the artwork we know as tragedy (*BT* §1; *KSA* 1, 25–26). Apollo represents the plastic arts and the artistic world governed by dream; his influence is characterized by beautiful semblance, form, consciousness, and the principle of individuation, adopted from Schopenhauer, which contributes fundamentally to a human being's sense of calm, security, and identity (*BT* §1; *KSA* 1, 26–28). Opposed to this world of calm appearances and the semblance of individual control is the Dionysian, which erupts as intoxication (*Rausch*) when the principle of individuation breaks down. Now it is unmitigated nature that asserts itself, sweeping aside the protective mechanisms of consciousness, inspired by either narcotic drink or the powerful stirrings of spring as they are collectively celebrated. With the principle of individuation suspended or temporarily disrupted, human beings renew their bond with nature; individuals abandon their sense of identity and become one with their neighbors, expressing themselves collectively through music and dance, merging into what Nietzsche called the primal unity (*BT* §1; *KSA* 1, 28–30). Thus Nietzsche juxtaposes and sets in play two opposing worlds whose temporary reconciliation forms the basis of tragedy, which represented the Greek form of public worship of Dionysus. It should be noted how universal, how fundamental and elemental are these opposites; conscious vs. unconscious, individual vs. primal unity, semblance vs. reality; order vs. chaos, stasis vs. dance, plastic art vs. music, knowledge vs. art, mind vs. body, and so on.

Nietzsche remained a dualistic thinker, because he cherished the state of tension created by the clash of forces, reflecting his profound interest in the Greek concept of *agon*. His earliest writings were characterized by the opposition between the Apollonian and the Dionysian, a model he applied not only to tragedy but to the whole of ancient Greek culture.[20] The early dichotomy of Apollo vs. Dionysus allowed him to express his general tendency to favor the body over the mind, a preference rooted so deeply in him that when he posited analogies for these two principles, he used dream and intoxication; cognition could not be used as a pole, since it is knowledge itself that requires an antidote in art, and art for Nietzsche arises from the coupling of Apollonian and Dionysian.[21] I agree with those scholars who emphasize the constancy of Nietzsche's use of these conceptual opposites, which he used throughout his career in language very similar to that of *The Birth of Tragedy*,[22] as well as those who underscore that later polarities such as Dionysus vs. Christ are not displacements of the earliest dichotomy but elaborations of further cultural differences rooted in the Apollo-Dionysus polarity.[23] When scholars speak of Nietzsche later abandoning the Apollonian, or abandoning the entire dichotomy, it is generally their way of explaining that Nietzsche abandoned the synthesizing of Apollonian and Dionysian as it occurs in *The Birth of Tragedy* along metaphysical, Schopenhauerian lines.[24]

The expression "primal unity" occurs already in the first chapter and is used throughout. I think it likely that Nietzsche adopted the term from his reading of Schopenhauer's *Parerga und Paralipomena II*, §190, where Schopenhauer refers to a lecture by Schelling on the Roman god Janus. According to Schopenhauer, Schelling described Janus as "the primal unity" (das Ur-Eins) and "chaos as primal unity" (das Chaos als Ureinheit).[25] Both expressions correspond with Nietzsche's in terms of grammar, meaning, and overall context. As mentioned above, when an individual's principle of individuation breaks down, she experiences the primal unity, joining with the primordial home where all human beings are at one with nature. In *The Birth of Tragedy* this primal unity purports to be both an enchanting and horrifying reality — depending on whether we are swept up in it or thinking of it — from which we are shielded by the principle of individuation and all the apparatus associated with the Apollonian, which gives us the world of semblance and appearances. On this reading, the primal unity would correspond with Schopenhauer's will. The primal unity is what is metaphysically most fundamental, possessing the ontological status of Kant's thing-in-itself; Nietzsche refers to it with many analogous expressions such as primal ground, innermost ground of the world, truly existing subject, eternal core of things, etc. However, Nietzsche himself had sharply criticized the metaphysics of both Kant and Schopenhauer as early as 1867/1868, and in *The Birth of Tragedy* he does not provide a theoretical grounding for his use of the term primal unity, unlike Schopenhauer, who provides such a grounding for his concept of the will.[26]

One explanation for why Nietzsche used a metaphysical concept whose validity he had already questioned is found in his appreciation of Heraclitus and that philosopher's understanding of Dionysus. By depicting the primal unity as primal contradiction and primal flux, Nietzsche could describe its creations as real, as more than mere appearance. The primal unity eternally creates and eternally destroys itself, as *causa sui*; it is appropriately associated with the Dionysian because Dionysus was simultaneously the eternally living and eternally dying god.[27] Later on, when it was no longer a matter of aesthetics with two opposing forces reconciling for a moment to create tragedy, Nietzsche could easily dispose of the dichotomy between semblance and reality by insisting that they are in fact one.[28] What then remains is a Dionysian conception of reality, for which Nietzsche famously coined the expression "will to power"; we find his concise argument for eliminating the distinction between a "false" and a "true" world in *Twilight of the Idols* (*Götzen-Dämmerung*; *TI* "How the 'True World' Finally Became a Fable"; *KSA* 6, 80–81), and we find him formulating the will to power on a Dionysian framework in *Beyond Good and Evil* (*BGE* §36; *KSA* 5, 21–22). I have elsewhere discussed this reworking of the Dionysian into the will to power on the basis of the published works and the unpublished notes.[29] Thus, while "primal unity" works well for Nietzsche, aesthetically, as a metaphor for the unconscious and nature in *The Birth of Tragedy*, its importance to his overall thought was magnified when he philosophically reworked it as the will to power during his later years as a "Dionysian philosopher."

What Nietzsche called the lyrical rests at the foundation of the tragic, and provides him with a new basis on which to discuss both subjectivity and the value of human existence. In section 5 of *The Birth of Tragedy*, he explains that the lyric poet is intimately associated with the musician in ancient Greek art. As a Dionysian artist, the lyric poet becomes one with the primal unity, producing a copy of it as music; this music is now channeled by means of the lyric poet's Apollonian dream function, resulting in symbolic dream images. These dream images, now visible to all in the form of dramatic dithyrambs and tragedies, are the closest we can come as human beings to expressing the essence of the primal unity, with its eternal contradiction and pain. Nietzsche reminds us at the same time that the lyric poet has surrendered his subjectivity, his ego or identity, upon first joining with the primal unity — the "I" of the poet has disappeared, and what he channels emanates from "the abyss of being" (dem Abgrunde des Seins). Nietzsche rightly asks us to juxtapose this lyrical ontological state with the vapid, modern aesthetic notion of "subjectivity" (*BT* §5; *KSA* 1, 43–44). Unlike the modern poet, whose subjectivity (read: individuality, personal preferences, idiosyncrasy, ego, etc.) influences and determines his poem, the ancient lyric poet is a medium of what is most real, the primal unity, and his poem remains unsullied by the merely personal, merely subjective character of the insignificant individual.

What is at stake here with the Dionysian union of poet and primal unity is nothing less than a re-examination of the status of subjectivity.[30] The mood in which the ancient lyric poet found himself, or into which he worked himself, was literally ecstatic, enabling him to dispossess his own subjectivity in order to enter a Dionysian state of disindividuation.[31] Nietzsche credits Archilochus with being the first lyric poet of the Greeks, the inaugurator of tragic drama itself,[32] and to underscore how universal was his function as poet, Nietzsche now describes him as no longer Archilochus, but the genius of the world expressing its primal pain in the symbolic likeness of Archilochus the man (*BT* §5; *KSA* 1, 45). Nietzsche was quite serious about this profound difference between ordinary individuality and the heightened Dionysian state, such that scholars have recognized in the Dionysian state an innovation that leaves behind both Kantian moral optimism and Schopenhauerian resigned pessimism; there is a degree of historical and psychological objectivity in the Dionysian.[33] Indeed, a human being's capacity to switch from the individuated, Apollonian state to the disindividuated, Dionysian state was central to Nietzsche's conception of the ancient Greeks during the tragic age; his later thinking was oriented along the line of this permanent practice of limitation and unlimitation.[34]

Having established the conceptual basis of Nietzsche's understanding of the lyrical, we can now proceed as he did in section 5 of *The Birth of Tragedy* to the celebrated notion of existence justified only as an aesthetic phenomenon. In a major departure from Schopenhauer, Nietzsche insists that dividing the arts into objective and subjective categories is misplaced, since the subject, as a willing individual following egoistic aims, can only be regarded as an obstacle to art, not its origin. To the extent that the subject is an artist, on the other hand, he has been freed of his individual will and has become a medium through which the truly existing subject (read: primal unity) celebrates its redemption in semblance or appearance. On this reasoning, he cautions, we human beings cannot see ourselves as the real creators of the world of art, but we can indeed see ourselves as artistic projections of the real creator (primal unity), leading to the conclusion that existence and the world are eternally justified only as an aesthetic phenomenon (*BT* §5; *KSA* 1, 47). This is a counterintuitive proposition, since moderns have accustomed themselves to regarding art as something invented by human subjects. By declaring the primacy of art as an expression of the primal unity, Nietzsche invites us to consider the fallacy — indeed, the hubris — underlying modern notions of subjectivity and creativity; what is authentic, real, and eternally justifiable about human beings, about existence, is the fact that we are artistic projections in the manner of Archilochus — in this scenario, the "real creator" (primal unity) creates humans. Note that the justification of existence here occurs on purely aesthetic grounds — there is no moral dimension whatsoever to mankind's relationship to the primal unity. Moreover, "aesthetics" (as it is used in "das Dasein als ästhetisches Phänomen" [existence as an aesthetic phenomenon]) cannot be understood in the limited, modernist sense associated with art and artworks. Instead, "existence as an aesthetic phenomenon" is Nietzsche's way of drilling down to the core, of expressing a view of existence free of idealism, metaphysics, and wishful thinking generally. It is precisely on this issue that *The Birth of Tragedy* decisively breaks with Kant and with Kant's self-appointed successor, Schopenhauer.

This early formulation resonates in the later works, helping to explain why Nietzsche needed to reject Schopenhauer's pessimism as well as Socrates's theoretical optimism, which rests on moral-Platonic grounds.[35] He rejects the notion of a fundamental truth to the world, and rejects making value judgments about life, as seen in both *The Gay Science* (*Die fröhliche Wissenschaft*) and *Twilight of the Idols*, but what is more, he continues to pursue theodicy as an existential project.[36] One scholar has identified a consistency between Nietzsche's unpublished note of 1885, where he discusses rare human types, transfigured existence, and mankind as the self-justification of nature in connection with the phrase in *The Birth of Tragedy* describing existence as justified only as an aesthetic phenomenon.[37] I have gone further in demonstrating that the celebrated phrase from *The Birth of Tragedy* undergoes a parallel reworking in *Zarathustra*, where Nietzsche's prophet offers his own justification of existence by proclaiming the superhuman to be the meaning of the earth (*Z* Prologue §3; *KSA* 4, 14).[38] The same theodicy-oriented strategy is used, with only slightly altered wording for the major concepts; "existence" becomes "the superhuman," "world" becomes "earth," and "justified"/"justification" becomes "meaning." Nietzsche sharpens the formulation "existence and the world are only justified eternally as an aesthetic phenomenon" into "the superhuman is the meaning of the earth." In order to give due credit to Nietzsche for this formulation and others that resemble "theodicy," namely, the defense of God's goodness in view of the existence of evil, we should really be referring to Nietzsche's strategy as a *geodicy*, since what he seeks to justify is not God's existence, but on the contrary, the meaning of the earth.

Nietzsche should also be properly credited with elevating the status of the tragic chorus beyond anything his predecessors had achieved. In section 7 of *The Birth of Tragedy* he reviews and critiques earlier theories on the origin of tragedy, noting that they are all correct insofar as they trace the emergence of tragedy to the chorus, but fail to comprehend the nature of the ancient chorus. He first dispenses with the notion that the chorus represented the common people versus the aristocracy, then with the Schlegelian notion that the chorus represented the ideal spectator (*BT* §7; *KSA* 1, 52–54). Nietzsche does credit Schiller with a more compelling explanation of the nature of the chorus, namely, that it served as a living wall around tragedy, in order to shut out the real world and preserve tragedy's ideal ground and poetic freedom (*BT* §7; *KSA* 1, 54). This definition of tragedy suited Nietzsche's interests quite well, since in all matters of art he was suspicious of naturalistic tendencies, that is, of efforts to equate art with mundane, day-to-day habits and events. The chorus is something "with which war should be openly and honestly declared against any kind of naturalism in art" (mit dem jedem Naturalismus in der Kunst offen und ehrlich der Krieg erklärt werde; *BT* §7; *KSA* 1, 55). By far the most innovative feature of Nietzsche's theory regarding the role of the chorus, however, is the elaboration of the satyr chorus and the nature of satyrs generally.

Original tragedy's chorus was composed of satyrs, those half-man, half-goat companions of Dionysus whom Nietzsche describes as fictitious creatures of nature acting in a fictitious state of nature. The satyr bridged the gulf between cultural man and natural man; he was immutable, powerful, and untouched by civilization. The cultured Greeks felt nullified when viewing the satyr chorus, deriving a metaphysical comfort from tragedy's message that life is indestructibly powerful and joyful despite the turmoil of appearances; behind the façade of all civilization, the Greeks could imagine these natural creatures living ineradicably, immune to the changes of generations and the history of nations (*BT* §7; *KSA* 1, 56). The satyrs relived the Dionysian experience of being torn to pieces and reconstituted, inspiring a religious reality despite their fictitious nature.[39] In "The Dionysian Worldview" Nietzsche described how, in the primitive springtime dithyramb, human beings did not express themselves as individuals, but as the species; now, the language of the satyr would come into play, a language consisting of gestures and dance. In the ancient Dionysian state of immanence as Nietzsche describes it, a human being's normal, cognitive channels are switched off, and human "speech" transforms into dance.[40]

The Dionysian world experienced by the cultured Greek was not an innocuous encounter, on the contrary, Nietzsche held that the Greeks were capable of the most delicate and severe suffering, by virtue of their insightful gaze into the horrific, destructive activity of world history, as well as their gaze into the cruelty of nature. What saved them from a reaction of Buddhistic denial of the will was art — art becomes the saving grace of life, and at this point in his argument Nietzsche details the transition from the Dionysian state back to mundane reality. There is a lethargic element to the Dionysian state of ecstasy, capable of suppressing all memory of one's individual past. Upon emerging from the ecstasy, however, mundane reality returns to fill the consciousness, resulting in nausea and an ascetic, will-negating mood. Now, Nietzsche applies his theory of tragedy to Shakespeare by comparing the nausea of the Dionysian Greek to the dilemma of Hamlet; both had gazed into the true essence of things, both had come to the realization that to act brings nausea upon them, since action would alter nothing in the eternal essence of things: "Knowledge kills action, action requires us to be veiled by illusion — this is the lesson of Hamlet" (Die Erkenntnis tödtet das Handeln, zum Handeln gehört das Umschleiertsein durch die Illusion — das ist die Hamletlehre; *BT* §7; *KSA* 1, 56–57). Art now arrives as the saving, healing sorceress, for it alone is capable of redirecting our nauseous thoughts about the horror or absurdity of existence into viable and life-sustaining representations. Tragic art addresses how we master horror with the sublime, while comic art addresses how we master the absurd. "The satyr chorus of the dithyramb is the saving act of Greek art" (Der Satyrchor des Dithyrambus ist die rettende That der griechischen Kunst; *BT* §7; *KSA* 1, 57).

What emerges from this detailed analysis of the function of the chorus is the vitality of tragedy as a physical and emotional response to a physical and emotional need. Art is not something dreamed up by human beings or added on as superficial dressing; instead, it is key to survival and it determines a given people's capacity for transforming suffering into life-affirmation and the style in which they do it. It is not by accident that Nietzsche elevated Archilochus and the lyrical, because this originator of lyric poetry both composed and led Dionysian choruses,[41] thereby initiating and practicing a brand of Dionysian wisdom that Nietzsche cherished as much as the fully-developed tragedies of Aeschylus, Sophocles, and Euripides. Whereas Aristotle ignored or diminished the importance of dance, mimicry, gestures, and music, dismissing them as ornamentation,[42] these are precisely the features of proto-tragedy that Nietzsche glorified in the tragic chorus, and he valued them for their ability to establish the link with and subsequently express the Dionysian essence. Moreover, the encounter with the Dionysian that is enabled by the ancient chorus not only "explains" the origin of tragedy, it provides an organic, physiological, and psychological framework for understanding art and its place in the human condition. Tragedy, Nietzsche argued, was of great historical consequence, and the loss of tragedy through the decline and death of myth could not be without historical consequences of its own.

In sections 1–9 of *The Birth of Tragedy* Nietzsche is indeed focused on providing an account of the rise of tragedy, exploring the significance of the mythology presented by Homer, juxtaposing the culture of the Titans and Olympians, and otherwise setting forth the consequences of the arrival of the cult of Dionysus in Greece, with its special myths relating to the resurrective god who rules over both life and death. Beginning in section 10, a marked transition takes place, according to which Nietzsche spends the next six sections discussing the death of tragedy, a process that unfolds primarily because the validity of the myths is interrogated until they eventually lose their appeal. Inasmuch as he had argued in the first nine sections for the existential importance of tragedy as a means of inculcating Dionysian wisdom and superior capacity for life affirmation, the middle part of *The Birth of Tragedy* argues just as strenuously, if not more so, for the deleterious effects of the loss of myth not only for the ancients but, in an unfortunate legacy, for moderns as well. A key ingredient to sustaining the viability of myth was suffering.

Nietzsche first explains that it is an unassailable historical fact that in its earliest form Greek tragedy dealt only with the suffering of Dionysus, who for a long time was the only hero depicted on the stage. Even when this hero adopted another identity, say that of Prometheus or Oedipus, essentially tragedy was working with a mask of the deity. It is crucial to stress this point because, according to Nietzsche, the Greeks simply could not tolerate the individual on the tragic stage, "the individual" here being the ordinary man or woman, the individual from the mundane world denounced by Schiller and Nietzsche as naturalistic. In fact, so averse were the Greeks to portraying the individual on stage that they used the Platonic distinction between Idea and idol to distinguish between the universal (Dionysus, the deity) and the individual (*BT* §10; *KSA* 1, 71).

Through the imagistic and representational powers of the Apollonian, Dionysus was represented to the spectators in a multiplicity of identities, but in truth, Nietzsche argues, "this hero is the suffering Dionysus of the mysteries, this god who experiences in himself the sufferings of individuation" (jener Held [ist] der leidende Dionysus der Mysterien, jener die Leiden der Individuation an sich erfahrender Gott; *BT* §7; *KSA* 1, 72). Here Nietzsche relates the myth of Dionysus who, as a boy, was torn to pieces by the Titans and was worshipped in his disindividuated state as Zagreus. The tearing to pieces of Dionysus is genuine Dionysian suffering, symbolizing his transformation into air, water, earth, and fire, prompting Nietzsche to adduce that the state of individuation per se is the source and primal cause of all suffering. This powerful myth conveys the doctrine of the ancient mysteries, according to which there is a unity to everything that exists, individuation is the primal cause of evil, and art is the joyful hope that the spell of individuation will be broken and unity restored (*BT* §10; *KSA* 1, 72–73). This is another formulation of the switching from Apollonian to Dionysian state that characterizes Nietzsche's description of the chorus, and here again we recognize the familiar juxtaposition of an ecstatic state with a state of nausea upon returning to mundane reality.

Nietzsche goes on to say that the Homeric age with its myths, which had represented the triumph of the Olympian gods and a prevalence of the Apollonian, imagistic and orderly principle, was challenged by a new spirit symbolized by the unruly Prometheus as depicted by Aeschylus. This Dionysian supplanting of the Homeric myths was powered by music, which infused the myths of the tragic age with new vitality, enabling the birth of tragedy. But at this point Nietzsche suddenly proclaims that it is the fate of every myth to slink away and hide in some historical reality; the Greeks had embarked on the path of transforming their entire mythical dream of youth into an arbitrary historical-pragmatic "history of youth" (Jugendgeschichte; *BT* §10; *KSA* 1, 74). Nietzsche explains the necessity of this transformative, sobering act of replacing faith with reason, myth with history, in language that reveals his dual status as a philologist intent on objectively portraying the customs and cultural transformations of an ancient people, as well as a philosopher concerned about the cultural consequences of this historical transition for the quality of life in his own day:

> For this is the manner in which religions tend to die out. The mythical prerequisites of a religion become systematized under the severe, rational gaze of orthodox dogmatism as a fixed sum of historical events, and people begin anxiously to defend the credibility of the myths, yet bristle at any natural continuation and propagation of them; then the feeling for myth dies and in its place arises the demand for religion on historical grounds.

> [Denn dies ist die Art, wie Religionen abzusterben pflegen: wenn nämlich die mythischen Voraussetzungen einer Religion unter den strengen, verstandesmässigen Augen eines rechtgläubigen Dogmatismus als eine fertige Summe von historischen Ereignissen systematisiert

> werden und man anfängt, ängstlich die Glaubwürdigkeit der Mythen
> zu vertheidigen, aber gegen jedes natürliche Weiterleben und Weit-
> erwuchern derselben sich zu sträuben, wenn also das Gefühl für den
> Mythus abstirbt und an seine Stelle der Anspruch der Religion auf
> historische Grundlagen tritt. (*BT* §10; *KSA* 1, 74)]

As any classical philologist will tell us, gods come and go. And as a later, more philosophical Nietzsche would tell us, "God is dead," and mankind itself is the collective culprit, having begun the process of killing all gods at that remote point in history when the Greeks began to lose faith in their myths.

Before concluding his pivotal section 10, Nietzsche named the individual he held responsible for the death of Dionysus and the spirit of music — Euripides, the third and last of the Greek tragedians, "sacrilegious Euripides" (frevelnder Euripides) who killed Dionysus with his own "violent hands" (gewaltsamen Händen; *BT* §10; *KSA* 1, 74). Nietzsche was quite serious about pagan religion's special capacity for life-affirmation,[43] and for that matter, his Romantic predecessor Novalis (Friedrich von Hardenberg) had similarly argued for the primacy of myth as it was embraced by Catholicism but spurned by Protestantism.[44] For Dionysian Greeks the power of myth was vivid and real, representing nothing less than a literal, if momentary, rebirth along the lines of the eternally-resurrecting Dionysus.[45] When he is finished heaping scorn on Euripides and his philosophical mentor Socrates (§10–§15), Nietzsche devotes the remainder of *The Birth of Tragedy* to discussing the new conditions under which a rebirth of tragic culture is possible, under the auspices of Wagnerian music. James I. Porter has even claimed that Nietzsche was not so much interested in the birth or death of Greek tragedy, and that he advertises the fictionality of his book by making it about a rebirth of German myth.[46] But, fictionality aside, Nietzsche was genuinely concerned about the loss of myth and mythic power in the modern age, and Porter himself concedes that Nietzsche was aware of modernity's — not just Germany's — need for myth. The historical birth of tragedy, Nietzsche maintained, had been a transformative experience enabling a heightened form of existence, for only tragic art is capable of filling the void left by optimistic, theoretically oriented myths of religions and philosophers.[47]

Myth continues to occupy a place of honor in Nietzsche's late thought, a fact that is illustrated in his relation to Plato, the enemy of myth and poets. While Nietzsche could agree with Plato that poets are liars, and that art is a form of lying, he does so with opposite intentions. Art may be far from truth, but this is no grounds for objection to art, on the contrary; art should have nothing to do with truth or reality, because it concerns life, which is of the utmost importance.[48] I have elsewhere formulated this major difference between the quotidian Nietzsche and the Platonists by demonstrating that Nietzsche distinguished his whole life long between *the furthest things*, such as truth, reality, the afterlife, the soul, ideals, etc., and *the closest things*, such as the body, nourishment, the environment, the earth, etc. In Nietzsche's view, myths that fuel our capacity for life-affirmation, for living embodied, grateful, and affirmative lives are more valuable than distant and indemonstrable "truths."[49] It is both a weakness of *The Birth of Tragedy* and its strength that existence can be justified as an aesthetic phenomenon: a weakness, because some would see art as a desperate justification; a strength, because others find it impossible to justify existence on moral grounds. The same can be said of Nietzsche's philosophy as a whole, since it is impossible to escape the psychological truth of his own dictum that philosophy is mythology.[50]

The middle sections of *The Birth of Tragedy*, §10–§15, constitute a powerful critique of modernity's reliance on reason and cognition. In keeping with his treatise on tragedy per se, Nietzsche tries to keep the focus on how this unique Athenian invention declined, but by taking on not only Euripides but his philosophical mentor, Socrates, the battle quickly becomes much larger and the modern readership feels itself implicated and drawn in. The gravest error committed by Euripides was his bringing the spectator onto the stage, which Nietzsche interprets as a popularization of tragedy. Art begins to mirror mundane reality, a voice is given to civic mediocrity, and the sublime degenerates to mere wit, levity, and caprice (*BT* §11; *KSA* 1, 76–78). Nietzsche's fundamentally antidemocratic instincts came into play as he condemned Euripides for pandering to something as lowly and fickle as "the public" (Publicum; *BT* §11; *KSA* 1, 79),[51] but we also know from his own understanding of tragic art that it emanated from a protected, ideal ground (the chorus) that served as a living wall against the naturalistic vagueness of the day-to-day. Nietzsche provides two reasons why Euripides deviated from his superior mentors Aeschylus and Sophocles: first, Euripides was not just a poet, he was also a critic, and second, Euripides dared to abandon the tragic conventions of his superior forerunners because he was emboldened by Socrates (*BT* §11; *KSA* 1, 80–81).

Whereas earlier tragedy dealt in the medium of Dionysian ecstasy and Apollonian contemplation, the new tragedy of Euripides, says Nietzsche, displays a popular, demystified style drawing on paradoxical ideas and fiery affects (*BT* §12; *KSA* 1, 84). The Dionysian aesthetics that had prevailed up to this time were supplanted by Socratic aesthetics, which Nietzsche reduced to two formulas: everything must be comprehensible in order to be beautiful, and only he who knows is virtuous (*BT* §12; *KSA* 1, 85). When Euripides applied Socratic aesthetics to his plays, one major change was the inclusion of a prologue, in which all the action of the drama was explained beforehand. Moreover, he intensified this demystifying and anti-mythical effect by adding the infamous "deus ex machina" to the conclusion of his dramas (*BT* §12; *KSA* 1, 86). These new devices of Euripides have appeal, to be sure, but by providing a sense of knowing and security to the audience, as well as a sense that all's well that ends well, they are mere contrivances that fly in the face of Dionysian wisdom and its profound, transcendental symbolism. Thus in Socrates we must recognize the opponent of Dionysus, the popular force who compels the god to flee (*BT* §88; *KSA* 1, 88).

Section 13 drills more deeply into the psychology of Socrates, with Nietzsche providing a modern psychobiography of one of western civilization's greatest teachers. He begins by asserting that, in the Greek mind, Socrates and Euripides were paired as the highest exemplars of wisdom. Wherever Socrates went in Athens, he encountered individuals who, unlike him, claimed to be knowledgeable, yet whose knowledge amounted to nothing more than a conceit. When he questioned them using his famous method, Socrates established that the illustrious men he interviewed practiced their professions merely out of instinct. Thus Socrates made it his goal in life to expose the fallacy of existing art and existing ethics, based as they were on instinct rather than knowledge, and he adopted the view that using knowledge he had a duty to correct existence (*BT* §13; *KSA* 1, 89). Nietzsche urges his readers at this point to consider how presumptuous this Socratic mission was, especially in light of his famous disclaimer that he did not know anything. What inspired Socrates to set himself above Homer, Pindar, Aeschylus, Phidias, Pericles, Pythia, and Dionysus? The explanation Nietzsche provides is clever enough to ensure some measure of sympathy for Socrates, even as he brands him a world-historical pervert. The key to understanding Socrates, Nietzsche argues, is his famous *daimonion*, the little voice that spoke to him. When his intellect failed him, Socrates's inner voice (read: instinct), would speak to him, but always in a dissuasive manner, therefore always negatively as opposed to creatively and affirmatively. When Socrates had a so-called gut feeling, it restrained him from doing something. Nietzsche pounces on this, asserting that in all productive human beings instinct is precisely the creative-affirmative force, while consciousness acts critically and dissuasively — Socrates is therefore "a veritable monstrosity *per defectum*!" (eine wahre Monstrosität per defectum; *BT* §13; *KSA* 1, 90), or a freak who is lacking something.

Socrates is further described as "the anti-mystic par excellence" (der spezifische Nicht-Mystiker), a type of human being incapable of mysticism and therefore — considering the importance of myth, mysticism, instinct, and pathos to the existence of tragedy — the polar opposite of a Dionysian human being. He is described as wielding an instinct-disintegrating influence, clearly a parallel expression by Nietzsche for the famous Socratic tool of dialectic with which he disarmed and humiliated his opponents. Socrates martyred himself by knowingly, calmly going to his death, and in dying became the hero of Athenian youths, most notably of Plato (*BT* §13; *KSA* 1, 91).

The hyperbole continues in section 14 with Nietzsche conjuring up the image of Socrates with a cyclops eye turned on tragedy — one imagines the instinct-disintegrating ray emanating from this single eye. Totally insensitive to poetry, Socrates spawned a new form of expression; whereas the earlier forms of epic and tragedy had absorbed and incorporated all previous types of art, now the Platonic dialogue would do so, but only begrudgingly, half-heartedly and without a hint of artistic inspiration. Nietzsche uses the metaphor of a ship piloted by Socrates on which all the older forms of poetry, ship-wrecked and subservient, have found tenuous asylum and are crowded into a narrow space (*BT* §13; *KSA* 1, 92–93). Philosophical thought now smothers art and forces it to cling to the trunk of dialectics. The Socratic formulas (virtue is knowledge, sin is committed only out of ignorance, the virtuous man is a happy man) become fundamental forms of optimism that embody the death of tragedy. Now the virtuous hero must be a dialectician, virtue and knowledge must be visibly connected, and the transcendental justice of Aeschylus must be debased to the insipid, impudent principle of poetic justice with its deus ex machina (*BT* §14; *KSA* 1, 94–95). The chorus becomes an afterthought — whereas for Nietzsche, of course, it was the very source of tragedy — and the musical-Dionysian substratum of tragedy fades into history, as demonstrated by Aristotle's dismissal of it as ornamentation (*BT* §14; *KSA* 1, 95).

Before Nietzsche dismisses the "despotic logician" Socrates (jener despotische Logiker) from the stage, he relates the saga of how Socrates, shortly before his death, began to play music and versify Aesopian fables, and this, too, he attributes to Socrates's imbalanced psyche. By making these gestures toward the deities Apollo and Dionysus, Nietzsche contends, Socrates was hedging his bets, acting to counter the possibility that he may have sinned against the gods by insisting that what is incomprehensible cannot be virtuous. Socrates was forced to consider these questions: "Perhaps there is a realm of wisdom from which the logician is banned? Perhaps art is even a necessary correlate and supplement of science?" (Vielleicht giebt es ein Reich der Weisheit, aus dem der Logiker verbannt ist? Vielleicht ist die Kunst sogar ein nothwendiges Correlativum und Supplement der Wissenschaft? *BT* §14; *KSA* 1, 96). Nietzsche's argument against Socrates is really at its best when he attempts to situate Socrates in the gray area, the middle zone where knowledge and logic reach the end of their efficacy and art becomes the only reliable human companion. But when Nietzsche only dehumanizes Socrates, he dehumanizes himself. I find a skillful formulation of the problem in Erich Heller's discussion of Nietzsche and the inarticulate.

Contradiction is a limited form of expression, Heller maintains, yet such as it is, it is fundamental to Nietzsche's thought. Nietzsche reclaimed the territory of contradiction in *The Birth of Tragedy*, and he did so again in *Zarathustra*, leading Heller to characterize his work as existential contradictoriness. Nietzsche's lifelong critique of Socrates was based on Socrates's virtuous pursuit of dialectics; using this method, he would entrap his interlocutors in logical contradictions, a strategy Nietzsche regarded as plebian. The fullness of life and its plenitudes of contradictions nourish the sense of tragedy, according to Heller, and it is this very contradictoriness that Socrates attacks.[52] In *The Birth of Tragedy* the Dionysian, and the primal unity, stand for eternal contradiction and pain, yet this state engenders tragedy, and tragedy in turn represents the highest affirmation of existence ever achieved on earth. It was not a matter of what tragedy said, but what tragedy was able to do for the ancients; this relationship was inverted by Socrates, who insisted on a degree of articulation circumscribed by logic, void of instinct, and as far as possible from any contradiction. In section 14 Nietzsche held out the hope for an alternative to disembodied logic, and in the following section he followed through by demonstrating that all science, all knowledge must reach the point of tragic insight.

Nietzsche refers to Socrates as a unique, unheard of form of existence, the world's first theoretical human being. Whereas Lessing, "the most honest theoretical human being" (der ehrlichste theoretische Mensch), claimed that the search for truth was more important to him than truth itself, Nietzsche juxtaposes him with the impudence and "profound *delusion* that first entered the world with Socrates, that unshakable belief that [. . .] thought is not only capable of knowing existence, but is even capable of *correcting* it" (eine tiefsinnige *Wahnvorstellung*, welche zuerst in der Person des Sokrates zur Welt kam, jener unerschütterliche Glaube, dass [. . .] das Sein nicht nur zu erkennen, sondern sogar zu *corrigieren* im Stande sei; *BT* §15; *KSA* 1, 98–99). This "sublime metaphysical illusion" (erhabene metaphysische Wahn) accompanies science as its instinct, leading it always to its limits, where it must transform into art (*BT* §15; *KSA* 1, 98–99). Meanwhile, Socrates spawns one school of philosophy after another, until the earth is covered by a common network of thought, and modernity has constructed an astonishingly tall pyramid of knowledge. Socrates thus becomes for Nietzsche the "turning point and vortex of so-called world history" (den einen Wendepunkt und Wirbel der sogenannten Weltgeschichte) and knowledge is regarded as a good in its own right, a force having the power of a panacea (*BT* §15; *KSA* 1, 99–100). But science's tendency, or as Nietzsche insists, its instinct, is to rush inexorably to its own limits, fueled by its powerful delusion, where its logocentric optimism founders. Nietzsche now explains that the theoretical individual who is noble and talented will begin to see the periphery of knowledge even before the midpoint of his life, and he will react with horror when he finally sees logic eating its own tail; "tragic insight" (tragische Erkenntniss) breaks out at this point, and in order to even be endured, this insight requires art as protection and medicine (*BT* §15; *KSA* 1, 101).

The remaining sections of *The Birth of Tragedy*, §16–§25, argue for the rebirth of tragedy, and at this point the argument becomes transparent that Wagnerian music will serve as the catalyst of a modern tragic revival. Some of these remaining sections contain worthwhile reformulations of the earlier argument. Section 16 discusses music as the highest enhancement of the ordinary, relying heavily on Schopenhauer's equation of music with the language of the will. Section 17 details what is lost when tragic wisdom and Dionysian music disappear, and section 18 offers a critique of modernity based on a comparison with tragic Greece. In section 18, Nietzsche also describes three different cultural types fueled by three different impulses: the Socratic type who loves knowledge, the artistic type who loves beauty, and the tragic type who loves eternal life beyond appearances. It is this section that resonates in the later essay "On the Uses and Disadvantages of History for Living" ("Vom Nutzen und Nachtheil der Historie für das Leben"), published in 1874 as the second of four *Untimely Meditations* (*Unzeitgemässe Betrachtungen*). Section 22 offers a persuasive critique of the modern audience in relation to art, including the important insight that the tragic is not in our domain, not even in Goethe's, because the ancients dealt with their deepest pathos aesthetically, whereas moderns need to get emotionally involved. Also of value in this section is the distinction between the critical and the aesthetic listener, with its recognition that a modern artist has to face critics because modern art attempts to appeal morally and to be topical, socially aware, engaged, and so on (*BT* §22; *KSA* 1, 142–44). As scholars have long pointed out, these later sections of *The Birth of Tragedy* compromise the original argument by linking the fortunes of tragedy to contemporary Germany and Wagnerian music, but there is nothing forced or compromised about the Dionysian itself, which Nietzsche continues to discuss even in these pro-Wagner sections. The last innovation I shall treat is therefore the primacy of the Dionysian as it emerges from *The Birth of Tragedy*.

By primacy of the Dionysian I mean simply that, although Nietzsche based his argument for the birth and flourishing of tragedy on the presence and interaction of both Apollonian and Dionysian elements, it is clear from the beginning that the Dionysian force is predominant and is infused with meaning far beyond the workings of the Apollonian. Consider, for instance, that when the death of tragedy needs to be chronicled, Nietzsche claims almost exclusively that Euripides, Socrates, and Plato banished Dionysus. Music, moreover, answering exclusively to the Dionysian and representing the substratum of proto-tragedy (lyrics, chorus, dithyramb), is relegated to mere ornamentation. Most important, however, it is the Dionysian nature or essence of the primal unity that upholds the primacy of the Dionysian;

the individuated world of semblance, order and security is a construct of the mind, a cultural product manifesting differently according to different peoples and different times, but the disindividuated, chaotic, eternally burgeoning world of the Dionysian is nature itself (or what Nietzsche later termed the "will to power"). Finally, the Dionysian takes on momentum and surpasses the Apollonian in scope and presence, because Nietzsche was correct in his assessment that moderns have constructed a massive pyramid of knowledge and suffer from a surfeit of faith in knowledge as a panacea. Whether one calls the Dionysian the unconscious, instinct, or the body, Nietzsche was responsible for elevating its role in relation to cognition. Allison formulates Dionysian priority as neither metaphysical, representational, nor productive, but analytic, testifying to the ever-present instinctual sources of human behavior.[53]

The Dionysian assumes primacy in *The Birth of Tragedy*, on the one hand, because it served as the heuristic key to understanding tragedy proper, but, on the other, because it evolved into a reliable, cultural-historical means for approaching all of ancient Greece. Thus while the Dionysian presence may be questioned, Nietzsche's lasting innovation was to put tragedy into a greater cultural context.[54] As Porter has documented, there is very little in Nietzsche's later Dionysian imagery that cannot be found in *The Birth of Tragedy*, including the material from sections 16–25; and though some later formulations of the Dionysian are not identical to those of *The Birth of Tragedy*, Nietzsche found it important to safeguard others throughout his career.[55] We have already discussed how, in *The Birth of Tragedy*, Nietzsche used a borrowed, metaphysical dichotomy based on Schopenhauer, even though he had seen through and dismissed the metaphysics of both Kant and Schopenhauer as early as 1867. When Nietzsche finally spoke unequivocally about his cherished concept of *amor fati* (love of fate) and affirmed all of existence — which I believe he did first and most systematically and consequentially in *The Gay Science*, then again more performatively in *Zarathustra*'s affirmation of the eternal recurrence of the same — this meant that the age-old division of real world and apparent world became moot; the world as it is, as it remains, as it concerns human beings, is Dionysian, and it is worthy of the highest affirmation.

Nietzsche's next work after *The Birth of Tragedy* is the series of four essays collectively entitled *Untimely Meditations*. The first essay is a polemic against David Strauss, the third is a panegyric on Schopenhauer, and the fourth a slightly less enthusiastic panegyric on Wagner; all these essays discuss influential Germans in the light of the first German unification and the new cultural circumstances of the *Gründerzeit* (founding years). The second essay, "On the Use and Disadvantage of History for Living," bears the closest resemblance to *The Birth of Tragedy*, and it is by far the most studied and substantive of the four essays. Two key factors in the "History" essay draw on the energy and innovation of *The Birth of Tragedy*; first, Nietzsche subjects contemporary historicism to a scathing critique reminiscent of the middle sections of *The Birth of Tragedy*, in which Socratic optimism is deconstructed; and second, Nietzsche holds out the alternative of life, vitality, vital force to a modern society of hollow, knowledge-driven automatons who rather resemble Socratic drones. One cannot help but juxtapose the vitality and affirmation of life of the tragic Greeks with the passive, spectator existence of moderns who venerate and consume knowledge for its own sake.

Nietzsche famously remarked on *The Birth of Tragedy* in the 1886 "Attempt at a Self-Critique" ("Versuch einer Selbstkritik") appended to the second edition, as well as in *Ecce Homo* where he "reviewed" all his published works in 1888. The general thrust of these much later revisitations of his first book is revisionist, that is, Nietzsche ascribes qualities and achievements to his early book that he really promulgated only later in his career. These later commentaries cannot be dismissed, however, and they have in fact set the tone for some critics who have relied on them perhaps all too trustingly. Given that his agenda had transformed so radically from that of a Romantic to an anti-Romantic in the intervening years, I shall sketch out some of the implications of his late claims.

Certain threads of "Attempt at a Self-Critique" ring true and are indeed credible as innovations or failings Nietzsche claimed were in the original book. He did, for instance, take on "the problem of science in itself" (das problem der Wissenschaft selbst) and did so by viewing science through the lens of art and art through the lens of life (*BT* "Attempt" §2; *KSA* 1, 13–14); this was abundantly demonstrated in the critique of Socratic optimism and the underscoring throughout of how the tragic Greeks triumphed over suffering to become extraordinary affirmers of life. Likewise Nietzsche was clearly sincere in discussing the stylistic inconsistencies of the book ("poorly written," "embarrassing," "rabid imagery," "uneven tempo," "lacking logical cleanliness" etc.), and in concluding that "it ought to have *sung*, this 'new soul' — and not spoken" (*BT* "Attempt" §3; *KSA* 1, 14–15). But we cannot validate his assertion from this same section that he had spoken in *The Birth of Tragedy* as a "disciple" of the unknown god (Dionysus), disguised as a scholar and a Wagnerian (ibid.). He does indeed transform into such a disciple, but at the time, he was a Wagnerian and he in fact wrote for a German-Wagnerian audience. On this issue compare Nietzsche's comments from *Ecce Homo* in the chapter on *Zarathustra*, where he claims about this book: "My concept 'Dionysian' here became *the highest deed*" (Mein Begriff "dionysisch" wurde hier *höchste That*) (*KSA* 6, 343); when it came to elevating his concept of the Dionysian, Nietzsche relied in *Ecce Homo* on *Zarathustra*, demonstrating that in his own mind he had become a disciple of Dionysus and a Dionysian spirit only later — his claims for the

Dionysian in *The Birth of Tragedy* are muted by comparison. This circumstance is even more apparent when we consider that the final section of the "Attempt" concludes with a lengthy quotation from *Zarathustra* to illustrate the Dionysian. I also ascribe validity to Nietzsche's claim (see §5 of his "Attempt") that in *The Birth of Tragedy* he maintained throughout a "hostile silence about Christianity," but even this must not be set on a par with his later philosophical critique of Christianity, and we have to question whether his instinct had at that time already "turned against" morality in the consequential manner he suggests. Finally, Dionysus did "speak differently" to him (*BT* "Attempt" §6; *KSA* 1, 20) than it had to earlier German thinkers, Schopenhauer in particular, and I have documented in this chapter how Nietzsche must be credited with expanding Europe's notions of "the classical" to include the powerful Dionysian phenomenon, which went far beyond the formulaic understanding of Greek art made famous by Winckelmann. That said, Dionysus also "spoke differently" to Nietzsche when he later *transformed* the artistic concept into a philosophical one (see note 59).

The claims Nietzsche made in behalf of *The Birth of Tragedy* in *Ecce Homo* reveal a similar pattern. We do not have to accept for instance that *The Birth of Tragedy* contributed mightily to the rise of Wagner's fame, or that it contributed to a higher estimation of the cultural value of Wagnerianism generally, although certainly these claims hold true in a limited sense. However, in the same section Nietzsche succinctly and reliably formulates the book's two major innovations: it delivered the first detailed understanding and psychology of the Dionysian phenomenon, and it identified Socrates as the chief cause of the dissolution of Greek culture by arguing for the first time that Socrates was a decadent (§1, *KSA* 6, 310). In section 3, Nietzsche conflates his early treatment of the Dionysian with the later philosophical treatment, and he uses hyperbole in section 4 by claiming that he really heard his own Dionysian music, not Wagner's. He gives a useful but audacious formulation to his own tendency to conflate the early and late Nietzsche when he writes: "The whole image of the *dithyrambic* artist is the image of the *pre-existent* poet of Zarathustra" (Das ganze Bild des *dithyrambischen* Künstlers ist das Bild des *präexistenten* Dichters des Zarathustra; §4, *KSA* 6, 313–14). It is of course undeniable that it was Nietzsche who wrote both *The Birth of Tragedy* and *Thus Spoke Zarathustra*, and that the former work provided him with the basis to write the latter, however, the Dionysian that Nietzsche claims to have translated into a deed with *Zarathustra* did not exist until that work came into being, in the early and mid-1880s. He cannot have it both ways; if he transformed the Dionysian into a philosophy, then the Dionysian was not yet a philosophy in *The Birth of Tragedy*. In addition to the chronology, in biographical and psychological terms, what Nietzsche had not yet experienced at the time he wrote *The Birth of Tragedy* was the shattering Dionysian effect of the relationship with Lou von Salomé. In philosophical terms, Nietzsche did not yet possess the lexicon, or the metaphors of the Zarathustran-Dionysian fusion; this began to manifest in Nietzsche's work only with *The Gay Science*, specifically in the aphorisms devoted to the madman (prophet of the death of God) and to the eternal recurrence of the same. We must also note that in *Ecce Homo* too, just as in "Attempt," Nietzsche was compelled to conclude his discussion of *The Birth of Tragedy* by invoking Zarathustra as the fulfillment of the Dionysian.

A final comment is necessary to explain why Nietzsche refrained from publicly discussing *The Birth of Tragedy* and the Dionysian after 1872, with the notable exceptions of "Attempt" and *Ecce Homo*, even though the Dionysian remained very much on his mind and he consolidated the innovations from *The Birth of Tragedy* and reapplied them to later works. The publication of *The Birth of Tragedy* brought Nietzsche ridicule and scorn from his rival classical philologist Ulrich von Wilamowitz-Möllendorf, who was not pleased with the extraordinary manner in which Nietzsche had been appointed professor of classical philology at Basel.[56] His review of *The Birth of Tragedy* zeroed in on its greatest weakness, namely the fact that it was not strict, scientific philology, but a hybrid of philosophy, Wagnerian aesthetics, and cultural criticism. While this scathing review by a fellow classicist and member of his own generation was not enough in itself to silence Nietzsche on the Dionysian, it was accompanied by the disapproval of his mentor and teacher Friedrich Ritschl, who had published Nietzsche's earliest articles and had intervened for him at Basel.[57] Add to this the personal enmity that soon arose between Nietzsche and the Wagnerians, once he made a clean break with them and launched his first truly independent work, *Human, All Too Human* (*Menschliches, Allzumenschliches*), in 1878, and quite clearly we have a host of reasons for Nietzsche to downplay his first book and the bitter associations it occasioned in him. Meanwhile, the concept of *amor fati*, which is celebrated in *The Birth of Tragedy*, section 3, where Nietzsche cautions that the Greeks deified all things, whether good or evil (*BT* §3; *KSA* 1, 35), emerges once again in *The Gay Science*, where it is the sustaining thread culminating in the first published version of the doctrine of the eternal recurrence of the same. Dionysus begins to receive explicit mention once again in the unpublished notes of 1885,[58] and scholars of Nietzsche's concept of the Dionysian have long pointed to the presence of Dionysian imagery and dithyrambs in *Zarathustra* and the emergence of an explicit Dionysian philosophizing in *Beyond Good and Evil*. Indeed, one of the protean features of *The Birth of Tragedy* has been its ability to transform with the times, engaging each new generation that searches for the values of creativity, just as Nietzsche transformed himself, under the mentorship of the deity he brought back to life, for a modernity hungry for life.[59]

Notes

The translations from Nietzsche in this essay are my own.

[1] The editors of the *Kritische Studienausgabe* in their commentary on all titles in the edition explain that Nietzsche published a second version with corrections in 1878, then a third version in 1886 with the new title and the "Versuch einer Selbstkritik." Both later versions made use of the original printing, and Nietzsche did not make changes to the text of the second edition (see KSA 14, 43).

[2] For Nietzsche's use of earlier German sources on tragedy, see Adrian Del Caro, *Nietzsche Contra Nietzsche* (Baton Rouge: Louisiana State UP, 1989), esp. 47–49, 78–80.

[3] Nietzsche referred to Wagner as both an arch-Romantic and as the epitome of modernity (see *CW* Vorwort; *KSA* 6, 12). For further discussion, see the chapter entitled "Wagner's Place in Nietzsche's Perception of Romanticism," in Del Caro, *Nietzsche Contra Nietzsche*, 144–60.

[4] M. S. Silk and J. P. Stern, *Nietzsche on Tragedy* (Cambridge: Cambridge UP, 1981), 28. See Nietzsche's letter to Erwin Rohde of 9 November 1868 and the subsequent letters to Rohde, which reveal great enthusiasm for Wagner (*KSB* 2, 335–42).

[5] Silk and Stern, *Nietzsche on Tragedy*, 52.

[6] The titles of these early lectures and essays are given in their entirety to demonstrate the evolution of Nietzsche's thoughts in the direction of tragedy and music (see *KSA* 14, 41–43).

[7] See *KSA* 14, 42.

[8] Silk and Stern, *Nietzsche on Tragedy*, 18.

[9] Silk and Stern, *Nietzsche on Tragedy*, 34; and Del Caro, *Nietzsche Contra Nietzsche*, 119–22.

[10] R. J. Hollingdale, *Nietzsche: The Man and His Philosophy* (Baton Rouge: Louisiana State UP, 1965), 69.

[11] Del Caro, *Nietzsche Contra Nietzsche*, 120–21, 154–55.

[12] Silk and Stern point out that Nietzsche was even involved in the preparation of Wagner's autobiography (*Nietzsche on Tragedy*, 202).

[13] Del Caro, *Nietzsche Contra Nietzsche*, 144. "Brothers *in Wagnero*" is an allusion to "brothers *in Christo*," brothers in Christ. Nietzsche's scathing condemnation of Wagner in *Der Fall Wagner* (*The Case of Wagner*) in 1888 repeatedly underscores how Wagner had been a mere Christian demagogue, a mesmerizing histrionic surrounded and worshipped by Christo-Germanic anti-Semites (see Del Caro, *Nietzsche Contra Nietzsche*, 154–60).

[14] For the text of "Homer's Contest," see Janet Lungstrum and Elizabeth Sauer, eds., *Agonistics: Arenas of Creative Contest* (Albany, NY: SUNY P, 1997), 35–45, and in the same volume Volney P. Gay's essay on agonistics and psychoanalysis (111–28), and Benjamin C. Sax's on the cultural history of the *agon* (46–69).

[15] See Rudolf Kreis, *Nietzsche, Wagner und die Juden* (Würzburg: Königshausen & Neumann, 1995), 19–21. Kreis's argument has a distinctly ecological dimension, insofar as he details how Nietzsche's earth-affirming and geocentric writings, in particular *Zarathustra*, are a direct counter to Wagner's Christological, nationalistic, and anti-Semitic works, which are disdainful of the earth and of all life on earth.

[16] See the section of *Ecce Homo* where Nietzsche discusses his first philological writings and the influence of Ritschl (*EH* "Why I Am So Clever" ["Warum ich so klug bin"] §9; *KSA* 6, 295).

[17] See Walter Kaufmann, "Translator's Introduction," in *The Basic Writings of Nietzsche*, ed. and trans. Walter Kaufmann (New York: Random House, 1968), 13.

[18] I am puzzled by Kaufmann's glib statement in his "Translator's Introduction," to the effect that the contrast of the Apollonian and Dionysian is not of lasting importance, since it smacks of Schopenhauer, etc. (*Basic Writings*, 9). Elsewhere I have shown that Kaufmann had a "tin ear" when it comes to the Dionysian (see Adrian Del Caro, "Symbolizing Philosophy: Ariadne and the Labyrinth," *Nietzsche-Studien* 17 (1988): 125–57), and in fact the contrast, or duality or dichotomy of Apollonian/Dionysian has profoundly influenced many different cultural spheres since Nietzsche set them into circulation. For that matter, it is partly on the strength of Nietzsche's growing centrality, and his application of Schopenhauerian principles in *The Birth of Tragedy* that interest in Schopenhauer is growing today, as seen in the comments of Christopher Janaway, editor and translator of Schopenhauer's *The Two Fundamental Problems of Ethics* (Cambridge: Cambridge UP, 2009), vii.

[19] James T. Porter, *The Invention of Dionysus: An Essay on "The Birth of Tragedy"* (Stanford: Stanford UP, 2000), 42–43. Nietzsche actually uses the word *Duplicität*, followed immediately by *Zweiheit*, both of which mean "duality."

[20] Koenraad Hemelsoet, Benjamin Biebuyck, Danny Praet, "'Jene durchaus verschleierte apollinische Mysterienordnung': Zur Funktion und Bedeutung der antiken Mysterien in Nietzsches frühen Schriften," *Nietzsche-Studien* 35 (2006): 1–28 (here: 2).

[21] Richard Schacht, *Nietzsche* (London: Routledge & Kegan Paul, 1985), 485–86.

[22] Schacht, *Nietzsche*, 509.

[23] Porter, *The Invention of Dionysus*, 24. See also Lionel Gossman's discussion of Burckhardt's understanding of the *polis* as based on an agon between nobility and measure, in which the latter reins in the energy of the former like the Apollonian reins in the Dionysian. Gossman, *Basel in the Age of Burckhardt: A Study in Unseasonable Ideas* (Chicago: U of Chicago P, 2000), 326–27.

[24] Robert Rethy, "The Tragic Affirmation of the *Birth of Tragedy*," *Nietzsche-Studien* (1988): 1–44 (here: 7); Benjamin C. Sax, "Cultural Agonistics: Nietzsche, the Greeks, Eternal Recurrence," in *Agonistics: Arenas of Creative Contest*, ed. Janet Lungstrum and Elizabeth Sauer (Albany: SUNY P, 1997), 46–69 (here: 49).

[25] Arthur Schopenhauer, *Parerga und Paralipomena II: Kleine philosophische Schriften*, in *Werke in zehn Bänden: Zürcher Ausgabe*, ed. Angelika Hübscher (Zurich: Diogenes, 1977), vol. 10, 442.

[26] See Hemelsoet, Biebuyck, and Praet, "'Jene durchaus verschleierte Mysterienordnung,'" 15–16.

[27] Margot Fleischer, "Dionysos als Ding an sich. Der Anfang von Nietzsches Philosophie in der ästhetischen Metaphysik der 'Geburt der Tragödie,'" *Nietzsche-Studien* 17 (1988): 74–90 (here: 81).

[28] Fleischer, "Dionysos als Ding an sich," 89.

[29] Adrian Del Caro, *Grounding the Nietzsche Rhetoric of Earth* (Berlin: Walter de Gruyter, 2004), 320–26.

[30] See David B. Allison, "Nietzsche Knows no Noumenon," in *Why Nietzsche Now?*, ed. Daniel O'Hara (Bloomington: Indiana UP, 1985), 295–310 (here: 298).

[31] Allison, "Nietzsche Knows no Noumenon," 306.

[32] Allison, "Nietzsche Knows no Noumenon," 307.

[33] Allison, "Nietzsche Knows no Noumenon," 304.

[34] See Enrico Müller, "'Aesthetische Lust' and 'Dionysische Weisheit': Nietzsches Deutung der griechischen Tragödie," *Nietzsche-Studien* 31 (2002): 134–53 (here: 153).

[35] See Daniel Came, "Nietzsche's Attempt at a Self-Criticism: Art and Morality in *The Birth of Tragedy*," *Nietzsche-Studien* 33 (2004): 37–67 (here: 38).

[36] Came, "Nietzsche's Attempt," 66. Although Came is right to point to *The Gay Science*, §107, as another expression of how existence is made bearable as an aesthetic phenomenon, he trivializes the thrust of *The Gay Science* by limiting its existential force to this single aphorism. In fact, the whole of *Gay Science*, in its structure and content, is a non-metaphysical rendering of *amor fati*, love of fate, which Nietzsche began in *The Birth of Tragedy* and developed philosophically in *The Gay Science*, which includes the first published formulation of the most life-affirming thought possible, viz., the eternal recurrence of the same.

[37] Schacht, *Nietzsche*, 393; see also Del Caro, *Grounding the Nietzsche Rhetoric of Earth*, 49–50.

[38] See Del Caro, *Grounding the Nietzsche Rhetoric of Earth*, 49–50.

[39] See Müller, "'Aesthetische Lust,'" 150.

[40] See Del Caro, *Grounding the Nietzsche Rhetoric of Earth*, 72–73.

[41] See Allison, "Nietzsche Knows no Noumenon," 305.

[42] See Müller, "'Aesthetische Lust,'" 138.

[43] See Del Caro, *Grounding the Nietzsche Rhetoric of Earth*, 161–67.

[44] See Del Caro, *Nietzsche Contra Nietzsche*, 58–59 and 134–38.

[45] See Allison, "Nietzsche Knows no Noumenon," 307.

[46] See Porter, *The Invention of Dionysus*, 149.

[47] See Schacht, *Nietzsche*, 497.

[48] See Schacht, *Nietzsche*, 511.

[49] See Del Caro, *Grounding the Nietzsche Rhetoric of Earth*, 212–21.

[50] See Porter, *The Invention of Dionysus*, 161.

[51] See Schacht, cited above, and Gossman's comment regarding the anti-plebian, aristocratic sympathies of Burckhardt and his contemporaries (*Basel in the Age of Burckhardt*, 326–27). Raymond Geuss also speaks persuasively of how Nietzsche and Wagner were virtual opposites on this issue, with Wagner (the Left Hegelian, egalitarian) colliding with Nietzsche (the proclaimer of order of rank); see Geuss, "Introduction," in *The Birth of Tragedy and Other Writings*, ed. Raymond Geuss, trans. Ronald Speirs (Cambridge: Cambridge UP, 2006), vii–xxx (here: xv–xvi).

[52] Erich Heller, "Nietzsche and the Inarticulate," in *Nietzsche: Literature and Values*, ed. Volker Dürr, Reinhold Grimm, and Kathy Harms (Madison: U of Wisconsin P, 1988), 3–13 (here: 6).

[53] Allison, "Nietzsche Knows no Noumenon," 308.

[54] Müller, "'Aesthetische Lust,'" 146, 148.

[55] Porter, *The Invention of Dionysus*, 23.

[56] Peter Bergmann, *Nietzsche, "The Last Antipolitical German"* (Bloomington, IN: Indiana UP, 1987), 92–94.

[57] Geuss, "Introduction," *The Birth of Tragedy*, xxviii.

[58] Del Caro, *Grounding the Nietzsche Rhetoric of Earth*, 163.

[59] See Adrian Del Caro, "Nietzschean Self-Transformation and the Transformation of the Dionysian," in *Nietzsche, Philosophy and the Arts*, ed. Salim Kemal, Ivan Gaskell, and Daniel W. Conway (Cambridge: Cambridge UP, 1998), 70–91.

Link to *Untimely Meditations*

The Birth of Tragedy was written in (and, in a sense, against) a number of contexts: the military context of the Franco-Prussian War; the political context of the proclamation of the German *Reich* in Versailles on 18 January 1871, of the declaration of the Paris Commune on 18 March of the same year, and of the growing revolutionary movement in Europe; and the academic-political context of Basel, especially the philological circles in which Nietzsche had to operate. As early as on 20 November 1868, after his first meeting with Wagner in the Brockhaus household, Nietzsche wrote a letter to Rohde in which his dissatisfaction with scholars and with his academic colleagues was expressed with some force. Here he speaks of "the teeming broods of philologists of today, [. . .] the entire molelike activity, with their full cheek-pouches and their blind eyes" (das wimmelnde Philologengezücht unserer Tage [. . .], das ganze Maulwurfstreiben, die vollen Backentaschen und die blinden Augen), and what upset him was not just "their joy at the captured worm and their indifference to the real, indeed the insistent problems of life" (die Freude ob des erbeuteten Wurms und die Gleichgültigkeit gegen die wahren, ja aufdringlichen Probleme des Lebens; *KSB* 2, 344).[1] This letter strikes one of the first notes in what will become a constant theme in Nietzsche's writings: the relationship between scholarly, academic activities and the tasks of the "real world"; ultimately, the relation of knowledge to life. His answer to this problem both returns Nietzsche to the tradition of philosophy conceived as *exercices spirituels*, as Pierre Hadot has called it, and marks him out as inaugurating, along with Schopenhauer, the body of thought known as *Lebensphilosophie*.

The wrong answer to the knowledge-life problem, as Nietzsche saw it, lay in scholarly activity *for its own sake*. As he put it in his third *Untimely Meditation* (*Unzeitgemässe Betrachtung*), "I consider every word written to be useless, unless it contains a call to activity" (ich erachte jedes Wort für unnütz geschrieben, hinter dem nicht eine solche Aufforderung zur That steht; *UM* III §8; *KSA* 1, 413), and in *Ecce Homo* he was even more trenchant, describing "the scholar" (der Gelehrte) as "a decadent" (ein Décadent): "His instinct of self-defense has become soft; otherwise he would defend himself against books" (Der Instinkt der Selbstvertheidigung ist bei ihm mürbe geworden; im andren Falle würde er sich gegen Bücher wehren). Nietzsche emphasized that his reflections were based on what he had himself seen: "Gifted, generously and liberally disposed natures 'read to ruins' in their thirties, mere matches requiring to be struck to make them emit sparks — or 'thoughts'" (Begabte, reich und frei angelegte Naturen schon in den dreissiger Jahren "zu Schanden gelesen", bloss noch Streichhölzer, die man reiben muss, damit sie Funken — "Gedanken" geben; *EH* "Why I Am So Clever" §8; *KSA* 6, 293).

Indeed, in his notes for a never-completed essay provisionally entitled "We Philologists" ("Wir Philologen"), Nietzsche went further: "Classical philologists are people who use the hollow feeling of inadequacy among modern people in order to earn money and put bread on their table. I know them, I'm one of them" (Philologen sind solche Menschen, welche das dumpfe Gefühl der modernen Menschen über ihr eigenes Ungenügen benutzen, um darauf hin Gold und Brod zu erwerben. Ich kenne sie, ich bin selber einer; *KSA* 8, 5[142], 76).[2] The reverse side of this dissatisfaction was his ideal of a secular monastery, an "educational institution of the future" (die zukünftige Bildungsanstalt), as his sister called it, which lay behind their plan in the summer of 1873 to purchase a small castle near Flims in the Swiss canton of Graubünden.[3] (The plan came to nothing, but the idea survived in Nietzsche's mind.) In contrast to the sad figures of conventional academics (of which, as he acknowledged, he himself was one) he opposed two men: the philosopher and the composer — Schopenhauer and Wagner.

Nietzsche had read Schopenhauer's *The World as Will and Representation* (*Die Welt als Wille und Vorstellung*, 1819; [2]1844; [3]1859) in late October 1865 and had been overwhelmed by the experience:

> One day I came across this book in Rohn's secondhand bookshop, picked it up as something completely strange, and flicked through it. I do not know which daimon whispered to me: "Take this book home with you." But I did, despite my habit of usually not being overhasty with book purchases. At home, I threw myself onto the sofa in the corner with the acquired treasure and began to allow this energetic, dark genius to work upon me. Here every line screamed of renunciation, denial, resignation, here I saw a mirror in which I glimpsed the world, life, and my own soul in terrible magnification. Here I looked at the completely disinterested solar eye of art, here I saw sickness and healing, exile and refuge, hell and heaven.

> [Eines Tages fand ich nämlich im Antiquariat des alten Rohn dies Buch, nahm es mir als völlig fremd in die Hand und blätterte. Ich weiß nicht welcher Dämon mir zuflüsterte: "Nimm Dir dies Buch mit nach Hause." Es geschah jedenfalls wider meine sonstige Gewohnheit, Büchereinkäufe nicht zu überschleunigen. Zu Hause warf ich mich mit dem erworbenen Schatze in die Sophaecke und begann jenen energischen düsteren Genius auf mich wirken zu lassen. Hier war jede Zeile, die Entsagung, Verneinigung, Resigna-

tion schrie, hier sah ich einen Spiegel, in dem ich die Welt, Leben und eigen Gemüt in entsetzlicher Großartigkeit erblickte. Hier sah mich das volle interesselose Sonnenauge der Kunst an, hier sah ich Krankheit und Zufluchtsort, Hölle und Himmel. (*BAW* 3, 298)]

In his third *Untimely Meditation*, "Schopenhauer as Educator" ("Schopenhauer als Erzieher"), Nietzsche's encomium demonstrates the principle enunciated in his essay: "I profit from a philosopher only inasmuch as he can be an example" (Ich mache mir aus einem Philosophen gerade so viel als er im Stande ist ein Beispiel zu geben; *UM* IV §3; *KSA* 1, 350).

A few years before his initiation in to the school of Schopenhauerian philosophy, in the autumn of 1862, Nietzsche had participated in "orgies of Wagner,"[4] and had become a committed supporter of the Wagnerian cause (and a close personal friend of the Wagners). Ironically, however, the publication of the fourth *Untimely Meditation*, "Richard Wagner in Bayreuth," which appeared in the summer of 1876 in time for the performance of the *Der Ring des Nibelungen* in Bayreuth, coincided with the very moment when Nietzsche realized that he and Wagner were on different paths. Nietzsche's notes from 1874 and 1875 document this gradual shift away from Wagner, which was to culminate in a complete breakdown in their friendship. (During the rehearsals for the first public performance of Wagner's tetralogy, for the inaugural festival held in the specially designed Festival Theater in Bayreuth in August 1876, Nietzsche became so ill that he had to flee to nearby Klingenbrunn to recover, but he managed to pull himself together to be in attendance for the performances.)

But the shift away from Wagner is tied up with other concerns, reflected in the other *Untimely Meditations*.[5] The first, "David Strauss, the Confessor and the Writer" ("David Strauss, der Bekenner und der Schriftsteller," 1873), is a polemical attack on the theologian and historian of religion, David Friedrich Strauss (1808–74). It reflects Nietzsche's unease about the triumphalist culture prevailing in the newly established *Reich* (*UM* I §1; *KSA* 1, 159–64): defining *Kultur* as "a unity of artistic style in all the vital expressions of a people" (Einheit des künstlerischen Stiles in allen Lebensäusserungen eines Volkes), in opposition to barbarism, *Barbarei*, which is seen as "the lack of style of a chaotic confusions of all styles" (die Stillosigkeit oder das chaotische Durcheinander aller Stile), or (in Goethe's words) the "resistance of the obtuse world" (Widerstand der stumpfen Welt) (*UM* I §1; *KSA* 1, 163).[6] The second, "On the Uses and Disadvantages of History for Life" ("Vom Nutzen und Nachtheil der Historie für das Leben," 1874), takes as its starting point Goethe's maxim "Übrigens ist mir Alles verhasst, was mich bloss belehrt, ohne meine Thätigkeit zu vermehren, oder unmittelbar zu beleben" (Anyway, I hate everything that merely instructs me, without increasing or directly invigorating my activity; *UM* II Vorwort; *KSA* 1, 245).[7] Distinguishing between the "monumental," the "antiquarian," and the "critical" kinds of history (*UM* II §2; *KSA* 1, 258), Nietzsche measures them against life — against "life alone, that dark, impulsive power, insatiably thirsting for itself" (das Leben allein, jene dunkle, treibende, unersättlich sich selbst begehrende Macht; *UM* II §3; *KSA* 1, 269). In this essay, Nietzsche argues that "the goal of humanity cannot lie in its end, but only in its highest exemplars" (das Ziel der Menschheit kann nicht am Ende liegen, sondern nur in ihren höchsten Exemplaren; *UW* II §9; *KSA* 1, 317).

All four essays, however, share a similar note of uncertainty in comparison with the exuberant and prophetic confidence of *The Birth of Tragedy*. That uncertainty is captured in a striking image in the third essay on Schopenhauer, when Nietzsche writes:

> A winter's day lies upon us, and we live in high mountains, dangerously and in need. Every joy is brief, and pale is every ray of sunlight that creeps down to us on the white mountains. Music sounds, an old man turns a barrel-organ, the dancers revolve — it astonishes the wanderer to see this: everything is so wild, so taciturn, so colorless, so hopeless, and now there resounds within it a note of joy, of sheer, unreflective joy! But already the mists of early evening close in, the music dies away, the wanderer's step crunches: as far as he can still see, there is nothing but the desolate and cruel face of nature.
>
> [Es liegt ein Wintertag auf uns, und am hohen Gebirge wohnen wir, gefährlich und in Dürftigkeit. Kurz ist jede Freude und bleich jeder Sonnenglanz, der an den weissen Bergen zu uns herabschleicht. Da ertönt Musik, ein alter Mann dreht ein Leierkasten, die Tänzer drehen sich — es erschüttert den Wanderer, dies zu sehen: so wild, so verschlossen, so farblos, so hoffnungslos ist Alles, und jetzt darin ein Ton der Freude, der gedankenlosen lauten Freude! Aber schon schleichen die Nebel des frühen Abends, der Ton verklingt, der Schritt des Wanderers knirscht; soweit er noch sehen kann, sieht er nichts als das öde und grausame Antlitz der Natur. (*UM* III §4; *KSA* 1, 367)]

This beautiful passage evokes the mood accompanying what, in the fourth essay, Nietzsche calls "a *sense for the tragic*" (eine *tragische Gesinnung*), which, if it could be retained, would constitute, in his view, "a guarantee for the future of what is human" (eine Gewähr für die Zukunft des Menschlichen): "A cry of distress such has never been heard would resound across the earth, if human beings should ever completely lose it; while, conversely, there is no joy more rapturous than to know what we know — that the tragic idea has been reborn into the world" (Es würde ein Geschrei sonder Gleichen über die Erde erschallen müssen, wenn die Menschen sie einmal völlig verlieren sollten; und wiederum giebt es keine beseligendere Lust als Das zu wissen, was wir wissen — wie der tragische Gedanke wieder hinein in die Welt geboren ist; *UW* IV §4; *KSA* 1, 453). The following discussion of the *Untimely Meditations* by Duncan Large brings out the extraordinary sense of ambivalence in these texts; an ambivalence captured in a passage from Nietzsche's letter to Carl von Gersdorff of 1 April 1874:

> Shall I ever reach it? Doubt upon doubt. The goal is too far, and if one manages to reach it, one has usually also consumed one's energies in the long searching and struggle: one attains one's freedom and is weary like a mayfly in the evening.

> [Werde ich's je erreichen? Zweifel über Zweifel. Das Ziel ist zu weit, und hat man's leidlich erreicht, so hat man meistens auch seine Kräfte im langen Suchen und Kämpfen verzehrt: man kommt zur Freiheit und ist matt wie eine Eintagsfliege am Abend. (*KSB* 4, 214)]

Notes

[1] Compare with Faust's scornful dismissal of the (lack of) intellectual ambition of his assistant, Wagner: "He's happy, if he can find some earthworms" (Und froh ist, wenn er Regenwürmer findet); Goethe, *Faust*, ed. Erich Trunz (Munich: Beck, 1972), 26, l. 605.

[2] See "We Classicists," trans. William Arrowsmith, in Friedrich Nietzsche, *Unmodern Observations*, ed. William Arrowsmith (New Haven and London: Yale UP, 1990), 305–87.

[3] Elisabeth Förster-Nietzsche, *Das Leben Friedrich Nietzsche's*, 3 vols. (Leipzig: Naumann, 1895–1904), 2.1:117–18.

[4] Förster-Nietzsche, *Das Leben Friedrich Nietzsche's*, 1:135.

[5] In all, Nietzsche planned to write a series of thirteen essays, but only completed four. Defining in his third essay the title-word *unzeitgemäß*, "untimely" or "unmodern," as "to be *simple* and *honest*, in thought and life" (*einfach* und *ehrlich*, im Denken und Leben) (*UM* III §2; *KSA* 1, 346), he echoes Schiller's observation that to concern oneself with aesthetics rather than with morality or politics is to be "ausser der Zeit" (Schiller, *Über die ästhetische Erziehung der Menschheit* [*On the Aesthetic Education of Humankind*], ed. and trans. Elizabeth M. Wilkinson and L. A. Willoughby (Oxford: Clarendon Press, 1982), 6 (Letter 2, §1); see Gary Brown, "Introduction" to "Richard Wagner in Bayreuth," in Friedrich Nietzsche, *Unmodern Observations*, ed. William Arrowsmith (New Haven and London: Yale UP, 1990), 227–52 (here: 233). Brown discusses in further detail Nietzsche's indebtedness to Schiller's cultural analysis ("Introduction," 233–34).

[6] See Goethe, "Epilogue zu Schillers 'Glocke,'" l. 52, in *Gedichte*, ed. Erich Trunz (Munich: Beck, 1974), 256–59 (here: 257).

[7] See Goethe's letter to Schiller of 19 December 1798.

3: *Untimely Meditations*

Duncan Large

THE *Untimely Meditations* (*Unzeitgemässe Betrachtungen*, 1873–76) are some of Nietzsche's most neglected works. They have attracted the attentions of translators less often than most of his other, more celebrated books — Walter Kaufmann, the doyen of postwar American Nietzsche translators, never got round to translating them, and he goes so far as to suggest that they merit translating last of all.[1] They have attracted relatively little scholarly interest, too, and are omitted from the canon established by Robert C. Solomon and Kathleen Higgins in their *Reading Nietzsche*,[2] while the term "untimeliness" has routinely been passed over in Nietzsche dictionaries.[3] The *Untimely Meditations* have indeed become unfashionable (as the title of one of the English translations has it),[4] although they represent some of the most impassioned statements of a number of Nietzsche's early philosophical positions.

Biographical and Intellectual Context

The period in which Nietzsche wrote the *Untimely Meditations* was a relatively stable and happy one in his personal life, even if he was periodically racked by debilitating illness. They are a product of the decade (1869–79) when he held down his "day job" as Professor of Classical Philology at the University of Basel in northern Switzerland, and they reflect the high-water mark in his crucially formative relationship with Richard Wagner. Indeed one can situate their composition between two great crises in Nietzsche's life: on the one hand the professional crisis occasioned by the publication of *The Birth of Tragedy* (*Die Geburt der Tragödie*) in 1872 and its aftermath (the shredding of his reputation as an academic), on the other the personal and intellectual crisis marked by his break with Wagner (triggered by the inaugural Bayreuth Festival in August 1876).

   The Birth of Tragedy precipitated out of an intellectual ferment that also produced a wealth of ideas for follow-up projects in Nietzsche's notebooks, so he was spoiled for choice, and it is not surprising if afterwards he pitched himself into shorter, less ambitious essayistic statements to work out some of this material. His projects from 1872 include a series of public lectures "On the Future of Our Educational Institutions" ("Ueber die Zukunft unserer Bildungsanstalten"; *KSA* 1, 641–752) and the "Five Prefaces for Five Unwritten Books" ("Fünf Vorreden zu fünf ungeschriebenen Büchern"; *KSA* 1, 753–92) presented to Cosima Wagner as a joint birthday/Christmas present that year, including the relatively well-known essays "The Greek State" ("Der griechische Staat"; *KSA* 1, 764–77) and "Homer's Contest" ("Homer's Wettkampf"; *KSA* 1, 783–92).[5] The following year he produced what have more recently become two of his best-known posthumous publications, "Philosophy in the Tragic Age of the Greeks" ("Die Philosophie im tragischen Zeitalter der Griechen"; *KSA* 1, 799–872) and "On Truth and Lie in an Extra-Moral Sense" ("Ueber Wahrheit und Lüge im aussermoralischen Sinne"; *KSA* 1, 873–90).

In the course of 1873 the outlines of a much bigger project began also to emerge, though: in response to promptings by Richard and Cosima Wagner, Nietzsche wrote and published an attack on the theological writer David Friedrich Strauss, but on its publication in the summer of that year Nietzsche was already making it clear that this was not just some lightweight occasional piece; rather, the Strauss essay was billed as the "first installment" of a series of essays in cultural criticism (the title page read: "Unzeitgemässe Betrachtungen Erstes Stück: David Strauss der Bekenner und der Schriftsteller"). In his notebooks of this period it is clear that from early in the planning process Nietzsche was aiming to publish no fewer than thirteen such installments, ideally at a rate of one every six months over six years.[6] Only four would eventually be completed: difficulties over the composition of the fourth led Nietzsche to draw the series to a premature close in early 1877, but only because by that stage he had attained a new conception of his philosophical task. By that stage, in other words, the *Untimely Meditations* had served their purpose.

"Untimeliness"

The German title Nietzsche gives to his series of essays, *Unzeitgemässe Betrachtungen*, is unusual and has proved quite resistant to English translation: the four different complete English translations of the work all take different titles. The key term "unzeitgemäss" was a relatively recent coinage — and not by Nietzsche, although the linguist R. M. Meyer ascribes it to him as a "subjective neologism" in the operative inflection Nietzsche favors[7] — and it could perhaps be translated most straightforwardly as "not in accordance with one's time." In the course of these essays Nietzsche gives the distinct impression that, to speak with Shakespeare's Hamlet (as he often does), his time is out of joint — with the corollary that it is incumbent on him to think and write in an oppositional, "untimely" fashion at odds with the *Zeitgeist*.

In the wider sociopolitical context of the 1870s, the *Untimely Meditations* are clearly intended as a cultural stock-taking exercise in the wake of Prussia's military victory in the recent Franco-Prussian War (1870–71) and the subsequent founding of a unified, resurgent German Empire: Nietzsche feels the need to adopt this gadfly role as a direct consequence of the *Gründerzeit* triumphalism which was in his view so catastrophically myopic. Although he never actually uses the term, he practices "*Kulturkritik*" *avant la lettre*: from his perch in Switzerland (a vantage point of Archimedean detachment that is as "unspacely" as it is "untimely"),[8] he tells the Germans the unpalatable truths that they don't want to hear, critiquing problematic aspects of German culture from the point of view of one who still loves and cares for it deeply.

In the third *Untimely* essay he encapsulates the modern world to which he takes exception, "the perversity of contemporary human nature" (die Verschrobenheit der jetzigen Menschennatur), in a series of fashionable buzzwords: "such bogus concepts as 'progress,' 'universal education,' 'national,' 'modern state,' 'cultural struggle'" (solche flausenhafte Begriffe wie 'Fortschritt', 'allgemeine Bildung', 'National', 'moderner Staat', 'Culturkampf'; *UM* III §7; *KSA* 1, 407).[9] In the second *Untimely* he describes an excess of historicism as a "malady of history" (historische Krankheit; *UM* II §10; *KSA* 1, 329), but this explicitly medical tone is often discernible elsewhere, too, with Dr. Nietzsche functioning as a "physician of culture" (Arzt der Cultur; *KSA* 7, 23[15], 545), diagnosing symptoms, then applying a cultural corrective.[10] In the preface to the second *Untimely* essay he gives us an explicit gloss on what the notion of "untimeliness" means to him: "untimely — that is to say, acting counter to our time and thereby acting on our time and, let us hope, for the benefit of a time to come" (unzeitgemäss — das heisst gegen die Zeit und dadurch auf die Zeit und hoffentlich zu Gunsten einer kommenden Zeit — zu wirken; *UM* II preface; *KSA* 1, 247). For this remarkably progressive classicist, then (and his close relation to Wagner was key in this respect), "untimeliness" does not mean returning to the "timeless" values of the classical age, but he appeals rather to the redemptive power of futurity.[11]

Formal and Stylistic Features

Formally speaking, with the *Untimely Meditations* Nietzsche continued in the same vein as with *The Birth of Tragedy*, and adopted the same procedures: thus, each of the essays is divided into a succession of numbered (but untitled) subsections of varying length. Overall, the four essays are roughly equal in length, around 25,000 words each in German,[12] although the briefest (*UM* IV) is approximately 15% shorter than the longest (*UM* III). Scandalously for a work by a German academic,

The Birth of Tragedy had lacked any scholarly apparatus and contained no footnotes; here, too, Nietzsche deliberately eschews what he considers to be the deadly dull writing style of standard German philosophy and cocks a snook at academic propriety in the interest (alas, largely frustrated) of securing for himself a wider readership. Although the *Untimely Meditations* are relatively early works, then, they are by no means apprentice pieces: the essays are undoubtedly highly readable and entertaining, and for all their youthful exuberance Nietzsche is already displaying a rhetorical accomplishment and assuredness of stylistic grasp. For example, he already demonstrates a striking ability to mobilize and manipulate extended metaphors such as his "master trope" of cultural sickness or the seafaring metaphor in *UM* II §10, and at the opening of the second essay — "Consider the cattle, grazing as they pass you by" (Betrachte die Heerde, die an dir vorüberweidet; *UM* II §1; *KSA* 1, 248) — he displays a gift for Biblical parody which will later bear rich fruit in *Thus Spoke Zarathustra* (*Also sprach Zarathustra*, 1883–85). Nor is he afraid to coin new terms, such as the notorious word "Bildungsphilister" (cultural philistine), a typically paradoxical formulation that is the centerpiece of the first essay's critique. In many ways the suppleness of Nietzsche's German and the creativity in his approach to the manipulation of (the German) language are experimental, and his experiments by no means always come off, leading to a certain stylistic unevenness when, for example, he occasionally gets carried away by his metaphors, but such lapses are rare.

When Nietzsche looks back on the *Untimely Meditations* in his late autobiography *Ecce Homo* (1888), the first aspect he emphasizes is their polemical character: "The four *Untimelies* are thoroughly warlike" (Die vier *Unzeitgemässen* sind durchaus kriegerisch; *EH UM* §1; *KSA* 6, 316). All four *Untimely* essays are exercises in polemic, then — even the third and fourth, which are *in addition* essays in advocacy (by contrast with the late work *Nietzsche contra Wagner*, one might dub them simply "Nietzsche pro Schopenhauer" and "Nietzsche pro Wagner"). The deliberately oppositional stance referred to above is reflected on every level of the texts' organization, so that there is a pointedness to their arguments and to their heightened rhetoric that is often far from fair (fairness was a value Nietzsche thought much overrated). Each of the essays is apparently a single-issue piece, although they are always also about much more, for Nietzsche cannot resist importing his wider preoccupations each time, often digressively.[13] These are "meditations" in the sense that they reveal what is on his mind at the time of composition, which is one reason why they are still so fascinating and rewarding to read, and it makes them surprisingly timely, as well: all are interventions in contemporary debates that were preoccupying him to a greater or lesser extent (i.e., the stance he adopts may be untimely, but the debate itself is not).

UM I: *David Strauss, the Confessor and the Writer*

The first of the *Untimely Meditations,* entitled "David Strauss, the Confessor and the Writer" (David Strauss der Bekenner und der Schriftsteller), was written quickly in April-May 1873 and published in the summer of that year. The "Young Hegelian" David Friedrich Strauss (1808–74) was not a figure to whom Nietzsche had previously paid much attention, but Strauss was one of the foremost exponents of the rationalist critique of religion, and his early work *The Life of Jesus* (*Das Leben Jesu,* 1835–36; translated by George Eliot) had scandalized Christian Europe by denying the divinity of the historical Jesus, rejecting the historical accuracy of the supernatural elements in the gospels and characterizing them instead as "mythical." One might have expected Nietzsche to be favorably disposed toward Strauss, and indeed initially he was — he had read *Das Leben Jesu* as a student of theology at Bonn University in 1864–65, and it had helped precipitate his loss of faith — but here Nietzsche turns on Strauss's latest work, *The Old Faith and the New Faith* (*Der alte und der neue Glaube,* 1872), which had again scandalized Europe (this time for its materialism) and, more especially, irritated Nietzsche's mentor Richard Wagner and his wife Cosima.[14] So Nietzsche wrote his *Untimely Meditation* at the Wagners' instigation (Wagner and Strauss had had a public feud some years before):[15] it is very much an occasional piece, an extended book review. Wagner was certainly using Nietzsche for his own purposes, but in turn the young scholar used the piece as a peg on which to hang a number of his contemporary concerns. It has no preface, but the opening pages serve the same purpose: Strauss is not mentioned until toward the end of the second section, and *Der alte und der neue Glaube* is not introduced until the third.

The essay adopts a contrarian position from the outset: Nietzsche recasts the recently fought (and, from the German perspective, recently won) Franco-Prussian War as a cultural conflict and seeks to correct the erroneous, commonly held view that Germany's military victory (cemented by the establishment of the new empire) somehow corresponded to a cultural victory as well. We can note in passing Nietzsche's respect for French culture, which will deepen into a positive Francophilia over the course of his career (cf. *EH* "Why I Am So Wise" §3);[16] at this stage, though, Nietzsche still cares about German culture and is more concerned to analyze what the problem is for Germany before proposing solutions. Contrary to the false complacency of "public opinion" (die öffentliche Meinung; *UM* I §1; *KSA* 1, 159), Nietzsche argues that "German spirit" (deutscher Geist) and "German Empire" (Deutsches Reich) are mutually exclusive terms, that in fact Germany doesn't currently have a culture worthy of the name. This of course raises the question of what Nietzsche means by "culture," and he duly defines it, in typically idiosyncratic fashion, as a marriage of art and life in the round: "Culture is, above all, unity of artistic style in all the expressions of the life of a people" (Kultur ist vor allem Einheit des künstlerischen Stiles in allen Lebensäusserungen eines Volkes; *UM* I §1; *KSA* 1, 163, cf. *UM* II §4). Instead of such unity, Germany today, as Nietzsche sees it, displays a "chaotic jumble of styles" (chaotischen Durcheinander aller Stile). The Germans may pride themselves on their so-called "Bildungsbürgerthum" (educated bourgeoisie), but in fact their "culture" (Bildung) is nothing but superficial "cultivatedness" (Gebildetheit) masking a more fundamental barbarism. In place of the truly (classically inspired) cultured individual, then, Germany can boast only *Bildungsphilister* or "cultural philistines" (*UM* I §2; *KSA* 1, 165), whom he will later describe as "the harassed slaves of the moment, opinion and fashion" (die geplagten Sklaven der drei M, des Moments, der Meinungen und der Moden; *UM* III §6; *KSA* 1, 392).[17]

At this point in the argument Nietzsche wheels out David Strauss as a prize specimen of what he means by the "Bildungsphilister," what has gone wrong with German culture. He picks on Strauss because of his popularity, and sees the favorable reception of Strauss's recent book as symptomatic of a more general cultural malaise. Typically, Nietzsche begins his assault by considering weaknesses in Strauss's character as revealed by his literary, musical, and philosophical tastes. Thus Strauss is attacked for misunderstanding Gotthold Ephraim Lessing (*UM* I §4) and Beethoven (*UM* I §5), for criticizing Schopenhauer and being too Hegelian in his "shameless philistine optimism" (schamloser Philister-Optimismus; *UM* I §6; *KSA* 1, 191). In turn this line of attack reveals Nietzsche's own allegiances of the time: interestingly, he defends Darwinism against Strauss's alleged misunderstanding of it (*UM* I §7), and of course he quotes Goethe repeatedly with approval. Strauss stands accused of intellectual cowardice and much else besides: ultimately Nietzsche turns away from him in "disgust" (Ekel; *UM* I §6; *KSA* 1, 193).

So far, so *ad hominem*. More substantive criticism is leveled at Strauss in section 8, the heart of the piece, where the deliberate provocation of calling Strauss "der Bekenner" in the ironic title of the essay becomes apparent. Whereas Strauss had in fact scandalized public opinion through his apparent godlessness, Nietzsche objects instead to his making science into a new religion:[18] he critiques the "paradox" of the "scientific man" (dieses Paradoxon, der wissenschaftliche Mensch; *UM* I §8; *KSA* 1, 202), and, correlatively, the kind of education currently on offer in German schools and universities. The critique of rationalism, now leveled at Strauss's "new criticism" in theology, is continued from the analysis of the origin of the scientific mentality in *The Birth of Tragedy*, where Nietzsche had vilified Euripides and Socrates for wiping away the mythical horizon of Greek tragic culture in their headlong desire to see everything explained. At this stage in his career Nietzsche is far from the sustained and aggressive irreligiosity of *The Anti-Christ* (*Der Antichrist*, 1888), yet even at this early stage the only point of religion in his eyes is its mystique, so for God's sake don't dispense with that!

The title of Nietzsche's first *Untimely* essay suggests two prongs to his attack on Strauss, namely ideological and stylistic. He duly devotes the final sections (*UM* I §9–§12) to style (which figures so importantly in his earlier definition of culture), and concludes (*UM* I §12) with an extended anthology of stylistic solecisms, excerpting from Strauss's book and poking fun in various ways.[19] Nietzsche quotes from another's work more in this essay than in any other of his books (even *The Case of Wagner* [*Der Fall Wagner*]), generally in order to subject it to crude lampooning. He criticizes Strauss's rhetorical "arts of seductions" (Verführungs-Künsten; *UM* I §9; *KSA* 1, 213) (a bit rich!) and mocks his sententiousness as unsubtle; his most general criticism is that Strauss's style is feigned — he tries too hard to be a "classic" — and lacks unity.[20] Implicitly defending his own move to Switzerland, Nietzsche concedes that it is difficult to write well in Germany any more, that German style has been ruined by the newspapers (*UM* I §11) and Hegelian philosophy (*UM* I §12). In Nietzsche's eyes, though, style is never merely accidental, but rather style maketh the man: it gives a good gauge of the character of a man and his philosophy. His stylistic criticism of Strauss, then, for all its knockabout elements, is a serious business, tantamount to moral censure, and the essay as a whole culminates in a curious quasi-mystical language nationalism where the stakes are as high as they can be: "For he who has sinned against the German language has profaned the mystery of all that is German: through all the confusion and changes of nations and customs, it alone has, as by a metaphysical magic, preserved itself and therewith the German spirit" (Denn wer sich an der deutschen Sprache versündigt hat, der hat das Mysterium aller unserer Deutschheit entweiht: sie allein hat durch alle die Mischung und den Wechsel von Nationalitäten und Sitten hindurch sich selbst und damit den deutschen Geist wie durch einen metaphysischen Zauber gerettet; *UM* I §12; *KSA* 1, 228).

It was not really Nietzsche's idea in the first place to attack David Strauss, and one could certainly argue that, for the only time in his career, he ranges his big guns against too soft a target, that his first *Untimely Meditation* is guilty of overkill (David Strauss actually died shortly after the essay appeared, and Nietzsche feared he might have finished him off).[21] In retrospect, Nietzsche viewed the first *Untimely* as the most important of all the essays, and he devotes most space to it when he reviews them in *Ecce Homo*, but posterity has not concurred. It is notable for Nietzsche's coinage of the term "Bildungsphilister" (ascribed to him in the Grimms' *Deutsches Wörterbuch*), for giving him practice in the polemical style (later to culminate in *On the Genealogy of Morals: A Polemic* [*Zur Genealogie der Moral: Eine Streitschrift*, 1887]), and for its critique of the scientific mentality. Its arguments also became very topical more recently, in the context of the 1990 Reunification of Germany and the ensuing debate over "core cultural values" (or "Leitkultur"), which closely mirrored the context of the composition of Nietzsche's essay.

UM II: *On the Uses and Disadvantages of History for Life*

The second *Untimely* essay, "On the Uses and Disadvantages of History for Life" (Vom Nutzen und Nachtheil der Historie für das Leben), was written between October 1873 and January 1874, and published in February 1874. As William Schaberg points out, this was the first Nietzsche book project not prompted by the Wagners, where he was striking out on his own,[22] and to mark the occasion he chose a topic of much greater personal concern than before. Whereas the first essay was a reaction to a contemporary trend in theology, with which Nietzsche otherwise had little to do, in the second essay he is reacting against contemporary currents in historiography, which was much closer to home given his professional life as an academic classicist. The title word "Historie" is relatively unusual in German (the standard word for "history" is "Geschichte"), and connotes "historiography," the writing of history as an academic discipline. This was another area in which nineteenth-century German culture prided itself, and where it was generally recognized as world-leading. At the hands of figures such as Leopold von Ranke (1795–1886), Ranke's successor to the chair of history at the University of Berlin Heinrich von Treitschke (1834–96), or the cultural historians Barthold Georg Niebuhr (1776–1831), Johann Gustav Droysen (1808–84), and Theodor Mommsen (1817–1903), German historiography had established many modern principles (for example, Ranke recommended using primary sources) and turned the discipline into a more scientific endeavor than hitherto, a "Wissenschaft." At the same time, though, German historiography had become drier, more impersonal, and (in Nietzsche's eyes) "infected" with Hegelianism and nationalism. Nietzsche preferred the more anecdotal style of classical historiography, but in the course of the essay he does not hold up individual favorites such as Thucydides, Plutarch, and Sallust as counterexamples — or for that matter the alternative models he favored in the contemporary period such as Bachofen and Burckhardt, Taine in Paris, or F. A. Lange's *History of Materialism* (*Geschichte des Materialismus*, 1866) — for by contrast with the Strauss essay he deliberately avoids focusing on specific historians, since he wants to paint historicism as a more general cultural malaise.[23]

As the title of the essay suggests, Nietzsche mounts an attack on contemporary historiography in the name of "life." He begins with a short preface in which, after the fact (that is, after designating the Strauss essay the first "Untimely Meditation"), he explains what he means by "untimeliness," and encapsulates the message of the second essay thus: "We want to serve history only to the extent that history serves life" (Nur soweit die Historie dem Leben dient, wollen wir ihr dienen; *UM* II preface; *KSA* 1, 245). This vitalistic strain in Nietzsche's philosophy — the appeal to "life" as ultimate criterion of value in the mode of *Lebensphilosophie* — will become particularly prominent in his later works, and for example his late critiques of religion will be mounted in the name of the same ("ascending" vs. "descending") "life," of what he calls already here (anticipating his later theory of "will to power"): "that dark, driving power that insatiably thirsts for itself" (jene dunkle, treibende, unersättlich sich selbst begehrende Macht; *UM* II §3; *KSA* 1, 269).[24] In the second *Untimely* essay historiography is treated as an exemplary "Wissenschaft" (*UM* II §4), and the essay as a whole seeks to determine what overall purpose(s) it should serve, in the context of the vital imperative. One can gloss its central questions as: How much history is good for you? To what extent is historiography life-affirming (or life-denying)? When is the time to put history aside and act? These are interesting questions indeed coming from a professional classicist.

The essay "proper" begins in quasi-Biblical fashion by considering the herd animals of the field, who are happy because they are oblivious to history. Forgetting can be a very good thing,[25] but historical awareness is part of what makes us human. First, then, Nietzsche establishes that a historical and an ahistorical attitude are equally valuable to an individual, a people, and a culture (*UM* II §1). How much historical awareness is needed? Currently we are oppressed by a "hypertrophied virtue" (hypertrophische Tugend; *UM* II preface; *KSA* 1, 246), too much of a good thing — a state that Nietzsche, introducing a metaphor from pathology, likens to sleeplessness. We moderns suffer from too much history, especially history of the wrong kind (modern historiography suffers from a surfeit of science), and a balance needs to be restored between different kinds of historical inquiry.

The most lasting contribution of the second *Untimely* essay is its tripartite categorization of historiography into "monumental" (monumental), "antiquarian" (antiquarisch) and "critical" (kritisch) modes of historical awareness. Each of these corresponds to a different aspect of the living man — respectively, "a being who acts and strives" (dem Thätigen und Strebenden) and thus requires inspirational examples; "a being who preserves and reveres" (dem Bewahrenden und Verehrenden); and "a [Schopenhauerian] being who suffers and seeks deliverance" (dem Leidenden und der Befreiung Bedürftigen) from the past altogether (*UM* II §2; *KSA* 1, 258). Nietzsche's conclusion is that all three modes are needed, but in moderation, whereas in fact modern man is hampered by a heavy weight of historical ballast: "Modern man drags around with him a huge quantity of indigestible stones of knowledge" (Der moderne Mensch schleppt zuletzt eine ungeheure Menge von unverdaulichen Wissens- steinen mit sich herum; *UM* II §4; *KSA* 1, 272). His is an age "over- saturated" with historical knowledge (*UM* II §5; *KSA* 1, 279), especially because "scientific" historiography prizes so-called "objectivity" (*UM* II §5–§6), which paralyzes judgment and deprives the historically informed agent of personal engagement. There is nothing that it is not fit to know or about which it is acceptable to be ignorant.

In addition to the modern excess of scientific historicity, Nietzsche objects to a certain prevalent way of doing history, and as in the first *Untimely* essay this amounts to a critique of Hegelianism in the form of an attack on the teleological historical model as applied in Eduard von Hartmann's *Philosophy of the Unconscious* (*Philosophie des Unbewussten*, 1869). Ultimately, Nietzsche defends a more monumental, elitist view of history, summarized in the claim "the goal of humanity cannot lie in its end but only in its highest exemplars" (das Ziel der Menschheit kann nicht am Ende liegen, sondern nur in ihren höchsten Exemplaren; *UM* II §9; *KSA* 1, 317),[26] which in turn prepares the way for the two exemplary portraits, of Schopenhauer and Wagner, that he draws in the next two *Untimely* essays. In the concluding section of this one (*UM* II §10) he returns to the opening contextualization of historicism and sug- gests that we need to restore the balance between the historical and its twin "antidotes" (Gegenmittel),[27] the unhistorical and what he calls the "suprahistorical" (das Ueberhistorische), by which he means art and reli- gion, "the powers which lead the eye away from becoming towards that which bestows upon existence the character of the eternal and stable" (die Mächte, die den Blick von dem Werden ablenken, hin zu dem, was dem Dasein den Charakter des Ewigen und Gleichbedeutenden giebt; *KSA* 1, 330). The essay as a whole then concludes with a paean to youth, rein- forcing the claim that one should concern oneself with history only out of a strong sense of the present and concern for the future.

Nietzsche was surprisingly self-conscious about the second *Untimely* essay, which he even sent to his friend Erwin Rohde for stylistic appraisal before publication, and initially it was poorly received, yet ironically it is now by far the best known and most commented of the four. For exam- ple, it is the only work of Nietzsche's that Heidegger explicitly treats in *Being and Time* (*Sein und Zeit*, 1927),[28] it is prominently discussed by Thomas Mann in his 1947 essay "Nietzsches Philosophie im Lichte unserer Erfahrung,"[29] and more recently it has continued to attract atten- tion from philosophers as diverse as Paul Ricoeur and Gilles Deleuze and Félix Guattari.[30] Nietzsche's analysis of the scientific imperative is all the more acute in our information(-saturated) age, and his categorization of different types of historiography has been widely influential. From the point of view of Nietzsche's own philosophical development the essay is important in that it lays the groundwork for the programmatically historical approach that he will soon be adopting (from the first section in the first volume of *Human, All Too Human* [*Menschliches, Allzumenschliches*] on) and developing into the practice of "genealogy."[31] It is also of abiding interest for Nietzsche's introduction of the trope of "self-overcoming" (Selbstüberwindung) with the claim that the current generation needs to overcome itself (*UM* II §4 and §10; *KSA* 1, 275, 328).

UM III: *Schopenhauer as Educator*

In the third and fourth *Untimelies* Nietzsche changes tack, switching his predominant tone from critique to affirmation. In his two portraits of Schopenhauer and Wagner, he presents two pictures of the exemplary, gifted individual: the philosophical and artistic genius, respectively, or as he later puts it in *Ecce Homo*: "two images of the harshest *egoism, self-discipline* [. . .], untimely types par excellence" (zwei Bilder der härtesten *Selbstsucht, Selbstzucht* [. . .], unzeitgemässe Typen par excellence; *EH UM* §1; *KSA* 6, 316–17).[32] The third essay, "Schopenhauer as Educator" ("Schopenhauer als Erzieher"), was written over the summer of 1874 and published in October that year, marking Nietzsche's thirtieth birthday. A French translation was produced in 1875 by Marie Baumgartner, mother of one of Nietzsche's students, but it remained unpublished. The second essay had concluded with an incitement to character formation, the claim that each of us "must organize the chaos within him" (muss das Chaos in sich organisiren; *UM* II §10; *KSA* 1, 333), and the third continues in this vein with a concrete example of one who has done this, who has "disciplined himself into a whole," as Nietzsche will later say of Goethe (*TI* Skirmishes of an Untimely Man §49).

As Nietzsche recounts in the essay's second section (*UM* III §2), he had first discovered and become infatuated with Schopenhauer nine years before — that is, in 1865 — when he came across Schopenhauer's magnum opus *The World as Will and Representation* (*Die Welt als Wille und Vorstellung*, 1819) in a Leipzig bookstore during his student days. Just as Aristotle was simply "the philosopher" to the Scholastics, Schopenhauer earns the same designation from the early Nietzsche (and from Wagner — indeed a love of Schopenhauer's work was one of the main interests the two men shared). The recently deceased Schopenhauer (1788–1860) had been deeply unfashionable for most of his life, but began to emerge from neglect in his final decade and would continue to gain in influence well into the twentieth century.[33] Again, then, it is a moot point to what extent Nietzsche was being "untimely" in advertising his devotion to a mentor whose star was at this stage already in the ascendant. In terms of Nietzsche's own development it was in any case hardly a surprise when he nailed his colors to the mast like this, since Schopenhauer had been heavily present in *The Birth of Tragedy*, and Nietzsche had made numerous favorable references in both previous *Untimely* essays (*UM* I §2, §6, §8, and §11; *UM* II §2 and §9).

What is it about Schopenhauer that so appealed to Nietzsche? One could point to a variety of key doctrines: what Miguel de Unamuno would later call the "tragic sense of life," his pessimism by contrast with the (glib) meliorism of the (neo-)Hegelian consensus; his vitalism, irrationalism, and concern with the psychology of the unconscious; his philosophical privileging of artistic and especially musical experience, and the rhetorical self-awareness of his philosophical prose style. All these features are rather taken as read, though, for Nietzsche gives us no exposition of Schopenhauer's actual philosophy. Instead, as the essay's title makes clear, he takes an oblique approach to his subject matter, emphasizing an unusual aspect of Schopenhauer's work that is not an aspect of the philosophy at all, but rather of the effect that philosophy and (his knowledge of) its originator had on Nietzsche himself: Schopenhauer's role "as educator." Nor is this analysis even derived from Schopenhauer's own biography or his educational philosophy: there is something perverse about Nietzsche's title if one considers, as Nietzsche well knew, that Schopenhauer was a failure as a university educator in the traditional sense, when in 1820 he hubristically scheduled his lectures at the University of Berlin at the same time as Hegel's, with disastrous results. Nietzsche admits that the subject of his essay — Schopenhauer as *Nietzsche's* educator — is a subjective concoction, what he himself calls "that ideal man who, as his Platonic ideal as it were, holds sway in and around him" (jenen idealen Menschen [. . .], welcher in und um Schopenhauer, gleichsam als seine platonische Idee, waltet; *UM* III §5; *KSA* 1, 376), or what we might call (following Max Weber) an ideal type, a projection. This is the view of Schopenhauer Nietzsche reached after reading him (and reading him very thoroughly), but he offers no guarantee that others will arrive at the same position.

Instead of presenting Schopenhauer as a historical teacher, then, Nietzsche presents him as a model, an exemplar (*Vorbild*) who taught by merely being, who indeed taught a mode of being — "be your self!" (sei du selbst!; *UM* III §1; *KSA* 1, 338) — and philosophy *as* a mode of being. Nietzsche's conception of exemplarity is crucial to the "identity education" at stake here, for he remarks: "I profit from a philosopher only insofar as he can be an example" (Ich mache mir aus einem Philosophen gerade so viel als er im Stande ist ein Beispiel zu geben; *UM* III §3; *KSA* 1, 350) (and the same might be said of anyone else, too, such as Wagner).[34] Schopenhauer, says Nietzsche, enjoins us to be our selves, but he also educates us as to what a self is and how we might each achieve it: "your true nature lies, not concealed deep within you, but immeasurably high above you, or at least above that which you usually take yourself to be. Your true educators and formative teachers reveal to you what the true basic material of your being is" (dein wahres Wesen liegt nicht tief verborgen in dir, sondern unermesslich hoch über dir oder wenigstens über dem, was du gewöhnlich als dein Ich nimmst; *UM* III §1; *KSA* 1, 340–41). In earlier works — especially his lectures "On the Future of Our Educational Institutions" and the first *Untimely* essay — Nietzsche had been concerned to critique the common (and in his view impoverished) conception of education as *Bildung*, a topic that grew naturally out of his professional concerns as a lecturer engaged in higher education. In the Schopenhauer essay, though, a different, more positive notion of education emerges, a distinctively Nietzschean concept of "education" (Erziehung) as "educement," as a drawing-one-out-of-oneself. Nietzsche here stresses the importance of heroic self-overcoming (the notion introduced in the previous essay), and lays the foundation for what J. P. Stern would term his "morality of strenuousness."[35]

Nietzsche takes his (typically Romantic) roster of exemplary educators from Schopenhauer's own "Holy Trinity" of favored types: "those true *men, those who are no longer animal, the philosophers, artists, and saints*" (jene wahrhaften *Menschen, jene Nichtmehr-Thiere, die Philosophen, Künstler und Heiligen*; *UM* III §5; *KSA* 1, 380). Such "great men" educate merely by being geniuses in their own ways: there is no point in their expounding how they became who they are; rather, by being solitary "peaks of achievement" towering above the rest of the mountain range that is humanity they demonstrate that there are such heights to scale, if not the ways of scaling them (which will always ultimately need to be via a unique personal route). Rehearsing an argument he will later use for the "free spirits" and the *Übermensch*, Nietzsche asserts that our role is to hasten the coming of these great men, both as outside agents and above all within ourselves. This kind of "existential imperative,"[36] the injunction to self-cultivation, complements the new definition of "culture" that Nietzsche gives in this essay, representing a task for nature herself. Culture is now defined as a task (*Aufgabe*): to prepare the ideal conditions for the production (*Erzeugung*) of genius, which in itself represents a fulfillment of nature (Vollendung der Natur; *UM* III §5; *KSA* 1, 382).[37]

Schopenhauer himself serves as the exemplary philosopher, demonstrating what philosophy can do and how best to practice it, by contrast with the dominant Hegelian school of German philosophy. For Nietzsche it was a positive boon that Schopenhauer was not an academic philosopher, and in his view this makes his philosophy all the stronger. Schopenhauer can teach German philosophy a different approach: "the philosopher in Germany has more and more to unlearn how to be 'pure knowledge': and it is to precisely that end that Schopenhauer as a human being can serve as an example" (die Philosophie in Deutschland es mehr und mehr zu verlernen hat, "reine Wissenschaft" zu sein: und das gerade sei das Beispiel des Menschen Schopenhauer; *UM* III §3; *KSA* 1, 351). Schopenhauer doesn't do this by dispensing discursive lessons, though; he represents an ideal of philosophy as *pathos* rather than *logos*.[38] As the terms suggest, this is an ideal that Nietzsche sees as the embodiment of a certain kind of Greek philosophy — "pre-Platonic" philosophy before it took the fateful Socratic wrong turn. Just as he will later argue that Wagner and his *Gesamtkunstwerk* represent a rebirth of the Greek ideal, so too he advances the same claim here about Schopenhauer. At the last, though, the essay swerves away from Schopenhauer and closes with a substantial quotation from Emerson, another of Nietzsche's educators.[39]

Richard Schacht advances some strong claims for "Schopenhauer as Educator," describing it as "Nietzsche's declaration of intellectual independence" and arguing that "among Nietzsche's writings, there is perhaps no better introduction to his thought."[40] This is not to say that the early work somehow eclipses, say, *Twilight of the Idols* (*Götzen-Dämmerung*, 1888) as a conspectus of his philosophical positions, but it is testament to the essay's rhetorical power and to the continuity of Nietzsche's thematic concerns. By the time he wrote the essay he had already broken with Schopenhauer's philosophy, as his contemporary notebooks attest, so that the whole piece is effectively a valediction, a testament to an overcoming. The crisis of confidence in Schopenhauer is reflected in the essay's lack of specifics about Schopenhauer's doctrines, and it is certainly not an exercise in unadulterated adulation, for the essay itself overtly admits that Schopenhauer has "scars and blemishes" (Narben und Flecken), that he is "all too human" (allzu menschlich) in some ways (*UM* III §3; *KSA* 1, 359). From the later 1870s Nietzsche's rejection of Schopenhauer — less spectacular than his repudiation of Wagner, but just as assured — becomes more apparent. He returns to Schopenhauer in the fourth part of *Zarathustra*, where he casts him as "the Soothsayer" (der Wahrsager), in the opening sections of the third essay of *On the Genealogy*, where he thematizes Wagner's and Schopenhauer's devotion to "ascetic ideals" (*GM* III §2–§8), and at several points in *Twilight of the Idols*, where he is at his most openly critical of his erstwhile mentor (*TI* "Morality as Anti-Nature" §5; *TI* "Skirmishes" §21–§22 and §36). The most lasting legacy of the third *Untimely* essay is in the persistence of its concept of self-education, which culminates in *Ecce Homo*, subtitled "How To Become What You Are" ("Wie man wird, was man ist"), where Nietzsche applies the lesson learned from Schopenhauer to an exposition of his own development.

UM IV: *Richard Wagner in Bayreuth*

In a literal sense, Wagner was the first untimely man in Nietzsche's philosophy, for he first uses the word "unzeitgemäss" to describe Wagner in a letter to his friend Rohde of 15 August 1869 (*KSB* 3, 42). It was inevitable, then, that he would devote one of the *Untimely* essays to his most important mentor and father-figure, especially since his adherence to the Wagnerian cause was even better known than his Schopenhauerianism, as he had made it very public in the latter stages of *The Birth of Tragedy*. What was less apparent when Nietzsche began working on the piece in August 1875, though, was that it would be the hardest of all to write, would take him a year to finish, and would bring the series to a premature close. For just as he harbored misgivings about Schopenhauer when writing the third essay, there is even more evidence in his notebooks (ultimately excised from the published text) of a more critical attitude toward Wagner as he was writing the fourth. He spent the first half of 1875 working on the *Untimely Meditation* that got away, "We Philologists" ("Wir Philologen"; *KSA* 8, 11–127), devoted to his own profession of classical philology, but left it incomplete. Instead, that summer he began an essay on Wagner, worked on it initially for a couple of months, then set it aside in October 1875 and only revived it the following year at the instigation of his new amanuensis Heinrich Köselitz (aka Peter Gast). He completed the piece under pressure to finish in time for the inaugural Bayreuth Festival of Wagner's works in August 1876, and it duly appeared with a month to spare. Like the Strauss essay, then, it is curiously timely, unwontedly topical, gratifying "Nietzsche's deep-seated desire [. . .] to have a best-seller."[41] It would prove to be his only work to have an initial print run in four figures (1,500 copies) and was once again quickly translated by Marie Baumgartner: this time the French version was published (by Schmeitzner in January 1877), as the only work of Nietzsche's to appear in translation during his mentally active lifetime.

The essay on Wagner may have been the most difficult to write; it is also now the most difficult to read. On the one hand it is difficult to put out of one's mind the knowledge of Nietzsche's imminent tergiversation: with hindsight, we know that this period represents a crucial turning point in Nietzsche's view of Wagner, and some tensions undoubtedly surface in the essay,[42] just as there is some evidence of padding with quoted material taken from Wagner himself. In places, though, the text strikes us now as positively cringeworthy on account of the depth of its hero-worship. Nietzsche makes it plain from the outset that he is preaching to the converted, addressing only initiates: "us with greater faith" (uns Vertrauensvolleren); "we disciples of art resurrected" (wir, die Jünger der wiederauferstandenen Kunst; *UM* IV §1; *KSA* 1, 432, 434). Only *fellow* "Unzeitgemäße" can possibly understand Wagner and his art, Nietzsche claims here, otherwise "we children of a wretched age" (wir Kinder eines erbärmlichen Zeitalters; *UM* IV §6; *KSA* 1, 464) are destined only to misunderstand the master, so we need to raise our game even just in order to appreciate the uniqueness of the man and his achievement adequately.

The basic premise of the text can be summed up in the immortal words, "we're not worthy!"

The fourth *Untimely* essay is monumental history in action: in *The Birth of Tragedy* the Wagner material had been bound into an intricate argument concerning the birth and rebirth of tragic drama, but here Nietzsche gives himself license to range more freely, celebrating the historical moment of Wagner at the apogee of his success in a kind of living obituary. Wagner is compared to Alexander the Great (*UM* IV §1), Goethe (*UM* IV §2 and §3), Schiller (*UM* IV §2), Luther, and Beethoven (*UM* IV §8); in its periodic religious language the essay verges on hagiography, combining Schopenhauer's categories of the artist and saint in its portrait of Wagner as wonder-worker (*UM* IV §6; *KSA* 1, 466). Like the Schopenhauer essay, though, the Wagner essay is *also* a narrative of the achievement of genius, of "[das] Werden Wagner's" (*UM* IV §8; *KSA* 1, 474), paying homage to his ability to learn (*UM* IV §3) and presenting his life retrospectively as a gradual unfolding, indeed "revelation" (Offenbarung; *UM* IV §8; *KSA* 1, 472).[43] It is no surprise when *Ecce Homo* remarks of the third and fourth *Untimely* essays together: "an unparalleled problem of education, a new concept of *self-discipline*, of *self-defense* to the point of harshness, a path to greatness and to world-historic tasks was clamoring for its first expression" (ein Problem der Erziehung ohne Gleichen, ein neuer Begriff der *Selbst-Zucht, Selbst-Vertheidigung* bis zur Härte, ein Weg zur Grösse und zu welthistorischen Aufgaben verlangte nach seinem ersten Ausdruck; *EH UM* §3; *KSA* 6, 319).

Perhaps the most telling characterization of Wagner in this essay is in section 4, which begins by attacking the Hegelian, progressivist view of history (again) and proposing instead a model of history as a swinging pendulum, privileging now one, now another tendency. In the age-old cultural conflict between Athens and Jerusalem Nietzsche views Wagner as a pagan, Hellenic influence in our time, and characterizes him (as in *The Birth of Tragedy*) as a modern Aeschylus (*UM* IV §7; *KSA* 1, 467). For the moment, though, Nietzsche's anti-Christian rhetoric remains subdued, and he develops instead a portrait of Wagner as what he calls a "counter-Alexander" (Gegen-Alexander), a great re-unifier, tying back together again the sundered Gordian knot of culture (*UM* IV §4; *KSA* 1, 447).

In the terms of the second *Untimely* essay Wagner *is* a culture, and one that can be contrasted with "the entire culture of the Renaissance" (aller Cultur der Renaissance; *UM* IV §10; *KSA* 1, 503):[44] Wagner's "renaissance" is, rather, a rebirth of tragedy (and many had been led by the Wagnerianism of Nietzsche's first book to mistake its title as precisely that).[45] In the midst of the Wagner adulation, Nietzsche even manages to be complimentary (in a backhanded way) about Wagner's writing style, of which he will later be particularly scathing in his mockery: "Wagner as a *writer* is like a brave man whose right hand has been cut off and who fights on with his left" (*Wagner als Schriftsteller zeigt den Zwang eines tapferen Menschen, dem man die rechte Hand zerschlagen hat und der mit der linken ficht*; *UM* IV §10; *KSA* 1, 501). Similarly, Nietzsche manages to thematize Wagner's politics in a positive light (*UM* IV §8), when he would later view Wagner's German nationalism as one of his most odious features. Ultimately, though, Wagner is lauded for having transcended his German identity and praised as "*supra-German*" (*überdeutsch*; *UM* IV §10; *KSA* 1, 505), as speaking to all nations, all humanity, of the future.

In "Richard Wagner in Bayreuth" Nietzsche serves as a Wagnerian propagandist: he himself takes practically no critical distance from his subject matter, so it is incumbent on us to do so. And as with all propaganda, the text's main interest now lies in its historical importance rather than in what it has to say about the subject matter itself. When Nietzsche gushes that nature realizes itself in Wagner's art (*UM* IV §6) one might counter (as Nietzsche himself says of *The Birth of Tragedy* in its later preface) that this "smells offensively Hegelian" and sounds like nothing so much as Hegel hailing the Prussian state as the fulfillment of history. Above all, then, we should read the essay symptomatically, as testament to the extent of his conflicted love for Wagner at this transitional stage in their relationship.

Aftermaths: What Remains

No sooner had the fourth *Untimely* essay been published than the inaugural Bayreuth Festival drove Nietzsche away, both physically and intellectually. The turbulent future course of his relation to Wagner is very well known, thanks to the late texts *The Case of Wagner* (1888) and *Nietzsche contra Wagner* (1889), but his series of *Untimely Meditations* had run its course. On leaving Bayreuth in August 1876 Nietzsche took refuge in the Bavarian Forest and started a notebook titled "Die Pflugschar" ("The Ploughshare"): he initially contemplated making this a fifth *Untimely* essay, but it quickly became apparent that the material was very different in tone and form from the preceding essays, and it would ultimately become *Human, All Too Human* (1878).[46] As late as the summer of 1876 one finds a redraft of the plan for thirteen *Untimely* essays in Nietzsche's notebook (*KSA* 8, 16[10], 289), but when his publisher Schmeitzner inquired about a fifth installment in late January 1877, Nietzsche replied on 2 February suggesting that they consider the series concluded (*KSB* 5, 219).[47] And indeed he would abandon the form of the continuous essay for a decade, before returning to it with renewed vigor in *On the Genealogy of Morals* and *The Anti-Christ*.

The *Untimely Meditations* were reissued, separately, in 1886, but (exceptionally) Nietzsche chose not to provide them with a retrospective preface, preferring to leave them as they were (however that is to be interpreted).[48] Nonetheless, there is other evidence of how he later felt about the works. For example, in a notebook entry from 1885–86 he finds the very notion of "untimeliness" itself (paradoxically) to have become dated (*KSA* 12, 2[201], 165). There are two main sources for his later view of the *Untimely* essays: in the preface to the second volume of *Human, All Too Human* (which effectively serves as the preface the *Untimely* essays never had) he sets them in the context of his self-overcomings, and sees them as being of historical interest only, although significantly he also claims that the first three essays predate even *The Birth of Tragedy* in their preoccupations. He treats the *Untimely* essays in the same vein in *Ecce Homo*, where he now openly admits that the latter two are self-portraits: "Schopenhauer and Wagner *or*, in one word, Nietzsche" (Schopenhauer und Wagner *oder*, mit einem Wort, Nietzsche; *EH UM* §1; *KSA* 6, 317).[49] It is for this reason, too, that he recommends the *Untimely* essays to Georg Brandes in a letter of 10 April 1888 (*KSB* 8, 287) as providing the key to an understanding of his development.

The *Untimely Meditations* were written and published piecemeal, so it is perhaps inevitable that they are disparate and to some extent uneven in quality, lacking an overriding theme and the integrity of a single work. In some ways they read as outdated (as Nietzsche himself clearly felt when he reissued them in the 1880s): from the point of view of his later development they show him to be still an admirer of Schopenhauer and Wagner, still a German patriot (in the cultural sphere, at least), still tinged with Romanticism, still very anti-science. They are unfamiliar in other ways, too, such as when the first essay concludes with Nietzsche rather conventionally boasting that he has the courage to tell the truth about Strauss (*UM* I §12; *KSA* 1, 242). Now the essays are seen as some of Nietzsche's least characteristic writings: we are more used to him as a waspish commentator rather than as the effusive, wide-eyed propagandist of the latter pieces. Yet they are also preparatory, with Nietzsche testing out forms and styles he would later perfect, and above all there are many thematic continuities with the later works that belie the sense of an absolute break that is otherwise often claimed for *Menschliches, Allzumenschliches*, not least by Nietzsche himself. Thus, although he may later claim the term "untimeliness" is jejune, it would remain an implicit watchword throughout the remaining fifteen years of his philosophical career. In 1888 he was still dismissing newspaper-reading and "modern ideas" (see, for example, *EH BGE*), and he devoted over half of *Twilight of the Idols* to a chapter explicitly titled "Reconnaissance Raids of an Untimely Man" (Streifzüge eines Unzeitgemässen). Nietzsche's early preoccupation with "untimeliness" draws attention to the importance of time and temporality in his work more generally, and the emphasis on historical development yields an apprenticeship in the later "genealogical" method. The recurrent medical metaphor used in "diagnosing" Germany's cultural ills will return strongly toward the end of Nietzsche's career, as when he remarks in *Twilight of the Idols*: "Morality is merely sign language, merely symptomatology" (Moral ist bloss Zeichenrede, bloss Symptomatologie; *TI* "Improvers" of Mankind §1; *KSA* 6, 98).[50] As we have seen, the *Untimely* essays also prefigure a number of the "grand doctrines" of Nietzsche's mature philosophy, such as the *Übermensch*, the will to power, and even the eternal return.

Notes

The translations from Nietzsche in this essay are cited from the version by R. J. Hollingdale.

[1] See Walter Kaufmann, *Nietzsche: Philosopher, Psychologist, Antichrist*, 3rd ed. (New York: Vintage, 1968), 488.

[2] Robert C. Solomon and Kathleen M. Higgins, eds., *Reading Nietzsche* (New York and Oxford: Oxford UP, 1988).

[3] To cite the two most recent such examples, it is omitted from Peter R. Sedgwick, *Nietzsche: The Key Concepts* (London and New York: Routledge, 2009) and Christian Niemeyer, ed., *Nietzsche-Lexikon* (Darmstadt: Wissenschaftliche Buchgesellschaft, 2009).

[4] Friedrich Nietzsche, *Unfashionable Observations*, ed. and trans. Richard T. Gray, *The Complete Works of Friedrich Nietzsche*, vol. 2 (Stanford, CA: Stanford UP, 1998).

[5] See Friedrich Nietzsche, *On the Future of Our Educational Institutions*, ed. and trans. Michael W. Grenke (South Bend, IN: St. Augustine's Press, 2004) and *Prefaces to Unwritten Works*, ed. and trans. Michael W. Grenke (South Bend, IN: St. Augustine's Press, 2005). For the *Nachlass* notes of this period, see *Philosophy and Truth: Selections from Nietzsche's Notebooks of the Early 1870's*, ed. and trans. Daniel Breazeale, 2nd ed. (Atlantic Highlands, NJ and London: Humanities Press International, 1990).

[6] See "Plans for the 'Untimely Meditations' (1873–6)" in Nietzsche, *Philosophy and Truth*, 162–65.

[7] R. M. Meyer, *Zeitschrift für deutsche Wortforschung* 15, 105 (cited in Grimm, *Deutsches Wörterbuch*, vol. 24, col. 2278).

[8] In his contemporary notebooks, Nietzsche repeatedly thematizes his status as "foreigner" ("Ausländer") and tries out "Unzeitgemässe Betrachtungen / eines / Ausländers" (A Foreigner's Untimely Meditations) as a draft subtitle to *UM* I (*KSA* 7, 27[57], 604).

[9] The *Untimely Meditations* are cited in this essay from R. J. Hollingdale's translation (Cambridge and New York: Cambridge UP, 1983; 2nd ed. 1997, ed. Daniel Breazeale).

[10] Cf. Daniel R. Ahern, *Nietzsche as Cultural Physician* (University Park: Penn State UP, 1995).

[11] See my essay "On 'Untimeliness': Temporal Structures in Nietzsche, or: 'The Day After Tomorrow Belongs to Me,'" *Journal of Nietzsche Studies* 8 (Autumn 1994): 33–53.

[12] *UM* I: ca. 25,000; *UM* II: ca. 27,000; *UM* III: ca. 28,500; *UM* IV: ca. 24,000.

[13] See, for example, the opening of *UM* III §5, where he pulls himself up and reminds himself of the task represented by the title of his essay, which he has hitherto failed to address (*KSA* 1, 375–76).

[14] To gauge the impact of Strauss's book more generally, see for example Hermann Ulrici, *Strauss as a Philosophical Thinker: A Review of His Book "The Old Faith and the New Faith," and a Confutation of Its Materialistic Views*, trans. Charles P. Krauth (Philadelphia: Smith, English; Edinburgh: Clark, 1874).

[15] Nietzsche begins to explain this in the sketch for a preface to the *Untimely Meditations* which he noted down in 1875 (*KSA* 8, 5[98], 66).

[16] In the midst of the conflict Cosima Wagner had presented Nietzsche with the collected *Essays* of Montaigne as a Christmas present in 1870.

[17] By coining this term, Nietzsche allies himself in residually Romantic fashion with the composer who had been his favorite before he discovered Wagner, namely Robert Schumann, who earlier in the century had fought the Philistines of his day in the name of the "League of David" (Davidsbündler).

[18] Later, in *Twilight of the Idols*, Nietzsche sharpens the invective even further and characterizes Strauss's book as a "barstool-gospel" (Bierbank-Evangelium; *TI* Skirmishes §2; *KSA* 6, 104–5), that is, suitable only for Germans whose brains had been addled by too much beer.

[19] Again this can be seen in the context of *The Anti-Christ*, where in §45 Nietzsche will give commented excerpts from the New Testament in similar fashion.

[20] Cf., much later, Nietzsche's attack on the decadent atomism of Wagner's style, borrowed from Paul Bourget, in *The Case of Wagner* (*CW* §7).

[21] See his letter to Carl von Gersdorff of 11 February 1874 (*KSB* 4, 200).

[22] Cf. William H. Schaberg, *The Nietzsche Canon: A Publication History and Bibliography* (Chicago and London: U of Chicago P, 1995), 36.

[23] Nietzsche mentions Ranke and Mommsen at *UM* I §3; in *UM* II he mentions only the ancient historian Niebuhr (*UM* II §1 and §3) and Burckhardt (*UM* II §3). Nietzsche will later return to the supposedly great age of German historiography in *Ecce Homo*, and pass unkind remarks about Treitschke et al. (*EH CW* §2). On the context of the history essay, see in particular Christian J. Emden, *Friedrich Nietzsche and the Politics of History* (Cambridge: Cambridge UP, 2008).

[24] Cf. Daniel W. Conway, *Nietzsche's Dangerous Game: Philosophy in the Twilight of the Idols* (Cambridge: Cambridge UP, 1997), chapter 2, "The Economy of Decadence," esp. 36–40.

[25] Nietzsche will return to this theme in *On the Genealogy of Morals* with the notion of "active forgetting" (*GM* II §1–§3).

[26] Cf. *UM* III §3, where Nietzsche describes "the procreation of genius" (die Erzeugung des Genius) as "the goal of all culture" (das Ziel aller Cultur; *KSA* 1, 358).

[27] For a rewarding reading of the essay in the light of the ambiguous motif of the *pharmakon* (poison/remedy) in Plato's *Phaedrus*, see Paul Ricoeur, *Memory, History, Forgetting*, trans. Kathleen Blamey and David Pellauer (Chicago and London: U of Chicago P, 2004), 287–92.

[28] See Martin Heidegger, *Sein und Zeit*, 18th ed. (Tübingen: Niemeyer, 2001), 396. Heidegger went on to devote a whole course of lectures to the text in Freiburg in 1938–39.

[29] Thomas Mann, "Nietzsches Philosophie im Lichte unserer Erfahrung," in *Essays 1945–1955*, ed. Hermann Kurzke and Stephan Stachorski (Frankfurt am Main: Fischer, 1997), 6:56–92.

[30] See Gilles Deleuze and Félix Guattari, *What is Philosophy?*, trans. Graham Burchell and Hugh Tomlinson (London: Verso; New York: Columbia UP, 1994), 96.

[31] See Alexander Nehamas, "The Genealogy of Genealogy: Interpretation in Nietzsche's Second *Untimely Meditation* and in *The Genealogy of Morals*," in *On Literary Theory and Philosophy*, ed. Richard Freadman and Lloyd Reinhardt (New York: St. Martin's, 1991), 236–52.

[32] On the role of the concept of genius in the *Untimely* essays, see Eugen Fink, *Nietzsche's Philosophy*, trans. Goetz Richter (London and New York: Continuum, 2003), 27–30.

[33] On Schopenhauer's reception by Nietzsche and others, see: Christopher Janaway, ed., *Willing and Nothingness: Schopenhauer as Nietzsche's Educator* (Oxford: Clarendon P, 1998); Thomas H. Brobjer, *Nietzsche's Philosophical Context: An Intellectual Biography* (Urbana and Chicago: U of Illinois P, 2008), 28–32; and the appendices to Bryan Magee, *The Philosophy of Schopenhauer* (Oxford: Clarendon P, 1983).

[34] See James Conant, "Nietzsche's Perfectionism: A Reading of *Schopenhauer as Educator*," in *Nietzsche's Postmoralism: Essays on Nietzsche's Prelude to Philosophy's Future*, ed. Richard Schacht (Cambridge: Cambridge UP, 2001), 181–257.

[35] J. P. Stern, *A Study of Nietzsche* (Cambridge: Cambridge UP, 1979), 156.

[36] See Bernd Magnus, *Nietzsche's Existential Imperative* (Bloomington and London: Indiana UP, 1978).

[37] See Sarah Kofman, "Le/les concept(s) de 'culture' dans les *Intempestives* ou la double dissimulation", in *Nietzsche et la scène philosophique* (Paris: UGE, 1979), 337–71; and Daniel Breazeale, "Becoming Who One Is: Notes on *Schopenhauer as Educator*," *New Nietzsche Studies* 2:3/4 (Summer 1998): 1–25.

[38] Cf. the early preface "On the Pathos of Truth" ("Ueber das Pathos der Wahrheit"; *KSA* 1, 755–60) and the later concept of "pathos of distance" (Pathos der Distanz; *BGE* §257).

[39] Brobjer, in *Nietzsche's Philosophical Context*, counts Emerson as Nietzsche's first significant philosophical mentor (22–25). See also George J. Stack, *Nietzsche and Emerson: An Elective Affinity* (Athens: Ohio UP, 1992).

[40] Richard Schacht, "Nietzsche's First Manifesto: On *Schopenhauer as Educator*," in *Making Sense of Nietzsche: Reflections Timely and Untimely* (Urbana and Chicago: U of Illinois P, 1995), 153–66 (here 155, 153).

[41] Schaberg, *The Nietzsche Canon*, 49.

[42] Although *Nietzsche contra Wagner* ignores the text and gathers its evidence only from the later 1870s onwards.

[43] By analogy with the "Bildungsroman" one might term it an "Erziehungs-märchen."

[44] This anti-Renaissance rhetoric will rapidly change in Nietzsche's work after the rejection of Wagner, from *HA* onwards. Cf. my *Nietzsches Renaissance-Gestalten: Shakespeare, Kopernikus, Luther* (Weimar: Verlag der Bauhaus-Universität Weimar, 2009).

[45] See *EH BT* §1 and Sarah Kofman, *Explosion II: Les enfants de Nietzsche* (Paris: Galilée, 1993), 77–99.

[46] See my article "Nietzsche's *Helmbrecht*; or, How to Philosophise with a Ploughshare," *Journal of Nietzsche Studies* 13 (Spring 1997): 3–22.

[47] In a letter to Georg Brandes of 10 April 1888 he offers a more contingent explanation: "they were to have been thirteen, but thankfully my health said 'no!'" (es sollten 13 werden: die Gesundheit sagte glücklicherweise Nein!; *KSB* 8, 287).

[48] See Nietzsche's letter to Ernst Wilhelm Fritzsch, 29 August 1886 (*KSB* 7, 238).

[49] See Kofman, "Accessories (*Ecce Homo*, 'Why I Write Such Good Books,' 'The Untimelies,' 3)," trans. Duncan Large, in *Nietzsche: A Critical Reader*, ed. Peter R. Sedgwick (Oxford and Cambridge, MA: Blackwell, 1995), 144–57.

[50] Cf. Daniel W. Conway, "Genealogy and Critical Method," in *Nietzsche, Genealogy, Morality: Essays on Nietzsche's "Genealogy of Morals,"* ed. Richard Schacht (Berkeley, Los Angeles, and London: U of California P, 1994), 318–33 (esp. 319–22, "Genealogy and Symptomatology").

Link to *Human, All Too Human*

In Leipzig Nietzsche had become friends with Heinrich Romundt (1845–1919), another classical philologist who joined the Philological Society, or Philologischer Verein, co-founded by Nietzsche. But both Nietzsche and Franz Overbeck, the theologian, were amazed by Romundt's decision in February 1875 to convert to Roman Catholicism and become a priest. Writing to Erwin Rohde on 28 February 1875, Nietzsche described Romundt as "a domestic problem, a house ghost" (ein Hausleiden, ein Hausgespenst), and expressed his indignation at Romundt's decision in a way that might surprise us: "Our good, pure, Protestant air! I have never felt my innermost dependence on the spirit of Luther more strongly than now, and this unfortunate fellow wants to turn his back on all these liberating spirits?" (Unsre gute reine protestantische Luft! Ich habe nie bis jetzt stärker meine innigste Abhängigkeit von dem Geiste Luther gefühlt als jetzt, und allen diesen befreienden Genien will der Unglückliche den Rücken wenden? *KSB* 5, 27–28).

Nietzsche's avowal of an affinity with Luther is surprising, but his attachment to the Protestant spirit is precisely because of its "liberating" (befreiend) effect. And 1875 and the following years stood very much under the sign of Nietzsche's search for liberation. First, his liberation from his sense of solitude, vividly expressed in another letter to Rohde — "we are all so solitary as we sit in our lighthouse — and if only it was just a lighthouse!" (wir sitzen alle so einsam auf unserem Leuchtturm — und wenn es nur immer ein Leuchtturm wäre! *KSB* 5, 6) — which explains his close friendship in 1875 with Marie Baumgartner, his proposal of marriage in spring 1876 to Mathilde Trampedach, and possibly later in 1876 to Louise Ott.[1] (Although it has been suggested that Nietzsche was homosexual, other accounts emphasize the charm Nietzsche held for women;[2] of course, the one is not incompatible with the other.) Second, his liberation from his ill health: suffering from headaches and migranes, Nietzsche described his state of health in a letter to Carl von Gersdorff of 26 June 1875 as explosive: "The machine seemed as if it wanted to fall apart, and I cannot deny that, sometimes, I wished it would" (Die Maschine schien in Stücke gehen zu wollen und ich will nicht leugnen, einige Male gewünscht zu haben, sie wäre es; *KSB* 5, 64). Third, liberation from Wagner and Bayreuth: after the débâcle in summer of 1876, relations with Tribschen could never recover their earlier joyful intensity. Fourth, liberation from his life as a professor in Basel:

on 14 July 1875, Nietzsche wrote to Marie Baumgartner: "I am trying to achieve the trick of combining this existence [as a scholar] and my personal destiny together in such a way that they do not harm each other, but even help each other" (ich versuche das Kunststück zu leisten, diese Existenz und meine persönliche Bestimmung so in einander zu verknüpfen, dass sie sich nicht schaden, sondern sogar nützen; *KSB* 5, 77), but the trick was proving increasingly hard to perform. Not least because of the repercussions of *The Birth of Tragedy*: Ritschl's successor in Bonn, Hermann Usener (1834–1905), had apparently declared the book to be "pure nonsense" (der bare Unsinn), and its author "in scholarly terms, dead" (wissenschaftlich todt; *KSB* 4, 70). Attendance at Nietzsche's classes had fallen drastically, and as one biographer has noted, "his professorial status was now practically reduced to that of an upper high-school teacher."[3] Finally, liberation from philology — not just from his life as a scholar, but from the scholarly arena as such — stimulated in part by his friendship with Paul Rée (1849–1901), a philosopher who had studied in Zurich and then moved to Paris, whose *Psychological Observations* (*Psychologische Beobachtungen*, 1875) Nietzsche much admired, and whose *The Origin of Moral Sensations* (*Der Ursprung der moralischen Empfindungen*, 1877) shared Nietzsche's critique of morality.[4] His friendship with the musician Heinrich Köselitz (1854–1918), to whom he gave the pseudonym Peter Gast, also broadened his horizons, as did his visits — on sick-leave — to Genoa in October 1876, then to Sorrento, where he stayed until May 1877 with Malwida von Meysenbug (1816–1903), Paul Rée, and one of his former pupils, Albert Brenner (1856–78).[5] Writing to Reinhart von Seydlitz on 24 September 1876, Nietzsche had expressed the desire to found with his friends in Sorrento "a sort of monastery for more free spirits" (eine Art Kloster für freiere Geister), planning afterward to return to Basel, "unless I build up somewhere my monastery, I mean 'the school of educators' (where these educate *themselves*) in a *higher* style" (es sei denn dass ich irgendwo mein Kloster, ich meine 'die Schule der Erzieher' (wo diese *sich* selbst erziehen) in *höherem* Style aufbaue; *KSB* 5, 188).

And it seems that, in Sorrento, Nietzsche came close to achieving these plans. Albert Brenner told his family in December 1876 that they were living "as if in a monastery" (wie in einem Kloster): his room, Nietzsche's, and Rée's were adjacent to each other, and each morning he got up at half past six, as Nietzsche encouraged him to do.[6] Nietzsche himself, writing a postcard from Sorrento to his sister on 20 January 1877, told her: "The 'school of educators' (also called the modern monastery, the ideal colony, the *université libre*) is in the air, who knows what will happen!" (Die "Schule der Erzieher" (auch modernes Kloster, Idealkolonie, université libre genannt) schwebt in der Luft, wer weiß was geschieht! *KSB* 5, 216).

But Nietzsche remained inwardly troubled, as he told — significantly enough — Cosima Wagner, in a letter written on the occasion of her birthday of 19 December 1876: "Almost every night I converse in dreams with long-forgotten people, yes, mainly with the dead. Childhood, the time when I was at school are as if present in my mind" (Fast alle Nächte verkehre ich im Traume mit längstvergessenen Menschen, ja vornehmlich mit Todten. Kindheit Knaben- und Schulzeit sind mir ganz gegenwärtig), and these nocturnal dialogues prompted him to think about what he had achieved — and what he hadn't: "When considering earlier goals and what has actually been achieved it strikes me that, in everything I have achieved, I have gone well beyond the hopes and general wishes of my youth; but then of everything I had deliberately chosen to do, I was on average able to achieve only a third" (Mir ist bei Betrachtung früherer Ziele und des thatsächlich Erreichten ausgefallen, daß ich in allem, was ich thatsächlich erreicht habe, bei Weitem über die Hoffnungen und allgemeinen Wünsche der Jugend herausgekommen bin; daß ich dagegen von allem, was ich mir absichtlich vorgenommen habe, durchschnittlich immer nur den dritten Thiel zu erreichen vermochte; *KSB* 5, 209). As well as visiting his own past in his dreams, Nietzsche visited in a very literal sense the historical past of humankind, making trips (in February/March 1877) to Pompeii and (in April 1877) to Capri, with its Mithraic grotto.[7] Nietzsche's imagination seems to have been caught by the Grotto Azzurra and the cult of Mithras: in the "madness of Mithraism" (Mithraswahn) he saw an appealing idea, "life as a *festival*" (das Leben als Fest; *KSA* 8, 28[22] and 28[34], 507 and 508).

In September 1876 Nietzsche had dictated to Köselitz part of a new work he was planning, called *The Ploughshare* (*Die Pflugschar*), and when Reinhold von Seydlitz visited him in Sorrento in March/April 1877, their aphoristic exchanges were taken over into this new work in progress (and they even espied, in an abandoned Capuchin monastery, a building for the projected "school of educators," if only the finances were available. . .).[8] In September 1877, back in Basel, Nietzsche resumed dictating the work to Köselitz, and there was still much in Nietzsche's life to confirm the implicit thesis of this new work's title — that human beings were "human, all-too-human." Healthwise Nietzsche had his ups and downs; his mother believed the solution lay in getting married, and she told him (see her letter of 31 August 1877) that she knew just the woman for him, "a delightful little lady, absolutely delightful, clever, pretty, well-off and at the same time extremely simple and clean" (ein köstliches Frauchen [. . .], höchst liebenswürdig, gescheidt, hübsch, wohlhabend und dabei höchst einfach und sauber; *KSB* II.6.1, 680). Maybe Nietzsche himself took this view: on 25 April 1877 he had shared with his mother a joke about his intention of marriage to a suitable, but wealthy woman — "'Good, *but* rich,' as Fräulein v[on] M[eysenbug] said, about the 'but' in which we laughed a lot" ('Gut, *aber* reich' wie Frl v M. sagte, über welches 'Aber' wir sehr lachten; *KSB* 5, 231), while in his letter to Malwida von Meysenbug herself of 3 September 1877, he asked: "Have you found the little fairy woman, who will set me free from the pillar to which I am attached?" (Haben Sie das Feenweibchen gefunden, welches mich von der Säule, an welche ich angeschmiedet bin, losmacht?; *KSB* 5, 284).[9]

Human, All Too Human (*Menschliches, Allzumenschliches*), subtitled "A Book for Free Spirits" (Ein Buch für freie Geister), appeared in three installments: what is now volume 1 was published in May 1878, followed by *Mixed Opinions and Maxims* (*Vermischte Meinungen und Sprüche*) in March 1879 and *The Wanderer and His Shadow* (*Der Wanderer und sein Schatten*) in December 1879. (Not until the second edition of 1886 were these three parts presented as two volumes of a single work.) In the period between the publication of the last two parts, Nietzsche liberated himself, as he came to think of it, from his professorship in Basel, and the concluding section of volume 1 offers a reworked (and, ultimately, more reassuring) version of the motif of the wanderer found in his *Untimely Meditation* on Schopenhauer:

> Then will come, as recompense, the joyful mornings of other places and times, when he shall see, even as the light dawns, the Muses as they dance by him amid the mountain mist, and when afterward, if he remains silent beneath the trees in the equanimity of the soul at morning, lots of good and bright things shall be showered down on him from the tree-tops and leafy nooks, the gifts of all those free spirits who are at home in mountain, wood, and solitude [. . .].

> [Dann kommen, als Entgelt, die wonnevollen Morgen anderer Gegenden und Tage, wo er schon im Grauen des Lichtes die Musenschwärme im Nebel des Gebirges nahe an sich vorübertanzen sieht, wo ihm nachher, wenn er still, in dem Gleichmaass der Vormittagsseele, unter Bäumen sich ergeht, aus deren Wipfeln und Laubverstecken heraus lauter gute und helle Dinge zugeworfen werden, die Geschenke aller jener freien Geister, die in Berg, Wald und Einsamkeit zu Hause sind [. . .]. (*HA* I §638; *KSA* 2, 363)]

It is through the delicate, delightful pages of the work that is conventionally held to mark the transition from Nietzsche's early to his middle period that the following contribution by Ruth Abbey now leads us.

Notes

[1] On the nature and outcome of this proposal, see Curtis Cate, *Friedrich Nietzsche* (London: Hutchinson, 2002), 219–20.

[2] See Jakob Wackernagel's account of Nietzsche as a high-school teacher, which emphasizes the seriousness of his pedagogy (see Sander L. Gilman, ed., *Conversations with Nietzsche: A Life in the Words of His Contemporaries*, trans. David J. Parent [New York and Oxford: Oxford UP, 1987], 35–37), but also his sociable side: "The young women were enchanted by him. We students liked to be told by them stories about his conversations with them. One of them reported to me, for instance, that he had told her how he had dreamed of being a camellia" (cited in *Chronik*, p. 333).

[3] Cate, *Friedrich Nietzsche*, 165.

[4] For a shrewd assessment of the common ground and the differences between Nietzsche and Rée, see Lou von Salomé's letter to Nietzsche of 4 June 1882 (Ernst Pfeiffer, ed., *Friedrich Nietzsche — Paul Rée — Lou von Salomé: Die Dokumente ihrer Begegnung* [Frankfurt am Main: Insel, 1970], 130).

[5] For an insight into Malwida von Meysenbug's ambition to bring about a radical change in social relations, see her letter to Lou von Salomé of 25 May 1882 (*Die Dokumente ihrer Begegnung*, 111–13). According to Meysenbug, this ambition could only be realized "on a larger basis, in communal studies at the universities, etc." (auf größerer Basis, im gemeinschaftlichen Studieren an den Universitäten etc; letter to Lou von Salomé of 6 June 1882; *Die Dokumente ihrer Begegnung*, 133).

[6] Carl Albrecht Bernoulli, *Franz Overbeck und Friedrich Nietzsche: Eine Freundschaft*, 2 vols. (Jena: Diederichs, 1908), 1:202. For further discussion of domestic arrangements in Sorrento, see 1:203–5; and Curt Paul Janz, *Friedrich Nietzsche: Eine Biographie*, 3 vols. (Munich and Vienna: Hanser, 1978), 1:748–51.

[7] See *KSA* 14, 610–11; Joachim Köhler, *Zarathustras Geheimnis: Friedrich Nietzsche und seine verschlüsselte Botschaft* (Reinbek bei Hamburg: Rowohlt, 1992), 192–96.

[8] See Reinhart von Seydlitz, "Friedrich Nietzsche: Briefe und Gespräche," *Neue Deutsche Rundschau* 10 (1899): 617–28.

[9] See Paul Janz, *Friedrich Nietzsche: Eine Biographie*, 1:758–59. See also *KSB* 5, 24 and 250.

4: *Human, All Too Human: A Book for Free Spirits*

Ruth Abbey

Introduction

ONE OF THE FIRST INTERPRETIVE WORKS about Nietzsche advanced the idea that three periods can be discerned in his writings. Lou Andreas-Salomé's *Friedrich Nietzsche in seinen Werken*, published in 1894, proposed that Nietzsche's middle period comprises the two volumes of *Human, All Too Human* (*Menschliches, Allzumenschliches*, 1878–80), *Daybreak* (*Morgenröthe*, 1881), and the first four books of *The Gay Science* (*Die fröhliche Wissenschaft*, 1882).[1] Nietzsche's middle period is thus demarcated at one end by contrast with his early writings and their enthusiasm for Wagner and Schopenhauer,[2] and at the other by *Thus Spoke Zarathustra* (*Also sprach Zarathustra*, 1883) and his subsequent writings. Salomé is too subtle a reader of Nietzsche to suggest that each period represents a clean and complete epistemological break with the earlier one. She points out, for example, that in his last phase Nietzsche returns to some of the concerns of his first, but approaches them differently. Thus it is possible to employ Salomé's tripartite periodization while acknowledging that the boundaries between Nietzsche's phases are not rigid, that some of the thoughts elaborated in one period were adumbrated in the previous one, that there are differences within any single phase, and that some concerns pervade his oeuvre.

According to Salomé's framework, Nietzsche's middle period is inaugurated by *Human, All Too Human*. The forces contributing to a change in his thinking at this time were several: his reassessment of Schopenhauer, his growing disenchantment with Wagner's religious tendencies, German nationalism, and towering egotism;[3] Nietzsche's burgeoning friendship with Paul Rée, who fostered his interest in the French moralists and in English thinkers like Darwin and Spencer; the deterioration of his health and his eventual resignation from his teaching post at the University of Basel. But Salomé diagnoses a constitutional compulsion to intellectual self-alienation and self-overcoming in Nietzsche: as she sees it, whatever the catalysts at any particular phase of his life, Nietzsche repeatedly felt impelled to distance himself from ideas with which he was familiar and to try on new possibilities.[4] This was a very productive time in Nietzsche's life, for having published a work each year for three years in succession, he went on to publish *Daybreak* in 1881, one year after "The Wanderer and His Shadow" ("Der Wanderer und sein Schatten"). Whatever the differences between *Human, All Too Human* and *Daybreak*, both are considered to be part of the middle period, and so they share many features in common.

The work currently known as *Human, All Too Human* amalgamates three of Nietzsche's writings. Its first volume was published in 1878 under the title eventually given to the work as a whole. Volume 2 comprises two shorter, contemporaneous writings, with "Assorted Opinions and Maxims" ("Vermischte Meinungen und Sprüche") appearing in 1879 and "The Wanderer and His Shadow" making its debut the following year. These three writings were fused into a single, two-volume work in 1886, when Nietzsche also composed a preface for each volume.[5] In its two-volume form, *Human, All Too Human* represents the longest publication in Nietzsche's corpus. As a chapter of this brevity cannot hope to do justice to this work's richness, it will isolate a selection of important themes for consideration. However, because part of the intellectual reward and sheer pleasure of this book comes from Nietzsche's fine-grained analyses, close readings of a number of passages are also offered. This chapter thus discusses the attraction of scientific knowledge that emerges in *Human, All Too Human* and outlines why Nietzsche values it over metaphysics, religion, and art. It underlines Nietzsche's ongoing concern with the effect that pursuing such knowledge will have on individuals' character and motivation. His relationship to the enlightenment tradition is considered, as is his experimentation with style. Nietzsche's presentation of himself as a psychologist is also discussed, and the contention that his apprenticeship as a genealogist of morality starts in *Human, All Too Human* is explained. Nietzsche is, further, shown to be reflecting on the rise of democracy in modern Western societies in this work. The chapter concludes with the claim that while *Human, All Too Human* endorses the scientific approach as the best path to knowledge, Nietzsche does not recoil from the dangers that seeking and finding such knowledge incur.

Science as a Vocation

Nietzsche entitled the first book of the first volume of *Human, All Too Human* "Of First and Last Things" ("Von den ersten und letzten Dingen"). He could be alluding here to a line in three of the New Testament's gospels, where Jesus predicts that in heaven, many who are first on earth will be last, while those who are last will be first.[6] Thus eternity could witness a dramatic reversal of the social hierarchy that prevails on earth. The hierarchy whose overturning Nietzsche is prophesying is not a social but an intellectual one, for he is reflecting on the tendency to value religious and metaphysical beliefs over the smaller, more modest and less pretentious truths that the natural sciences, and inquiries modeled after them, can reveal. What Nietzsche means by the term science is the careful, dispassionate quest for knowledge and the possibility of seeing the world as it really is, without wishful thinking or need imputing or imposing meaning.[7] Book 1's thirty-four sections thus juxtapose religion and metaphysics on the one hand with science on the other, accusing the former of constructing a fantasy world, in much the same way that humans do when we dream (*HA* 5, §12–§13; *KSA* 2, 31–35).[8] With religion and metaphysics, however, the fabricated world does not disappear when we wake up: on the contrary, belief in this world orders and arranges values in ordinary, waking life.

Nietzsche also poses a fundamental challenge to the way the Western philosophical tradition privileges that which is unchanging and enduring over that which becomes and develops. We get a good sense of how philosophy prioritizes permanence from this work's opening words, which observe that philosophy's key questions have remained unchanged for two millennia (see *HA* §37; *KSA* 2, 59–61). Philosophers have refused to see that humans change over time, as does their capacity for knowledge. Nietzsche, by contrast, firmly rejects any belief in eternal facts or absolute truths (*HA* §2, §16, §107 and WS §43; *KSA* 2, 24–25, 36–38, 103–6, and 572–73). He has Kant and Schopenhauer in particular in mind when launching this attack on metaphysics and its dream world of permanence, of things in themselves and of boundlessly compassionate or contemplative individuals (*HA* §21; *KSA* 2, 42–43; cf. *HA* §33; *KSA* 2, 52–53). But this wake-up call is also an exercise in self-criticism, for at the halfway point of book 1 we encounter what is effectively a confessional statement. The passage entitled "Metaphysical Explanations" ("Metaphysische Erklärungen") explains why a (supposedly generic) young person values these (*HA* §17; *KSA* 2, 38). Their attraction lies in the sense they give to things that had seemed undesirable or repellent. If, moreover, the young person feels dissatisfied with himself, metaphysics can offer the comforting knowledge that he is not responsible for those elements of the self that disturb or distress him (see *HA* §108 and §117; *KSA* 2, 107 and 119). The young person is thus drawn to metaphysical inquiry for reasons extraneous to the love of knowledge and the clear-eyed quest to understand the world. With time the youth comes to realize, however, just as Nietzsche did, that science is a better path to knowledge (*HA* §17; *KSA* 2, 38; cf. *HA* §272–§273; *KSA* 2, 224–25). In *Human, All Too Human* Nietzsche seeks to show why a maturing youth would prefer science to religion and metaphysics.

One advantage of a scientific approach is that it opens the door to historical awareness. Such an approach does not assume either that real things do not change or that things that do not change are more real than those that do. Science sees and accepts becoming, in nature, in humans, in societies, cultures, and moralities. Thus one of the ways in which the practice of philosophy should become more scientific is by acquiring a sense of history: what is needed is historical philosophy (*HA* §1 and §2; *KSA* 2, 13–15; cf. *HA* AOM §10, §17 and WS §16; *KSA* 2, 384, 386, and 550–51). As this indicates, Nietzsche is not pitting science against philosophy in any implacable sense: rather, he is urging philosophers to become more scientific. As well as acknowledging change and becoming, the sort of scientific thinking he champions contents itself with small, unpretentious truths, encouraging modesty and humility in its practitioners (*HA* §2, §6, §588, §609, §635 and AOM §25; *KSA* 2, 15, 20–21, 338, 345, 360–61, and 388–89). Yet this need not doom a scientific approach to trading only in isolated points of information: it can, on the contrary, move incrementally toward a fuller picture of nature or the person. But it does this with a caution and rigor alien to high-flying, undisciplined metaphysical speculation (*HA* §16 and §22; *KSA* 2, 36–38 and 43–44).

But book 1 is not simply an encomium to the scientific model of knowledge, for Nietzsche remains cognizant of the continuing appeal of religion and metaphysics, and asks himself hard questions about what might be lost should science come to enjoy the cultural preeminence that religion and metaphysics have hitherto exercised. Thus from section 22 until the end of book 1, he reflects on the consequences for human motivation and action of pursuing his preferred approach to knowledge. He wonders, for example, whether the demise of religion with its gaze toward the eternal and the subsequent refocusing of attention toward change, becoming, and small truths will dissuade people from looking to the long term and from forging enduring institutions. He ponders whether the sort of scientific approach to knowledge he advocates can inspire individuals to think beyond themselves and their immediate needs and interests (*HA* §22; *KSA* 2, 43–44). This is an especially pressing question given his belief that most people are already inclined toward self-absorption (*HA* §33; *KSA* 2, 52–53).[9]

Yet book 1's answer to these questions about the consequences that adopting Nietzsche's preferred path to knowledge might have for human action and motivation is ultimately hopeful. Nietzsche concludes that progress, while not guaranteed, is possible, and imagines the sort of large-scale improvements that could be ushered in if the scientific approach to knowledge were applied to society. Section 24, entitled "Possibility of Progress" ("Möglichkeit des Fortschritts"), declares that from now on, progress can be based on a willed, conscious decision by individuals to move their culture and society forward. Its expansive vision embraces "better conditions for the generation of humans, their nourishment, upbringing, instruction; they can administer the earth as a whole economically, can weigh the strengths of humans, one against the other, and employ them [. . .] progress is *possible*" (bessere Bedingungen für die Entstehung der Menschen, ihre Ernährung, Erziehung, Unterrichtung schaffen, die Erde als Ganzes ökonomisch verwalten, die Kräfte der Menschen überhaupt gegen einander abwägen und einsetzen [. . .] den Fortschritt, — er ist möglich; *KSA* 2, 45; cf. WS §183 and §189; *KSA* 2, 631 and 635–36). In answering his own questions about the social and cultural ramifications of the scientific approach, Nietzsche seems also to hope that such a vision of the future will galvanize others to work for the advancement of learning and to turn their backs upon the meretricious charms of religion and metaphysics. Indeed, at one point he seems to suggest that improvements in living conditions will loosen the hold of religion over people's emotions, for when living conditions improve, they will no longer seek the anesthetizing effects of religion or art (*HA* §108; *KSA* 2, 107; cf. §148 and §234; *KSA* 2, 143 and 195–96).[10]

This optimistic accent on progress in section 24 makes it less surprising that in section 26, Nietzsche explicitly aligns himself with the Enlightenment tradition, invoking Petrarch, Erasmus,[11] and Voltaire, while regretting that the promising scientific elements of Schopenhauer's thought were eclipsed by its metaphysical ones.[12] Indeed, the first edition of *Human, All Too Human* included a dedication to Voltaire on the centenary of his death as "one of the greatest liberators of the human spirit" (einem der grössten Befreier des Geistes).[13] Further evidence of Nietzsche's affinity with the Enlightenment project appears in his later enthusiastic references to progress and improvement for humanity as a whole (*HA* §25, AOM §179; *KSA* 2, 46 and 457–58).[14] He seems to have sloughed off the preoccupation with national greatness that characterized *The Birth of Tragedy* and to be concerned now with the world — or at the very least with Europe — rather than with any particular national culture or society (see *HA* §475; *KSA* 2, 309–11). As he explains in section 25, however, a concern with universal progress need not demand universalization of methods. He questions Kant's assumption that truly moral action is that which can be replicated by all others, suggesting instead that sometimes the most beneficial course requires a division of labor, with different groups or collectivities doing different things that ultimately redound to the benefit of all (*KSA* 2, 46).[15] Nietzsche presents the challenge of devising the best means for advancing human progress as the enormous task facing the great minds (or spirits — he calls them "die grossen Geister") of the twentieth century (*HA* §25; *KSA* 2, 46).[16]

Book 1 culminates with a portrait of the sort of personality Nietzsche envisages as the scientific person par excellence. Such a figure sees religion and metaphysics for the beautiful illusions they are, and can live unaided by them without descending into despair at life's meanness or meaninglessness. Although believing in and working for the improvement of humanity, his learning also lends a certain distance and detachment from this world. He relishes this "free, fearless hovering over people, customs, laws and the traditional evaluations of things" (jenes freie, furchtlose Schweben über Menschen, Sitten, Gesetzen und den herkömmlichen Schätzungen der Dinge; *HA* §34; *KSA* 2, 55). The knowledge such a person is committed to acquiring simplifies his temperament and cleanses him of the push and pull of clashing desires (*HA* §34; *KSA* 2, 54–55; cf. *HA* §56, §288, and §291; *KSA* 2, 75, 234, and 234–35).[17] Although Nietzsche has not yet deployed this signature expression, there is also a "joy" in this person's "wisdom." Such "a secure, mild, and basically cheerful soul" (eine gefestete, milde und im Grunde frohsinnige Seele) neither is offended to be part of, nor aspires to rise above nature (*HA* §34; *KSA* 2, 55; cf. *HA* §254 and WS §327; *KSA* 2, 211 and 696).[18] He is, instead, content to count himself among the human, all too human.

This summary of the first book of *Human, All Too Human* gives the lie to the commonplace that Nietzsche held truth to be unattainable, for he maintains that truth can and should be pursued and prescribes ways in which this should be done (see *HA* §225 and §609; *KSA* 2, 189 and 345). The sort of truths whose pursuit he commends are the more provisional, falsifiable truths of science rather than the permanent, unconditional truth sought by traditional philosophers, but he repeatedly portrays it is a form of truth nonetheless (AOM §7, §20 and WS §16, §213; *KSA* 2, 383 and 387, 550–51 and 645–46). This brief summary of book 1 also gives the lie to those who label the middle period writings aphoristic, for there is not an aphorism in the strict sense to be seen in this first book.[19] Instead we have thirty-four numbered and titled passages, most of which are paragraph length, while a few occupy a page or more (*HA* §13, §16 and §18; *KSA* 2, 32–35, 36–38, and 38–40).[20] While aphorisms do make their debut in *Human, All Too Human*, it is misleading to call the work as a whole aphoristic. Perhaps their relative paucity is because Nietzsche finds them so hard to compose (*HA* §35; *KSA* 2, 57–58), but it is more likely due to the fact that many of the points he wishes to communicate are simply unsuited to the aphoristic form. Because the aphorism is just one of a variety of styles Nietzsche uses henceforth, what *Human, All Too Human* really inaugurates is his stylistic diversity. This is further enhanced when "The Wanderer and His Shadow" stages brief dialogues — between the wanderer and his shadow (*KSA* 2, 537–39 and 703–4), between Pyrrho and the old man (WS §213; *KSA* 2, 645–46), and between unnamed speakers (WS §71, §90; *KSA* 2, 584 and 593–94). That most manifold art of style upon which he prides himself in *Ecce Homo*[21] thus begins with the volumes of *Human, All Too Human*. Finally, this synopsis of book 1 also gives the lie to those who emphasize the disjointed and discontinuous nature of Nietzsche's writings, for a number of key themes are raised and pursued coherently and consistently throughout this first book. Interestingly, the more aphoristic *Human, All Too Human* becomes — as at the start of book 6, for example — the more the ideas seem, prima facie at least, to be disjointed and discontinuous.

This first book also contains the volume's first reference to its dedicated addressees: free spirits (*HA* §30: *KSA* 2, 50). Nietzsche refers to the free spirit or *der Freigeist* in the second part of a passage that warns of the mistakes that a critic of traditional philosophy might make. It would be unwise for such a critic to simply reverse or negate standard views. Take for instance the view, which Nietzsche traces to ancient Greek thinkers influenced by Socrates, that if a belief brings happiness, it must be true (*HA* §7; *KSA* 2, 27–28; cf. *HA* §120, §227, §229 and §517; *KSA* 2, 120, 191, 192–93, and 323). In rejecting this equation, the free spirit should not fall into the obverse error of holding that if a belief causes pain, it must be correct (see *HA* §56; *KSA* 2, 75). Free spirits must practice a more radical skepticism about, and more thorough revision of, the foundations of philosophical thinking. That *Human, All Too Human*'s first substantive reference to free spirits comes in the context of errors they might incur further reinforces its emphasis on the scientific thinker's modesty and humility. Whatever their talents and qualities, free spirits are still human, all too human, and can remain in the thrall of the philosophical tradition even as they think they are escaping it. This warning against errors to which critics are heir also shows that Nietzsche knows what a battle he is fighting in attempting to lessen the sway of traditional habits of thinking.[22]

Just as Nietzsche introduces the figure of the free spirit in the context of error, so *Human, All Too Human*'s second and third references to the free spirit also arise in connection with mistakes they might make or lapses they might commit. In book 3 we read that not just the "less thoughtful free spirits" (die weniger bedachtsamen Freigeister) but all practitioners of "scientific philosophy" (wissenschaftliche Philosophie) must beware of the emotional appeal religion can exert even when its cognitive content has been rejected (*HA* §131; *KSA* 2, 124). A parallel point is made in book 4's account of the blandishments of art, for art soon joins religion and metaphysics as a force antagonistic to science. Consider Nietzsche's warning that art "makes the sight of life bearable by laying over it the veil of unclear thinking" (die Kunst macht den Anblick des Lebens erträglich, dadurch dass sie den Flor des unreinen Denkens über dasselbe legt; *HA* §151; *KSA* 2, 154; cf. *HA* §150, §159, §220, §251, and §264; *KSA* 2, 144, 149, 180, and 219–20). The person in quest of scientific knowledge must, therefore, eschew art's temptations too, not least because of the metaphysical illusions they can nourish. In what must be another quasi-confessional passage, Nietzsche magically describes how a passage from

Beethoven can inspire other-worldly religious-cum-metaphysical fanta-
sies, putting the free spirit's intellectual probity to the test (*HA* §153;
KSA 2, 145). Given that the first three references to the free spirit in a
book ostensibly written for free spirits warn of errors, dangers, and temptations, it is hard to avoid the conclusion that whatever such a figure's
talents, abilities, and potential, the free spirit's progress toward truth is as
fraught as any Christian's path to heaven!

Psychological Rée-alism

Just as young people are attracted to metaphysics for the consolations
it offers, so Nietzsche opens book 2 of *Human, All Too Human* with
the declaration that psychological observation can provide relief from the
burdens of living and comfort in disagreeable phases of one's life, to say
nothing of presence of mind in difficult moments and diversion in dull
ones (*HA* §35; *KSA* 2, 57). So although psychological observation is,
or at least can be, scientific in Nietzsche's sense, it resembles religion and
metaphysics in yielding more than purely intellectual dividends. However,
unlike religion and metaphysics, psychological observation aims for per-
spicuous encounters with the depths and complexity of the human psyche
and produces small, unpretentious (but not insignificant) truths about the
self. Indeed, Nietzsche equates psychological observation with reflection
on the human, all too human (*HA* §35; *KSA* 2, 57), implying that a work
ostensibly about this must pay considerable and careful attention to the
psyche. But it will do so without any presupposition of original sin, which
has informed and infected the Christian approach to psychology that has
dominated Western culture for centuries (*HA* §141; *KSA* 2, 135–36).

It is in this opening passage of book 2 that Nietzsche first mentions
the aphorism, and its introduction here is not accidental. With its delivery
of short, sharp sentences that penetrate the heart and puncture the pride,
the aphorism is the ideal vehicle for conveying petite but potent truths
about human psychology. It warrants attention that Nietzsche's explanation of the aphorism's value is not conveyed in aphoristic form, indicating
anew that not all of his purposes in this work can be served by this genre.
Book 2 thus ushers in two additional, related features of Nietzsche's work
that begin in the middle period and persist for the rest of his oeuvre.
The first is his sense of himself as a psychologist who is committed to the
unblinking examination of the human psyche, especially as it pertains to
moral life.[23] The second is his experiment with the aphorism.

These new dimensions of Nietzsche's thought did not come out of
the blue: instead, in moving in this direction he was influenced by Paul
Rée, who was a close friend at the time. Nietzsche and Rée read the work
of the French moralists — La Rochefoucauld and Chamfort, among others — who wrote aphorisms that often sought to disabuse people of their

illusions about themselves and human motivation more generally.[24] In equating the art, or rather the science, of psychological observation with the human, all too human, Nietzsche is also echoing the title of Rée's first book, *Psychological Observations* (*Psychologische Beobachtungen*), a collection of aphorisms published in 1875. The title of book 2 of *Human, All Too Human*, "On the History of the Moral Sensations" ("Zur Geschichte der moralischen Empfindungen"), is, moreover, an allusion to another of Rée's works, for his *The Origins of Moral Sensations* (*Der Ursprung der moralischen Empfindungen*) had been published in 1877. In section 36, Rée is placed in the company of the French moralists, as "skilful marksmen who again and again hit the bullseye [. . .] of human nature" (zielenden Schützen, welche immer und immer wieder in's Schwarze treffen [. . .] der menschlichen Natur; KSA 2, 59).[25] The very next passage calls Rée "one of the boldest and coldest of thinkers" (einer der kühnsten und kältesten Denker; HA §37; KSA 2, 61), while shortly thereafter Nietzsche explains that his age needs such cold intellects (HA §38; KSA 2, 61–62). With Rée's companionship and the education supplied by the French moralists,[26] Nietzsche was able to steer a course away from Wagner and Schopenhauer[27] to become one of those wintry thinkers, one of the more spiritual figures in "an age which is visibly becoming more and more ignited" (die geistigeren Menschen eines Zeitalters, welches ersichtlich immer mehr in Brand geräth; HA §38; KSA 2, 62).[28] The first few pages of book 2 thus testify to Nietzsche's close intellectual affinity with Rée at this stage of his development.[29]

Nietzsche associates the sort of incisive, clairvoyant psychological analysis he finds in the work of Rée and the French moralists with a scientific approach to human personality in general and in particular to the moral life. In "Assorted Opinions and Maxims" he points out that in propagating temporary, provisional truths, the work of moralists avoids one of the philosopher's original sins ("eine Erbsünde der Philosophen") of transforming every particular observation into a general and permanent truth (AOM §5; KSA 2, 541; cf. WS §37; KSA 2, 569). When this more scientific approach to psychology is combined with the historical approach to philosophy adumbrated in book 1, it becomes possible to analyze the origins and trajectory of morality at two levels: at the level of individual motivation by penetrating the mystery and complexity of the psyche, and at the larger sociocultural level by recording the ways in which understandings of moral life have changed over time (see, for example, WS §40, §44, and §48; KSA 2, 570–71, 573, and 574–75). With this new approach, Nietzsche begins his apprenticeship as a genealogist of morality.[30]

As book 2 unfolds we witness once again that several sections follow one another in a logical fashion. Section 35, for example, speaks of the "advantages of psychological observation" (Vortheile der psychologischen Beobachtung), while section 36 raises an "objection" (Einwand), considering as it does the threats that psychological perspicacity might pose to human happiness and wellbeing. A passage entitled "Nevertheless" (Trotzdem) follows, contending that whatever distress such psychological probings might generate, it is necessary in the interests of truth and the advancement of science (*HA* §37; *KSA* 2, 59–61). Section 38 weighs up "to what extent" (inwiefern) psychology is "useful" (nützlich), and concludes, once again, that such an approach is necessary, whatever discomfort it might engender (*KSA* 2, 61). Having defended his method in book 2's first four passages, Nietzsche launches into a discussion of the history of morality, identifying the changing things for which individuals have been held responsible. He declares (but does not demonstrate) that the history of accountability in morality has moved through four stages, from people being deemed responsible for (1) the consequences of their actions, (2) the actions themselves, (3) the act's motivations, and (4) the nature of the actor him- or herself (*HA* §39; *KSA* 2, 62–64). This question of accountability is bound up with the issue of free will that had been flagged in book 1 (*HA* §18; *KSA* 2, 38–40), for if a person is not free in some way to choose how or whether to act, she cannot legitimately be held responsible for her actions or their effects. Here Nietzsche is casting doubt upon a premise that has characterized Western thinking about morality and personal responsibility at least since St. Augustine. In several of the passages to follow, Nietzsche continues to underscore some of the ways in which moral thinking changes over time (*HA* §42, §43, and §45; *KSA* 2, 65–66 and 67–68) and to reflect critically on the themes of free will and responsibility.[31] Space does not permit a careful elaboration of all of Nietzsche's claims and concerns in *Human, All Too Human*, but even this brief tasting reveals anew that it possesses a unity and coherence that should not be underestimated.[32]

Democracy in Europe

On the face of it, book 8, entitled "A Glance at the State" ("Ein Blick auf den Staat"), exhibits great variety in style and topic. One theme that does come through clearly, however, is Nietzsche's dislike of socialism (*HA* §451–§452, §473; *KSA* 2, 293–94 and 307–8; cf. WS §285 and §292; *KSA* 2, 679–80 and 683–84). And just as he rejects socialism, so he criticizes the other major force of political opposition at that time — nationalism (*HA* §480; *KSA* 2, 314). Instead of the latter, Nietzsche looks forward to the growth of pan-European sentiment, with book 8 containing his first invocation of the "good European" (*HA* §475; *KSA* 2, 309), a phrase he later associates with "free spirits" (WS §87; *KSA* 2, 593). This ideal of the good European is, moreover, carried into the later works. This passage, entitled "The European and the Abolition of Nations" ("Der europäische Mensch und die Vernichtung der Nationen"), also conveys his hope that a more transnational perspective will dissolve the plague of anti-Semitism, for once the goal of preserving distinct nations is eclipsed by that of producing a robust European race, the Jews with their many strengths and talents will be welcomed.

Another unifying thread in book 8 is provided by Nietzsche's reflections on the rise of democracy in modern Western societies and its replacement of older, more hierarchical forms of politics. He asks what it means that the masses are now entering politics and expecting the state to serve their interests. He ruminates on the implications of this for authority relations and the relationship between religion and politics. Indeed, the longest passage of *Human, All Too Human*'s two volumes appears in this book, as Nietzsche examines religion's role in a democratic polity (*HA* §472; *KSA* 2, 302–7). He anticipates not just the demise of civic religion and the privatization of religion in its stead, but also the contracting out of certain supposedly core state functions such as the protection of some of its citizens from the predation of others. He speculates that, in the service of self-interest, people might seek to abolish the state and replace it with other institutions. In accordance with this work's praise for science, with its more incremental and modest approach to knowledge, Nietzsche fears rather than applauds such dramatic and radical efforts at reform or revolution. Indeed, in an earlier passage from book 8 he had inveighed against the spirit of the French Revolution, seeing it as a betrayal, rather than a corollary, of the Enlightenment. A true student of Voltaire and admirer of his moderate nature would not endorse revolution. Nietzsche thus redirects the Voltairean catch-cry, "Ecrasez l'infâme," toward Rousseau's revolutionary followers (*HA* §463; *KSA* 2, 299).[33]

Nietzsche returns to this theme of Europe's democratization in WS §275, declaring the process to be "irresistible" (unaufhaltsam; *KSA* 2, 275; cf. WS §292; *KSA* 2, 683–84). By comparison with some of the remarks in his later works, he is not contemptuous of this but portrays it in a fairly positive light and points out some of its advantages. Shortly after he describes democratic institutions as useful because they keep tyranny in check, but very boring (WS §289; *KSA* 2, 683). But for Nietzsche at this time, the ethos and institutions of politics are important not just in themselves but also because they provide a template for other human relationships. As he declares in the section entitled "New and Old Conception of Government" ("Neuer und alter Begriff der Regierung"):

> The relationship between people and government is the most pervasive ideal relationship upon which commerce between teacher and pupil, lord and servants, father and family, general and soldier, master and apprentice have unconsciously been modeled. All these relationships are now, under the influence of the dominant constitutional form of government, altering their shape a little: they are becoming compromises.

[Das Verhältniss zwischen Volk und Regierung ist das stärkste vor-
bildliche Verhältniss, nach dessen Muster sich unwillkürlich der
Verkehr zwischen Lehrer und Schüler, Hausherrn und Dienerschaft,
Vater und Familie, Heerführer und Soldat, Meister und Lehrling bildet. Alle diese Verhältnisse gestalten sich jetzt, unter dem Einflusse
der herrschenden constitutionellen Regierungsform, ein Wenig
um — sie werden Compromisse. (*HA* §450; *KSA* 2, 292)]

It is hard to imagine a stronger statement about the importance and influence of politics, and its power poses a challenge to those who insist that
Nietzsche was uninterested in the political.[34]

First Things Last

By culminating in a portrait of the new person of knowledge ("der Erkennende"), book 2 of *Human, All Too Human* mirrors book 1. Nietzsche
admits there that the critique he has been mounting of the idea of moral
accountability, which is founded on the myth of free will, could be debilitating for those persuaded by it, for at the end of this critique we find that
it is "the individual's sole desire for self-enjoyment (together with the fear
of losing it) that gratifies itself in every instance, let a man act as he can, that
is to say as he must" (das einzige Verlangen des Individuums nach Selb-
stgenuss (sammt der Furcht, desselben verlustig zu gehen) befriedigt sich
unter allen Umständen, der Mensch mag handeln, wie er kann, das heisst
wie er muss; *HA* §107; *KSA* 2, 104). This desire for self-enjoyment, this
pleasure in self-assertion that is the font of all action is, in Nietzsche's estimation, both original and innocent. Be they good or bad, actions are not
freely chosen and their agents can neither be credited with nor blamed for
them. Such a perspective on moral life and motivation must surely throw
habits of moral evaluation into complete disarray, for not just blame but
also praise for individuals and their actions is ruled out by this doctrine (see
HA §588; *KSA* 2, 338). The same goes for forgiveness (WS §68; *KSA*
2, 582). Recognizing that the moral disorientation this creates is painful,
Nietzsche strives to assure his readers that such pain should be understood
as giving birth to a new form of human being, one who is not moral but
knowing. This will be a long slow gestation, but a new sort of person awaits
at its end, one habituated to "comprehending, not-loving, not-hating,
surveying" (eine neue Gewohnheit, die des Begreifens, Nicht-Liebens,
Nicht-Hassens, Ueberschauens), one who is "a wise, innocent (conscious
of innocence) person" (den weisen, unschuldigen (unschuld-bewussten)
Menschen; *HA* §107; *KSA* 2, 105). Once again then, Nietzsche moots
the image of individuals freed by knowledge from their passions, for their
understanding gradually educates them to detach themselves from emotions and judgments that currently seem so natural.[35]

In the last (untitled) passage of book 3, Nietzsche proposes that the scientific insight that humans are not responsible for their actions can free everyone to feel like Jesus, because all can see themselves as sinless, as he saw himself (*HA* §144; *KSA* 2, 139–40). This suggests a further continuation of the pattern detected in books 1 and 2 where the last passage of each book envisages the sort of person one can become if one internalizes scientific teachings. Book 5 likewise concludes with the injunction, "Forward on the path of wisdom with a bold step and full of confidence" (Vorwärts auf der Bahn der Weisheit, guten Schrittes, guten Vertrauens! *HA* §292; *KSA* 2, 235). The individual in quest of such wisdom should not regret any earlier allegiance to religion or art, for, seen from the correct perspective, they afford greater insight into history. Indeed, Nietzsche concludes that these are not regrettable but rather necessary stages in the wise person's formation. What matters is not to have once been immersed in these media but to go beyond them. In a strange mix of metaphors, he urges that any distress the thinker experiences should be seen as a source of nourishment, with "hanging clouds of sadness" (die hängenden Wolken der Trübsal) becoming "udders from which you milk the milk for your refreshment" (zum Euter [. . .] aus dem du die Milch zu deiner Labung melken wirst; *KSA* 2, 237). In a more conventional combination of images, along with this milk, the thinker can feast on knowledge, for "no honey is sweeter" (kein Honig süsser als der der Erkenntniss ist; *KSA* 2, 237).[36] So the last things in books 1, 2, 3, and 5 — Nietzsche's vignettes of the person pursuing the sort of scientific knowledge he advocates — take us to matters of first priority for him, that is to say, the ramifications of particular doctrines and intellectual positions for the character, temperament, and outlook of those holding them.

Yet despite the extended answers offered at the end of these books, Nietzsche does not seem wholly persuaded by his own claims about how to going on living in an affirmative way with knowledge of the truth as disclosed by scientific inquiry. This question haunts *Human, All Too Human*. In the passage "Sorrow is Knowledge" ("Gram ist Erkenntniss") he turns, paradoxically perhaps, to the poet Byron for a formulation of this problem. Early in act 1, scene 1 of the play *Manfred*, its eponymous hero announces that "Sorrow is knowledge: they who know the most / Must mourn the deepest o'er the fatal truth, / The tree of knowledge is not that of life" (*HA* §109; *KSA* 2, 108; cf. WS §1; *KSA* 2, 540). In the face of this fatal truth, a return to religious or metaphysical edification is not on the cards for Nietzsche, for he finds such a prospect unconscionable for one versed in the ways of science and its commitment to a clairvoyant pursuit of the truth (see *HA* §110 and §248; *KSA* 2, 109–11 and 206). He consoles himself that only the person who has endured "the worst hours and eclipses of the soul" (die schlimmsten Stunden und Sonnenfinsternisse der Seele) that are induced by this problem of how to live with the truth can "become a leader and educator of mankind" (einem Führer und Erzieher der Menschheit; *HA* §110; *KSA* 2, 108–9). Such torment seems, then, to be a necessary stage in the free spirit's education. Indeed, the line from *Manfred* immediately before those quoted by Nietzsche recommends that grief "be the instructor of the wise." But the fact that Nietzsche returns again and again to this dilemma of how to live with the knowledge generated by science suggests that those who read him as a wholehearted enthusiast for science or positivism in the middle period neglect the existential shadow science casts in these works. While he does endorse the scientific approach as the best path to knowledge, he does not shy away from the dangers and debilitations that seeking and finding such knowledge generate. Rather than being a poster boy for modern science, he is better read as conducting an honest, searching, and troubled conversation with himself about the implications of treading the scientific path to knowledge.

It is also relevant to note that book 4's penultimate passage permits a form of art to persist into the future, one that appreciates change rather than permanence. This suggests that the antagonism between art and science usually staged in *Human, All Too Human* is not insurmountable: art can be put on a non-metaphysical footing just as science can learn from art that humans are part of nature and that life is replete with pleasure and interest (*HA* §222; *KSA* 2, 185–86). While *HA* §239 seems to reconsider this conclusion (*KSA* 2, 201), *HA* §251 warns of the dangers that would follow if science expunged metaphysics, religion, and art (*KSA* 2, 208–9). *HA* §276, §278, and §486 as well as AOM §173 and §180 also gesture toward the fruitful co-existence of art and science (or knowledge) (*KSA* 2, 227–38, 228–29, and 317; 453 and 458). "Assorted Opinions and Maxims" contains a section entitled "By What Kind of Philosophy Art is Corrupted" ("An welcher Art von Philosophie die Kunst verdirbt"; §28; *KSA* 2, 392), implying again that art is not intrinsically incompatible with science, just as its later section, "The Poet as Signpost to the Future" ("Der Dichter als Wegzeiger für die Zukunft"), anticipates a future characterized by "knowledge and art blended to a new unity" (das Wissen und die Kunst zu neuer Einheit zusammengeflossen; AOM §99; *KSA* 2, 420). Incidentally, this section also holds that "many a path to this poetry of the future starts out from *Goethe*" (von *Goethe* aus führt mancher Weg in diese Dichtung der Zukunft; *KSA* 2, 420; cf. AOM §114; *KSA* 2, 426).[37] Given that the cultural eras Nietzsche so admires for their scientific achievements — Ancient Greece (AOM §220; *KSA* 2, 473–74) and the Renaissance — also displayed spectacular artistic achievements, it would be strange for him to insist that art and science could not flourish together. It must be said, however, that his position on their relationship is not developed in any linear way throughout these volumes; see, for example, AOM §30, §32 and §109, as well as WS §123, which remain critical of art and/or see it as incompatible with science (*KSA* 2, 393, 394, 423, 605–6). Nietzsche's twists and turns make it appropriate to consider the role of art in a more scientific or enlightened age as another of those issues that churns throughout this work.[38]

Human All Too Human's first volume ends on an upbeat note. Continuing to grapple with this question of what sort of person the pursuer of knowledge will be, in a series of sections starting with "Of Conviction and Justice" ("Von der Ueberzeugung und der Gerechtigkeit"; *HA* §629–§637; *KSA* 2, 354–62), Nietzsche elaborates a point made aphoristically about convictions as impediments to truth (*HA* §483; *KSA* 2, 317). Anti-dogmatic practitioners of science are ever willing to reconsider the things they hold to be true. Possessed of "the virtue of cautious reserve" (der Tugend der vorsichtigen Enthaltung), they are contrasted with the person of conviction (*HA* §631; *KSA* 2, 357). Schooled by science in disciplined and methodical inquiry (*HA* §633–§634; *KSA* 2, 358–60) and always willing to learn and examine anew, the person of science looks upon committed and noisy dogmatists as a relic of the past. Those times did, to be sure, inadvertently contribute to the growth of science, for the incompatible claims of those convinced of their truth had to be mediated in some way, and this often involved one party challenging the methods and procedures of others (*HA* §634; *KSA* 2, 359–60). But one thing is indisputable: the person of knowledge will not cleave to settled convictions. Having established this, it is not surprising that book 9's final passage casts the seeker after truth as a wanderer ("der Wanderer") and, in so doing, anticipates the title of the second part of volume 2. Indeed, the wanderer, the free spirit, and the philosopher seem to be interchangeable labels in this passage.[39] The wandering seeker after truth does not know his final destination, but journeys on, taking in all he sees around him, without becoming attached to any place. This journey will know its share of difficulties, and there will be times when the wanderer longs to cease moving, but to compensate for this, there will also be joyful mornings. The fact that such mornings disclose dancing muses, combined with the highly artistic, almost operatic way in which Nietzsche paints this final vignette of the free spirit, suggests once again that art has not been banished from his vision of a more enlightened future.[40] But if the person of science is a wanderer, and the wanderer casts a shadow, then we witness here again Nietzsche's powerful and ongoing awareness of both the uses and the disadvantages of science for life.[41] This is a theme that concerned him in *The Birth of Tragedy* and in the essay on the "Uses and Disadvantages of History for Life" in the *Untimely Meditations*.

Conclusion

The move into what some scholars consider Nietzsche's middle period, initiated by *Human, All Too Human*, does not entail a complete and clean break from every aspect of his previous writings. Some questions continue to preoccupy him, while others — such as how to redeem German culture — fall by the wayside, being replaced by a focus on Europe rather than any single national unit within it. I have also argued that *Human, All Too Human* inaugurates the stylistic diversity, that most manifold art of style, that characterizes Nietzsche's writing from here onwards. But we should be wary of inferring thematic discontinuity from this diversity, and throughout this chapter I have pointed to a handful of key themes that are raised and pursued coherently and consistently throughout *Human, All Too Human*. Of course, it could be objected that a brief treatment of such a substantial work is bound to underscore its thematic unity and thus to marginalize the variety of Nietzsche's interests in this text. This is a valuable caution, and a fuller treatment of *Human, All Too Human* would no doubt do more justice to the variety of its concerns. But even then, Nietzsche's injunction "Against the Shortsighted" (Gegen die Kurzsichtigen) should be kept in view:

> Do you think this work must be fragmentary because I give it to you (and must give it to you) in fragments?

> [Meint ihr denn, es müsse Stückwerk sein, weil man es euch in Stücken giebt (und geben muss)? (AOM §128; *KSA* 2, 432)]

Notes

The translations from Nietzsche in this essay are based on R. J. Hollingdale's, with occasional emendations.

[1] The fifth book of *The Gay Science* was composed after *Jenseits von Gut und Böse* (*Beyond Good and Evil*) in 1887.

[2] I don't mean to suggest that Nietzsche's attitude to Wagner or Schopenhauer was invariant at this time. Richard Schacht thinks that his unpublished essays of this period show him moving away from his preoccupation in *The Birth of Tragedy* (*Die Geburt der Tragödie*) with Wagner and with art (see preface to Christa Davis Acampora, trans., *Homer's Contest: Translation and Introductory Essay* [*Nietzsche-ana*, vol. 5; Urbana, IL: North American Nietzsche Society, 1996]). Nietzsche's critique in "Homer's Contest" ("Homer's Wettkampf") of the modern idea that the genius is an exclusive being and his clear preference for the ancient notion that geniuses thrive on agonistic competition could be directed at Wagner!

[3] Nietzsche emphasizes his growing disillusionment with Wagner in section 3 of the preface to volume 2 of *Human, All Too Human* (*KSA* 2, 372–73) and in his remarks on *Human, All Too Human* in *Ecce Homo*, sections 2–3 and 5 (*KSA* 6, 323–25 and 327).

[4] See Lou Andreas-Salomé, *Nietzsche*, ed. and trans. Siegfried Mandel (Urbana and Chicago: U of Illinois P, 2001), 52. If Salomé is right, Nietzsche is speaking from personal experience when he says that the free spirit hates "everything

enduring and definitive, that is why he sorrowfully again and again rends apart the net that surrounds him [. . .]. He has to learn to love where he formerly hated, and the reverse" (alles Dauernde und Definitive, desshalb reisst er, mit Schmerz, das Netz um sich immer wieder auseinander [. . .]. Er muss dort lieben lernen, wo er bisher hasste, und umgekehrt; *HA* I §427; *KSA* 2, 280). See also his remarks about himself in sections 4–5 of the preface to volume 2 of *Human, All Too Human* (*KSA* 2, 373–75).

[5] In recognition of the work's original tripartite nature, this chapter signals which of the three sections is being cited. *HA* refers to the 638 passages in the first volume, AOM to the first part of volume 2, which comprises 408 sections, and WS to the second part of volume 2, which contains 350 passages. I quote from R. J. Hollingdale's translation *Human, All Too Human* (Cambridge: CUP, 1986), but make emendations. I recommend against reading the prefaces as part of *Human, All Too Human* (or any of the middle period writings), because not only were they written during a later period, but Nietzsche typically uses them to re-write the history of his ideas, trying to shape the way we read these works and to fit them into his later vision of himself and his corpus.

[6] See Matthew, 19:30; Mark 10:31; Luke 13:30. The phrase "first and last things" recurs in *HA* WS §16, in the context of waiting to see science's revelations about these things.

[7] As Robin Small points out, "when Nietzsche refers to 'science' (*Wissenschaft*) in these writings, he is invoking a concept of disciplined inquiry which applies to classical philology as much as to the investigation of natural phenomena" (*Nietzsche and Rée: A Star Friendship* [Oxford: Oxford UP, 2005], 9). For illustrations of this claim, see *HA* §266 and §270 (*KSA* 2, 220–21 and 223).

[8] On the contrast between science and metaphysics, see also AOM §12 and WS §16 (*KSA* 2, 385 and 550–51). For other passages contrasting religion unfavorably with science, see *HA* §110 and §134–§135 (*KSA* 2, 109–11 and 128–29). Notwithstanding his repeated generalizations about religion, Nietzsche does recognize that religions differ from one another. See *HA* §114, for example, which contrasts Hellenic religion with Christianity (*KSA* 2, 109–11) and *HA* §144's acknowledgment that Indian saints might not fit the profile of Christian saints just sketched (*KSA* 2, 139–40).

[9] But from this it should not be inferred that most people know, or are able to care for, themselves well; see WS §5–§6 (*KSA* 2, 541–42).

[10] A later passage suggests that religion appeals to those whose daily lives are "empty and monotonous" (leer und eintönig; *HA* §115; *KSA* 2, 118, cf. *HA* §139–§141; *KSA* 2, 133–37). Because it is not clear that improvements in material conditions could ever eliminate such emptiness and monotony, he would have to accept that religion could be around for a while.

[11] These two thinkers — the first from the fourteenth century and the second who lived from the mid-fifteenth to mid-sixteenth century — would not normally be classified as part of the Enlightenment. But Nietzsche takes a long view, linking the Age of Enlightenment and the Renaissance as progressive phases in Western thought because of their shared respect for of scientific thinking (see *HA* §237; *KSA* 2, 199–200). See *HA* §219 for a variation on this theme (*KSA* 2, 179–80).

[12] One of the points of this passage — that Enlightenment thinkers fail to fully understand religion — is reiterated in *HA* 110, while AOM 33 also points to the tussle between scientific and metaphysical elements in Schopenhauer's thought.

[13] See note on the reverse of the title page of the first edition (*KSA* 2, 10). Further praise for Voltaire appears in *HA* §221 (*KSA* 2, 181–82), but this time it is for his skill as a playwright and for representing French thinking, which continues some of the best aspects of ancient Greek thinking. Here Voltaire also provides an opportunity for Nietzsche to chastise German thinkers. Voltaire is mentioned again in §240 (*KSA* 2, 201), is quoted as a critic of democracy in §438 (*KSA* 2, 285), and is contrasted as a figure of moderation and reform by comparison with the revolutionary Rousseau in §463 (*KSA* 2, 299). In AOM, by contrast, the view that error has its merits is attributed to Voltaire to show how free-spirited thinking has moved on (AOM §4; *KSA* 2, 382). Nietzsche emphasizes the presence of Voltaire in this work in *Ecce Homo*'s retrospective remarks on *Human, All Too Human*, section 1 (*KSA* 6, 322–23). For an illuminating account of the Voltairean aspects of Nietzsche's thought, see Nicholas Martin, "Aufklärung und kein Ende': The Place of Enlightenment in Friedrich Nietzsche's Thought," *German Life and Letters* 61 (2008): 79–97.

[14] AOM §171 casts Wagner's music as a reaction, destined to fail, against the spirit of the Enlightenment (*KSA* 2, 450–52).

[15] He could have in mind here something like the Ricardian doctrine of comparative advantage. But his further point, that this is a challenge for great minds of the next century, suggests that he didn't have a well-worked-out position in mind but was, instead, more invested in criticizing Kant.

[16] Elsewhere I have argued that in the middle period, Nietzsche situates himself as both legatee and vehicle of enlightenment and have shown the powerful parallels between his thinking in this period and Kant's "What is Enlightenment?" See my "So Polyphonous a Being: Friedrich Nietzsche in His Middle Works," presentation at the conference "Nietzsche and the Philosophical Life," Texas Christian University, April, 2008.

[17] *HA* §287 evokes a similar image of detachment, but this time the person alternates between joy and sorrow, just as nature moves through seasons (*KSA* 2, 233). The goal of transforming, rather than either extirpating or submitting to the passions, is also articulated in WS §37 (*KSA* 2, 569).

[18] Wisdom is also associated with joy in *HA* §292 and §486 (*KSA* 2, 237 and 317), while in the former it is tied up once again with the ideal of being in synch with nature. Science is also associated with the joy of knowledge in AOM §98 (*KSA* 2, 418).

[19] Indeed, I would argue that the first real aphorism does not appear until passage 66, nearly halfway through book 2. Aphorisms dot the work from then on until the first sustained run of them appears at the start of book 6. Nietzsche returns to the practice of opening the book with a string of aphorisms in books 7 and 9. The latter contains the most aphorisms in *Human, All Too Human*.

[20] In this sense Nietzsche's so-called aphorisms resemble Schopenhauer's, who also wrote short passages and paragraphs. Nietzsche nowhere, to my knowledge, draws attention to the fact that he shares this element of style with Schopenhauer.

[21] See *EH* "Why I Write Such Excellent Books," section 4 (*KSA* 6, 304–5).

[22] He ruminates further on this in book 5, §230 as part of a cluster of passages contrasting free and "fettered" (gebundenen) spirits and emphasizing the free spirit's challenge of thinking outside what is customary (*HA* §225–§231; *KSA* 2, 189–94).

[23] In *Ecce Homo*, for example, he says that "out of my writings there speaks a *psychologist* who has not his equal" (dass aus meinen Schriften ein *Psychologe* redet, der nicht seines Gleichen hat; *EH* "Warum ich so gute Bücher schreibe" §5; *KSA* 6, 305; emphasis in original).

[24] For Nietzsche's admiration of this tradition, see WS §214 (*KSA* 2, 646–47). Note, too, that he describes this section as being about "European" rather than "French" books.

[25] Moralists (in general) are associated with astute psychological insights in WS §19 (*KSA* 2, 553), while the following passage distinguishes what we might call deflationary moralists from those who recognize and try to understand greatness and purity (WS §20; *KSA* 2, 554).

[26] In the preface to *Human, All Too Human*, by comparison, Nietzsche portrays himself as friendless and alone during this period. See also *Ecce Homo*, where he not only discounts Rée's contribution to his intellectual development but makes himself the author of "On the Origin of the Moral Sentiments" (*EH HA* §6; *KSA* 6, 328).

[27] This is not to suggest that Schopenhauer became irrelevant to Nietzsche's intellectual development. Despite his many claims about overcoming Schopenhauer's influence, he remained an important philosophical interlocutor throughout Nietzsche's career. See, for example, Julian Young, *Nietzsche's Philosophy of Art* (Cambridge: Cambridge UP, 1993), 3; Michael Gillespie, *Nihilism Before Nietzsche* (Chicago: U of Chicago P, 1996), 183; and the essays in *Willing and Nothingness: Schopenhauer as Nietzsche's Educator*, ed. Christopher Janaway (Oxford: Clarendon P, 1998).

[28] See also *HA* §244, where Nietzsche writes that "the spirit of science [. . .] on the whole makes one somewhat colder and more skeptical" (der Geist der Wissenschaft [. . .] welcher im Ganzen etwas kälter und skeptischer; *KSA* 2, 204). See *HA* §195 (*KSA* 2, 165–66), but note there, too, Nietzsche's warning against excesses of heat or cold, which is part and parcel of this work's praise of moderation (*HA* §463–§464, §631, AOM §196, §230, §326 and WS §41, §212; *KSA* 2, 299–300, 357–58, 464, 484, 514, 571–72, 645) and awareness of the risks of respecting supposed antitheses (WS §67, §285; *KSA* 2, 582 and 679–81). Consider, too, his claim in "Assorted Opinions and Maxims" that a cold book need not be chilling; if read properly, "the sunshine of spiritual cheerfulness" (die Sonnenscheine der geistigen Heiterkeit) can be seen to surround it (§142; *KSA* 2, 437).

[29] Thanks to Small's *Nietzsche-Rée* (cited above, note 7), we have a fascinating and detailed study of their nexus.

[30] See chapter 1 of my *Nietzsche's Middle Period* (Oxford: Oxford UP, 2000). As Keith Ansell-Pearson and Duncan Large say, with *Human, All Too Human*

"begins Nietzsche's commitment to an examination of the origins of morality, which was now to become a feature of all his work and constitutes one of its most essential tasks" (*The Nietzsche Reader* [Malden, MA: Blackwell, 2006], 155). See also Iain Morrisson, "Nietzsche's Genealogy of Morality in the Human, All too Human Series," *British Journal for the History of Philosophy* 11 (2003): 657–72.

[31] See *HA* §70, §81, §99, §101–§102, §104–§107, §133, AOM §33, §50, and §51, WS §9–§12, §23, and §28; *KSA* 81, 85–86, 95–96, 97–99, 100–106, 127–28, 395–96, 401–2, 545–48, 557–58, and 561–62.

[32] The issue of whether egoism can be transcended recurs in AOM §37 and §62 (*KSA* 2, 397–98 and 405). Deception is the thread uniting sections 51 to 55 (*KSA* 2, 71–75), while book 3, "The Religious Life" ("Das religiöse Leben"), comprises passages on exactly that theme. Within a long series of reflections on art, WS provides a sequence of passages on music in sections 149 to 169 (*KSA* 2, 614–23). Sections 133 to 135 and 137 to 144 are the first in *Human, All Too Human* to appear without subtitles, which could be a reflection of their thematic unity (*KSA* 2, 126–29 and 130–40). The only other untitled passages in the two volumes appear in *HA* §630–§637, where once again they are marked by a strong unity of theme (*KSA* 2, 356–62). Many of the sections in "Assorted Opinions and Maxims" take up the question of artistic creation, which was a focus of book 4 of *Human, All Too Human*. "Assorted Opinions and Maxims" also reflects repeatedly on art's interpretation. In fact, the themes of all of *Human, All Too Human*'s book titles are revisited in "Assorted Opinions and Maxims" and "The Wanderer and His Shadow."

[33] Jonathan Israel's distinction between moderate and radical Enlightenment thinkers is illuminating here, for he places Voltaire in the moderate school, which opposes sweeping reform and prefers a gradualist, incremental approach to social change. Nietzsche deviates from the moderate eighteenth-century Enlightenment thinkers Israel discusses, however, by refusing to underpin his faith in reason and hope for progress with religious belief. See chapter 1 of Israel's *A Revolution of the Mind: Radical Enlightenment and the Intellectual Origins of Modern Democracy* (Princeton: Princeton UP, 2009).

[34] For one recent expression of this view, see Thomas H. Brobjer, "Critical Aspects of Nietzsche's Relation to Politics and Democracy," in *Nietzsche, Power and Politics: Rethinking Nietzsche's Legacy for Political Thought*, ed. Herman W. Siemens and Vasti Roodt (Berlin and New York: Walter de Gruyter, 2008), 205–30.

[35] Some of the Stoic resonances that Melissa Lane detects in Nietzsche's works from *Daybreak* to *Beyond Good and Evil* seem also to be present in *Human, All Too Human*, albeit without the organizing concept of "Redlichkeit," to which she attributes such importance. See her "Honesty as the Best Policy?: Nietzsche on Redlichkeit and the Contrast between Stoic and Epicurean Strategies of the Self" in *Histories of Postmodernism: The Precursors, The Heyday, The Legacy*, ed. Mark Bevir, Jill Hargis, and Sara Rushing (New York: Routledge, 2007), 25–51.

[36] Canaan, the land into which Moses is to lead the Israelites, is described in the Old Testament as a "land of milk and honey." R. J. Hollingdale's translation omits the "hanging" before clouds, rendering the udder comparison even stranger.

[37] Consider too "Assorted Opinions and Maxim's" paean to the free spiritedness of the English writer Laurence Sterne (§113; *KSA* 2, 424–26). WS §170 also sees a place in the future for art (*KSA* 2, 623–24).

[38] *The Birth of Tragedy* turned over a version of this question, with chapter 14 asking whether an artistic Socrates was possible (*KSA* 1, 92–96).

[39] Although WS §171 suggests that philosophers are not full-blown scientists (*KSA* 2, 624–26).

[40] I assume that Nietzsche is alluding to "The Wanderer" ("Der Wanderer") by Friedrich von Schlegel, a text set to music by Schubert. We hear only of the twilight movements of Schlegel's wanderer — the morning scene is Nietzsche's invention. It might be relevant here that a nocturnal wanderer cannot cast a shadow. *HA* §638's image of the person pursuing scientific knowledge as a wanderer, who wanders sometimes in the desert, who sometimes longs for relief and its references to his travails and sorrows, is reiterated in AOM §31, "In the Desert of Science" ("In der Wüste der Wissenschaft"; *KSA* 2, 393).

[41] One of Nietzsche's four *Untimely Meditations* was "On the Uses and Disadvantages of History for Life." Michael Tanner's reference to *Human, All Too Human*'s "naïve ideas about how science could function as an end as well as a means" strikes me as misplaced when Nietzsche's remarks are viewed in the round (see his "Introduction" to *Daybreak*, trans. R. J. Hollingdale [Cambridge: Cambridge UP, 1982], xi). Moreover, *HA* §128 contains a seemingly pejorative remark about modern science seeking a long, painless life for people, which is much more in tune with sentiments sometimes expressed about science in Nietzsche's later writings (*KSA* 2, 123). For just one expression of such sentiment, see the chapter on *Beyond Good and Evil* in *Ecce Homo* (*EH BGE* §2; *KSA* 6, 350–51).

Link to *Daybreak*

Against the wishes of his mother and his sister (*KGB* II.6.1, 501), and against the advice of his friend Erwin Rohde (*KGB* II.6.1, 595) — which may, ever since Rohde's marriage in August 1877, have counted for much less (cf. *KSB* 5, 277) — Nietzsche decided to give up his professorship at Basel, and he applied to be released from the post on grounds of ill-health on 2 May 1879 (*KSB* 5, 411–12). He had developed, as he told Franz Overbeck on 3 April 1879, "a phobia about Basel, a veritable anxiety and inhibition about the bad water, the bad air, the entire depressed essence of this unholy breeding-ground of my sufferings!" (die *Basileophobie*, eine wahre Angst und Scheu vor dem schlechten Wasser, der schlechten Luft, dem ganzen gedrückten Wesen dieser unseligen Brütestätte meiner Leiden!; *KSB* 5, 402).

Yet, as we have seen, this dissatisfaction with his life in Basel had deep roots, and it constantly emerged during his time as professor there, sometimes in ways that must have been unsettling for those who met him. Clara Thurneysen, for example, recalled how he told her at a dinner party:

> "I recently dreamed that my hand, which was resting in front of me on the table, suddenly acquired a glassy, transparent skin; I saw clearly into its bone structure, into its tissue, into its muscles. Suddenly I saw a fat toad sitting on my hand and at the same time I felt the irresistible urge to swallow the animal. I overcame my terrible revulsion and gulped it down."

> ["Mir hat kürzlich geträumt, meine Hand, die vor mir auf dem Tische lag, bekam plötzlich eine gläserne, durchsichtige Haut; ich sah deutlich in ihr Gebein, in ihr Gewerbe, in ihr Muskelspiel hinein. Mit einen Male sah ich eine dicke Kröte auf meiner Hand sitzen und verspürte zugleich den unwiderstehlichen Zwang, das Tier zu verschlucken. Ich überwand meinen entsetzlichen Widerwillen und würgte sie herunter."][1]

His dining partner laughed — well, what else was she meant to do? — but Nietzsche's response cannot have made the situation easier for her to deal with: "'And you laugh at that?' Nietzsche asked with terrible seriousness and kept his eyes, half questioning, half sad, fixed on the woman sitting next to him" ("Und darüber lachen Sie?" fragte Nietzsche mit furchtbarem Ernste und hielt seine tiefen Augen halb fragend, halb traurig auf seine Nachbarin gerichtet).[2] For Jung, the toad was "the expression of the loathsomeness of life, or of the lower man," and more specifically it was, as a "poisonous creature," "the quintessence of what the world did to Nietzsche."[3] For Joachim Köhler, the dream expresses Nietzsche's loathing of the feminine, confirming his thesis that Nietzsche was homosexual.[4] And what about Clara Thurneysen? She interpreted the dream as follows: "[Nietzsche] experienced the transparency of his hand as a great suffering, from which he could only be healed if he swallowed down a living toad" (Er empfand die Durchsichtigkeit seiner Hand als ein schweres Leiden, von dem er nur geheilt werden konnte, wenn er eine lebendige Kröte verschluckte).[5]

Yet his most recently published book, *Human, All Too Human* (*Menschliches, Allzumenschliches*) had demonstrated his ability to transform the insights of his suffering into brilliant, gemlike aphorisms, of the kind that — as Jacob Burckhardt told Nietzsche — the likes of such French *moralistes* as La Rochefoucauld, La Bruyère, and Vauvenargues would have envied him (*KSB* II.6.2, 1071). Another admirer of *Human, All Too Human* was Paul Rée (KGB II.6.2, 1057), who remained an enthusiastic supporter of Nietzsche's idea for a "secular monastery." In a letter to Nietzsche from Berlin sent at the end of November 1877, Rée had even gone so far as to encourage Nietzsche to think of himself as "the head of an invisible church" (das Haupt einer unsichtbaren Kirche), and amid "the outlines of the modern monastery" (die Umrisse des modernen Klosters) that took shape in his mind's eye, he could imagine Nietzsche as its "chief pontiff, pope, or prior" (Pontifex maximus, Papst, Prior; *KSB* II.6.2, 769). Now, writing to Nietzsche, who had gone to St. Moritz in Switzerland for three months in June 1879 in the wake of resigning his post, Rée linked the project with Goethe's novel *Wilhelm Meister* and its mysterious, shadowy *Turmgesellschaft*: "The conservatoire of the spirit, our monastery [. . .] is in fact the most complete realization of the "Tower" in Wilh[elm] Meister: a union of people who strive for the completion of their own personality and thereby contribute to the development of others" ([das] Konservatorium des Geistes, unser[ ] Kloster [. . .] [ist] die vollkommenste Realisierung des 'Thurms' in Wilh. Meister [. . .]: eine Vereinigung von Menschen, welche selbst nach Vollendung der eigenen Persönlichkeit streben und dabei die Entwickelung anderer fördern; *KSB* II.6.2, 1142).

The search for the secular monastery continued in early 1880, when Nietzsche and his sister, after their earlier plan had fallen through in Flims, considered buying a farmhouse in Naumburg in order to provide a location for his project to bring about nothing less than a revival of the Epicurean garden.[6] The change from Rée's earlier religious (if parodic) vocabulary to the pagan ideal of Epicurus reflects Nietzsche's description of his project as "my 'Epicurean Garden'" (mein "Garten Epikurs") in his letter to Rée of 31 October 1879 (*KSB* 5, 460), echoing his question to

Köselitz on 26 March 1879: "*Where* are we going to renew the garden of Epicurus?" (*Wo* wollen wir den Garten Epicurs erneueren? *KSB* 5, 399) and one of the aphorisms in "The Wanderer and His Shadow" ("Der Wanderer und sein Schatten") in the second volume of *Human, All Too Human*: "A small garden, figs, little cheeses and, in addition, three or four good friends — that was the sensual pleasure of Epicurus" (Ein Gärtchen, Feigen, kleine Käse und dazu drei oder vier gute Freunde, — das war die Ueppigkeit Epikur's; *HA* WS §192; *KSA* 2, 638).[7]

But in March 1880, Nietzsche was tempted by Heinrich Köselitz to go and stay with him in Venice, where at one point Nietzsche stayed in a room with a direct view of the city's graveyard island (*KSB* 6, 13). While Köselitz's projects included a setting of Goethe's *Singspiel*, entitled "Scherz, List und Rache" (Jokes, Cunning and Revenge) — the title of which Nietzsche was to use as his title for the prefatory poems in *The Gay Science* (*Die fröhliche Wissenschaft*) — Nietzsche continued to work on *Die Pflugschar* (*The Ploughshare*), a work whose title he subsequently changed in February 1881, inspired by Köselitz's allusion to a passage from the *Rig Veda*, to *Daybreak* (*Morgenröthe*) (*KSB* 6, 60–61; cf. *KSA* 14, 203). Yet this title had also been anticipated in the closing section of the first volume of *Human, All Too Human*: "Born out of the mysteries of the dawn, [wanderers and philosophers] consider how, between the sound of the bell at the tenth and at the twelfth hour, the day can have such a pure, transfigured and cheerful face, flooded with light: — they are searching for the *philosophy of the morning*" (Geboren aus den Geheimnissen der Frühe, sinnen sie darüber nach, wie der Tag zwischen dem zehnten und zwölften Glockenschlage ein so reines, durchleuchtetes, verklärt-heiteres Gesicht haben könne: — sie suchen die *Philosophie des Vormittages*, *KSA* 2, 363).

Moreover, attention to light and shade seems to have become an important principle determining how Nietzsche, perhaps because of his continuing ill-health, spent his day. Spending the winter of 1880/1881 in Genoa, Nietzsche wrote on a postcard to his mother and his sister on 8 January 1881 about how he tried to relieve his headaches: "When the sun shines I always go to a secluded cliff by the sea and lie there in the open under my sunshade quite still, like a lizard" (Wenn die Sonne scheint, gehe ich immer auf einen einsamen Felsen am Meer und liege dort im Freien unter meinem Sonnenschirm still, wie eine Eidechse; *KSB* 6, 56–57), an image to which he returned in the section on *Daybreak*, when he described the book as lying "in the sun, round and happy, like a sea-creature sunning itself among the rocks" (in der Sonne [. . .], rund, glücklich, einem Seegethier gleich, das zwischen Felsen sich sonnt), then identified himself with this sea-creature, and finally associated his work's contents with special moments, moments in which he practiced "the art [. . .] of making things which easily slip by without a sound [. . .] stay still for a little while" (die Kunst, [. . .] Dinge, die leicht und ohne Geräusch vorbeihuschen, [. . .] ein wenig fest zu machen) — "moments" (Augenblicke) he called "divine lizards" (göttliche Eidechsen; *KSA* 6, 329) . . .[8]

In Genoa Nietzsche lived simply — and cheaply (*KSB* 6, 65) — but well. He enjoyed eating tripe and fish, and his landlady helped him prepare a dish of artichokes and eggs (*KSB* 6, 84), using the small spirit stove his sister had given him (*KSB* 6, 41). Nietzsche got on well with his fellow guests, who used to call him *il piccolo santo* — "the little saint."[9] At Köselitz's suggestion, Nietzsche moved on in May 1881 to Recoaro, a town in the Tyrolean Alps, where he and Köselitz corrected the proofs of *Daybreak*, which was published in the summer of 1881. Rebecca Bamford discusses the intricacies and subtleties of the book with which, as Nietzsche said in retrospect in *Ecce Homo*, he began "my campaign against *morality*" (mein Feldzug gegen die *Moral*), "the struggle against the morality of unselfing" (den Kampf gegen die Entselbstungsmoral; *EH D* 1–§2; *KSA* 6, 329 and 332):

> Not that there is the slightest whiff of gunpowder about it: one will perceive quite different and much more pleasant odors in it, providing that one has some subtlety to one's nostrils.

> [Nicht dass es den geringsten Pulvergeruch an sich hätte: — man wird ganz andre und viel lieblichere Gerüche an ihm wahrnehmen, gesetzt, dass man einige Feinheit in den Nüstern hat. (*EH D* §1; *KSA* 6, 329)]

Notes

[1] Carl Albrecht Bernoulli, *Franz Overbeck und Friedrich Nietzsche: Eine Freundschaft*, 2 vols. (Jena: Diederichs, 1908), 1:72.

[2] Bernoulli, *Franz Overbeck und Friedrich Nietzsche*, 1:73.

[3] C. G. Jung, *Nietzsche's "Zarathustra": Notes of the Seminar given in 1934–9*, ed. James L. Jarrett, 2 vols. (London: Routledge, 1989), 1:255 and 610.

[4] Joachim Köhler, *Zarathustra Geheimnis: Friedrich Nietzsche und seine verschlüsselte Botschaft* (Reinbek bei Hamburg: Rowohlt, 1992), 215–18.

[5] Bernoulli, *Franz Overbeck und Friedrich Nietzsche*, 1:74.

[6] See Paul Rée's letters to Elisabeth Nietzsche of late January and early February 1880 in Ernst Pfeiffer, ed., *Friedrich Nietzsche, Paul Rée, Lou von Salomé: Die Dokumente ihrer Begegnung* (Frankfurt am Main: Insel, 1970), 74–75; and for further discussion, 389 and 402.

[7] See *Die Dokumente ihrer Begegnung*, 402n69.

[8] For further discussion of this image in Nietzsche, see Babette E. Babich, "Nietzsche's *göttliche Eidechsen*: 'Divine Lizards,' Greene Lyons, and Music," in *A Nietzschean Bestiary*, ed. Christa David Acampora and Ralph Acampora (Lanham, MD: Rowman and Littlefield, 2004), 204–68.

[9] See *Chronik*, 485.

5: *Daybreak*

Rebecca Bamford

NIETZSCHE BEGAN TO MAKE PREPARATORY NOTES for *Daybreak: Thoughts on the Prejudices of Morality* (*Morgenröthe: Gedanken über die moralischen Vorurteile*) in January 1880, and performed most of the main work of composing it in Genoa between November 1880 and May 1881; the preface was added in 1886.[1] In *Ecce Homo* (published 1908), Nietzsche claims that the particular pathologies of his existence provided the necessary conditions for *Daybreak*. He writes that during the winter of 1880, spent at Genoa, a "sweetening and spiritualization" (Versüssung und Vergeistigung) almost inseparable from an "extreme poverty of blood and muscle" (extremen Armuth an Blut und Muskel) produced *Daybreak* (*EH* "Why I Am So Wise" §1; *KSA* 6, 265). He claims that *Daybreak* is characterized by a perfect cheerfulness and exuberance of spirit compatible with profound physiological weakness and pain. This combination of convalescence and relapse enabled Nietzsche to look from the perspective of the sick toward healthier concepts and values, and to scrutinize the "secret work of the instinct of decadence" (heimliche Arbeit des Décadence-Instinkts) from the possible perspective of a rich and healthy existence (*KSA* 6, 266). In the text, as I will show, he engages with three main questions, drawing thematic connections between physical and psychological health on the one hand and ethics on the other, in order to develop a foundation for his project of critical transvaluation of values. First, what is the nature of, and relationship between psycho-physiological and cultural health? Second, by which method of critical engagement may our health be diagnosed and promoted? And third, what virtues are required for such work?

Exploratory threads of medical narrative initiating these questions are evident in several of Nietzsche's letters from the *Daybreak* period. Writing to his mother, Franziska Nietzsche, on 21 July 1879, Nietzsche speculates on gardening as a helpful activity, writing that he was becoming more and more committed to a more simple and natural way of living for the sake of his health, and that what might benefit him most would be time-consuming, physically tiring labor that would not demand significant psychological exertion (*KSB* 5, 427–28). In a letter to Heinrich Köselitz (later known as Peter Gast) from Naumburg on 5 October 1879, Nietzsche reported some success in limiting his intellectual activity in order to minimize his headaches and other physiological symptoms of poor health (*KSB* 5, 450–52). Nietzsche goes on in *Daybreak* to make similar recommendations of a change of diet and hard physical labor as a treatment for affliction or distress of the soul, while also counseling against resorting to means of intoxication such as art in such circumstances (*D* §269; *KSA* 3, 211). He also draws an analogy between the labor of gardening and the act of philosophizing, describing how philosophical conclusions tend to sprout seemingly overnight like fungus, and warning that the thinker must be a gardener as well as soil to the flora growing in him (*D* §382; *KSA* 3, 248).

In a letter of 14 January 1880, Nietzsche remarks to Malwida von Meysenbug that the degree of his martyrdom to his health problems was almost sufficient to make him welcome the end of his life (*KSB* 5, 4–6). He also speaks of his satisfaction in having produced work during this period that outlines one way in which peace of mind may be attained, claiming this philosophical development as a direct outcome of his suffering owing to his poor health. He identifies truthfulness as a virtue, characterizing his efforts by suggesting that no pain has been, or ought to be, able to make him represent life untruthfully. He also claims to share with von Meysenbug the virtue of courage in the face of distressing or disparaging experiences — these experiences being ones Nietzsche had certainly had in the preceding five years in the form of his serious health problems, the necessity of his resignation from Basel, his break with Wagner, and the unfortunate critical reception of *The Birth of Tragedy* (*Die Geburt der Tragödie*, 1872) and *Human, All Too Human* (*Menschliches, Allzumenschliches*, 1878). In another letter to Köselitz written on 18 July 1880, Nietzsche comments on the connections he has been exploring between character, virtue, moral emotions, psychology, and health (*KSB* 6, 28–30). He describes his aphoristic exploration of moral psychology in *Daybreak* as akin to digging in a moral mine, remarking that as a result of his project he has begun to seem almost wholly subterranean to himself, and explaining his progress in writing the book by drawing a cautious, though still optimistic, analogy to the feeling of having found the main gallery of the mine.

In this same letter to Köselitz, Nietzsche remarks that he had recently been reading Prosper Mérimée's "The Etruscan Vase." The tone, style, and psychological focus of this text, which is also rich in careful descriptions of the health and physiology of the characters, all resonate strongly in *Daybreak*.[2] Mérimée anatomizes the psychology of his characters in order to diagnose their cultural condition, thereby uncovering the moral psychology of nineteenth-century European upper-middle-class society. Mérimée's text exposes the ways in which what Nietzsche terms the morality of custom, or *Sittlichkeit der Sitte* (*D* §9, §38, §103, §109 and

§132; *KSA* 3, 21, 45, 91, 96 and 123), generates Saint-Clair's wholly unfounded and pathetic jealousy of Mathilde's former lover, Massigny, a source of emotional frustration that Saint-Clair ultimately vents in a moment of rage and irritation, using his riding crop to strike at the nose of Alphonse de Thémines's horse — thereby provoking a pointless, yet unavoidable, duel of honor with Thémines that costs Saint-Clair his life and Mathilde her health and the promise of happiness.

Nietzsche's description of himself as almost entirely subterranean raises the specter of Dostoyevsky's Underground Man in the form of the "mole" (Maulwurf) and "subterranean man" (einen "Unterirdischen"), a "seeming Trophonius" (scheinbare Trophonios) who speaks to us in the preface (*D* preface §1; *KSA* 3, 11). As Nietzsche explains, his subterranean activities created the necessary space for his attack on morality to commence; he tells us that he descended into the depths, tunneled into the foundations, and excavated our ancient faith in morality (*D* preface §2; *KSA* 3, 12). As with Mérimée, we should note the medical narrative of *Notes from Underground*, which resonates with Nietzsche's interest in health. Dostoyevsky's Underground Man speaks of his "respect for medicine and for doctors," identifies himself as a "sick" man who has something wrong with his liver, and refuses treatment "out of spite."[3] He claims that to think too much is "a real, actual disease" (17) and that "we all show off with our diseases," himself perhaps more than anyone else (18). In addition to anatomizing nineteenth-century society, and in the spirit of Nietzsche's experimental philosophical psychology in *Daybreak*, Dostoyevsky's Underground Man anatomizes himself even while he operates as a vector of disease, and particularly the disease of intellectual activity: "But I will explain myself. I'll go on to the end. That is why I took up my pen . . ." (19).

Despite these thematic connections, it is not clear whether or not Nietzsche had completed his work on *Daybreak* prior to reading Dostoyevsky in French translation for the first time, and as such, it is not immediately clear how much of a Dostoyevskyan influence we should observe at work in *Daybreak*'s preface. As Eric von der Luft and Douglas G. Stenburg discuss, the preface to *Daybreak* is dated "Ruta bei Genua, im Herbst des Jahres 1886" (Ruta, Genoa, Fall 1886; *KSA* 3, 17); however, Nietzsche could not have read the French translation of *Notes from Underground* before 20 November 1886, as it was not published until then.[4] Given the deep connection between the subterranean talk in the preface and Dostoyevsky's text, von der Luft and Stenburg suggest a simple and plausible explanation to resolve the apparent problem of dates: Nietzsche drafted the preface of *Daybreak* at the same time as he worked on the preface to *The Gay Science* (*Die fröhliche Wissenschaft*, 1882; 1887), amending some sentences in *Daybreak*'s preface to reflect his reading of, and enthusiasm for, the French translation of *Notes from*

Underground — but he did not change the date of the preface before mailing it to his publisher via Köselitz (443).

Nietzsche tells us in *Ecce Homo* that he had conceived of *Daybreak* as a series of thoughts on the prejudices of morality (*EH D* §1; *KSA* 6, 329). The campaign against "the morality of unselfing" (die Entselbstungs-Moral) targets selflessness and degeneration as conflicting with the exuberance of strength and overflowing energy that Nietzsche as physiologist considers natural and essential to human flourishing (*EH D* §2; *KSA* 6, 332). Previous scholarship is clear that Nietzsche's attack on morality in *Daybreak* is different from his attack on morality in *Human, All Too Human*; in section 103 of *Daybreak*, Nietzsche admits the existence of moral motives and denies the equivalence between the moral and the unegoistic that he presented in *Human, All Too Human* (*KSA* 3, 91–92).[5] He engages critically with philosophical methodology based purely on abstraction from sensation and prioritization of pure reason (e.g. *D* preface §3, §52, §251, §370, §395, §490, §493, §500, §542–45; *KSA* 3, 12–14, 56, 205, 244, 251, 289, 290, 294, and 309–16). At the same time, he provides a performative demonstration of how the renewal of health can only emerge from out of the current state of illness (for instance, *D* §27–§28; *KSA* 3, 37–38).

Nietzsche's campaign against morality is already well-known; he accounts for moral judgments as erroneous motives for action and counsels encouraging moral actions and avoiding immoral actions for other reasons than hitherto, in order for us to learn to think differently and perhaps also to feel differently (*D* §103; *KSA* 3, 91–92). For Nietzsche, different thinking and feeling involves the imagination of possible virtues of the future (*D* §551; *KSA* 3, 321–22) as well as a strange, though sacred, pregnancy with the secret hope for something greater than we are (*D* §552; *KSA* 3, 322–23). As Keith Ansell-Pearson remarks, this state is one of purification and consecration in anticipation of the task of humanity's self-overcoming as well as of the determination of rank of greatness of all past mankind.[6] The particular focus of my discussion here is how Nietzsche thinks *Daybreak* contributes to the transvaluation project. As I will show, Nietzsche conceives of the transvaluation of values as emergent via the text through our intersubjective performance of "the self-sublimation of morality" (die Selbstaufhebung der Moral; *D* Preface §4; *KSA* 3, 16).

The epigraph to *Daybreak* announces the transvaluation project to readers, and yet it does so perplexingly. "There are so many days that have not yet broken" (Es giebt so viele Morgenröthen, die noch nicht geleuchtet haben; *KSA* 3, 10) is a free adaptation of the *Rig Veda*, book 7, hymn 76, entitled "Dawn" — but what is the significance of this free adaptation?[7] Dorothy Figueira notes that the German and English translations of this passage available to Nietzsche clearly translated the relevant passage in a contrary sense to that expressed by the epigraph, as "there are so many dawns that have already dawned."[8] With regard to this question, Schaberg has shown that it was Heinrich Köselitz, not Nietzsche, who was chiefly responsible for the epigraph. While making the fair copy of the text, Köselitz wrote the epigraph on the title page; Nietzsche liked the suggestion so much that he kept it, and changed the intended title of the book from *The Ploughshare* (*Die Pflugschar*) — which had also been the intended title of *Human, All Too Human*. However, this does not entirely solve the puzzle. Why did Nietzsche so appreciate Köselitz's suggestion, and how might knowing this help to frame our reading of the text productively?

Some evidence from *Ecce Homo* helps to clarify this point. Referring to the epigraph, Nietzsche suggests that he sought the new morning — indeed "a whole series, a whole world!" (eine ganze Reihe, eine ganze Welt neuer Tage!) — of new days in the "transvaluation of all values" (Umwerthung aller Werthe), which he describes as a liberation from all moral values; a saying "Yes" to, and having confidence in, all that has hitherto been forbidden, despised, and damned (*EH D* §1; *KSA* 6, 330). Drawing a clearer connection between *Daybreak* and *Ecce Homo* also helps to explain the striking difference between two sets of imagery at work in the text: that of the dawn, which suggests the possibility of transcendence and of redemption, and that of the ploughshare, with its obvious connection to the notion of groundbreaking, and more generally, to the earth and to the subterranean. It is not immediately clear why Nietzsche employs this diversity of images to carry forward the philosophical work of this text. In his preface of 1886, Nietzsche emphasizes the importance of the mole's subterranean tunneling work, while the epigraph, the final selection of *Daybreak* as the work's title, and the redemptive possibility of the transvaluation project pursued in this text suggest a countervailing emphasis on the transcendent. But the subterranean investigation of the psyche is required in order to create the possibility of transvaluation: thus the mole's groundbreaking engagement in psychological earthworks is commensurate with the notion that the breaking of new days would be groundbreaking for human psychology and for the morality emerging from this, as Nietzsche's epigraph from the *Rig Veda* suggests.

In a letter written from Naumburg to Heinrich Köselitz on 5 October 1879, Nietzsche explicitly describes how his health dictated his approach to writing *Daybreak*. His headaches and other health concerns forced him to write while out walking, and made it impossible for him to return to a note and revise it. Every aphorism in each of the five books of *Daybreak* begins with a title that strikes the critical tone for the remarks to follow, thus acting as a prompt for the reader's engagement with the text.[9] One class of aphorism titles summarizes the conclusion to a complex discussion while also representing that conclusion and opening it for readers' interpretations. For example, the title of the aphorism entitled

"The Many Forces that Now Have to Come Together in the Thinker" (Wie viele Kräfte jetzt im Denker zusammenkommen müssen) summarizes Nietzsche's argument in this section (and, indeed, throughout *Daybreak*) on the new, experimental, type of philosophical activity required for the proposed transvaluation project (*D* §43; *KSA* 3, 50). Nietzsche identifies various means to knowledge that the thinker of transvaluation must incorporate, and further notes the mistake of conceiving of these means to knowledge as ends, or goals, thereby suggesting that we can no longer abstract ourselves from sensory perception and engage in a feeling of exaltation at the contemplation of abstractions.

The thought is continued in a subsequent section entitled "'Know Yourself,' is the Whole of Science" ("Erkenne dich selbst" ist die ganz Wissenschaft), in which Nietzsche simultaneously summarizes, represents, and opens for our experiential interpretative engagement the argument that humanity is distributed into the world rather than being abstracted from it. Humanity's self-knowledge is contingent upon a final knowledge of all things, he contends, because "things are only the boundaries of man" (die Dinge sind nur die Gränzen des Menschen; *D* §48; *KSA* 3, 53). Another class of aphorism titles prefaces key claims with ironic humor, animating the text; for example, Nietzsche uses the title "Thinking about Illness!" (Die Gedanken über die Krankheit!) to prompt distinctively cheerful reflections about the morbidity of modern culture (*D* §54; *KSA* 3, 57).

Graham Parkes observes that Nietzsche's poor health prompted him to make sustained use of aphorism in his works from *Human, All Too Human* onwards: in practical terms, using aphorisms meant that Nietzsche did not need to spend sustained periods of time writing; conceptually, the aphorism was ideally suited to experimental philosophical engagement with human psycho-physiology.[10] Volker Gerhardt has argued that Nietzsche understood himself first and foremost as an experimental philosopher, and this experimentalism is evident in *Daybreak*.[11] Writing from a possible future in which he imagines that humans submit only to laws that they themselves have given for both great and small things, Nietzsche makes two joyful exclamations: first, that there are "so many experiments still to make!" (es müssen so viele Versuche noch gemacht werden!); and second, that there are "so many futures still to dawn!" (es muss so manche Zukunft noch an's Licht kommen!; *D* §187; *KSA* 3, 160).

Two further sections of the text substantiate this link between experimental philosophical method and his transvaluation project. The first relevant section provides Nietzsche's diagnosis of our living in a state of moral interregnum, which is either "prelude or postlude" (vorläufiges Dasein oder ein nachläufiges Dasein; *D* §453; *KSA* 3, 274). Nietzsche's subterranean burrowings throughout *Daybreak* have, so he thinks, enough evidence to suggest that in this state, the foundations and superstructure of our moral feelings and judgments are defective (*D* §453; *KSA* 3, 274). He contends that since the sciences of physiology, medicine, sociology, and solitude are not yet sufficiently sure of themselves to construct the laws of life and action anew, the best thing for us to do is to "be as far as possible our own *reges* (kings) and found little experimental states" (unsere eigenen reges zu sein und kleine Versuchsstaaten zu gründen; *D* §453; *KSA* 3, 274). As he exhorts us: "We are experiments: let us also want to be them!" (Wir sind Experimente: wollen wir es auch sein! *D* §453; *KSA* 3, 274). The second section makes the psychological dimension of transvaluation apparent. Previously, the type and scale of reflections on morality and moral psychology that Nietzsche thinks are necessary would have counted as blasphemous because belief in the immortal soul made the need for protection of the moral purity of each such soul paramount (*D* §501; *KSA* 3, 294). Now, however, having abandoned belief in the immortal soul, Nietzsche contends that humanity has gained the time and freedom for ethical reflection on a social, cultural, and intergenerational scale, rather than on a personal moral scale (*D* §501; *KSA* 3, 294). We have the right to experiment with ourselves because we may do so open-endedly, having reclaimed our courage for error, for experimentation, and for the continuously provisional nature of the moral-experimental results (*D* §501; *KSA* 3, 294).

Nietzsche claims that *Daybreak* is at once a diagnostic and a corrective text, incorporating and performing both decadent and transformative physiological perspectives, and ultimately constituting a Yes-saying book (*EH D* §1; *KSA* 6, 330). His experimental medicine does not neatly encapsulate conceptual nuggets of moral philosophy for dutiful patients to swallow obediently. Given the twin features of aphorism and experimentalism, an explanation of how the text achieves both diagnosis and therapy is required. My suggestion is that Nietzsche performs philosophical work *in the text* while at the same time also prompting open-ended philosophical engagement with the issues at hand, by himself and other readers, *through the medium of the text*. One of the ways in which this is made possible is through the musical structuring of the text, which depends on the use of aphorism; another way is by means of Nietzsche's matching of style and structure with his conception of our psychological functioning. I will account for each of these aspects of Nietzsche's methodology in turn.

In bright daylight, Nietzsche contends, the ear — which he names the organ of fear — is less necessary than it is in darkness; he suggests that the ear could only have evolved in night, twilight, and the long age of human timidity, and suggests that this is why music as an art has acquired the character of night and twilight (*D* §250; *KSA* 3, 205). Nietzsche's subterraneanism in *Daybreak* thus recognizes and requires the twilight art of music to help bring about the dawn of the new days of transvalu-ation from the obscurity of moral mines or, as he writes in this section, caves (*D* §250; *KSA* 3, 205). The cave imagery in section 250 also recalls Plato's cave allegory, a reference that is supported by Nietzsche's demon-strated respect for Plato and ancient philosophy in *Daybreak*.[12] Nietzsche celebrates the musical, joyful dimension of Platonic and Socratic dia-logue alongside the rigorous and sober dimension by acknowledging their authors as "contrapuntal composers" (Contrapunctiker der Musik; *D* §544; *KSA* 3, 314–15). The conversation, or dialogue, about music, which happens halfway through the text, is a good example of how apho-rism presents *Daybreak* both as a diagnostic and as a therapeutic text, musically as well as physiologically (*D* §255; *KSA* 3, 206–8).

The two interlocutors in the conversation are "A," who describes some of the aims of the text and its author/composer, and "B," who is perhaps one of the perfect readers mentioned in the preface to *Daybreak* (*D* preface §5; *KSA* 3, 17). "A" describes the musical structuring of the text in physi-ological terms of hearing, vision, and bodily movement, indicating that up until now, what we are hearing has not been what he wants to say to us: we have received only promises that "something unheard-of" (etwas Uner-hörtes) will be said, and hints of this something via "gestures" (Gebärden; *D* §255; *KSA* 3, 206). Gesture and color work together to generate pos-sible variations on the overarching theme of health. "A" remarks that the author/composer knows what color health is and knows how to make it appear, making this a sign of the author's self-knowledge. As "A" then sug-gests, there is a drama to the music of the text, which unfolds as follows. After the author/composer has used gesture and color to indicate the pre-viously-unheard, he believes that he has convinced his hearers of his mes-sage, then presents his ideas as though they have the greatest importance by means of "stormy and thunderous rhythms" (stürmischer und donnernder Rhythmen), and finally takes advantage of the effect of these rhythms to introduce his theme at such a point that we are convinced that our stupe-faction and convulsion are direct consequences of this theme. The readers/ hearers, according to "A" in this section, react accordingly . . . and then the music stops (*D* §255; *KSA* 3, 207). "B" reacts with the claim that the readers/hearers would rather let themselves be deceived than even once know the truth in this way; "A" retorts that this reaction, though com-monplace and evident even in the best, signifies a loss of conscience in the art of hearing and a loss of the finest part of honesty, meaning that it may no longer be possible to distinguish between innocent music, defined as music that thinks only of and believes in itself, and guilty music (both of which, according to "A," include what we commonly call good and bad music). In case we may have begun to suspect the text of performing guilty music, "A" confirms that what we have been hearing is innocent music. The conversation between "A" and "B" tracks the relationship between the author/composer and the reader/hearer of *Daybreak* that has been unfolding thus far, while also once again performatively re-engaging readers/hearers in this relationship.

The performative engagement of readers, and this account of *Daybreak* as enacted by the critical-experimental performances of author and readers, is central to the work; yet this experimentalism should not suggest a lack of objectivity or of discipline. Objectivity, Nietzsche claims, is the child of habit and of discipline (*D* §111; *KSA* 3, 99–100). He maintains that asceticism remains the appropriate discipline only for those whose sensual drives are "raging beasts of prey" (wüthende Raubthiere) requiring extermination (*D* §331; *KSA* 3, 234). This point on asceticism and discipline has been made several times in the scholarly literature. Most recently, Horst Hutter has emphasized the existence of a positive role for asceticism as distinct from Christian asceticism in Nietzsche, and Bruce Ellis Benson has defended a claim for the positive role of ascetic discipline in explicitly musical terms; for Benson, if decadence for Nietzsche is literally de-cadence, "falling out of rhythm with life," then there is a sense of musical *askesis* for Nietzsche that constitutes the "special discipline" through which he resists this decadence.[13] Taken together, these accounts supply sufficient room to claim that the aphoristic structure of *Daybreak* enables the emergence of de-cadence and resistance in and through the text, disciplining and facilitating our ethical experimentation.

Daybreak facilitates independent resistance to the decadence of Christian asceticism while also affording readers an opportunity to develop a new sense of themselves as natural creatures comprised of natural drives. An interesting and relevant experiment in critical moral imagination is presented in section 333 (*KSA* 3, 234), where Nietzsche points out that we do not regard animals as moral beings, and then invites us to question whether we should assume that animals regard *us* as moral beings — in so doing, prompting us to rethink our preconceptions about our human and our animal status, and thereby to reflect more critically upon our status as moral beings. Jokingly, but also seriously, he presents us with an animal's response to the question at hand to prompt our questioning: " — An animal which could speak said: 'Humanity is a prejudice of which we animals at least are free'" (Ein Thier, welches reden konnte, sagte: "Menschlichkeit ist ein Vorurtheil, an dem wenigstens wir Thiere nicht leiden"; *D* §333; *KSA* 3, 234). This experiment facilitates the reader's critical engagement with our values. If this leads readers to develop the same conclusion as Nietzsche (which, as Nietzsche acknowledges, is not certain), then perhaps readers may ultimately end up as round and happy as one of Nietzsche's basking "sea animals" (Seegethier; *EH D* §2; *KSA* 6, 329).

The importance of self-knowledge and self-discipline is emphasized in section 322, where Nietzsche exhorts us to live without a physician if possible, in order to take responsibility for our own psychophysical and cultural health, and avoid the heights of abandonment and destructiveness that he imagines would result from all abdicating responsibility for their health and leaving everything in the hands of a "divinity as physician" (Gottheit als [. . .] Arzte; D §322; KSA 3, 230). He suggests that taking responsibility for doctoring ourselves will lead to better health insofar as we will be less likely to engage in frivolous dismissal of our own prescriptions, where we may dismiss the concerns and prescriptions of some other physician. This point about self-rule and responsibility is developed in Carl B. Sachs's recent account of Nietzschean autonomy and freedom in *Daybreak*. Sachs shows that four key aspects of self-knowledge of the material conditions of subjectivity, "the organization of drives and affects, the sediment of interpretations, one's personal past and the past of one's culture," are required for an autonomous Nietzschean subject's self-transformation.[14] As Sachs notes, self-transformation is dependent upon and limited by raw materials, namely body, drives, affects, and discursive and non-discursive practices (93). By this account, the self-determining behaviors of a Nietzschean autonomous subject do not logically conflict with Nietzsche's naturalistic drive-psychology (90–91).

Following Sachs, we can note that Nietzsche makes two important claims concerning the psychological conditions required for transvaluation in *Daybreak*: first, that we have abandoned belief in the immortal soul (D §501; KSA 3, 294); and second, that our being is composed of a totality of drives (D §119; KSA 3, 111–14). How we read section 119 is of particular importance in understanding Nietzsche's strategy in *Daybreak* of relating aphoristic experimentalism to the functioning of our moral drives. Nietzsche remarks that we have a seriously incomplete image of the totality of drives that comprise each of our beings. The laws of nutriment governing these drives are unknown: our everyday experiences nourish some of our drives, but any nourishment is accidental and is not allocated with reference to drive-hunger and drive-superfluity. When a drive requires nourishment, it displays intentionality.[15] Nietzsche uses a number of metaphors to illustrate that drives consistently require some form of nourishment unless satiated within this economy, including drives as desiring gratification, exercising or discharging strength, and saturating an emptiness (D §119; KSA 3, 111–14). Drive intentionality involves each drive regarding each daily event or experience as a route to attaining its goal; it will either go on waiting if the experience in question does not nourish it, ultimately withering away for lack of nourishment, or in some cases, given an appropriate combination of drive and experience, the drive will be nourished. While we may distinguish between a drive such as hunger as satisfied by food and not by dream-food, we are not generally aware of the nourishing or starving of drives that are "not as much in earnest as is *hunger*" (wenn alle Triebe es so gründlich nehmen wollten, wie der

Hunger), or of the developmental effects of the general economy of drive nutrition. This includes the moral drives: as such, Nietzsche can contend, by means of this sketch of our drive psychology, that just as other cognitive behavior is contingent on drives, so too are our moral judgments and evaluations. Consciousness, as he puts it, is a more or less fantastic commentary on an unknown but felt text (*D* §119; *KSA* 3, 113). As Nietzsche goes on to state the same point in the subsequent aphorism, we do not know how we are acting and we do not know how to act, but we may be sure that we are being acted upon (*D* §120; *KSA* 3, 115).

The title of section 119, "Experience and Invention" ("Erleben und Erdichten"), needs to be read with special care in order for us to appreciate the more general argument on human psychology being made here. At the beginning of the aphorism, experience and invention seem to be disparate concepts, as Nietzsche renders by means of describing differences between a man and the drives that motivate and structure him, but at the end of the aphorism, Nietzsche tentatively raises the question of the role of invention in experience. In raising this question at the end of the aphorism, Nietzsche facilitates our engagement with the philosophical possibility that all experience is already invention on our part. Notice that Nietzsche is quite open with us about this: he uses the example of the text of *Daybreak* to illustrate the point. The text is, he says, much the same on one night as on another; however, it receives such diverse commentary that "inventive reasoning faculty" (die dichtende Vernunft) imagines two different causes for the same nervous stimuli, where in fact, a difference in drive nourishment explains the difference in commentary (*D* §119; *KSA* 3, 113).

The consequences of this account for the concept of subjectivity are clearly articulated by Sachs: we are never merely a bundle of drives and affects, we are interpreted and interpreting drives and affects (85). According to Sachs, this means that for Nietzsche, our first-person (autonomous, agential) and third-person (drive-based) accounts of subjectivity may be reconciled (85). While considerations of space prohibit a full account of the contemporary relevance of Nietzsche's drive psychology, it is worth briefly translating the type of argument that Nietzsche is putting forward with respect to subjectivity into the language of contemporary cognitive science: this account is emergentist, in Andy Clark's sense that emergent phenomena are phenomena whose roots involve uncontrolled variables.[16]

Nietzsche's remarks on the moral interregnum indicate that he thinks we live within a period that is "a prelude or a postlude," in which the sciences of physiology, medicine, sociology, and solitude are not yet sufficiently self-assured to reconstruct the existing laws of life and action that will, he contends, be knocked down by his campaign on morality (*D* §453; *KSA* 3, 274). Ultimately, Nietzsche argues that his mastery of inverting psycho-physiological perspectives is why a "transvaluation of values" (Umwerthung der Werthe) is possible for him alone (*EH* "Why I Am So Wise" §1; *KSA* 6, 266). Mastery is attained when one neither goes wrong nor hesitates in the performance (*D* §357; *KSA* 3, 306). However, Nietzsche had not attained mastery when writing *Daybreak*. Given some of the autobiographical inspiration for the text to which I drew attention at the beginning of this chapter, and the autobiographical dimensions of the text, it is important to note that even while Nietzsche begins to express hope for a possible, positive future for humanity, he does also recognize some of the limitations of his anatomical excavation of human moral psychology. Ruminating on its circuitous paths, Nietzsche wonders exactly where it is that his diagnosis of, and critical engagement with, modern morbidity is heading. He questions whether it is really anything more than a personal drive or *Trieb* toward his personal prejudices concerning health, weather, and diet (*D* §553; *KSA* 3, 323).

David Owen and Keith Ansell-Pearson have identified this self-critical feature of the text.[17] Seeking to account for Nietzsche's reasons for developing his genealogical mode of inquiry, Owen identifies three key problems with *Daybreak* of which Nietzsche is aware, and which he only resolves from *The Gay Science* onwards (253). These self-acknowledged problems are: first, the assumption that loss of belief in God would lead to Christian moral beliefs losing their authority; second, the assumption of the authority of scientific knowledge requires supplementation by an account of "how we come to value truth and why this should lead us to reject Christian morality"; and third, the failure to provide any basis for re-evaluating moral values that did not simply express Nietzsche's personal commitments (252–53). According to Owen, the first of these problems is more precisely one of not inferring or of failing to draw appropriate conclusions because — using the language of Wittgenstein's well-known claim in section 115 of his *Philosophical Investigations* — the conceptual picture of God holds us captive (253).[18] As Owen (253) argues, Nietzsche himself articulates the problem of not inferring by using the language of "new struggles" (neue Kämpfe) against the authority of Christian moral beliefs, acknowledging that we still need to vanquish the shadow of God (*GS* §108; *KSA* 3, 467); he supplements this initial articulation with the infamous dramatization of the problem in section 125 of *Gay Science* (*KSA* 3, 480–82).

With respect to the question of the philosophical trajectory of *Daybreak*, Ansell-Pearson appeals to section 335 of *The Gay Science* (*KSA* 3, 560–61), arguing that the direction of the philosophy of the morning of *Daybreak* is already fixed on purification of our opinions and evaluations and on the creation of our own new tables of what is good, meaning that the ultimate goal of Nietzsche's "philosophy of the morning" is "authenticity" or "the task of becoming one's own lawgiver" (26–27). Ansell-Pearson claims that, for this reason, section 553 of *Daybreak* (*KSA*

3, 323) is a particularly important example of intellectual integrity on Nietzsche's part (26). It is worth noting that the point from *The Gay Science* (§335) to which Ansell-Pearson draws our attention is already clearly expressed in *Daybreak* when Nietzsche, writing from a possible future, describes what it might mean to be able to exercise the lawgiver's power over oneself. As Nietzsche puts it, although the malefactors may have committed an offense by calling themselves to account, publicly dictating their own punishment, and voluntarily accepting punishment, the malefactors raise themselves above their offense through "freeheartedness, greatness and imperturbability" (Freimüthigkeit, Grösse und Ruhe), while also thereby performing a public service (*D* §187; *KSA* 3, 160). Yet as Ansell-Pearson recognizes (24–25), even given such a sketch of self-rule, Nietzsche admits that many will struggle to achieve the experiences required for a drive-psychological account of self-rule, or, having achieved them, accomplished philosophers may ultimately falter in their experimental vigor and seek instead to become institutions (*D* §539, §542 and §547; *KSA* 3, 308, 311 and 317).

Concerning Owen's first problem of failure to infer, Nietzsche's suggestion that the circuitousness of his writing is not a problem for the coherence of his philosophy, but that it is rather a demonstration of its coherence and rigor, helps to identify more clearly how his responses to this problem in *The Gay Science* and in such later texts as *On the Genealogy of Morals* (*Zur Genealogie der Moral*) is built upon work already done in *Daybreak* (*D* §530, *KSA* 3, 303). Attending to Nietzsche's use of the metaphor of water supports this point.[19] Commenting on thinkers' digressions, Nietzsche draws an analogy between the trajectory of his new philosophy and the type of work it may accomplish, and water courses (*D* §530; *KSA* 3, 303). He suggests that while the whole course of thought of many thinkers is bold and rigorous, the detail of such thought is gentle and flexible, circling the same item multiple times before resuming its trajectory; similarly, he says, there are rivers with many meanderings that play hide-and-seek with themselves, but which ultimately (like Zarathustra's unbreakable will) break their way through the hardest stone (*D* §530; *KSA* 3, 303, cf. *KSA* 4, 145). Thinkers who dwell in great streams of thought and feeling will, Nietzsche suggests, desire rest and silence of life because their philosophy is fundamentally a part of life; he contrasts this with the work of thinkers who take a rest from life when engaging in their meditations (*D* §572; *KSA* 3, 330). These latter types of thinkers are characterized by a way of thinking that closely resembles the cognitive cause of the problem of not inferring: a picture holds them captive. Nietzsche had earlier used the example of a man who is thirsty and cannot get water, but whose thoughts produce pictures of water immediately before his eyes as though water were easily obtainable, in order to demonstrate that we tend to assume that the realm of thought is free in comparison to the realms of willing, acting, and experiencing, whereas in genuine comparison to experience and action, thought is superficial (*D* §125; *KSA* 3, 116–17).

The same problem of deception of the eyes is raised in Nietzsche's discussion of rococo horticulture, in which Nietzsche makes an analogy from the visual horticultural deceptions of grottos, mazes, and waterfalls to the type of philosophy that seeks to entertain an exalted audience rather than seeking truth. He has an alternative conception of philosophical activity in mind, however, as is suggested in section 572 (*KSA* 3, 330) as well as in section 491. Here Nietzsche, once again analogizing the action of thinking to that of water, employs a brief dialogue to show that solitude fosters the kind of independence in philosophical activity that is born out of "the well of the self" (dem Brunnen meines Selbst) rather than from "drinking out of everyone's cistern" (aus den Cisternen für Jedermann zu trinken; *D* §491; *KSA* 3, 290). Ultimately, as Ansell-Pearson shows, the water of new thinking turns to the sea in, for example, section 423 and section 575 (*KSA* 3, 259 and 331), where Nietzsche uses the sea as a metaphor for a new sublime of human self-overcoming (8).

Owen's second problem shows how Nietzsche identifies the need for supplementation of the authority of scientific knowledge by providing an account of how we come to value truth and why this should lead us to reject Christian morality (252). Nietzsche's critique of rococo horticulture warns against the intoxicating effect of art as it applies to the beautification of science; further, he contends that the inspiration for rococo horticulture — the feeling that nature is ugly, savage, and boring, therefore we should beautify it — is the same as the feeling that inspires philosophy — the feeling that science is ugly, dry, challenging, and cheerless, and that we should therefore beautify it (*D* §427; *KSA* 3, 263). According to Ansell-Pearson, Nietzsche is using the sublime in section 427 to explain the activity and function of philosophy in light of the new science of knowledge; Ansell-Pearson combines this with evidence from section 429 to argue that, in book 5 of *Daybreak*, Nietzsche has essentially developed the concept of the "gay science" project, which combines poetry, song, aphorism, and affirmation of science and which will receive more complete attention in *The Gay Science* (21–22).

With respect to Owen's third problem, Nietzsche's self-critical concern is fully in keeping with the four cardinal virtues — honesty, bravery, magnanimity, and politeness — that he specifies in section 556 (*KSA* 3, 325). It is also continuous with an important feature of his experimental approach to philosophy in *Daybreak*: virtues in thinkers, their conceptual ideologies, as well as their reflective outputs and — factoring in drive psychology — subjectivities, are always works in progress. Here it is important to attend to Nietzsche's claim that honesty, the youngest, most immature, and most misunderstood and mistaken of the virtues, is among neither the Socratic nor the Christian virtues: it is a virtue in the process of becoming (*D* §456; *KSA* 3, 275). While Robert Solomon counts Nietzschean honesty as an emotion, Clancy Martin suggests that we should think of honesty as a drive or impulse, appropriate in some circumstances and inappropriate in others, and dependent on a person's internal compulsion toward truth-telling on a case-by-case basis; however, both Solomon and Martin do agree that honesty is a Nietzschean virtue.[20]

Discussing the relationship between life and truth through the example of the pricked pride that Rousseau and Schopenhauer must have suffered when the truth as each of them understood it did not harmonize with their lives, Nietzsche identifies magnanimity or *Grossmüthigkeit* as the fairest virtue of the thinker because it involves the offering of the thinker's self and life as a sacrifice (*D* §459; *KSA* 3, 276). Following up on the consequences of his experimental method for his own extolling of honesty as a virtue, Nietzsche contends that virtuousness is not a matter of identifying the personal virtues one happens to possess and playing on these to the detriment of others who happen to lack them, but of acting humanely in light of our particular virtues (*D* §536; *KSA* 3, 306). Honesty, he suggests, gives us a kind of thumbscrew that we could use to torture those who wish to impose their beliefs on the world; but, having tested this thumbscrew on ourselves, we should perhaps be careful — judicious, even, in the language of the lawgiver (*D* §187; *KSA* 3, 160) — in directing it toward others (*D* §536; *KSA* 3, 306). He uses his water analogy to strengthen his case for virtues, and self-criticism, as works in progress. While he claims to love those who are "transparent water" (durchsichtiges Wasser) and who, alluding to Alexander Pope, "do not hide from view the turbid bottom of their stream" (die Unreinlichkeit auf dem Grunde ihres Stromes sehen lassen), he also cautions against the sin of vanity in hiding virtues such as that of transparency (*D* §558, *KSA* 3, 325).[21] Though he does not yet have a full or satisfactory answer to Owen's third problem, Nietzsche recognizes the scope of the problem and begins to grapple with it.

Ruth Abbey identifies a different aspect of Nietzsche's self-critique as incomplete in *Daybreak*: his redemption of the ad hominem strategy.[22] Abbey defines the ad hominem strategy in Nietzsche as the contention, first, that argument is not ignored but, second, that no position can be evaluated on solely intellectual merits — the psyche of the author, advocates, and adherents must also be considered for the position to receive fuller appreciation (150). She argues that in works from the so-called "middle period," including *Daybreak*, the ad hominem strategy does not play a significant role in Nietzsche's approach; moreover, she contends that Nietzsche advises against using such a strategy (150). She takes her evidence for this argument from section 431, where Nietzsche claims that it is advisable to use interpretation and reproduction of the opinion of opponents in order to take the measure of the opponent's intellect: a perfect sage will purge an opponent's work of error prior to embarking upon sustained disagreement (*D* §431; *KSA* 3, 265). Abbey links this unwillingness to engage in caricature of opponents on Nietzsche's part in *Daybreak* with his general admiration and emulation of scientific virtues during this period of his work (152).

Abbey does, however, note a concession on Nietzsche's part with respect to the type of writing that can transcend the self-expression presupposed by the type of symptomatic reading that accompanies the ad hominem strategy (152). This concession, which renders our readings of *Daybreak* more compatible, is based on Nietzsche's distinction between types of thinkers such as Plato, Spinoza, and Goethe, in whom the spirit seems to be sufficiently tenuously connected to the character and temperament that it can detach itself and soar above these, and types of thinkers such as Schopenhauer, in whom the spirit could never get free from the temperament (*D* §497; *KSA* 3, 292–93). According to Nietzsche, Schopenhauerian genius is great in that such geniuses believe that wherever they fly they discover and rediscover themselves, whereas geniuses of the Platonic, Spinozan, or Goethean type better deserve the title of genius because they possess "the pure, purifying eye" (das reine, reinmachende Auge) that, free from temperament and character and usually in opposition to these, looks down on the world as on a god that they love (*D* §497; *KSA* 3, 292–93).

In addition to these remarks, three additional sections support my view that Nietzsche does include some role for the ad hominem in *Daybreak*. First, Nietzsche points out that there are no scientific methods that alone lead to knowledge; he contends that we need to tackle things experimentally and affectively, giving examples of modes of critical-experimental engagement that include the policeman, the father confessor, and the inquisitive wanderer, as well as listing sympathetic, forceful, reverent, and roguishly indiscreet approaches that mean investigators like us (and Nietzsche is explicitly inclusive of readers in this aphorism) will be considered audacious and evil (*D* §432; *KSA* 3, 266). Second, with respect to the question of the ad hominem, and hearkening back to his gardening metaphor in section 382, Nietzsche remarks that at one time (and presumably no longer) he was the kind of fool who refuses the philosophical fruit he finds most tasty simply because it was growing on his own tree (*D* §493; *KSA* 3, 290–91). Third, supporting the previous point, he argues that if a thinker forces himself to think against the grain — for example, to think the thoughts necessary to an office or a prescribed schedule rather than those that come from within — he will fall sick (*D* §500; *KSA* 3, 294). Such chronic sicknesses of the soul require a slow cure (*D* §462; *KSA* 3, 278).

Nietzsche's personal medical narrative, and his reading of texts by Mérimée and Dostoyevsky that anatomize human moral psychology, spur his engagement with key themes of psycho-physiological and cultural health in *Daybreak*. As I have discussed, his campaign against morality is initiated by means of aphorism and experimental philosophical engagement. His drive psychology, combined with abandonment of belief in the immortal soul, creates the necessary critical-imaginative space to facilitate a possible transvaluation of values. Nietzsche also uses aphorism to create the necessary conditions for readers' own performative engagements in and through the medium of the text: we are not to be passive recipients of his wisdom, but rather, fellow dancers to Nietzsche's new music, which demands of us, "Hic Rhodus, hic salta!" (*D* §461; *KSA* 3, 277).[23] However, as I have also suggested following work by Abbey, Ansell-Pearson, and Owen, and as Nietzsche recognized, the promise of the transvaluation project remains subject to problems of intellectual and moral virtue, subjectivity, self and character, and scientific and personal authority. Nietzsche continues to grapple with these problems in *The Gay Science*.[24]

Notes

Translations from Nietzsche in this essay are from *Daybreak: Thoughts on the Prejudices of Morality*, ed. Maudemarie Clark and Brian Leiter, trans. R. J. Hollingdale (Cambridge: Cambridge UP, 1997).

[1] On the chronology of *Daybreak*'s composition, see William H. Schaberg, *The Nietzsche Canon: A Publication History and Bibliography* (Chicago and London: U of Chicago P, 1995), 77.

[2] Mérimée uses a direct reference to act 3 scene 5 of Shakespeare's *Romeo and Juliet* to introduce the events leading to the separation of the characters of Mathilde and Saint-Clair: "*The lark, the herald of the morn*, was beginning to sing, and long streaks of pale light tinged the clouds in the east. It was at this hour that Romeo bade farewell to Juliet. It is the moment when lovers traditionally take their leave of one another." (Prosper Mérimée, "The Etruscan Vase," in *Carmen and Other Stories*, ed. and trans. Nicholas Jotcham [Oxford: Oxford UP, 1998], 108).

[3] Fyodor Dostoevsky, *Notes from Underground*, trans. Jessie Coulson (London: Penguin, 1972), 16.

[4] Eric von der Luft and Douglas G. Stenberg, "Dostoevskii's Specific Influence on Nietzsche's Preface to Daybreak," *Journal of the History of Ideas* 52/3 (July–September 1991): 441–61 (here 443).

[5] Maudemarie Clarke and Brian Leiter, "Introduction," in *Daybreak: Thoughts on the Prejudice of Morality*, ed. Maudemarie Clark and Brian Leiter (Cambridge: Cambridge UP, 1997), xxiv–xxvi; and David Owen, "Nietzsche, Re-evaluation, and the Turn to Genealogy," *European Journal of Philosophy* 11/3 (2003): 249–72 (here 250–52).

[6] Keith Ansell-Pearson, "On the Sublime in *Dawn*," *The Agonist* 2/1 (March 2009): 5–30 (here 6–7). An extended and revised version appears in Keith Ansell-Pearson, "Nietzsche, the Sublime, and the Sublimities of Philosophy: An Interpretation of *Dawn*," *Nietzsche-Studien* 39 (2010): 201–32.

[7] This is Mervyn Sprung's translation of the epigraph in "Nietzsche's Trans-European Eye," in Graham Parkes (ed.), *Nietzsche and Asian Thought* (Chicago, IL: U of Chicago P, 1991), 76–90 (78–79).

[8] Dorothy Matilda Figueira, *Aryans, Jews, Brahmins: Theorizing Authority through Myths of Identity* (Albany, NY: SUNY P, 2002), 170.

[9] *Daybreak* is comprised of 575 aphorisms divided into five books, and a preface composed in five sections; book 1 contains 96 aphorisms, book 2 contains 52, book 3 contains 59, book 4 contains 215, and book 5 contains 153. For a detailed discussion of Nietzsche and the aphorism, see Jill Marsden, "Nietzsche and the Art of the Aphorism," in *A Companion to Nietzsche*, ed. Keith Ansell-Pearson (Oxford: Blackwell, 2006), 22–38.

[10] Graham Parkes, *Composing the Soul: Reaches of Nietzsche's Psychology* (Chicago, IL: U of Chicago P, 1994), 116.

[11] Volker Gerhardt, "'Experimental Philosophy': An Attempt at a Reconstruction," trans. Peter S. Groff and Herbert Möller, in *Nietzsche: Critical Assessments*, ed. Daniel W. Conway and Peter S. Groff, 4 vols. (London and New York: Routledge, 1998), vol. 3, 79–94 (here 82).

[12] On Nietzsche's use of Platonic cave imagery in later works, see Martha Kendal Woodruff, "Untergang und Übergang: The Tragic Descent of Socrates and Zarathustra," *Journal of Nietzsche Studies* 34 (Fall 2007): 61–78.

[13] Horst Hutter, *Shaping the Future: Nietzsche's New Regime of the Soul and Its Ascetic Practices* (Lanham, MD: Lexington Books, 2006); and Bruce Ellis Benson, "Nietzsche's Musical *Askesis* for Resisting Decadence," *Journal of Nietzsche Studies* 34 (Fall 2007): 28–46 (here 28–29).

[14] Carl B. Sachs, "Nietzsche's Daybreak: Toward a Naturalized Theory of Autonomy," *Epoché* 13/1 (Fall 2008): 81–100 (here 96).

[15] See, for example, John Richardson, "Nietzsche on Time and Becoming," in *A Companion to Nietzsche*, ed. Ansell-Pearson, 208–29.

[16] Andy Clark, *Being There: Putting Brain, Body and World Together Again* (Cambridge, MA: MIT Press, 1997), 110.

[17] David Owen, "Nietzsche, Re-evaluation, and the Turn to Genealogy," *European Journal of Philosophy* 11:3 (2003): 249–72; and Ansell-Pearson, "On the Sublime in *Dawn*."

[18] See Ludwig Wittgenstein, *Philosophical Investigations*, trans. G. E. M. Anscombe, 3rd ed. (Oxford: Blackwell, 2001), 80.

[19] Ansell-Pearson includes a sustained discussion of the use of the water/ocean metaphor in Nietzsche and in the broader history of the sublime (see "On the Sublime in *Dawn*," 7–8).

[20] Robert C. Solomon, *Living with Nietzsche: What the Great "Immoralist" Has to Teach Us* (New York: Oxford UP, 2003); and Clancy W. Martin, "Nietzsche's

Homeric Lies," *Journal of Nietzsche Studies* 31 (2006): 1–9 (here 6–7). For further discussion of Nietzsche and virtue, see Michael Slote, "Nietzsche and Virtue Ethics," *International Studies in Philosophy* 30/3 (1998): 23–27; Christine Swanton, "Outline of a Nietzschean Virtue Ethics," *International Studies in Philosophy* 30/3 (1998): 29–38; Lester H. Hunt, *Nietzsche and the Origin of Virtue* (London: Routledge, 1991); and Christine Daigle, "Nietzsche: Virtue Ethics . . . Virtue Politics?" *Journal of Nietzsche Studies* 32 (Fall 2006): 1–21.

[21] Nietzsche claims to be alluding to Alexander Pope, but does not specify his source. This has caused some confusion, as it is not immediately clear whether Nietzsche is indeed referring to Pope, or to which text by Pope Nietzsche might be referring. Thomas H. Brobjer has suggested that the "origin of or inspiration for" Nietzsche's allusion to Pope in this section is "probably . . . the reading of Taine's discussion of Pope in his *Geschichte der Englischen Literatur*, which Nietzsche read in 1879" (Brobjer, *Nietzsche and the "English": The Influence of British and American Thinking on his Philosophy* [Amherst: Humanity Books, 2008], 85). John J. Sullivan (personal correspondence) suggests that Nietzsche may be referring to Pope's letter to Congreve of 16 January 1714–15. There, Pope writes: "Methinks, when I write to you, I am making a confession, I have got, I cannot tell how, such a custom of throwing myself out upon paper without reserve. You were not mistaken in what you judged of my temper of mind when I writ last. My faults will not be hid from you, and perhaps it is no dispraise to me that they will not. The cleanness and purity of one's mind is never better proved than in discovering its own fault at first view; as when a stream shows the dirt at its bottom, it shows also the transparency of the water" (Alexander Pope, *The Works of Alexander Pope*, vol. 6, *Correspondence*, vol. 1, ed. John Wilson Croker [London: John Murray, 1871], 411).

[22] Ruth Abbey, *Nietzsche's Middle Period* (Oxford: Oxford UP, 2000), 149–53.

[23] Compare Nietzsche here with Hegel's *"Hic Rhodus, hic saltus"* in the *Preface to the Philosophy of Right*, and Marx's *"Hic Rhodus, hic salta"* in *The Eighteenth Brumaire of Louis Bonaparte* (G. W. F. Hegel, *Philosophy of Right*, trans. S. W. Dyde (New York, NY: Cosimo, 2008), xx; and Karl Marx, *The Eighteenth Brumaire of Louis Bonaparte*, trans. Daniel De Leon, 3rd ed. (Chicago, IL: Kerr, 1913), 15). It seems that Nietzsche is following Marx here, with an emphasis upon dance that will become even more significant in later works.

[24] I would like to thank the following people: Paul Bishop and an anonymous reviewer for their helpful remarks on earlier versions of this chapter; Marcia D. Nichols (University of Minnesota Rochester) for helping me to seek fruitful assistance from eighteenth-century English literature scholars with respect to Nietzsche's allusion to Alexander Pope; Thomas H. Brobjer and Nicholas Martin for taking time to discuss Nietzsche's reading of Pope and of Hippolyte Taine; John Jeremiah Sullivan (*New York Times Magazine*) for suggesting a source for this allusion; and Mary Beth Sancomb-Moran (University of Minnesota Rochester) and Michelle Twait (Gustavus Adolphus College) for helping me to access research materials.

Link to *The Gay Science*

In June 1881, Nietzsche traveled on from Recoaro into the Engadin, staying first in St. Moritz and the moving on, in July 1881, to a small town in the mountains, where he was to stay for three months, and return time and again: Sils Maria. Here Nietzsche read Spinoza,[1] went for walks by the lake — noting, in particular, the existence of a large, pyramid-shaped rock by the water, close to Surlei — and wondered about whether to buy a typewriter. Externally, Nietzsche's life looked dull, even boring: he stayed in a small house near the woods, ate a cheap lunch from the tourist menu at a nearby hotel, and sometimes chatted with the other visitors.[2] His inner life, however, was rich, intense, and exciting, even dangerous, as he told Heinrich Köselitz on 14 August 1881: "Actually I am leading an extremely dangerous life, for I am one of those machines that might *explode*! The intensity of my feeling makes me shudder and laugh" (daß ich eigentlich ein höchst gefährliches Leben lebe, denn ich gehöre zu den Maschinen, welche *zerspringen* können! Die Intensitäten meines Gefühls machen mich schaudern und lachen; *KSA* 6, 112).

From Sils Maria, Nietzsche traveled to Genoa, where he spent the winter and undertook to live under the protection of three local "patron saints": Columbus, Paganini, and Mazzini (*KSB* 6, 134). A letter to Paul Rée gives us an insight into the kind of cures used by Nietzsche for his constant ill-health: they included phosphoric magnesia and kali phosphoricum (*KSB* 6, 139). Nietzsche even began to play the lottery, but his greatest comfort was in his discovery of a new musical aesthetic, embodied in Bizet's *Carmen* (*KSB* 6, 144–46).[3] In *The Case of Wagner* (*Der Fall Wagner*), Nietzsche would cite Bizet's opera as an alternative to Wagnerian music.

First by hand, and then using a typewriter, Nietzsche began work in Genoa on a continuation of *Daybreak* (*Morgenröthe*), which turned into a new work — *The Gay Science* (*Die fröhliche Wissenschaft*). Not simply the title of the work, but its quotation on the title page of the first edition — "To the poet, to the philosopher, to the saint, all things are friendly and sacred, all events profitable, all days holy, all men divine" — and arguably its entire ethos, demonstrate Nietzsche's indebtedness to Ralph Waldo Emerson (1803–82), the American philosopher, essayist, and poet.[4] In Schulpforta, Nietzsche had read a selection of Emerson's *Essays*, and when his copy was lost in a stolen bag in 1874, he soon replaced it. A note from his *Nachlass* of autumn 1881 testifies to Nietzsche's rereading of Emerson's *Essays* at this time, and to his sense of proximity with the American philosopher: "Never has a book made me feel so much at home and in my own home — it is not proper for me to praise it, it is too close to me" (Ich habe mich nie in einem Buch so zu Hause und in meinem Hause gefühlt als — ich darf es nicht loben, es steht mir zu nahe; *KSA* 9, 12[68], 588). Among other things, an admiration for Goethe was common to both.[5]

Rée's visit in February/March 1882 simultaneously delighted and exhausted Nietzsche; his new typewriter kept breaking. But through Rée, after he had moved on to Rome, Nietzsche heard about a beautiful, intelligent Russian aristocrat: Lou von Salomé. (This extraordinary woman, a former student of theology at Zurich University, went on to become a close friend of Rilke and a prominent member of the psychoanalytic circle around Freud in Vienna; in 1887, she married Friedrich Carl Andreas, a professor of oriental studies at Göttingen.)[6] Writing to Rée from Genoa, Nietzsche told him: "I lust after this kind of soul" (Ich bin nach dieser Gattung von Seelen lüstern), and he pondered the possibilities of marriage with her — even if only a two-year marriage, in view of all that Nietzsche planned to do in the next ten years (*KSB* 6, 186–86). In March/April 1882, Nietzsche moved to Messina, where he worked intensively on poetic texts.[7] Rée was insistent that Nietzsche meet Lou von Salomé (KGB II.2, 251), so Nietzsche accepted his and Malwida von Meysenbug's invitation to Rome for a week in the spring. On 24 April 1882, in front of the massive basilica on St. Peter's Square, Nietzsche met Lou von Salomé for the first time, when he greeted her with the words: "From which stars have we fallen to meet each other here?" (Von welchen Sternen sind wir hier einander zugefallen?).[8]

In her book on Nietzsche, published in 1896, Lou von Salomé recalls her first impression of him: "something hidden, the sense of a silenced solitude — that was the first, strong impression with which Nietzsche's appearance seized one" (dieses Verborgene, die Ahnung einer verschwiegenen Einsamkeit, — das war der erste, starke Eindruck, durch den Nietzsches Erscheinung fesselte), and she noted his moustache, his gentle laugh, his quiet way of speaking, and his beautiful, noble hands.[9] Between von Salomé, Rée, and Nietzsche, a bond of friendship was formed: von Salomé and Rée had a plan for a scholarly microcommunity,[10] which Nietzsche — his plan for a revival of the Epicurean garden still in mind,[11] perhaps, or what he also called the "Pythagorean friendship" (pythagoreische Freundschaft)[12] — wished to join as the "Dritter im Bund,"[13] and the three of them considered studying together in Vienna, or Paris, or Munich.[14] But did Nietzsche want more, especially from Lou? According to von Salomé, Nietzsche asked Rée to make her a proposal on his behalf; she refused on principle.[15] When the three of them, accompanied by her mother, visited Orta on their way to Lucerne, they went on a boat trip up the lake to the Sacro Monte. As Rée looked after the mother, Lou von Salomé and Nietzsche wandered off up the mountain together. On their walk, Nietzsche discussed with her his central philosophical ideas, including one which had come to him in Sils-Maria and which he would later discuss with the Overbecks: the eternal recurrence of all things, which he told her about "in a quiet voice and with every sign of the deepest horror" (mit leiser Stimme und mit allen Zeichen des tiefsten Entsetzens).[16] From Nietzsche's point of view, this initiation into his philosophical thoughts was a moment of great trust and intimacy.[17] (It would be inappropriate to ask about other kinds of intimacy; in other words, did they kiss? When thinking about it later, Lou von Salomé tactfully said she could not remember — *ich weiß es nicht mehr.*[18])

From Lucerne, Nietzsche took her on a visit to Triebschen, where the Wagners had lived. Playing with his stick in the sand by the lake, and speaking in a low voice about past time, von Salomé records, Nietzsche looked up, crying — "da weinte er."[19] After a short visit to the Overbecks in Basel, Nietzsche returned to Lucerne, and made what may have been a second proposal to Lou von Salomé while they were walking together in a public park, the Löwengarten.[20] But the playfulness and passion that characterized Nietzsche's relationship with Lou von Salomé is captured by the picture, whether taken at his or her behest is unclear, in a photographer's studio in Lucerne. This remarkable visual document, depicting Lou, whip in hand, in a cart pulled by Rée and Nietzsche, is difficult to interpret; but the heavy-handed reading that Elisabeth Förster-Nietzsche applied to the notorious passage in *Zarathustra*, "Are you going to women? Don't forget your whip!" (Du gehst zu Frauen? Vergiss die Peitsche nicht! *Z* I 18; *KSA* 4, 86), shows what happens when the dimension of humor is removed from the interpretation of Nietzsche.[21]

Over May and June, Lou von Salomé was the recipient in Hamburg of numerous affectionate, even intimate letters from Rée — "Now, my dear dear Lu, *be reassured that you are the only person in the world whom I love dearly*" (Nun, meine liebe liebe Lu, *sei versichert, daß Du der einzige Mensch auf der Welt bist, den ich lieb habe*)[22] — while in his letters, Nietzsche addressed her in the formal *Sie*, took as their common motto lines from Goethe's poem "Generalbeichte,"[23] and said that something in which he had ceased to believe, "finding a friend of my *ultimate joy and suffering*" (einen Freund meines *letzten Glücks und Leidens* zu finden), now seemed possible "as the *golden* possibility on the horizon of my future life" (als die *goldene* Möglichkeit am Horizonte alles meines zukünftigen Lebens).[24] Looking for someone to whom he could be a "teacher" (Lehrer), and conversely for people to be his "heirs" (Erben),[25] Nietzsche's attitude toward von Salomé implied no disrespect: to Köselitz, he described her as being "as astute as an eagle and as courageous as a lion" (scharfsinnig wie ein Adler und muthig wie ein Löwe).[26]

Then, in July 1882, Lou von Salomé visited Nietzsche in Tautenburg, a village in the Thuringian forest, where he was spending the summer. Not far away from Nietzsche's birthplace, Röcken (and not far away either, as he realized, from Dornburg, the small town north of Weimar where Goethe had stayed from time to time in the later years of his life).[27] The village was, as Nietzsche put it, "a half hour away from Dornburg, where the elderly Goethe enjoyed his solitude, lies in the midst of lovely forests Tautenburg" (eine halbe Stunde abseits von der Dornburg, auf der der alte Goethe seine Einsamkeit genoß, liegt inmitten schöner Wälder Taut-enburg; *KSB* 6, 210). Here, he told von Salomé, his sister Elisabeth had arranged for him "an idyllic little nest" (ein idylles Nestchen), although the arrival of Lou in Tautenburg was to make this quiet, secluded village rather less than idyllic, thanks to her endless quarrels with Elisabeth.

During his time with Lou in Tautenburg, Nietzsche made a reso-lution that would be echoed by Zarathustra: "Ich will nicht mehr ein-sam sein und wieder lernen, Mensch zu werden" (I no longer want to be lonely and want to learn again to be human; *KSB* 6, 217).[28] But Elisabeth preferred to see her brother lonely, rather than with Lou. The two women had met in Bayreuth earlier that year, and on the journey to Tautenburg, they had fallen out over Nietzsche in Jena.[29] In Elisabeth, Lou now had an enemy. Although both Nietzsche and Lou von Salomé displayed enor-mous psychological acuity, not least in their shared project of a collection of aphorisms, initiated by Lou in the form of her "Stibbe Nest-Book" (Stibber Nest-Buch), to which Nietzsche responded by rewriting some of them in "On High Seas: A Book of Aphorisms" (Auf hoher See: Ein Sentenzen-Buch);[30] neither was able to see the powerful psychological and emotional dynamic at work in their own case.

Nietzsche and von Salomé talked and talked and talked; he set some of her poems to music, including "To Pain" ("An den Schmerz") and "Hymn to Life" ("Hymnus an das Leben");[31] he believed that he and she were, in terms of their intelligence and their tastes, "profoundly *related*" (im Tiefsten *verwandt*), or so he told Franz Overbeck (*KSB* 6, 255). Yet when it became clear that Rée had continued to court her and the two of them were growing closer together; when it turned out that Rée had not been "a better friend" (ein *besserer* Freund), as Nietzsche had believed him to be;[32] when Elisabeth continued to cast aspersions against Lou, arousing Nietzsche's suspicion about her motives; and when Lou's own intuition that Nietzsche still "secretly wanted something else" (im geheimen anderes wollte),[33] that he was trying to criticize Rée behind his back,[34] and that there was something sensual about his idealistic love for her,[35] began to prevail, then the "Trinity" (Dreieinigkeit) — as Lou referred to herself, Nietzsche, and Rée[36] — began to drift, then fall, apart. (Malwida von Meysenbug's skepticism about the likely outcome of such a constellation turned out to have been justified.)[37] The atmosphere became poisonous; feeling abandoned and misunderstood by family and friends alike, Nietzsche saw von Salomé and Rée for the last time on 5 November 1882, when they took leave of him in Leipzig.

Yet in the midst of the relationship with Lou, Nietzsche had corrected the proofs of *The Gay Science*, completed earlier in the year in Genoa,[38] and the work was published in the summer of 1882, containing four sections; the fifth section, the preface, and the appendix of poems, "Songs of Prince Free-As-A-Bird" ("Die Lieder des Prinzen Vogelfrei") were added in the second edition, published in 1887. The contrast between the circumstances in which it had been written and its presentation of "a new image and ideal of the free spirit" (ein neues Bild und Ideal des Freigeistes; *KSB* 6, 213) is one of which Nietzsche himself would have been well aware. If it concludes the series of works begun with *Human, All Too Human* and continued in *Daybreak*, it also anticipated the future direction of his thought — not least in its presentation of the idea of eternal recurrence (*GS* §341; *KSA* 3, 570) and in the section that concluded the first edition, entitled "*Incipit tragoedia*," which began: "When Zarathustra was thirty years old, he left his home and Lake Urmi, and went into the mountains" (Als Zarathustra dreissig Jahr alt war, verliess er seine Heimath und den See Urmi und gieng in das Gebirge; *GS* §342; *KSA* 3, 571). Keith Ansell-Pearson here discusses this work, in which Nietzsche encourages us to learn from artists, and ask: "What means do we have to make things beautiful, attractive, and desirable for us, when they are not?" (Welche Mittel haben wir, uns die Dinge schön, anziehend, begehrenswerth zu machen, wenn sie es nicht sind? *GS* §299: *KSA* 3, 538).

Notes

[1] See Nietzsche's note of autumn 1881: "When I talk about Plato, Pascal, Spinoza, and Goethe, I know that their blood is mixed with mine" (Wenn ich von Plato Pascal Spinoza und Goethe rede, so weiß ich, daß ihr Blut in dem meinen rollt; *KSA* 9, 12[52], 585). In another note, Nietzsche offers an even more impressive roll-call: "In what moved Zoroaster, Moses, Mohammed, Jesus, Plato, Brutus, Spinoza, Mirabeau, there I am already living, and in some things there is only now properly coming to light what required a few millennia as an embryo" (In dem, was Zarathustra, Moses, Muhamed Jesus Plato Brutus Spinoza Mirabeau bewegte, lebe ich auch schon, und in manchen Dingen kommt in mir erst reif an's Tageslicht, was embryonisch ein paar Jahrtausende brauchte; *KSA* 9, 15[17], 642). In the spring of 1884, Nietzsche restated: "My predecessors: Heraclitus, Empedocles, Spinoza, Goethe" (meine Vorfahren *Heraclit Empedocles Spinoza Goethe*; *KSA* 11, 25[454], 134).

[2] Eugen Diederichs, "Sils-Maria und Friedrich Nietzsche," *Berliner Tageblatt*, 8 August 1906; cited in *Chronik*, 489.

[3] In *The Case of Wagner* (*Der Fall Wagner*) Nietzsche explained his preference for Bizet as follows: "And I really seemed to myself, every time I heard *Carmen*,

more a philosopher, a better philosopher, than I usually consider myself to be" (Und wirklich schien ich mir jedes Mal, dass ich *Carmen* hörte, mehr Philosoph, ein besserer Philosoph, als ich sonst mir schiene; *CW* §1; *KSA* 6, 13), a phrase later quoted by Ernesto Grassi to exemplify the transpositional, metaphorical activity of the philosopher or the artist (*Die Macht der Phantasie: Zur Geschichte abendländischen Denkens* [Königstein im Taunus: Athenäum, 1979], 170).

[4] In "The Scholar," Emerson says: "I think the peculiar office of scholars in a careful and gloomy generation is to be (as the poets were called in the Middle Ages) Professors of the Joyous Science, detectors and delineators of occult symmetries and unpublished beauties; heralds of civility, nobility, learning and wisdom; affirmers of the one law, yet as those who should affirm it in music and dancing; expressors themselves of that firm and cheerful temper; infinitely removed from sadness, which reigns through the kingdom of chemistry, vegetation, and animal life" (Ralph Waldo Emerson, *Lectures and Biographical Sketches* [London: Waverley Book Company, 1883], 249–71 [here: 250]). Emerson, "History," in Ralph Waldo Emerson, *Essays and Lectures*, ed. Joel Porte (New York: Library of America, 1983), 237–56 (here: 242). For Nietzsche's ironic use of this quotation in his correspondence, see his letters to Paul Rée of end of August 1882 and to Erwin Rohde of 25 December 1882 (*KSB* 6, 247 and 312).

[5] See, for example, the lecture entitled "Goethe; or, the Writer," in *Representative Men* (1850), in which Emerson concludes: "Goethe teaches us courage, and the equivalence of all times; that the disadvantages of any epoch exist only to the faint-hearted. Genius hovers with his sunshine and music close by the darkest and deafest eras" (Emerson, *Essays and Lectures*, 746–61 [here: 761]).

[6] See H. F. Peters, *My Sister, My Spouse: A Biography of Lou Andreas-Salomé* (London: Gollancz, 1963); Rudolph Binion, *Frau Lou: Nietzsche's Wayward Disciple* (Princeton, NJ: Princeton UP, 1968); and Angela Livingstone, *Lou Andreas-Salomé* (London: Gordon Fraser, 1984).

[7] See the "Idyllen aus Messina," first published in *Internationale Monatsschrift: Zeitschrift für allgemeine und nationale Kultur und deren Literatur* 1/5 (May 1882): 269–75; *KSA* 3, 333–42.

[8] Lou Andreas-Salomé, *Lebensrückblick: Grundriß einiger Lebenserinnerungen* [1951], ed. Ernst Pfeiffer (Frankfurt am Main: Insel, 1974), 79.

[9] Lou Andreas-Salomé, *Friedrich Nietzsche in seinen Werken* [1896], ed. Ernst Pfeiffer (Frankfurt am Main: Insel, 2000), 37. As a contemporary account of Nietzsche's life and thought, this work remains one of insight and value.

[10] Ernst Pfeiffer, ed., *Friedrich Nietzsche, Paul Rée. Lou von Salomé: Die Dokumente ihrer Begegnung* (Frankfurt am Main: Insel, 1970), 97.

[11] In her turn, Lou von Salomé applies the image of the garden, and more specifically of the plant, to her friendship with Rée in her letter to Rée of New Year's Eve 1882/1883 (*Die Dokumente ihrer Begegnung*, 282).

[12] See Nietzsche's letter to Rée of 29 May 1882: "I often laugh about our Pythagorean friendship, with its very strange '*philois panta koiná*'" (Ich lache öfter über unsre pythagoreische Freundschaft, mit dem sehr seltsamen "*philois panta koiná*")

(*Die Dokumente ihrer Begegnung*, 128). The quotation from the *Golden Words* of Pythagoras means "friends hold everything in common."

13 *Die Dokumente ihrer Begegnung*, 107.

14 Andreas-Salomé, *Lebensrückblick*, 79.

15 Andreas-Salomé, *Lebensrückblick*, 80.

16 Andreas-Salomé, *Friedrich Nietzsche in seinen Werken*, 255.

17 *Die Dokumente ihrer Begegnung*, 264 and 266.

18 Andreas-Salomé, *Lebensrückblick*, 236.

19 Andreas-Salomé, *Nietzsche in seinen Werken*, 116.

20 Lou Andreas-Salomé, *Lebensrückblick*, 81.

21 Elisabeth Förster-Nietzsche, *Das Leben Friedrich Nietzsche's*, 3 vols. (Leipzig: Naumann, 1895–1904), 2.2:559–61. According to Resa von Schirnhofer, for Förster-Nietzsche the photograph was "an immodest but very comical picture," while Malwida von Meysenbug spoke of it as "a hideous photograph" (Sander L. Gilman, ed., *Conversations with Nietzsche: A Life in the Words of His Contemporaries*, trans. David J. Parent (New York and Oxford: Oxford UP, 1987), 147).

22 *Die Dokumente ihrer Begegnung*, 116.

23 *Die Dokumente ihrer Begegnung*, 125. The lines cited are: "Uns vom Halben zu entwöhnen / Und im Ganzen Guten Schönen / *Resolut zu leben*" (to free ourselves from half-heartedness, and in the whole, in goodness, and in beauty *to lead our lives resolutely*) (Goethe, *Gedichte in zeitlicher Folge*, ed. Heinz Nicolai [Frankfurt am Main: Insel, 1982], 528). According to Resa von Schirnhofer, Malwida von Meysenbug knew these lines, but Nietzsche did not (*Conversations with Nietzsche*, 155), but this is clearly not the case, and Carl von Gersdorff had told Nietzsche about Goethe's authorship of these lines in his letter of 8 November 1871 (*KGB* II.2, 452). See also "Preface to Richard Wagner" (Vorwort an Richard Wagner) of 1871 (*KSA* 7, 356).

24 *Die Dokumente ihrer Begegnung*, 135.

25 *Die Dokumente ihrer Begegnung*, 152; cf. *Die Dokumente ihrer Begegnung*, 266.

26 *Die Dokumente ihrer Begegnung*, 159.

27 See the so-called "Dornburger Gedichte," "Dem aufgehenden Vollmonde" (Dornburg, 25 August 1828) and "Früh wenn Thal Gebirg und Garten" (Dornburg, September 1828) (Goethe, *Gedichte in zeitlicher Folge*, 1150–51).

28 Compare with Zarathustra's resolution in his prologue: "Siehe! Dieser Becher will wieder leer werden, und Zarathustra will wieder Mensch werden" (Look! This cup wants to become empty again, and Zarathustra wants to become human again; *Z* I preface §1; *KSA* 4, 12).

29 For Elisabeth Nietzsche's perspective, see *Die Dokumente ihrer Begegnung*, 251–58.

30 See Nietzsche, Rée, Salomé, *Die Dokumente ihrer Begegnung*, 190–211; *KSB* 6, 242–45; *KSA* 10, 3[1], 53–107.

31 In his letter to Lou of 16 September 1882, Nietzsche described the possibility of the Leipzig Musik-Verein performing his setting of her text as "a little path on

which we both *together* would reach posteriority — not excluding other paths" (Das wäre so ein kleines Weglein, auf dem wir Beide *zusammen* zur Nachwelt gelangten — andre Wege vorbehalten; KB 6, 260).

[32] See *Die Dokumente ihrer Begegnung*, 119, 126, and 127.

[33] Lou Andreas-Salomé, *Lebensrückblick*, 241.

[34] See *Die Dokumente ihrer Begegnung*, 239.

[35] See *Die Dokumente ihrer Begegnung*, 239.

[36] See *Dokumente ihrer Begegnung*, 123.

[37] See Malwida von Meysenbug's letter to Lou von Salomé of 6 June 1882 (*Die Dokumente ihrer Begegnung*, 133).

[38] According to Nietzsche in his letter to Hippolyte Taine of 4 July 1887 (*KSB* 8, 107).

6: *The Gay Science*

Keith Ansell-Pearson

Introduction

The Gay Science (*Die fröhliche Wissenschaft*) was originally published in four parts or books, with a prelude in German rhymes in 1882; a fifth part, together with an appendix of songs and a preface, was added and published in 1887. Nietzsche began to compose notes for what would become *The Gay Science* in the summer of 1881, drafting a set of remarkable notes that have yet to be translated into English, many anchored around his experience of the thought of eternal recurrence.[1] Nietzsche's initial plan was for an addition to his previously published book, *Daybreak* (*Morgenröthe*), and he conceived it as his last book.[2] He wrote to his amanuensis Heinrich Köselitz, whom he called Peter Gast, at the end of January 1882 that he had recently completed books 6–8 of *Daybreak*, with the two final parts, books 9–10, to be reserved for the following winter because, as he put it, "I have not yet matured enough for the prime ideas which I shall present in these books" (ich bin noch nicht *reif* genug für die elementaren Gedanken, die ich in diesen Schluß-Büchern darstellen will; *KSB* 6, 159).[3] In particular, Nietzsche confides that there is one idea that requires a "thousand years" to mature and that he needs the strength to express it: a clear reference to the doctrine of eternal recurrence. Approximately two weeks later, however, he reported to Gast that a draft of the new book was well in process. Nietzsche was still resident in Genoa at this time, where he received a visit from his friend Paul Rée in February of 1882. Upon Rée's departure in March he made a trip to Messina in Sicily, where he wrote more poetry than prose. His return from this trip and his journey to Rome toward the end of April 1882 coincided with the beginning of his "fateful encounter" with Lou Salomé.[4] There now followed a five-month period of intense activity in Nietzsche's personal life that also involves the editing, proofreading, and publication of *The Gay Science*. Nietzsche received his first four copies of the book on 20 August 1882.

Nietzsche clearly saw the book as the final installment of his "free spirit" trilogy, for he had written on the back cover, "With this book we arrive at the conclusion of a series of writings by FRIEDRICH

NIETZSCHE, whose common goal is to erect a new image and ideal of the free spirit" (Mit diesem Buche kommt eine Reihe von Schriften FRIEDRICH NIETZSCHE'S zum Abschluss, deren gemeinsames Ziel ist, eine neues Bild und Ideal des Freigeistes aufzustellen), and then listed the two volumes *Human, All Too Human* (*Menschliches, Allzumenschliches*), *Daybreak,* and the new text. The title of the book is a rich and fertile one, suggesting the idea of a science — as well as a practice of knowledge and scholarship and an intelligence — that is gay, cheerful, and joyous. Like its predecessor *Daybreak, The Gay Science* covers myriad topics, but it differs in that it contains some of Nietzsche's grandest ideas, such as the death of God and the eternal recurrence. Indeed, Richard Schacht has argued that *The Gay Science* goes beyond the other volumes that make up the "free spirit" trilogy "in both coherence and content."[5] Schacht is surely right in his suggestion that in the book we ultimately encounter something more than the disjointed collection of aphorisms and meditations that it appears to be at first glance. "In this work," Schacht writes, "the philosopher emerges with greater clarity than in any of his previous works."[6] The book is a sustained effort to sketch the outlines of a reinterpretation of nature and humanity, one that brings Nietzsche into rapport with Spinoza's remarkably modern attempt to demystify both. Indeed, Nietzsche claimed to have discovered in the early 1880s a precursor in Spinoza. In a letter to Franz Overbeck from the end of July 1881 — close to the time when he began work on materials that would eventually find their way into *The Gay Science* — Nietzsche enumerates the points of doctrine he shares with Spinoza, such as the denial of free will, of a moral world order, and of evil, and also mentions the task of "making knowledge the most *powerful affect*" (die Erkenntniß zum *mächtigsten Affekt* zu machen; *KSB* 6, 111).[7] Indeed, a Spinozist inspiration hovers over his first remarkable sketch of eternal recurrence, which, like Spinoza's *Ethics,* is a plan for a book in five parts, culminating in a meditation on "blessedness" or beatitude.[8]

As Pierre Klossowski notes, the gay science is the fruit of "the greatest imaginable solitude,"[9] and seeks to address those rare and few solitary spirits who have seceded from society. Indeed, in the book Nietzsche invites his imagined free spirits to practice a specific "morality":

> Live in seclusion so that you *can* live for yourself. Live in *ignorance* about what seems most important to your age. [. . .] And the clamor of today, the noise of wars and revolutions should be a mere murmur for you. You will also wish to help — but only those who distress you *understand* entirely because they share with you one suffering and one hope — your friends — and only in the manner in which you help yourself. I want to make them bolder, more persevering, simpler, gayer. I want to teach them what is understood by so few today, least of all by these preachers of pity: *to share not suffering but joy.*

[Lebe im Verborgenen, damit du dir leben *kannst*! Lebe *unwissend* über Das, was deinem Zeitalter das Wichtigste dünkt! [. . .] Und das Geschrei von heute, der Lärm der Kriege und Revolutionen, soll dir ein Gemurmel sein! Du wirst auch helfen wollen: aber nur Denen, deren Noth du ganz *verstehst*, weil sie mit dir Ein Leid und Eine Hoffnung haben — deinen *Freunden*: und nur auf die Weise, wie du dir selber hilfst: — ich will sie muthiger, aushaltender, einfacher, fröhlicher machen! Ich will sie Das lehren, was jetzt so Wenige verstehen und jene Prediger des Mitleidens am wenigsten: — *die Mitfreude*! (*GS* §338; *KSA* 3, 568)]

It seems clear, as Horst Hutter has pointed out, that Nietzsche sought to found a philosophical school modeled on Plato's Academy and Epicurus's garden.[10] For some commentators, such as Hutter, Nietzsche's ultimate goal is the shaping of the future of European humanity and society, and in this conception of his philosophy the retreat into an Epicurean-inspired community of friends is merely a temporary expedient in which free spirits work on themselves so as to become philosophical legislators of a future culture. As Hutter has written, "such fraternities of free spirits would be necessary to traverse the period of nihilism until a future point in time, when direct political action would again become possible."[11]

At same time, it is clear that Nietzsche is first and foremost writing for himself. As he reveals in a letter to Erwin Rohde of 15 July 1882: "*Mihi ipsi scripsi* [I have written for myself] — and there it stands; and thus everyone should do for himself his best in his own way — that is my morality, the only remaining morality for me" (Mihi ipsi scripsi — dabei bleibt es; und so soll Jeder nach seiner *Art* für sich *sein* Bestes thun — das ist meine Moral: — die einzige, die mir noch übrig geblieben ist; *KSB* 6, 226).[12] In large part this is connected to what Nietzsche felt about questions of health, namely, that one must become one's own doctor, in the sense that one treats "soul, mind and body all at once and with the same remedies" (Seele Geist und Leib auf Ein Mal und mit denselben Mitteln; *KSB* 6, 226–27).[13] It is quite possible, Nietzsche reflects, that "others may perish using the same remedies" (Andere an meinen Mittel *zu Grunde* gehen könnten), and this is why, he continues, he exerts so much energy in warning others against him: "Especially this latest book, which is called 'the gay science,' will scare many people away from me" (Namentlich dieses letzte Buch, welches den Titel führt "die fröhliche Wissenschaft" wird Viele von mir zurückschrecken; *KSB* 6, 227).[14] In a letter of August 1882 to his former colleague at Basel, the great Swiss historian Jacob Burckhardt, Nietzsche confides that *The Gay Science* is a highly "personal" (zu persönlich) book, noting that "everything personal is indeed comic" (alles Persönliche ist eigentlich *komisch*; *KSB* 6, 234).[15]

With *The Gay Science* Nietzsche believed he had "crossed a tropic" (einen *Wendekreis* überschritten):

Everything that lies before me is new, and it will not be long before I catch sight also of the *terrifying* face of my more distant life task. This long, rich summer was for me a testing time; I took my leave of it in the best of spirits and proud, for I felt that during this time at least the ugly rift between willing and accomplishment had been bridged. There were hard demands made on my humanity, and I have become equal to the highest demands I have made on myself. This whole interim state between what was and what will be, I call "in media vita" [. . .].

[Alles liegt neu vor mir, und es wird nicht lange dauern, daß ich auch das *furchtbare* Angesicht meiner ferneren Lebens-Aufgabe zu sehen bekomme. Dieser lange reiche Sommer war für mich eine *Probe-Zeit*; ich nahm äußerst muthig und stolz von ihm Abschied, denn ich empfand für diese Zeitspanne wenigstens die sonst so häßliche Kluft zwischen Wollen und Vollbringen als *überbrückt*. Es gab *harte* Ansprüche an meine Menschlichkeit, und ich bin mir im Schwersten genug geworden. Diesen ganzen Zwischenzustand zwischen sonst und einstmals nenne ich "in media vita" [. . .]. (*KSB* 6, 255)][16]

Of course, Nietzsche did have a powerful need to write to and communicate and share with others. In a letter of December 1882, he confesses to Heinrich von Stein that he wishes to remove from human existence "some of its heartbreaking and cruel character" (etwas von seinem herzbrecherischen und grausamen Charakter; *KSB* 6, 288).[17] By the end of 1882, the ill-fated *ménage à trois* with Rée and Salomé was in tatters, and Nietzsche felt deeply bruised by the experience and the betrayals. As he confided to his friend Franz Overbeck on Christmas Day of this remarkable year in his life, he now had the chance to prove to himself what he preached, namely, that all experiences are useful, all days holy, and all people divine. Unless he could discover the alchemical trick of turning the muck into gold he would be lost.[18]

"La gaya scienza"

According to Walter Kaufmann, the title of the book has deliberate polemical overtones, for "it is meant to be anti-German, anti-professorial, anti-academic,"[19] and it goes well with the idea of the free-minded "good European" Nietzsche had been promoting since the time of *Human, All Too Human*. The title also suggests, as Kaufmann remarks, light feet, dancing, and laughter, as well as a ridicule of the "spirit of gravity." But there is also, as Robert Pippin has pointed out, in Nietzsche's project as a whole, a complicated combination of lightheartedness or cheerfulness and a sort of heaviness or gravitas. As Pippin observes, such paradoxical formulations commence early in Nietzsche's writings and continue late into them.[20] For his part, Schacht notes that, both in tone and in content, the volume merits its cheerful, even optimistic (certainly affirmative) title.[21] Thus the gay science is "a comprehensive philosophical enterprise" that considers traditional matters of philosophical inquiry (truth, knowledge, logic), revitalizes ancient philosophical concerns with ethical health and human flourishing, and extends to the domains of art, culture, religion, and morality and its value.[22] As Schacht rightly says, Nietzsche's approach to these topics is "avowedly experimental, multi-perspectival, and interpretive," while also being "cognitive in intent."[23]

"La gaya scienza" — Nietzsche added this subtitle to the text for its second edition in 1887 — draws its inspiration from a number of influences. First, there is the example of the troubadours of the Middle Ages, the Provençal poet-knights, who roamed across Europe singing, dancing, and practicing the art of poetry and who invented courtly love. In *Ecce Homo* Nietzsche reveals he chose the term "la gaya scienza" to demonstrate the unity of singer, knight, and free spirit that characterized early Provençal culture (*EH GS*; *KSA* 6, 334). In *Beyond Good and Evil* (*Jenseits von Gut und Böse*) he draws attention to the aristocratic or noble origins of "*passionate* love" (die Liebe als *Passion*), referring to the Provençal poet-knights as those "splendid, inventive people of the '*gai saber*' to whom Europe owes so much — virtually its very self" (jenen prachtvollen erfinderischen Menschen des "gai saber," denen Europa so Vieles und beinahe sich selbst verdankt; *BGE* 260; *KSA* 5, 212). Second, there is the influence of Ralph Waldo Emerson (1803–82), whom Nietzsche first read as a young schoolboy and came to cherish. For the first edition of the frontispiece of the text he used the following quotation from Emerson as an epigraph: "To the poet and the sage all things are friendly and hallowed, all experiences profitable, all days holy, and all human beings divine" (see the thirteenth paragraph of Emerson's "On History"). In a journal entry of 1841 Emerson had even referred to himself as a "professor of joyous science," but it is very doubtful that Nietzsche knew of this.[24] Third, there is the influence of the "cynical" philosopher, Diogenes of Sinope (ca. 404–423 BCE), evident in striking form, for example, in aphorism 125 on the death of God. Nietzsche is influenced by the literary style of cynicism that "mixes humor with earnestness in a serio-comic vein that is marked by caricature, sarcasm, mockery, sharp-witted wordplay, and multi-layered meanings fraught with a moral intensity that presses its message to the limits of obscenity."[25]

The gay science has two key principles: first, life as a means to knowledge; and second, knowledge as the most powerful passion (that is, a form of superior spiritual mastery). The utilization of the word "gay" is a reference to the desire to live in defiance of morality, that is, not to accept and conform to existing conventions and customs regarding how one is expected to live and love. The love that the gay scientist seeks — of life and knowledge — is a learning kind of love (see *GS* §334, entitled "One must learn to love" [Man muss lieben lernen; *KSA* 3, 559–60]). Robert Pippin has emphasized the extent to which the gay science is a knowledge of erotics, describing it as "not so much a knowledge of what love is as how to love and live so well [. . .] in some way that 'does justice' to the requirements of love and life."[26] "La gaya scienza" is, then, a kind of "love poetry," one that is intended to call to mind "an extremely idealized love and [is] engaged in not for purely aesthetic reasons but for the sake of some conversion, or seduction, and the attachments and commitments it inspires are a 'condition of life.'"[27] The book endeavors to bring together, then, the art of poetry and a new conception, light and cheerful, of disciplined knowledge. In the tradition of courtly love, the lover does not seek to transcend the ordinary, empirical world of transient things, but instead practices love as an art capable of valuing mortal objects with no contemplation of transcendence. It is this revaluation of mortal *eros* that appeals to Nietzsche when he draws inspiration from the Provençal troubadours. The gay science aims to "re-channel all the force of *eros*, all its poetic powers of idealization, into those fleeting appearances that the Platonic and Christian tradition had devalued."[28] The task is to love the empirical world of time and mortality as a world of becoming and to commit oneself to an ungodly reality and eschew the aesthetic or religious desire for "some Apart, Beyond, Outside, Above" (Abseits, Jenseits, Ausserhalb, Oberhalb; *GS* preface 2).

Both in this text and in the next, *Thus Spoke Zarathustra* (*Also sprach Zarathustra*), Nietzsche asks: how light or heavy do we feel with regard to ourselves and life? This is such a pressing question for us to determine because of what we are in the process of overcoming and becoming. The task of the gay science is to promote the scientific study of moral matters — basically, the conditions of existence of the human animal to date, including the reason, the passion, and the superstition involved in them — and to ask whether "science" can now furnish and fashion goals of existence after it has demonstrated that it can take away goals and annihilate them. Then, Nietzsche writes, "experimentation would be in order that would allow every kind of heroism to find satisfaction — centuries of experimentation that may eclipse all the great projects and sacrifices of history to date" (und dann würde ein Experimentiren am Platze sein, an dem jede Art von Heroismus sich befriedigen könnte, ein Jahrhunderte langes Experimentiren, welches alle grossen Arbeiten und Aufopferungen der bisherigen Geschichte in Schatten stellen könnte; *GS* §7; *KSA* 3, 379–80, cf. the opening aphorism of the book on the "hero" of the gay science). In short, can science build its "cyclopic buildings" (Cyklopen-Bauten) into the future and help prepare for the future? Nietzsche is in search of a "joyful" science in which there is the promise of the future and new possibilities of life and in which different energies of thinking and knowledge will find a new level of integration and synthesis, and this involves artistic energies and the practical wisdom of life joining forces with scientific thinking in an effort to cultivate "a higher organic system in relation to which scholars, physicians, artists, and legislators — as we know them at present — would have to look like paltry relics of ancient times" (ein höheres organisches System sich bildet, in Bezug auf welches der Gelehrte, der Arzt, der Künstler und der Gesetzgeber, so wie wir jetzt diese kennen, als dürftige Alterthümer erscheinen müssten!; *GS* §113; *KSA* 3, 474).

Nietzsche clearly wishes to see the cultivation of a spiritual maturity that will enable us to deal adequately with the new post-metaphysical situation in which we find ourselves and not be overcome by disillusionment and despair. In *Human, All Too Human* he had already mentioned the need in a post-metaphysical age for the requisite temperament, namely, a cheerful soul (*HA* I §34; *KSA* 2, 55). Indeed, throughout his writings, from first to last, Nietzsche can be found wrestling with the meaning of cheerfulness. The German word used in section 343 is *Heiterkeit* (*KSA* 3, 573), a word that is often used ironically in the sense, for example, of "that's going to be fun" (*das kann ja heiter werden*), as when one goes out for a walk, sees a big black cloud coming and foresees getting drenched. One takes the walk, even though one knows that risks are involved. The way in which Nietzsche presents his cheerfulness in *The Gay Science* clearly contains something of this sense, indicating a spirit of adventure and fearlessness with regard to the pursuit of knowledge. His cheerfulness has hidden depths and dimensions. In particular, it explains the peculiar sense of distance he himself feels in relation to the monstrous event of the death of the Christian God.

We find echoes of this argument in the preface to the second edition of *The Gay Science*, which Nietzsche composed in the autumn of 1886. Here he speaks as a convalescent for whom the gay science signifies the "saturnalia of a spirit" (die Saturnalien eines Geistes), a convalescent who has patiently resisted a terrible, long pressure without submitting and without hope, but who suddenly finds himself attacked by hope, including the hope for health (*GS* preface §1; *KSA* 3, 345). He states that a philosopher who has traversed many different kinds of health has gone through an equal number of philosophies, and that philosophy is nothing other than this "art of transfiguration" (Kunst der Transfiguration) by which the thinker transposes his states into a spiritual form and distance (*GS* preface §3; *KSA* 3, 349). It is certain that our trust in life has gone, and gone forever, simply because life has become a problem for us. Nietzsche counsels us, however, that we should not jump to the conclusion that this problem necessarily makes us gloomy. Love of life is still possible, only it is now like the love of a beloved object that causes doubts in us. Taking delight in the problem of life entails a highly spiritualized thinking that has overcome fear and gloominess. Nietzsche's cheerfulness stems from his experiences of knowledge, including the experience of disillusionment and despair that can result from the practice of the love of knowledge — this is the "long pressure" that needs to be resisted. Nietzsche's love of knowledge embraces the demands of this love and represents a victory, something that one has won. He will, in fact, frequently speak of gay or joyful science as a reward, for example, "a reward for a long, brave, diligent, subterranean seriousness [. . .]" (ein Lohn für einen langen, tapferen, arbeitsam und unterirdischen Ernst [. . .]; *GM* preface §7; *KSA* 5, 255). Knowledge is to be conceived in terms of a "world of dangers and victories in which heroic feelings [. . .] find places to dance and play" (eine Welt der Gefahren und Siege, in der auch die heroischen Gefühle ihre Tanz- und Tummelplätze haben; *GS* §324; *KSA* 3, 553). He posits as a principle, "*life as a means to knowledge*" (*Das Leben ein Mittel der Erkenntniss*), in which the pursuit of knowledge is not to be conducted in a spirit of duty or as a calamity (Verhängniss) or trickery (*GS* §324; *KSA* 3, 552–53). He speaks of the human intellect as "a clumsy, gloomy, creaking machine" (eine schwerfällige, finstere und knarrende Maschine), and of how the human being always seems to lose its good spirits when it thinks by becoming too serious (*GS* §327; *KSA* 3, 555). He wants to teach the intellect that it does not have to be such a machine, and to challenge the prejudice that would hold that thinking informed by laughter and gaiety is good for nothing. In a note from 1881, as he was preparing *The Gay Science*, he wrote of the need to love and promote life for the sake of knowledge and to love and promote illusion for the sake of life:

> The fundamental condition of all passion of knowledge is to give existence an aesthetic meaning, *to augment our taste for it*. Thus, we discover here a night and a day as the conditions for *our* lives: desiring knowledge and desiring error are ebb and flow. Ruled by *one* absolute, mankind would perish and *with it its capacities*.

> [Dem Dasein eine ästhetische Bedeutung geben, *unseren Geschmack an ihm mehren*, ist Grundbedingung aller Leidenschaft der Erkenntniß. So entdecken wir auch hier eine Nacht und einen Tag als Lebensbedingung für *uns*. Erkennen-wollen und Irren-wollen sind Ebbe und Fluth. Herrscht *eines* absolute, so geht der Mensch zu Grunde; und *zugleich die Fähigkeit*. *KSA* 9, 11[162], 504]

We might say that what Nietzsche came to develop and name as "gay science" is knowledge about what it is to have knowledge or to know; and this involves having our wits about us with respect to knowledge. *Wissenschaft* is the noun corresponding to the verb *wissen*, to know, and has the connotations of the ways or conduits of knowing. This is captured in the archaic English word "wis" ("to show the way"), from which we get the word "wit."[29] We also need to understand the passion (*Leiden-schaft*) that informs science (*Wissenschaft*). For Nietzsche, there has to be wisdom about science, and what he is promoting in his middle period is philosophically-minded science. Heidegger described this science as "the passion of a well-grounded mastery over the things that *confront* us and over our own way of *responding to* what confronts us" (die Leiden-schaft des gegründeten Herrseins über das, was uns *be*gegnet, ebenso wie darüber, *wie* wir dem Begegnenden *ent*gegnen).[30] For Nietzsche in *The Gay Science*, as in the previous texts of the trilogy, the emphasis is on new kinds of knowledge, including physiology, sociology, and solitudinol-ogy (see *D* §453; *KSA* 3, 274). It might be said that, while the content of Nietzsche's project is recognizable as an essential component of intel-lectual and scientific modernity, its form is something completely novel. The form of a work, however, is for Nietzsche an essential element in the teachings of a philosophical educator and innovator. *The Gay Science* con-tains some of the most beautifully crafted and thought-provoking apho-risms in Nietzsche's corpus.

The Death of God

The Gay Science is Nietzsche's first and his most complete attempt to reckon with the death of God and its consequences for Occidental humanity, although the idea is presaged in *Daybreak* (*D* §96; *KSA* 3, 87–88). It is the theme that hovers over the text as a whole, being the explicit beginning of the third and fifth books. The death is referred to in the third book's opening short aphorism, §108, and it is given a dramatic presentation in section 125. The long aphorism §109 seems to provide vital clues as to what Nietzsche thinks follows on from this death as our specific task; but it is not until the opening aphorism of book five (§343), added in 1887, that Nietzsche makes explicit which God is meant and focuses on the question of *Sinn*: what is the meaning of this event?

Aphorism 343 is devoted to the topic of Nietzsche's kind of "cheer-fulness" (Heiterkeit; *KSA* 3, 573). It carries the title "We Fearless Ones" ("Wir Furchtlosen"), which names those who pursue philosophical ques-tions free of moral prejudices and fears. It affords valuable insight into how Nietzsche positioned himself as a philosopher, namely, in the con-text of the event of God's death and the opportunities and challenges this event — which signals the collapse of the old metaphysical and moral order — presents for fearless lovers of knowledge. The aphorism speaks of an event that can fairly be considered the greatest of all recent ones, and in order to convey the full impact of it Nietzsche deploys some highly colorful imagery: a setting sun, an eclipsed sun, and a world becoming more autumnal. This event will cast a shadow; its actual eventful character will not be perceived and recognized as such by everyone, as there are many for whom it will still appear as distant; and the meaning of the event is for many still harder to grasp. It is not only that a religious faith has collapsed; rather, everything that has been built on this faith will now be shaken to the core.

However, Nietzsche says that the free-spirited philosopher can greet the news of God's death with expectation and anticipation, even hope, simply because all the daring of the true lover of knowledge is now permitted once again. Nietzsche seems to be indicating that the philosophers and free spirits have been patiently waiting for this event and are in some deep sense prepared for it. He speaks, for example, of their particular love of knowledge being possible once again. Nietzsche draws the aphorism to a close by wondering whether there has ever been such a sea as that which now opens up before us. Yet a note of caution is immediately sounded in the very next aphorism of the text, which is entitled "How we are still too pious" ("Inwiefern auch wir noch fromm sind"), where he makes clear that some new and highly demanding tasks now face all free-spirited philosophers and lovers of knowledge. How much "truth" can we now endure? What new knowledge can we now dare? What can we now "attempt"? Can we still be lovers of knowledge once the idealization and moralization of the world has been undermined and we confront a universe that is now devoid of meaning and purpose?

Let me seek to clarify the nature of the death of God and illuminate further the sense of Nietzsche's cheerfulness. It could be said that the Christian religion is built upon the death of God. It is not simply that Christ, as the Son of God, died on the cross for our sins but that God himself died on it too. Ever since, a Christian-moral culture and civilization has been mourning the death of God and has been bound to him in terms of an infinite debt. Nietzsche is not the first philosopher to speak of the death of God. Hegel writes of this death in his *Lectures on the Philosophy of Religion* (*Vorlesungen über die Philosophie der Religion*, 1827), referring to a Lutheran hymn of 1641 that contains the phrase "God himself is dead" (Gott selbst ist tot).[31] For Hegel, this expresses an awareness that the distinctively human — the finite, the fragile, and the negative — is itself a moment of the divine and is within God himself. On the one hand, Hegel says, there is the death of Christ, which means principally "that Christ was the God-man, the God who at the same time had human nature, even unto death. It is the lot of human finitude to die" (daß Christus der Gottmensch gewesen ist, der Gott, der zugleich die menschliche Natur hatte, ja bis zum Tode. Es ist das Los der menschlichen Endlichkeit, zu sterben).[32] On the other hand, a further determination is brought into play: that "*God has died, God is dead*" (Gott ist gestorben, Gott ist tot), which is "the most frightful of all thoughts" (der fürchterlichste Gedanke), since it means that "everything eternal and true *is not*, that negation is found in God" (daß alles Ewige, alles Wahre nicht ist, die *Negation selbst in Gott* ist).[33] Nietzsche's figuration of the death of God is obviously very different from Hegel's, being rooted in a different epoch and in different philosophical commitments. Gilles Deleuze, for example, says that in Nietzsche the death of God is to be understood not as a "speculative" proposition, but as a "dramatic" one. The difference is this: Nietzsche's statement contains no essential meaning, no speculative truth about the unfolding and becoming of *Geist*, but is an event or a rupture within which the statement that God is dead enjoys multiple meanings or senses, since everything depends on the forces that are brought to bear on this statement.[34]

How has this death come about, and what is its meaning for Nietzsche? In section 125 he speaks of a violent death: we have *killed* him. But this can mislead. We humans may have simply killed God in the very act of trying to understand him and subject him to practices of truth and interpretation. This, for example, is what takes place in the work of medieval thinkers such as Thomas Aquinas. Here God is held to be the source of universal intelligibility, but he himself is inscrutable and unknowable. Medieval thought sought to overcome the problem by conceiving the workings of the divine by analogy. This is our only source of knowledge of God. They called this the analogy of "proper proportionality": we can conceive of God and his products — the creation of the world — in terms of man and his products. This only works if we assume that which is fatal to assume: that the two orders are equivalent. But clearly the relation between the finite and the infinite is not continuous; the orders are different in kind. If not, then God's craftsmanship has been reduced to that of man's, and he is dead.[35] Other arguments can be evinced. God may have died from atrophy — the need for the old God is no longer felt: perhaps modern science can explain to us all we need to know about how things work. (Here one thinks of the undermining role played by Darwin's discovery of evolution by natural selection, which deeply influenced Nietzsche in his free spirit period: the most complex forms of life emerge from the most simple, and what we take to be well-designed organisms and life forms are simply the result of a blind, mechanical, and algorithmic process.)[36] Nietzsche sees God's death as being bound up with the development of truth and intellectual conscience: we reach a point when the discipline of truth forbids itself the lie of faith in God. Thus, what really triumphs over the Christian God is Christian morality itself and its concept of truthfulness, which comes to be understood more and more rigorously, in Nietzsche's words "the father confessor's refinement of the Christian conscience, translated and sublimated into scientific conscience, into intellectual cleanliness" (die Beichväter-Feinheit des christlichen Gewissens, übersetzt und sublimirt zum wissenschaftlichen Gewissen, zur intellektuellen Sauberkeit; *GS* §357; *KSA* 3, 600). Nietzsche lists what he takes to be now over for us moderns: looking at nature as if it were

proof of the goodness and governance of a divine force; interpreting history in honor of a divine reason and a testimony of a moral world order;
and interpreting one's experiences as if they were informed and guided by
providence and ordained for the salvation of one's soul (*GS* §285; *KSA*
3, 527–28). What stands against all of these things is our modern intellectual conscience: such articles of faith have simply become unbelievable
for us.

In Nietzsche the death of God means two things. On the one hand, it
means the death of the "symbolic God," that is, the death of the particular God of Christianity. Although this God has held European humanity
in bondage for two millennia and helped to breed a pathological hatred
of the human and the earth, it has also served to protect the human will
from theoretical and practical nihilism. On the other hand, it also means
that the God of theologians, philosophers, and even some scientists is also
dead, that is, the God that serves as a guarantor that the universe is not
devoid of structure, order, and purpose. In section 109, a long aphorism
that comes immediately after the very short section where, for the first
time in the book, Nietzsche mentions the death of God (§108: *KSA* 3,
467), he makes clear that there are shadows of God that must now be
vanquished. There are a number of things we now need to beware of,
such as, for example, thinking of the universe as either a living being or
a machine, thinking that there are laws of nature when there are only
necessities, thinking that death is opposed to life when what is living is
simply a rare type of what is dead, replacing the fiction of God with a cult
of matter, and so on. The world is simply, and in all eternity, "chaos."
Nietzsche argues, in short, that we now face a situation of difficult knowledge simply because we realize that none of our aesthetic and moral judgments apply to the universe. At the end of this aphorism, he calls for these
shadows of God to stop darkening the human mind, but says that this can
only come about through a thoroughgoing de-deification of nature.[37]

For Nietzsche, then, humanity has reached a point in history where
belief in God has become unbelievable. Although, as we have seen,
Nietzsche is not the first philosopher to speak of the death of God, it is
clear that he seeks to give this death a new meaning. When he speaks of
a thing's "meaning" (*Sinn*), he is speaking of its sense and direction. For
him, the death has the status of an event: the humanity that emerges in
the wake of it, and that now has the task of giving it a sense and meaning,
will be very different from the humanity that preceded it. For Nietzsche,
there is a sense in which we have to become equal to this event, hence his
emphasis on new tasks, and ultimately on a new philosophy conceived as a
"philosophy of the future" (the subtitle of *Beyond Good and Evil* of 1886
is "Prelude to a Philosophy of the Future" ["Vorspiel auf eine Philosophe
der Zukunft"]). As Schacht has noted, although the pathos of the parable
on the crazy man (*der tolle Mensch*; *GS* §125; *KSA* 3, 480–82) may have

been one Nietzsche experienced himself, it is a pathos that he overcame and left behind.[38] Moreover, as Robert Pippin has recently argued, in section or aphorism 125 Nietzsche is suggesting that the madman is "pathologically wrong" to regard the absence of God as a loss and mistaken to take on the burden of a "self-lacerating guilt," and that the "village atheists" addressed in it are too easily satisfied with a secular materialism, failing to understand "the erotic aspirations and ideals Nietzsche elsewhere treats as 'a condition of life.'"[39] Thus, two forms of pathological reaction are shown to be faulty: a melancholic theatrical guilt and the smug pose of enlightened free thinking.[40]

The Incorporation of Truth

Although Nietzsche boasted of writing on the death of God as "a godless one and an anti-metaphysician" (Gottlose und Antimetaphysiker; *GS* §344; *KSA* 3, 577), he was also careful to take himself to task for being such a monstrous thing. This is why he goes on to pose a challenge to science: what if science still rests on a metaphysical faith, for example, the faith that holds "truth" to be something divine that cannot be questioned? Nietzsche's statements on truth have perplexed many commentators on his work. He is notorious for claims such as that life is not an argument in favor of truth, since "the conditions of life might include error" (unter den Bedingungen des Lebens könnte der Irrthum sein; *GS* §121; *KSA* 3, 478), and that man's truths might simply be his "his *irrefutable* errors" (die *unwiderlegbaren* Irrthümer; *GS* §265; *KSA* 3, 518). Nietzsche himself thinks there are no stronger convictions than the ones bound up with our belief in truth. Too often he has been read insensitively on this topic, with commentators seeking to make him conform to some existing and established theory of truth and paying little attention to the distinctive manner in which he questions truth. One of Nietzsche's earliest meditations on truth is entitled "On the Pathos of Truth" ("Ueber das Pathos der Wahrheit," 1872), the very title of which shows the extent to which he always sought to approach the issue of truth in terms of our belief in truth, our desire for truth, and our will to truth. What are we doing with "truth"? What do we want from it and what do we do with it? Nietzsche takes "truth" to denote an unconditional power of knowledge and questions it on this basis.

In an important aphorism in *The Gay Science* on the "origin of knowledge" (Ursprung der Erkenntniss; *GS* §110; *KSA* 3, 469), we find Nietzsche developing an evolutionary account of the emergence of truth and asking some novel questions concerning our valuation of it. We exist today in a situation where knowledge itself has now become a part of life. A preoccupation with truth actually appeared late in the evolution of human life and was for a long time held to be the weakest form of knowledge because humans found it hard to endure it as a practice of living. In the story Nietzsche tells in this aphorism, for the greater part of its evolutionary history the human animal has survived, prospered even, by incorporating a set of basic errors that became for it a set of erroneous articles of faith, such as that there are enduring things and that things are what we at first take them to be. In the section that immediately comes after *GS* §110, he presents a quasi-Darwinian account of the origins and development of our basic ways of thinking. For example, to be able to think always in terms of identity proves helpful in the struggle for survival because it means things in the environment can be recognized and acted upon quickly. To see only a perpetual becoming everywhere would be disastrous for the evolution of a species. As Nietzsche points out, "the beings who did not see exactly had a head start over those who saw everything 'in a flux'" (die nicht genau sehenden Wesen hatten einen Vorsprung vor denen, welches Alles 'im Flusse' sahen; *GS* §111; *KSA* 3, 472). What has so far determined the strength or power of knowledge is not its degree of truth, as we might suppose, but rather its character as a condition of life. And wherever life and knowledge came into conflict, denial and doubt were taken to be expressions of madness. However, a new situation has come into being in which the quest for knowledge and the striving for the true have taken their rightful place among the most fundamental needs, to the point where we now have techniques and disciplines of scrutiny, of denial, and of suspicion. Nietzsche brings the aphorism to a close by saying that the thinker today is "the being in whom the drive to truth and those life-preserving errors are fighting their first battle" (das ist jetzt das Wesen, in dem der Trieb zur Wahrheit und jene lebenerhaltenden Irrthümer ihren ersten Kampf kämpfen; *GS* §110; *KSA* 3, 471). Such a battle is now taking place because the striving for the true has also shown itself to be a life-preserving and life-enhancing force. In order to make further progress with truth, it is necessary to conduct an experiment in a new kind of incorporation (*Einverleibung*).

The German word *Einverleibung* literally means a taking-into-the-body (*Leib*). The experiment Nietzsche has in mind is one of finding out just what is involved in learning to live in the space or horizon of truth. Incorporating or ingesting truth does not so much mean incorporating a set of specific or actual truths. Rather, it involves denoting "truth" as a practice and grasping what is involved in this practice, namely, permanent skepticism, suspension of belief, doubt, holding things at a distance and subjecting them to scrutiny, etc. Can there be a diet of truth and knowledge? Hitherto human beings have incorporated only errors, errors that are rooted in conditions of adaptive existence. The question Nietzsche now poses for us is whether we can learn to incorporate truth as a style of living and a form of human practice, and in this respect Nietzsche is continuing a line of reflection he had already broached in his previous book, *Daybreak*. There he had reflected on the reason for our ambivalent stance toward errors. On the one hand, it is through errors that humanity has been elevated and has excelled itself again and again, for example, through errors as to its descent, uniqueness, and destiny (*D* §425; *KSA* 3, 261, cf. *HA* I §29; *KSA* 2, 49–50). On the other hand, it has to be noted that it is through the same errors that unspeakable amounts of suffering, persecution, suspicion, and misery have come into the world. Our moralities and modes of thought do not wed us to the earth as a site of dwelling and thinking; rather, we consider ourselves "too good and too significant for the earth" (zu gut und zu bedeutend für die Erde), as if we were paying it only a passing visit. At the same time as alerting us to the dangers of our errors, Nietzsche also asks why it should be considered desirable that truth *alone* should rule and be omnipotent. Although we can esteem it as a force, even a great one, we should not allow it to rule over us in some tyrannical fashion. Much healthier is to allow truth to have opponents, and for us to find relief from it from time to time and be at liberty to reside knowingly in "untruth." Failure to place truth within a rich economy of life will make it, and ourselves in the process, "boring, powerless, and tasteless" (langweilig, kraft- und geschmacklos; *D* §507; *KSA* 3, 297, cf. *GS* §107 on our "ultimate gratitude to art" [unsere letzte Dankbarkeit gegen die Kunst; *KSA* 3, 464]).

With his question and experiment in *The Gay Science* concerning the incorporation of truth, Nietzsche posed a major challenge to humankind. Perhaps, as Rüdiger Safranski has hinted, it will take a significant period of time before the ultimate truth can be incorporated by humankind, namely the extent to which everything is implicated in becoming, and that becoming is devoid of purpose, substance, and meaning: "Although we may have a Copernican worldview — and in our era an Einsteinian one — when it comes to incorporation, we are still Ptolemaists."[41]

Ethics

Nietzsche seems to have laid special importance on book 4 of *The Gay Science*, which can, I think, be read as constituting Nietzsche's ethics. In the aforementioned letter to Burckhardt of August 1882, Nietzsche was keen that Burckhardt read book 4 "to see if it *communicates itself* as a coherent whole" (um zu wissen, ob er als Ganzes *sich mittheilt*; *KSB* 6, 235).[42]

Nietzsche expresses his opposition to any ethics that would draw its inspiration from the negative virtues. He says that he abhors every morality that says "Do not do this! Renounce! Overcome yourself!" (Thue diess nicht! Entsage! Ueberwinde dich!; *GS* §304; *KSA* 3, 542). What he is well disposed toward, he continues, is a morality that impels one "to do something again and again from morning till evening, and to dream of it at night" (Etwas zu thun und wieder zu thun und von früh bis Abend, und Nachts davon zu träumen), but to think of nothing else other than doing it well, "as well as *I* alone can" (so gut als es eben *mir* allein möglich ist! *GS* §304; *KSA* 3, 542). When we live this way, he says, the things that do not belong to such a life drop off without hate or reluctance. The task, then, is not to strive for an impoverishment of our lives with open eyes, as the negative virtues teach. Rather, we should fix our eyes forwards, not sideways, backwards, or downwards, and in living like this we will not even notice those things in our lives that have taken their leave. Nietzsche invites us to reflect on the history of our everyday life by considering the habits it is made up of: are they the product of innumerable little cowardices and lazinesses or of our courage and innovative reason? We cannot find out the answer to the question by relying upon the judgment we may receive from other people, since it is possible to imagine receiving doses of praise, and such praise is only of benefit for those who merely want a good conscience (*GS* §308; *KSA* 3, 545). Nietzsche writes of making our experiences a matter of conscience for our knowledge, which entails practicing a type of honesty (*Redlichkeit*) that is quite alien to founders of religion and moral systems. It requires being conscientious through knowledge: "What did I really experience? What happened in me and around me at the time? Was my reason bright enough?" (Was habe ich eigentlich erlebt? Was gieng damals in mir und um mich vor? War meine Vernunft hell genug? *GS* §319: *KSA* 3, 551). Those who are thirsty for reason and knowledge want to face their experiences as sternly as a scientific experiment; they want to be their own experiments and guinea-pigs.

In section 335 Nietzsche focuses attention on how difficult it is for us to follow the Delphic oracle's admonition, "know thyself," and to observe ourselves adequately. The aphorism is entitled "Long live physics!" ("Hoch die Physik!") and its opening questions make it clear that, by physics, Nietzsche simply means the methods and techniques of observation and self-observation. In becoming the ones that we are — unique, singular, and incomparable, as Nietzsche puts it — we need to become discoverers of how things actually work, since the ethical task of self-creation and self-legislation cannot be one of romantic fantasy. At the end of the aphorism he argues that we can no longer posit valuations and ideals either in ignorance of or in contradiction to what we discover to be lawful and necessary in the world. This "compulsion" (Zwang) to physics places a constraint on creation, and what binds us to it is our honesty or probity (*GS* §335; *KSA* 3, 560–64).

Nietzsche has already spoken of this virtue of probity in section 319 (*KSA* 3, 550–51), and he says that it names the voice of a superior form of conscience behind our conscience (in *Daybreak*, *Redlichkeit* — that is, honesty — is said to be our youngest virtue [*D* §456; *KSA* 3, 275]). In section 319, Nietzsche subjects our claim to being sincere and upright to the scrutiny of the intellectual conscience (the conscience of scientific reason in part). We need to put our claims to sincerity to the test, and in part this test is physics, where "physics" denotes learning the character of our moral judgment and evaluations (for example, their prehistory in the instincts, the likes and dislikes, and so on). Nietzsche invites us to consider the way in which we often declare ourselves to be good because we have judged a course of action to be right, which we then think entitles us to label the action as "moral." To justify that we have done the right action, one that we can label as moral, we often appeal to our conscience. But this is to assume that our conscience is infallible and that it always speaks morally (truthfully) to us. Moreover, do we not require another conscience to assess the adequacy of this belief, an intellectual conscience, which would be the conscience behind our conscience? Any judgment we make that "this is right" has a prehistory in our drives, inclinations, aversions, and experiences to date, as well as what we have failed to experience. As Nietzsche points out, there are many different ways we can listen to our conscience, and among them, the method of relying upon the firmness of our moral judgment is inadequate, because this firmness could be evidence of our personal abjectness or lack of a personality. Moreover, our so-called moral strength might have its source in our stubbornness or in our inability to envisage new ideals.

For Nietzsche, reliance upon a universal law in order to acquire a firm moral judgment, as in Kant's categorical imperative, shows that one has neither discovered oneself nor created for oneself one's own ideal. Self-knowledge consists in learning that every act we perform is unique and unrepeatable: every act we perform is done in a unique and unrepeatable way, and all prescriptions of action cover only their rough exterior and so yield only a deceptive appearance of sameness. He insists that, while our opinions and valuations constitute powerful levers in the machinery of our actions, the actual law of the mechanism of each action is unknowable. It is here that knowledge reaches a limit. At this point in his argument Nietzsche proposes a change in how we conceive of ourselves and relate to others. This will involve purifying ourselves of our opinions and value judgments and creating our own new tables of good. These tasks are to become our new limit, and should lead to a situation where we cease to brood over the moral value of our actions. And when we hear people engaging in moral chatter about others, sitting in moral judgment, it will offend our taste to the point where we experience nausea.

Nietzsche is saying in this aphorism that when we become ourselves, we are, in fact, existing beyond morality, but only where morality is understood in an all-too-easy manner: as that which makes assumptions about its universally binding character, about its claim to knowledge when, in fact, it has very little knowledge to support its command (the "ought"), and so on. If, however, morality is taken to mean attention and devotion to the practice of "continual self-command and self-overcoming" in both great and small things (see *HA* WS §45 and §212; *KSA* 2, 573–74 and 645), then Nietzsche is advocating the importance of being moral or ethical (the need to practice self-command, for example, and achieve mastery of oneself and one's affects).

Eternal Recurrence

Section 341 is the penultimate aphorism of the fourth and final book of the original edition of the text (*KSA* 3, 570). It is sandwiched between an aphorism on the last words of Socrates ("The dying Socrates" ["Der sterbende Sokrates"; *GS* §340; *KSA* 3, 569]) and one entitled "The Tragedy Begins" (*"Incipit tragoedia"*; *GS* §342; *KSA* 3, 571), where the figure of Zarathustra is first introduced in Nietzsche's writings. It is Nietzsche's first published presentation of the idea of the eternal recurrence of the same (later presentations can be found in *Zarathustra*, in "Of the Vision and the Riddle" ["Vom Gesicht und Räthsel"; *KSA* 4, 197–202] and "The Convalescent" ["Der Genesende"; *KSA* 4, 270–77], in *Beyond Good and Evil*, §56 [*KSA* 5, 74–75], and in *Twilight of the Idols* [*Götzen-Dämmerung*], "What I Owe to the Ancients," §4–§5 [*KSA* 6, 158–60]). Aphorism 342 signals the next move in Nietzsche's thought, namely the *Untergang* (or descent) of Zarathustra (*KSA* 3, 571). So the presentation of eternal recurrence in *The Gay Science* comes at the end or as the culmination of a number of projects: the end of book 4 of the text — indeed, the end of the first edition of the text itself — and the final destination point of the "free spirit" trilogy as a whole.

The aphorism announces a thought experiment: what if some day or night a demon were to steal after us and into our most solitary solitude, and say to us: "This life, as you now live it, and have lived it, you will have to live once more and innumerable times more" (Dieses Leben, wie du es jetzt lebst und gelebt hast, wirst du noch einmal und noch unzählige Male leben müssen), with every pain and every joy and everything great and small in our life returning to us in the same succession and sequence, including the spider and moonlight that appears for us as we experience this moment. "The eternal hourglass of existence is turned upside down again and again, and you with it, speck of dust!" (Die ewige Sanduhr des Daseins wird immer wieder umgedreht — und du mit ihr, Stäubchen vom Staube!; *GS* §341; *KSA* 3, 341). Towards the end of the aphorism it is suggested that if this thought gained "possession" of us, it would either change us as we are or perhaps even crush us, for a weighty question would lie upon our actions: do we desire this once more and innumerable times more? How well disposed to ourselves and to life would we have to become to desire nothing more ardently than this "ultimate eternal confirmation and seal" (letzten ewigen Bestätigung und Besiegelung)?

With respect to this aphorism, several things need to be thought about. First, the title in German is literally "The Greatest Heavyweight" ("Das grösste Schwergewicht"), and Nietzsche intends the boxing reference: it is as if we are to come to blows with the thought and so test ourselves in relation to it. Second, the opening gambit, "what if?," makes it clear that eternal recurrence is being offered as an experiment or trial. In a note from the 1880s, Nietzsche says: "This is now the epoch of experiments: I am conducting a great trial: *who can stand the thought of eternal recurrence?* Whoever is not crushed by the proposition, 'there is no redemption,' should die out" (Zeitalter der Versuche. Ich mache die grosse Probe: *wer hält den Gedanken der ewigen Wiederkunft aus?* — Wer zu vernichten ist mit dem Satz 'es giebt keine Erlösung', der soll aussterben; KSA 11, 25[290], 85). Third, why is it a demon who brings the thought? It is important to note that the demon catches us by surprise; we do not will the coming of this terrifying thought. Fourth, the imagery of the spider and the moonlight is typical death-imagery in Nietzsche associated with sleep, tombs, Hades, and so on. Fifth, the way the human is addressed as a speck of dust implies cognizance of our cosmic insignificance and that the challenge is to be equal to this, not to wail in despair and be crushed by it, to lament that "all is in vain." The task, as hinted at in the conclusion to the aphorism, is instead to become well disposed toward life and ourselves (which has already been figured in several aphorisms in book 4 prior to this point; see, for example, the aphorism entitled "Will and Wave" ["Wille und Welle"; GS §310; KSA 3, 546]).

In its initial articulation, eternal recurrence is Nietzsche's response to the set of problems that he has worked through in his free-spirit period of 1878–82, especially the death of God. Nietzsche speaks of our having lost the center of gravity — the heaviest weight — that allowed us to live. The old teaching offered by the Christian-moral hypothesis placed the center of gravity outside life, in a beyond and in an otherworldly God. The new teaching seeks to provide a new center of gravity focused on the immanent conditions and form of life, whereas religion has hitherto taught human beings to despise this life as merely transitory and to cast their hopes on an indeterminate other life. For Nietzsche, however, we cannot now rest content with a shallow atheism that encourages us to devote all our energies of knowledge and being to a fleeting life. Rather, the task, he says, is to impress the likeness of eternity on our lives. Nietzsche offers a teaching that says that the task is to live one's life in such a way that one wants to live it again, and to do this it is necessary to find out what gives one the highest feeling (KSA 9, 11[163], 504–5). The doctrine is a charitable one: it has no hell and no threats; it apportions neither merit nor blame (KSA 9, 11[144], 496). The most ordinary instinct of life is the first to give its assent. In *The Gay Science* §341, Nietzsche chose a particular form of address to communicate his thought. The words come from the strange voice of a demon who "steals" into our life at a particular hour, that of our most solitary solitude, and addresses us as specks of dust. Perhaps the strongest connection to be made is with the well-known demon of Socrates. The Greek term *daimon* means divider or allotter, and from Homer onward it refers to the operator of unanticipated and intrusive events in life; the adjective *daimonios* means strange and uncanny. Later, the word came also to acquire the meaning of a guardian or protector, a spirit who accompanies a person's life and brings either luck or misfortune. In Plato, the *daimon* operates as an intermediary between God and human beings, and this conception was taken up by all subsequent demonologies. Indeed, Socrates spoke of his demon in terms of being subject to a divine or supernatural experience, in which a voice came to him to dissuade him from what he was proposing to do. In Nietzsche's aphorism the words of the demon are designed neither to persuade nor dissuade; rather, they give us the means to find out something essential concerning our disposition toward life and the things we desire to will.

It has been suggested that Nietzsche conceived eternal return as working as a kind of deathbed revelation in which the loneliest loneliness refers to the actual hour of one's death. The fact that this aphorism on the eternal return comes after one on the last words of Socrates gives, I think, good grounds for this interpretation.[43] Would we be able at the end of our lives to look back and affirm everything great and small that has taken place in them, to the point where we would want to live those lives again and would be willing to live them in exactly the same sequences? Could we die happy, facing the prospect of life's eternal recurrence? Or would our desire express itself in the wish to escape from life and be relieved of it?

Nietzsche was intrigued by the image of the dying Socrates. He deals with it in his first work, *The Birth of Tragedy* (*Die Geburt der Tragödie*; see §15; *KSA* 1, 97–102) and returns to it in one of his last texts, *Twilight of the Idols*, in the section entitled "The Problem of Socrates" ("Das Problem des Sokrates"; §1 and §12; *KSA* 6, 67–68). In *The Gay Science* §240, Nietzsche states that he admires Socrates for his courage and wisdom in everything he said — and did not say. However, he says that he also wishes Socrates had remained taciturn at the last moment of his life when he is said to have uttered the words: "O Crito, I owe Asclepius a rooster; pray do not forget to pay the debt" (Plato, *Phaedo*, 118). Asclepius was the Greek god of healing and medicine, and the customary way of expressing thanks to him for the curing of an illness would have been to offer a rooster in sacrifice. There have been several different interpretations of the meaning of Socrates's last words; for example, as indicating that his soul has been healed, or that he is presenting a challenge to the Pythagoreans he is addressing, Simmias and Cebes, who would have objected to any maltreatment of animals, whose souls may be one's own ancestors. Socrates's challenge consisted in claiming that one is only injuring the body. Nietzsche reads the last words of the dying Socrates as expressing a terrible complaint against life: life is one long illness, and death offers a release from it.

In the *Phaedo*, Socrates has no problem accepting his death and not being intimidated by it, simply because he conceives the philosopher as one who lives in a state as close as possible to death. The true profession of the philosopher is that of dying (*Phaedo*, 67e). This is because the philosopher devotes his life to the attempt to free the soul from the body — from its loves, desires, fears and fancies — and to divorce true knowledge from the deceptions of our sense perception. To devote oneself to philosophy consists in nothing other than preparing the self for dying and death. It is thus wholly appropriate that Socrates mark the end of his life with a thanksgiving sacrifice to the god of medicine. By contrast, Nietzsche says in *The Gay Science* that *his* focus is on life, not death, and that with regard to human beings, "I should like very much to do something that would make the thought of life even a hundred times more appealing to them" (Ich möchte gern Etwas dazu thun, ihnen den Gedanken an das Leben noch hundertmal *denkenswerther* zu machen; *GS* §278; *KSA* 3, 523).

There are two main parts to Nietzsche's presentation in section 341. In its first part, a demon tells us that we shall have to re-live the life we have lived not just once more, but innumerable times with nothing new in it, and everything (however small or great) that has marked it will come back to us in the same sequence. We are then asked in the aphorism's second part to consider how we would respond. To perceive the promise of this aphorism's thought, however, two things are needed. First, we must once have experienced a moment so tremendous that it would be possible for us to greet the thought as a divine one worthy of being affirmed. Second, there is the quite different issue of the thought of eternal recurrence gaining power over us, and for this we need to want to discover ourselves and become the ones that we are. Supposing it did, a peculiar kind of question in each and every thing would come to lie upon our actions as the heaviest weight.

In one sketch from 1881 it is clear that Nietzsche conceived the idea as working as a kind of regulating practical rule, one that can play a supervening role in all our other thoughts. In another sketch, for example, which seems to be an early version of what becames the second part of *The Gay Science* §341, he offers the thought as a response to a well-known philosophical problem: if everything is necessary, how can I exert some influence on my actions? He writes in a clear conception of eternal recurrence as an ethical doctrine:

> Thought and belief are a weight pressing down on you as much as and even more than any other weight. You say that food, a place, air,

society transform and condition you: well your opinions do so even more, since it is they that determine your choice of food, place, air, society. If you incorporate this thought within you, amongst your other thoughts, it will transform you. The question "am I certain I want to do it an infinite number of times?" will become for you the *heaviest* weight in everything that you will.

[Der Gedanke und Glaube ist ein Schwergewicht, welches neben allen anderen Gewichten auf dich drückt und mehr als sie. Du sagst, dass Nahrung Ort Luft Gesellschaft dich wandeln und bestimmen? Nun, deine Meinungen thun es noch mehr, denn diese bestimmen dich zu dieser Nahrung Ort Luft Gesellschaft. — Wenn du dir den Gedanken der Gedanken einverleibst, so wird er dich verwandeln. Die Frage bei allem, was du thun willst: "ist es so, dass ich es unzählige Male thun will?" ist das *grösste* Schwergewicht. *KSA* 9, 11[143], 496]

Finally, what of the ultimate eternal confirmation and seal? Why the *eternal*?[44] If we truly love something, then we want it again and again; if we do not want its repetition, then we do not really want it, not fully and unreservedly (examples of this might be the little pleasures of life, the half-satisfactions, the world of semi-wants). We all know the saying "See Rome and die," which names the experience of being in the presence of something of such enchanting beauty that we no longer desire anything else. We are so fulfilled that we are prepared to die. Nietzsche wants us, however, to attain a state where we can say of life: "Was that it? Well then, once more and innumerable times more!" This is what is at work in the presentation Nietzsche provides in *Beyond Good and Evil*, §56, of seeing a drama or hearing a musical performance, and declaring loudly "da capo" (from the beginning) not just to ourselves but to the whole drama. To say "yes" as the highest formula of affirmation attainable is to include the repetition of the "yes." It is this "again and again" that confirms and seals.

Conclusion

The Gay Science has long been admired as one of Nietzsche's most beautifully composed books, with one commentator declaring it to be "probably his most important."[45] It is a highly congenial and personal work, one that Nietzsche refers to as "his most *medial* book," standing as it does at the midpoint of his life and serving as a fulcrum for much of his subsequent thought.[46] Nietzsche reached a crisis in his life at the end of 1882, but he was indeed soon to turn the muck of his life into gold — in the form of the extraordinary philosophical riches of his next book, *Thus Spoke Zarathustra* (1883–85). This work, which Nietzsche himself regarded as his most important, represents in many ways a dramatic working out of much that he had accomplished in the free-spirit trilogy, including the announcement of the death of God and the search for a new center of gravity to existence (eternal recurrence) and a new goal for existence (the *Übermensch*). *The Gay Science* thus brings to a close an immensely fertile period in Nietzsche's writing, with multiple transformations taking place and new dawns presaged. After *The Gay Science*, as Pippin notes, Nietzsche's themes become even broader, with the conditions relevant to becoming a free spirit more comprehensive, as he turns to write the books most responsible for his reputation, notably, *Zarathustra, Beyond Good and Evil*, and *On the Genealogy of Morality (Zur Genealogie der Moral)*.[47] *The Gay Science* displays, like the previous texts of the free-spirit trilogy, Nietzsche the brilliant psychologist at work, mining and undermining humankind's prejudices and fears. Pippin is surely right in suggesting that it is this Nietzsche, and not Heidegger's bombastic designation of him as "the last metaphysician of the West" (der *letzte Metaphysiker des Abendlandes*) that needs to occupy our attention today,[48] and this makes *The Gay Science* all the more important as a text to read and to study closely.

In his appreciation of the text, Richard Schacht suggests that it is a mystery why it has not received more attention and why it does not figure more centrally in interpretations of Nietzsche's philosophy.[49] In it, he thinks, we find the essential philosophical Nietzsche. Moreover, he suggests that the cause of understanding Nietzsche would be significantly advanced if the rest of his corpus were read in relation to it and construed in the light of what he does and writes in it. However, there are clear signs that this situation is changing, with the publication of the first guide to the text in 2010, and with more such guides on their way.[50] In terms of both its content and coherence, *The Gay Science* represents the attainment of a new intellectual and personal maturity on Nietzsche's part: he seeks to embrace the love of fate, to be one of those who "learn more and more to see as beautiful what is necessary in things" (immer mehr lernen, das Nothwendige an den Dingen als das Schöne sehen; *GS* §276: *KSA* 3, 521), and he refuses to be disappointed by life, but rather finds it more desirable and mysterious every year (*GS* §324; *KSA* 3, 552–53). However, even greater tasks lay ahead of him at this stage in his intellectual odyssey, and many more philosophical and literary riches were to follow in the wake of this remarkable, enigmatic, and beautiful book.

Notes

[1] For a small selection of these notes translated into English, see Keith Ansell-Pearson and Duncan Large, *The Nietzsche Reader* (Malden, MA: Blackwell, 2006), 238–41.

[2] See Walter Kaufmann, "Translator's Introduction" to *The Gay Science*, trans. Walter Kaufmann (New York: Random House, 1974), 3–26 (here: 19).

[3] Cited in William H. Schaberg, *The Nietzsche Canon: A Publication History and Bibliography* (Chicago: U of Chicago P, 1995), 83; see also Kaufmann, "Translator's Introduction," *Gay Science*, 18.

[4] See Schaberg, *The Nietzsche Canon*, 84. For insight into Nietzsche's relationship to Salomé, see the biographies by Curtis Cate, *Friedrich Nietzsche* (London: Hutchinson, 2002), 320–43, and Julian Young, *Nietzsche: An Intellectual Biography* (Cambridge: Cambridge UP, 2010), 339–57.

[5] Richard Schacht, "How to Naturalize Cheerfully: Nietzsche's *Fröhliche Wissenschaft*," in Schacht, *Making Sense of Nietzsche* (Urbana: U of Illinois P, 1995), 187–206 (here: 187).

[6] Schacht, "How to Naturalize Cheerfully," 187.

[7] *Selected Letters of Friedrich Nietzsche*, trans. and ed. Christopher Middleton (Indianapolis: Hackett, 1996), 177. As Yirmiyahu Yovel points out, there are important differences between Spinoza and Nietzsche in their conceptions of knowledge. For Spinoza the immediate affective tone of knowledge is joy (a feeling of the enhanced power of life), whereas in Nietzsche the painful nature of knowledge is repeatedly stressed (indeed, Nietzsche measures the worth of a person by how much "truth" he or she can bear and endure). For Nietzsche, then, knowledge — in the sense of critical enlightenment and disillusionment — is a source of suffering and primarily a temptation to despair, and this means that the gay science, or joyful knowledge, is "a task and goal," not the "normal outcome." See Yirmiyahu Yovel, *Spinoza and Other Heretics: The Adventures of Immanence* (Princeton, NJ: Princeton UP, 1989), 106.

[8] See *The Nietzsche Reader*, 238–39; and for further insight, see Keith Ansell-Pearson, "The Incorporation of Truth: Towards the Overhuman," in *A Companion to Nietzsche*, ed. Ansell-Pearson (Malden, MA: Blackwell, 2006), 230–50.

[9] Pierre Klossowski, "On Some Fundamental Themes of Nietzsche's *Gaya Scienza*," in Klossowski, *Such a Deathly Desire*, trans. Russell Ford (New York: SUNY Press, 2007), 16.

[10] Horst Hutter, *Shaping the Future: Nietzsche's New Regime of the Soul and Its Ascetic Practices* (Lanham, MD: Lexington Books, 2006), 4.

[11] Hutter, *Shaping the Future*, 5.

[12] Nietzsche, *Selected Letters*, 187.

[13] Nietzsche, *Selected Letters*, 187.

[14] Nietzsche, *Selected Letters*, 187.

[15] Nietzsche, *Selected Letters*, 190.

[16] Letter to Franz Overbeck, September 1882, in *Selected Letters*, 193.

[17] Nietzsche, *Selected Letters*, 197.

[18] Nietzsche, *Selected Letters*, 199.

[19] Kaufmann, "Translator's Introduction," in *The Gay Science*, 7.

[20] Robert B. Pippin, *Nietzsche, Psychology, and First Philosophy* (Chicago: U of Chicago P, 2010), 36.

[21] Schacht, "How to Philosophize Cheerfully," 188.

[22] Schacht, "How to Philosophize Cheerfully," 191.

[23] Schacht, "How to Philosophize Cheerfully," 191.

[24] For some details see Kaufmann, Introduction, *The Gay Science*, 7–13; see also Pippin, who refers to Thomas Carlyle's contrast between a "gay science" and the "dismal sciences" as a possible influence (*Nietzsche, Psychology, and First Philosophy*, 34).

[25] Charles Bambach, "Nietzsche's Madman Parable: A Cynical Reading," *American Catholic Philosophical Quarterly* 84:2 (2010): 441–57 (443).

[26] Pippin, *Nietzsche, Psychology, and First Philosophy*, 35.

[27] Pippin, *Nietzsche, Psychology, and First Philosophy*, 41.

[28] Michael Ure, *Nietzsche's "The Gay Science": An Introduction* (Cambridge: Cambridge UP, forthcoming).

[29] On these points see Babette E. Babich, "Nietzsche's 'Gay' Science," in Ansell-Pearson, *A Companion to Nietzsche*, 97–115.

[30] Martin Heidegger, *Nietzsche*, ed. David Farrell Krell, trans. David Farrell Krell et al., 4 vols. in 2 (San Francisco: Harper and Row, 1979–87), 2 (vols. 1 and 2): 20; *Nietzsche*, 2 vols. (Pfullingen: Neske, 1961), 1:271.

[31] G. W. F. Hegel, *Werke in 20 Bänden*, ed. Eva Moldenhauer and Karl Markus Michel, 20 vols. (Frankfurt am Main: Suhrkamp, 1986), 17:297.

[32] Hegel, *Werke*, 17:289; *The Hegel Reader*, ed. Stephen Houlgate (Oxford: Basil Blackwell, 1998), 497–98.

[33] Hegel, *Werke*, 17: 91; *The Hegel Reader*, ed. Houlgate, 497–98.

[34] Gilles Deleuze, *Nietzsche and Philosophy*, trans. Hugh Tomlinson (London: Continuum, 1983), 152–56.

[35] For further insight on these points, see the analysis in David B. Allison, "The Gay Science," in Allison, *Reading the New Nietzsche* (Lanham, MD: Rowman and Littlefield, 2001), 71–111 (esp. 94–95).

[36] For Darwin's influence on Nietzsche in his "free spirit" trilogy period, see Dirk S. Johnson, "On the Way to the 'Anti-Darwin': Nietzsche's Darwinian Meditations in the Middle Period," *Tijdschrift voor Filosofie* 65 (2003): 657–79.

[37] For further insight into section 109, see Heidegger, *Nietzsche*, trans. David Farrell Krell, 2 (vols. 3 and 4): 90–97; *Nietzsche*, 1:342–54; Jill Marsden, *After Nietzsche* (Basingstoke: Palgrave Macmillan, 2002), 11–13; and Christoph Cox, *Nietzsche, Naturalism, and Interpretation* (Berkeley: U of California P, 1999), 101–5.

[38] Compare Nietzsche on nihilism, where he presents himself as "the first perfect nihilist of Europe who, however, has even now lived through the whole of nihilism, to the end, leaving it behind, outside himself" (der erste vollkommene Nihilist Europas, der aber den Nihilismus selbst schon in sich zu Ende gelebt hat, — der ihn hinter sich, unter sich, außer sich hat; *WP* preface §3; *KSA* 13, 11[411], 190).

[39] Pippin, *Nietzsche, Psychology, and First Philosophy*, 51.

[40] Pippin, *Nietzsche, Psychology, and First Philosophy*, 54.

[41] Rüdiger Safranski, *Nietzsche: An Intellectual Biography*, trans. Shelley Frisch (New York: Norton, 2002), 237.

[42] Nietzsche, *Selected Letters*, 191.

[43] See Paul S. Loeb, "The Moment of Tragic Death in Nietzsche's Dionysian Doctrine of Eternal Recurrence: An Exegesis of Aphorism 341 in *The Gay Science*," *International Studies in Philosophy* 30/3 (1998): 131–43.

[44] In this part of my treatment of eternal recurrence I draw on the essay by Eric Oger, "The Eternal Return as Crucial Test," *Journal of Nietzsche Studies* 14 (1997): 1–18 (here: 13).

[45] See Allison, "The Gay Science," 71.

[46] Allison, "The Gay Science," 71.

[47] Pippin, *Nietzsche, Psychology, and First Philosophy*, 33n18.

[48] Pippin, *Nietzsche, Psychology, and First Philosophy*, 9; see Heidegger, *Nietzsche*, trans. David Farrell Krell, 2 (vols. 3 and 4): 8; *Nietzsche*, 1:480.

[49] Schacht, "How to Philosophize Cheerfully," 189.

[50] See Monika. M. Langer, *Nietzsche's "The Gay Science": Dancing Coherence* (Basingstoke: Palgrave Macmillan, 2010); and Michael Ure, *Nietzsche's "The Gay Science": An Introduction* (Cambridge: Cambridge UP, forthcoming). See also Kathleen Higgins, *Comic Relief: Nietzsche's "Gay Science"* (Oxford: Oxford UP, 2000).

Link to *Zarathustra*

The catastrophic breakdown in relations with family and friends alike after the débâcle with Lou von Salomé and Paul Rée left Nietzsche isolated from almost everyone in his life. After his mother accused him of having besmirched the name of his father, Nietzsche packed his bags and left Naumburg for Leipzig in September 1882 (cf. *KSB* 6, 256 and 326); his sister, Elisabeth, was seemingly unable to understand why Nietzsche was so upset by this remark, but we should remember Nietzsche's identification with his father, following his early death. Although the Pindaric imperative, "become who you are" that Nietzsche had earlier drawn to Lou von Salomé's attention (*KSB* 6, 203) was one that he continued to urge upon her in the form of her "emancipation from her emancipation" (*schließlich muß man sich noch von dieser Emancipation emancipiren*; *KSB* 6, 247–48), his discovery that Lou was, as he told Malwida von Meysenbug, "almost a caricature of what I admire as an ideal" (beinahe die Caricatur dessen, was ich als Ideal verehre; *KSB* 6, 315), had led to complete disillusionment; Nietzsche's attitude became increasingly grim and bleak. Consumed by his emotions "in the *school of the affects*" (in der *Schule der Affekte*), and plagued by bad headaches and migraines, he turned to opium for relief (*KSB* 6, 306–7).

After a little more than two months in Leipzig (from 9 September to 15 November 1882), he returned to Rapallo for the winter. Not far from Rapallo lies Portofino, and in the autumn of 1882 Nietzsche gave the name of this town on the Genovese and Ligurian coast to a short poem as its title:

Portofino.

Here I sit, waiting — waiting? But for nothing,
Beyond good and evil, and for the light
No more longing than for the darkness.
To midday a friend, and a friend of eternity.

[Hier sitz ich wartend — wartend? Doch auf nichts,
Jenseits von gut und böse, und des Lichts
Nicht mehr gelüstend als der Dunkelheit.
Dem Mittag Freund und Freund der Ewigkeit.
(*KSA* 10, 3[3], 107–8)]

In the light of a revision of this poem, however,[1] the moment this text was composed can be seen as when Nietzsche's most famous book was born:

All sea, all midday, all time without aim
A child, a plaything
And suddenly one turns into two
And Zarathustra walked into my view.

[Ganz Meer, ganz Mittag, ganz Zeit ohne Ziel
Ein Kind, ein Spielzeug
Und plötzlich werden Eins zu Zwei
Und Zarathustra gieng an mir vorbei.
(*KSA* 10, 4[145], 157)]

Nietzsche himself uses the language of gestation. Writing to Hans von Bülow at the beginning of December 1882, he commented: "Enough, I am a hermit again, and more so than ever; and I am — as a result — planning something new. It seems to me that only the condition of *pregnancy* binds us to life again" (Genug, ich bin wieder Einsiedler und mehr als je; und denke mir — folglich — etwas Neues aus. Es scheint mir, daß allein der Zustand der *Schwangerschaft* uns immer wieder an's Leben bindet; *KSB* 6, 290). And from Rapallo, on Christmas Day, he wrote to Franz Overbeck, "If I cannot pull off the alchemists' trick of turning this — *filth* into gold, then I am lost" (Wenn ich nicht das Alchemisten-Kunststück erfinde, auch aus diesem — *Kothe* Gold zu machen, so bin ich verloren; *KSB* 6, 312).[2] And on New Year's Eve 1882/1883, again writing to Overbeck, he says that the previous ten years have turned him into a machine about to break: "I have become too much a *machine*, and there is no small danger, with such violent movements, that the spring will *snap*" (ich bin zu sehr *Maschine* dadurch geworden, und die Gefahr ist nicht gering, bei so heftigen Bewegungen, daß die Feder *springt*; *KSB* 6, 313, cf. *KSB* 6, 112).

Yet Nietzsche, to use his own alchemical imagery, succeeded in finding the Philosophers' Stone. At any rate, toward the end of January 1883, *something happened*. Nietzsche wrote intensively, with the result that, at the end of the month, *Thus Spoke Zarathustra* (*Also sprach Zarathustra*) was born. In his letter to Heinrich Köselitz (his friend, whom he called Peter Gast) of 1 February 1883, Nietzsche suddenly, and jubilantly, announced its completion: "It is quite a small book — about a hundred printed pages. But it is my *best*" (Es handelt sich um ein ganz kleines Buch — hundert Druckseiten etwa. Aber es ist mein *Bestes*; *KSB* 6, 321, cf. to Overbeck on 1 February 1882; *KSB* 6, 324). Later, on 17 April 1883, he admitted to Köselitz: "Seine Entstehung war eine Art *Aderlaß*, ich verdanke ihm, daß ich nicht erstickt bin. Es war etwas Plötzliches, die Sache von 10 Tagen" (Its composition was a kind of *blood-letting*, I owe to it that I did not suffocate. It was something sudden, a matter of 10 days; *KSB* 6, 361). On 13 February 1883 Nietzsche proceeded to contact his publisher in Chemnitz, Ernst Schmeitzner, to discuss publication of the work, describing it as "a 'work of literature,' or a 'fifth gospel,' or something for which there is as yet no name" (eine "Dichtung", oder ein fünftes "Evangelium" oder irgend Etwas, für das es noch keinen Namen giebt), and predicting for it a wide audience as "by far the most serious and *also* the most cheerful of my productions, and accessible to everyone" (bei weitem das Ernsteste und *auch* Heiterste meiner Erzeugnisse, und Jedermann zugänglich; *KSB* 6, 327).

Now although Nietzsche emphasized that *Zarathustra* — or, rather, what was to become part 1 of *Zarathustra* — was written in ten days in Rapallo in January 1883, its roots lie in his experiences in Sils Maria in the summer of 1881. In his notebooks for summer 1881 we find a lengthy note, entitled "*The Recurrence of the Same.* Sketch" (*Die Wiederkunft des Gleichen.* Entwurf; *KSA* 9, 11 [141], 494). This note includes a paragraph with the phrase "the new weight," which is echoed in the title for the section about eternal recurrence in *The Gay Science* (*Die fröhliche Wissenschaft*), "The Heaviest Weight" ("Das grösste Schwergewicht"; *GS* §341; *KSA* 3, 570). (In Paul S. Loeb's recent study of *Zarathustra*, the concept of eternal recurrence provides the clue to solving the riddles scattered throughout the text,[3] and in an earlier analysis, Robert Gooding-Williams discerns in eternal recurrence the essence of Zarathustra's "Dionysian modernism.")[4]

Three further sketches in his notebook for this period demonstrate Nietzsche's plans for the concluding section of *The Gay Science*, which introduces the figure of Zarathustra (*KSA* 9, 11[195], 519); show that Nietzsche had already begun to consider the imagery and literary style of the work (*KSA* 9, 11[196], 519);[5] and make clear that he had developed a conception for this project as a series of four books (*KSA* 9, 11[197], 519–20). Thus, although part 1 of *Zarathustra* was written in Rapallo, Nietzsche was entirely justified when, in his letter to Köselitz of 3 September 1883, he referred to the Engadine as "die Geburtsstätte meines Zarathustra" (the birthplace of my Zarathustra), and when, in his final revision of the poem "Portofino," Nietzsche transposes this moment to Sils Maria — to the town where he had had the intuition of the idea of eternal recurrence next to a large pyramidal rock along the lake:

Sils-Maria

Here I sat, waiting — not for anything —
Beyond Good and Evil, fancying
Now light, now shadows, all a game,
All lake, all noon, all time without aim.

Then, suddenly, woman-friend, one turned into two —
And Zarathustra walked into my view.

[Hier sass ich, wartend, wartend, — doch auf Nichts,
Jenseits von Gut und Böse, bald des Lichts
Geniessend, bald des Schattens, ganz nur Spiel,
Ganz See, ganz Mittag, ganz Zeit ohne Ziel.

Da, plötzlich, Freundin! wurde Eins zu Zwei —
— Und Zarathustra gieng an mir vorbei . . .

(*KSA* 3, 649)[6]]

Why did Nietzsche choose the figure of Zarathustra (or, in English, Zoroaster)? The original Zoroastrian texts (dating back to the third century CE, although reflecting a centuries-old oral tradition) were appearing in translation in the 1850s and 1860s, coinciding with Nietzsche's time as a student at Bonn.[7] Nietzsche's most likely source of information about the historical figure of Zoroaster was probably *Symbolism and Mythology of Ancient Peoples, Especially the Greeks* (*Die Symbolik und Mythologie der alten Völker, besonders der Griechen*), published in 4 volumes (1810–12; second ed., 1819–21) by Georg Friedrich Creuzer (1771–1858), which he had consulted during his work on *The Birth of Tragedy* (*Die Geburt der Tragödie*), and from which, according to a letter to Köselitz of 23 April 1883, he later noted the etymological origin of the name, while disclaiming all knowledge of this at the time of composition: "Today I learned by chance *what* 'Zarathustra' means: namely, 'Gold-Star.' This coincidence made me happy. One might think that the whole conception of my little book has its root in this etymology: but until today I knew nothing about it" (Heute lernte ich zufällig, *was* "Zarathustra" bedeutet: nämlich "Gold-Stern". Dieser Zufall machte mich glücklich. Man könnte meinen, die ganze Conception meines Büchleines habe in dieser Etymologie ihre Wurzel: aber ich wußte bis heute nichts davon; *KSB* 6, 366).[8] (Equally, on the basis of another etymology, found in Johann Joseph von Görres, Wagner had chosen the name "Parsifal" for the central figure of his eponymous opera, which premiered in 1882, because the name allegedly derived from "foolish Parsee" or "pure fool."[9] The parodic allusions to *Parsifal* and the *Ring* operas in *Zarathustra* have been studied in detail by Roger Hollinrake.)[10] Finally, another source for the figure of Zarathustra is Emerson, who, in his essay on "Character," refers to Zoroaster in a passage that Nietzsche marked in his personal copy (*KSA* 14, 279).[11] Equally, the celebrated phrase that features in the title and with which most chapters conclude may also have its source in Emerson, whose essay entitled "Prospects" includes the following words: "Thus my Orphic poet sang."[12]

To the extent that Nietzsche had become estranged from family and friends alike, *Zarathustra* represents a substitute family that Nietzsche was creating for himself: on several occasions, he refers to *Zarathustra* as his son (*KSB* 6, 367–69, 406 and 460). (If Nietzsche was the father, would it be an exaggeration to see von Salomé has having been its mother? Ida Overbeck believed Lou had played an important part in the text's genesis.)[13] And as his son (*Zarathustra*) was born, Nietzsche's (symbolic) father died: on 13 February 1882, Wagner passed away in Venice, and Nietzsche only heard the news by chance. He described its effect as "a deep, muffled thunder" (einen tiefen, dumpfen Donner; *KSB* 6, 336), and despite the remaining bitterness over the parting of their ways, he nevertheless recognized Wagner as "by far the *most complete* human being I ever knew" (bei weitem der *vollste* Mensch, den ich kennen lernte; *KSB* 6, 337). In another respect, the very conception and production of *Zarathustra* was confirmation of Nietzsche's own philosophical theses. If, in Leipzig, Nietzsche's ambition had been to fashion for himself "a life of my own that suits me" (ein eignes anpassendes Leben; *BAW* 3, 297), *Zarathustra* itself was part of Nietzsche's existential project: "My life is gradually taking shape, not without convulsions — but it *shall* take shape!" (Mein Leben gestaltet sich allmählich und nicht ohne Krämpfe — aber es *soll* Gestalt bekommen!; *KSB* 6, 339).

After ten weeks in Genoa (where he had arrived from Rapallo at the end of February 1883, staying until the beginning of May), followed by a visit at the suggestion of Malwida von Meysenbug to Rome (from 3 May until 14 June 1883), where a reconciliation with his sister took place, Nietzsche found himself back in Sils Maria in June 1883: at "a kind of end of the world" (eine Art Ende der Welt; *KSB* 6, 389), as he put it in a letter to Elisabeth. Yet he also told Carl von Gersdorff in June 1883: "Here *my* Muses dwell" (Hier wohnen *meine* Musen; *KSB* 6, 387); it was a place where he experienced the *Doppelgänger*-like nature of Nature, to which he felt "related by blood" (blutsverwandt; cf. *HA WS* §338; *KSA* 2, 699). And in the same letter there is the hint that there might be more of *Zarathustra* to come: "Oh, how everything still lies hidden in me and wants to become word and form! It cannot be still and high and solitary enough around me, so I can hear my inmost voices!" (Ach, was liegt noch Alles verborgen in mir und will Wort und Form werden! Es kann gar nicht still und hoch und einsam genug um mich sein, daß ich meine innersten Stimmen vernehmen kann!; *KSB* 6, 386).

Indeed, by mid-July 1883, the manuscript of the second part of *Zarathustra* was complete (*KSB* 6, 442). Although he still presented parts 1 and 2 as the product of spontaneous inspiration, Nietzsche's earliest sketches for *Zarathustra* in summer 1881 had envisaged a work in no less than four parts. As soon as part 2 was completed, Nietzsche was already contemplating part 3, as he told Köselitz on 13 July 1883 (*KSB* 6, 397; cf. *KSB* 6, 442–43). And after the first of what would be four winters spent in Nice, from December 1883 to April 1884, Nietzsche announced to his publisher, Ernst Schmeitzner, that part 3 was complete (*KSB* 6, 465).

In Nice, Nietzsche was sought out by Josef Paneth (1857–90), an Austrian physiologist who was interested in his writings, and who has left an account of his conversations with Nietzsche in early 1884.[14] In April, he was visited by a student from Zurich, Resa von Schirnhofer (1855–1948), on whom he left the impression of being "of exquisite sensitivity, tenderness, and refined courtesy in attitude and manners toward the female sex" (von exquisiter Sensibilität, zartfühlend und von ausgesuchter Höflichkeit in Gesinnung und Manieren dem weiblichen Geschlecht gegenüber); although she found in his recitation of a scene from *Zarathustra* (*Z* III 15 §2; *KSA* 4, 285) and his presentation of the doctrine of the eternal recurrence "something bizarre, indeed eerie" (etwas Bizarres, ja Unheimliches) — "A different Nietzsche was suddenly standing before me and had frightened me" (Ein anderer Nietzsche stand plötzlich vor mir und hatte mich erschreckt).[15]

After Nice, Nietzsche stayed in Venice (with Köselitz), then in Basel (where he visited the Overbecks), then in Zurich (where he met Meta von Salis [1855–1929]), and then — "*At last* in Sils-Maria! At last a return to — reason!" (*Endlich* in Sils-Maria! Endlich Rückkehr zur — Vernunft!; *KSB* 6, 515). In Sils Maria he received visits from Resa von Schirnhofer and from the philosopher Heinrich von Stein (1857–87); then, after a stay in Zurich, accompanied by his sister, Nietzsche went back to Nice for the winter. As he began to look for a different publisher for part 4 of *Zarathustra*, he sought to recover from his previous publisher, Schmeitzner, the rights to the three previous parts. Although he suffered badly from headaches and migraines over the winter, having frequent recourse to chloral hydrate to relieve his pain, by February he had completed work on part 4, "as the '*fruit*' of this winter" (als "*Frucht*" dieses Winters; *KSB* 6, 604), provisionally entitled *The Temptation of Zarathustra* (*Die Versuchung Zarathustra's*; *KSB* 7, 12; *KSB* 8, 228). In March he sent the manuscript to his new publisher, Constantin Georg Naumann, explaining that part 4 was not for the general public, but to be published privately for a select circle of friends.

Nietzsche planned further installments, parts 5 and 6 — "It's no use, I must first help my son Zarathustra to his beautiful *death*, otherwise he will give me no peace" (Es hilft nichts, ich muß meinem Sohne Zarathustra erst zu seinem schönen *Tode* verhelfen, er läßt mir sonst keine Ruhe; *KSB* 6, 557), and his notebooks contain various sketches for the death of Zarathustra, some of which envisage the introduction of a mysterious female figure called Pana (*KSA* 10, 13[3], 446–47). They were never written. In an entry in his notebooks from the period autumn 1884 to the beginning of 1885, Nietzsche saw Nice as the place where *Zarathustra* came to an end: "To the Engadine I am indebted for *life*, Zarathustra"

(Dem Engardin verdanke ich *Leben, Zarathustra*), he wrote, "to Nice I am indebted for the *completion* of Zarathustra" (Nizza verdanke ich die *Beendigung* des Zarathustra; *KSA* 11, 29[4], 337). And so it is as a work in four parts that we know *Thus Spoke Zarathustra* today: in his contribution, Laurence Lampert guides us through the complex yet rewarding text of what is now by common consent regarded as Nietzsche's philosophical masterpiece.

Notes

[1] For a discussion of the dating, see Philip Grundlehner, *The Poetry of Friedrich Nietzsche* (New York and Oxford: Oxford UP, 1986), 134–36.

[2] For further discussion of alchemical imagery in Nietzsche's writings, see Richard Perkins, "Nietzsche's *opus alchymicum*," *Seminar* 23 (1987): 216–26; Graham Parkes, *Composing the Soul: Reaches of Nietzsche's Psychology* (Chicago and London: U of Chicago P, 1994), 133–34, 141, 158, 166, and 418; and Paul Bishop, "The Superman as Salamander: Symbols of Transformation or Transformational Symbols?," *International Journal of Jungian Studies* 3/1 (2011): 4–20.

[3] Paul S. Loeb, *The Death of Nietzsche's Zarathustra* (Cambridge: Cambridge UP, 2010).

[4] Robert Gooding-Williams, *Zarathustra's Dionysian Modernism* (Stanford, CA: Stanford UP, 2001).

[5] As Gary Brown has pointed out, "among the many reflections in *Zarathustra*, a careful reader can catch glimmers of Schiller, especially in images such as the storm-tossed boat, receding horizons, companion animals, preferences for the slopes of Vesuvius, etc." ("Introduction" [to "Richard Wagner in Bayreuth"], in Friedrich Nietzsche, *Unmodern Observations*, ed. William Arrowsmith [New Haven and London: Yale UP, 1990], 227–52 [here: 241]).

[6] For the genesis of this text, see Manfred Riedel, "Nietzsches Gedicht *Sils-Maria*: Entstehungsgeschichte und Deutung," *Nietzsche-Studien* 27 (1998): 268–82. For further analysis and references, see Paul Bishop, "'Creation — That is the Great Redemption from Suffering, and Life's Easement,'" Parts 1 and 2, in Stacy Wirth, Isabelle Meier, and John Hill (eds), *Destruction and Creation: Facing the Ambiguities of Power* (New Orleans, LA: Spring Journal Books, 2010), 31–43 and 45–58.

[7] For further discussion, see Michael Stausberg, *Faszination Zarathushtra: Zoroaster und die europäische Religionsgeschichte der frühen Neuzeit*, 2 vols. (Berlin: Walter de Gruyter, 1998).

[8] For further discussion, see Manfred Mayrhofer, "Zu einer Deutung des Zarathustra-Namens in Nietzsches Korrespondenz," in *Beiträge zur Alten Geschichte und deren Nachleben: Festschrift für Franz Altheim zum 6.10.1968*, ed. Ruth Stiehl and Hans Erich Stier, 2 vols. (Berlin: Walter de Gruyter, 1969), 2:369–74.

[9] Richard Wagner, *Das braune Buch: Tagebuchaufzeichnungen 1865 bis 1882*, ed. Joachim Bergfeld (Zurich and Freiburg im Breisgau: Atlantis, 1975), 22; cf. Johann Joseph von Görres, ed., *Lohengrin, ein altteutsches Gedicht* (Heidelberg: Mohr & Zimmer, 1813), vi. See *Parsifal*, act 2, scene 2: "You I named,

you foolish pure one, / 'Fal parsi' — / You, the pure fool, 'Parsifal'" (Dich nannt' ich, tör'ger Reiner, / "Fal parsi" / — Dich, reinen Toren "Parsifal") (Richard Wagner, *Sämtliche Schriften und Dichtungen: Volks-Ausgabe*, 16 in 8 vols. [Leipzig: Breitkopf & Härtel/Siegel, 1911], 10:355.)

[10] Roger Hollinrake, *Nietzsche, Wagner, and the Philosophy of Pessimism* (London: Allen & Unwin, 1982).

[11] See Emerson, "Character," in Ralph Waldo Emerson, *Essays and Lectures*, ed. Joel Porte (New York: Library of America, 1983), 495–509 (here: 505).

[12] See Emerson, "Prospects," in *Essays and Lectures*, ed. Joel Porte (New York: Library of America, 1983), 43–49 (here: 46).

[13] See "Erinnerungen von Frau Ida Overbeck," in Carl Albrecht Bernoulli, *Franz Overbeck und Friedrich Nietzsche: Eine Freundschaft*, 2 vols. (Jena: Diederichs, 1908), 1:234–51 (here: 336).

[14] Richard Frank Krummel, "Josef Paneth über seine Begegnung mit Nietzsche in der Zarathustra-Zeit," *Nietzsche-Studien* 17 (1988): 478–95.

[15] Resa von Schirnhofer, "Vom Menschen Nietzsche," in Hans Lohgerber, "Friedrich Nietzsche und Resa von Schirnhofer," *Zeitschrift für philosophische Forschung* 22 (1969): 250–60 and 441–58 (here: 255 and 260); *Conversations with Nietzsche*, 148 and 157.

7: *Thus Spoke Zarathustra*

Laurence Lampert

Introduction

"A MONG MY WRITINGS my *Zarathustra* stands alone" (Innerhalb meiner Schriften steht für sich mein *Zarathustra*; *EH* preface §4; *KSA* 6, 259). But Nietzsche never thought that *Thus Spoke Zarathustra* (*Also sprach Zarathustra*) should be studied alone. While it is strikingly unique, it fulfills and extends the relatively more conventional books that preceded it and is supplemented by those that followed it. It stands alone because Nietzsche chose a unique vehicle to introduce a unique thought, one that came to him suddenly but only as a consequence of the gathering understanding acquired across decades of study and writing. The oddness of that thought and the change it signified in the human disposition toward things required a unique introduction. *Thus Spoke Zarathustra* stands alone as the introduction to Nietzsche's thought of eternal return.

"I have not been asked, as I should have been asked, what 'Zarathustra' means in my mouth" (Man hat mich nicht gefragt, man hätte mich fragen sollen, was gerade in meinem Munde [. . .] der Name *Zarathustra* bedeutet; *EH* "Why I Am a Destiny" §3; *KSA* 6, 367). When Nietzsche wrote this four years after completing his *Zarathustra*, he explained what it meant. "Zarathustra" was the name of the Persian prophet who first viewed time as history, the locus of a continuous struggle between good and evil that would culminate at the end of history in an apocalyptic victory for the good, assigning good human beings an eternity of well-being and evil ones an eternity of suffering. Who is Zarathustra in Nietzsche's mouth? The founding teacher of the meaning of life that was taken over by the monotheistic religions of Judaism, Christianity, and Islam that shaped Middle-Eastern and Western civilization; the founding teacher of the view that entered Western philosophy as Platonism and that is still present in modern views of history as progress. When Zarathustra returns in Nietzsche's book, he is, as is fitting, the first to see through his own original teaching and see beyond the ruins it had left in the slow demise of its millennial rule, beyond the coming nihilism. "Zarathustra" means in Nietzsche's mouth the post-Platonic, post-Christian, postmodern thinker, whose new teaching promises to be as consequential, as world-ordering, as the teaching he brought the first time.

When Nietzsche reviewed *Thus Spoke Zarathustra* while reviewing all his books in *Ecce Homo*, he began by stating simply, "I relate now the history of *Zarathustra*" (Ich erzähle nunmehr die Geschichte des Zarathustra; *EH Z* §1; *KSA* 6, 335). As a prelude to that personal history he gave "the basic conception of the work, the *thought of eternal return*" (die Grundconception des Werks, der *Ewige-Wiederkunfts-Gedanke*), describing it as the "highest formula of affirmation that can ever be attained" (diese höchste Formel der Bejahung, die überhaupt erreicht werden kann; *EH Z* §1; *KSA* 6, 335). The history of *Zarathustra* that Nietzsche relates in *Ecce Homo* describes a personal odyssey that ties his thought to place and action, summoning a precise geography of mountain lakes and sea bays where on strenuous hikes and climbs over a period of three years he "found" the ideas of *Zarathustra* and the images and events indispensable to their communication.

The thought of eternal return "belongs in August of the year 1881" (gehört in den August des Jahres 1881), and was first "sketched on a sheet of paper with a notation underneath, '6000 feet beyond man and time'" (auf ein Blatt hingeworfen, mit der Unterschrift: "6000 Fuss jenseits von Mensch und Zeit"; *EH Z* §1; *KSA* 6, 335). If the thought itself transcended human things, its place of appearing was embedded in them: "I was walking that day by the lake of Silvaplana through the woods; at a powerful pyramidal block of stone not far from Surlei I came to a halt. There this thought came to me" (Ich gieng an jenem Tage am See von Silvaplana durch die Wälder; bei einem mächtigen pyramidal aufgethürmten Block unweit Surlei machte ich Halt. Da kam mir dieser Gedanke; *EH Z* §1; *KSA* 6, 335). These exact objects naming the thought and giving it its spiritual and physical place of arrival contrast dramatically with the manner in which Nietzsche chose to present it to the world in *Thus Spoke Zarathustra*.

Six months after the thought first appeared to him, Nietzsche was still preparing the last book he wrote before *Zarathustra*, *The Gay Science* (*Die fröhliche Wissenschaft*). He told his young friend and assistant, Heinrich Köselitz (to whom he gave the name Peter Gast), in a letter of 25 January 1882 that "I have not yet *matured* enough for the prime ideas I shall present in [*The Gay Science*]. Among them there is one idea which needs a thousand years to mature properly. How will I find the strength to express it!" (ich bin noch nicht *reif* genug für die elementaren Gedanken, die ich in diesen Schluß-Büchern darstellen will. Ein Gedanke ist darunter, der in der That 'Jahrtausende' braucht, um etwas zu *werden*. Woher nehme ich den Muth, ihn auszusprechen!; *KSB* 6, 159). *The Gay Science* was published in July 1882, and in its penultimate section (§341) the thought of eternal return made a first sudden and calculated appearance. Entitled "The Heaviest Weight" ("Das grösste Schwergewicht"), the section sketched an ominous scene of the loneliest loneliness with moonlight between the trees and a demon who whispers that the thought of greatest weight would either transform or crush the person taken over by it (*KSA* 3, 570). Nietzsche then closed his book with a section entitled "*Incipit tragoedia*" ("The Tragedy Begins") that opens, "When Zarathustra was thirty years old he left his home and Lake Urmi and went into the mountains" (Als Zarathustra dreissig Jahr alt war, verliess er seine Heimath und den See Urmi und gieng in das Gebirge), continued with the rest of what would turn out to be the first section of the first part of *Thus Spoke Zarathustra*, and ended: " — Thus began Zarathustra's going-under" (— Also begann Zarathustra's Untergang; *GS* §342; *KSA* 3, 571). Those two final sections can have been only a complete mystery to the first readers of *The Gay Science*, a book on the historic gains of science as opposed to teachings of purpose that Enlightenment, now the modern Enlightenment, always laughed out of existence.

When *The Gay Science* first appeared, an announcement on its back cover marked it as an epoch in Nietzsche's life: "With this book a series of writings by FRIEDRICH NIETZSCHE comes to a conclusion; their common goal is to erect *a new image and ideal of the free mind*" (Mit diesem Buche kommt eine Reihe von Schriften FRIEDRICH NIETZSCHE'S zum Abschluss, deren gemeinsames Ziel ist, *ein neues Bild und Ideal des Freigeistes* aufzustellen).[1] Nietzsche announced this ending while preparing the book his final two sections mysteriously heralded. That book would in no way set aside the ideal of the free mind, but would show how one particularly free mind had attained insights that needed a completely different art of writing to be properly introduced. The audience for these new insights was the one created by the series of books just completed: minds freed by the modern Enlightenment and deepened in that freedom by Nietzsche's indispensable series on the free mind. The new book takes the decisive step beyond freemindedness, a step that he knew could not be welcomed by modern minds who thought the skeptical free mind the highest possible human attainment. After completing *Zarathustra* Nietzsche stated exactly how he understood its relation to his earlier writings. In a letter of 29 August 1886, he told the publisher, Ernst Wilhelm Fritzsch, who was reissuing most of those earlier writings with new prefaces: "The essential thing is that to have the prerequisite for understanding *Zarathustra*, *all* my earlier writings must be genuinely and profoundly understood; also the *necessity* of the sequence of these writings and the development expressed in them" (Das Wesentliche ist, daß, um die Voraussetzungen für das Verständniß des *Zarathustra* zu haben [. . .] *alle* meine früheren Schriften ernstlich und tief verstanden sein müssen; insgleichen die *Nothwendigkeit* der Aufeinanderfolge dieser Schriften und der in ihnen sich ausdrückenden Entwicklung; *KSB* 7, 237).

But for students of Nietzsche's earlier books, *Zarathustra* presents difficulties because of its different form. Not only does it feature characters, setting, and a plot, it does not present its thoughts through an examination of concepts weighed by arguments for and against. Rather, as a "return of language to the nature of imagery" (diese Rückkehr der Sprache zur Natur der Bildlichkeit; *EH Z* §6; *KSA* 6, 344), it has a logic all its own that never abandons the rigors of the intellectual conscience but invites it to different challenges. Exacting, flamboyant, drawing on the great traditions of Greece and the Bible plus the literary masters Nietzsche had absorbed, it demands, as Graham Parkes has written, that its readers pursue "a train of thought through fields of imagery, and participate in a play of imagination that engages the whole psyche rather that the intellect alone."[2] Doing the book justice requires permitting it its form and reading it not as a treatise but as rigorous philosophy in the form of a literary fable. Nietzsche alludes to another feature of *Zarathustra* in one of its chapters, "On Reading and Writing" ("Vom Lesen und Schreiben"): *Zarathustra* practices an art of writing that does as little as possible for the reader (*Z* I 7; *KSA* 4, 48–50). Though the book is long, it employs abbreviation or concision, the art of the aphorism. It is a frugal art that does its reader the favor of allowing him or her to experience the exhilaration of discovery by coming to possess, through interpretation, what the artist-author already possesses and wants to share, knowing that it can be shared only by being co-discovered and not by dictation. Nietzsche, like Socrates, adheres to the ancient principle that the things that need to be learned cannot be taught — but they can be learned.

Nietzsche wrote *Zarathustra* in order to present the thought of eternal return but in the first part of the book, which was published on 26 August 1883, Zarathustra completes his teaching with eternal return totally absent. That hundred page book was only the beginning, although there was no way for its first readers to know that. A second part was published separately shortly thereafter, perhaps as early as September 1883, in exactly the same format with only a large "2" added to the front cover and title page. It contained at its center a series of chapters in which Zarathustra attained a fundamental new insight, but still gave no inkling of the thought for which the book existed. Then, in a pivotal chapter toward the end of "2," Zarathustra discovered how his new insight required an unprecedented and almost intolerable thought to complete it. Finally, in April 1884, a third part was published, again with an identical cover and title page except for a large "3" and the date 1884 instead of 1883. Here, finally, after all that preparation, Zarathustra approached the thought of eternal return, first in a "vision and riddle," and then, after further preparations, in the climax of the book, its final four chapters. Only in 1886 did Nietzsche reissue the three little volumes together in a single volume. He had written a fourth part, intending it to be followed by two more parts, but it was the last one that he completed. He had it privately printed in forty copies, nine of which he distributed to selected friends. As interesting and worthy of study as it is — Zarathustra meets in it the few "superior humans" of Nietzsche's time, but they all prove unequal to his thought of eternal return — part 4 conflicts with the ending of part 3 and, without the other two intended parts, which describe Zarathustra's descent to create worthy hearers of his thought, it leaves Zarathustra's new task unfinished. The present form of the book in four parts is therefore a whole, parts 1–3, plus a fragment, part 4, of a larger whole that does not exist. In the account that follows, instead of brief summaries of each chapter I give more extensive interpretations of those chapters that seem most important.

Part 1

The first part consists of "Zarathustra's Prologue" ("Zarathustra's Vorrede"), which proves to be a false start, and "The Speeches of Zarathustra" ("Die Reden Zarathustra's"), twenty-two separate chapters that successfully convey Zarathustra's teaching at this point in his career. The prologue begins with Zarathustra's ascent to a ten-year solitude and his descent to teach what he learned there. His first speeches are given to a crowd assembled in the marketplace of a city. These initial proclamations to the multitude contain some of the most famous words in Nietzsche's writings, but they must be treated with caution because Zarathustra himself undergoes a process of change. His primary imperative in the prologue, however, stands as a constant throughout his — and Nietzsche's — career: "*Stay true to the earth*" (*Bleibt der Erde treu*; *Z* prologue §3; *KSA* 4, 15). He issues this as the imperative for a new age because "God died" and loyalty to anything transcendent has become meaningless. If God is dead, then the whole array of human beliefs and practices must be centered on the new principle of loyalty to the earth. But who shall legislate that order? "*I teach to you the Overhuman*" (*Ich lehre euch den Übermenschen*), Zarathustra says repeatedly (*Z* prologue §3; *KA* 4, 14): the Overhuman (*Übermensch*) is that singularity who will establish the needed principles and ordinances of a new humanity true to the earth.

Zarathustra commands the multitude to live in a way that prepares the coming of the Overhuman. When they scorn his new ideal, he changes his strategy; instead of appealing to their pride with the Overhuman, he appeals to their shame by describing "the last human" (der letzte Mensch), modern global humanity as the final goal of historical progress (*Z* prologue §5; *KSA* 4, 19). The last human lives in the comfortable, calculated self-interest made possible by the modern technological mastery of nature: above all else, the last human values equality and the end of suffering. The crowd reacts as it must: "Give us this last human [. . .] you can have the Overhuman!" (Gieb uns diesen letzten Menschen [. . .] So schenken wir dir den Übermenschen!; *Z* prologue §5; *KSA* 4, 20). Zarathustra draws a lesson from his failure: he will have to alter his manner of speaking and attempt to lure a few followers from the multitude by challenging and persuading them. That will make him a wolf to the crowd, he recognizes, a teacher of evil who seeks to win their best offspring to a view that is destructive to theirs. The Zarathustra of the twenty-two "Speeches" (Reden) is a Zarathustra changed: the teaching with which he descended from his mountain cave is intact, but his strategy is altered: he now speaks in order to win disciples dedicated to the coming of the Overhuman, the founding teacher of loyalty to the earth.

"The Speeches of Zarathustra" implement the new strategy and prove successful in gaining him the desired disciples. Zarathustra begins with an appealing description of the nature of those he seeks. "On the Three Transformations" ("Von den drei Verwandlungen") describes a "camel" spirit becoming a "lion" spirit and then a "child" spirit (*Z* I 1; *KSA* 4, 29–31). A camel spirit is a prerequisite in those Zarathustra seeks, something he cannot teach: a spirit passionately wanting to take upon itself the hardest task, to prove to itself that it is equal to any burden. To these, the spiritually adventurous, Zarathustra teaches the transformation to the lion spirit, the breaking free of the burden of the revered, of tradition, of "one's own." That lion spirit is driven by its own imperative, its intellectual conscience, into a wasteland of valuelessness, into nihilism. But there it can experience, Zarathustra promises, new birth as a child. The child, at play in its creative freedom, creates a home for itself, an affirmative, yes-saying home.

In the following six speeches Zarathustra entices young listeners to rebel against the old teachings. He argues that what tradition held to transcend mere body — gods and transcendent worlds, reason and spirit, the virtues — are in fact rooted in body as products of a hatred or revulsion against the earthly body. The Overhuman, the primary concern of his teaching, he now introduces gradually as the antidote to the old teachings he discredits. This series of speeches ends with "On Reading and Writing," a chapter on the art of communication Zarathustra adopts. He aphoristically describes his art of aphorism: "In the mountains the shortest way is from peak to peak; but for that you must have long legs" (Im Gebirge ist der nächste Weg von Gipfel zu Gipfel: aber dazu musst du lange Beine haben; *Z* I 7; *KSA* 4, 48). The little peaks of his aphorisms, in their coiled brevity, practice an art of selection that singles out and educates those to whom he especially wants to speak. In this context of challenge he speaks briefly and beautifully of matters whose centrality emerges only later: *Wisdom*, a woman he loves who always loves only a warrior; *Life*, a woman he also loves; *God*, but he could believe only in a God who dances; *Devil*, his devil, the Spirit of Gravity.

"On the Tree on the Mountainside" ("Vom Baum am Berge") shows that Zarathustra's speeches are having their desired effect (*Z* I 8; *KSA* 4, 51–54). In a dramatic dialogue Nietzsche raises a theme from Greek antiquity that had occupied him since his youth: the challenge of contest, of individual vying and competing, and the passions of envy and emulation they incite. Zarathustra's speeches have incited admiration and envy in a gifted young man who outstrips his contemporaries and knows it. In a subtle dialogue, Zarathustra induces him to confess his mix of passions in order to free him from guilt at the envy and despair he experiences in the face of someone he may not be able to surpass. Zarathustra's private lesson to him aims to replace Christian humility with Greek pride and the Christian curse on envy with the Greek blessing on emulation that strives to outdo the emulated, to be the best and to know it. Lessons in the noble and the base are needed to prepare the youth to resist the temptation to merely indulge his passions. Only such a victory-loving spirit can embrace the challenge Zarathustra offers, a spiritual challenge to reach for the highest insight and the most glorious action.

In the next six chapters Zarathustra speaks more openly of the demands that discipleship will place on those attracted by the liberation his opening speeches promise. He counsels solitude to develop the warrior discipline necessary to break the hold of public temptations to politics or commerce. "On the New Idol" ("Vom neuen Götzen") and "On the Flies of the Marketplace" ("Von den Fliegen des Marktes") sketch a new and grand politics that prepares his hearers for large-scale undertakings on behalf of humanity (*Z* I 11 and 12; *KSA* 4, 61–64 and 65–68).

"On the Thousand Goals and One" ("Von tausend und Einem Ziele") develops these themes, making it the high point of the first part (*Z* I 15; *KSA* 74–76). It is the chapter richest in implication for the coming parts because it names the fundamental element of human social order and defines the intellectual and political labors of the Overhuman. The title means to be exact: the "thousand" goals represent the thousand peoples that have existed on earth; the "one" represents a new people with a new goal, the people Nietzsche anticipated as postmodern global humanity, a humanity first made global by the power of modern science and technology to fuse all particular peoples into one. Presenting himself as an Odysseus who has seen many peoples and known their minds, Zarathustra relates his basic discoveries. Each of the thousand peoples possesses and is possessed by its own "good and evil" (gut und böse), its own evaluation of "the praiseworthy [. . .], the good [. . .], and the holy" (löblich [. . .], gut [. . .], heilig), an ascending series of things thought difficult (*Z* I 15; *KSA* 4, 74). "There is no greater power on earth than good and evil" (Keine grössere Macht fand Zarathustra auf Erden, als gut und böse; *Z* I 15; *KSA* 4, 74), a power that organizes populations into unitary forces each in conflict with its neighbors, each united by its different evaluations of good and evil.

By announcing this knowledge of good and evil, Zarathustra offers the forbidden fruit to all, as he builds up to a rhetorical peak to announce an element still deeper than good and evil: the single source of this greatest power on earth is "will to power" (Wille zur Macht; *Z* I 15; *KSA* 4, 74). With this phrase Nietzsche pronounces for the first time in his published writings words that take a central place in all his thinking and writing till the end, a dangerous phrase easily misunderstood, a phrase frequently used to denounce him. Nietzsche was aware of the dangers of his phrase and of the need to set out its full sense along with its implications: a key purpose of the dramatic development of *Thus Spoke Zarathustra* is to show a thinker gradually entertaining that thought and even more gradually accepting its full implication. From this point on — from the single mention of will to power in the first part — the odyssey of Zarathustra is in large measure an odyssey into the deeper meaning of what he already understands as the foundation of the greatest power on earth. Nietzsche's artful economy in presenting the full implications of this thought offers a fine example of his art of writing: Zarathustra's acceptance of the thought of will to power blazes the trail his reader is invited to follow.

Nietzsche builds up to the end of this chapter by emphasizing that what created the tablets of good that hangs over every people is love and that the evaluations exhibited in such tablets is a creating. In the history of value-creating that created peoples, peoples came first and only later was the individual a creator, a creator of individuality; "the individual is itself the latest creation" (wahrlich, der Einzelne selber ist noch die jüngste Schöpfung; *Z* I 15; *KSA* 4, 75). This late creation of a mass global humanity of individuals occasions Zarathustra's final image and final question. The thousand peoples are likened to a beast with a thousand necks. "Who will throw the shackles over the thousand necks of this beast?" (Sagt, wer wirft diesem Thier die Fessel über die tausend Nacken?; *Z* I 15; *KSA* 4, 76). It fits Zarathustra's rhetoric *not* to state simply that this is the task of the Overhuman, to provide that one goal that will unite humanity into one people, a new good and evil that will create humanity for the first time. That creation too will be a creation of love that springs from the will to power.

Six more speeches follow, each defining conventions that will contribute to the coming of the Overhuman, each stating some hardness or discipline required of Zarathustra's followers. Ending on a new teaching on death, they prepare the final chapter of the first part, a set of three speeches that Zarathustra gives outside the city to those he has won to his new teaching, those he now calls "disciples" (Jünger). These speeches provide the most revealing statement of who the Zarathustra of the first part is, because they describe at last his particular virtue, the bestowing or gift-giving virtue that gives oneself as a gift to humanity's future. His disciples are to surpass him in the gift-giving virtue by sacrificing themselves in the task of preparing the way for the coming Overhuman.

The teaching of the first part is progressive and implies a linear view of time: the Overhuman is the meaning of the earth, and human life in the present is meaningful only as a gift given for his future coming. This teaching must be treated with the caution due the teaching of a mere herald. The something greater Zarathustra heralds in the first part in fact appears in the second and third parts. There, Nietzsche shows Zarathustra attaining an understanding of being and time wholly absent from the first part: the herald becomes the one heralded.

Part 2

The second part opens with Zarathustra's joy at being permitted to return to his disciples. It closes with Zarathustra leaving his disciples again, but leaving transformed in a way that is acted out without being stated. The second part of *Thus Spoke Zarathustra* is the most important part for understanding Nietzsche's philosophy; here he indicates just where his own long odyssey of thought led him.

When Zarathustra returns to his disciples after years in his cave, he returns to speak to them only, disciples of his teaching who have spent years pondering and discussing it. He returns with a wisdom more radical and exclusive, a "wild wisdom" (wilde Weisheit) won by his own years of reflection (*Z* II 1; *KSA* 4, 107). His first six speeches of this part emphasize how uncompromising that wisdom is, how little it can be harmonized with the reigning teachings — his disciples must have "denied" him by reconciling his views with the prevailing ones. The teachings he criticizes remain nameless, but they are clearly those of the modern heirs of Christianity, which Zarathustra condemns as carrying forward the spirit of Christianity while seeming to oppose it.

This critique of modern moral teachings peaks with the final speech in the series, "On the Tarantulas" ("Von den Taranteln"), a speech on justice, condemning modern justice (*Z* II 7; *KSA* 4, 128–31). Employing a method of psychological unmasking, it challenges the disciples by criticizing those whose teaching attracts them, modern "preachers of *equality*" (Prediger der *Gleichheit*), moral tarantulas, Zarathustra charges, who preach equality out of the passion of revenge. Hurt by the unfair portions meted out by nature, they have translated their repressed envy into a teaching of equality that has become the dominant doctrine of modern justice. Brandishing this charge that the preachers act out of revenge, Zarathustra himself holds that "the bridge to the highest hope" (die Brücke zur höchsten Hoffnung) is *"that humanity might be redeemed from revenge"* (*dass der Mensch erlöst werde von der Rache*; *Z* II 7; *KSA* 4, 128). He claims provocatively that justice says to him, "Humans are not equal" (die Menschen sind nicht gleich), and that the way to the future is through "war and inequality" (Krieg und Ungleichheit; *Z* II 7; *KSA* 4,

130). Claiming to be moved by love while accusing his enemies of being moved by revenge, Zarathustra ends picturing a tarantula biting his finger and charging that he is stirred by revenge.

Is Zarathustra, is Nietzsche, a teacher of revenge? This challenge ends "On the Tarantulas," and many interpreters of Nietzsche, led by Martin Heidegger, have answered yes.[3] But the whole movement of the argument of *Zarathustra* answers no, beginning with the end of this chapter. For Zarathustra elaborates his image of the ruins of an ancient temple in which the tarantula had spun its web. That temple is Greek, and its ultimate architect is Homer, the educator of Greece, creator of a culture of agonistic striving that Nietzsche viewed as the highest yet. Christianity and modernity claim to advance the Greek heritage, but the tarantula's web in the ancient ruins gives Zarathustra's judgment on that claim. He claims to be its true heir: asking to be tied to a column in the ancient ruins in order that he not swirl with revenge, he asks what Odysseus, wisest of Homer's Greeks, asked: that his companions tie him to the mast so that he might hear the Sirens' song and not be ruined by it. Zarathustra had not used the words *wisdom* or *wisest* in his speeches on Christianity and modernity, but introduces them in alluding to Homer, and the five linked chapters that follow have wisdom as their theme.

Two separate acts of solving the riddles of the wise occur in these chapters, as Zarathustra solves those of the most famous of the wise in the first and the wisest of the wise in the last. The most famous are moved by a passion for fame, but something different moves the wisest, for there is, Zarathustra claims, a wisdom free of the need for glory or recognition, the wisdom of the free mind celebrated in the first of these chapters. That free mind, embodied in Zarathustra, can solve the riddle of the wisest only after undergoing a profound act of learning in the intervening three chapters, three songs that are among the most important chapters of the book.

The songs open with "The Night-Song" ("Das Nachtlied"), a song of Zarathustra's inwardness, an unexpected lament for being what he is, a pure gift-giver incapable of receiving (Z II 9; *KSA* 4, 136–38). The crisis of the Night-Song, the dark night of the gift-giving soul, is answered in the next song, "The Dance-Song" ("Das Tanzlied"), which sings of an unexpected receiving of the highest possible gift (Z II 10; *KSA* 4, 139–41). The disciples are present as Zarathustra, walking in the evening in search of a spring, happens across a meadow where young girls are dancing. Correcting their mistaken impression of him that led them to stop their dance, he commends himself to them as a friend of dancing and an advocate of their favorite god, Cupid or Eros. "God's advocate am I before the Devil: but he is the Spirit of Gravity" (Gottes Fürsprecher bin ich vor dem Teufel: der aber ist der Geist der Schwere; Z II 10; *KSA* 4, 139). He sings a song for their dance with their god, "a dance- and mocking-song on the Spirit of Gravity" (ein Tanz- und Spottlied auf den

Geist der Schwere), whom he identifies as his own "supreme and most powerful Devil, of whom they say he is 'Lord of the World'" (allerhöchsten grossmächtigsten Teufel, von dem sie sagen, dass er "der Herr der Welt" sei; *Z* II 10; *KSA* 4, 140). Taking up these images from "On Reading and Writing," Zarathustra sings of his own dance with Life and with Wild Wisdom, his two great loves.

This second song opens with Zarathustra addressing Life: "Into your eye I looked of late, O Life! And into the unfathomable I seemed then to be sinking" (In dein Auge schaute ich jüngst, oh Leben! Und in's Unergründliche schien ich mir da zu sinken; *Z* II 10; *KSA* 4, 140). This report on the Night-Song draws a response from Life, who pulls him out of the unfathomable with her golden fishing rod and laughs mockingly at being called unfathomable: "'So runs the talk of all fish,' you said; 'What *they* do not fathom is unfathomable'" ("So geht die Rede aller Fische, sprachst du; was *sie* nicht ergründen, ist unergründlich"; *Z* II 10; *KSA* 4, 140). Life then describes herself for him:

"But changeable am I only and wild and in all things a woman, and not a virtuous one:
　Even though you men call me 'the Profound' or 'the Loyal,' 'the Eternal,' 'the Mysterious.'
　But you men always confer on us your own virtues — ah, you virtuous ones!"

["Aber veränderlich bin ich nur und wild und in Allem ein Weib, und kein tugendhaftes:
　"Ob ich schon euch Männern 'die Tiefe' heisse oder 'die Treue', 'die Ewige', 'die Geheimnisvolle'.
　"Doch ihr Männer beschenkt uns stets mit den eigenen Tugenden — auch, ihr Tugendhaften!" (*Z* II 10; *KSA* 4, 140)]

Zarathustra cannot accept Life's gift that she can be fathomed, and he adds a name to what men call her — "the Incredible" (die Unglaubliche) — saying: "I never believe her and her laughter when she speaks wickedly of herself" (ich glaube ihr niemals und ihrem Lachen, wenn sie bös von sich selber spricht; *Z* II 10; *KSA* 4, 140). Has Life spoken wickedly of herself in suggesting that she can be fathomed? That an unvirtuous male could fathom her? His song goes on to report a private meeting with his Wild Wisdom, who angrily berated him: "You will, you desire, you love, for that alone you *laud* Life!" (Du willst, du begehrst, du liebst, darum allein *lobst* du das Leben! *Z* II 10; *KSA* 4, 140). He "almost answered wickedly and told the Angry One the truth" (fast [. . .] bös geantwortet und der Zornigen die Wahrheit gesagt) — the truth that these are the best of reasons for lauding Life though they are not Wild Wisdom's reasons (*Z* II 10; *KSA* 4, 140).

Reflecting on the lovers' triangle in which he is caught, Zarathustra confesses that he loves only Life from the ground up and that he is often too fond of Wild Wisdom because she reminds him so much of Life. But Life has a final way of appealing to him. "Who is that then, this Wisdom?" (Wer ist denn das, die Weisheit?), she asks, and Zarathustra answers eagerly, as rash with Life as he is sparing of Wild Wisdom, confessing his love for Wisdom to her rival (Z II 10; KSA 4, 141). Life is not angry with him, and acts as if he had spoken of her when he said, "Changeable she is and stubborn [. . .] Perhaps she is wicked and false, and a female in every way; but when she speaks ill of herself, precisely then is she most seductive" (Veränderlich ist sie und trotzig [. . .] Vielleicht ist sie böse und falsch, und in Allem ein Frauenzimmer; aber wenn sie von sich selber schlecht spricht, da gerade verführt sie am meisten; Z II 10; KSA 4, 141). Wisdom is most seductive when she speaks a skepticism or even ignorance — Zarathustra's love for his skeptical Wild Wisdom kept him from believing Life when she offered herself to be fathomed. But he will learn to believe Life after all. The third song, "The Grave-Song" ("Das Grablied"), ends on a resurrection, a recovery of what is deepest in him and most his own but that had almost been killed in him (Z II 11; KSA 4, 145). And that leads to "On Self-Overcoming" ("Von der Selbst-Ueberwindung"), the chapter that records the successful resolution of the songs: the pure gift-giver of the Night-Song receives the gift Life offered in the Dance-Song; fathoming Life, Zarathustra recovers his own nature as promised in the Grave-Song (Z II 12; KSA 4, 146–49). And gaining that, he can solve the riddle of the wisest.

In "On Self-Overcoming" Zarathustra reaches the deepest point in his odyssey; appropriately, he addresses the fewest, "you wisest" (ihr Weisesten), the philosophers who bestowed virtuous names on unvirtuous Life (Z II 12; KSA 4, 146). (When Nietzsche approached the same point in *Beyond Good and Evil* (*Jenseits von Gut und Böse*), he said that the rest of us listen in without permission.)[4] Life's gift to Zarathustra is the truth about herself, about *life*, which in *Thus Spoke Zarathustra* stands for all that is. He uses that truth about the whole, the fundamental fact, for a single purpose here, to solve the riddle of the wisdom of the wisest, to persuade them that he has understood them.

"Will to truth" (Wille zur Wahrheit) — these first words of the chapter state the virtuous name the philosophers gave their passion (Z II 12; KSA 4, 146). Zarathustra calls it "will to the thinkability of all beings" (Wille zur Denkbarkeit alles Seienden), the desire of philosophers that the whole be rational, thinkable by the human intellect and, Zarathustra charges, subject to mastery and control (Z II 12; KSA 4, 146). Will to truth is a "*will to power*" (*Wille zur Macht*; Z II 12; KSA 4, 146). Zarathustra used this term once before: in "On the Thousand Goals and One," it named the power behind the greatest power on earth, good and evil. Here too he connects it with good and evil: the valuations of the philosophers, the content they gave to *good* and *evil*, created the world within which "the unwise" (die Unweisen) dwelt. Zarathustra is on familiar ground for philosophers, for he puts in his own imagery Plato's teaching, seriously meant and actually practiced, of the philosopher-king. Philosophers ruled through creative acts of naming the good, that for the sake of which everyone does what one does. Zarathustra puts this Platonic thought in an image: the unwise, the people, are like a river directed in its forward streaming by an ark of values invented by the wisest. Opposition to the ruling ark may rise out of the river, but "not the river is your danger and the end of your will to power, you who are wisest, but that will itself, the will to power — the unexhausted procreative life-will" (nicht der Fluss ist eure Gefahr und das Ende eures Guten und Bösen, ihr Weisesten: sondern jener Wille selber, der Wille zur Macht, — der unerschöpfte zeugende Lebens-Wille; *Z* II 12; *KSA* 4, 147). Who is Nietzsche's Zarathustra? He is the wise rival of the wisest who ruled through their creative power to name the good; their rival brings a new good and evil that promises to redirect the river of humanity. Life's gift of insight led Zarathustra to this action; the deepest insight sparks the most comprehensive act; in Platonic language, philosophy leads to political philosophy.

Zarathustra makes an unusual effort to persuade his exclusive audience. He presents himself as a most canny student of the most reluctant subject, "the way of all the living" (von der Art alles Lebendigen), the way of all beings: with a hundred-fold mirror he caught the look of the living, when its mouth was closed, that its eye might speak to him (*Z* II 12; *KSA* 4, 147). Imploring the wisest to "test in earnest whether I have crept into the very heart of Life" (prüft es ernstlich, ob ich dem Leben selber in's Herz kroch und bis in die Wurzeln seines Herzens!), he reports a fabulous deed of stealthy entry into Life's fortress to steal her unchangeable secret to her changeable ways (*Z* II 12; *KSA* 4, 147). He reports to the wisest her private words to him alone, "'Behold,' she said, 'I am *that which must always overcome itself*'" ("Siehe, sprach es, ich bin das, *was sich immer selber überwinden muss*"; *Z* II 12; *KSA* 4, 148). Privately revealing herself as will to power, she claims victory over him and his will to truth, and ends by saying "where Life is, there too is will: [. . .] will to power!" (wo Leben ist, da ist auch Wille: [. . .] Wille zur Macht!; *Z* II 12; *KSA* 4, 149). "Thus did Life once teach me" (Also lehrt mich einst das Leben), says Zarathustra to the wisest, the Zarathustra whose Dance-Song reported that his Wild Wisdom prohibited believing that Life was fathomable (*Z* II 12; *KSA* 4, 149). Now he knows that Life was not speaking wickedly of herself when she said she could be fathomed.

Zarathustra's claim to have stolen into Life's fortress and won her secret from her makes no claim to some miraculous harmony between the mind of man and the nature of things, only that the path into the way of all beings is not completely closed. The elusive secret of beings lies in the secret heart of the highest or most spirited beings, the wisest: the soul is "the ladder of a hundred rungs on which to climb to knowledge" (eine Leiter mit hundert Sprossen, auf welchen du zur Erkenntnis steigen kannst; *HA* I §292; *KSA* 2, 236). This ontological claim based on psychological insight is itself only an interpretation, but Zarathustra's invitation to the wisest makes it an interpretation that can certify itself as true to the phenomena, including the phenomenon of wisdom. For Zarathustra breaks off his speech challenging the wisest, saying "Let us at least *talk* of this" (Reden wir nur davon), talk among ourselves knowing that "there is many a house still to build!" (manches Haus giebt es noch zu bauen!; *Z* II 12; *KSA* 4, 149). With these last words, the second chapter to mention the will to power, and the only one to analyze and defend it, points back to the first — humanity is "housed" by the greatest power on earth, good and evil — and points ahead to the third and last — the first glimpse of the new good and evil that aspires to house humanity ("On Redemption" ["Von der Erlösung"]). The economy with which Nietzsche employs his most basic phrase demonstrates its singular importance: *will to power* names the fundamental fact, names it for philosophers, directs them toward what it founds, the moral evaluations of good and evil, and looks to a new founding — let that be the subject of philosophers' talk.

Zarathustra's next seven speeches, some of his greatest, analyze forms of modern wisdom and include an analysis of the poet, the modern revolutionary, and the modern nihilism soon to be pervasive. The disciples return to the narrative for these speeches on poetry, revolution, and nihilism, and they prove themselves unequal to the tests Zarathustra administers; he shakes his head three times, first at one, then at all, last at the most beloved. Then, in an unguarded speech in "On Redemption," Zarathustra reveals his own failure, his inadequacy for the task he has only now glimpsed, the path he himself must take (*Z* II 20; *KSA* 4, 177–82).

"On Redemption," Zarathustra's single most important speech, begins as he is crossing the great bridge. In a speech to cripples who accompany him, he refuses to heal them, to redeem them from their ills, and he reflects on the crippled, fragmentary character of even those thought most whole, the geniuses. Turning to his disciples, he speaks in profound dismay, *Unmut*, the feeling of being deprived of moral courage in the face of peril. In this uncharacteristic mood he speaks with increasing inwardness until he ends speaking only to himself. In revelatory forgetfulness of his audience, Zarathustra betrays how he is still fragmentary and crippled and what it would take to be redeemed. The importance of the speech lies in the fact that in his mood of dismay Zarathustra glimpses for the first time the thought for the sake of which Nietzsche wrote *Thus Spoke Zarathustra*.

Zarathustra's dismay focuses on a universal crippledness: "the Now and the Formerly on earth" (das Jetzt und das Ehemals auf Erden) offer only "fragments and severed limbs and dreadful accidents — but no human beings!" (Bruchstücke und Gliedmaassen und grause Zufälle — aber keine Menschen!; *Z* II 20; *KSA* 4, 179). The future alone offered promise to him. Standing on the bridge, himself "a bridge to the future" (eine Brücke zur Zukunft), but also a cripple, he asks on behalf of his disciples, "Who is Zarathustra to us?" (wer ist uns Zarathustra?; *Z* II 20; *KSA* 4, 179). Answering with questions, he ends by saying that all his thought and endeavor have aimed to compose into one the fragmentary character of the human, the promise that human being could be "the redeemer" (der Erlöser) of the accident and chance that has governed the human till now. He then defines redemption in a formula: "To redeem that which has passed away and to re-create all 'It was' into a 'Thus I willed it!' — that alone should I call redemption!" (Die Vergangenen zu erlösen und alles 'Es war' umzuschaffen in ein 'So wollte ich es!' — das hiesse mir erst Erlösung!; *Z* II 20; *KSA* 4, 179). There is only one possible agent of such redemption — human will. But whereas Zarathustra taught when he first returned to his disciples that the will is the liberator, he teaches now that the will is still imprisoned — he interprets for his disciples the nightmare of the previous speech, "The Soothsayer" ("Der Wahrsager"), that his most beloved disciple could not interpret (*Z* II 19; *KSA* 4, 173–74). The liberating will is chained by the "It was" (Es war), the unwillable past peering out of glass coffins in the nightmare. The will cannot break "time's desire" (der Zeit Begierde) — Zarathustra's phrase for the temporality lived by humans in which all future promise passes through the present into an unwillable past from which it governs or pre-determines all futures (*Z* II 20; *KSA* 4, 180).

Zarathustra's speech of dismay now reports the reaction of the creative will to its imprisonment in time. At issue is not the will of everyman, but the creative will of those few geniuses whom Zarathustra described to the cripples: *they* created the worlds of images and concepts within which the rest of humanity dwell, *they* fashioned the tablets of good and evil that rule humanity. But what directed them in their creating and fashioning? *Revenge* is Zarathustra's answer as he defines a cardinal point in Nietzsche's historical study of the human soul. "This, yes this alone, is what *revenge* itself is, the will's ill will toward time and its 'It was'" (Diess, ja diess allein ist *Rache* selber: des Willens Widerwille gegen die Zeit und ihr "Es war"; *Z* II 20; *KSA* 4, 180). Zarathustra earlier accused the preachers of equality of acting out of revenge and informed the wisest that their will to truth is a will to power; here he unites revenge and will to power in a comprehensive accusation against traditional wisdom. For the imprisoned creative will, turned sick with revenge for its imprisonment, "acquired spirit" (lernte Geist) — it devised spiritual ways of expressing itself, teachings that cursed the world and invented mad forms of redemption from it. "*The spirit of revenge*: that, my friends, has been up to now humanity's best reflection" (*Der Geist der Rache*: meine Freunde, das war bisher der Menschen bestes Nachdenken; *Z* II 20; *KSA* 4, 180). That reflection began with a primary fact of human existence, suffering, interpreted here by Nietzsche as taking its most spiritual form in the will's suffering of imprisonment. Suffering demands to be interpreted as meaningful, and meaning was given: "Wherever there was suffering, there was always supposed to be punishment. [. . .] Willing itself and all life were supposed to be — punishment! And then cloud upon cloud rolled across the spirit" (Wo Leid war, da sollte immer Strafe sein. [. . .] also sollte Wollen selber und alles Leben — Strafe sein! Und nun wälzte sich Wolke auf Wolke über den Geist; *Z* II 20; *KSA* 4, 180). These clouds are the moral and religious interpretations of life that have dominated Western culture, and Zarathustra lists four historic teachings of cosmic or divine justice from Greek philosophy, Christianity, modernity, and the nihilism that followed. He calls each a preaching of madness, without mentioning the mad redemption each promised. His accusation is comprehensive: the ontological and theological forms of justice in traditional philosophy and religion spring from the passion of revenge.

When Zarathustra's speech of dismay turns finally to the possibility of redemption it turns completely inward, as he traces the logic of his thought to its only possible conclusion, the only form of redemption possible, redemption grounded in a will with a different disposition toward life, toward beings and time. "All 'It was' is a fragment, a riddle, a cruel coincidence — until the creating will says to it: 'But thus I willed it!' [. . .] 'But thus do I will it! Thus shall I will it!'" (Alles "Es war" ist ein Bruchstück, ein Räthsel, ein grauser Zufall — bis der schaffende Wille dazu sagt: "aber so wollte ich es!" [. . .] "Aber so will ich es! So werde ich's wollen!"; *Z* II 20; *KSA* 4, 181). Zarathustra gives two ways in which the creative will could perform this redemptive act of willing that turns the fragments into a desired and loved whole: "who has taught [the will] reconciliation with time, and something higher than any reconciliation?" (Wer lehrte [den Willen] Versöhnung mit der Zeit, und Höheres als alle Versöhnung ist?; *Z* II 20; *KSA* 4, 181). Reconciliation with time would end the enmity between the will and time's desire, marking a historic gain for humanity by replacing revenge with acceptance of "It was." Zarathustra says nothing more about this great gain, instead immediately adding to the already mentioned "something higher" the essential thought. "Something higher than any reconciliation the will that is the will to power must will — yet how shall this happen?" (Höheres als alle Versöhnung muss der Wille wollen, welcher der Wille der Macht ist —: doch wie geschieht ihm das?; *Z* II 20; *KSA* 4, 181). The conclusion that is present, but not stated, as Zarathustra falls silent, is this: the will to power must will the eternal return of everything that was and is — only *that* is higher than reconciliation. Zarathustra ends his speech on redemption without speaking the redeeming conclusion to its argument, the thought for which *Thus Spoke Zarathustra* exists.

Such is the writerly thrift Nietzsche was able to master in presenting the thought that had first come to him two years earlier, the thought for which he composed this book. Thrift also governs his speech about the fundamental thought, will to power: Zarathustra first named it as the ground of the greatest power on earth, good and evil; he next used it in a private speech to the wisest ones where he pronounced it nine times to expound the highest, most spiritual form it could take as the source of the teachings of the wise; and he names it now, once and for the last time, making it the source of the thought for which the book exists. The final naming of *will to power* is the first intimation of *eternal return*. Not merely being *reconciled* to everything that was and is, but *wanting*, passionately desiring, the eternal return of life just as it is — *that* is the redeeming teaching that leads humanity beyond the historic teachings of revenge founded, like it, on the will to power of the wise.

A glimpse is not a teaching — the content and implications of eternal return are the theme of part 3. But one thing is clear: the insight gained in "On Redemption" glimpses the ultimate teaching that is true to the earth, the teaching Zarathustra had said must await some Overhuman for whose arrival all must be sacrificed. We watch as Zarathustra finds the task of the Overhuman thrust on him. The chapter answers its question, Who is Zarathustra?: he is the herald of the Overhuman on the way to becoming the very one he heralded. In the two final speeches of part 2 Zarathustra reflects on the necessary prudence he must practice now that he knows what his destiny is.

Part 3

The third part has sixteen chapters, not twenty-two like the first two parts. But chapter 16 is "The Seven Seals (or: The Yea- and Amen-Song)" (Die sieben Siegel [Oder: das Ja- und Amen-Lied]), an image taken from the Book of Revelation, the Apocalypse, the last book of the Bible, a book with twenty-two chapters that is the sixty-sixth book of the Bible. The image of seven seals (and many other images from the Book of Revelation) seals the point: fifteen chapters and seven seals make twenty-two and three sets of twenty-two make sixty-six. Nietzsche made the final chapter of the final part of *Thus Spoke Zarathustra* indicate his ambition — what is revealed in the third part of *Zarathustra* is apocalyptic, a new teaching that means to defeat the teaching of the Bible and all teachings like it, teachings of revenge on life that Zarathustra the Persian once bequeathed to the future monotheisms of Judaism, Christianity, and Islam.

The third part opens on the night the second closed. Zarathustra ascends the mountain at midnight after leaving his disciples, speaking to himself of his resoluteness in facing his coming task. Standing at the summit, he says he knows his lot. Having descended to the sea on the other side, he first speaks to the sea, but laughs at himself for speaking consolation even to the sea — "*love* is the danger of the loneliest — love of anything *if only it is alive!*" (die *Liebe* ist die Gefahr des Einsamsten, die Liebe zu Allem, *wenn es nur lebt!*; Z III 1; *KSA* 4, 196). With that recognition of his love and its dangers he sets sail; the next three chapters take place on board ship, as Zarathustra sails away from the Blessed Isles of hope for his disciples and takes up the task he once assigned to them.

The first explicit appearance of the teaching for which the book exists occurs in "On the Vision and the Riddle" ("Vom Gesicht und Räthsel"; Z III 2; *KSA* 4, 197–202). Zarathustra there relates his "vision of the loneliest" (das Gesicht des Einsamsten) to awed sailors, the right audience: "You bold searchers, tempters, experimenters [. . .] where you can *guess*, you hate to *deduce*" (euch, den kühnen Suchern, Versuchern [. . .] wo ihr *errathen* könnt, da hasst ihr es, zu *erschliessen*; Z III 2 §1; *KSA* 4, 197). His vision has two scenes. In the first, he uses the thought of eternal return as a club to banish the "Spirit of Gravity," called here "my Devil and arch-enemy" (meinem Teufel und Erzfeinde; Z III 2 §1; KA 4, 198). In the second, the embrace of the thought by a "young shepherd" (jungen Hirten) sparks in him the joyous laughter that Zarathustra wants for himself (Z III 2 §2; *KSA* 4, 201). This first presentation of eternal return in *Zarathustra* enacts in these dramatic scenes the two reactions Nietzsche had pictured in his first-ever presentation of the thought, in *The Gay Science*: "If this thought gained possession of you, it would transform you as you are or perhaps crush you" (Wenn jener Gedanke über dich Gewalt bekäme, er würde dich, wie du bist, verwandeln und vielleicht zermalmen; *GS* §341; *KSA* 3, 570). The thought crushes Zarathustra's enemy, the world-hating Spirit of Gravity, when it takes possession of him: this hated world, from which it had devised historic forms of escape through otherworldly dreams, is not just the only world, it is a world that in its smallest details returns exactly as it was and returns eternally. The gateway "Moment" (Augenblick) with its eternal path backward into the past and eternal path outward into the future becomes unbearable when Zarathustra's reasoning persuades him that the paths meet in the circle of time and that every moment recurs an infinite number of times, including this horrifying moment of defeat for a spirit that hates earthly life. When the scene switches to the young shepherd, he is choked by a heavy black snake that has crawled into his throat, but he is transfigured when the thought takes possession of him: he bites its head off, spits it out, and laughs the transformed laugh of his happiness.

Being crushed by the thought or being transfigured in joy depends on one thing only, according to the *Gay Science*: "How well disposed would you have to become to yourself and to life *to crave nothing more fervently* than this ultimate eternal confirmation and seal?" (Oder wie müsstest du dir selber und dem Leben gut werden, um nach Nichts *mehr zu verlangen*, als nach dieser letzten ewigen Bestätigung und Besiegelung?; *GS* §341; *KSA* 3, 570). The thought is therefore a "selective principle" (*auswählendes* Princip; *KSA* 10, 24[7], 646), "the great *cultivating* idea" (den großen *züchtenden* Gedanken; *KSA* 11, 25[227], 73); it does what Nietzsche said religions do: encourage and enhance particular dispositions and types while discouraging and making shameful their opposites (*BGE* §61; *KSA* 5, 80). If, as Zarathustra claimed, the dominant religions have had their source in revenge against earthly life, they encouraged and enhanced a disposition that would find the thought of eternal return crushing. Given the historic cultural dominance of the passion of revenge, its inventive, poetic power to create worlds of human habitation, the opposite passion of love of the earth, potentially no less inventive or poetic, would create a world for human habitation built on affirmation of self and world, and there is no more world-affirming thought than the thought of, the desire for, the eternal return of self and world. Raised and educated in that thought, humans with a natural disposition to love self and world would have their disposition cultivated, made strong and proud; those with the opposite disposition would have their disposition starved and condemned, made weak and shameful. The vision and riddle that Zarathustra announces to bold adventurers means to re-make a world through re-educating the world, founding it on the passion of love, not revenge.

The first of the other two chapters on the sea voyage has Zarathustra look back in affirmation of the course he has followed and look ahead to his embrace of his abysmal thought, followed by another return to his disciples. The second chapter, "Before Sunrise" ("Vor Sonnen-Aufgang"), is the secret speech of Zarathustra's aspiration, of his "godlike desires" (göttlichen Begierden), the most rash and perhaps most beautiful of his speeches (*Z* III 4; *KSA* 4, 207). On the open sea he stands before the sky in the pure abyss of light at the passing moment between the starry blackness of night and the sun-dominated brightness of day. Speaking to the open sky, he affirms its openness and emptiness, its depth and silence, as a blessing. In the past, the open sky had been slandered: interpretations of the heavens made them the source of punishment and reward, home to watchful gods who exercised the vengeance desired of them by humans. Other clouds obscured the sky's openness: "necessity, purpose, and guilt" (Zwang und Zweck und Schuld; *Z* III 4; *KSA* 4, 208), "human constructs of domination" (menschliche Herrschafts-Gebilde; *KSA* 13, 11[99], 49), were invented by creative humans to cloud the open sky, to read the purposes of some "rational spider" (Vernunft-Spinne) into the actual innocence of becoming (*Z* III 4; *KSA* 4, 209). Emulating the most enviable, Zarathustra aspires to the creative act that replaces those curses with a blessing. His teaching of eternal return blesses every earthly thing by providing a sheltering vault of blue sky over it, saying to it: be what you are, be eternally what you are. Following the long curse of earth-enclosing teachings on necessity, purpose, and guilt, Zarathustra's blessing is a letting be, an allowing, a sparing. Deriding any sovereign rationality, Zarathustra hymns the open and indeterminate universe of modern science. "God is dead, everything is permitted" is not an expression of moral horror or of mere liberation; it is the pandemonium of allowing each thing to be what it is. Humans thus "raise [themselves] *to justice*" (erhebt sich *zur Gerechtigkeit*; *KSA* 11, 26[119], 182), exhibiting what Nietzsche required of the new thinker, "justice and love for all that exists" (Gerechtigkeit und Liebe gegen Alles, was da ist; *D* §43; *KSA* 3, 51). Justice allows them to be what they are, and love exults in them, saying, be eternally what you are. Zarathustra's hymn to the sky expresses a core element of Nietzsche's project, "the dehumanization of nature and then the naturalization of the human after it has achieved the new concept of nature" (die Entmenschung der Natur und dann die Vernatürlichung des Menschen, nachdem er den reinen Begriff "Natur" gewonnen hat; *KSA* 9, 11[211], 525); it puts into poetry Nietzsche's thought as a comprehensive ecological philosophy in love with the earth.

The end of "Before the Sunrise" prepares the following four chapters, for Zarathustra learns a final lesson from the silent sky as it reddens with the coming sunrise: he makes a pact of silence with the sky, a silence that does not betray itself with silence but covers itself with speech. The coming speeches in daylight, addressed to many audiences, seem open and reckless, but maintain silence on the things spoken to the open sky. Traveling on the mainland after his sea voyage, Zarathustra is an observer of what he now knows the history of the next two centuries will be: the long twilight of nihilism (*KSA* 13, 11[411], 189). He makes speeches criticizing modern virtue even as he is aware of the uses of silence and the art of seeming as forms of concealment. Hearing a supposed follower who has turned his teaching into an instrument of his own vengeance, Zarathustra learns in "On Passing By" ("Vom Vorübergehen") that "where one can no longer love, there one should — *pass by!* —" (wo man nicht mehr lieben kann, da soll man — *vorübergehen!* —; *Z* III 7; *KSA* 4, 225). Finally, Zarathustra returns to the city where he first made disciples and finds in "On Apostates" ("Von den Abtrünnigen") that they have all embraced new beliefs (*Z* III 8 §1; *KSA* 4, 226). His speech describes the coming age of the death of the Christian God as an age of new pieties and old skepticisms. The death of the Christian God is different from the death of the Greek gods that that God caused — and this allows Zarathustra to tell Nietzsche's best joke, one of hundreds: One of the gods announced one day, "There is only one God, thou shalt have no other gods before me!" And all the other gods — died laughing. Thus there was only one God (*Z* III 8 §2; *KSA* 4, 230).

Zarathustra returns to his cave in "The Return Home" ("Die Heimkehr"), a chapter celebrating the solitude that lasts till the end of the book. In solitude, says Zarathustra, "the words and word-shrines of all Being spring open for me: all Being wants to become word here, all Becoming wants to learn from me here how to speak" (alles Seines Worte und Wort-Schreine [springen] auf: alles Sein will hier Wort werden, alles Werden will hier von mir reden lernen) — Being as Becoming comes to word in his speech (*Z* III 9; *KSA* 4, 232). The next three chapters, the last before he definitively and finally confronts the thought of eternal return, have special importance as Zarathustra's review of his public teaching and his final formulation of it. Schooled by his errors and his audience, he gives speeches that are a guide to what he has become; correcting the errors and excesses of the first and second parts, they state what will be required of friends of his teaching. The new measure that his speech will give to all things revalues all values from the perspective that to be is to be will to power. Zarathustra's revaluation aims to give a new weight to things in which even evil, especially evil, is re-evaluated. In "On the Three Evils" ("Von den drei Bösen"), Zarathustra can bless the three most accursed things — sensuality, the lust to rule, and selfishness — because he understands them in a way that is true to the earth and true to the human (*Z* III 10; *KSA* 4, 235–40). "On the Spirit of Gravity" ("Vom Geist der Schwere") — which is about the one they say is the master of the world — shows how the new center of gravity, eternal return, can give all things a new weightiness in accord with nature (*Z* III 11; *KSA* 4, 241–45). "On Old and New Tablets" ("Von alten und neuen Tafeln"), the longest chapter of the book and one that Nietzsche singled out as "decisive" (entscheidend; *EH Z* §4; *KSA* 4, 341), anticipates a new political order honoring a "new nobility" (neuer Adel) of leaders and teachers true to the earth, the alternative to the two types of tyranny that rule modern times, the single tyrant who views himself as the meaning of history and the tyranny of mass democracy that praises itself as the end of history (*Z* III 12 §11–§12; *KSA* 4, 254–55).

Then come the last four chapters, containing the event which needs the whole book to be interpreted, the final chapters, or so Nietzsche thought while writing them. Zarathustra's previous speeches and discourses show that the wise create the ark of values carried forward by the people, the thousand peoples so far carrying forward values based on revenge against mortal life. The one thing now needed and now possible is a wise teacher to redirect the river of humanity with values true to the earth. That would be "redemption." Redemption occurs in "The

Convalescent" ("Der Genesende"), an event that the speeches and songs following it interpret.

"The Convalescent" solves the easy riddle of "The Vision and the Riddle": Zarathustra is the young shepherd who redeems himself from the universal sickness, the madness of the teachings of revenge inspired by the Spirit of Gravity. Zarathustra, "the advocate of life, the advocate of suffering, the advocate of the circle" (der Fürsprecher des Lebens, der Fürsprecher des Leidens, der Fürsprecher des Kreises), summons his "most abyss-deep thought" (abgründlichsten Gedanken) and then collapses (Z III 13 §1; KSA 4, 271). When he comes to himself, his animals, his eagle and snake, minister to him as seven days pass. On the seventh day the animals speak, and in a dialogue Zarathustra and his animals give different interpretations of what has happened. The animals speak for "all things" (alle Dinge) to say that the world awaits Zarathustra like a garden (Z III 13 §2; KSA 4, 272). For "those who think as we do" (solchen, die denken wie wir), they say, "all things themselves are dancing" (tanzen alle Dinge selber), and they speak of Being in a way Zarathustra never had: "Eternally rolls the wheel of Being [. . .] eternally runs the year of Being [. . .] eternally is built the same house of Being [. . .] eternally true to itself remains the ring of Being" (Ewig rollt das Rad des Seins [. . .] ewig läuft das Jahr des Seins [. . .] ewig baut sich das gleiche Haus des Seins [. . .] ewig bleibt sich treu der Ring des Seins; Z III 13 §2; KSA 4, 273). They speak ontologically of a non-teleological coming and going of all things, a celebratory dance of beings of which they are part. Does Zarathustra think as they do? He keeps his distance, speaking first of language, not of "all beings" (alle Dinge); "words and tones" (Worte und Töne) are "seeming-bridges" (Schein-Brücken) that bridge what is eternally separated, the soul and the world; with words and tones "human beings can dance over all things" (damit tanzt der Mensch über alle Dinge; Z III 13 §2; KSA 4, 272). Every time he speaks, he playfully disparages what the animals said. Still, he acknowledges that they well knew what had to be fulfilled as the monster crawled down his throat and he bit its head off and spat it out. He states precisely what it was that nearly choked him on the thought of eternal return: willing the return of what takes revenge on life, willing the return of the small human being.

His animals put a stop to his long central speech, telling him that he must find new songs to heal his soul. They know well, he says, "what comfort I devised for myself in those seven days! That I should have to sing again, *that* is the comfort I devised for myself" (welchen Trost ich mir selber in sieben Tagen erfand! Dass ich wieder singen müsse, — *den* Trost erfand ich mir und *diese* Genesung; Z III 13 §2; KSA 4, 275). In their final speech his animals claim to know much more: who Zarathustra is — "*you are the teacher of eternal return*" (*du bist der Lehrer der ewigen Wiederkunft*); what he teaches — "that all things recur eternally" (dass alle Dinge ewig wiederkehren); and "if you wanted to die now [. . .] how you would then speak to yourself" (wenn du jetzt sterben wolltest, [. . .] wie du da zu dir sprechen würdest; *Z* III 13 §2; *KSA* 4, 275–76). The animals then state the most literal vision of eternal return that ever occurs in Nietzsche's writings: "The knot of causes in which I am entwined recurs [. . .] I come again [. . .] *not* to a new life or a better life or a similar life [. . .] I come eternally again to the self-same life, in the greatest and smallest respects" (Der Knoten von Ursachen kehrt wieder [. . .] Ich komme wieder [. . .] *nicht* zu einem neuen Leben oder besseren Leben oder ähnlichen Leben: — Ich komme ewig wieder zu diesem gleichen und selbigen Leben, im Grössten und auch im Kleinsten; *Z* III §2; *KSA* 4, 276).

Zarathustra cannot comment on their words when they fall silent, for he did not hear that they were silent; he lay still with his eyes closed, "conversing with his soul" (unterredete sich eben mit seiner Seele; *Z* III 13 §2; *KSA* 4, 277). That conversation of Zarathustra's self and soul constitutes the last three chapters, a solitude made complete when his animals discreetly steal away, honoring the great stillness around him. The book thus offers the two forms of redemption it has led its reader to expect. The animals speak and sing as part of "all things" redeemed under the shelter of the open sky that permits them to be the things they are; Zarathustra speaks and sings as the shepherd, the thinker and singer who does not think as they do but as the solitary one the book has prepared: the wise creator of values that redirect the stream of humanity, the founder of the new teaching on life that redeems things from revenge. What that self says to its soul in the final three chapters is the culmination of Zarathustra's course in his private account of his redemption.

The first of these three songs, "On the Great Yearning" ("Von der grossen Sehnsucht"), is the key to the others because it defines their setting (*Z* III 14; *KSA* 4, 278–81). Twenty-two times he says "O my soul" (Oh meine Seele); the first eleven recount his past gifts that made his soul what she is, the second eleven describe her present state and — after his soul speaks for the only time in the book — a prophecy of what her songs will bring. His redemption is in his past but demands future acts, songs of his soul, which is like a vine weighted with grapes awaiting the harvester. The yearning of "On the Great Yearning" is the longing of Zarathustra's soul for the harvester who will arrive from across the sea, a vintner with the vintner's knife; the seas will quiet as his bark floats in, a "golden wonder, around whose gold all good and bad and wonderful things now frolic" (das güldene Wunder, um dessen Gold alle guten schlimmen wunderlichen Dinge hüpfen; *Z* III 14; *KSA* 4, 280). The master of the golden wonder is the harvesting vintner, "your great releaser, O my soul, the Nameless — for whom only future songs will find names" (dein grosser Löser, oh meine Seele, der Namenlose — dem zukünftige Gesänge erst

Namen finden; *Z* III 14; *KSA* 4, 280). Those future songs begin with the next two, the songs of Zarathustra's soul for the coming Nameless. The Nameless has a name, not spoken at the culmination of this book, though all *but* spoken, and actually spoken at the culmination of Nietzsche's next book, *Beyond Good and Evil* (*BGE* §295; *KSA* 5, 237–39). For the one who arrives from across the sea to celebrants of all kinds is Dionysos, god of arriving and dying, of intoxication, of the sap and flow of life. And he arrives to Ariadne, the title Nietzsche gave to this chapter as he was writing it, Ariadne, a name for the mother goddess of all life. Dionysos's arrival to Ariadne prepares the final two chapters of the book, the first a song for a dance whose successful outcome turns the second into a marriage song. These three songs ("Von der grossen Sehnsucht," "Das andere Tanzlied," Die sieben Siegel") therefore resolve and close the three songs on which the whole book turns, the songs at the center of the second part ("Das Nachtlied, "Das Tanzlied," "Das Grablied").

Thus Spoke Zarathustra, a fable of the becoming of a philosopher, ends on songs of celebration heralding a religion. Nietzsche, like Plato, held that philosophy must superintend religion, the means of cultivating and educating a population that cannot by its very nature be philosophical. The religion of Dionysos and Ariadne, embodying in image the truth, holding procreating life highest under the open sky, would generate practices and celebrations true to the earth while recognizing that gods too philosophize, that the whole is a wonder worthy of a god's awe and investigation.

The dissonance of "The Dance-Song" from part 2 is resolved in "The Other Dance-Song" ("Das andere Tanzlied"), for three characters have become two: Zarathustra's Wild Wisdom has been transformed into love of Life. But is his love genuine? Proving that it is makes this song prelude to a marriage song. Zarathustra no longer sinks into the unfathomable when gazing into Life's eye but sees there a Dionysian vision. Inviting him to dance, Life draws him on while eluding his attempts to possess her. Zarathustra finally takes command but she resists, needing proof that he loves her from the ground up. Confessing that she loves him for his wisdom, she is suspicious because the wise have always imposed names on her that are untrue to her. Hearing the midnight bell, she forces him to think of his mortality: does he think death means Life is untrue to him? And does that lead him to be untrue to her? "You think, O Zarathustra, well I know, of how you want to leave me soon!" (du denkst daran, oh Zarathustra, ich weiss es, dass du mich bald verlassen willst!; *Z* III 15 §2; *KSA* 4, 285). "Yes" (Ja), he answers, "but you also know that —" (aber du weisst es auch —; *Z* III 15 2; *KSA* 4, 285). What he whispers in her ear for her alone can only be what the book as a whole makes necessary — that he will return to her eternally. She responds: "You *know* that, O Zarathustra? No one knows that —" ("Du *weisst* Das, oh Zarathustra?

Das weiss Niemand. —; *Z* III 15 §2; *KSA* 4, 285). No one can *know* that life eternally returns but one cannot love life more than to *desire* its eternal return exactly as it is. For a knower like Zarathustra to affirm eternal return proves to Life that he loves her. She yields to this highest affirmation of her, as the next and final song, the marriage song, shows. In "The Seven Seals (or The Yea- and Amen-Song)," Zarathustra sings the song of his marriage to "Eternity" (Ewigkeit): as befits a marriage he gives "Life" (das Leben) her married name, a name that proves that this wise man loves her.

By borrowing a final symbol — seven seals — from the old revelation and by sealing the ending in its own way — the Yea- and Amen-Song — Nietzsche proclaims, as the Book of Revelation had done, a new battle for the earth, spiritual warfare against the Spirit of Gravity in all its forms. The seven stanzas of the final song gather a portrait of Zarathustra from his chief features of his portrayal in the book — soothsayer, destroyer, creator, bringer of harmony, seafarer, dancer, and finally, supremely, flier — and declare his fitness to marry Life and bestow on her the name Eternity (*Z* III 16; *KSA* 4, 287–91). Children will spring from that marriage, spiritual offspring who will live within the earthly garden of mortal things wanting nothing more than their eternal return just as they are. This consummating act of Nietzsche's fable of Zarathustra completes what he called "the entrance way" (Vorhalle) to his philosophy:[5] it traces the way into his philosophy as insight into the way of all beings, will to power, and as the highest affirmation of that totality that can ever be attained, the desire that it eternally return exactly as it is.

Part 4 and Beyond

The fourth part is fascinating and instructive, for it shows that Zarathustra's now complete entry into his teaching is not the end: he must descend again with it. But the fourth part only prepares that descent, for it presumes parts that would follow it, showing Zarathustra's descent to teach eternal return. The fourth part's great fascination is its exhibition of how advanced Nietzsche knew his own thought to be in relation to his greatest contemporaries, "the superior humans" (die höheren Menschen; *Z* IV 13; *KSA* 4, 356–68). But instead of publishing the fourth part and then going on to write the fifth and sixth parts, Nietzsche decided to speak in his own voice, rather than in Zarathustra's. The books he actually published after *Zarathustra* are all polemics, acts of war engaging contemporary topics while looking back to *Zarathustra* for the deeper points those books only approach. While writing them, Nietzsche was looking forward to another *Hauptwerk*, *The Revaluation of All Values* (*Die Umwerthung aller Werthe*), sometimes titled *The Will to Power* (*Der Wille zur Macht*), and sketching it in extensive notes. Those now-published notes preparing the *Revaluation* contain matters of great interest, but they lack what Nietzsche always gave his published thoughts, a setting within a process of thinking that assigned them their necessary context, nuance, and depth. The landscape of Nietzsche's completed authorship therefore takes this shape: ten years of great books ascending in insight to peak in *Thus Spoke Zarathustra*, then four more years of great polemical books preparing a second peak he never got to write. The absence of that other peak makes Nietzsche's words more true than he could know while writing them: "Among my writings my *Zarathustra* stands alone."

Notes

In this essay, translations from Nietzsche's *Zarathustra* are taken from the version by Graham Parkes, *Thus Spoke Zarathustra: A Book for Everyone and Nobody* (Oxford: Oxford UP, 2005) with minor modifications; translations from other texts are my own.

[1] William H. Schaberg, *Nietzsches Werke: Eine Publikationsgeschichte und kommentierte Bibliographie*, trans. Michael Leuenberger (Quellen, Studien und texte zu Leben, Werk und Wirkung Friedrich Nietzsches, vol. 4) (Basel: Schwabe, 2002), 121.

[2] Graham Parkes, "Introduction," in Friedrich Nietzsche, *Thus Spoke Zarathustra: A Book for Everyone and Nobody* (Oxford: Oxford UP, 2005), pp. ix–xxxiv (here: xvii). In this contribution I have used Parkes's translation, with occasional changes, because of its superiority compared with other available translations.

[3] Martin Heidegger, "Who is Nietzsche's Zarathustra?," trans. Bernd Magus, in *The New Nietzsche: Contemporary Styles of Interpretation*, ed. David B. Allison (Cambridge, MA and London: MIT Press, 1985), 64–79; "Wer ist Nietzsches Zarathustra?" in *Vorträge und Aufsätze* (Pfullingen: Neske, 1954), 101–26.

[4] See *BGE* §30; *KSA* 5, 48.

[5] See Nietzsche's letters of 8 March 1884 and 7 April 1884 to Franz Overbeck, and end of March 1884 and beginning of May 1884 to Malwida von Meysenbug (*KSB* 6, 485 and 496; 490 and 499).

Link to *Beyond Good and Evil*

Although Nietzsche had sought, and found, solitude in Sils Maria, he had not given up on his project for a secular monastery. Before leaving Nice, he had written to Franz Overbeck about his hope, when he returned next winter, to establish "a society" (eine Gesellschaft) in which he would not be completely in hiding: possible members included the poet Paul Lanzky (1852–?), whom Nietzsche had gotten to know in Nice, and Heinrich Köselitz (known as Peter Gast), his trusted friend, perhaps even (as unlikely as it sounds) Paul Rée and Lou von Salomé (*KSB* 6, 494–95). And in a postcard to his mother and his sister in November 1884, he had envisaged Nice as the site of his "future 'colony'" (zukünftige "Colonie"), which would consist of "pleasant people to whom I can teach my philosophy" (sympathische Menschen, vor denen ich meine Philosophie doziren kann; *KSB* 6, 563) — as we shall see, a very different colony from the one his sister had in mind . . .

But Nietzsche was aware that he needed to create a community of readers for his ideas. For, now that it was complete, *Zarathustra* was intended to act as "an entrance-way" (eine Vorhalle; *KSB* 6, 496 and 499) — or, to use a Goethean term, a propylaeum — to his philosophy as a whole, and in 1883, while he was completing part 3 of *Zarathustra*, he was working on "a larger philosophical project" (eine größere philosophische Arbeit; *KSB* 6, 414; cf. *KSB* 6, 427 and 429), provisionally entitled "The Innocence of Becoming: A Guide to Redemption from Morality" ("Die Unschuld des Werdens: Ein Wegweiser zur Erlösung von der Moral"; *KSA* 10, 8[26], 343) or "Morality for Moralists" ("Moral für Moralisten"; *KSA* 10, 7[201], 305–6 and 24[27], 660–61). And Nietzsche felt the need for a stylistic change: despite his enthusiasm for Zarathustra, he also had his doubts (*KSB* 6, 443), and in his notebooks for spring 1884 we find the note that reads: "*Decision*: I want to speak, and no longer Zarathustra" (*Entschluß*. Ich will reden, und nicht mehr Zarathustra; *KSA* 11, 25[277], 83).

In 1885 Nietzsche maintained the life of the wanderer that he had made his own. In April he visited Köselitz again in Venice, where Köselitz found a room for Nietzsche to stay in, not realizing that it was in the house of a prostitute.[1] When his sister announced her engagement to Bernhard Förster, an Orientalist with strong anti-Semitic views who planned to establish an Aryan colony (to be called Nueva Germania) in Paraguay, relations between her and Nietzsche became tense again; he did not attend her wedding in Naumburg, held on 22 May 1885 (the same day, in other words, as Wagner's birthday).[2] Back in Sils Maria for the summer, one of the hottest for many years, Nietzsche began writing the prefaces for new editions of his previous works, with the aim of giving them a new lease on life.[3] It is perhaps revealing that he batted away questions from fellow guests about the kind of books he wrote, although he always did so very politely, or tried to introduce his ideas in a disguised form. (The Fynns — an elderly Englishwoman and her daughter — are a case in point. On one occasion Nietzsche complimented the daughter on the quality of her paintings, her favorite subject being flowers, but advised her to include something ugly, which would serve to intensify the beauty of the flowers; and the next day he showed her a small toad he had caught. But when Emily Fynn, the mother, asked him about his works, Nietzsche's eyes filled with tears, and he begged her, a committed Catholic, not to read the books he had written, since there "so much in them that was bound to hurt her feelings.")[4]

In September, Nietzsche visited Leipzig for negotiations with his old publisher, Schmeitzner. Sales of Nietzsche's works had never been strong (in fact, he never sold many more than a hundred copies),[5] so the new prefaces for the revised editions of his works were part of his efforts to establish a reputation for himself as a recognized philosopher. His choice of subject — morality — was not exactly new, inasmuch as he had begun his psychological dissection of it in 1878 with *Human, All Too Human* (*Menschliches, Allzumenschliches*) and was later to state that his "campaign" (Feldzug) against morality began with *Daybreak* (*Morgenröthe*), published in 1881 (*EH D* §1; *KSA* 6, 329). Yet his style was new — for Zarathustra no longer spoke, but Nietzsche, the "free spirit" — or at any rate different. This mixture of old and new resulted in *Beyond Good and Evil* (*Jenseits von Gut und Böse*), published in August 1886, a book that, as Nietzsche — back in Sils Maria again for the fifth time in the summer of 1886 — told Jacob Burckhardt, "says the same things as *Zarathustra*, but in a different way, in a very different way" (dieselben Dinge sagt, wie mein Zarathustra, aber anders, sehr anders; *KSB* 7, 254).

For instance, the ideal of the *Übermensch* taught by Zarathustra as "a choice kind of being" (eine ausgesuchte Art Wesen) that seeks to lift itself "to its higher task and to a higher state of *being*" (zu ihrer höheren Aufgabe und überhaupt zu einem höheren *Sein*)[6] is symbolized here by the *Sipo matador*, a kind of sun-seeking vine-plant found in Java, that takes hold of trees and climbs up them, in order "to be able to unfold its crown in the open light and openly to display its happiness" (in freiem Lichte ihre Krone entfalten und ihr Glück zur Schau zu tragen; *BGE* §258; *KSA* 5, 207).[7] In other words, the *Sipo matador* illustrates the drive revealed by Zarathustra as present wherever life is (*Z* II 12: *KSA* 4, 149) — the will to power (*BGE* §259; *KSA* 5, 208). For Nietzsche, "the 'tropical man'" (der "tropische Mensch") is also "a beast of prey and a man of prey" (das Raubthier und der Raubmensch), embodied in the figure of the Renaissance *condottiere*, Cesare Borgia (*BGE* §197; *KSA* 5, 117), harking back to his discussion in his essay on Schopenhauer of "subtle beasts of prey" (die verfeinerten Raubthiere; *UM* III §5; *KSA* 1, 378), and anticipating one of the most famous images of his next work, *On the Genealogy of Morals* (*Zur Genealogie der Moral*), the notorious "blond beast" (blonde Bestie) or "beast of prey" (das Raubthier; *GM* I §11; *KSA* 5, 275). Nietzsche does not so much champion "the primeval forest and the tropics" (der Urwald und die Tropen) as urge the recognition of their legitimate existence, drawing the same conclusions that, in his "Tribute to Shakespeare" (Zum Shakespeares-Tag, 1771), Goethe did: "What we call evil is only the other side of good; evil is necessary for good to exist and is part of the whole, just as the tropics must be torrid and Lapland frigid for there to be a temperate zone" (Das, was wir bös nennen, ist nur die andre Seite vom Guten, die so notwendig zu seiner Existenz und in das Ganze gehört, als Zona torrida brennen und Lappland einfrieren muß, daß es einen gemäßigten Himmelsstrich gebe).[8] And he shared with Goethe, and with others, the concern that the "temperate" (*gemässig*) would degenerate into the "mediocre" (*mittelmäßig*),[9] so that, in the image he would use in his next book, there was a risk that the entire world would turn into a vast hospital (*GM* III §14).[10]

In his letter to Burckhardt, Nietzsche wrote that among the problems addressed in *Beyond Good and Evil* were "the unsettling conditions for all growth in culture, that extremely dubious relation between what is called the 'improvement' of humankind (or even 'making it humane') and making the human species great, above all the contradiction between every moral concept and the scientific concept of *life*" (die unheimlichen Bedingungen für jedes Wachsthum der Cultur, jenes äußerst bedenkliche Verhältniß zwischen dem, was "Verbesserung" des Menschen (oder geradezu "Vermenschlichung") genannt wird, und der *Vergrößerung* des Typus Mensch, vor Allem der Widerspruch jedes Moralbegriffs mit jedem wissenschaftlichen Begriff des *Lebens*; *KSB* 7, 254). Yet far from being a dark book, *Beyond Good and Evil*, as Martine Prange shows, dazzles with wit, insight, and intelligence, and proposes a reordering of philosophers depending on the rank of their laughter, "all the way up to those capable of *golden laughter*" (bis hinauf zu denen, die des *goldenen* Gelächters fähig sind; *BGE* §294; *KSA* 5, 236). Fittingly, then, its penultimate section depicts Dionysos, or "the genius of the heart" (das Genie des Herzens), as a god who smiles a halcyon smile (*BGE* §295; *KSA* 5, 239).

Notes

[1] Goethe- und Schiller-Archiv, Weimar, Peter-Gast-Nachlaß; cited in *Chronik*, 610.

2 For an outline of Förster's program for which Elisabeth was so enthusiastic, see her letter to Heinrich Köselitz of 7 January 1883: "Pity, heroic self-denial, Christianity, heroism, vegetarianism, Aryanism, southern colonies etc. etc. I like the sound of all this and in these ideas I feel so completely at home" (Mitleid, heroischen Selbstverleugnung, Christenthum[,] Heldenthum, Vegetarismus, Arierthum[,] südliche Colonien usw. usw. Das ist mir Alles so sympathisch und in diesen Vorstellungen fühle ich mich so zu Hause") (Ernst Pfeiffer, ed., *Friedrich Nietzsche, Paul Rée, Lou von Salomé: Die Dokumente ihrer Begegnung* (Frankfurt am Main: Insel, 1970), 284). For Nietzsche's response to these ideas, see his letter to Elisabeth of December 1887 (*KSB* 8, 218–20).

3 See the texts collected with an extensive introduction in Friedrich Nietzsche, *Ecce auctor: Die Vorreden von 1886*, ed. Claus-Artur Scheier (Hamburg: Meiner, 1990).

4 See Sander L. Gilman, *Conversations with Nietzsche: A Life in the Words of His Contemporaries*, trans. David J. Parent (New York and Oxford: Oxford UP, 1987), 213 and 195.

5 See, for instance, Nietzsche's discontent with the fact that, after the Leipzig Book Fair in 1887, only 114 copies of *Beyond Good and Evil* had been sold (*KSB* 8, 87); or that, by the autumn of 1887, only 106 copies of *Zarathustra* had been sold (*KSB* 8, 140).

6 Compare with Nietzsche's comments about the moment when a species is about to make a "transition into a higher species" (Übergang in eine höhere Art) in "Schopenhauer as Educator" ("Schopenhauer als Erzieher"; *UM* III §6; *KSA* 1, 384). Similarly, what Zarathustra calls the *Übermensch* is described in that essay as the product of *Kultur* — as "the human who feels perfect and unbounded in knowledge and love, in contemplation and ability, and in this completeness is at one with and in nature, as the judge and evaluator of things" (der Mensch [. . .], welcher sich voll und unendlich fühlt im Erkennen und Lieben, im Schauen und Können, und mit aller seiner Ganzheit an und in der Natur hängt, als Richter und Werthmesser der Dinge; *UM* III §6; *KSA* 1, 385).

7 In his *Nachlass* for 1885–86, Nietzsche associates this plant, *Sipo matador*, with his *Zarathustra* project (*KSA* 12, 2[71], 93).

8 Goethe, *Werke: Hamburger Ausgabe*, ed. Erich Trunz, 14 vols. (Hamburg: Wegner, 1948–60; Munich: Beck, 1981), 12:224–27 (here: 227). Similarly, and, in his review of Sulzer's *Die schöne Künste* (*The Fine Arts*) in 1772, Goethe stated that, in nature, "beautiful and ugly, good and evil, all exist side by side with equal rights" (schön und häßlich, gut und bös, alles mit gleichem Rechte nebeneinander existierend; Goethe, *Werke*, 12:15–20 [here: 18]).

9 Compare with the view expressed by C. G. Jung that "to be 'normal' is the ideal aim for the unsuccessful" (der "Normalmensch" ist das ideale Ziel für die Erfolglosen) (C. G. Jung, "Problems of Modern Psychotherapy" (Die Probleme der modern Psychotherapie, 1929/1950), in *Collected Works*, ed. Sir Herbert Read, Michael Fordham, Gerhard Adler, and William McGuire, 20 vols. (London: Routledge and Kegan Paul, 1953–83), 16:70, §161; *Gesammelte Werke*, ed. Lilly Jung-Merker, Elisabeth Ruf, Leone Zander, 20 vols. (Olten and Freiburg im Breisgau: Walter, 1960–83), 16:80, §161).

[10] Compare with Goethe's letter to Charlotte von Stein of 8 June 1781, where he writes, apropos of Herder's *Ideas towards a Philosophy of History of Mankind* (*Ideen zur Philosophie der Geschichte der Menschheit*, 1784–91): "He will certainly have expounded splendidly the ideal dream of humankind that things one day will get better for them. And I must say myself that I believe it to be true that the principle of humanity will one day be victorious, only I fear that at the same time the world will become one great hospital and everyone will be everyone else's humane sick-attendant" (Er wird gewiß den schönen Traumwunsch der Menschheit daß es dereinst besser mit ihr werden möge trefflich ausgeführt haben. Auch muß ich selbst sagen halt ich es für wahr, daß die Humanität endlich siegen wird, nur fürcht ich daß zu gleicher Zeit die Welt ein großes Hospital und einer des andern humaner Krankenwächter werden wird; Goethe, *Briefe*, ed. Kurt Robert Mandelkow, 4 vols. [Hamburg: Wegner, 1962–67], 1:359).

8: *Beyond Good and Evil*

Martine Prange

Toward the end of June 1885, Nietzsche wrote to Resa von Schirn-hofer that he was dictating to Louise Röder-Wiederhold for several hours a day his "thoughts on the dear Europeans of today and — *tomorrow*" (meine Gedanken über die lieben Europäer von heute und — *Morgen*; KSB 7, 59). Thirteen months later, these thoughts were published as the "dangerous" book *Beyond Good and Evil* (*Jenseits von Gut und Böse*, 1886).[1] The book developed out of a reworking of *Human, All Too Human* (*Menschliches, Allzumenschliches*), and it was originally conceived as a companion volume to *Daybreak* (*Morgenröthe*). Toward the end of March, Nietzsche baptized it *Beyond Good and Evil*, a title adopted from the section "Retired" (Ausser Dienst) in *Thus Spoke Zarathustra* (*Also sprach Zarathustra*; KSA 4, 324, cf. BGE §153; KSA 5, 99). After a difficult series of negotiations with potential publishers, he decided to bring out the book himself and to print it with C. G. Naumann in Leipzig. The proofing and printing took place in June and July 1886; his friend, Peter Gast, was closely involved in the editorial process. On 4 August 1886, Nietzsche received the first printed copies.

Nietzsche wrote *Beyond Good and Evil* while he was staying in Sils-Maria, Naumburg, Leipzig, and Nice. Prompted by recurring eye problems and migraines, he had been an ever more passionate visitor of "the South" since 1876 (especially Genoa, Venice, and Nice), searching for haunts where the atmosphere was not too "electric" and cloudy. In line with this, climatologically and medically charged terms such as "southern," "northern," "health," and "sickness" began to play an increasingly vital role in his philosophical works, especially from his second stay in Genoa (in the winter of 1881–82) onwards. "Southern" became the equivalent of "healthy" against "northern" or "sick." These are metaphors for the clear (healthy) or clouded (sick) judgment of religious, moral, aesthetic, epistemological, scientific and political matters. A "healthy" judgment includes the condemnation of Christian morality, German music, philosophical idealism, and cultural and political nationalism. In contrast to the latter, Nietzsche — from *Human, All Too Human* onward and especially in *Beyond Good and Evil* — proclaims "good Europeanism."

The terms "north," "south," "free spirit," "good European," "health" and "sickness" form the conceptual skeleton of Nietzsche's philosophy from *Human, All Too Human* onward. This is especially clear in *Beyond Good and Evil*; in the prefaces Nietzsche wrote in 1886 for reprints of *Human, All Too Human, Daybreak*, and *The Gay Science* (*Die fröhliche Wissenschaft*); in Book 5 of *The Gay Science*, its *The Songs of Prince Vogelfrei* (*Lieder des Prinzen Vogelfrei*); and in the late essay, *The Case of Wagner* (*Der Fall Wagner*). By utilizing a climatological, geographical, and medical terminology as a framework in all these works, Nietzsche links *Beyond Good and Evil* conceptually (and, as it were, in its spirit) with the "free-spirit" or "travel books" *Human, All Too Human, Daybreak*, and *The Gay Science*. More than any other work, however, *Beyond Good and Evil* discloses Nietzsche's critique of modern-day Europe and his expectations with regard to Europe's future.[2] As "philosopher with the hammer," Nietzsche's criticism is not only theoretical, but is also meant to bring about this future.[3] More than in any other book, Nietzsche explicitly does so by introducing a new philosophy of "revaluation of values," claiming that philosophical views form the basis of any culture, because philosophers are "creators of values."

In what follows, I explore *Beyond Good and Evil* from the perspective of Nietzsche's delineation of Europe's future, before discussing the primary intellectual innovations and stylistic features of *Beyond Good and Evil* with regard to Nietzsche's previous work and philosophy in general. Finally, I show how *Beyond Good and Evil* links in with *On the Genealogy of Morals* (*Zur Genealogie der Moral*), which appeared as the follow-up to it in 1887.

A Book on the Future of Europe

In *Beyond Good and Evil*, Nietzsche describes himself as one of the "Europeans of the day after tomorrow (Europäer von Übermorgen; *BGE* §215; *KSA* 4, 151), explaining that "*good* Europeans" (*gute* Europäer) are "*very* free spirits" (*sehr* freie Geister), as opposed to the present-day Europeans he criticizes elsewhere (*BGE* preface; *KSA* 5, 13).[4] These future Europeans are not the inhabitants of the European federation of nation-states of today, but the ones that are "awake" in contrast to the "dogmatic" philosophers.[5] The "dogmatists" are Plato and Kant and all philosophers that operate in their wake.[6] In Nietzsche's view, Plato and Kant lie at the root of the long history of humankind's metaphysical, idealist, rationalist, universalist, and moral view of life; namely, the belief in the human soul and the universally applicable concept of "the good" (that is, life under "the shadow of God"). Plato and Kant have been "standing truth on its head" (die Wahrheit auf den Kopf stellen), by neglecting life's "perspectivism," ignoring that the appearance of things is all there is, and discounting the fact that the body and reason cannot be divided (*BGE* preface; *KSA* 5, 12).

Having been given the task of "wakefulness" (Wachsein; *BGE* preface; *KSA* 5, 12), "the good Europeans" or "very free spirits" bear responsibility for protecting Europe from Platonism and Christianity (which Nietzsche regards as "Platonism for the people").[7] According to Nietzsche, philosophers have the power to rule — and they *have* ruled. For they are the creators of values, of worldviews, that are subsequently spread around the world via religion, economics, politics, science, and art. The "good Europeans" are seen as the new philosopher-kings, the creators of a new worldview revolving around the idea that *"perspectivism* [. . .] is the fundamental condition of all life" (das *Perspektivische*, die Grundbedingung alles Lebens; *BGE* preface; *KSA* 5, 12).[8] This new ontology, which includes the notion of the "will to power," will — if Nietzsche has anything to do with it — form the basis of a new, "truthful" European spirit.[9] He suggests indeed that "Europe breathes a sigh of relief after this nightmare" (Europa von diesem Alpdrucke aufathmet), the "nightmare" referring to "Plato's invention of pure spirit and the Good in itself" (Plato's Erfindung vom reinen Geiste und vom Guten an sich; *BGE* preface; *KSA* 5, 12). Despite breathing a sigh of relief, Europe is still under a "magnificent tension of spirit" (eine prachtvolle Spannung des Geistes), as a result of its immense "struggle against Plato [. . .] the struggle against the Christian-ecclesiastical pressure of millennia" (Kampf gegen Plato [. . .] Kampf gegen den christlich-kirchlichen Druck von Jahrtausenden; *BGE* preface; *KSA* 5, 12–13).[10] Never has there been, he writes, such a strong tension within Europe. Platonism, like its Kantian form of a priori knowledge, is almost overcome: the new philosophers are already coming to bring us alternative modes of thought, hence this is a time of transition marked by the collision of old and new views.

The benefit here is that a great promise for Europe's future awaits us; thanks to this intense tension in our bow "we can now shoot at the furthest goals" (mit einem so gespannten Bogen kann man nunmehr nach den fernsten Zielen schiessen; *BGE* preface; *KSA* 5, 13). Jesuitism and Democratic Enlightenment, Nietzsche explains, were two earlier attempts "to unbend the bow," or to set a new course for Europe by setting new values. *Beyond Good and Evil* is now the third attempt to "unbend the bow":

> We, who are neither Jesuits nor Democrats, nor even German enough, we good Europeans, and free, very free spirits — we still have it, the whole need of spirit and the whole tension of its bow! And perhaps the arrow, too, the task, and — who knows? The goal . . .

> [Wir, die wir weder Jesuiten, noch Demokraten, noch selbst Deutsche genug sind, wir guten Europäer und freien, sehr freien Geister — wir haben sie noch, die ganze Noth des Geistes und die ganze Spannung seines Bogens! Und vielleicht auch den Pfeil, die Aufgabe, wer weiss? Das Ziel . . . (BGE preface; KSA 5, 13)]

To which "goal" or "goals" — to which values far away from Platonism, Christian, and Kantian values — to which *golden dream* will the good Europeans' arrow shoot Europe?

The good Europeans' arrow shoots Europe, first, beyond the idea that "truth remains the truth when one pulls off the veil" (dass Wahrheit noch Wahrheit bleibt, wenn man ihr die Schleier abzieht; *GS* preface §4; *KSA* 3, 352);[11] second, beyond the belief that "good" and "evil" are natural values; and third, beyond nationalism. It shoots to a perspectivist view of life revolving around the idea of "will to power," replacing metaphysical approaches with naturalistic and historical-cultural views, taken from new sciences such as ethnography, sociology, moral psychology, and linguistics. These are approached from an (evolutionary) biological perspective in order to understand humanity "psycho-physiologically," in other words, in its naturalness, including its natural (or necessarily normative) "order of rank."

The New Philosophers versus the Dogmatists: The Value of Truth and the Will to Power

In the first section of *Beyond Good and Evil*, entitled "On the Prejudices of the Philosophers" ("Von den Vorurtheilen der Philosophen"), and its second, entitled "The Free Spirit" ("Der freie Geist"), Nietzsche expounds his idea that new, free-spirited philosophers are about to come to rule in Europe in place of the "dogmatists," launching an extra-moral period in history conveying new values.[12] The vantage point of these new philosophers is the question of the "value of truth" (*BGE* §1–§4 and §16; *KSA* 5, 15–18 and 29–30), their task "the overall development of humanity" (die Gesammt-Entwicklung des Menschen; *BGE* §61; *KSA* 5, 79). Despite the fact that this "new breed of philosophers" or "philosophers of the future" are also lovers of truth, they are not dogmatic, because their truth is not "a truth for everyone" (*BGE* §43; *KSA* 5, 60). Instead, their philosophy revolves around "perspectivism," the idea of the "will to power," and the "revaluation of values." (In fact, solitude and danger are important conditions or characteristics of the new philosophers. The main condition for Nietzsche's "very free spirit" is "danger," because only through danger and pressure can humanity grow [see *BGE* §42; *KSA* 5, 59].) Essential to their perspectivism is the recognition that "appearance, the will to deception, and craven self-interest" as well as "instinct" and "evil" may be just as or even more valuable to life than truth, truthfulness, selflessness, consciousness, and goodness (*BGE* §2; *KSA* 5, 16–17; cf. *BGE* §23 and §44; *KSA* 5, 38–39 and 60–63).[13] In other words, feelings of hatred, envy, greed, and power-lust may be just as important for the growth of humanity and the "total economy of life."

These new philosophers necessarily also question the metaphysical *"belief in oppositions of values"* (*der Glaube an die Gegensätze der Werthe*; *BGE* §2; *KSA* 5, 16), declaring war on the metaphysical neglect of the senses (*BGE* §12; *KSA* 5, 26–27) and assuming that "the moral (or immoral) intentions in every philosophy constitute the true living seed from which the whole plant has always grown" (die moralischen (oder unmoralischen) Absichten [machen] in jeder Philosophie den eigentlichen Lebenskeim aus [. . .], aus dem jedesmal die ganze Pflanze gewachsen ist; *BGE* §6; *KSA* 5, 19–20). Hence, while philosophy needs to question morality, it simultaneously always expresses a morality itself and, when researching the history of philosophy, Nietzsche seeks to understand the morality that a philosophy is seeking to inculcate.[14] In order to understand this morality, he uses psychology, which can reveal "in what order of rank the innermost drives of his nature stand with respect to each other" (in welcher Rangordnung die innersten Triebe seiner Natur zu einander gestellt sind; *BGE* §6; *KSA* 5, 20).

Subsequently, and conscious of the order of values and the needs and sufferings that drive them, philosophers can set new values. According to Nietzsche, philosophy is the most powerful tool for such value creation. In fact, philosophy *is*, he claims, the (psychological-historical, that is, genealogical) investigation and creation of new values. Philosophy "creates the world in its own image" (die Welt nach ihrem Bilde), so that philosophy is "this tyrannical drive itself, the most spiritual will to power, to the 'creation of the world,' to the *causa prima*" (dieser tyrannische Trieb selbst, der geistigste Wille zur Macht, zur "Schaffung der Welt," zur causa prima; *BGE* §9; *KSA* 5, 21–22). Both old and new philosophers, like all life, are driven by the will to power, but only the new philosophers are conscious of this. As part of the creation and spread of new values for Europe, they will also circulate the doctrine of the will to power against the old philosophical idea that humans are subjects with — and defined by — a free will.

This fact prompts one to ask: what is the "will to power"? In *Beyond Good and Evil*, Nietzsche famously writes that "life itself is will to power" (Leben selbst ist Wille zur Macht; *BGE* §13; *KSA* 5, 27–28). His primary assumption is that "a living will wants to *discharge* its strength" (Vor Allem will etwas Lebendiges seine Kraft *auslassen*), and that, because "every drive craves mastery" (jener Trieb ist herrschsüchtig) it discharges its strength in physiological and social ways (*BGE* §6; *KSA* 5, 20). Nietzsche understands subjectivity or the individual will — which elsewhere he also calls *soul* (*BGE* §12; *KSA* 5, 27) — to be a "'subject-multiplicity'" and a "'society constructed out of drives and affects'" ("Seele als Subjekts-Vielheit" und "Seele als Gesellschaftsbau der Triebe und Affekte") rather than an instance of identity marked by metaphysical slogans such as "I think" or "I will" (*BGE* §12; *KSA* 5, 27). Willing, to Nietzsche, is not an act carried out by some subject. It involves "a plurality of feelings" (eine

Mehrheit von Gefühlen), "commandeering thought" (einen comman-direnden Gedanken), and is "fundamentally an *affect*" (vor Allem noch ein *Affekt*; *BGE* §19; *KSA* 5, 32). As an affect, willing is explained as "specifically the affect of the command" (zwar jener Affekt des Commando's), arguing that "what is called 'freedom of the will' is essentially the affect of superiority with respect to something that must obey" (das, was "Freiheit des Willens" genannt wird, ist wesentlich der Überlegenheits-Affekt in Hinsicht auf Den, der gehorchen muss; *BGE* §19; *KSA* 5, 32).

Hence, rather than believing in the causality of the will (or, in other words, actions as conscious decisions made from free will), Nietzsche ventures the hypothesis that reality is the reality of our drives, and that a will only affects other wills: "'Will' can naturally have effects only on 'will'" ("Wille" kann natürlich nur auf "Wille" wirken; *BGE* §36; *KSA* 5, 55). He even goes so far as to build a hypothetical ontology, centered on the will to power:

> Assuming, finally, that we succeeded in explaining our entire life of drives as the organization and outgrowth of one basic form of will (namely of the will to power, which is my claim); assuming we could trace all organic functions back to this will to power and find that it even solved the problem of procreation and nutrition (which is a single problem); then we will have earned the right to clearly designate all efficacious force as: will to power. The world seen from inside, the world determined and described with respect to its "intelligent character" — would be just this "will to power" and nothing else. —
>
> [Gesetzt, dass man alle organischen Funktionen auf diesen Willen zur Macht zurückführen könnte und in ihm auch die Lösung des Problems der Zeugung und Ernährung — es ist Ein Problem — fände, so hätte man damit sich das Recht verschafft, alle wirkende Kraft eindeutig zu bestimmen als: Wille zur Macht. Die Welt von innen gesehen, die Welt auf ihren "intelligiblen Charakter" hin bestimmt und bezeichnet — sie wäre eben "Wille zur Macht" und nichts ausserdem. — (BGE §36; KSA 5, 55)]

Willing, therefore, is a "multifarious thing" ([ein] vielfaches Ding), and hence to call this whole process a matter of "I will" is to commit a grammatical and philosophical error: "'Freedom of the will' — that is the word for the multi-faceted state of pleasure of one who commands and, at the same time, identifies himself with the accomplished act of willing" ("Freiheit des Willens" — das ist das Wort für jenen vielfachen Lust-Zustand des Wollenden, der befiehlt und sich zugleich mit dem Ausführenden als Eins setzt), or in other words, with success and the feeling of power that accompanies success (*BGE* §19; *KSA* 5, 32). Moreover, what happens in this society of drives and affects "is what happens in every well-constructed and happy community: the ruling class identifies itself with the successes of the community. All willing is simply a matter of commanding and obeying on the groundwork [. . .] of a society constructed out of many 'souls'" (was sich in jedem gut gebauten und glücklichen Gemeinwesen begiebt, dass die regierende Klasse sich mit den Erfolgen des Gemeinwesens identificirt. Bei allem Wollen handelt es sich schlechterdings um Befehlen und Gehorchen, auf der Grundlage [. . .] eines Gesellschaftsbaus vieler "Seelen"; *BGE* §19; *KSA* 5, 33).

For Nietzsche, "real life is only a matter of *strong* and *weak* wills" (im wirklichen Leben handelt es sich nur um *starken* und *schwachen* Willen; *BGE* §21; *KSA* 5, 36). Consequently, *psychology* or "physio-psychology" is the "queen of the sciences" (Herrin der Wissenschaften; *BGE* §23; *KSA* 5, 39), inasmuch as it is a science that studies morality "as a doctrine of the power relations under which the phenomenon of "life" arises" (als Lehre von den Herrschafts-Verhältnissen [. . .] unter denen das Phänomen 'Leben' entsteht; *BGE* §19; *KSA* 5, 34). Hence, despite the good Europeans' immoralism, there is always some perspective under which life is perceived, and this perspective attests to some morality, even if it is a very nihilistic one. For this reason, psychology is "again the path to the fundamental problems" (Psychologie ist nunmehr wieder der Weg zu den Grundproblemen; *BGE* §23; *KSA* 5, 39); the fundamental problem being "the problem of morality itself" (die eigentliche Probleme der Moral; *BGE* §186; *KSA* 5, 106).

These strong and weak wills, these commanding and obeying wills, lead to a dual typology that comes to play an important role in Nietzsche's thought: the distinction between *slave* and *master* morality. The *new* philosophers, it seems, start their rule in Europe with the "revaluation and reversal" of the old values and by breaking down the *herd* morality, which has caused the steady mediocratization and degeneration of humanity. The question is whether this new future then will be "extra-moral," as is suggested by Nietzsche's division of history into a "pre-moral," a "moral," and an "extra-moral" period (*BGE* §32; *KSA* 5, 50–51), or whether it will instead express an aristocratic *master* morality, as suggested by the title of section nine, "What is Noble?" ("Was ist vornehm?"; *KSA* 5, 205).

Europe's Herd Morality: Slaves and Masters

"Will to power" is the fundamental concept with which the "born psychologist" (geborenen Psychologen) approaches the "history" of the human "soul" (*BGE* §45; *KSA* 5, 65). This psychologist perceives the workings of the human soul as depending on drives, which, by combatting one another, seek to gain mastery of the soul. These workings express themselves in philosophical ideas or "moralities" that these drives unconsciously seek to fulfill. Hence, understanding the (pre-moral, moral, and extra-moral) history of the human soul comes down to the question about the creative and oppressive relations between drives (or *affects*), knowledge, and values, that have formed human identity, morality, culture, and history. This basic question can be broken down into many subquestions. In section 3 of *Beyond Good and Evil*, entitled "The Religious Character" ("Das religiöse Wesen"), for example, Nietzsche focuses on the "problem of *science and conscience*" (das Problem von *Wissen und Gewissen*) of religious characters (*BGE* §45; *KSA* 5, 65). He goes on to examine the *cruelty* that, in his view, is at the root of Christianity. By "cruelty," Nietzsche is thinking of the way in which, according to his account, human reason was suppressed in order to subjugate the ideas that dominated the beginnings of Christianity and to replace "science" with "conscience." This event, he continues, meant the first drastic "revaluation of all values" in human history. Nietzsche characterizes it as the "slave-revolt" (Sklaven-Aufstand) against "a skeptical, southern, free-spirited world" (einer skeptischen und südlich-freigeisterischen Welt) and the concomitant rise of Christianity (*BGE* §46; *KSA* 5, 66). He further explains this "inversion" (Umwerthung) of values as arising from what he calls an "Oriental" need for something deeply unattractive to Nietzsche — for *revenge*:

> This was the revenge of the Orient, the deep Orient, this was the revenge of the oriental slave on Rome with its noble and frivolous tolerance, on Roman "Catholicity" of faith. And what infuriated the slaves about and against their masters was never faith itself, but rather the freedom from faith, that half-stoic and smiling nonchalance when it came to the seriousness of faith. Enlightenment is infuriating. Slaves want the unconditional; they understand only tyranny, even in morality. They love as they hate, without nuance, into the depths, to the point of pain and sickness — their copious, hidden suffering makes them furious at the noble taste that seems to deny suffering.

> [Es ist der Orient, der tiefe Orient, es ist der orientalische Sklave, der auf diese Weise an Rom und seiner vornehmen und frivolen Toleranz, am römischen "Katholicismus" des Glaubens Rache nahm: — und immer war es nicht der Glaube, sondern die Freiheit vom Glauben, jene halb stoische und lächelnde Unbekümmertheit um den Ernst des Glaubens, was die Sklaven an ihren Herrn, gegen ihre Herrn empört hat. Die "Aufklärung" empört: der Sklave nämlich will Unbedingtes, er versteht nur das Tyrannische, auch in der Moral, er liebt wie er hasst, ohne Nuance, bis in die Tiefe, bis zum Schmerz, bis zur Krankheit, — sein vieles verborgenes Leiden empört sich gegen den vornehmen Geschmack, der das Leiden zu leugnen scheint. (BGE §46; KSA 5, 67)]

To understand the different types of humanity, and the "revaluation of values" that underlies the landmark changes in history, which are characterized by the emergence of new "types" of humanity, Nietzsche seeks to grasp the physiological or psychological need for certain values by looking at the kind of pain that drove men to these need and values. In this regard, he is especially interested in the cruelty of asceticism, the self-inflicted pain and discipline, as we see for example in "solitude, fasting, and sexual abstinence" (Einsamkeit, Fasten und geschlechtlicher Enthaltsamkeit; *BGE* §47; *KSA* 5, 67), in other words, the kind of suffering that man chooses to sublimate his "*hidden* suffering" (*verborgenes* Leiden) that drives him to revenge. Nietzsche, alluding to Schopenhauer, reformulates this interest into another subquestion: "How is negation of the *will* possible? How is the saint possible?" (Wie ist Willensverneinung möglich? wie ist der Heilige möglich? *BGE* §46 and §47; *KSA* 5, 67 and 68).

Nietzsche appreciates asceticism, the cruelty or tyranny against the self, as a form of passive nihilism, of life- or will-negation, which is a psychologically very different state of affairs from the one of Greek affirmation and gratitude (see *BGE* §49; *KSA* 5, 70). He wants to understand how this ascetic and cruel "religious neurosis" or "religious character" came about and developed, and what its modern expression looks like. In other words, what kind of need and pain lay behind Christian values and made them so strong that they were able to usher in the change in culture and history from its "pre-moral" to its "moral" period? And how does this need show itself today, in a time of "magnificent tension"?

"From the beginning, Christian faith has been sacrifice: sacrifice of all freedom [...], cruelty" (Der christliche Glaube ist von Anbeginn Opferung: Operfung aller Freiheit [...], Grausamkeit), he writes, and "its presupposition is that the subjugation of spirit *causes indescribable pain*" (seine Voraussetzung ist, dass die Unterwerfung des Geistes unbeschreiblich *wehe thut*; *BGE* §46; *KSA* 5, 66). On this account, Christians sacrificed to their god "the strongest instincts they had, their 'nature'" (die stärksten Instinkte, die man besass, seine "Natur"; *BGE* §55; *KSA* 5, 74). Modern people can no longer relate to the image of a "God on the Cross"; so instead, the modern form of this pain, need, and cruelty, he continues, expresses itself in Schopenhauer's nihilism, in the sacrifice of God for nothingness, in the negation of the will by the saint (*BGE* §47; *KSA* 5, 67–69, cf. *BGE* §55; *KSA* 5, 74). Nietzsche considers Schopenhauer's "half-Christian, half-German" (halb christlichen, halb deutschen) pessimism (*BGE* §56; *KSA* 5, 74) — and Wagner's opera *Parsifal* — to be "the latest epidemic outbreak" (letzten epidemischen Ausbruch) of "the religious neurosis" (die religiöse Neurose) before history progresses to the extra-moral period, which, like the pre-moral religions of antiquity, revolves around *gratitude* (rather than Christian *fear*) (*BGE* §47; *KSA* 5, 68; cf. *BGE* §49; *KSA* 5, 70).

The historical transgression of morality, Nietzsche claims, started with Descartes, the father of modern philosophy. Since Descartes, philosophy has been out "to assassinate the old concept of the soul [. . .] the fundamental presupposition of the Christian doctrine" (ein Attentat auf den alten Seelen-Begriff [. . .] die Grundvoraussetzung der christlichen Lehre; *BGE* §54; *KSA* 5, 73). As a form of "epistemological skepticism," modern philosophy is fundamentally *"anti-Christian"* (*antichristlich*; *BGE* §54; *KSA* 5, 73). Looking "beyond good and evil," that is, no longer being "under the spell and delusion of morality" (im Bann und Wahne der Moral), involves the inverse ideal of Schopenhauerian world-negation, or "the ideal of the most high-spirited, vital, world-affirming individual" (das Ideal des übermüthigsten lebendigsten und weltbejahendsten Menschen; *BGE* §56; *KSA* 5, 75). Nietzsche expects that for someone who looks "beyond good and evil," "the concepts of 'God' and 'sin,' which are the most solemn concepts of all and have caused the most fighting and suffering, will seem no more important to us than a child's toy and a child's pain seem to an old man" (die Begriffe "Gott" und "Sünde," nicht wichtiger, als dem alten Manne ein Kinder-Spielzeug und Kinder-Schmerz erscheint; *BGE* §57; *KSA* 5, 75). Such a person will have "looked deeply into the world" (tief in die Welt gesehen) and come to understand "the wisdom that lies in human superficiality" (welche Weisheit darin liegt, dass die Menschen oberflächlich sind; *BGE* §59; *KSA* 5, 78). Those who, in the magnificent words of *The Gay Science*, are "superficial — *out of profundity!*" (oberflächlich — *aus Tiefe*; *GS* preface §4; *KSA* 3, 352) experience an Epicurean joy in superficiality and in forms, to which "an instinct of preservation" (erhaltender Instinkt) attracts them (*BGE* §59; *KSA* 5, 78).

Looking at the history of Christianity, the Epicurean person regards this history as a great "comedy," as one long attempt at "the *deterioration of the European race*" (*Verschlechterung der europäischen Rasse*), as an "almost willful degeneration and atrophy of humanity" (fast willkürliche Entartung und Verkümmerung des Menschen), prompting the following question: "Doesn't it seem as if, for eighteen centuries, Europe was dominated by the single will to turn humanity into a *sublime miscarriage?*" (Scheint es denn nicht, dass Ein Wille über Europa durch achtzehn Jahrhunderte geherrscht hat, aus dem Menschen eine *sublime Missgeburt* zu machen? *BGE* §62; *KSA* 5, 83). By this, Nietzsche means that because Christianity has turned the human beings into a "herd animal" (ein Heerdenthier), into "something mediocre" (Mittelmässiges), "the European of today" (der heutige Europäer; *BGE* §62; *KSA* 5, 83) is someone who knows how to obey, but does not use his full potential and capacities to express himself as human being:

> The oddly limited character of human development [. . .] is due to
> the fact that the herd instinct is inherited best, and at the cost of

the art of commanding [. . .]. This is in fact the situation in Europe today; I call it the moral hypocrisy of the commanders [. . .]. The herd man of today's Europe gives himself the appearance of being the only permissible type of man.

[Die seltsame Beschränktheit der menschlichen Entwicklung [. . .] beruht darauf, dass der Heerden-Instinkt des Gehorsams am besten und auf Kosten der Kunst des Befehlens vererbt wird. [. . .]. Dieser Zustand besteht heute thatsächlich in Europa: ich nenne ihn die moralische Heuchelei der Befehlenden. [. . .] Auf der anderen Seite giebt sich heute der Heerdenmensch in Europa das Ansehen, als sei er die einzig erlaubte Art Mensch. (BGE §199; KSA 5, 119)]

A morality of pity and "neighborly love" helps tame humans, as do all representative constitutions, by replacing "the commander with an agglomeration of clever herd men" (durch Zusammen-Addiren kluger Heerdenmenschen die Befehlshaber zu ersetzen; *BGE* §199; *KSA* 5, 120). As a consequence of all of which Nietzsche arrives at the following conclusion: "*Morality in Europe these days is the morality of herd animals*" (*Moral ist heute in Europa Heerdenthier-Moral*; *BGE* §202; *KSA* 5, 124).

Having investigated various kinds of morality throughout the history of humankind, Nietzsche concludes that there are, in fact, only two types of morality: a "slave" (or "herd") morality" and a "master morality," a *Herren-Moral* and a *Sklaven-Moral* (*BGE* §260; *KSA* 5, 208). Again, we must consider how this view of morality relates to Nietzsche's diagnosis of his own age as being in a historical transition stage from the moral period to the extra-moral. Then, we must explore how the different kinds of morality relate to Nietzsche's medical, geographical, and philosophical differentiation between "northern sickness" and "southern health."

Northern Barbarians and Southern Schools of "Convalescence"

In his description of the religious character provided in section 3 of *Beyond Good and Evil*, Nietzsche associates first Christianity and then antiquity with a spirituality formed by climatological and geographical circumstances. He seeks to explain the different kind of pains, needs, and emotions underlying religion and morality as a function of their "native soil." It makes a difference whether one is born in "the north," stemming from barbarians, or in the south, where a noble gratitude to life and aristocratic "freedom from faith" (Freiheit vom Glauben) are, he suggests, more common (*BGE* §49 and §46; *KSA* 5, 70 and 66). Nietzsche makes a link between, on the one hand, "gratitude" and, on the other, "aristocracy" and "free-spiritedness," suggesting that a "southern" affirmative approach to life is both aristocratic and extra-moral. For the "skeptical, southern, free-spirited world," Nietzsche explains, had experienced "a centuries-long struggle between schools of philosophy" (einen Jahrhunderte langen Kampf von Philosophenschulen) and undergone an "education in tolerance" (die Erziehung zur Toleranz), which makes it "*not* the simple, rude, laborer's faith with which a Luther or Cromwell or some other northern barbarian of spirit clung to its God and its Christianity" (*nicht* jener treuherzige und bärbeissige Unterthanen-Glaube, mit dem etwa ein Luther oder ein Cromwell oder sonst ein nordischer Barbar des Geistes an ihrem Gotte und Christenthum gehangen haben; *BGE* §46; *KSA* 5, 66).[15] The northern faith does not, in fact, run that deep: "The Latin races seem to have much more of an affinity to their Catholicism than we Northerns do to Christianity in general" (Es scheint, dass den lateinischen Rassen ihr Katholicismus viel innerlicher zugehört, als uns Nordländern das ganze Christentum überhaupt), Nietzsche claims, adding that "we Northerns are descended from barbarian races, even as far as our talent for religion goes — it is a *meager* talent" (wir Nordländer stammen unzweifelhaft aus Barbaren-Rassen; *BGE* §48; *KSA* 5, 69). When it comes to religion, "the whole of Protestantism is devoid of any southern *delicatezza* [. . .] lacking any nobility of demeanor and desire" (der ganze Protestantismus entbehrt der südlichen delicatezza; aller Vornehmheit der Gebärden und Begierden ermangelt; *BGE* §50; *KSA* 5, 70). Hence, where the south is "deep," "sophisticated," "delicate," "aristocratic," "free-spirited," and "life-affirmative," the north is shallow, barbarian, and backward-looking. He suggests that, in the south, humanity has explored more of its powers and therefore attained a higher level of culture there than in the north, where early barbarism developed directly into the obedient type of human, without the intervention and resulting sophistication of centuries of philosophical education.[16]

This image of the "barbarian," unfree north and "delicate," free-spirited south is reiterated in section 8, entitled "Peoples and Fatherlands" ("Völker und Vaterländer"), where Nietzsche applies his genealogical method to the historical and psychological development of a people in more detail. Once again, he takes climatological and geographical aspects as his starting point, in order to draw more general and ahistorical conclusions about what can be identified as "northern" (or "German") and "southern" (or "Mediterranean") spirit. He does so to acquire insight into the role that geographic and demographic changes may play with regard to the future of Europe: in other words, what effect they have on *affects*, the constellations and tensions between *drives*, the *pains* and *needs* behind them, and indeed the philosophical thought that emerges from the combination of all these.

In his (ultimately, highly negative) judgment on German music, German language and literature, German style, and the German soul, the

South stands out as a positive counter-example. In his analysis in this section, the North and the South are considered (in Shapiro's words) two "interdependent and antagonistically related zones of intensity."[17] They are interdependent, because Europe, in its democratization and unification, is increasingly becoming a "mix of cultures." Due to "their increasing independence from that *determinate* milieu where for centuries the same demands would be inscribed on the soul and the body" (ihre zunehmende Unabhängigkeit von jedem *bestimmten* milieu, das Jahrhunderte lang sich mit gleichen Forderungen in Seele und Leib einschreiben möchte), people are, Nietzsche believes, gradually becoming more and more alike (*BGE* §242; *KSA* 5, 182). In the long run, however, Nietzsche expects that because of (or despite) democratization and globalization, there will arise a "new type," or the "good European." This good European is a mix of north and south, a mix of cultures, someone who is no longer plagued by relapses into "fatherlandishness" (Vaterländerei), and who is "an essentially supra-national and nomadic type of person who, physiologically speaking, is typified by a maximal degree of the art and force of adaptation" (einer wesentlich übernationalen und nomadischen Art Mensch, welche, physiologisch geredet, ein Maximum von Anpassungskunst und -kraft als ihre typische Auszeichnung besitzt; *BGE* §242; *KSA* 5, 182).[18]

At the same time, however, the process of "becoming European" as a result of democratization and globalization further entrenches the typological distinction between two kinds of people: the slaves and the masters, or the ones that obey and the ones that command.[19] These are, throughout history, the types of individual to which Nietzsche reduces humanity, but he also speaks of "the hybrid mixed man of Europe" (der europäische Mischmensch; *BGE* §223; *KSA* 5, 157). So what is Nietzsche really looking for when he thinks about the new, extra-moral period, and of the good European as an exponent of this period? The ideal, it seems, is a commanding type of individual: but someone who commands and obeys *only himself*, a truly *autonomous* person. This person is "a kind of chaos" (eine Art Chaos) or a multitude, consisting of a mix of affects, of wills, of tastes, of values, of cultures (*BGE* §224; *KSA* 5, 158). What matters is that there is one commanding will to give this variety — of wills, tastes, values, and cultures — *one style*. This style, however personal and unique, is characterized by gratitude, by a surplus of life-energy, and the (moral and aesthetic) values created by this autonomous philosopher are an expression of a master-morality.

In other words, both kinds of morality, that of the slave and that of the master, could result from democratization, globalization, and the mix of cultures. Rather disdainfully, Nietzsche remarks that Europe has been plunged into a state of "half-barbarism" (Halbbarbarei), thanks to "the democratic mixing of classes and races" (die demokratische Vermengung der Stände und Rassen; *BGE* §224; *KSA* 5, 158). Here as elsewhere, it must be said, Nietzsche seems to be on dangerous ground, using a Lamarckian biological perspective of humankind to justify anti-democratic politics. Yet his anti-democratic politics, it should be noted, do not involve him in an argument for an authoritarian state and a nationalist politics. On the contrary, they lead him precisely to propagating "good Europeanism" as a cosmopolitan, nomadic lifestyle. He does not clarify, however, how these *nomads* relate to or will form a "new caste to rule Europe" (einer neuen über Europa regierenden Kaste) (*BGE* §251; *KSA* 5, 195). This lacuna has shown itself to be a dangerous aporia in Nietzsche's thought.

Nietzsche's Philosophical Achievement and Style

Beyond Good and Evil is another book in the series of Nietzsche's mature works written by someone who saw himself as a *free spirit*, starting with *Human, All Too Human*. *Ecce Homo* describes the stylistic expression of his *Freigeisterei* as "hard, cruel," and "halcyonic" (*EH* preface §4, *Z* §4 and §8, *BGE* §2; *KSA* 6, 259, 341 and 349, 351). Like the other "free-spirited" books, *Beyond Good and Evil* is written in aphorisms (totaling 296), which are grouped in nine chapters. The chapters carry titles, while most of the aphorisms do not have titles. The book bears the subtitle "Prelude to a Philosophy of the Future" ("Vorspiel einer Philosophie der Zukunft"), and includes a preface and an "aftersong" or *Nachgesang*, entitled "From High Mountains" ("Aus hohen Bergen"). The title of this aftersong refers to the distance with which Zarathustra looked upon the world, as opposed to the author of *Beyond Good and Evil*, who finds himself forced to "focus on things that are closest to it, the age, our *surroundings*" (das Nächste, die Zeit, das *Um-uns* scharf zu fassen; *EH BGE* 2; *KSA* 6, 351), and it reminds us that after the "*no-doing*" part of the revaluation of values, we have to return to the "yea-saying" part.

A passage from Nietzsche's *Nachlass* helps us appreciate his ambitions in *Beyond Good and Evil*, and his achievements in it as well. Nietzsche's description of his own writings as "travel-books" (or *Reisebücher*), as books that one can read "on the way" (unterwegs), indicates that he saw himself as writing for the "health" (Gesundheit) and "alteration of public opinion" (Veränderung der allgemeinen Ansichten) of modern-day working people. Rather than "stretched systems of thought" (lang gesponnene Gedankensysteme), Nietzsche offers "the hasty and turbulent soul of traveling" (dem beflügelten und unruhigen Wesen der Reise): not so much a book *to read* as a book to which one *can turn*:

> One clings to some sentence today, and to another tomorrow and one thinks finally again with the heart: back and forth, up and down, as the mind drives one, in such a way that one finds pleasure and

well-being every time again. Gradually, a certain general reconsideration of opinions emerges out of such excited — genuine, because unforced — reflection: and with it that general feeling of spiritual recovery, as if the bow has been given a new string and is strung even tighter than ever before. One has traveled with benefit.

[An irgend einem Satze bleibt man heute, an einem anderen morgen hängen und denkt einmal wieder heute aus Herzensgrunde nach: für und wider, hinein und drüber hinaus, wie einen der Geist treibt, so dass es einem dabei jedesmal heiter und wohl im Kopfe wird. Allmählich entsteht aus dem solchermaassen angeregten — ächten, weil nicht erzwungenen — Nachdenken eine gewisse allgemeine Umstimmung der Ansichten: und mit ihr jenes allgemeine Gefühl der geistigen Erholung, als ob der Bogen wieder mit neuer Sehne bespannt und stärker als je angezogen sei. Man hat mit Nutzen gereist. (KSA 8, 23[169], 473–74)]

As a physician of culture, Nietzsche wrote *Beyond Good and Evil* for the recovery of Europe. Compared to his other "free-spirited" books, it displays a more urgent sense of tension. This tension spans a creativity that leads Europe's arrow to new lands, horizons, and values, bringing about a radical change and a new orientation toward a healthy future. One of the ways in which Nietzsche gives form to this "magnificent tension," as well as to his perspectivism (the outcome of his anti-Platonic stance, which forms the substance of the tension) and hence to his "good Europeanism," is precisely by writing aphoristic "travel books."

Beyond Good and Evil is generally described as one of Nietzsche's most "lyrical" books, connecting all the significant features of his philosophy, and therefore constituting the best introduction to it.[20] However, apart from connecting the themes of Nietzsche's wider philosophy, it is a major philosophical achievement in its own right. For *Beyond Good and Evil* deals more explicitly than his other books with the future of Europe, and it conveys more strongly than his previous writings the thought that the whole history of Europe is a matter of philosophy — philosophy, that is, as a set of values created by a struggle of drives craving for mastery within the "total economy" (Gesammt-Haushalt) of the philosopher's soul (*BGE* §20; *KSA* 5, 34).

Hence, more than any of Nietzsche's other books before this one, *Beyond Good and Evil*'s analysis is cast in sociopolitical and physiological terms in an attempt to understand modern and future humanity in terms of its interactions and the cultural values that result from those interactions. "The will to power" is tied to "perspectivism," a much older term in Nietzsche's writing, but now more clearly physiologically labeled and assigned the huge task of forming the content of Europe's future philosophy and system of values or "worldview." Culture owes to *values* the acquisition of *meaning*, and it is only through *meaning* that an era will establish for itself its place in history. For Nietzsche, Europe's future meaning depends on the values of the "will to power" and "perspectivism" that the new anti-Platonic, anti-Christian, and anti-Kantian philosophers will create for Europe.

By focusing on philosophy's task of creating new values, *Beyond Good and Evil* re-establishes Nietzsche's claim that philosophy *is* the creation of values, as well as his definition of historical periods in terms of their respective sets of values. But the new philosopher is also a "good European." This "good European," as has become clear from the discussion above, is a successful "mix of cultures," that is, an individual in whom the democratization and globalization process has not led to slavery (that great danger of democracy), but to the kind of autonomy that is typically Nietzschean: in other words, to the self as the expression of the struggle with his own will to power, arising out of his "war with the self," leading to someone who commands and obeys himself only.

These new philosophers will start their task of preparing us "good Europeans" for the future by insisting on a "revaluation of values," an idea that is strongly emphasized in *Beyond Good and Evil*. Such a revaluation consists above all in questioning, rather than protecting and strengthening (as the old Platonic and Kantian philosophers did), the "value of values." More than in his previous books, Nietzsche here emphasizes the need for "in-depth psychology," for "physio-psychology" or "morphology," to unmask the history of philosophy as having been shaped by certain values, in order to set new values and launch a new philosophy (one free from Christian moral values) that will shape the future of Europe — a Europe inhabited by "good Europeans." These "good Europeans" are to be found in the pages of *Beyond Good and Evil* more than anywhere else in Nietzsche's work, set up against the current, narrow-minded, xenophobic people that identify themselves by way of their national identity and are conservative ("asleep"), inasmuch as they are not open to change.

For the change that is to come is a radical, even dangerous one: nothing less than the entire transformation of Europe and European humanity. This coming change is the hallmark, Nietzsche believes, of contemporary culture, and he investigates the nature of this change while helping to bring the change about, first and foremost by showing us that, in order to change and prepare for the future, we must confront ourselves with the unknown — that is, with ourselves.

Notes

The translations from Nietzsche in this essay are my own.

[1] It was reviewed by Josef Victor Widmann in *Der Bund* (vol. 37, no. 256–57, 16–17 September 1886) under the title "Nietzsche's Dangerous book" (Nietzsches gefährliches Buch) (Raymond J. Benders and Stephan Oettermann,

Friedrich Nietzsche: Chronik in Bildern und Texten [Munich and Vienna: Hanser, 2000], 641–42).

2 *Beyond Good and Evil* is about "the problem Europe or the problem of Europe" (das Problem Europa oder das Problem Europas). See Andreas Urs Sommer, "Skeptisches Europa? Einige Bemerkungen zum Sechsten Hauptstück: wir Gelehrten (Friedrich Nietzsche, *Jenseits von Gut und Böse*, Aphorismen 204–213)" in *Nietzsche und Europa* ed. Volker Gerhardt and Renate Reschke (Berlin: Akademie-Verlag, 2007), 67–78 (here: 68). As Vivetta Vivarelli has remarked, "In *Beyond Good and Evil* Nietzsche considers an 'increasing liberation' as the fate of the 'becoming Europeans'" (in *Jenseits von Gut und Böse* betrachtet Nietzsche eine "wachsende Loslösung" als das Schicksal des "werdenden Europäers") (Vivetta Vivarelli, "Der freie Geist, die amerikanische Rastlosigkeit und die Verschmelzung der Kulturen," in *Nietzsche-Philosoph der Kultur(en)?*, ed. Andreas Urs Sommer [Berlin and New York: Walter de Gruyter, 2008], 529–44 [here: 530]).

3 In *Ecce Homo*, Nietzsche presents *Beyond Good and Evil* as "*no-doing*" (*neinthuend*) in relation to *Thus Spoke Zarathustra*'s "yea-saying" (jasagend), and as on the lookout "for anyone related to me, for anyone who [. . .] would give me a hand with *destruction*" (nach Verwandten, nach Solchen, die [. . .] *zum Vernichten* mir die Hand bieten würden; *EH BGE* §1; *KSA* 6, 350). *Beyond Good and Evil* is further described as "in essence a *critique of modernity*" (in allem Wesentlichen eine *Kritik der Modernität*), pointing to "an opposite type who is as un-modern as possible, a noble, affirmative type" (einem Gegen-Typus, der so wenig modern als möglich ist, einem vornehmen, einem jasagenden Typus; *EH BGE* §2; *KSA* 6, 350).

4 Like Maudemarie Clark and David Dudrick ("The Naturalisms of *Beyond Good and Evil*," in *A Companion to Nietzsche*, ed. Keith Ansell-Pearson [Malden, Oxford, and Carlton: Blackwell, 2006], 148–67), and Laurence Lampert (*Nietzsche's Task: An Interpretation of "Beyond Good and Evil"* [New Haven and London: Yale UP, 2001], I consider *Beyond Good and Evil* to constitute one single whole.

5 See Marco Brusotti, "'Europäisch und Über-Europäisch': Nietzsches Blick aus der Ferne," *Tijdschrift voor Filosofie* 66 (2004): 31–48 (here: 41); and Gert Mattenklott, "Der 'werdende Europäer' als Nomade. Völker, Vaterländer und Europa," in *Nietzsche — Philosoph der Kultur(en)?*, ed. Urs Sommer, 125–48 (here: 129). Nietzsche uses a trope here from Kant, who, in his critical philosophy, linked the "rotten dogmatism" of Leibniz's and Christian Wolff's rationalist metaphysics to the "dogmatic slumber" of Christian doctrine and authoritarian politics. Nevertheless, Nietzsche includes Kant in the pool of "dogmatic philosophers" because of his doctrine of the "thing-in-itself," his attempt to salvage the metaphysical ideas of God and the (immortal) soul, and his moral philosophy based on the categorical imperative.

6 Nietzsche criticizes both Cartesian rationalism and British empiricism, next to German Idealism and forms of what he calls "weak" skepticism (which are, in fact, nihilistic). What these different approaches to reality and knowledge have in common is their (according to Nietzsche, moral) belief in something real and the belief in the possibility of attaining knowledge of that reality. For an analysis of Nietzsche's skepticism in *Beyond Good and Evil*, see Paul van Tongeren, "Nietzsche's Symptomatology of Skepticism," in *Nietzsche's Epistemology and Phi-*

losophy of Science, ed. Babette Babich and Robert C. Cohen (Dordrecht: Kluwer, 1999), 61–72.

[7] The term "guardians of Europe" with which Nietzsche addresses the good Europeans (the anti-Platonist, anti-Kantian philosophers that "put the truth straight") alludes ironically to the "philosopher-kings," the rulers and guardians of Plato's ideal republican city-state in *The Republic*.

[8] Compare with *BGE* §34 (*KSA* 5, 53). "Perspectivism" results from a "radical" or "strong" skepticism, which focuses on the linguistic construction of and naturalistic need for scientific knowledge to point out "the deceptive nature of knowledge" (van Tongeren, "Nietzsche's Symptomatology of Skepticism," 64). See, too, *BGE* §16–§18 and *BGE* §20 (*KSA* 5, 29–31 and 34–35).

[9] Nietzsche thus divides modern Europe in two: into the "good Europeans" who are the guardians that keep watch and into the dogmatists that slumber, lulled by their doctrinaire beliefs. This philosophical division is also a historical division: the dogmatists are the philosophers from Plato to Schopenhauer, the new philosophers are Nietzsche and his followers.

[10] This nightmare is also referred to as "most dangerous of all errors" (gefährlichste aller Irrthümer; *BGE* preface; *KSA* 5, 12). To Nietzsche, man must be translated back to nature (see *BGE* §230 and *GS* §109; *KSA* 5, 169 and *KSA* 3, 469). This includes understanding the essential animality of humankind. From *Twilight of the Idols* (*Götzen-Dämmerung*), it becomes clear that Nietzsche does not imply Rousseau's moral "return to nature," but rather a Goethean, pagan understanding of nature (*TI* "Skirmishes" §48; *KSA* 6, 150–51). Richard Schacht has pointed out the parallel with Hume's naturalism, observing that this does not imply that Nietzsche has a simple, biological understanding of humanity ("Nietzsche and Philosophical Anthropology," in *A Companion to Nietzsche*, ed. Ansell-Pearson, 115–32 [here: 115–17]). But, as Gary Shapiro remarks, this naturalism does imply a *methodological* discussion of ethnocentric principles in historiography and our moral self-understanding ("Geophilosophy and Geoaesthetics," in *A Companion to Nietzsche*, ed. Ansell-Pearson, 477–94 [here: 478]).

[11] I shall not offer another interpretation of the famous phrase with which the preface starts: "Suppose that truth is a woman" (Vorausgesetzt, dass die Wahrheit ein Weib ist; *BGE* preface; *KSA* 5, 11). I should, however, like to note that the German word for truth, "die Wahrheit," is a feminine noun, and that the Greek "sophia" (or wisdom) as the truth that philosophers love and seek, is also female. Is it too superficial to understand this as a joke on Nietzsche's part, where he mocks male scientists and philosophers for their bad manners when it comes to the truth? Note, too, how Nietzsche's phrase is hypothetical, setting the tone for the rest of the book.

[12] Nietzsche distinguishes between a "pre-moral" period of history, a "moral" period, and an "extra-moral" or "immoral" period of history (*BGE* §32; *KSA* 5, 50–51).

[13] Nietzsche calls this "dangerous knowledge," because "we are sailing straight over and *away from* morality; we are crushing and perhaps destroying the remnants of our own morality by daring to travel there [. . .]. Never before have intrepid voyagers and adventurers opened up a *more profound* world of insight" (wir fahren

geradewegs über die Moral *weg*, wir erdrücken, wir zermalmen vielleicht dabei unsren eignen Rest Moralität, indem wir dorthin unsre Fahrt machen und wagen [. . .]. Niemals noch hat sich verwegenen Reisenden und Abenteurern eine *tiefere* Welt der Einsicht offenbart; *BGE* §23; *KSA* 5, 38–39). Clearly, this perspectivism is a result of a radical skepticism that confronts reason with the body (taking the body as source of philosophical knowledge and activity), and objectivity with subjectivity (and the historical, cultural, linguistic and physiological conditions of valuation).

[14] That this is not an easy task becomes clear in the section where Nietzsche asks: "Don't people write books precisely to keep what they hide to themselves?" (Schreibt man nicht gerade Bücher, um zu verbergen, was man bei sich birgt?), and concludes: "Every philosophy is a foreground philosophy" (Jede Philosophie ist eine Vordergrunds-Philosophie; *BGE* §289: *KSA* 5, 234).

[15] Elsewhere, Nietzsche describes Luther's passion for God as one of "the peasant types, naïve and presumptuous" (bäurische, treuherzige und zudringliche Arten; *BGE* §50; *KSA* 5, 70).

[16] Nietzsche's interest in the cultural and spiritual differences between Northern and Southern Europeans is not new. Neither are the associations with "shallowness" and "depth," barbarianism and development. The division between northern, or German, and southern, or Italian, music is already a key framework in *The Birth of Tragedy* (*Die Geburt der Tragödie*), where Italian opera is dismissed as "idyllic" and "moral," and Wagner's music-drama presented as the savior of European musical culture, because of its more successful rejuvenation of Greek art and metaphysical "depth" (see *BT* §21; *KSA* 1, 134–39). For further discussion, see Martine Prange, "Nietzsche's Ideal Europe: Aestheticization and Dynamic Interculturalism from 'The Birth of Tragedy' to 'The Gay Science'" (diss., University of Groningen, 2007), chapter 4; and "Nietzsche's Artistic Ideal of Europe in the Spirit of Wagner's Beethoven-essay," in *Nietzsche und Europa*, ed. Gerhardt and Reschke, 91–117.

[17] As Shapiro also remarks: "However much Nietzsche acknowledges the power of physical geography, he does not endorse any form of geographical reductionism or determinism" ("Geophilosophy and Geoaesthetics," 478).

[18] Elsewhere, Nietzsche argues that "the source of great culture" (der Quell großer Cultur) is "where races are mixed" (wo Rassen gemischt sind; *KSA* 12, 1[153], 45, cf. *HA* I §475 and *BGE* §230; *KSA* 2, 309–11 and *KSA* 5, 167–70, cf. further *KSA* 12, 7[67], 321. As far as Nietzsche's discourse on "race" (or, in German, *Rasse*) in *Beyond Good and Evil* is concerned, I follow van Tongeren's principle that "classes and races in Nietzsche's writings always refer to a physiological and societal way of valuing" ("Nietzsche's Symptomatology of Skepticism," 68). For further discussion of the vexed question of "race" in Nietzsche's thought as a whole, see Gerd Schank, *"Rasse" und "Züchtung" bei Nietzsche* (Berlin and New York: Walter de Gruyter, 2000).

[19] To this already heady brew, Nietzsche introduces considerations of gender, in one passage making a link between commanding and masculinity (*BGE* §209; *KSA* 5, 140).

[20] For an excellent account of Nietzsche's writing style, see Paul van Tongeren, *Reinterpreting Modern Culture: An Introduction to Friedrich Nietzsche's Philosophy* (West Lafayette, IN: Purdue UP, 2000), 51–104.

Link to *On the Genealogy of Morals*

Of Nietzsche's publications to date (i.e., to 1886), *Beyond Good and Evil* (*Jenseits von Gut und Böse*) had enjoyed arguably the best critical reception. In a review for the Swiss journal *Der Bund*, Josef Victor Widmann described it as Nietzsche's "dangerous book" (gefährliches Buch), pointing out that the dynamite used in the construction of the Gotthardbahn, the railway line that traverses the Swiss Alps, always bore a black warning-flag to alert people to its danger — and that Nietzsche's book deserved a similar warning.[1] Nietzsche was delighted by the review, both for commercial reasons (*KSB 7*, 249 and 256) and because, in essence, it said his book was dynamite (*KSB 7*, 251–52 and 258); in *Ecce Homo*, he would allude to Widmann's review and playfully apply his description of *Beyond Good and Evil* to himself: "I am not a man, I am dynamite" (Ich bin kein Mensch, ich bin Dynamit; *EH* "Why I Am a Destiny" §1; *KSA* 6, 365). Other reviews were positive, too, but Nietzsche's old friend, Erwin Rohde, was not impressed.[2] The two friends were reunited when Nietzsche visited Leipzig again in 1886, but the encounters left both disappointed. Rohde told Franz Overbeck that there was "something totally uncanny" (etwas mir damals völlig unheimliches) about Nietzsche, "as if he came from a country where no one else lived" (als käme er aus einem Lande, wo sonst Niemand wohnt);[3] for *his* part, Nietzsche wrote to Overbeck that Rohde's case simply proved that "the best go to seed in the atmosphere of the university" (in dieser Universitäts-Luft entarten die Besten), so that even with someone like Rohde he discovered "an accursed general attitude of I-couldn't-care-less and a complete lack of belief in what he is doing" (eine verfluchte allgemeine Wurschtigkeit und den vollkommenen Mangel an Glauben zu ihrer Sache; *KSB 7*, 208).

While *Beyond Good and Evil* was published with C. G. Naumann, this year also saw the re-issue of a number of Nietzsche's previous works with his other new publisher, E. W. Fritzsch: *The Birth of Tragedy* (*Die Geburt der Tragödie*) acquired its "Attempt at a Self-Criticism" (Versuch einer Selbstkritik); *Human, All Too Human* (*Menschliches, Allzumenschliches*) was re-issued as two-volume work (each with its own new preface), incorporating *Assorted Opinions and Maxims* (*Vermischte Meinungen und Sprüche*) and *The Wanderer and His Shadow* (*Der Wanderer und sein Schatten*); in 1887, a second edition of *Daybreak* (*Morgenröthe*) would be published; and a preface, a fifth section, and an appendix of songs, the "Songs of Prince

Free-As-A-Bird" (Lieder des Prinzen Vogelfrei), would be added to the second edition of *The Gay Science* (*Die fröhliche Wissenschaft*).

Returning from Venice to Naumburg, in May 1886 Nietzsche stopped over in Munich for a couple of days. While he was in the Bavarian city, he received a letter from a local art historian, who expressed an intense interest in meeting Nietzsche. Although the meeting never took place, the art historian would follow Nietzsche's work in the coming years, and following Nietzsche's collapse, now only four years away, would contact his sister. The art historian's name was Julius Langbehn (1851–1907). Nietzsche spent the summer of 1886 once again in Sils Maria, where Widmann's review of *Beyond Good and Evil* made everyone in the small town look at him with different eyes — or so Nietzsche believed (*KSB* 8, 101–2). As usual he was suffering from headaches and migraines, a weak stomach, and poor eyesight,[4] despite all of which he would maintain that "suffering" (Leiden) was never among "the arguments *against* existence" (unter den Argumenten *gegen* das Dasein; *GM* II §7; *KSA* 5, 303). After four weeks visiting the Ligurian coast, spent in the company of Paul Lanzky and W. E. Altsmann, a teacher from the Technical Institute in Genoa, at the end of October he went back to Nice for the winter. Nietzsche's mood was gloomy, and he told Franz Overbeck in a letter of 14 November 1886 that he saw his life in terms of "much sickness and melancholy" (viel Krankheit und Melancholie; *KSB* 7, 282). His existence, he told Overbeck, was founded on a fundamental antinomy: what was *necessary* for his task as a *philosophus radicalis* (his freedom from a job, a wife, a child, social obligations, patriotic duties, religious belief, etc.) was also a source of *deprivation*, of *Entbehrung*, for him — "insofar as I am, fortunately, a living being, and not simply an analytical machine or an apparatus for objective measurement" (insofern ich glücklicher Weise ein lebendiges Wesen und nicht bloß eine Analysirmaschine und ein Objektivations-Apparat bin; *KSB* 7, 282).

The winter in Nice was harsh (*KSB* 7, 294; *KSB* 8, 3 and 9), but Nietzsche was less worried about the fact that the cold weather was turning his fingers blue, and more about the negative effect of Stoicism, of Christianity, and — above all — of Plato. He had been reading, he told Overbeck, Simplicius's commentary on Epictetus, and he found in it the entire philosophical schematic on which Christianity had based itself. Here, he wrote, "the *falsification* through morality of everything factual stands there in its full glory" (die *Fälschung* alles Thatsächlichen durch Moral steht da in vollster Pracht): its psychology was miserable, the philosopher was reduced to a country parson — "And all of it is *Plato's* fault! — he *is still* Europe's greatest misfortune" (Und an alledem ist *Plato* schuld! er *bleibt* das größte Malheur Europas!; *KSB* 8, 9).[5]

So despite his critique of morality in *Beyond Good and Evil*, Nietzsche felt the need to return to the attack on morality; just as *Beyond Good and*

Evil had said "the same things" (dieselben Dinge) as *Zarathustra*, but very differently (*KSB* 7, 254), so in turn he prepared *On the Genealogy of Morals* (*Zur Genealogie der Moral*) as, so the words on the reverse of its title-page explained, a "supplement and clarification" (zur Ergänzung und Verdeutlichung) of *Beyond Good and Evil* (*KSB* 14, 377), and he was insistent that his publisher, C. G. Naumann, produce his new book to look *exactly* like his previous one (*KSB* 8, 111 and 116). Yet *On the Genealogy* maintains its own relation to *Zarathustra* by placing a passage from "On Reading and Writings" ("Vom Lesen und Schreiben") — "Courageous, unconcerned, sarcastic, violent — thus wisdom wants us: she is a woman and always loves only a warrior" (Unbekümmert, spöttisch, gewaltthätig — so will *uns* die Weisheit: sie ist ein Weib, sie liebt immer nur einen Kriegsmann; *Z* I 7; *KSA* 4, 49; cf. *GM* III; *KSA* 5, 339)[6] — at the beginning of the third essay, although the precise relation between this text and the "commentary" (Commentar; *GM* preface §8; *KSA* 5, 256) remains a matter for debate.[7]

Nietzsche composed the text, as he later told the Danish critic, Georg Brandes (1842–1927), between 10 and 30 July 1887 (*KSB* 8, 287), when he was yet again in Sils Maria; he hoped that *On the Genealogy of Morals*, which he subtitled "A Polemic" ("Eine Streitschrift"), would not just make *Beyond Good and Evil* more comprehensible — "everyone complains that one 'can't understand' me" (alle Welt hat sich beklagt, daß man "mich nicht verstehe") — but would also boost the sales of his previous writings, or so he told Köselitz (*KSB* 8, 112–13). Likewise, when writing to Franz Overbeck, he emphasized that the aim of his new book was to make his previous one more (in quotation marks) "comprehensible" (verständlich); and now, he added, he intended to wait for the final fruit to fall from his tree . . . (*KSB* 8, 140). Certainly, *On the Genealogy of Morals* is written with an intensity and an urgency, even a fury, remarkable even for Nietzsche; but as Michael Allen Gillespie and Keegan F. Callanan show in their contribution, its combination of intellectual insight and stylistic passion make it one of Nietzsche's most compelling works.

Notes

[1] Josef Victor Widmann, "Nietzsche's gefährliches Buch," *Der Bund* 37, no. 256–57 (16–17 September 1886), in *Nietzsche und die deutsche Literatur*, 1: *Texte zur Nietzsche-Rezeption 1873–1963*, ed. Bruno Hillebrand (Munich and Tübingen: Deutscher Taschenbuch Verlag; Niemeyer, 1978), 58–61 (here: 58).

[2] Rohde wrote: "I have read most of it with great displeasure. By far the greater part of it is the conversation of someone who has had too much to eat after the meal, lifted here and there through the stimulus of the wine, but completely full of a repulsive disgust at everything and everybody" (Das Meiste habe ich mit großem Unmuthe gelesen. Allermeist sind das doch Discurse eines Uebersättigten nach

dem Essen, durch die Weinanregung hie und da gehoben, aber voll einer widerlichen Verekelung an Allem und Jedem) (Andreas Patzer, ed., *Franz Overbeck — Erwin Rohde: Briefwechsel* (Berlin and New York: Walter de Gruyter, 1990), 108).

3 Letter from Erwin Rohde to Franz Overbeck of 24 January 1889, in *Franz Overbeck — Erwin Rohde: Briefwechsel*, 135.

4 See Pia Daniela Volz, *Nietzsche im Labyrinth seiner Krankheit: Eine medizinisch-biographische Untersuchung* (Würzburg: Könighausen & Neumann, 1990). For the suggestion that Nietzsche used hashish, see Resa von Schirnhofer's remarks, cited in Sander L. Gilman, ed., *Conversations with Nietzsche: A Life in the Words of His Contemporaries*, trans. David J. Parent (New York and Oxford: Oxford UP, 1987), 163.

5 Compare *KSA* 12, 10[150], 539. Simplicius of Cilicia was a sixth-century neo-Platonist who wrote several commentaries on Aristotle and a commentary on the *Manual* of Epictetus, the great Stoic philosopher of the mid-first to the second century. Simplicius's commentaries adopt an anti-Christian stance, particularly toward the Christian neo-Platonist John Philoponus.

6 Nietzsche, *Thus Spoke Zarathustra*, ed. Adrian Del Caro and Robert Pippin, trans. Adrian Del Caro (Cambridge: Cambridge UP, 2006), 28.

7 See Christopher Janaway, *Beyond Selflessness: Reading Nietzsche's "Genealogy"* (Oxford: Oxford UP, 2007), chapter 10, "Nietzsche's Illustration of the Art of Exegesis," 165–85.

9: *On the Genealogy of Morals*

Michael Allen Gillespie and Keegan F. Callanan

FROM HIS YOUTH NIETZSCHE WAS CONCERNED with the problem of German culture and the possibilities for cultural renewal. In his early work his hopes for renewal centered on Wagner and the rebirth of a tragic age out of the spirit of (Wagnerian) music.[1] After his break with Wagner, he gave up the idea of an immediate transformation of culture through a public festival or performance, and sought instead to provide the foundations for a new European cultural elite. This vision of cultural renewal gave way after 1881 to a more apocalyptic notion of cultural transformation that he connected to the advent of nihilism, the idea of eternal recurrence, the figure of Zarathustra, and the "Great Noon" (der grosse Mittag; *Z* I 22 §3; *KSA* 4,102).[2] Nietzsche was convinced that the Christian values that had guided European humanity for the last 1,500 years had become unbelievable. Present-day Europeans had to make a fateful choice between the last man and the superman, between a consumer-oriented, utilitarian society dedicated to universal happiness like that of Denmark or America, or a higher but tragic culture with superhuman possibilities.[3] In this final period of his thought Nietzsche became convinced that these superhuman possibilities depended on the proclamation of the doctrine of eternal recurrence. He believed this doctrine was essential because it was the only way toward a positive future free from resentment and the desire for revenge. To think and affirm eternal recurrence for him meant to accept, indeed to will, everything that had ever occurred or that would occur. While it thus demanded the acceptance of the most abysmal possibilities, it was also the basis for absolute affirmation (*EH Z* §6; *KSA* 6, 343–44). Nietzsche was convinced that if most men came to believe in eternal recurrence there would be a complete break with existing European spiritual life.[4] He constructed the character of Zarathustra as the teacher of this doctrine (*EH Z* §8; *KSA* 6, 348). Zarathustra was thus not just a literary character but in Nietzsche's view the supreme deed (höchste That), a world-governing spirit and a creator of truth (*EH Z* §6; *KSA* 6, 343). Zarathustra in this sense was his ideal of a playful, benevolent superhuman being, but one who would often seem inhuman to his contemporary readers (*EH Z* §2; *KSA* 6, 339). By creating Zarathustra to proclaim the doctrine of eternal recurrence, Nietzsche hoped to reinvigorate myth in the midst of a positivistic and materialist world.[5] However, this task filled him with a terrifying feeling of responsibility.[6] Indeed, while he hoped to "pressure humanity to decisions, which will decide all of the human future" (die Menschheit zu Entschlüssen drängen, welche über die ganze menschliche Zukunft entscheiden), he knew that the path he laid out led to a cataclysm of such tremendous proportions that "it could come to be that sometime in millennia men will swear by my name" (es kann so kommen, daß einmal ganze Jahrtausende auf meinen Namen ihre höchsten Gelübde tun).[7] Swear, not pray.

We cannot discuss the Zarathustra project in detail but it is essential that we say something about it and particularly about the idea of the Great Noon that guided Nietzsche's thought in the remaining years of his creative life. For a millennium and a half European humanity had been preeminently characterized by what Nietzsche calls the camel-spirit, the spirit of the believer who has organized his passions according to the commandments of a transcendent God. With the death of this God, this organization of the self is no longer tenable. Humanity thus must choose between the disintegration of all hierarchy among the passions and a consequent effort to satisfy whichever one is most pressing without any repression or sublimation, or the establishment of a new hierarchy of passions and a new notion of self. This latter choice leads to the superman but also entails the destruction of the old (Platonic/Christian) tablet of values, the hardening of humans and the elimination of pity by prolonged warfare, and the breeding of extraordinary human beings with the capacity to embrace the doctrine of eternal recurrence. Or to put this in the allegorical language of *Zarathustra*, the camel-spirit must first become a lion before it becomes a child or a superman (*Z* I 1; *KSA* 4, 11–12). The Great Noon is the moment of transition from the camel-spirit to the lion-spirit, from the believer to the warrior and destroyer.[8] It is thus the first step in the direction of the superhuman. Nietzsche asserts that this step will produce war and destruction that will last "two hundred years" and end with the establishment of "a thousand year" Dionysian Empire.[9]

In the aftermath of *Zarathustra*, his great Yes-saying work, all of his efforts, Nietzsche tells us in *Ecce Homo*, were directed toward bringing to fruition the teaching that is announced in that work, beginning with the Great Noon. He began this effort by writing new prefaces for his earlier works to align them with what he now saw as his true task.[10] He then began what he called the No-saying part of his project, which was meant to culminate in his great magnum opus, variously entitled in his notes *The Will to Power* (*Der Wille zur Macht*) and *The Revaluation of All Values* (*Die Umwerthung aller Werthe*). The first work in this No-saying series was *Beyond Good and Evil* (*Jenseits von Gut und Böse*), which Nietzsche describes as a critique of modernity that aimed to conjure up a day of decision as the beginning of the great war (*EH BGE* §1; *KSA* 6, 350). All of his writings from this point on, he tells us, are fishhooks.[11] The works from *Beyond Good and Evil* to *Ecce Homo* thus are part of one effort to attract those who will bring about the Great Noon, a new elite, a cadre of resolute warriors willing to carry out the destruction of existing European civilization. In his view, this elite will destroy the prevailing notions of good and evil, clearing the ground for the revaluation.[12]

On the Genealogy of Morals (*Zur Genealogie der Moral*) was originally conceived as a continuation of *Beyond Good and Evil*, and it used the same graphic layout.[13] Indeed, the verso of the title page carried the notice: "An addition to the last-published *Jenseits von Gut und Böse* that is meant as a supplement and clarification," and Nietzsche clearly intended it to show how the principles of the previous book might be applied in specific cases.[14] The *Genealogy* was written, drawing on existing material, in about twenty days.[15] Although it appears to be relatively straightforward, Nietzsche warns us against accepting appearances too readily. He explains in *Ecce Homo* that, in expression, intention, and art of surprise, the *Genealogy* is uncannier than anything he has written to date, pointing out that Dionysos is the god of darkness (*EH GM; KSA* 6, 352). He explains that the beginning of each essay is intended to mislead, and that an explosive new truth is revealed at the end of each essay. The three "truths" revealed by the work are the birth of Christianity out of spirit of *ressentiment*, the revelation that the voice of conscience is not the voice of God in man but cruelty turned back on the self, and that the ascetic ideal has triumphed in history, not because God is behind it, but because it has had no competition so far. The net consequence of all this for Nietzsche is nihilism, which he describes as the decision to will nothing rather than not to will. This horrifying conclusion, he claims, is the inevitable consequence of the pursuit of the ascetic ideal. *Zarathustra*, he argues, opens up the possibility for overcoming nihilism and establishing a higher, healthier, and more meaningful human existence.

In order to understand Nietzsche's rhetorical strategy in the *Genealogy*, we need to understand its intended audience. While Nietzsche hoped his books would be read widely (and at least in his literary persona never admitted to any doubts that this would ultimately occur), he clearly imagined after 1881 that his thought would have a more varied reception and effect. This is foreshadowed in the subtitle to *Zarathustra*, which declares it to be a book for all and none. Nietzsche thereby indicates that while his books may be vitally important for all, they were likely in the present to appeal to no one. In short, he had no obvious audience, and had yet to attract those who would help him complete his task. His early work had been generally well received only by Wagnerians, and even after his break with the composer, Wagner's followers remained his most loyal readers and supporters. Part of the problem he thus faced, especially after the poor reception of *Zarathustra*, was how to write in order to gain or create an audience.[16]

The No-saying spirit of Nietzsche's late works points to an effort to dispirit the weak and inspire the strong by demonstrating that all adherence to the moral project of Christianity, whether in its explicit form or behind a Kantian veil, is useless and absurd. He clearly hopes to attract those he called higher men in *Zarathustra* to join him in his no-saying and no-doing project. In this context he addresses these potential higher men, "the last to believe in God," as he puts it in *Zarathustra*, with a view to convincing them to assist him in bringing about the Great Noon, the moment of decision in which humanity will turn decisively away from both Christian morality and utilitarian eudaimonism to the pursuit of superhuman possibilities.[17] He wants to convince some of them to become lion-spirits who will destroy the old tablets. Here he was clearly thinking of the active nihilists who were seeking at the time to destroy contemporary civilization.[18] He also hopes to engage a second group, those who have faith in modern science.[19] He is particularly interested in helping these "men of knowledge" come to know themselves and to provoke them to abandon their faith in science and ask the crucial question he raised at the beginning of *Beyond Good and Evil* concerning the value of truth. They are the honest, unconditional atheists who do not yet understand that the ascetic ideal has arrived at its strictest, purest, and final form *in them*. While they believe they have shaken free of Christianity, Nietzsche is convinced they still have faith in truth, and thus have not become conscious of the will to truth as a problem. These are the "readers of the kind I need" (Leser, wie ich sie brauche) — those who doubt Christian dogma (*GM* III §16; *KSA* 5, 376). The "Note" (*Anmerkung*) at the end of the first essay suggests Nietzsche wants to employ their scholarly efforts in the project of revaluation. In the third essay, Nietzsche explicitly attempts to awaken *in them* the process whereby the will to truth becomes conscious of itself as a problem, and thus to make possible the final self-overcoming of the ascetic ideal (*GM* III §27; *KSA* 5, 409). Insofar as they come to recognize that their science is not compatible with their atheism and is in fact a manifestation of the ascetic ideal, he hopes they will come to see that art is the only thing that can give meaning to life.

The title of the work directly targets those concerned with genealogical accounts of morals given within the British tradition that culminated in Darwin, Spencer, and Mill and that were defended in Germany by Nietzsche's one-time friend Paul Rée in his book, *The Origin of Moral Sensations* (*Der Ursprung der moralischen Empfindungen*, 1877).[20] In this work Rée argues on a quasi-Darwinian basis that there are two basic instincts, one egoistic and the other unegoistic or altruistic and that what tends to the preservation of the species is called good and what leads to its destruction evil.[21] Here Rée accepts Schopenhauer's notion of the centrality of altruistic impulses to morality, but also echoes David Friedrich Strauss, claiming that Darwin's theory of evolution applies to not just to the physical origins of the species but to morality as well.[22] He was apparently convinced that in their interpretation of Darwin, Rée and Spencer were deeply indebted to Hegel's notion of progress.[23] However, while Rée's book occasioned the writing of the *Genealogie* and was its rhetorical target, the ideas in Nietzsche's book predated his reading of Ree's work. They were originally conceived as part of a consideration of the question of the value of morality (*GM* preface §3–§4; *KSA* 5, 249–50). The study of the origin of morality is merely one way to address the question of morality's value (*GM* preface §5; *KSA* 5, 251–52). The aim of the project is thus not merely to correct Rée et al. on the origins of morality but to push toward the Great Noon and the revaluation of values.

The basic structure of Nietzsche's argument about the origins and development of morality can perhaps be brought more clearly to light by comparison to Hegel. For Hegel the advent of self-consciousness leads to the desire to make the suddenly alien world one's own either by consuming it or appropriating it as one's property. When two self-consciousnesses face one another they each seek to make the other their own and are thus thrown into a life and death struggle that ends either in the death of one or both or the submission of one to the other. Those who submit give up their claim to universal ownership and become the property of the victors. As slaves, they are then forced to transform the natural world through work on behalf of their masters. For Hegel, however, this transformation of nature is the true road to liberation. The history of the development of humanity is thus the history of the development of the slave through art, religion, and philosophy to create the modern world of universal freedom, human rights, Kantian morality, an efficient and productive market, the rational state, and the realm of absolute knowledge and science.

It was precisely this rational world that Nietzsche saw collapsing around him as a result of the death of God. The end of history that Hegel proclaimed was thus in Nietzsche's view not a triumph but a disaster, the final victory of slave morality (and the worker) over master morality (and the warrior). This nihilistic process then was the self-undermining of the Christian morality, and left man with a choice between the eudaimonistic world of the last man and the tragic path to the superman.

For Nietzsche human beings are characterized not by consciousness but by instincts. Nietzsche suggests that most humans originally hunted and gathered together, guided by a herd instinct without the development of rational faculties. In contrast to these herds, other men were essentially predators, "blond beasts" who conquered and ruled these herds as masters. There was no original equality among men but a natural inequality, which was the source of what Nietzsche calls the pathos of distance, which he believes was the original basis for morality. The masters saw themselves as a different kind of being than the slaves. In contrast to Hegel's claim that masters are originally driven by a need for recognition, Nietzsche believes they act solely on the basis of their predatory instincts.[24] Originally, they did not even think of themselves as individuals (needing anything like recognition) but as a part of a people, hunting in packs like wolves rather than like solitary cats, coordinating their actions instinctually to capture their prey. Singly, they were all merely appendages of their people, powerfully shaped and bound together by custom, by the morality of mores as Nietzsche called it in his earlier work. They became what they were because of their success as a people, and their freedom consisted in their power and their independence of other peoples.

In contrast to the masters, who lived an active life according to their customs, slaves only reacted to the masters. Their lack of freedom was a reflection of their weakness. The distinctions within the morality of mores reflected these social distinctions. The good were the powerful, the clean, the beautiful, everything that distinguishes the nobles from their slaves. Bad was everything that characterized the weak, the unclean, the ugly. In contrast to Schopenhauer, Rée, and the utilitarians, Nietzsche thus argues that morality begins in instinctual, self-aggrandizing action and not in reactive altruism.

Nietzsche's alternative moral history thus begins as an attack upon Rée's genealogy, but this is not his ultimate goal. He is more interested in undercutting reverence for the still-dominant slave morality and its ideal human type. He also sketches the contours of a project to bring about the final demise of slave morality while calling the higher men to join him. Nietzsche thus seeks to prepare the way for a second revaluation of values in the aftermath of the Great Noon. The revaluation will be modeled formally but not substantively on the slaves' revaluation of noble values. Like the slave revolt in morality, it will follow from the self-overcoming of the regnant morality and will in part represent an inversion of it, although not without adopting some of its most important features.

The slave morality of good and evil arose as a reaction to the noble morality of good and bad. It does not consist in but springs from *ressentiment*, the slave's psychic experience of "imaginary revenge" (imaginäre Rache; *GM* I §10; *KSA* 5, 270). This experience compensates for the slave's inability to exact actual revenge upon his masters. *Ressentiment* is thus the child of vengefulness and impotence. Slave morality emerges when this repressed desire for revenge becomes creative and fabricates values. Yet, Nietzsche explains, this creative act is simply a denial of the master morality (*AC* §24; *KSA* 6, 191–93). Animated by unsatisfied hatred, the slave condemns *in toto* his master's station and distinguishing qualities.

Nietzsche describes this creative deed as an "inversion" for two reasons. First, all that the noble morality considered "good" the slave now deems "evil," and all that it considered "bad" the slave deems "good." The substantive moral judgments are inverted. But more importantly, the process of value creation is itself inverted when *ressentiment* begets slave morals. The basic concept of noble morality was positive, with the masters affirming themselves as good (*GM* I §10; *KSA* 5, 270). The corollary negative judgment against slave qualities arose later and incidentally, as a moral parenthesis. But in the creation of slave morality, *ressentiment* inverts the "value-positing eye" (werthesetzenden Blick; *GM* I §10; *KSA* 5, 270). Slave morality begins not with an affirmation of the slave but with a judgment against the master. The slaves define good only subsequently, as a function of evil: whatever is *not evil* is good (*GM* I §13; *KSA* 5, 280). Nietzsche explains that this valuation springs from impotence, which leads the slave to call patience, meekness, and mercy good. While the noble first affirms all that he is and does as good, the slave regards as evil all that he cannot do and cannot be. Impotence thus dons "the ostentatious garb of the virtue of quiet, calm resignation" (Prunk der entsagenden stillen abwartenden Tugend; *GM* I §14; *KSA* 5, 280). In this way, slave morality inverts both the substance and the creative mode of noble morality.

Nietzsche's initial account of this inversion in *Beyond Good and Evil* makes no mention of slave morality's original authors.[25] In the *Genealogy*, he claims that not all enslaved peoples but the Jews were the originators of the slave revolt in morality. *Ressentiment* abides in the bosom of all dominated races, but it was with the Jews that it first became creative and manufactured new values by inverting noble values (*GM* I §7; *KSA* 5, 266–67). Their vengefulness took this hitherto unexampled form because they were, Nietzsche explains, a priestly people that divided the world between pure and impure, rather than good and bad (*GM* I §6; *KSA* 5, 265). This priestly mode of evaluation makes the priestly type physically weaker. The priest's aversion to uncleanness turns him away from action and perverts his instinctual drives. In this way he becomes impotent and unhealthy.

When the Jews found themselves under the thumb of knightly-aristocratic masters, they became the most dangerous enemies of the noble ideal. As a priestly people, they were especially incapable of meting out actual revenge, so their desire for revenge was more 'deeply repressed' (zurückgetreten) and therefore more incendiary than that of other enslaved races (*GM* I §7; *KSA* 5, 267). The more completely a people's desire for revenge is stanched, the more inflamed is their *ressentiment*. Subdued by their aristocratic Roman conquerors, the Jews inverted the master morality's value equation of "good = noble = powerful = beautiful = happy = beloved of God" (gut = vornehm = mächtig = schön = glücklich = gottgeliebt; *GM* I §7; *KSA* 5, 267).[26] In this way the slave revolt in morality began and continued apace with the advent of Christianity, which won adherents to the slave morality among the master races themselves (*GM* I §8; *KSA* 5, 268–69).

This is the "very disagreeable truth" (sehr unangenehme Wahrheit) of the first essay: Christianity was born out of the spirit of *ressentiment* (*EH GM*; *KSA* 6, 352). But this genealogical tale also casts doubt upon the sustainability of the noble ideal, which was finally unable to maintain its integrity in the face of the slaves' cleverness and psychic resources. The master races had no ideal other than themselves and thus were unable to provide a meaning for their existence (as Socrates demonstrated to them time and again). Nietzsche is thus not unequivocal in his praise of the noble ideal.

Indeed, for Nietzsche, modern Europe's "higher natures" (höhere Naturen) are not followers of the noble ideal, but rather men torn between the demands of noble and slave morality (*GM* I §16; *KSA* 5, 286). They have internalized the definitive struggle of human history.[27] As spiritual hosts to this struggle, they are uniquely prepared to join Nietzsche in bringing about the Great Noon.[28] These higher natures are part of Nietzsche's most important audience, the "unknown friends" (unbekannte Freunde) he urges to follow the lion path and to become no-saying destroyers of Christian values (*GM* III §17; *KSA* 5, 410).

The second essay offers what Nietzsche calls a psychology of the conscience (*EH GM*; *KSA* 6, 352). Whereas the first essay assaults European humanity's faith in the objective basis of morality by revealing its origin, the second essay attacks faith in conscience, the source of *subjective* sanction for slave values. But even as Nietzsche uncovers the animal psychology of conscience, he also suggests that these psychic experiences provided a depth to the human soul that was absent in the blond beasts. Like the first essay, the second thus not only undercuts Christian morality but also points to spiritual deficits of the master races.

Nietzsche approaches the problem of conscience by examining two psychological phenomena: guilt and bad conscience. He initially gives the impression that conscience and guilt grow together as the fruit of the relationships of credit, of buyer and seller, or debtor and creditor that are the most ancient human relationships, predating the formation of human communities and alliances, including noble tribal communities (*GM* II §8; *KSA* 5, 305–6). Through exchange, man gains a sense of value, contract, and right. He experiences the feeling of being in debt. From this sphere, the world of guilt and conscience seems to have originated (*GM* II §6; *KSA* 5, 300).

Yet we find that this account of the origin of conscience is incomplete. The most significant manifestations of conscience occur not in these pre-social exchanges but within walled communities. Basic to all peoples according to Nietzsche is a natural instinct for cruelty. This instinct is synonymous with the "instinct for freedom" (*Instinkt der Freiheit*) and the will to power (*GM* II §18; *KSA* 5, 326). It is a drive to impose form upon nature and human nature, an unconscious artist's instinct (*GM* II

§17–18; *KSA* 5, 324–26). The physical and customary bounds of human society limited the discharge of this instinct, so the most primitive tribal societies compensated for these limits by undertaking murderous conquests (*GM* II §11; *KSA* 5, 274). Unlike these noble tribes, subdued nomadic peoples were incapable of seeking *external* compensation for their confinement — they could not vent their instinct for form-imposing cruelty upon others. Instead, this instinct was internalized, inflicting suffering upon the self in the form of bad conscience.

Nietzsche notes that because these acts of conquest were sudden and without protracted struggle, all *ressentiment* was initially precluded.[29] He thus claims that the development of bad conscience preceded the emergence of *ressentiment.* The spiritual resources developed through the experience of bad conscience were therefore available to Nietzsche's man of *ressentiment.* This begins to illuminate more fully the means of his victory over the masters.

The psychological changes surrounding the development of bad conscience were deep and lasting. Naturally, the inner world of the human animal is as "thin as if it were stretched between two membranes" (ursprünglich dünn wie zwischen zwei Häute eingespannt; *GM* II §16; *KSA* 5,322). With the growth of bad conscience, the slave's inner world expanded enormously. Unable to discharge his instincts, the slave was forced to rely upon and develop his inner resources (*GM* II §16; *KSA* 5, 322). He attained a capacity for imagination, self-awareness and self-styling that did not exist in the wild (*GM* III §16; *KSA* 5, 375). While unhealthy and painful in itself, the experience of bad conscience serves as "the womb of all ideal and imaginative phenomena [. . .] and perhaps beauty itself" (der eigentliche Mutterschooss idealer und imaginativer Ereignisse [. . .] und vielleicht überhaupt erst die Schönheit; *GM* II §18; *KSA* 5, 326). In this light, one can more readily discern the source of the slave's psychological advantage over the master. Likewise, one sees more clearly why Nietzsche aims not at a straightforward revival of the classical type but rather at a fusion of the master's physiological vigor with the slave's spiritual resources and depth.

Nietzsche sees the convergence of guilt and bad conscience in Christian theology. The first step toward this convergence was the establishment of the most primitive tribal communities. The establishment of these communities of course predates their subjugation of weaker peoples — and so predates bad conscience. Within these primitive tribes, the relationship of the tribe to its founders comes to be understood in terms of personal relationships of credit. The founders are the creditors; the succeeding generations develop a sense of debt to them (*GM* II §19; *KSA* 5, 327–28). Through sacrifices, festivals, music, and finally obedience to the customs of the founders, successive generations seek to pay back their debt. The greater and more powerful the tribe becomes, the more fearsome and worthy of reverence their ancestral founders appear. In the most powerful tribes, the ancestor steadily acquires divine attributes and is counted a god (*GM* II §19; *KSA* 5, 328). The Christian God finally appears as the greatest god, engendering the greatest burden of guilt.

There is, however, no essential connection between the experience of indebtedness to God and bad conscience. Bad conscience merely reinterprets this debt in order to transform it into an instrument of psychological torture. This, Nietzsche argues in the third essay, was the work of the ascetic priest and his doctrine of sin, which put an end to the pagan hope of redemption through repayment. The ascetic priest enlisted the psychology of debt to increase psychic torment, and thus turned it against life itself.[30] In this way, he uses bad conscience to hijack religion and turn it to his own ends (*GM* II §21–22; *KSA* 5, 331–33).

The union of conscience with the concept of God was thus for Nietzsche a marriage of convenience. When man hears "conscience" speak on behalf of life-denying values, he does not hear the voice of God. Yet beyond this unmasking, Nietzsche has revealed the raw spiritual power developed by bad conscience. Unlike the razor-thin inner world of the blond beasts, souls cultivated by bad conscience produced an ideal: the ideal of the holy God before whom all are maximally guilty. While Nietzsche regards the substance of this ideal as madness, he means to employ and redirect the ideal-creating capacity formed in the cauldron of bad conscience to a higher end.

This is why he turns to the Greek pantheon in the penultimate section of the second essay. In contradistinction to the makers of the Christian God, the Greeks established their gods to numb the sting of conscience (*GM* II §23; *KSA* 5, 333–34). While bad conscience cannot simply be eradicated through the gradual spread of modern atheism, the spiritual and imaginative capacities developed among the subject peoples can be put to healthier use in the production of life-affirming ideals. The Greeks represent this hope. In Nietzsche's view, Christian theology ascribes the guilt of sin to man, while God bears the punishment. But Greek theology ascribes the guilt itself to the gods. When a man commits an atrocity, he has been deceived by the Olympians. He is at worst a fool, not a sinner. The Greeks thus viewed the tragic nature of life through the lens of an ideal that allowed them to vindicate themselves (*GM* II §23; *KSA* 5, 334).

Though the Greeks suggest the possibility of life-affirming ideals, Nietzsche concludes the essay with a disavowal of any creative intentions of his own. It falls to him to destroy the existing temple to make way for the new one. But for such a creative project to be possible today, great health would be necessary. However, even today's higher men and honest unconditional atheists would oppose this creative project (*GM* III §27; *KSA* 5, 409). While these good Europeans might believe themselves to be Nietzsche's allies in his assault on Christian morality, they are not yet capable of creation because they are not sufficiently free of metaphysical temptation to partake in the creative project (*GM* II §24; *KSA* 5, 398–99). These higher men are, however, fit to serve as warriors against the old values by virtue of their very entanglement with the old tablet of values. They must follow the lion-spirited path.

The theme of the third essay — the ascetic ideal — is mentioned just once in each of the previous essays. But it turns out that the ascetic priest was lurking in the shadows throughout (*GM* I §6 and II §3; *KSA* 5, 264–65 and 294–95). The ascetic priest was behind the moralization of guilt as well as the doctrine of sin. In the third essay Nietzsche reveals that the ascetic ideal was the "organizing term for counternatural values."[31] This concept unifies all the ostensibly life-denying psychological forces — slave values, bad conscience, moralized guilt — described earlier in the work. Nietzsche in this essay examines the *meaning* of the ascetic ideal in order to show his best readers (the higher men) that they themselves are still loyal to it. In this way, Nietzsche hopes to inspire a few such men to become warriors against the ascetic ideal, in preparation for the work of a creative and life-affirming posterity that may someday affirm a new ideal.

Nietzsche explains that the ascetic ideal springs from the "*protective instinct of a degenerating life*" (*dem Schutz- und Heil-Instinkte eines degenerirenden Lebens*; *GM* III §13; *KSA* 5, 366). Because man is a futural being, he is filled with "restless energies that never leave him in peace" (von seiner eignen drängenden Kraft keine Ruhe mehr findet; *GM* III §14; *KSA* 5, 367). He experiments with his nature and innovates more than any other animal. But this daring makes him weary, disgusted with himself, unable to affirm life.[32] The terminus of this downward spiral would have been suicidal nihilism, had not degenerating life itself engendered what Nietzsche calls the ascetic ideal. The ascetic ideal is not a single way of life but an interpretation of life. Confronting the pain of life, the ascetic ideal imagines an alternative sphere of existence and reinterprets life as a byway to this other existence (*GM* III §11; *KSA* 5, 361). In this way, the ascetic ideal offers man *meaning* for suffering and a goal to *will* — nothingness.[33] It turns the human will against life in order to fill the void within the human will (*GM* III §28; *KSA* 5, 411–12). It appears to deny life, but this denial is in service of life.[34]

While different human types adopt ascetic valuations and habits, the primary agent of this "protective instinct of degenerating life" is the ascetic priest. The ascetic priest works to deaden the pain of the sick and to separate them from the healthy with the doctrine of sin. The *ressentiment* of the sick threatens to destroy the integrity of the herd. Through the doctrine of sin, the priest seeks to persuade the sick man that he is to blame for his own suffering, rendering him less harmful. He is less likely to infect the healthy with his cries for pity. The doctrine of sin also redirects the patient's attention away from his pain. As he gazes inward, his dull melancholy is punctuated by paroxysms of guilt. These treatments make him sicklier, but they also make life bearable by giving his suffering meaning.[35]

The ascetic ideal is powerful, Nietzsche argues, not because God is behind it but because it has had no competition. Even science, he argues, is only the latest manifestation of the ascetic ideal. For Nietzsche, those who believe that science is an alternative to Christianity are partly correct but fail to see both as manifestations of the deeper ascetic instinct. They assume that modern science can offer man an alternative meaning or goal simply because it has dared to challenge religious dogma and certain tenets of Christian morality. Most scholars, however, are merely modest laborers, toiling away in their nooks in order to hide from the pain of a meaningless existence. In Nietzsche's view, science itself possesses no goal, will, or ideal. A merely scientific view of the world would be meaningless. The skepticism and rationalism of modern science provide no alternative to nihilism.[36] A second kind of scholar — the rare exception — embodies the ascetic ideal in its latest form. These "last idealists left among philosophers and scholars" (die letzten Idealisten, die es heute unter Philosophen und Gelehrten giebt) style themselves as the sternest opponents of the ascetic ideal and Christian faith (*GM* III §24; *KSA* 5, 398). But their unconditional will to truth and their faith in its metaphysical value betray them as the purest expression of the ascetic ideal. Opposed to the trappings of religion and tradition, these last idealists have simply sloughed off the outer layer of the ascetic ideal while remaining devoted to its inner core. But exactly how does faith in truth and the will to truth implicate these "pale atheists" (blasse Atheisten) and "anti-Christians" (Antichristen) in the ascetic ideal (*GM* III §24; *KSA* 5, 398)?

Nietzsche refers his readers to the aphorism "How We Too Are Still Pious" ("Inwiefern auch wir noch fromm sind") in *The Gay Science* (*Die fröhliche Wissenschaft*) for a more elaborate treatment of the subject.[37] Here, he frames the discussion of truth's value in terms of the desire *not* to be deceived. The man who wills truth unconditionally, who possesses an absolute faith in the value of truth, also possesses an unconditional and absolute desire not to be deceived. In other words, he is unconditionally distrustful of all mere convictions. For such a man, all convictions must prove themselves before they count as knowledge. The unconditional desire not to be deceived presupposes that it is better for me to know the truth *no matter what*. But is this so? Nietzsche suggests that we *know* nothing that warrants our adherence to the principle of unconditional distrust. As he argues in *Human, All Too Human* (*Menschliches, Allzumenschliches*), "there is no pre-established harmony between the furtherance of truth and the well-being of mankind" (es giebt keine prästabilirte Harmonie zwischen der Förderung der Wahrheit und dem Wohle der Menschheit; *HA* I §517; *KSA* 2, 323).[38] Therefore, if we *will* the truth unconditionally, we will it not with an eye to well-being in this world but rather as a *metaphysical value* — with reference to some other sphere of existence in which truth is valuable *absolutely* (*GM* III §11; *KSA* 5, 361). In this world, its value is not absolute. Precisely because they are beholden to the ascetic ideal, the last idealists fail to ask this final and decisive terrestrial question: "*value* for *what?*" (*werth wozu? GM* I §17; *KSA* 5, 289).

In *The Gay Science* Nietzsche clarifies the inner connection between the ascetic ideal and the unconditional will to truth (*GS* §344; *KSA* 3, 574–77). But this same aphorism has fueled debate over Nietzsche's relationship to the last idealists. In the *Genealogy*, Nietzsche inserts an extended quotation from this aphorism that suggests that he himself maintains a metaphysical faith in truth.[39] He appears to signal to his best readers that he counts himself among the atheistic scholars who retain faith in the truth. But Nietzsche's relationship to this group is ambiguous. Much of what he says about the last idealists could not be said of himself. He suggests that the last idealists do not recognize their faith in truth. They cannot see themselves. But Nietzsche could not intelligibly say such a thing about himself. He sympathizes with the last idealists and knows himself susceptible to similar bouts of faith in truth. Even his present attempt to explain the meaning and power of the holy man in non-miraculous terms suggests Nietzsche's affinity with the scientist, whose irreverent pursuit of truth indicates reverence for truth alone (*HA* I §136; *KSA* 2, 130). Nietzsche sees the will to truth at work in himself, but unlike his potential collaborators, he is also conscious of the problem of the value of truth. He considers himself different from these last idealists only because he arrived at this consciousness *before them*. Like Hegel, he counts himself not primarily wiser but *first*.

Nietzsche calls upon these men of knowledge to approach truth *experimentally*, to search out the truth about truth.[40] In effect, Nietzsche aims to harness the unconditional will to truth of the last idealists in service of a project that will finally undermine the unconditional will to truth — and so, the ascetic ideal. The will to truth operates on a principle of unconditional distrust. This is its law. Nietzsche urges them to apply this principle to their last unchallenged conviction — faith in the absolute value of truth. In this way, Christian truthfulness will draw its "*most striking inference* [. . .] against itself" (ihren *stärksten Schluss* [. . .] gegen sich selbst; *GM* III §27; *KSA* 5, 410). The ascetic ideal will overcome itself.

In the first essay, Nietzsche had invited a cadre of scholars to examine experimentally the worth of various moral values. He knows that the last idealists will initially respond with pleasure to this daring and irreverent research project. But here in the closing sections of the third essay, he exposes the scientist's will to truth as *just another moral value* and thereby adds it to their research agenda. He serves these scholars notice that the project cannot be completed with the detachment of the scientist, for it will require an attack on the foundations of their very identity. Since this project involves self-criticism, it will be exceedingly painful for the last idealists (including Nietzsche himself).[41] The third essay, according to Nietzsche (*GM* Vorrede §8; *KSA* 5, 256), is thus a meditation on its opening epigram: "Unconcerned, mocking, violent — thus wisdom wants *us*: she is a woman and always loves only a warrior" (Unbekümmert, spöttisch, gewaltthätig — so will uns die Weisheit: sie ist ein Weib, sie liebt immer nur einen Kriegsmann; *KSA* 5, 339). As warriors against the ascetic ideal, those Nietzsche wants to inspire must be unconcerned for themselves — for they attack their own ideal.[42] In their assault upon the kernel of Christian morality, they will be partially driven by their native scientific conscience, which itself is a sublimated form of Christian morality (*GM* III §27; *KSA* 5, 409). The ascetic ideal will thus meet its match in the purest manifestation of its own power.[43]

The *Genealogy* is preeminently a No-saying work that seeks to undermine Platonic-Christianity morality in order to prepare the ground for the Great Noon. This does not mean, however, that Nietzsche does not give us some positive images of the future he imagines. These are almost invariably associated with the role of art and the artist in the new world he hopes to bring into being. The artist, in contradistinction to the scientist, as Nietzsche tells us in the third essay, is not subservient to the ascetic ideal. When he seems to be, as in the case of Wagner (and presumably also Tolstoy and others), he is actually only an actor playing the role of the ascetic. Art in Nietzsche's view is essentially creative and life-affirming. The world-affirming individual who plays such an important if understated role in Nietzsche's late work is preeminently an artist, although he is not only an artist. He is also in some sense a philosopher, a lover, and a ruler in addition to being a creator.[44]

In Nietzsche's view, we need such artists to guide us lest we perish of the truth.[45] To seek to live by the truth in the time of the death of God and all the ideals that were founded on God leads to nihilism. If nothing is true, and everything, as Nietzsche tells us, is permitted, then only the artist can give us a new goal. By affirming his own existence the philosopher/lover/artist/ruler of the future redeems not only his own existence but also the historical process that produced him.[46]

Nietzsche points to this artist-tyrant of the future (as he calls him elsewhere) at the end of the first two essays in the *Genealogy*. In the first essay he describes him using Napoleon as an example, "this synthesis of the *inhuman* and the *superhuman*" (diese Synthese von *Unmensch* und *Übermensch*) as a rebirth of the noble ideal (as opposed to the slave or ascetic ideal). He asks, "Must the ancient fire not someday flare up much more terribly, after much longer preparation? Moreover, must one not desire it with all one's might? Even will it? Even promote it?" (Sollte es nicht irgendwann einmal ein noch viel furchtbareres, viel länger vorbereitetes Auflodern des alten Brandes geben müssen? Mehr noch: wäre nicht gerade das aus allen Kräften zu wünschen? selbst zu wollen? selbst zu fördern?; *GM* I §16 and §17; *KSA* 5, 288). But as a *synthesis*, Napoleon points not simply backward to the "ancient fire" of the inhuman beast of prey, but forward — to the as-yet-undefined superman. Napoleon, in Nietzsche's view, was a throwback to the military adventurers, usurpers, founders, and men of action of the fifteenth century, such as Borgia, Dante, Michelangelo, Castruccio Castracani (as described by Machiavelli, Stendhal, and Madame de Staël).[47] Napoleon, for Nietzsche, as described in *Twilight of the Idols* (*Götzen-Dämmerung*), was a return to nature, not in Rousseau's sense, but to the naturalness of the Renaissance (*TI* "Skirmishes" §44 and §48–§49; *KSA* 6, 145–46 and 150–52). What particularly attracted him to Napoleon, however, was Napoleon's artistic approach to government and his lack of constraint with respect to conscience and tradition.[48] While Nietzsche recognized that Napoleon himself was a lucky accident, he was convinced that conditions were ripe for such men due to the democratization of Europe, which he believed was preparing Europeans for slavery and tyranny.[49] Here he had much in common with Tocqueville.

Napoleon is not the only model Nietzsche employed during this period. Perhaps even more important for him as a representative of a higher possibility and a different ideal was Caesar. In part Nietzsche has in mind the historical Caesar, but in *Ecce Homo* he credits the creation of such an ideal to Shakespeare, thus emphasizing the connections of artist and tyrant.[50] According to Holzer, "Nietzsche did not perceive Caesar primarily as an imperialist politician, military and political tyrant or symbol of a political principle of state organization. Instead, he associated him with the convalescent Zarathustra, a figure that unites creativity and clemency, or with the 'richest, most independent, and bravest' humans, like 'the hero, the prophet, the Caesar, the redeemer, or the shepherd.'"[51] In *Twilight of the Idols*, Caesar is held up as the exemplar of what Nietzsche means by freedom, the freedom of the warrior, illiberal, close to tyranny and servitude, and always in the midst of danger. Among such men, Caesar is, for Nietzsche, the most beautiful type (*TI* "Skirmishes" §38; *KSA* 6, 140).

At the end of the second essay, Nietzsche also points to the need for a spirit different from that of today, strengthened by war and victory, for whom conquest has become a need, a redeeming man of great love and contempt, a "man of the future, who will redeem us not only from the hitherto reigning ideal but also from that which was bound to grow out of it, the great nausea, the will to nothingness, nihilism; this bell-stroke of noon and of the great decision that liberates the will again and restores its goal to the earth and his hope to man; this Antichrist and antinihilist; this victor over God and nothingness — *he must come one day.* —" (Dieser Mensch der Zukunft, der uns ebenso vom bisherigen Ideal erlösen wird, als von dem, was aus ihm wachsen musste, vom grossen Ekel, vom Willen zum Nichts, vom Nihilismus, dieser Glockenschlag des Mittags und der grossen Entscheidung, der den Willen wieder frei macht, der der Erde ihr Ziel und dem Menschen seine Hoffnung zurückgiebt, dieser Antichrist und Antinihilist, dieser Besieger Gottes und des Nichts — *er muss einst kommen* . . .; *GM* II §24; *KSA* 5, 336). This figure, who makes possible the Great Noon, is identified in the succeeding aphorism as Zarathustra.

This man (or more likely these men) of the future will *will* a day of decision (*EH CW* §3–§4 & "Why I Am a Destiny" §1; *KSA* 6, 360–66). Nietzsche believes that such a man will come into being over the next two centuries as the result of war and victory, by means of "a hundred acts" (hundert Akten; *GM* III §27; *KSA* 5, 410), that will, Nietzsche fears, leave his name associated with a crime without equal.[52] Crucial to the production of such a heroic human being in Nietzsche's view is the acceptance of the doctrine of eternal recurrence, or what Nietzsche also calls *amor fati.* He can come to be only by affirming everything that has been or will be, thus affirming and willing everything horrible and terrifying. Insofar as this superhuman being is creative, he hearkens back to and calls upon the primordial human instinct for world-forming that Nietzsche associated with the cruelty of the blond beasts (*GM* II §17; *KSA* 5, 324–25), but he combines this creative cruelty with the self-understanding capacity for giving meaning to life that arises out of the ascetic spirit. This creative and affirming individual, whom Nietzsche describes in *Beyond Good and Evil* as shouting *da capo*, gives a new meaning to life in its most abysmal depths and thus makes possible an ascent to the greatest heights (*BGE* §56; *KSA* 5, 75).

Nietzsche's initial attempt to proclaim this doctrine to humanity in *Zarathustra* was a failure. He was not heard; indeed, his lack of success with the public mirrored that of Zarathustra when he tried to address the people of the Motley Cow (*Z* I §22; *KSA* 4, 97–99). Nietzsche certainly hoped to attract some followers away from this indifferent public, but he did not stop there. His works after *Zarathustra,* the *Genealogy* among them, were intended to eliminate the obstacles that prevented such an understanding and to create an audience for Nietzsche's message. In particular, he hoped to create a group of lion-spirited individuals who were dedicated not merely to his No-saying but to his No-doing project as the first step on the path to the superman. The creation of this cadre of No-sayers and No-doers and the beginning of the destructive period Nietzsche both foresees and longs for is the meaning of the Great Noon. The No-saying of all the works after *Zarathustra* is thus the beginning of a great Yes-saying, which can only, however, be heard by an audience able to understand and accept his final teaching.

The *Genealogy* is a polemic directed against Christian morality. Its goal is not merely critique but a complete revaluation of all Christian values. These values in Nietzsche's view have led Europe to the brink of nihilism, and they must be overturned in order to found a new code of values that will make possible a superhuman future. The *Genealogy* is principally aimed at the men of knowledge Nietzsche addresses at the beginning of the work, and is an attempt to convince them that contrary to their own understanding of themselves as men of science and honest atheists, they are in fact the culmination of the ascetic ideal and thus of Christian morality (*GM* preface §1; *KSA* 5, 247–48). Or to put it in other terms, Nietzsche seeks to convince them that they are complicit in the process that has produced nihilism. The argument of the *Genealogy* is thus an extension of the argument presented in *Beyond Good and Evil*, which calls into question the value not just of morality but of truth itself. The work in this sense clearly has a rhetorical purpose in the context of Nietzsche's final project, but this fact should not blind us to the profound philosophical challenges it poses to almost everything that has hitherto been imagined to constitute moral theory.

In the preface to the work, Nietzsche states that he wants to raise the question of the value of morality. The value of reigning moral values — whether Kantian or utilitarian — has, he says, been taken as a "given." Both these reigning schools of value seek simply to reground morality upon what they take to be "rational" (rather than theological) foundations (*BGE* §186; *KSA* 5, 105–7). Nietzsche understands himself to be the first major thinker to break this pattern. Before him, he asserts, moral thinkers "never doubted or hesitated in the slightest degree in supposing the good man to be of greater value than the evil man" (man hat bisher auch nicht im Entferntesten daran gezweifelt und geschwankt, 'den Guten' für höherwerthig als 'den Bösen' anzusetzen; *GM* preface §6; *KSA* 5, 253). As we have shown, Nietzsche turns almost all of the key concepts that have been imagined to characterize our moral lives on their head — cruelty, conscience, asceticism, pity, honesty, altruism, and charity are all revealed to be the opposite of what we have hitherto imagined.

At the core of his argument is the revolutionary claim that all Western morality from the time of Socrates is merely a reaction to an earlier and original master morality that characterized the ancient world. As such our morality is not something new and positive but something entirely negative, constructed as the mirror image of what it rejects. Morality's presumed high and noble purposes in this way are shown to be the result of weakness, vengefulness, and self-interest. This critique is carried out by means of a novel approach to the study of morality that combines a historical investigation of origins with a revolutionary understanding of the psychology of moral beliefs and actions. This approach leads to "knowledge of a kind that has never yet existed or even been desired" (wie eine solche Kenntniss weder bis jetzt da war, noch auch nur begehrt worden ist), as Nietzsche puts it (*GM* preface §6; *KSA* 5, 253).[53] Nietzsche is not the first to deny the supernatural foundations of the reigning moral outlook — the English psychologists had done so before him. But he claims that he is the first to approach the question of the origin of moral values through a historical method, with a historical spirit. Specifically, what Nietzsche means is that he rejects the assumption that a value's *present-day* utility provides a sure indication of its cause or origin. This *ahistorical* confusion of origin and utility, cause and purpose, has plagued all putative historical approaches to morality before Nietzsche, and the superiority of his study stems largely from his rejection of this error (*GM* II §12–§13; *KSA* 5, 313–18). The purpose of any human value or practice is not transmitted from its origin but rather is imposed by the will. This is why values and practices (Nietzsche's leading example is punishment) acquire so many competing meanings over time. So to practice the historical method in his sense is to understand the role of the will in the creation of meaning.

At the core of his critique of morality is the *Entlarvungspsychologie,* the "psychology of unmasking," that Nietzsche developed in his earlier works beginning with *Human, All Too Human.* This psychological approach is an attempt to show that everything we take to be high or spiritual has a low or bodily origin; that all altruism and self-sacrifice is rooted in a self-interested effort to promote oneself, one's progeny, and one's people; and that what we consider morality is decidedly unmoral in its origins and intentions. Nietzsche thus rejects not merely Kantian universalism but also the optimistic utilitarianism that, building on Darwin, imagines there is progress in moral development. His critique of morality thus does not require moral argument in the traditional sense but rather a "psychologically plausible and historically truthful" account of the emergence of the Western moral outlook, which makes the adherence to that moral outlook more difficult to maintain.[54]

Nietzsche's account treats man as essentially no different than any other form of life, and indeed uses the terminology of herds, beasts, predators, and prey to describe human beings and to account for the origins of morality. In this way he opened up an approach that played a tremendous role in the analysis of human moral behavior in the twentieth century. He had an obvious influence on Freud, on Jung, and on the development of modern psychology, as well as on the anthropological investigations of Claude Lévi-Strauss, Konrad Lorenz, Ruth Benedict, and many others. Despite the disregard of Anglo-American philosophy for his thought (and German thought in general) in the aftermath of the two world wars, his work on moral thought has become more popular with analytic philosophers who have seen in his naturalism a solution to moral questions that arise as a result of their acceptance of Darwin's evolutionary theory.

It is perhaps no accident that when Nietzsche accounted the successes of the year 1887 in *Ecce Homo,* he pointed not just to the *Genealogy* but to his "Hymn to Life" ("Hymnus an das Leben"), published the same year.[55] This work was partially composed in August and September of 1882, based on a poem by Lou Salome, and then revised by Nietzsche's friend, the composer Heinrich Köselitz (or, as Nietzsche called him, Peter Gast). Nietzsche believed that if it were performed in public it would seduce people to his philosophy. The hymn resembles the "Yes and Amen Song" of *Zarathustra* in its proclamation of an eternal love for life in both its deepest joy and its deepest pain. Like the *Genealogy* it does not merely accept the tragic, but wills, loves, and thus seeks to redeem it.

This love of life that Nietzsche believes will characterize the highest men plays a central role in his appeal to his unknown friends to join him in his questioning, in his rejection of the ascetic ideal, and in the self-overcoming of truth. But it is also evident that he puts such emphasis on the love of life, even in pain, because he is convinced that the future that leads to the superman is only possible on the basis of such pain. As Nietzsche urges his potential followers onto a path toward the superman, he also tries to prepare and harden them for the unavoidable suffering of the Great Noon.

Notes

Unless otherwise noted, the translations from Nietzsche in this essay are our own.

[1] Nietzsche did not see the importance of the political, as opposed to the cultural, question for Europe. For further discussion, see Curt Paul Janz, *Friedrich Nietzsche: Biographie,* 3 vols. (Munich: Hanser, 1978–79), 2:417.

[2] Janz, *Friedrich Nietzsche,* 2:79, 82, 108–9. See also *Z* III §3; *KSA* 4, 217; *Z* III 10 §1 and §2; *KSA* 4, 236 and 240; and *Z* IV §13; *KSA* 4, 357.

[3] Janz, *Friedrich Nietzsche,* 2:616.

[4] Janz, *Friedrich Nietzsche,* 2:291.

[5] Janz, *Friedrich Nietzsche,* 2:164.

[6] Janz, *Friedrich Nietzsche,* 2:198.

[7] Cited in Janz, *Friedrich Nietzsche,* 2:289.

[8] For a fuller discussion of this point, see Michael Allen Gillespie, "Nietzsche and the Anthropology of Nihilism," *Nietzsche-Studien* 28 (1999): 141–55.

[9] *GM* III §27; *KSA* 5, 409; and *KSA* 12, 9[82], 377; *KSA* 13, 11[50] and 11[411], 71, and 189. For further discussion, see Elizabeth Kuhn, *Nietzsches Philosophie der europäischen Nihilismus* (Berlin: Walter de Gruyter, 1992), 26.

[10] Janz, *Friedrich Nietzsche,* 2:485.

[11] *EH BGE* §1; *KSA* 6, 350. Nietzsche is fishing for followers (see *Z* IV 1; *KSA* 4, 295–99); the parallel to Christ is obvious.

[12] Janz, *Friedrich Nietzsche*, 2:453–55.

[13] Janz, *Friedrich Nietzsche*, 2:543.

[14] William H. Schaberg, *The Nietzsche Canon: A Publication History and Bibliography* (Chicago: U of Chicago P, 1995), 149 and 153. Nietzsche also planned a second volume with sections on "The Herd Instinct in Morality," "The History of Morality — Denaturing," and "Among the Moralists and Moral Philosophers" (Janz, *Friedrich Nietzsche*, 2:562; see *KSA* 12, 9[83], 377).

[15] Janz, *Friedrich Nietzsche*, 2:541.

[16] Owen recognizes this problem when he sees Nietzsche's task as akin to the Hellenistic effort at a therapeutic ethical re-formation; see David Owen, "Nietzsche's Genealogy Revisited," *Journal of Nietzsche Studies* 35–36 (2008): 141–53 [here: 146–47].

[17] These "higher men" are the "higher natures" whose souls are torn between the slave ideal and the noble ideal (*GM* I §16; *KSA* 5, 286).

[18] On the connection between the higher men and activive nihilists, see Gillespie, "Nietzsche and the Anthropology of Nihilism." Nietzsche remarked that if he lived in St. Petersburg he would be a nihilist (Janz, *Friedrich Nietzsche*, 2:586).

[19] For Nietzsche, science included the natural sciences (*Naturwissenschaften*) and the human sciences (*Geisteswissenschaften*).

[20] Janz, *Friedrich Nietzsche*, 2:549. The *Genealogy's* rhetorical target is the British utilitarian tradition that Nietzsche saw as a manifestation of the drift of European culture toward the last man; see Bernd Magnus and Kathleen M. Higgins, "Nietzsche's Works and Their Themes," in *The Cambridge Companion to Nietzsche* ed. Bernd Magnus and Kathleen M. Higgins (Cambridge: Cambridge UP, 1996), 21–69 (here: 49). On Nietzsche's account of the implausibility of the basic assumptions of the genealogists, see Catherine Zuckert, 'Nietzsche on the Origin and Development of the Distinctively Human,' *Polity* 16 (1983): 48–71 (here: 52); and Elijab Millgram, 'Who Was Nietzsche's Genealogist?,' *Philosophy and Phenomenological Research* 75 (2007): 92–110 (here: 93). Jacqueline Stevens believes that Nietzsche actually seeks to debunk the whole idea of genealogy in favor of an actual history of morality ("On the Morals of Genealogy," *Political Theory* 31 (2003): 558–88 [here: 558, 560, 570]).

[21] Stevens, "On the Morals of Genealogy," 562. While the title of Rée's first chapter promises a discussion of "good and evil," the text refers only to "good" and "bad." For Nietzsche, this oversight revealed one of Rée's most fundamental errors; see Paul Rée, "Origin of the Moral Sensations," in *Basic Writings*, ed. and trans. Robin Small (Chicago: U of Illinois P, 2003), 85–168 (here: 89–99); and Christopher Janaway, "Beyond Selflessness in Ethics and Inquiry," *Journal of Nietzsche Studies* 35–36 (2008): 124–40 (here: 78).

[22] Janaway, "Beyond Selflessness in Ethics and Inquiry," 125; Stevens, "On the Morals of Genealogy," 556.

[23] Stevens, "On the Morals of Genealogy," 562 and 570. As Stevens points out, Rée takes the problems of Hobbes, Locke, Hume, and Smith (including the war of all against all) and hands them back to Darwin.

[24] Zuckert, "Nietzsche on the Origin and Development of the Distinctively Human," 54.

[25] Friedrich Nietzsche, *Beyond Good and Evil*, ed. Rolf-Peter Horstmann and Judith Norman (Cambridge: Cambridge UP, 2002), §260; *KSA* 5, 208.

[26] Nietzsche says the slave revolt "has a history of two thousand years," which may seem odd, but he is referring not to the birth of Christ but to the Roman occupation of Israel, which began in ca. 64 BCE (cf. *AC* §24–§26; *KSA* 6, 191–97).

[27] *GM* I §16; *KSA* 5, 285–86. In *Beyond*, Nietzsche similarly comments that "all higher and more mixed cultures" (allen höheren und gemischteren Culturen) are marked by an effort to reconcile these two moralities (*BGE* §260; *KSA* 5, 208).

[28] Compare these "higher natures" to the "higher men" (höheren Menschen) of *Zarathustra* (Z IV 13 §1–§15; *KSA* 4, 356–65).

[29] Nietzsche apparently does not mean to suggest that *ressentiment* would *never* develop in these enslaved races. Indeed, earlier in the second essay, he claims that the man of *ressentiment* was the inventor of bad conscience (*GM* II §18; *KSA* 5, 324). Unless we are to take this as a simple contradiction, we must assume he means to suggest that the human type that would become the man of *ressentiment* was the inventor of bad conscience.

[30] Finally, as a means of "temporary relief" from this torment, Christianity offers a doctrine of atonement — the debt is imputed to the creditor himself. This is also the work of the ascetic priest.

[31] Lawrence J. Hatab, "How Does the Ascetic Ideal Function in Nietzsche's Genealogy?," *The Journal of Nietzsche Studies* 35–36 (2008): 106–23 (here: 107).

[32] Elsewhere, Nietzsche suggests other causes of widespread psycho-physiological sickness (see *GM* III §17; *KSA* 5, 378).

[33] See Zuckert, "Nietzsche on the Origin and Development of the Distinctively Human," 69.

[34] As Hatab puts it, "[W]hen some forms of life are degenerating, are losing a more original natural vitality, life itself will engender different strategies [. . .] to prevent an utter abnegation of life" ("How Does the Ascetic Ideal Function in Nietzsche's Genealogy?," 109).

[35] See Hatab, "How Does the Ascetic Ideal Function in Nietzsche's Genealogy?," 110.

[36] Zuckert, "Nietzsche on the Origin and Development of the Distinctively Human," 69.

[37] *GS* §344; *KSA* 3, 574–77. Hatab focuses unduly on the distinction between perspectival and binary truth, missing the clearer explanation in *Gay Science* §344, to which Nietzsche refers his readers ("How Does the Ascetic Ideal Function in Nietzsche's Genealogy?," 113).

[38] Friedrich Nietzsche, *Human, All Too Human*, trans. R. J. Hollingdale (Cambridge: Cambridge UP, 2001), 182. In *Beyond Good and Evil*, Nietzsche insists that some judgments must "be believed to be true, for the sake of preservation of creatures like ourselves, though they might, of course, be false judgments for all

that" (dass zum Zweck der Erhaltung von Wesen unsrer Art solche Urtheile als wahr geglaubt werden müssen; weshalb sie natürlich noch falsche Urtheile sein könnten!; *BGE* §11; *KSA* 5, 25).

[39] *GM* III §24; *KSA* 5,398. See Daniel Conway, *Nietzsche's "On the Genealogy of Morals": A Reader's Guide* (London: Continuum, 2008), 139.

[40] Conway, *Nietzsche's "On the Genealogy of Morals,"* 144.

[41] As Conway notes, Nietzsche had become increasingly convinced that self-critique was a sign of strength (*Nietzsche's "On the Genealogy of Morals,"* 140).

[42] Conway, *Nietzsche's "On the Genealogy of Morals,"* 176.

[43] Conway goes so far as to describe this as a "suicide mission" for Nietzsche and his collaborators. They will engage in a final act of self-cancellation as they oppose the precondition of their own existence. Yet Conway's view assumes that the last idealists are finally incapable of distancing themselves from the ascetic ideal. Here, the better part of wisdom seems to be with Hatab's suspicion that this reading is too polarized. The closing section of the second essay, which anticipates the struggle outlined in the third essay, suggests that through the experience of war and victory and "winter journeys to ice and mountains in every sense" (winterliche Wanderungen, an Eis und Gebirge in jedem Sinne), the higher men of the modern age might acquire a "different kind of spirit" (einer andern Art Geister), prepared to accept and even flourish under a new life-affirming, nature-affirming tablet of values — the inversion of the ascetic ideal (*GM* III §24; *KSA* 5, 336).

[44] *KSA* 10, 16[49], 514; see Henning Ottmann, *Philosophie und Politik bei Nietzsche* (Berlin: Walter de Gruyter, 1987), 387.

[45] Hatab, "How Does the Ascetic Ideal Function in Nietzsche's Genealogy?," 117.

[46] Zuckert, "Nietzsche on the Origin and Development of the Distinctively Human," 70.

[47] *TI* "Skirmishes" §44; *KSA* 6, 145–46. On this point see Don Dombrowski, "Nietzsche as Bonapartist," in *Nietzsche, Power and Politics: Rethinking Nietzsche's Legacy for Political Thought*, ed. Herman W. Siemens and Vasti Roodt (Berlin: Walter de Gruyter, 2008), 347–69 (here: 352). Resa von Schirnnhofer asserted that Napoleon was the only person who fascinated Nietzsche as a transition type to the overman (ibid., 357).

[48] Dombrowski, "Nietzsche as Bonapartist," 368.

[49] *BGE* §242; *KSA* 5, 182–83. See Dombrowski, "Nietzsche as Bonapartist," 365.

[50] *EH* "Why I Am so Clever" §4; *KSA* 6, 286–87; and *TI* "Skirmishes" §38; *KSA* 6, 139–40. On this point, see also Angela Holzer, "'Nietzsche Caesar': The Turn against Dynastic Succession and Caesarism in Nietzsche's Late Works," in *Nietzsche, Power and Politics*, 371–91(here: 374).

[51] Holzer, "'Nietzsche Caesar,'" 388.

[52] Nietzsche was deeply disturbed by the prospect of an actual war as opposed to a spiritual one, which he clearly longed for. He knew how terrible such a war would be, and yet he saw clearly that it was the necessary consequence of his doctrine.

It thus stood as a terrifying specter in front of him. See Janz, *Friedrich Nietzsche*, 2:266 and 576–77.

[53] This claim is not incontestable; see, for example, David Owen, *Nietzsche's "Genealogy of Morality"* (Stocksfield, UK: Acumen, 2007), 3.

[54] Owen, *Nietzsche's Genealogy*, 150.

[55] See Janz, *Friedrich Nietzsche*, 2:540.

Link to *The Case Of Wagner* and *Nietzsche Contra Wagner*

While he and Heinrich Köselitz were still correcting the proofs of *On the Genealogy of Morals* (*Zur Genealogie der Moral*), Nietzsche told Meta von Salis that the work indicated everything essential that should be known about him: from the preface to *The Birth of Tragedy* (*Die Geburt der Tragödie*) to the preface of his latest work there was revealed, he said, "a kind of 'evolution'" (eine Art "Entwicklungsgeschichte"; *KSB* 8, 151). Before Nietzsche returned to Nice for his fifth winter, E. W. Fritzsch published a composition by Nietzsche, his setting of Lou von Salomé's "Hymn to Life" (Hymnus an das Leben), arranged for choir and orchestra. Amid the evolutionary unfolding of Nietzsche's thought, one thing remained constant: his passion for music.

After all, his first book examined the birth of tragedy *out of the spirit of music*, where he associated music with the Dionysian (*BT* §1; *KSA* 1, 25 and 29–30). In his fourth and final *Untimely Meditation* (*Unzeitgemäße Betrachtung*), he described "the primally-determined nature through which music speaks to the world of appearance" (die ur-bestimmte Natur, durch welche die Musik zur Welt der Erscheinung spricht), as "the most mysterious thing under the sun, an abyss in which power and goodness dwell together, a bridge between the Self and the Non-Self" (das räthsel-vollste Ding unter der Sonne, ein Abgrund, in welchem Kraft und Güte gepaart ruhen, eine Brücke zwischen Selbst und Nicht-Selbst; *UM* IV §6; *KSA* 1, 465). In *Twilight of the Idols* (*Götzen-Dämmerung*), he followed up a brief meditation on the sound of bagpipes with the beautiful aphorism, "without music life would be an error" (ohne Musik wäre das Leben ein Irrthum; *TI* "Sayings and Arrows" §33; *KSA* 6, 64). And in *Ecce Homo* he confessed, "I do not know how to distinguish between tears and music" (Ich weiss keinen Unterschied zu machen zwischen Thränen und Musik; *EH* "Why I Am So Clever" §7; *KSA* 6, 291).[1]

Furthermore, Nietzsche himself was a pianist and a composer, to an extent that cannot be considered with any thoroughness within the confines of this volume. If one samples, however, some of the tracks from a basic discography of Nietzsche's music, one can hear that, if lacking in sophistication (especially compared with Wagner!), the simplicity, even naiveté, of his compositions are not lacking in charm.[2] Following Richard Wagner's gift to Cosima of his *Siegfried Idyll*, written for her birthday after the birth of their son, Siegfried, in 1869, and performed on the morning of Christmas Eve in 1870, in 1871 Nietzsche had dedicated one of his compositions, *Reminiscences of a New Year's Eve* (*Nachklang einer Sylvesternacht*), to Cosima as a personal gift.[3] In 1872, his piano duet, the *Manfred-Meditation*, was performed in front of the Wagners in Bayreuth, on the occasion of their visit to lay the foundation stone of the Festspielhaus.[4] Perhaps it would be fairest to describe Nietzsche as a *frustrated musician*: writing to his friend, the musician and composer Köselitz (whom he called Peter Gast) on 22 June 1887, he admitted: "There is no doubt that, right deep down, I would have liked to be able *to write* the very music that you do — and that I have only written my music (including books) *faute de mieux . . .*" (Es ist nämlich kein Zweifel, daß ich im alleruntersten Grunde *die* Musik *machen können* möchte, die Sie machen — und daß ich meine eigne Musik (Bücher eingerechnet) immer nur gemacht habe faute de mieux . . .; *KSB* 8, 95).

As we have already seen, Nietzsche had first met Wagner in Leipzig in 1868, and Julian Young has suggested that this encounter and the ensuing friendship with the composer led to the birth of *The Birth of Tragedy* (*Die Geburt der Tragödie*).[5] According to Rudolf Steiner, in the 1860s Wagner became nothing less than an "epistemological problem," an *Erkenntnisproblem*, for Nietzsche: "How could one live with what had, in the sense of contemporary spiritual development, or the new worldview, taken shape in Richard Wagner — how could one live with that in a human soul that wanted to experience for itself the inspiring powers of life?" (Wie läßt sich mit dem, was gerade im Sinne der neueren Geistesentwickelung, der neueren Weltanschauung in dem Musiker Richard Wagner geworden war, wie läßt sich mit dem leben in einer Menschenseele, die die befruchtende Kräfte des Lebens in sich erfahren will?).[6] (It will come as no surprise to learn that, for Steiner, Wagner's soul was steeped in "mysticism" [Mystik], inasmuch as his art looked back to a remote human past — a point, Steiner believed, that was on Wagner's mind when he realized his mission, and on Nietzsche's, too, when he tried to describe it in *The Birth of Tragedy*.)[7] The desire to find a connection between art and life — to see art as an enhancement, intensification, and profound expression of life — runs throughout Nietzsche's writings.

Although Nietzsche later dismissed one of Wagner's chief compositional devices, the leitmotiv, describing it as "an ideal toothpick, as an opportunity to get rid of *what is left over* from meals" (als idealen Zahnstocher [. . .], als Gelegenheit, *Reste* von Speisen los zu werden; *GS* §8; *KSA* 6, 32), it would be no exaggeration to see *Thus Spoke Zarathustra* (*Also sprach Zarathustra*) as a response to Wagner's music: as an anti-*Ring*,[8] an anti-*Parsifal*.[9] Wagner is also present in other ways in *Zarathustra*: the chapter in part 2 entitled "The Grave Song" ("Das Grablied") is, in part, a reflection on the death of Wagner, which coincided with the completion of part 1, as well as a reference to the isle of the dead on the lagoon in Venice, onto which Nietzsche's room looked when he visited in 1880 (*KSB* 6, 13) — the various layers of cultural and autobiographical references are one of the reasons why the text is so difficult to interpret[10] — while the figure of the Magician in part 4 is widely held to be a representation of Wagner.[11]

When Nietzsche fled the first Bayreuth Festival in 1876, he disassociated himself from Wagner as a person (and, perhaps, a substitute father-figure) and from Wagnerianism as a cultural project. One might argue that the break was inevitable, given not just the differences in their intellectual and cultural trajectories, but their respective Faustian identifications: in his letter accompanying his birthday gift of roses on 21 May 1870, Nietzsche addressed Wagner as "Pater Seraphice," signing the letter as "one of the 'blessed youths" (Einer "der seligen Knaben"), an allusion to the closing scene of *Faust*, Part Two, which Wagner acknowledged in his reply of 23 May 1870.[12] But the "blessed youths," the children who have died young, whom the Pater Seraphicus takes into himself, soon beg to be released from him, and circle upward ever higher, accompanying Faust's soul until it reaches the highest sphere of the Mater Gloriosa. This playful allusion to Goethe presages Nietzsche's eventual desire to "go beyond" Wagner.

After his intensive work on *On the Genealogy of Morals* (*Zur Genealogie der Moral*) in Sils Maria in the summer of 1887, Nietzsche decided to spend the autumn of that year in Venice, in the company of Köselitz. During his stay Nietzsche entertained a strange fantasy, as he narrated in a letter to Reinhart von Seydlitz:

> Yesterday I invented an image of a *moralité larmoyante*, as Diderot would say. Winter landscape. An old coachman who, with an expression of the most brutal cynicism, harder than even the winter all around, is urinating against his own horse. The horse, a poor, flayed creature, looks around, gratefully, so very gratefully —
>
> [Gestern dachte ich mir ein Bild aus von einer moralité larmoyante, mit Diderot zu reden. Winterlandschaft. Ein alter Fuhrmann, der mit dem Ausdruck des brutalsten Cynismus, härter noch als der Winter ringsherum, sein Wasser an seinem eignen Pferde abschlägt. Das Pferd, die arme geschundne Creatur, blickt sich um, dankbar, *sehr* dankbar — (*KSB* 8, 314)][13]

If, in Venice, Nietzsche encountered an imaginary horse, in December 1888 in Turin he would encounter a real horse, and enter a state where the border between reality and fantasy began to blur.

For winter, Nietzsche returned to Nice, where he was able to rent a cheap but commensurately cold room. To combat the "blue-fingered frostiness" (blaufingrige Fröstelei) of the winter, he told Köselitz, he had set up a small oven, a "fire-idol" or *Feuergötze*, in his room, around which, presumably to keep warm, he admitted he had already made "a number of pagan leaps" (einige heidnische Sprünge; *KSB* 8, 202). Similarly, in view of later events in Turin, Nietzsche's behavior — here, charmingly eccentric — was to take a more alarming turn.

Perhaps it was his return to Venice, the city where Wagner had died in February 1883 exactly at the time when Nietzsche was finishing what became part 1 of *Zarathustra* (*KSB* 6, 429); perhaps it was because, as he told Franz Overbeck, he had suffered such a strong sense of deprivation in the years subsequent to their break, because Wagner had been "by far the most *complete* individual" (bei weitem der *vollste* Mensch) he had known (22 February 1883; *KSB* 6, 337); perhaps it was because of the publication of his "Hymn to Life," confirming (in his own eyes, at least) his abilities as a composer — but for whatever reason, after his fifth winter spent in Nice and his move to Turin in the spring of 1888, Nietzsche began work on a short book about Wagner. Praising Turin in his letter to Köselitz of 20 April 1888, Nietzsche talked about "a small pamphlet about music" (ein kleines Pamphlet über Musik) that was keeping his fingers busy (*KSB* 8, 299), and he completed the text, back in Sils Maria, in June 1888. (Was this the summer in which, so Theodor W. Adorno was later told, the local children would fill Nietzsche's umbrella with tiny stones, so that when he opened it, they dropped onto his head — in response to which he would give chase?)[14]

When he sent the manuscript of *The Case of Wagner* (*Der Fall Wagner*) to his publisher, C. G. Naumann, in June 1888, Nietzsche asked that the publication should look "*as aesthetic as possible*" (*so ästhetisch wie möglich*) — as the rest of the letter shows, Nietzsche had very precise suggestions, down to the choice of font, for its appearance (*KSB* 8, 342–43 and 344).[15] Following its publication in September 1888, Nietzsche sent a copy to Georg Brandes in Copenhagen, together with an accompanying letter in which he described the style of the book's writing as "almost French" (beinahe französisch), and alerted Brandes to two other current projects: one called *A Psychologist at Leisure* (*Müßiggang eines Psychologen*) and another called *Revaluation of All Values* (*Umwerthung aller Werthe*; see *KSB* 8, 419–20). And when he sent a copy in October 1888 to Malwida von Meysenbug in Rome, he again emphasized its French style, described the work as "a declaration of war *in aestheticis*" (eine Kriegserklärung in aestheticis), and referred to his larger project, to "the first book of my *Revaluation of All Values*" (das erste Buch meiner *Umwerthung aller Werthe*; *KSB* 8, 447). Thus, while *The Case of Wagner* should be seen against the background of Nietzsche's other projects of his final year and a half, it is also a work that stands on its own, deserving appreciation for its stylistic excellence.

Shortly before his death in Venice in 1883, Wagner is reported to have told Elisabeth Förster-Nietzsche, "Tell your brother that, since *he* left me, I have been alone" (Sagen Sie es Ihrem Bruder, seit *er* von mir gegangen ist, bin ich allein).[16] That this sense of isolation after their break was mutual is confirmed by Nietzsche's letter to Overbeck of 22 February 1883, in which he claimed that he had been suffering such a great privation because of Wagner's completeness (*KSB* 6, 337) — a remark that casts an interesting light on Nietzsche's claim in *Ecce Homo* that Wagner had been "by far the man most closely related" (der [. . .] bei Weitem verwandteste Mann) to him (*EH* "Why I Am So Wise" §3; *KSA* 6, 268). Ultimately, the dynamics of the Nietzsche-Wagner story testify to the uniqueness of all such friendships, as encapsulated in Montaigne's famous remark about his own with Étienne de La Boétie: *parce que c'était lui; parce que c'était moi* (because it was he, because it was I).[17] In the following chapter, Daniel Conway discusses in further detail both this work and *Nietzsche contra Wagner* (1888), Nietzsche's own selection of his writings on Wagner, and reads them not simply in the light of Nietzsche's intense, yet complex, relationship to the composer but in relation to his philosophical project as a whole.

Notes

[1] For further discussion of Nietzsche's relation to music, see Anthony Storr, *Music and the Mind* (London: HarperCollins, 1992), 150–67.

[2] For further discussion of Nietzsche's relation to music, see Georges Liébert, *Nietzsche and Music*, trans. David Pellauer and Graham Parkes (Chicago and London: U of Chicago P, 2004); and Christoph Cox, "Nietzsche, Dionysus, and the Ontology of Music," in *A Companion to Nietzsche*, ed. Keith Ansell-Pearson (Chichester, West Sussex: Wiley-Blackwell, 2005), 495–513. Various recordings of Nietzsche's compositions are available, and the following constitutes a basic discography: *Friedrich Nietzsche: Piano Music*, performed by John Bell Young and Constance Keene, recorded in 1992, Newport Classic NPD 85513; *Friedrich Nietzsche: Lieder — Piano Works — Melodrama*, performed by Dietrich Fischer-Dieskau, made in 1995, available on Philips 426 863-2; a two-disc Canadian recording produced at Concordia University, Montreal, entitled *The Music of/La Musique de Friedrich Nietzsche*, Atma classique ACD 1998; and *Friedrich Nietzsche "Ohne Heimat": Lieder und Texte des jungen Nietzsche*, recorded in 2006, HörZeichen 37-1.

[3] See Curt Paul Janz, *Friedrich Nietzsche: Eine Biographie*, 3 vols. (Munich and Vienna: Hanser, 1978), 1:427–28.

[4] Janz, *Friedrich Nietzsche*, 1:477–83.

[5] Julian Young, *Friedrich Nietzsche: A Philosophical Biography* (Cambridge: Cambridge UP, 2010), 112–34.

[6] Rudolf Steiner, "Nietzsches Seelenleben und Richard Wagner: Zur deutschen Weltanschauungsentwickelung der Gegenwart" [1916], in *Aus dem mitteleuropäischen Geistesleben: Fünfzehn öffentliche Vorträge gehalten zwischen dem 2. Dezember 1915 und dem 15. April 1916 im Architektenhaus zu Berlin* [*Gesamtausgabe*, vol. 65], ed. Wolfram Groddeck and Paul Jenny (Dornach: Rudolf Steiner Verlag, 2000), 497–542.

[7] Rudolf Steiner, "Richard Wagner und sein Verhältnis zur Mystik" [1907], in *Die okkulten Wahrheiten alter Mythen und Sagen: Griechische und germanische Mythologie — Richard Wagner im Lichte der Geisteswissenschaft: Sechzehn Vorträge, gehalten in Berlin, Köln und Nürnberg in den Jahren 1904, 1905 und 1907 (Hörernotizen)* [*Gesamtausgabe*, vol. 92], ed. Helmuth von Wartburg und Ulla Trapp (Dornach: Rudolf Steiner Verlag, 1999), 158–78 (here: 162–63).

[8] For further discussion, see Roger Hollinrake, *Nietzsche, Wagner, and the Philosophy of Pessimism* (London: Allen and Unwin, 1982).

[9] Indeed, exactly at the same time as Wagner had sent Nietzsche the libretto of *Parsifal*, Nietzsche had sent Wagner a copy of *Menschliches, Allzumenschliches* (*Human, All Too Human*) — a coincidence and a contrast on which, in retrospect, Nietzsche reflected in *Ecce Homo* as follows: "The crossing of these two books — it seemed to me I had heard an ominous sound. Didn't it sound as if two *swords* had crossed? . . ." (Diese Kreuzung der zwei Bücher — mir war's, als ob ich einen ominösen Ton dabei hörte. Klang es nicht, als ob sich *Degen* kreutzen? . . .; *EH HA* §5; *KSA* 6, 327).

[10] For further discussion of this chapter, see Paul Bishop, "'Yonder lies the grave-island, the silent island; yonder, too, are the graves of my youth': A Commentary on Zarathustra's Grave-Song," *Orbis Litterarum* 57 (2002): 317–42.

[11] Compare with Nietzsche's description in his fourth *Untimely Meditation* of Wagner as a "dithyrambic dramatist" (dithyrambischer Dramatiker) and, in turn, such a dramatist as "the greatest magician and benefactor among mortals" (der größte Zauberer und Beglücker unter den Sterblichen; *KSA* 1, 467 and 472).

[12] Dieter Borchmeyer and Jörg Salaquarda, eds., *Nietzsche und Wagner: Stationen einer epochalen Begegnung*, 2 vols. (Frankfurt am Main and Leipzig: Insel, 1994), 1:83–84.

[13] For discussion of Nietzsche's mobilization of Cynic themes, see Heinrich Niehues-Pröbsting, "The Modern Reception of Cynicism: Diogenes in the Enlightenment," in *The Cynics: The Cynic Movement in Antiquity and Its Legacy*, ed. R. Bracht Branham and Marie-Odile Goulet-Cazé (Berkeley: U of California P, 1996), 329–65 (esp. 353–63).

[14] Theodor W. Adorno, "Aus Sils Maria," in *Ohne Leitbild: Parve Aesthetica*, in *Kulturkritik und Gesellschaft I* [*Gesammelte Schriften*, vol. 10.1] (Frankfurt am Main: Suhrkamp, 1977), 326–29 (here: 328–29).

[15] Nietzsche's instructions to his publisher on the choice of font should be seen in the context of the nineteenth-century debate over *Fraktur* (or Gothic) and Roman type; for further discussion, see Silvia Hartmann, *Fraktur oder Antiqua: Der Schiftstreit von 1881 bis 1941* (Frankfurt am Main: Lang, 1998).

[16] Elisabeth Förster-Nietzsche, *Wagner und Nietzsche zur Zeit ihrer Freundschaft* (Munich: Müller, 1915), 279.

[17] Montaigne, "On Friendship," in *Essays*, book 1, chapter 28; see Montaigne, *Œuvres complètes*, ed. Albert Thibaudet and Maurice Rat (Paris: Gallimard, 1962), 187.

10: *The Case of Wagner* and *Nietzsche contra Wagner*

Daniel Conway

> My greatest experience was a *recovery*. Wagner is merely one of my illnesses.
>
> [Mein grösstes Erlebniss war eine *Genesung*. Wagner gehört bloss zu meinen Krankheiten. (*CW* preface; *KSA* 6, 12)][1]

THE YEAR 1888 WAS NOT ONLY Nietzsche's most productive as an author, but also his final year of sanity. In May of that year he completed a first draft of *The Case of Wagner* (*Der Fall Wagner*), to which he subsequently added a preface, two postscripts, and an epilogue.[2] The first edition was published by C. G. Naumann in September of that year.[3] Later that year, responding in part to reviews of *The Case of Wagner*,[4] Nietzsche quickly prepared *Nietzsche contra Wagner* for print. He excerpted the contents from his earlier books, lightly editing these selections and adding a very brief preface. By design, this book contains very little that is new. The preface to *Nietzsche contra Wagner* is dated Christmas, 1888,[5] and the book was published in February of 1889.[6] By that time, of course, Nietzsche had surrendered to the madness that would envelope him for the remainder of his life.

In general, we find that Nietzsche's treatment of Wagner in these two books consistently touches on the following themes: first, his aversion to Wagner was neither recent nor opportunistic; second, his early enthusiasm for Wagner was symptomatic of a more basic illness, which he associated with the moral and cultural demands of "selflessness"; third, as a decadent artist, Wagner is responsible for making art and music sick; fourth, Wagner is to be praised for his true talents and genuine accomplishments, which, it turns out, are very different from those that are popularly attributed to him; fifth, Nietzsche's enmity for Wagner's music is directed most vehemently against his final opera, *Parsifal*, which he regards as irredeemably Christian in character; sixth, Nietzsche's break with Wagner allowed him to emerge from the Master's shadow and establish for himself a fully individuated and authentic existence; and, seventh and finally, embracing one's destiny — in Nietzsche's terms, *becoming what one is* — may require one to retreat from the scene of one's most painful contestations.

Biographical Background

Friedrich Nietzsche and Richard Wagner met for the first time in November of 1868.[7] Wagner was visiting his sister in Leipzig, where Nietzsche had resumed his doctoral studies following a period of military service. Wagner was in fine form on the evening they first met, and he made an extremely favorable impression on Nietzsche.[8] They were able to nurture their budding friendship when, in April of 1869, Nietzsche relocated to Basel to begin an appointment as extraordinary professor of classical philology. Basel was situated in relatively close proximity to Tribschen, Wagner's villa near Lake Lucerne, where Nietzsche was a frequent visitor.[9] By all accounts, including his own (*EH* "Why I Am So Clever" §5; *KSA* 6, 288), this was an unusually happy period in Nietzsche's life.[10] Flattered by the attention Wagner paid him, Nietzsche embraced his role as the composer's philosophical protégé. As several scholars have noted, Wagner soon became a kind of father figure to Nietzsche, whose own father, born in the same year as Wagner, had died in 1849.[11]

Nietzsche also appreciated the warmth with which he was welcomed into Wagner's family life.[12] He became especially close to Wagner's mistress and future wife, Cosima (*née* Liszt) von Bülow, whom he greatly admired. Much later, gripped by madness, Nietzsche would declare his love for Wagner's widow, referring to her as Ariadne and to himself as Dionysos (*KSB* 8, 572–73). Wagner's relocation to Bayreuth in 1872 marked the beginning of the end of his friendship with Nietzsche.[13] The intimate familial bonds of Tribschen were not to be recreated in Bayreuth, and Nietzsche's assertion of his independence from Wagner was at that point overdue.[14] Wagner's move to Bayreuth took on additional (and ominous) significance for Nietzsche, who regarded it as a capitulation to the philistinism of the Reich (*EH* "Why I Am So Clever" §5; *KSA* 6, 289). Nietzsche may have been rudely divested of his familial happiness, but the German people had been swindled out of their future (*CW* postscript 1; *KSA* 6, 40–42; cf. *EH* "Why I Am So Clever" §5; *KSA* 6, 288–89).

Notwithstanding the tumultuous course of Wagner's life, rich in accomplishments, reversals, triumphs, and controversies, the *case* of Wagner, in Nietzsche's eyes, rests on a single, decisive development. Nietzsche observes that Wagner began his career as an optimist, a revolutionary, and a libertine. Influenced by Feuerbach and emboldened by his "cry of 'healthy sensuality'" (Feuerbach's Wort von der "gesunden Sinnlichkeit"; *GM* III §3; *KSA* 5, 342), Wagner developed his central mythic themes in tandem with his dreams of revolution (*CW* §4; *KSA* 6, 19–20). While living in exile following the Dresden uprising, however, Wagner discovered the German philosopher Arthur Schopenhauer (1788–1860), whose notorious pessimism quickly infused Wagner's art.[15] Under the influence of Schopenhauer, Wagner was obliged to renounce his revolutionary optimism — deemed "infamous" (ruchlos) by Schopenhauer — in favor of the nihilistic pessimism that, according to Nietzsche, informs his later writings and compositions (*CW* §4; *KSA* 6, 20).

When he learned of Wagner's death in 1883, Nietzsche initially suffered a physical breakdown, from which he soon, however, recovered.[16] In his letter to Köselitz (or Peter Gast) of 19 February 1883, he identified the "aged" (altgewordne) Wagner, the author of *Parsifal*, as his antagonist, while renewing his allegiance to the "real" Wagner (den eigentlichen Wagner), whose "*heir*" (sein *Erbe*) he would, to some extent, become (*KSB* 6, 333–34).[17] As we shall see, he presents himself in *The Case of Wagner* as inheriting from Wagner, and subsequently perfecting, the regimen of "lifelong self-discipline" that enabled each of them, in turn, to become what he was.

Relationship to Preceding Works

The profound influence of Richard Wagner is evident from the very beginning of Nietzsche's philosophical career. His first book, *The Birth of Tragedy* (*Die Geburt der Tragödie*, 1872), not only was dedicated to Wagner, but also included an extended paean to the redemptive power of Wagner's music. Convinced that Wagner would succeed in reviving the "spirit of music" that had enlivened Greek tragedy (*BT* §20; *KSA* 1, 130–31), he dared to think that he might provide a philosophical narrative in support of the innovations and aspirations of Wagner's art.[18]

Looking back on *The Birth of Tragedy*, first in his 1886 preface to the new edition, which he called "An Attempt at Self-Criticism" ("Versuch einer Selbstkritik"), and again in *Ecce Homo*, in his surprisingly insightful survey of the "good books" he had written, Nietzsche was unsparing in his criticism of his youthful enthusiasm for all things Wagnerian. In the former text he expressed his deep regret that he had mistakenly heard in Wagner's music the rejuvenation of the German spirit (*BT* "Attempt" §6; *KSA* 1, 20), while in the latter text he urged his readers "to forget a few things" (Einiges vergessen) about *The Birth of Tragedy*, most notably its proposal to interpret the spread of Wagnerism as a "symptom of *ascent*" (ein *Aufgangs*-Symptom; *EH BT* §1; *KSA* 6, 309).

Nietzsche once again addressed the cultural importance of Wagner in the fourth installment of his *Untimely Meditations* (*Unzeitgemäße Betrachtungen*), which he called "Richard Wagner in Bayreuth" (1876). Despite intending to remain both complimentary and respectful of Wagner, Nietzsche nevertheless managed in this essay to convey a sense of the rift growing between them.[19] In particular, this essay introduces Nietzsche's concern, expressed far less charitably in *The Case of Wagner*, that in Bayreuth Wagner was in danger of disappearing into his role as

Schauspieler — an actor or showman. Notwithstanding Nietzsche's apparent ambivalence, Wagner claimed to be delighted with the essay, and forwarded a copy to his patron, King Ludwig of Bavaria.[20]

Nietzsche's estrangement from Wagner is reflected in the themes addressed in the books that represent the "middle" period of his writing career. In these books — *Human, All Too Human* (*Menschliches, Allzumenschliches*, 1878–79), *Daybreak* (*Morgenröthe*, 1881), and *The Gay Science* (*Die fröhliche Wissenschaft*, 1882) — Nietzsche turned his attention to a cluster of issues pertaining to the underexplored field of moral psychology. This shift in focus was neither academic nor accidental, for these investigations were integral to his efforts to lead an authentic and fully individuated existence. (Just in case his readers had somehow overlooked this theme, Nietzsche underscored it for them in the prefaces he wrote in 1886 for the new editions that appeared in 1886–87.) Tracing the origins of *Human, All Too Human* to his experience of "alienation" (Fremdheit) at the inaugural Bayreuth Festival, Nietzsche confides that he felt compelled to explain how Wagner had allowed himself to be defined by the narrow ambitions of the Reich (*EH HA* §2; *KSA* 6, 323).

Reminiscing in *Ecce Homo*, Nietzsche allows that his troubled friendship with Wagner, like his ill-starred tenure at Basel, was symptomatic of a more basic personal crisis, involving, as he put it, "a total aberration of [his] instincts" (eine Gesammt-Abirrung [s]eines Instinkts; *EH HA* §3; *KSA* 6, 324). Instead of blaming Wagner for causing or precipitating his aberrancy, Nietzsche interprets his attraction to Wagner, like his pursuit of academic philology, as indicative of a more fundamental loss or displacement of his center of gravity. He identifies as the common root of these kindred afflictions the "'selflessness'" (Selbstlosigkeit) that hitherto had been allowed to govern his upbringing and moral development (*EH HA* §4; *KSA* 6, 326). In short, he now believes, he was compelled by his unpleasant visit to Bayreuth to call himself to order.

Nietzsche's next book, *Daybreak*, was meant to unearth the origins of the "selflessness" that had led him, he now realized, to embrace Wagner.[21] As he recalls, this investigation was distinctly personal, involving him in a "fight against the morality that would unself humankind" (den Kampf gegen die Entselbstungs-Moral; *EH D* §2; *KSA* 6, 332). In *The Gay Science*, Nietzsche mentions Wagner only infrequently, but his preface to the 1887 edition places the book in the context of his convalescence from the illness that he associated with his affiliation with Wagner. In book 5 of this new edition, Nietzsche offers several observations that anticipate the diagnosis he advances in *The Case of Wagner*. One observation in particular warrants mentioning. Acknowledging the faulty analysis that informed his early estimation of Wagner, he identifies the "*romantic pessimism*" of Schopenhauer and Wagner as "the last *great* event in the fate of our culture" (der romantische Pessimismus, das letzte *grosse Ereigniss im Schicksal unsrer Cultur*; *GS* §370; *KSA* 3, 622). Still, Wagner's music should not be confused with the music of the future, which, Nietzsche tantalizingly suggests, will bespeak an as-yet-unarticulated "*Dionysian* pessimism" (den *dionysischen* Pessimismus; *GS* §370).

Nietzsche's greatest work, *Thus Spoke Zarathustra* (*Also sprach Zarathustra*; 1883–85), followed next. As several scholars have noted, references and allusions to Wagner appear throughout this book. According to Roger Hollinrake, for example, Nietzsche is deeply indebted to Wagner's *Ring*, and in particular to *Siegfried*, for the drama, plot, and imagery of his *Zarathustra*.[22] As Paul S. Loeb has recently observed, Nietzsche's debts to the figure of Siegfried are even greater than Hollinrake reckoned, as evidenced by the articulation of Zarathustra's quest in part 3.[23] According to Loeb, in fact, Nietzsche's allusions to the figure of Siegfried are central to a proper interpretation of the famous riddle posed by Zarathustra toward the beginning of part 3 (*Z* III 2 §2; *KSA* 4, 202).[24] As Hollinrake has suggested, moreover, part 4 of *Zarathustra* may be interpreted as a parody of Wagner's *Parsifal*.[25]

In his first post-Zarathustrian book, *Beyond Good and Evil* (*Jenseits von Gut und Böse*, 1886), Nietzsche closes his discussion of "Peoples and Fatherlands" ("Völker und Vaterländer") by situating Wagner among "the more profound and comprehensive men of this century" (allen tieferen und umfänglicheren Menschen dieses Jahrhunderts), a group that includes the likes of Napoleon, Goethe, Beethoven, Stendhal, Heine, and Schopenhauer (*BGE* §256; *KSA* 5, 201). Notwithstanding these words of praise, Nietzsche reiterates his enmity for Wagner's *Parsifal*, which, he suggests, expresses "*Rome's faith without the text*" (*Rom's Glaube ohne Worte!*; *BGE* §256; *KSA* 5, 204). Wagner re-appears again in the third essay of *On the Genealogy of Morals* (*Zur Genealogie der Moral*; 1887), where Nietzsche proposes to treat Wagner as exemplary of how artists in general derive meaning from the ascetic ideal. As we shall see, the profile he develops in the *Genealogy* of the ascetic priest informs the diagnosis he delivers in *The Case of Wagner*.

Nietzsche's next year, 1888, which was also his final year of sanity, was very much influenced by Wagner. While continuing to labor over the *Hauptwerk* that was not to be, Nietzsche produced several short books (including the two books under explicit consideration in this chapter), in which he measured the progress of his recovery from the "selflessness" that his earlier infatuation with Wagner had signified. Although Nietzsche barely mentions Wagner in *Twilight of the Idols* (*Götzen-Dämmerung*), he devotes an entire chapter of the book to his diagnosis of the Germans. What the Germans lack, among other things, is a commitment to the kind of education that would encourage and honor genuine *thought* (*Denken*; *TI* "What the Germans Lack" §7; *KSA* 6, 109). Nietzsche also reiterates that he has largely given up on the German "spirit," though one suspects that here, as elsewhere, he protests too much.

Wagner is named only once in *The Anti-Christ* (or *The Antichristian*, as *Der Antichrist* may also be translated), as an exemplar of "aesthetic décadence" (artistischen décadence; *AC* §7; *KSA* 6, 174), but the Germans, for whom Wagner had come to stand in Nietzsche's mind and words, are subjected to more regular ridicule (cf. *AC* §10, §52, §61; *KSA* 6, 176–77, 233–34; 250–52). As we have seen, Wagner figures prominently in *Ecce Homo*, which relates a richer version of the basic story of self-overcoming that he tells in his preface to *The Case of Wagner*. Here we learn that Nietzsche became what he was through, and as a consequence of, the various contestations and struggles in which he had been entangled over the course of his life. In addition to providing a more detailed (albeit idealized) account of his life, *Ecce Homo* also treats *The Case of Wagner*, identified as one of his "good books," in some detail. This review rehearses Nietzsche's profound sense of disappointment with the Germans, for whom, in his mind, the Wagner of Bayreuth had become emblematic.

The Theme of Decadence

Nietzsche's case rests squarely on his claim that Wagner is best appreciated and understood as a *decadent* artist (*CW* §5; *KSA* 6, 21). According to Nietzsche, Wagner's relocation to Bayreuth marked a critical juncture, a point of no return, in the decay of German culture. Anyone hoping that Germany (or Wagner) might spark a renascence of European culture, as Nietzsche once did, was obliged henceforth to abandon that hope and look elsewhere for inspiration. For his own part, Nietzsche sought refuge in the south of Europe, in Turin, and in the carnal naturalism of Bizet's *Carmen*.

Nietzsche's diagnosis of Wagner's decadence is clearly meant to be decisive in the case he presents. But what, exactly, does Nietzsche mean for this diagnosis to convey? In *The Case of Wagner*, as elsewhere, Nietzsche helps himself to this diagnosis with very little explanation. He proceeds, in fact, as if he simply expected his readers to be familiar with the more general account of decadence that his diagnosis presupposed, such that they would naturally share his sense of the gravity of the case of Wagner. In this light, it may be valuable to review some of the most salient elements of Nietzsche's diagnosis of European decadence.[26]

In general, Nietzsche traced the decline of culture to the inevitable deterioration of the mores, customs, traditions, and institutions that collectively serve to shape the prevailing ethos of a nation, people, or tribe. He regarded modern societies as uniquely (and perhaps unrealistically) dependent on institutions to instill into diverse individuals of various backgrounds the norms and expectations of the culture in question.

When assessing the relative health (or decay) of a modern society, he was especially concerned to examine the structural integrity of those institutions that were entrusted with the administration of law, education, religion, and morality (cf. *TI* "Skirmishes" §39; *KSA* 6, 140–42). According to Nietzsche, the collapse of a society's signature institutions necessarily results in an irreparable estrangement between the culture in question and the individuals whom it formerly guided and nurtured.

The breakdown of institutional order in turn precipitates the instinctual disarray, or *laisser aller*, that is celebrated, to Nietzsche's chagrin, as modern freedom (*TI* "Skirmishes" §41; *KSA* 6, 143). Deprived of the acculturation formerly provided to them, individuals increasingly come to experience a clash of competing directives, as instincts formerly held in check battle blindly, as they must, for preponderance. The result of this clash is a depletion of the will itself, as individuals are obliged to distribute ever more broadly the limited volitional resources at their disposal. No longer able to marshal the resources needed to muster an undivided will, these individuals suffer the loss of their formerly assured sense of meaning, direction, and orientation. In this light, it is not surprising that Nietzsche associates the onset of decadence with the experience of what might be called a weakness of will.[27] Bereft of the clarity, focus, and direction formerly granted them, tempted by an ever-expanding tangle of competing instincts and conflicting goals, individuals find themselves unable to sustain the will to carry out the kinds of tasks that ensure the long-term survival of a culture.

The depletion of the will eventually yields a condition in which individuals have no choice but to elect and embrace precisely what is least likely to enhance their prospects for flourishing (*CW* §5; *KSA* 6, 21; cf. *EH* "Why I Am So Wise" §2; *KSA* 6, 266). At such a point, Nietzsche observes, individuals are no longer apt recipients of institutional guidance, for their battered instincts are no longer amenable to the imposition of a single principle or rule of order. Nothing can be done to or for them to restore the instinctual focus they have lost (*GS* §356; *KSA* 3, 595–96). In that event, the project of culture, by means of which a people or nation endeavors to assert its will into the future, comes to an end (*TI* "Skirmishes" §39; *KSA* 6, 140–41). Against this backdrop of systemic decay, cultures, nations, peoples, families, tribes, and individuals may be observed to forfeit the structural integrity that formerly made them whole.

According to Nietzsche, moreover, the problem of advanced decay admits of no political solution. While the natural process of decay can be accelerated or protracted via artificial means (*TI* "Skirmishes" §33; *KSA* 6, 132), it cannot be suspended or reversed. Lacking the instincts that would orient them productively to the future (*TI* "Skirmishes" §39; *KSA* 6, 140–41), late modern Europeans are now powerless to combat the decadence that grips them. All supposed responses, including the mighty Reich, are but alternate expressions of the decadence they are said and believed to address (*TI* "Skirmishes" §37; *KSA* 6, 136–37). In short, Nietzsche's critique of modernity yields a terminal diagnosis. The decadence of late modern European culture must be suffered to run its course (*TI* "Skirmishes" §43; *KSA* 6, 144).[28]

While it may be tempting to *pity* decadents, for example, by providing them with the stimulants and distractions they typically crave, Nietzsche cautions his readers to resist this temptation, which he and Zarathustra both acknowledge as their *final* temptation. (As we shall see, it is also a distinctly *priestly* temptation, inasmuch as the priest expands his clientele, thereby extending the reach of his empire, by disseminating the gospel of pity.) The appropriate response to protracted decay, according to Nietzsche, is that of the "physician," who, responding to a "new responsibility" reflecting "the highest interest of life," endeavors to arrange a timely and dignified demise for those superannuated decadents whom the priests have cruelly exploited ("Eine neue Verantwortlichkeit schaffen, die des Arztes, für alle Fälle, wo das höchste Interesse des Lebens, *des aufsteigenden* Lebens, das rücksichtsloseste Nieder- und Beiseite-Drängen des *entartenden* Lebens verlangt . . ."; *TI* "Skirmishes" §36; *KSA* 6, 134). Although decadence itself is both inevitable and irresistible, the *surplus* decadence encouraged by the priests (and Wagner) may be mitigated by the healing intervention of the physician. Short of actually wielding the physician's scalpel, however, one has no choice but to retreat from the scene and the stench of protracted decay — hence Nietzsche's relocation to Turin.

This general account of decadence has obvious implications for Nietzsche's prosecution of the case of Wagner. In pronouncing Wagner a *decadent* artist, Nietzsche means to claim that Wagner's art both expresses and promotes the decay of German culture, as reflected in the philistinism that he regards as characteristic of the Reich. Rather than elevate, challenge, or edify his audiences, Nietzsche alleges, Wagner exacerbates their advancing decay. Indulging their need to be overwhelmed and distracted, he feeds them the kinds of falsehoods that satisfy (and validate) their wish not to think (*CW* §8; *KSA* 6, 30–31). He does so, moreover, not as a musician, but as an *actor* (*Schauspieler*), which Nietzsche reveals as the true ambit of Wagner's genius (*CW* §8; *KSA* 6, 30). This particular revelation is meant, in turn, to explain why Wagner's musicianship simply does not measure up (*CW* §8; *KSA* 6, 31), notwithstanding the chorus of protestations to the contrary.

Nietzsche's diagnosis of Wagner's decadence thus informs his intentionally provocative account of Wagner's most enduring accomplishments. As a decadent artist, Wagner was incapable of imposing upon his art the "organic form" that would make it whole ("seine Unfähigkeit zum organischen Gestalten"; *CW* §7; *KSA* 6, 28). Despite his fascination with drama, in fact, Wagner never managed to develop or establish a coherent dramatic style of his own (*CW* §7; *KSA* 6, 27). As in all cases of decadent art and artists, that is, Wagner simply failed to develop an overarching vision that would unify his operas (and their respective parts) in a comprehensive totality. That this failure is not generally noticed is attributable, Nietzsche reveals, to the "bold habit that accompanied Wagner through his whole life: he posits a principle where he lacks a capacity" (einer kühnen Gewohnheit, die Wagnern durch's ganze Leben begleitet hat: er setzt ein Princip an, wo ihm ein Vermögen fehlt; *CW* §7; *KSA* 6, 28). As a result, Wagner's greatest accomplishments cannot possibly reside in the grand ideas, motifs, gestures, and flourishes for which he is best known. According to Nietzsche, these at best yield a motley patchwork of themes drawn from various artistic, mythic, and philosophical traditions. Wagner's true legacy lies instead in the bittersweet details he embroiders onto this motley patchwork (*CW* §7: *KSA* 6, 28). Relegated by the degradation of the larger whole to the smallest spaces available to him, Wagner fills these spaces with an exquisite range of subtle colors, shades, emotions, and sensibilities (*CW* §7; *KSA* 6, 28). Ostensibly granting Wagner his due, Nietzsche recommends him "as a master of the first rank, as our greatest *miniaturist* in music" (als einen Meister ersten Ranges [. . .], als unsern grössten *Miniaturisten* der Musik; *CW* §7; *KSA* 6, 28). Elaborating on this assessment, Nietzsche endeavors to open his readers' eyes to *another* Wagner —

> a Wagner who lays aside small gems: our greatest melancholiac in music, full of glances, tendernesses, and comforting words [. . .] the master in tones of a heavy-hearted and drowsy happiness . . .
>
> [einen Wagner, der kleine Kostbarkeiten bei Seite legt: unsern grössten Melancholiker der Musik, voll von Blicken, Zärtlichkeiten und Trostworten [. . .] den Meister in Tönen eines schwermüthigen und schläfrigen Glücks . . . (*CW* §7; *KSA* 6, 29)]

This evaluation will no doubt strike many readers as ludicrous and even perhaps as resentful.[29] In any event, let us note that Nietzsche has attempted to bestow upon Wagner the highest compliment that can be paid to a decadent artist. When judged by the standards to which he claimed to adhere, Wagner must be deemed a failure. When judged by the standards to which he was obliged to adhere, however, he is deemed an unparalleled master of his craft. By way of contrast, Nietzsche is unsparing in his criticism of Brahms, whom he considers undeserving of the title of Wagner's antagonist (*CW* postscript, 2; *KSA* 6, 47–48).

Perhaps the most surprising aspect of Nietzsche's diagnosis of European decadence is his willingness to situate himself within its scope. Rather than exempt himself from the crisis he sought to document — a typical dodge practiced by philosophers and social critics — he placed himself at its center. Very early in *The Case of Wagner*, by way of introducing himself and presenting his credentials for review, he announces that, like Wagner, he too is a decadent (*CW* preface; *KSA* 6,11). He does so, moreover, in an attempt to explain why *his* consideration of the case of Wagner should be esteemed above all others. Rather than disqualify him from this case, his share in the decadence that afflicts late modern European culture in fact recommends the critical perspective he adopts.

To be sure, however, Nietzsche's case differs from the more typical cases of decay and, more importantly, from the case of Wagner. Although Nietzsche was a decadent, he was also (and simultaneously) the "*opposite* of a decadent*" (das *Gegenstück* eines décadent; *EH* "Why I Am So Wise"; *KSA* 6, 267). As he explains, this internal opposition in turn afforded him a productively divided perspective on all matters pertaining to health and sickness. Unlike other decadents, that is, Nietzsche has recovered from his illness and now employs his decadence in the service of his larger critical engagement with late modernity. So it was, for example, that he could sincerely express his sympathy for those who prefer "Wagner's problem" to Bizet's (*CW* §3; *KSA* 6, 16), while simultaneously resisting Wagner and distancing himself from the sickness this preference betrays.

The Theme of the Psychological Profile

Nietzsche contra Wagner is advertised by its subtitle as a document assembled from "the files of a psychologist" (Aktenstücke eines Psychologen; *KSA* 6, 413). While the intended impact of this subtitle is largely rhetorical, its implication — namely, that Nietzsche is (now) a psychologist — accurately reflects the focus of his scholarly interests in 1888. By the time he assembled the materials for *Nietzsche contra Wagner*, he had been involved for several years in a serious study of the various psychological types that he judged to be emblematic of the decadence of late modern European culture. Whether or not he was a psychologist "without equal" (der nicht seines Gleichen hat; *EH* "Why I Write such Good Books" §5; *KSA* 6, 305) is perhaps debatable. That he was a psychologist whose files merit our attention, however, is beyond dispute.

In addition to the specific files he reproduces for our perusal, Nietzsche also provides his readers with profiles of the psychological types that either fascinated or vexed him. One such profile figures prominently in his diagnosis of Wagner: that of the *ascetic priest*, whom Nietzsche discussed at some length in the third essay of *On the Genealogy of Morals*.[30] In building his case against Wagner, as we shall see, Nietzsche borrows liberally from this profile. Although he stops short of calling Wagner an ascetic priest,[31] he leads us to believe that Wagner exerted an unhealthy influence over his German audiences while conducting a quasi-priestly assault on what remained of German culture.

As he did in *Genealogy*, Nietzsche emphasizes the decisive, counter-revolutionary influence of Schopenhauer, who, he claims, brokered Wagner's transformation from optimistic libertine to pessimistic prophet of nihilism (*CW* §4; *KSA* 6, 20). As in *Genealogy*, moreover, Nietzsche's point in emphasizing the influence of Schopenhauer is to discredit any claim to the originality or independence of Wagner's artistic aspirations. What one encounters in Wagner's music, notwithstanding its pretensions, is in fact the romantic pessimism that he inherited, happily, from Schopenhauer (*CW* §4; *KSA* 6, 20; cf. *BT* "Attempt" §7; *KSA* 1, 21). This point in turn positions Nietzsche to declare his own independence from Wagner *and* Schopenhauer. Like Wagner, to be sure, Nietzsche famously fell under the spell of Schopenhauer's pessimism. Unlike Wagner, however, Nietzsche recovered from this illness, as his buoyant cheerfulness in *The Case of Wagner* is meant to demonstrate.

As in *On the Genealogy of Morals*, Nietzsche becomes serious only after exposing Wagner as the artist of decadence (*CW* §5; *KSA* 6, 21). His seriousness manifests itself in the sensational claim, all joking aside, that Wagner "makes sick whatever he touches — *he has made music sick —*" (er macht Alles krank, woran er rührt, — *er hat die Musik krank gemacht —*; *CW* §5; *KSA* 6, 21). Here we are immediately put in mind of the ascetic priest, who, as Nietzsche explained in *Genealogy*, involuntarily sickens everyone to whom he ministers, including those whom he supposedly saves (*GM* III §15; *KSA* 5, 372–73). As in *Genealogy*, that is, Nietzsche is primarily concerned here to clear up a persistent misunderstanding, to which the Germans, in their decay, are acutely vulnerable. Just as the ascetic priest is widely believed to be a genuine physician, a true healer, so Wagner is received by his German audiences as a genuine redeemer, emblematic of the cultural ascendancy of the German people and the Reich. In both cases, however, the reverse is true: the ascetic priest cannot be considered a genuine physician, and Wagner actually redeems (or improves) no one. In both cases, in fact, the origin of the misunderstanding in question may be traced to the decadence of the clientele these would-be redeemers serve. The sick, we are meant to understand, are not competent to judge the quality of the care they receive.

As Nietzsche made clear in *On the Genealogy of Morals*, moreover, the advantage afforded him by his new, physiological perspective lies in the facility with which he may enter and exit his rival's native perspective (*GM* III §13; *KSA* 5, 365–66). Much as he did in *Genealogy*, that is, he sympathetically inhabits Wagner's perspective, thereby granting Wagner his due, before stepping back to identify the conditions under which this perspective may claim its limited validity. Although he regards his physiological perspective as demonstrably superior, he is not concerned to make his case either to those who are sick or to those who tend the sick. Nor is he particularly concerned to save the sick from the swindle in which they are enrolled, as if such a thing were even possible. As in *Genealogy*, in fact, his intended audience comprises those like-minded psychologists and physiologists who will not need to be persuaded of the need to check the spread of decay (cf. *NCW* preface; *KSA* 6, 415).

With this audience in mind, Nietzsche proceeds to explain why Wagner is so regularly misunderstood, especially by the Germans. Like the ascetic priest, we learn, Wagner is widely hailed for an expertise that he only *appears* to possess. Wagner's true genius lies *not* in his musicianship, which Nietzsche sharply criticizes, but in his unprecedented breadth and plasticity as an *actor* (*CW* §8; *KSA* 6, 30). On *this* point, in fact, Nietzsche is positively effusive in his praise of Wagner, lauding him as "an inventor and innovator of the first rank" (als Erfinder und Neuerer ersten Ranges; *CW* §8; *KSA* 6, 30). Much as he did in *On the Genealogy of Morals*, however, Nietzsche praises his rival only in order to gain credence for the withering critique he proceeds to launch. Disarmed by Nietzsche's praise of Wagner as an actor, his readers may be willing to consider his explanation of why the more customary praise of Wagner as a musician is both unwarranted and dangerous.

As in *On the Genealogy of Morals*, this critique rests on the assertion that decadence has become the norm for Wagner's German audiences, such that they are no longer able to discern the actual limits of his genius. Borrowing from his profile of the ascetic priest, he depicts Wagner as an imposter — a veritable "Cagliostro of modernity" (der Cagliostro der Modernität; *CW* §5; *KSA* 6, 23) — who both dupes and exploits his needy, redemption-seeking audiences. Like the ascetic priest, whose affect-medication treats only the outward signs and symptoms of depression (*GM* III §15; *KSA* 5, 373–74), Wagner is limited in his expertise to the world of appearances, that is, the realm of fleeting images, pleasing falsehoods, and other ephemera (*CW* §8; *KSA* 6, 30–31). This means, according to Nietzsche, that Wagner can produce only the *experience* or *feeling* of redemption, and not redemption itself. Like the ascetic priest, moreover, Wagner exacerbates the nervous exhaustion of his disciples (*CW* §5: *KSA* 6, 23), who invariably crave progressively stronger stimulants so as to gain the desired relief from their suffering (*CW* §6; *KSA* 6, 24). He does so, of course, while insisting — above all, to himself — that his music evinces a *higher taste*, an assertion that his increasingly pliant audiences meekly accept "as law, as progress, and as fulfillment" (als Gesetz, als Fortschritt, als Erfüllung; *CW* §5; *KSA* 6, 21).

Although Nietzsche is careful to document the harm done by Wagner to the German youths among his audiences (*CW* §10; *KSA* 6, 36), this is not his main objection to Wagner's music. (Nor, we recall, was he primarily concerned in *On the Genealogy of Morals* to object to the ascetic priest's mistreatment of the sickly sheep entrusted to his care.) In general, we might say, Nietzsche is far more concerned to assess the *collateral damage* caused by the priests and their ilk as they consolidate their power and extend the reach of their dominion. In the case of Wagner, Nietzsche is most deeply concerned to document the collateral damage done to *art and music*. Wagner has prevailed, we learn, by founding what Nietzsche calls a *theatrocracy*, wherein the theater is granted "the right [. . .] to *lord it* over the arts, over art —" (an ein Recht auf *Herrschaft* des Theaters über die Künste, über die Kunst . . .; *CW* postscript, 1; *KSA* 6, 42). Having identified the true victims of Wagner's priestly mischief, Nietzsche unloads his harshest invective:

> *This is precisely what is proved by the case of Wagner:* he won the crowd, he corrupted taste, he spoiled even our taste for opera! —

> [*Dies eben beweist der Fall Wagner:* er gewann die Menge, — er verdarb den Geschmack, er verdarb selbst für die Oper unsren Geschmack! — (*CW* postscript, 1; *KSA* 6, 42)][32]

In this light, the charge of *Schauspieler* — showman, huckster, manipulator of forms and images — is meant to appear especially damning.[33] As in *On the Genealogy of Morals*, where he revealed the physiological secrets of the ascetic priest's various prescriptions for salvation (*GM* III §17–§19; *KSA* 5, 377–87), Nietzsche is concerned here to expose Wagner's stagecraft as serving no end, no truth, beyond itself. Ever and only a showman, Wagner aims at nothing more, nothing higher, than to impassion and over-stimulate his audiences for a span of several hours. So long as his audiences remain sheltered in the space of his theater, the magician Wagner — "this Klingsor of all Klingsors!" (dieser Klingsor aller Klingsore!; *CW* postscript, 1; *KSA* 6, 43) — may sustain the illusion of their redemption. Beyond the sturdy walls of the Festspielhaus, however, he is largely powerless to project his magic. The faithful will need to return to Bayreuth, as many do, year after year, to renew the illusion (cf. *NCW* §2; *KSA* 6, 420).

If this were the extent of Wagner's showmanship, if the victims of his priestly mischief were limited to those poor pilgrims who voluntarily make their way to Bayreuth, then it would be difficult to take seriously Nietzsche's larger concerns in *The Case of Wagner*. If Wagner's sphere of influence were restricted to those who already share in his illness, that is, those who suffer further debilitation in order to feel redeemed in his music, then he would hardly qualify as the scourge of German (and European) culture. On this point, Nietzsche's profile of the ascetic priest is especially helpful to us. As he explains in *On the Genealogy of Morals*, the true victims of the ascetic priest are those (relatively) healthy, noble individuals whom the priest has sworn to destroy. Waging a war of cunning against his noble enemies (*GM* III §15; *KSA* 5, 372–73), the priest dispatches an army of sufferers whose mission it is to spread their decay, to consume scarce resources, and, thereby, to starve and crowd out any and all remaining specimens of healthy nobility (*GM* III §21; *KSA* 5, 391–92).[34]

Nietzsche has in mind something similar, or so I propose, in *The Case of Wagner*. As a *Schauspieler*, we know, Wagner exerts a direct influence only over those who are already sick enough to seek him out. The reach of his *indirect* influence, however, is far more extensive (and dangerous). Much like those sickly sheep whom the ascetic priest infects with his hatred of nobility (*GM* III §15; *KSA* 5, 372–73), Wagner's disciples serve, unwittingly, as weaponized agents of contagion. As they depart Bayreuth, they carry with them the gospel of romantic pessimism, which celebrates their decadence as a desirable cultural norm. While the price each disciple pays is enormous (*CW* postscript, 1; *KSA* 6, 40), the cost of their discipleship to German culture — in particular, to art and music — is prohibitive. Against the increasingly anti-intellectual backdrop of the Reich, that is, Wagner's disciples enable him to project his own decadence — or, as he would demur, his "higher taste" (höheren Geschmack; *CW* §5; *KSA* 6, 21) — well beyond the walls of the Festspielhaus. As the case of Nietzsche confirms, in fact, those who would escape the toxic spread of Wagner's decadence are obliged to take drastic measures, including seeking refuge outside Germany. Like the ascetic priest, that is, Wagner conducts his leveling assault on German culture via indirect means, by loosing an army of decadents convinced of the genius of Wagner and committed to the glory of the Reich.

Finally, Nietzsche depicts Wagner as playing a decisive, catalytic role similar to that assigned in *On the Genealogy of Morals* to the ascetic priest. Just as the ascetic priest unwittingly nurtures the growth and individuation of his supposed nemesis, namely, the new "philosopher" (*GM* III §10; *KSA* 5, 360), so Wagner is pronounced "indispensible" (unentbehrlich) for philosophers in general (*CW* preface; *KSA* 6, 12) and a "*windfall*" (ein *Glücksfall*) for the particular philosopher who presses this case (*CW* epilogue; *KSA* 6, 53). In both cases, moreover, the catalysis in question is identified as born of *impotence*: unable to develop further in their own right, the ascetic priest and Wagner both participate, unwittingly and indirectly, in the ongoing articulation of the human spirit. By virtue of the suffocating, contractionary measures they impose, they inadvertently preside over the incubation of a fortified human type who may yet warrant the future of humankind. In both cases, moreover, the struggle in question is presented as both necessary and non-negotiable: The path toward a fully individuated existence, whether for Nietzsche himself or for the philosophical type in general, requires a confrontation with the most powerful exemplar of the priestly type. It is here, Nietzsche insists, that Wagner's assault on German culture becomes personal, for Wagner, like the ascetic priest, is obliged to "wage war against *us*! Us, the free spirits" (Wie er *uns* damit den Krieg macht! Uns, den freien Geistern!; *CW* postscript, 1; *KSA* 6, 43).

The Theme of Recovery (*Genesung*)

In his extremely brief preface to *Nietzsche contra Wagner*, Nietzsche declares that he and Wagner are *antipodes*, standing strictly opposed to (i.e., contra) one another. He furthermore claims that their antipodal relationship is clearly established throughout the period represented by the writings excerpted in *Nietzsche contra Wagner*. (Leaving nothing to chance, he titles the fifth chapter "We Antipodes" ("Wir Antipoden"; *NCW* §5; *KSA* 6, 424].) While this may be true of the period in question, he and Wagner certainly did not begin as antipodes.[35] Initially, we know, they were sufficiently close that Wagner's genius threatened to eclipse Nietzsche's efforts to carve out for himself a reputation and task of his own. He eventually emerged from Wagner's shadow, but only as a result of the grueling process of "self-overcoming" (Selbstüberwindung) that he describes in the preface to *The Case of Wagner* (*CW* preface; *KSA* 6, 11). As we have seen, moreover, Nietzsche's achievement of self-overcoming was also — and perhaps more impressively — an achievement of self-individuation. He became what he is — Wagner's antipode — by resisting what he was — Wagner's sympode.

As Nietzsche confirms, he too is a "child" of his age, that is, a decadent (*CW* preface; *KSA* 6, 11). As he goes on to explain, however, he is also more than that, for he has *comprehended* and *resisted* his share in the decadence that grips late modernity. (As we have seen, he remarks elsewhere that he is both a decadent and the "*opposite*" [*Gegenstück*] of a decadent [*EH* "Why I Am So Wise" §2; *KSA* 6, 267].) Although he does not say so explicitly, I take him to mean that he now stands in a similarly dual relationship to Wagner. As a decadent, he remains moved by Wagner's music and wary of its seductions (*CW* §3; *KSA* 6, 16–17). As the "opposite" of a decadent, however, he comprehends the destructive power of Wagner's music and resists its influence over him. In doing so, he gains a protective measure of critical distance from the decadence he carries within himself. By dint of striking this balance, in fact, Nietzsche is able to sustain the fully individuated existence that he has managed to secure, at great expense, for himself. Indeed, his self-directed resistance has culminated in his emergence as a novel and unique species of Wagnerian, which we might call a *recovering* Wagnerian.

As he does elsewhere in his writings from 1888, Nietzsche presents himself in *The Case of Wagner* as *productively* at odds with himself. The modern soul may evince the legacy of "*a contradiction of values*"

(*Widerspruch der Werthe*; *CW* epilogue; *KSA* 6, 53), but this contradiction need not prove debilitating, as the case of Nietzsche is meant to demonstrate. Far from the corrosive self-loathing that afflicts his contemporaries, Nietzsche's self-directed resistance is in fact the key to his recovery. He remains a decadent, and a Wagnerian to boot, but he is reducible to neither. As *The Case of Wagner* is meant to demonstrate, he came to understand modernity both from the *inside*, that is, as a fellow traveler through the lowlands of European decadence, and from the *outside*, that is, as a diagnostician and critic of European decadence. As we shall see, moreover, he credits the success of his self-overcoming to an improbable source: none other than Wagner himself, from whom he claims to have learned the technique of self-directed resistance that has secured his recovery.

Although Nietzsche is explicitly concerned to reckon the costs absorbed by the disciples of Wagner (*CW* postscript, 1; *KSA* 6, 40–41), he is also concerned to acknowledge the benefits that he has reaped from his relationship with Wagner. As we learn toward the (initial) conclusion of *The Case of Wagner*, Nietzsche is most deeply indebted (and grateful) to Wagner for teaching him the art of "lifelong self-discipline" (die lebenslängliche Zucht an sich; *CW* §11; *KSA* 6, 39), which he has employed, or so we are meant to understand, in the service of his own labors of self-overcoming. (Here we may detect echoes of his earlier encomium to Schopenhauer, whom he similarly honored, in the third of his *Untimely Meditations*, as his "educator," or *Erzieher*.) Nietzsche is also grateful to Wagner for teaching him how a regimen of self-discipline might authorize the kind of reckless experiments in "self-violation" (Selbstvergewaltigung) that are called for in desperate, decadent times (*CW* §11; *KSA* 6, 39). In short, Nietzsche claims to have learned from Wagner how to place himself at odds with the reigning idols of late modernity, and, in so doing, to become the "bad conscience" of his age (*CW* preface; *KSA* 6, 12).

This is not to suggest, however, that Nietzsche approves of what Wagner's commitment to "lifelong self-discipline" allowed him to make of himself. His point here is not to recommend the "actor's genius" (Schauspieler-Genie) that tyrannized Wagner, but to praise Wagner for surrendering to his dominant instinct, regardless of its specific character (*CW* §8; *KSA* 6, 30). As we know from both *On the Genealogy of Morals* and *Ecce Homo*, yielding to one's dominant instinct, whatever it turns out to be, is a *sine qua non* for becoming what one is and assuming (limited) responsibility for one's destiny (*GM* III §8; *KSA* 5, 352–53; cf. *EH* "Why I Am So Clever" §8–§9; *KSA* 6, 291–95).

Of course, the point of this story is that Nietzsche ultimately outgrew his teacher, employing (and adapting) a Wagnerian regimen to overcome the influence of Wagner. Whereas Wagner's dominant instinct led him to perfect himself in his decadence, Nietzsche's dominant instinct steered him toward the recovery that *The Case of Wagner* and *Nietzsche contra Wagner* are meant to commemorate. In the end, that is, Nietzsche owes it to Wagner that he is now a recovering Wagnerian, able to weigh this case from afar and to speak with good cheer about such a serious matter.[36]

Nietzsche thus presents himself, in all seriousness, as a legitimate and worthy heir to Wagner.[37] In his prosecution of the case of Wagner, or so we are meant to believe, he carries forward everything that is vital and worthwhile in Wagner's art, discarding or setting aside all that is not. Most notably, as we have seen, he demonstrates the value for recovering Wagnerians of the "lifelong self-discipline" that was practiced by Wagner himself. Also notable in this respect is Nietzsche's appreciation for the genius of Wagner's miniaturism, especially in an age in which aspirations to totality remain chronically frustrated. For his own part, we know, Nietzsche boasted of a kindred mastery of "the 'little' things" (die "kleinen" Dinge), citing his unprecedented attention to matters of nutrition, place, climate, and recreation as evidence of his abundant prudence (*EH* "Why I Am So Clever" §10; *KSA* 6, 295–96). It also bears noting in this context that he soon would abandon for good his oft-promised *Hauptwerk*, which meant that his readers would be obliged to receive in its place the sparkling little books he composed in the halcyon year of 1888.

"What is it to us that Herr Nietzsche has become well again?" (was geht es uns an, dass Herr Nietzsche wieder gesund wurde? . . .; *GS* preface §2; *KSA* 3, 347). It all depends on who *we* are or turn out to be. If we count ourselves among the psychologists and physiologists for whom Nietzsche intended his Turinese letter, his recovery marks an important and potentially exhilarating milestone in the diagnosis and treatment of advanced decadence. His recovery means that some remnant of the old European order, along with its defining order of rank, may yet survive the decay of late modern European culture. What is more, Nietzsche's regimen of self-discipline may serve some of his readers as a useful model for resisting the decadence that afflicts them.

Although Nietzsche's condition should not be confused with the "great health" or *die grosse Gesundheit* that he occasionally claims to glimpse on the horizon (*GS* §382; *KSA* 3, 635–36), his recovery is sufficiently impressive as to encourage others to entertain the possibility that they, too, may aspire to similar progress in their own efforts to convalesce. Simply by virtue of invoking the ideal of the "great health," as if such an ideal were even remotely relevant to the circumstances of his late modern readers, he may succeed in persuading some of them to follow in his footsteps, perhaps even to retrace his path to Turin. For such readers, the cheerful tone he strikes in *The Case of Wagner* may prove infectious, as they too look forward to a future brightened and ennobled by exemplars of the "great health." In short, Nietzsche's grateful account of his improbable recovery also serves to announce his discovery of a potentially reproducible treatment program for those kindred decadents who remain, at bottom, healthy. For them, or so it would seem, all is not lost.

The Theme of Authenticity

Although Nietzsche rejects the idea that redemption is a viable goal for late modern Europeans (*CW* postscript, 2; *KSA* 6, 49), *The Case of Wagner* neither strikes nor recommends a pessimistic tone. Now recovered from the illness that induced the perceived *need* for redemption, he cheerfully introduces his readers to a goal that is both laudable and attainable in late modernity. He does so, moreover, by presenting himself, in his Turinese incarnation, as exemplifying the attainment of this goal.

Having exposed Wagner as an *actor* or *Schauspieler*, Nietzsche alludes to the possibility that others, himself included, may be considered, and especially by way of contrast, *authentic* (*CW* §12; *KSA* 6, 39). Although this is not a term that enjoys wide currency in Nietzsche's writings, the notion or concept of individual authenticity is generally understood to stand at or near the center of his philosophy.[38] The key to a meaningful life, he is widely held to have maintained, lies in fashioning for oneself an existence whose authenticity would compel one's assent and, perhaps, one's unconditional affirmation. Doing so will not be easy, of course, for an authentic existence must be pursued in opposition to the countervailing forces exerted by popular opinion, prevailing trends, and the general tyranny of the majority. (Here we recall that Wagner poses a threat to the "integrity" [*Rechtschaffenheit*] and "'authenticity'" [*"Echtheit"*] of musicians, precisely insofar as he mobilizes the masses against them [*CW* §11; *KSA* 6, 37]). It is probably fair to say, in fact, that only those who have secured for themselves an authentic existence will be tempted to embrace Nietzsche's notoriously stringent teachings of eternal recurrence and *amor fati*.

Despite the popular association of Nietzsche's philosophy with a teaching or ideal of authenticity, readers of *The Case of Wagner* may be surprised to learn that he presents *himself* — decadent, displaced, homeless, wounded, scarred, and prone to debilitating illness — as exemplary of an authentic existence.[39] To be sure, *this* Nietzsche will put no one in mind of either the pre-moral, rampaging beasts of prey (*GM* II §17; *KSA* 5, 324) or the post-moral, commanding philosophers of the future (*BGE* §211; *KSA* 5, 144–45). As several commentators have noted, however, Nietzsche gradually distanced himself from the model of human flourishing for which he is best known — namely, the willful, amoral, autarkic, masterly *Übermensch* — while promoting a model of human flourishing that more faithfully reflects the unique historical conditions of late modern European culture.[40] As the writings from his post-Zarathustran period confirm, this emergent model of human flourishing places greater emphasis on the value of the challenges one has faced, the obstacles one has overcome, the debts one has borne, the injuries one has endured, the parasites one has hosted, and the illnesses one has survived.

If the more familiar Nietzschean model of flourishing may be described as predicated on an ideal of *activity*, that is, of spontaneous, willful transformation of the external world, this post-Zarathustran model may be described as predicated on an ideal of *patiency*, that is, on the self-fashioning that takes place when one opens oneself to the blind impresses of an amoral cosmos.[41] It is this latter model of human flourishing that Nietzsche presupposes when he presents himself as *authentic* in *The Case of Wagner*. He has become what he is by suffering the cosmos to mark him as it will and, subsequently, by narrating his existence in such a way that merits his unequivocal affirmation.

Here it bears noting, in fact, that Nietzsche's achievement of authenticity is fully consistent with his continued vulnerability. Indeed, this may help to explain why he feels compelled to issue the three demands with which he marks the original conclusion of *The Case of Wagner* (*CW* §12; *KSA* 6, 39). He must press these demands because he knows from experience just how seductive Wagner's music is to those who aspire to, or have attained, an authentic existence. He thus reminds us, in fact, that he too remains susceptible to the spectacles that Wagner has staged (*CW* §3; *KSA* 6, 16–17). Although he now stands *contra* Wagner, facing the Master in opposition and reproach, he does so only from the safe (and healthy) distance afforded him by his retreat to Italy. Notwithstanding his love for his new life and home in Turin, he is ever reminded that he did not initially choose to relocate from Germany. That decision was made for him, by virtue of his continued vulnerability to Wagnerism and the more general pathology (namely, of "selflessness") it expressed.

Finally, we should note that Nietzsche's achievement of authenticity confirms his understanding of the *selective* power of decadence. Quite simply put, not everyone will be devastated by the death of God, the demise of morality, and the collapse of late modern European culture. Some individuals will thrive amid the ruins, owing to the traces of order and discipline that continue, anachronistically, to structure their bodies and souls. Against the increasingly bleak backdrop of pandemic decay, moreover, the authenticity of these individuals will emerge in progressively sharper relief. This means, of course, that some critics of modernity, confident in their basic attunement to health, may acquire an incentive to cheer, perhaps even to facilitate, the spread of decay. Was Nietzsche one of those who stood to profit from the intensification of European decadence?

This possibility was not lost on Nietzsche's first champion of international note, Georg Brandes (1842–1927), who found in Nietzsche the inspiration to stand firm in his commitment to "aristocratic radicalism."[42]

Nor was this possibility lost on one of Nietzsche's earliest critics, Max Nordau (1849–1923), who regarded Nietzsche's apparent embrace of European decadence as a chilling expression of "ego-mania."[43] If some individuals believed their native greatness to be obscured by the projects and pursuits of culture, Nordau advised, they would naturally find themselves in an antagonistic relationship to culture itself. In extreme cases, he warned, these individuals would pull for, and perhaps work toward, the destruction of culture.[44] One such individual, he feared, was Nietzsche himself.[45]

Notes

I am grateful to Nick Martin and Christa Davis Acampora for their very helpful discussions of Nietzsche's relationship to Wagner.

[1] I rely throughout this chapter on the translation of *Der Fall Wagner* found in Friedrich Nietzsche, *The Birth of Tragedy* and *The Case of Wagner*, trans. Walter Kaufmann (New York: Vintage, 1967), as well as Friedrich Nietzsche, *On the Genealogy of Morals*, trans. Walter Kaufmann and R. J. Hollingdale, and *Ecce Homo*, trans. Walter Kaufmann (New York: Vintage, 1989); *The Gay Science*, trans. Walter Kaufmann (New York: Vintage, 1974); *Beyond Good and Evil: Prelude to a Philosophy of the Future*, trans. Walter Kaufmann (New York: Vintage, 1989); *Twilight of the Idols* and *The Antichrist*, in *The Portable Nietzsche*, ed. and trans. Walter Kaufmann (New York: Viking Penguin, 1982).

[2] Kaufmann includes with his translation a sampling, in chronological order, from those letters in which Nietzsche requests and/or announces the various additions to, and emendations of, this text (193–97).

[3] Kaufmann in his translation, 199; and Ronald Hayman, *Nietzsche: A Critical Life* (Oxford: Oxford UP, 1980), xxii.

[4] Hayman, *Nietzsche*, 332–34; and Julian Young, *A Philosophical Biography of Friedrich Nietzsche* (Cambridge: Cambridge UP, 2010), 524.

[5] Friedrich Nietzsche, *Nietzsche contra Wagner*, in *The Portable Nietzsche*, ed. and trans. Walter Kaufmann (New York: Viking Penguin, 1982).

[6] Young, *A Philosophical Biography*, 524.

[7] Hayman, *Nietzsche*, 96–100; Young, *A Philosophical Biography*, 74–78.

[8] Hayman, *Nietzsche*, 97–100; Rüdiger Safranski, *Nietzsche: A Philosophical Biography*, trans. Shelley Frisch (New York: Norton, 2002), 56–57; Young, *A Philosophical Biography*, 77–78.

[9] Hayman, *Nietzsche*, 107–8; Young, *A Philosophical Biography*, 105–8.

[10] Walter Kaufmann, *Nietzsche: Philosopher, Psychologist, Antichrist*, 4th ed. (Princeton, NJ: Princeton UP, 1974), 34–35; Hayman, *Nietzsche*, 110–12; Safranski, *Nietzsche*, 56–58; Young, *A Philosophical Biography*, 105–10.

[11] Kaufmann, *Nietzsche*, 30–38; Hayman, *Nietzsche*, 122–23; Young, *A Philosophical Biography*, 105–11.

[12] Kaufmann, *Nietzsche*, 33–34; Safranski, *Nietzsche*, 57–58; Young, *A Philosophical Biography*, 110–11.

[13] Kaufmann, *Nietzsche*, 37–38; Hayman, *Nietzsche*, 150–52; Young, *A Philosophical Biography*, 110–11.

[14] Kaufmann, *Nietzsche*, 35–36; Safranski, *Nietzsche*, 133–39; Young, *A Philosophical Biography*, 157–58.

[15] Hayman, *Nietzsche*, 98–100; Young, *A Philosophical Biography*, 76.

[16] Hayman, *Nietzsche*, 261; Young, *A Philosophical Biography*, 359–60.

[17] Cited by Hayman in *Nietzsche*, 261; see also Young, *A Philosophical Biography*, 359–60.

[18] See Safranski, *Nietzsche*, 57–58.

[19] In the words of J. P. Stern, "The essay [. . .] is clearly designed as an act of homage; yet it does not read easily" ("Introduction," in Friedrich Nietzsche, *Untimely Meditations*, trans. R. J. Hollingdale [Cambridge: Cambridge UP, 1983], xxv).

[20] Hayman, *Nietzsche*, 186; Young, *A Philosophical Biography*, 222.

[21] Nietzsche's campaign to overcome selflessness is the focus of Christopher Janaway's *Beyond Selflessness: Reading Nietzsche's "Genealogy"* (Oxford: Oxford UP, 2007), especially 245–67.

[22] Roger Hollinrake, *Nietzsche, Wagner, and the Philosophy of Pessimism* (London: Allen & Unwin, 1982), 38–39, 91–92, 103–4.

[23] Paul S. Loeb, *The Death of Nietzsche's Zarathustra* (Cambridge: Cambridge UP, 2010), 148–49.

[24] Loeb, *The Death of Nietzsche's Zarathustra*, 150–51.

[25] Hollinrake, *Nietzsche, Wagner*, 140–41, 166–71.

[26] For my understanding of Nietzsche's preoccupation with decadence, I am indebted to Brian Domino, "Nietzsche's Republicanism" (Doctoral Thesis, Pennsylvania State University, 1993), especially 133–44. My own efforts to make sense of this preoccupation may be found in Daniel Conway, *Nietzsche's Dangerous Game: Philosophy in the Twilight of the Idols* (Cambridge: Cambridge UP, 1997), chapters 2–3.

[27] A cogent interpretation to this effect is found in Mark Warren, *Nietzsche and Political Thought* (Cambridge, MA: MIT UP, 1988), 157–89.

[28] I discuss at greater length the political implications of advanced decadence in my essay, "The Birth of the State," in *Nietzsche, Power and Politics: Rethinking Nietzsche's Legacy for Political Thought*, ed. Herman W. Siemens and Vasti Roodt (Berlin and New York: de Gruyter, 2008), 37–67.

[29] See, for example, Aaron Ridley, "Introduction," in Friedrich Nietzsche, *The Anti-Christ; Ecce Homo; Twilight of the Idols; and Other Writings*, ed. Aaron Ridley and Judith Norman (Cambridge: Cambridge UP, 2005), vii–xxxiv (here: xxxiii–iv); and Young, *A Philosophical Biography*, 496–97.

[30] Nietzsche's reliance in *The Case of Wagner* on his profile of the ascetic priest is explored productively by David Wellbery in "Nietzsche — Art — Postmodern-

ism: A Reply to Jürgen Habermas," in *Nietzsche in Italy*, ed. Thomas Harrison (Saratoga, CA: Anma Libri, 1988), 77–100; here: 92–98.

[31] Nietzsche is considerably less circumspect in *On the Genealogy of Morals*, where he insists that Wagner's success in promoting the "extraordinary rise in the value of music" (diese ausserordentliche Werthsteigerung der Musik) had the effect of turning "*the musician* himself" (*der Musiker* selbst) into "an oracle, a priest, indeed, more than a priest, a kind of mouthpiece of the 'in itself' of things, a telephone from the beyond — henceforth he uttered not only music, this ventriloquist of God — he uttered metaphysics: no wonder he one day finally uttered *ascetic ideals*" (ein Orakel, ein Priester, ja mehr als ein Priester, eine Art Mundstück des 'An-Sich' der Dinge, ein Telephon des Jenseits, — er redete fürderhin nicht nur Musik, dieser Bauchredner Gottes, — er redete Metaphysik: was Wunder, dass er endlich eines Tages *asketische Ideale* redete? . . .; *GM* III §5; *KSA* 5, 346).

[32] Nietzsche uses similar language in summing up his investigations of the ascetic priest and the ascetic ideal: "The ascetic priest has ruined spiritual health [*hat die seelische Gesundheit verdorben*] wherever he has come to power; consequently, he has also ruined taste *in artibus et litteris* — he is still ruining it" (*GM* III §22; *KSA* 5, 392–93); and: "The ascetic ideal has not only ruined health and taste [*hat nicht nur die Gesundheit und den Geschmack verdorben*], it has also ruined a third, fourth, fifth, sixth thing as well" (*GM* III §23; *KSA* 5, 395).

[33] Here I follow Ridley, "Introduction," xxxii–xxxiii. See also Wellbery, "Nietzsche — Art — Postmodernism, 97–100.

[34] I make this interpretive case in greater detail in Daniel Conway, *Nietzsche's "On the Genealogy of Morals": A Reader's Guide* (London: Continuum, 2008), 131–34.

[35] Although some entries date as far back, as he says, to 1877, *Nietzsche contra Wagner* includes no excerpts from *The Birth of Tragedy* and none from "Richard Wagner in Bayreuth."

[36] Ridley, "Introduction," Nietzsche, *The Anti-Christ . . . and Other Writings*, xxix.

[37] Young thus concludes that "the Wagnerian ideal remained with Nietzsche to the very end of his thinking" (*A Philosophical Biography*, 360). See also Hayman, *Nietzsche*, 61. Thomas Mann famously maintained that "There is *no* breach in Nietzsche's relationship to Wagner, no matter what one might say" (*Nietzsche's Philosophy in the Light of Contemporary Events* [Washington: Library of Congress, 1947], 11).

[38] See, for example, the interpretations advanced by Richard Rorty in *Contingency, Irony, and Solidarity* (Cambridge: Cambridge UP, 1989), 26–43; and Jacob Golomb in *In Search of Authenticity: From Kierkegaard to Camus* (London: Routledge, 1995), 68–87.

[39] Ridley, "Introduction," Nietzsche, *The Anti-Christ . . . and Other Writings*, xxvi.

[40] See, for example, Kaufmann, *Nietzsche*, 307–16; Alexander Nehamas, *Nietzsche: Life as Literature* (Cambridge, MA: Harvard UP, 1985), 170–99; Rorty, *Contingency, Irony, and Solidarity*, 96–108; and T. K. Seung, *Nietzsche's Epic of the Soul: "Thus Spoke Zarathustra"* (Lanham, MD: Lexington Books, 2005), 346–59.

[41] I am indebted here for the term and concept of "patiency" to Fiona Jenkins, "Performative Identity: Nietzsche on the Force of Art and Language," in *Nietzsche, Philosophy, and the Arts,* ed. Salim Kemal, Ivan Gaskell, and Daniel W. Conway (Cambridge: Cambridge UP, 1998), 212–38; and Seung, *Nietzsche's Epic,* 335–46.

[42] George [*sic*] Brandes. *Friedrich Nietzsche,* trans. A. G. Chater (London: Heinemann, 1914), 63–64.

[43] Max Nordau, *Degeneration* (Lincoln, NE: U of Nebraska P, 1993), 469.

[44] Nordau, *Degeneration,* 470–72.

[45] I discuss at greater length these competing responses to Nietzsche in "Whither the 'Good Europeans'?," *South Central Review* 26.3 (Fall 2009): 40–60.

Link to *Twilight of the Idols,*
The Anti-Christ, and *Ecce Homo*

Turin forms the backdrop to Nietzsche's most productive year, and his last year of sanity: in addition to *The Case of Wagner* (*Der Fall Wagner*), published in September 1888, and *Nietzsche contra Wagner* (a series of selections from his earlier writings, first published in 1889 and then again in 1895), 1888 saw the preparation of three new works, *Twilight of the Idols* (*Götzen-Dämmerung*), *The Anti-Christ* or *The Anti-Christian* (*Der Anti-Christ*), and *Ecce Homo*, all published posthumously — all of which stand in some relation or another to Nietzsche's final philosophical project. This work is (or a part of it) is referred to variously as *The Will to Power* (*Der Wille zur Macht*), *The Innocence of Becoming* (*Die Unschuld des Werdens*), or *The Revaluation of All Values* (*Die Umwerthung aller Werthe*), to name the texts that have been published in various (and controversial) selected forms and are available in their raw, unedited state in the final volumes of the *KGW* or the *KSA*.

When Nietzsche first visited Turin in the spring of 1888, he was delighted: "This is really the city I need *now!*" (Das ist wirklich die Stadt, die ich jetzt brauchen kann!), he enthused to his friend Heinrich Köselitz (or Peter Gast) on 7 April 1888, "in the evening on the *bridge over the Po*: magnificent! Beyond Good and Evil!!" (Abends auf der *Pobrücke*: herrlich! Jenseits von Gut und Böse!!; *KSB* 8, 285–86). Moreover, Turin was considerably cheaper than Nice, Venice, or Switzerland (*KSB* 8, 292). On 21 May the Teatro Carignano put on "a superb performance" (eine glänzende Aufführung) of *Carmen*, featuring the soprano Erminia Borghi-Mamo;[1] superb, although not as excellent as the performances in Nice with a singer called De Reims as Don José and Lison Frandin as Carmen (*KSB* 8, 317). Turin had good bookshops, too: Nietzsche got to know one of the managers of the bookshops owned by Ermanno Löscher, Carlo Clausen (1838–1902), a Buddhist, an enthusiast for the philosopher Philipp Mainländer (1841–76),[2] and a vegetarian (*KSB* 8, 316), and perhaps it was Clausen who introduced Nietzsche to the *Lawbook of Manu*, in an edition published in French by Louis Jacolliot (1806–90), a work in which Nietzsche took especial interest (*KSB* 8, 692).

In June Nietzsche returned to Sils Maria for the seventh — and last — time. As well as completing work on *The Case of Wagner*, he finished work during the long, hot August on his *Twilight of the Idols*, whose title was originally planned to be *A Psychologist at Leisure* (*Müssiggang eines Psychologen*; *KSB* 8, 411), but was changed (at Köselitz's suggestion) when Nietzsche was back in Turin, hence at the last minute — one admires the publisher's patience — to its current title. In his letter to Heinrich Köselitz of 27 September 1888, Nietzsche described *Twilight* as the first part of a larger work, the *Revaluation*, and as consisting of "terrible detonations" (horrible Detonationen; *KSB* 8, 443). This larger project, the *Revaluation*, was going to be "the greatest philosophical event of all times" (das größte philosophische Ereignis aller Zeiten), he told Malwida von Meysenbug, "with which the history of humankind will be split into two. . ." (mit dem die Geschichte der Menschheit in zwei Hälften auseinander bricht. . .; *KSB* 8, 447). Almost immediately after the completion of *Twilight* and the publication of *The Case of Wagner*, Nietzsche began work on the autobiographical text *Ecce Homo* (*KSB* 8, 462 and 470), while another text — presumably what became *The Anti-Christ* — was in turn now described as the first part of the *Revaluation* (*KSB* 8, 470), and later in November 1888 as the entirety of that work (*KSB* 8, 492). In his letter to Paul Deussen, with whom he was now reconciled, of 26 November 1888, Nietzsche presents the ambitions and function of *Twilight* and *Ecce Homo*, describing the former as "a cheerful book" (ein heiteres Buch) and the latter as a work that casts light on *Zarathustra*, which he called "the first book of all millennia, the bible of the future, the most supreme outburst of human genius in which the fate of humankind is included" (das erste Buch aller Jahrtausende, die Bibel der Zukunft, der höchste Ausbruch des menschlichen Genius, in dem das Schicksal der Menschheit einbegriffen ist; *KSB* 8, 492).

As in Nice, Sils Maria, and so many other locations, Nietzsche sought in Turin relief from his headaches, migraines, and other painful symptoms. Throughout his correspondence over the years, we find complaints about his physical condition, despite (or because) of which his philosophy prized health — and "great health" (die grosse Gesundheit; *GM* II §24; *KSA* 5, 336) — above all. While the precise source of his illness and eventual dementia remains a matter for debate, attributed variously to tertiary syphilis, a brain tumor, or manic depression and psychosis,[3] Nietzsche knew as well as anyone that their source was not purely physiological. In a letter to Malwida von Meysenbug of 11 August 1875, he had written that "people like us [. . .] never suffer *purely physiologically*, but everything is deeply intertwined with spiritual crises" (Unsereins [. . .] leidet *nie rein körperlich*, sondern alles ist mit geistigen Krisen tief durchwachsen; *KSB* 5, 104). Writing to Franz Overbeck on 30 June 1887, Nietzsche went so far as to admit: "There is some deep physiological inhibition whose cause and location I am unable to determine, and thanks to which my average sensation [. . .] is constantly below zero" (es giebt irgend eine tiefe physiologische Hemmung, deren Ursache und Sitz ich nicht nachzuweisen vermag, Dank welcher die Durchschnittsempfindung [. . .] beständig unter dem Nullpunkte ist; *KSB* 8, 104); and a year later, again to Overbeck, Nietzsche suggested his illness was, in part, hereditary: "It is *not* my head that hurts, *not* my stomach: but under the pressure of nervous exhaustion (which is, in part, inherited — from my father, who also died of only the *effects* of a complete lack of vital energy — in part, acquired) its consequences appear in all different forms" (Ich bin durchaus *nicht* kopfleidend, *nicht* magenleidend: aber unter dem Druck einer nervösen Erschöpfung (die zum Theil *hereditär*, — von meinem Vater, der auch nur an *Folgeerscheinungen* des Gesammt-Mangels an Lebenskraft gestorben ist — zum Theil erworben ist) erscheinen die Consequenzen in allen Formen; *KSB* 8, 348). In his epilogue to *The Case of Wagner*, Nietzsche even expressed gratitude for being so ill: to it, he suggested, he owed his entire philosophy, and he cited an idea expressed in the preface to the second edition of *The Gay Science* (*Die fröhliche Wissenschaft*). Great pain, he said, is "the ultimate liberator of the spirit, being the teacher of the *great suspicion*" (der letzte Befreier des Geistes, als der Lehrmeister des *grossen Verdachts*) — and lest we be complacent about such a thesis, Nietzsche compared this insight-generating pain to "that long, slow pain that takes its time, in which we are consumed, as if with green wood" (jener lange langsame Schmerz, der sich Zeit nimmt, in dem wir gleichsam wie mit grünem Holze verbrannt werden; *NCW* epilogue §1; *KSA* 6, 436, cf. *GS* preface §3; *KSA* 3, 350).[4]

So many years of pain, combined with a rigorous intellectual honesty and a clear foresight into what the future held for Western civilization, might be sufficient to explain what happened to Nietzsche during his last days in Turin, without recourse to complex pathologies that are unprovable in the end. Was Nietzsche right, for example, to think at Christmas 1888 that when he entered a shop, everyone's faces changed; that women on the street were looking at him; or that the woman running the stall where he brought his grapes would set aside the juiciest ones — and reduce the price — for him (*KSB* 8, 549)? In his correspondence, Nietzsche's formulations, already notable for a certain eccentricity of style, became even more cryptic, their tone increasingly strident, so that he refers to himself as being considered in Paris as "the most ingenious animal that has ever been on earth and, perhaps, as something more" (das geistreichste Thier, das auf Erden dagewesen ist und, vielleicht, noch als etwas mehr; *KSB* 8, 564) and describes "Ruhm und Ewigkeit" ("Fame and Eternity"), one of the *Dionysos-Dithyramben* (an anthology of poetic fragments from the time of the composition of *Zarathustra*) as "my *non plus ultra*, [. . .] composed beyond all seven heavens" (mein non plus ultra [. . .], jenseits von aller sieben Himmel gedichtet; *KSB* 8, 566).

As Christmas approached, a season associated in Nietzsche's mind "with the annual 'going-under' (*Untergang*) of the dying year and rich with nostalgic memories of Naumburg celebrations with the Krug and Pinder families" — that is, the families of his Schulpforta friends Gustav Krug and Wilhelm Pinder — "and, most irretrievable of all, of the unforgettable *Siegfried Idyll* surprise staged for Cosima's birthday in 1870,"[5] Nietzsche was working on the proofs of *Ecce Homo* (published posthumously in 1908), completing the preface to *Nietzsche contra Wagner*, and finishing work on *The Anti-Christ*. Then, on 3 January 1889, there took place the famous event in Nietzsche's biography, with which he is so often associated to the detriment of engaging seriously with his philosophy.

It is reported that, while crossing the Piazza Carlo Alberto, Nietzsche saw a horse being beaten by its driver, and threw his arms around the animal's neck. He was carried away from the scene down the Via Po by two policemen, and this incident is regarded as marking the onset of his insanity.[6] That analysis is supported by the letters that Nietzsche began sending over the next few days, known as the *Wahnsinnszettel*. On 3 January 1889, he wrote to Meta von Salis: "I have just taken possession of my kingdom, am throwing the pope into jail, and am having [Kaiser] Wilhelm [II], Bismarck, and [Adolf] Stöcker shot" (Ich habe eben Besitz ergriffen von meinem Reich, werfe den Papst ins Gefängniß und lasse Wilhelm, Bismarck und Stöcker erschießen), signing his letter "The Crucified" (Der Gekreuzigte; *KSB* 8, 572); on 4 January, he wrote to Paul Deussen: "After it has irrevocably turned out that I have in fact created the world, my friend, Paul, is provided for in the scheme of things: together with [the French poet] M. Catulle Mendès, he is meant to be one of my great satyrs and festive animals" (Nachdem sich unwiederruflich herausgestellt hat, daß ich eigentlich die Welt geschaffen habe, erscheint auch Freund Paul im Weltenplan vorgesehen: er soll, zusammen mit Monsieur Catulle Mendès, einer meiner großen Satyrn und Festthiere sein; *KSB* 8, 574); and on the same day, he wrote to Heinrich Köselitz the following hymnic note: "Sing me a new song: the world is transfigured, and all the heavens rejoice" (Singe mir ein neues Lied: die Welt ist verklärt und alle Himmel freuen sich; *KSB* 8, 575).

Reportedly Nietzsche's behavior became worryingly bizarre:[7] the family from whom he was renting a room discovered that he was tearing up his letters, even paper money; his landlady is said to have peered through the keyhole and seen her tenant dancing naked;[8] he was shouting, raving, and banging on the piano keyboard. In Basel, Franz Overbeck and Jacob Burckhardt, two of Nietzsche's oldest friends, who had both received a *Wahnsinnszettel*, consulted each other, and Overbeck traveled to Turin and witnessed Nietzsche's behavior: as Carl Albrecht Bernoulli, the editor of the Nietzsche-Overbeck correspondence, put it in his commentary, it was "a sight that embodied in a terrible way the orgiastic representation of sacred madness that lay at the roots of ancient tragedy."[9] Overbeck took his friend, wearing his Turin landlord's nightcap, to the railway station, and brought him, the man who described himself as dynamite (*KSB* 8, 492, 500 and 537), through the Gotthardtunnel that had been dynamited through a few years earlier, and back to Basel. From the psychiatric clinic in Basel, Nietzsche was moved, at his mother's request, to the psychiatric clinic of the university in Jena, under the charge of the Swiss neurologist, Otto Binswanger (1852–1929). Thence in May 1890 he was moved to his mother's house in Naumburg: after his many years of wandering, Nietzsche, or what was left of him — had come home.

Among notes in the *Nachlass* from spring-summer 1875, we find a note headed "Plans for Life" (Pläne für das Leben): for his thirties, Nietzsche scheduled his *Unzeitgemässe Betrachtungen* (*Untimely Meditations*), which appeared between 1873 and 1875, with a further eleven or so planned; then, for his forties, Nietzsche would work on the Greeks; while, for the fifth decade of his life, Nietzsche planned to turn to "Discourses to Humankind" ("Reden an die Menschheit"; *KSA* 8, 5[42], 52). Nietzsche fulfilled the first part of this schedule; although he left his career as a philologist, one might argue that his philosophical texts sought to embody a vision that brings the values and experiential qualities of ancient Greece alive again. But for urgent reasons of ill-health, Nietzsche brought forward his plans to address humankind directly, and did so with remarkable rhetorical brilliance in these later writings: *Twilight of the Idols, The Anti-Christ,* and *Ecce Homo,* all of which show Nietzsche's linguistic gifts at their most scintillating, and which are examined in turn by Carol Diethe, Martin Liebscher, and Paul Bishop. Although it would be easy to read these works against the biographical background of Nietzsche's collapse, to do so would be to ignore their rhetorical skepticism, their powerful analysis, and the way in which they transcend Nietzsche's physical and mental condition, illustrating his fundamental ambition: "Out of my will-to-health, will-to-*life*, I made my philosophy. . ." (ich machte aus meinem Willen zur Gesundheit, zum *Leben*, meine Philosophie . . .; *EH* "Why I Am So Wise" §2; *KSA* 6, 267).

Notes

[1] Did Nietzsche attend this performance? The commentary in the critical edition states categorically that he did not, and that he must have taken the information from the *Gazzetta Piemontese* (KGB III.7/3.1, 317).

[2] Philipp Mainländer (1841–76) was the author of *Philosophie der Erlösung* (vol. 1, 1876; vol. 2, 1886), a work of radical pessimism and a systematic exposition of nihilism. For an introduction to Mainländer's thought, presented in the form of an extensive preface and extracts from his *magnum opus* of some 1,300 pages, see Philipp Mainländer, *Philosophie der Erlösung,* ed. Ulrich Horstmann (Frankfurt am Main: Insel, 1989).

[3] For further discussion of Nietzsche's illness and the cause of his collapse, see Erich F. Podach, *Nietzsches Zusammenbruch: Beiträge zu einer Biographie auf Grund unveröffentlichter Dokumente* (Heidelberg: Kampmann, 1930); Paul Cohn, *Um Nietzsches Untergang: Beiträge zum Verständnis des Genies mit einem Anhang von Elisabeth Förster-Nietzsche: Die Zeit von Nietzsches Erkrankung bis zu seinem Tode* (Hanover: Morris, 1931); Pia Daniela Volz, *Nietzsche im Labyrinth seiner Krankheit: Eine medizinisch-biographische Untersuchung* (Würzburg: Königshausen & Neumann, 1990); and Sander L. Gilman, *Inscribing the Other* (Lincoln, NE, and London: U of Nebraska P, 1991), chap. 6, "Nietzsche's Writings and Conversations in His Madness: The Other Unravels Himself," 143–71 (esp. "Clinical Evaluation of Nietzsche's Illness," 159–63). For the most recent medical analysis of the evidence, see Dimitri Hemelsoet, Koenraad Hemelsoet, and D. Devreese, "The Neurological Illness of Friedrich Nietzsche," *Acta Neurologica Belgica* 108 (2008): 9–16, who argue that a diagnosis of "cerebral autosomal dominant arteriopathy with subcortical infarcts and leukoencephalopathy" (or CADASIL) accounts for Nietzsche's symptoms.

[4] Compare with his earlier aphorism in *Human, All Too Human* (*Menschliches, Allzumenschliches*) (*HA* I §289; *KSA* 2, 234). In *On the Genealogy of Morals* (*Zur Genealogie der Moral*) Nietzsche explores the generative role of pain and suffering. In one of this work's most memorable passages, he cites Thomas Aquinas (*Summa Theologiae*, III, *Supplementum*, q. 94, art. 1) and Tertullian (*De Spectaculis*) to the effect that the bliss of the blessed in the kingdom of heaven is made more delightful by the sight of the punishments of the damned (*GM* I §15; *KSA* 5, 283–85).

[5] Curtis Cate, *Nietzsche*, 546.

[6] This account is given in Ugo Pavia, "La bizarrie del filosofo nei recordi torinesi," *Stampa Sera*, 26 July 1932, reprinted in Anacleto Verrechia, *Zarathustras Ende: Die Katastrophe Nietzsches in Turin*, trans. Peter Pawlowsky (Vienna, Cologne, Graz: Böhlau, 1986); cited in *Chronik*, 725–26.

[7] See Lesley Chamberlain, *Nietzsche in Turin: The End of the Future* (London: Quartet Books, 1997), who offers an account of these final weeks in Turin. See also Verrecchia, *Zarathustras Ende*, 107–8, citing Kurt Liebmann, *Nietzsches Kampf und Untergang in Turin: Nietzsche und Mussolini* (Leipzig: Möhring, 1934).

[8] For the implications of Nietzsche's behavior, see Kenneth King, "The Dancing Philosopher," *Topoi* 24/1 (2005): 103–11.

[9] Carl Albrecht Bernoulli, *Franz Overbeck und Friedrich Nietzsche: Eine Freundschaft*, 2 vols. (Jena: Diederichs, 1908), 2:251.

11: *Twilight of the Idols*

Carol Diethe

The Preamble to Nietzsche's Mental Collapse

The great tragedy of Nietzsche's mental breakdown is compounded by the fact that, by the time of his last year of sanity, he had severed his connections with those formerly nearest to him (Wagner, his mother Franziska, and his sister Elisabeth): he was free at last to concentrate on what he intended to publish as his *magnum opus, The Will to Power* (*Der Wille zur Macht*). His sister, with whom he had had a fraught relationship ever since her involvement in his attempt at a rapprochement with Lou Salomé in 1882, had married the anti-Semitic agitator and Wagnerian acolyte, Bernhard Förster, on 22 May 1885 (the late Wagner's birthday). Nietzsche had not attended the wedding, though he had accepted a family invitation to Naumburg for his birthday on 15 October.[1] The newlyweds emigrated to Paraguay in 1886. Nietzsche was, at first, worried about the precariousness of the colonial venture, but he gradually closed the book on his relationship with his mother and sister — until his catastrophic collapse on 3 January 1889 threw him into their care.

An abiding aftereffect of his sister's *mésalliance* was that Nietzsche found anti-Semitism even more loathsome than before. In a fragment of a letter to his mother dated 29 December 1887 (probably truncated by Elisabeth after her brother's collapse), Nietzsche accuses the anti-Semitic party of having systematically ruined "my publisher, my reputation, my sister, my friends" (meinen Verleger, meinen Ruf, meine Schwester, meine Freunde; *KSB* 8, 216). And he spelled out, in a trenchant draft of a letter that he wrote to Elisabeth at the end of December 1887 — but probably never sent — his disgust at her husband's anti-Semitic propaganda:

> After reading the name Z[arathustra] in the *Anti-S[emitic] Correspondence*[2] my patience is at an end — I now adopt a state of *self-defense* against your husband's political party. [. . .] How I have suffered already from the fact that our name is mixed up with this movement through your marriage!

[Nachdem ich gar den Namen Z[arathustra] in der anti-s[emitischen]
Correspondenz gelesen habe, ist meine Geduld am Ende — ich bin
jetzt gegen die Partei Deines Gatten im Zustand der *Notwehr*. [. . .]
Daß unser Name durch Deine Ehe mit dieser Bewegung zusammen
gemischt ist, was habe ich daran schon gelitten! (*KSB* 8, 218–19)]

Nietzsche goes on to upbraid his sister for having paid no heed either to
his poor health or to his "most painful and surprising experience" (mein
schmerzhaftes und überraschendstes Erlebniß): namely, "the fact that
the man whom I had most admired had degenerated so disgustingly into
what I had always most despised, into a fraudster peddling moral and
Christian ideals" (daß der Mann, den ich am meisten verehrt hatte, in
einer ekelhaften Entartung gradwegs in das überging, was ich immer am
meisten verachtet hätte, in den Schwindel mit moralischen und christlichen Idealen; *KSB* 8, 218).

So much for Wagner.

If Nietzsche had, at last, organized his life to the point where there
were few ties to disrupt his concentration, it was not without an inner
struggle; indeed, it had contributed to his wretched state of health.
Even the news relayed by Franziska in May 1888 that Elisabeth had
entered the colony in Paraguay on 5 March 1888 in a triumphant pro-
cession — ostensibly, a joyous relief for all — was calculated to open old
wounds. In a letter to his mother dated 27 May 1888, Nietzsche concedes that he is beginning to think the Paraguay scheme might work for
the Försters, but he swiftly moves on to describe the minutiae of his life
to her in a neutral fashion: Franziska was not someone he could now trust
with his thoughts.

In a way, Nietzsche's books were now his family; he had been producing a major text roughly once a year. *Beyond Good and Evil* (*Jenseits
von Gut und Böse*, 1886) had received mixed reviews, possibly because of
its apparent lack of direction, which is, however, manifest in most of his
writings. The nearest Nietzsche had come to writing systematically was in
On the Genealogy of Morality: A Polemic (*Zur Genealogie der Moral: Eine
Streitschrift*), published in 1887. It is glaringly obvious that this was not
his favorite work: he did not have a copy of it when he needed it in 1888,
and had to borrow one from a friend, as we shall see below. And in the
section of *Ecce Homo* devoted to a critique of his own works, he could
find nothing to say about *On the Genealogy of Morality* beyond platitudes
that cover just over a page. However, that brief section does end with the
comment that "this book contains the first psychology of the priest" (dies
Buch enthält die erste Psychologie des Priesters; *EH GM*; *KSA* 6, 353),
a timely reminder that, by 1888, Nietzsche had elevated himself to the
position of psychologist, as witnessed by much of the contents of *Twilight
of the Idols* and *Ecce Homo*.

Nietzsche held to the advantages of his peripatetic lifestyle: by October 1887, he had quit Sils for Nice via Venice, arriving in Nice on 23 October. He spent the winter there, with a demonstrably miserable New Year, before proceeding to Turin for the two months from 7 April to the beginning of June, relishing (in his letter to Franziska of 20 April 1888) the dry air there (*KSB* 8, 300). This did not deter him from his summer sojourn in Sils (from early June to late September). At first he found it difficult to make headway with his work there. The problem did not lie entirely in the fact that he was ill that summer and the weather was poor. The real problem was that Nietzsche had set aside the year 1888 for classifying his notes for *The Will to Power*, often — though not always — subtitled the *Revaluation of All Values* (*Umwerthung aller Werte*), yet, as autumn approached, all he had achieved was the penning of *The Case of Wagner* (*Der Fall Wagner*). That work ranked with him as a pleasant diversion, as he told Meta von Salis in a letter dated 22 August 1888, attributing the work "in all essentials to Turin" (in allem Wesentlichen nach Turin; *KSB* 8, 397). He also thanked Meta von Salis for the loan of the complimentary copy of *On the Genealogy of Morality* he had sent her on its publication so that he could refresh his memory of it, commenting: "I discovered a long foreword to the *Genealogy*, the existence of which I had *forgotten* . . ." (Ich entdeckte eine lange *Vorrede* zur der "Genealogie," deren Existenz ich *vergessen* hatte . . .; *KSB* 8, 396).

He wrote to his mother on 30 August with the same complaint he had made in his letter to Meta von Salis eight days earlier: the summer in Sils had been a washout in terms of work, prompting his decision to publish everything that was ready for print: in other words, the material earmarked for *The Will to Power*. In spite of his dissatisfaction with his progress, Nietzsche worked intensively in the latter part of his stay in Sils, no doubt making up for lost time. Having relinquished the struggle to expand the material for *The Will to Power*, his immediate task was to redirect some of it into a shorter, light-hearted introduction to his philosophy, provisionally entitled *A Psychologist at Leisure* (*Müßiggang eines Psychologen*) and now known as *Twilight of the Idols* (*Götzen-Dämmerung*). He dispatched the manuscript to his publisher, C. G. Naumann, on 7 September 1888, remarking: "I need to publish this now because at the end of next year, we shall probably be busy printing my main work *Revaluation of All Values*" (Ich habe es nöthig, sie jetzt noch herauszugeben, weil wir Ende nächsten Jahres wahrscheinlich daran gehen müssen, mein Hauptwerk die *Umwerthung aller Werthe* zu drucken; *KSB* 8, 411). As we see, the *Revaluation* rather than the *Will to Power* was now to be his "main work."

By mid-September 1888, Nietzsche had also written most of what would become *The Anti-Christ* or *The Anti-Christian* (*Der Antichrist*). In a letter to Meta von Salis, also dated 7 September 1888 and occasioned by his return of her book, Nietzsche described his state of euphoria on 3 September, the day when he rose early to write the foreword to the *Revaluation/Anti-Christian*. He told Meta it was the most beautiful day he had ever experienced in the Engadine, and he went on to add:

> Next year I am resolved to publish my *Revaluation of all Values,* the most independent book there is . . . not without a great deal of hesitation. For example, the *first* book is called *The Anti-Christian.*

> [Im nächsten Jahre werde ich mich dazu entschließen, meine *Umwerthung aller Werthe*, das unabhängigste Buch, das es giebt, in Druck zu geben . . . *Nicht* ohne große Bedenken! Das *erste* Buch heißt zum Beispiel *der Antichrist.* (*KSB* 8, 411)]

Nietzsche's departure from Sils, planned for 15 September, had been delayed because of an upset stomach; in addition, the heavy rain had created floods, so that he did not arrive in Turin until 21 September. The extra few days in Sils enabled him to take stock of the *Revaluation* project. "Such an undertaking necessitates deep pauses and distractions for hygienic reasons alone" (Ein solches Unternehmen macht tiefe Pausen und Distraktionen selbst hygienisch nöthig), he announced to Franz Overbeck in a letter dated 14 September 1888 (*KSB* 8, 434), adding that the first book of the *Revaluation of all Values* was half finished and bore the title *The Anti-Christian* (as *Der Antichrist* may be translated). On the same day, he wrote to Paul Deussen with much the same message about the *Revaluation*: "Its *first* book" (Das *erste* Buch davon) — that is, what would ultimately be *The Anti-Christian* — "is half finished" (ist zur Hälfte vollendet), adding that *Nietzsche contra Wagner* and *Twilight of the Idols* were a true convalescence in the midst of the "immeasurably difficult and decisive task" (einer unermeßlich schweren und entscheidenden Aufgabe) posed by the *Revaluation* (*KSB*, 426). So difficult, in fact, that he was moved to divert his attention to writing his literary autobiography, *Ecce Homo*. In addition, he arranged poems old and new into the *Dithyrambs of Dionysos* (*Dionysos-Dithyramben*), and by 15 December was able to dispatch *Nietzsche contra Wagner*, a pugnacious farewell to his antagonist, to the Leipzig printers.[3]

So we can say with some confidence that, by 3 September 1888, Nietzsche's aspiration to write a book called *The Will to Power* had been dropped, with the favored title for his main project emerging as *Revaluation of All Values*, and with some *Will to Power* material having been enlarged into the manuscript drafts of *Twilight of the Idols*. Nietzsche continued with plans for the *Revaluation* until late November, when he bowed to the reality that *The Anti-Christian* was not just the first book of the *Revaluation of all Values* but the whole of it. His letter to Georg Brandes of 20 November reveals the relation of *Ecce Homo* to the *Revaluation of All Values* (and hence to *The Anti-Christian*): "All of it" — that is, *Ecce Homo* — "is," he wrote, "a curtain raiser for the *Revaluation of all Values,* the work that lies completed before me" (Das Ganze ist das Vorspiel der *Umwerthung aller Werthe,* das Werk, *das fertig vor mir liegt; KSB* 8, 482). At that point he had already drafted what is known as the "October version" of *Ecce Homo* and, during December, he had assembled the printer's manuscript for Naumann. After prevaricating about when it should be published, Nietzsche decided that there was no need for delay, telling Naumann on 2 January 1889: "Forwards with *Ecce!*" (Vorwärts mit *Ecce!*; *KSB* 8, 571). The next day, he collapsed in the street. *Ecce Homo* was published posthumously in 1908.

Twilight of the *Will to Power*

Roaring ahead with his work in the autumn of 1888, Nietzsche viewed his recent *Nietzsche contra Wagner* and the following work, *A Psychologist at Leisure* (now known as *Twilight of the Idols*), as "light-hearted works" (nur wirkliche Erholungen) when set against *the Revaluation of All Values,* as he told Paul Deussen in a letter of 14 September 1888 (*KSB* 8, 426). However, *Twilight of the Idols* has little to say specifically on Wagner; nor is it particularly "light," having emerged as a cluster of sections culled from the *Will to Power* material. That close relationship between *Twilight of the Idols* and *The Will to Power* must now be examined.

At the end of *On the Genealogy of Morality,* Nietzsche had directed his readers to "a work I am writing, *The Will to Power: Attempt at a Revaluation of All Values*" (ein Werk, das ich vorbereite: **Der Wille zur Macht,** *Versuch einer Umwerthung aller Werthe; GM* III §27; *KSA* 5, 409). He made various lists of contents in his notebooks, and in mid-February 1888, he categorized 372 notes (or 374, if two double entries are counted as two each) in two quarto notebooks and one folio volume, using another notebook for an index of key words. The first three hundred key words were also categorized according to which of the four intended sections they related to, but the book headings for this collection have been lost. More or less at random, Heinrich Köselitz (whom Nietzsche called Peter Gast) and Elisabeth Förster-Nietzsche, when compiling *The Will to Power* in 483 sections for volume 15 of the *Großoktavausgabe* (published in 1901 and translated into English as *The Will to Power* by R. J. Hollingdale and Walter Kaufmann, first published in 1967), selected Nietzsche's scheme for a work in four books that he had jotted down in Nice on 17 March 1887 (*KSA* 12, 7[64], 318). Nietzsche's final plan for the *Will to Power* (as opposed to the *Revaluation*) was drafted on "the last Sunday of the month of August 1888" (am letzten Sonntag des Monat August 1888) — that is, 26 August 1888 (*KSA* 13, 18[17], 537–38).

Nietzsche wrote a number of draft titles for the "summary" of his philosophy (i.e., what would eventually be *Twilight of the Idols*) (*KSA*

13, 19[3], 542). There were twelve chapter divisions connected to the plan for this work (*KSA* 13, 19[4], 543). A number of these chapter titles — "The Problem of Socrates" ("Das Problem des Socrates"), "Reason in Philosophy" ("Die Vernunft in der Philosophie"), "How the True World Finally [Became] A Myth" ("Wie die wahre Welt endlich zur Fabel [wurde]"), "Morality as Anti-Nature" ("Moral als Widernatur"), "The Four Great Errors" ("Die vier großen Irrthümer"), and "Sayings and Arrows" ("Sprüche und Pfeile") — did finally appear in *Twilight of the Idols* under the same headings, while one — "Among Artists and Writers" ("Unter Künstlern und Schriftstellern") — is the original title of what would eventually end up as "Forays of an Untimely One" ("Streifzüge eines Unzeitgemässen") in *Twilight of the Idols*. Other items were diverted to *The Anti-Christian* and correspond to various sections in the text of *The Anti-Christian* as it stands today: "We Hyperboreans" ("Wir Hyperboreer"), see §1–§7; "For Us — Against Us" ("Für uns — wider uns"), see §8–§14; "Concept of a Décadence-Religion" ("Begriff einer Décadence-Religion"), see §15–§19; and "Buddhism and Christianity" ("Buddhismus und Christenthum"), see §20–§23 (*KSA* 6, 169–74, 174–81, 181–85 and 186–91).

At the end of August 1888 Nietzsche was now able to proceed with his new version of the former planned master work, *The Will to Power*, planning it in four sections, the first of which, as discussed above, was to be *The Anti-Christian*, by that time one-third complete (and consisting of the above 23 sections). There were a further six versions of the plan for the *Revaluation of all Values* in four books.[4] Clearly, Nietzsche was writing *Twilight of the Idols* and *The Anti-Christian* in tandem in the early autumn of 1888. According to the commentary on *Twilight of the Idols* by Giorgio Colli and Mazzino Montinari, one notebook (designated *Mappe* XVI 4 in the *Nachlass*) contained two similar fragments for a foreword to the *Revaluation*, the more mature of which was dated "Sils Maria, beginning of September 1888," from which emerged the version "Sils Maria, 3 September 1888," mentioned in Nietzsche's letter to Meta von Salis of 7 September 1888 discussed above (*KSA* 14, 410–11). In the period from 7 to 11 September 1888, however, Nietzsche changed his mind and attached that foreword to *A Psychologist at Leisure*, although on 13 September 1888 he sent Naumann a substitute for its third paragraph (*KSB* 8, 422). By 18 September 1888 he had enlarged the "foreword" material into the penultimate seven-section chapter of *Twilight of the Idols*, "What the Germans Lack" ("Was den Deutschen Abgeht"; *KSA* 6, 103–10), necessitating a brand new foreword for *Twilight*. As he told Naumann in a letter dated 18 September 1888, "the *foreword* is now much shorter — *and* much more suitable" (das *Vorwort* ist jetzt viel kürzer — *und* zweckentsprechender; *KSB* 8, 442). The final foreword to *Twilight of the Idols*, dated "Turin 30 September 1888, on the day the first book of the *Revaluation of all Values* was finished" (Turin, am 30. September 1888, am Tage, da das erste Buch der *Umwerthung aller Werthe* zu Ende kam; *KSA* 6, 58), is nothing short of publicity for *The Anti-Christian.*

After Köselitz's (or Gast's) letter of 20 September 1888 urging Nietzsche to adopt a more appropriate title for his current work (that is, *A Psychologist at Leisure*; (see below), Nietzsche experimented with various titles — "*Idols' Hammer.* Or Frolics of a Psychologist" (*Götzen-Hammer.* Oder Heiterkeiten eines Psychologen); "*Idols' Hammer.* Or: How a Psychologist Asks Questions" (*Götzen-Hammer.* Oder: wie ein Psycholog Fragen stellt); "*Idols' Hammer.* A Psychologist at Leisure" (*Götzen-Hammer.* Müssiggang eines Psychologen) — until he came up with the one he finally adopted:

Twilight of the Idols
or:
How One Philosophizes with a Hammer.
by
Friedrich Nietzsche.

[*Götzen-Dämmerung.*
Oder:
wie man mit dem Hammer
Philosophirt.
Vom
Friedrich Nietzsche. (*KSA* 13, 22[6], 586)]

Nietzsche sent off the final version in a letter to Köselitz (or Gast) dated 27 September 1888, very pleased with the substitute title (*KSB* 8, 443). The subtitle in this version invites a comparison with its final section, "The Hammer Speaks" ("Der Hammer redet"), which is lifted verbatim from part 3 of *Thus Spoke Zarathustra,* "Of Old and New Tablets" ("Von alten und neuen Tafeln," §29; *KSA* 4, 268). Yet that final section had been intended as the ending to *The Anti-Christian.* The compositional procedure was bizarre in the extreme.

No wonder, then, that the reader's first impression of *Twilight of the Idols* is often that it is a hastily thrown together patchwork, however much one also admires Nietzsche's industry during the last few months prior to his mental collapse. Not only does Nietzsche make a collage of certain passages and chapters: concepts, too, can seem to be thrown in at random. However, his single-minded industry paid off, so that, on 25 November 1888, after he had received his four author's copies of *Twilight of the Idols* from Naumann, he was able to reply to his publisher: "I really like *Twilight of the Idols*" (die "*Götzen-Dämmerung*" gefällt mir sehr; *KSB* 8, 486). Though printed in December 1888, the flyleaf is dated 1889, and so this is the date normally given for the publication of *Twilight of the Idols*.

Intellectual Innovations in Relation to Philosophical and Stylistic Features

Given that Nietzsche first conceived of this work as a leisure activity, the reader has to accept that it has no clear line of thought, in stark contrast to *The Anti-Christian*, which without deviation vilifies religion, especially Christianity. Yet Nietzsche's claim to have fashioned *Twilight of the Idols* into a summary of his philosophy is valid, as we shall see. The new title *Twilight of the Idols* was a rather good joke at Wagner's expense.[5] Nor, with such a heavyweight subtitle — "How One Philosophizes with a Hammer" — can the influence of *Zarathustra* on *Twilight of the Idols* be overlooked: it presages a sledgehammer approach that is echoed in the final passage of the work, which consists verbatim of a section from *Zarathustra*, part 3, §29, "Of Old and New Tablets" (*KSA* 6, 161; cf. *KSA* 4, 268).

Of course, Nietzsche had first mooted the concept of the will to power in *Zarathustra*, as will be discussed below. What is completely lacking in *Twilight of the Idols* is any mention of the *Übermensch*, whose début also belongs to *Zarathustra*, though Nietzsche does include a brief, yet trenchant, allusion to eternal return (also first mooted in *Zarathustra*) in the penultimate section of *Twilight of the Idols*, which ends with the words: "— I, the last disciple of Dionysos, — I, the teacher of eternal return . . ." (— ich, der letzte Jünger des Philosophen Dionysos, — ich, der Lehrer der ewigen Wiederkunft . . .; *TI* "What I Owe" §5; *KSA* 6, 160). His reference here to Dionysos harks back to his first attempt at describing the Dionysian in *The Birth of Tragedy*, and provides a certain symmetry in this rather anarchic assemblage.

Twilight of the Idols contains many references to power, in line with the portioning out of the material intended for the never-written *Will to Power*. However, the full weight of this trope is to be found more clearly in *The Anti-Christian*, which flaunts the concept of "the will to power" with no little exuberance (*AC* 23, §6, §16 and §17; *KSA* 6, 170, 172, 182–83 and 183–84), though its argument mainly criticizes the "power of the Church" (*AC* §37; *KSA* 6, 208–9) and the power of religion in general terms. In particular, Nietzsche in *The Anti-Christian* outlines the pursuit of power in religious movements, as in the cruel aspects of the *Laws of Manu* (*AC* §57; *KSA* 6, 241–42) and the aspirations for power in religious priests such as St. Paul: "His requirement was power" (*Sein* Bedürfniss war die *Macht*; *AC* §42; *KSA* 6, 216). Even Yahweh is not spared (*AC* §25; *KSA* 6, 193–94).

Hence, Nietzsche's central insight of the will to power is implicit rather than explicit in *Twilight of the Idols*, where he treats the topic of "power" in the round, and especially the power exercised by the state — "power *stupefies*" (die Macht *verdummt*; *TI* "What the Germans Lack" §1; *KSA* 6, 103) — as well as by liberal institutions that "undermine the will to power" (sie unterminiren den Willen zur Macht; *TI* "Forays" §38; *KSA* 6, 139). But he is careful to include the metaphysical dimension of power as well: "Where there is a struggle, it is a struggle for power" (wo gekämpft wird, kämpft man um *Macht*; *TI* "Forays" §14). For the Greeks, power was "their strongest instinct" (ihren stärksten Instinkt; *TI* "What I Owe" §3), while Nietzsche considers the aesthetics of human beauty as they relate to power and warns us about the loss of power that results from degeneration:

> Wherever the human is oppressed, he senses himself to be in the presence of something "ugly." His feeling of power, his will to power, his courage, his pride — all of this deflates with the ugly and inflates with the beautiful . . .

> [Wo der Mensch überhaupt niedergedrückt wird, da wittert er die Nähe von etwas "Hässlichem." Sein Gefühl der Macht, sein Wille zur Macht, sein Muth, sein Stolz — das fällt mit dem Hässlichen, das steigt mit dem Schönen . . . (*TI* "Forays" §20; *KSA* 6, 124)]

The above reference to the "will to power" as a *psychological* factor is vital to Nietzsche's argumentation in *Twilight of the Idols*, notwithstanding the more universal claim for the will to power in *Thus Spoke Zarathustra*,[6] and in spite of the culling of *Will to Power* material corresponding to the concept for use in *The Anti-Christian*. Nietzsche claimed to be a psychologist in *Twilight of the Idols* and the works that followed; he was delighted to have found this niche, and made great efforts to exploit it.

Possibly Nietzsche's mental state was such that he had a heightened sense of sound and sight prior to the months before his collapse; at all events, he created himself as psychologist (literally, "scholar of the soul"), establishing a platform from which he could make comments on the psyche.[7] "Peace of soul" (Frieden der Seele), Nietzsche tells us, describes many innocent human pleasures as well as vices, and as such is wrongly named; for example, it can herald fatigue — "the first shadow cast by evening" (der erste Schatten, den der Abend [. . .] wirft) — or damp air — "south winds are approaching" (dass Südwinde herankommen) — it can also be "the expression of maturity and mastery in the midst of doing, creating, effecting, and willing, a quiet breathing, *achieved* 'freedom of will'" (der Ausdruck der Reife und Meisterschaft mitten im Thun, Schaffen, Wirken, Wollen, das ruhige Athmen, die *erreichte* "Freiheit des Willens"; *TI* "Morality as Anti-Nature" §3; *KSA* 6, 84–85). As this passage shows, Nietzsche used poetic fallacy as well as emotional terms to establish a particular kind of truth — a truth of experience rather than fact.

In his *Nietzsche, Biology and Metaphor*, Greg Moore has suggested that Nietzsche was interested in Charles Féré's *Dégénérescence et criminalité* (1888), which appeared in Paris in 1888 and was thus "hot off the press" when he was writing his late works.[8] Féré had also co-authored, with Alfred Binet, a study of hypnosis entitled *Le Magnétisme animal* (1887).[9] Nietzsche referred to the power of Wagner's hypnotic charisma on a number of occasions, but not in *Twilight of the Idols*, where the accusation of "fascination" is leveled at Socrates, who "discovered a new form of *agon* in which he was the first fencing master for the noble circles of Athens" (dass er eine neue Art *Agon* entdeckte, dass er der erste Fechtmeister davon für die vornehmen Kreise Athen's war; *TI* "Problem of Socrates" §8; *KSA* 6, 71). Nietzsche feels it incumbent upon himself to clarify how Socrates "fascinated" people. Using a psychosexual argument, he states that the fascination — a sort of mesmerism — exercised by Socrates not only brought out the spirit of competition in Greek youth of the day, but had sexual overtones as well: "Socrates was also a great *erotic*" (Sokrates war auch ein grosser *Erotiker*; *TI* "Problem of Socrates" §8; *KSA* 6, 71). Nietzsche is no doubt hinting that Socrates was a pederast, yet in Plato's *Symposium*, the handsome Alcibiades lusts after Socrates rather than the other way round. In *The Birth of Tragedy*, Nietzsche deplores Socrates's rationalism and heralds Dionysian abandonment as its antidote. In *Twilight of the Idols*, however, Nietzsche deliberately raises the question of Socrates's supposed sexual frustration, as he believes it to be linked to the denial of the instincts; thus he jeers with disgust at this "cesspit of all evil lusts" (Höhle aller schlimmen Begierden; *TI* "Problem of Socrates" §9; *KSA* 6, 71), thereby undermining his own credentials as a psychologist.

The difference between Nietzsche and a sexologist like Sigmund Freud, the founder of psychoanalysis (1856–1939), his junior by a dozen years, must now be examined. Freud and Nietzsche never met, and Freud in later life avoided reading Nietzsche's works because he feared they might influence him too strongly, while Nietzsche seems to have known Freud only as the translator of four of John Stuart Mill's essays.[10] A key departure is that Freud made some pretense at medical authenticity for his theories on psychoanalysis,[11] while Nietzsche did nothing of the kind, relying wholly on the perceptions of his own faculties: eyes, ears, nose, mouth, fingers. This allowed Nietzsche to deride Socrates's sexuality (we have the spectacle of Nietzsche haranguing Socrates for his putative homosexual leanings toward young boys), whereas Freud would seek to be a neutral observer. However, there is coherence in this vehemence, in much the same way that Nietzsche's antifeminist diatribes are — and I speak as a feminist! — both insulting and refreshingly lucid. It is typical of Nietzsche that he turns this form of argumentation to his advantage, declaring that the true psychologist is a politician, whereas "the 'objective' psychologist is a *despiser* of humans" (dieser "Unpersönliche" ist ein Menschen-*Verächter*; *TI* "Forays" §15; *KSA* 6, 121) and should therefore be shunned.

The Contents of *Twilight of the Idols*

With regard to the division of this work into chapters, readers are entitled to feel somewhat mystified by the drastic variation in their length; in the rest of this essay, the contents of each chapter will therefore receive due comment and discussion in turn, there being no overall pattern for the work as a whole.

After the briefest of forewords, Nietzsche plunges into his collection of forty-four "Sayings and Arrows" ("Sprüche und Pfeile"), some of them echoing thoughts set down in his collection of two hundred aphorisms bearing the title "Evil Wisdom"/"Arrows" ("Böse Weisheit"/"Pfeile"), written in 1883 (*KSA* 10, 12[1], 383–400). As that year had also seen the publication of *Thus Spoke Zarathustra*, parts 1 and 2, it was natural for Nietzsche to use a number of those aphorisms for *Zarathustra*, while a further eighteen were inserted into *Beyond Good and Evil* (published in 1886). Although Nietzsche certainly did not pillage the 1883 cohort of two hundred aphorisms for inclusion in *Twilight of the Idols*, there are some similarities of theme. Compare, for example, "Woman is the creator's leisure on that Seventh Day" (Das Weib ist der Müssiggang des Schöpfers an jedem siebenten Tage) (aphorism 39 of "Evil Wisdom"/"Arrows"; *KSA* 10, 12[1], 386) with "The male created woman — but from what? From a rib of his God — of his 'ideal' . . ." (Der Mann hat das Weib geschaffen — woraus doch? Aus einer Rippe seines Gottes, — seines "Ideals" . . .; *TI* "Sayings and Arrows" §13; *KSA* 6, 61). Clearly, both aphorisms deal with the Genesis story of human creation; in addition, the reference to "leisure" in "Evil Wisdom"/"Arrows," §39, finds a resonance in Nietzsche's original intentions in regard to the prototype title of *Twilight of the Idols*. It is perhaps true to say that the "Evil Wisdom"/"Arrows" aphorisms are more straightforward than those in *Twilight of the Idols*, where Nietzsche sets out his stall as a psychologist and speaks to the reader in a disconcertingly direct manner, all of a piece with the new style he wishes to embrace in this work.

"The Problem of Socrates" ("Das Problem des Sokrates") has twelve brief sections and is a pithy condemnation of the Greek philosopher, who needed "to make a tyrant out of *reason*" (aus der *Vernunft* einen Tyrannen zu machen; *TI* "Problem of Socrates" §10; *KSA* 6, 72). Nietzsche's argument is that philosophers through the ages have conspired to use "reason" as an exemplar of morality, at the cost of denying healthy human instincts. Nietzsche accuses Socrates of arousing revulsion, perhaps deliberately, with his dialectic. He asks: "is dialectic just a form of *revenge* with Socrates?" (ist Dialektik nur eine Form der *Rache* bei Sokrates? *TI* "Problem of Socrates" §7; *KSA* 6, 70). Unpopular though Socrates may have been with the Greek nobility, however, the latter were fascinated by him too: for all Greece was in danger of anarchy with regard to the instincts: "Having to fight against the instincts: that is the formula for *décadence*" (Die Instinkte bekämpfen *müssen* — das ist die Formel für décadence; *TI* "Problem of Socrates" §11; *KSA* 6, 73).

The following six-section chapter, "'Reason' in Philosophy" ("Die 'Vernunft' in der Philosophie"), continues the critique of Socratic rationalism, while broadening the argument into a discussion of the "apparent" (scheinbare) world as opposed to the "real world" (wahre Welt), which is "just *an added lie*" (nur *hinzugelogen*; *TI* "'Reason' in Philosophy" §2; *KSA* 6, 75). In applauding the place given to the world of appearance by the tragic actor, Nietzsche validates the latter as "Dionysian." At the same time, he highlights the metaphysics of language, which can never truly say what is meant: "Reason in speech: oh what a treacherous old crone! I fear we shall not get rid of God because we still believe in grammar . . ." (Die "Vernunft" in der Sprache: oh was für eine alte betrügerische Weibsperson! Ich fürchte, wir werden Gott nicht los, weil wir noch an die Grammatik glauben . . ."; *TI* "Reason' in Philosophy" §5; *KSA* 6, 78). Nietzsche's criticism of reason threads through the rest of the work, so that the initial Socratic equation "reason = virtue = happiness" (*TI* "Problem of Socrates" §4 and §10; *KSA* 6, 69 and 72) is deconstructed, and we finally arrive at the psychologist's assessment:

> Morality and religion completely belong to the *physiology of error*: in every single case, cause and effect are mixed up; or truth is confused with the effect of what is *believed* to be true; or a state of consciousness is confused with the causation of this state.

> [Die Moral und Religion gehört ganz und gar unter die *Psychologie des Irrthums:* in jedem einzelnen Falle wird Ursache und Wirkung verwechselt; oder die Wahrheit mit der Wirkung des als wahr *Geglaubten* verwechselt; oder ein Zustand des Bewusstseins mit der Ursächlichkeit dieses Zustands verwechselt. (*TI* "Four Great Errors" §6; *KSA* 6, 95)]

An astonishingly fresh and witty summary of philosophical error follows the chapter on "Reason in Philosophy" in the form of a six-point polemic entitled "How the Real World Finally Became a Fable" ("Wie die 'wahre Welt' endlich zur Fabel wurde"), subtitled "History of an Error" ("Geschichte eines Irrthums"; *KSA* 6, 80–81).

Its argument can be summarized as follows: (1) for the Ancient Greeks, the real world is "attainable for the wise, devout, virtuous person" (erreichbar für den Weisen, den Frommen, den Tugendhaften), in other words, for Plato; (2) the emergence of Christianity moves the goalposts so that the real world, though unattainable for the moment, is promised "for the sinner who does penance" (für den Sünder, der Busse thut); (3) the real world in Kant's scheme "cannot be attained, proved or promised" (unerreichbar, unbeweisbar, unversprechbar), but is nevertheless a reassuring "idea turned sublime" (Idee sublim geworden); (4) the dawn of positivism throws cold water on the reassuring aspects of the "unattainable" (unerreichbar) real world; (5) the idea of any "real world" (wahre Welt) is refuted; (6) everyone wakes up to the fact that we have gotten rid of the apparent world as well as the real world. The time line for these mock formulae is: (1) Antiquity; (2) Christianity; (3) the Enlightenment; (4) the "grey morning" (grauer Morgen) of positivism; (6) the "broad daylight" (heller Tag) of reason or "*bon sens*"; (6) Zarathustra's "noon" (Mittag). It goes without saying that this particular section is an unheard-of departure from normal philosophical inquiry.

There now follows the short six-section chapter entitled "Morality as Anti-Nature" ("Moral als Widernatur"), the title of which says in a nutshell what the argument is about. Here Nietzsche's opening remarks set the tone of this section: "Church *praxis* is hostile to life . . ." (die Praxis der Kirche ist *lebensfeindlich* . . .; *TI* "Morality as Anti-Nature" §1; *KSA* 6, 83), while his conclusion defines morality as a "specific error with which nobody should have compassion, a *degenerated idiosyncrasy* that has caused an unspeakable amount of harm! . . ." (ein spezifischer Irrthum, mit dem man kein Mitleiden haben soll, eine *Degenerirten-Idiosynkrasie*, die unsäglich viel Schaden gestiftet hat! . . .; *TI* "Morality as Anti-Nature" §6; *KSA* 6, 87). The arguments in between these declarations consist of pithy rhetoric tempered by psychological observations, especially in Nietzsche's evaluation of "peace of soul." This can be the calm after either a good or bad experience, as Nietzsche demonstrates, leading up to the final declaration in this section: "*Twilight of the Idols:* who knows? Perhaps just another kind of 'peace of soul' . . ." (*Götzen-Dämmerung:* wer weiss? vielleicht auch nur eine Art "Frieden der Seele" . . .; *TI* "Morality as Anti-Nature" §3; *KSA* 6, 85). In this way, Nietzsche shows that "peace of soul" has its place in the human psyche and is not an exclusively Christian reserve. In this section, Nietzsche fully deserves his self-endowed epithet "knower of the soul," or in other words, psychologist.

In the following section, Nietzsche formulates the principle that "all naturalism [. . .] is dominated by an instinct of life" (jeder Naturalismus [. . .] ist von einem Instinkte des Lebens beherrscht; *TI* "Morality as Anti-Nature" §4; *KSA* 6, 85), in contrast to Schopenhauer's "denial of the will to life" (Verneinung des Willens zum Leben; *TI* "Morality as

Anti-Nature" §5; *KSA* 6, 86). The sixth and final section outlines the "immoralist" who sees and acts correctly in accordance with what is natural — all of a piece with Nietzsche's first intention of writing a summary of his philosophy while "at leisure," incorporating personal observations not usual in philosophical texts: "we immoralists are the answer here" (wir Immoralisten sind hier die Antwort; *TI* "Morality as Anti-Nature" §6; *KSA* 6, 87).

In the next chapter, "The Four Great Errors" ("Die vier grossen Irrthümer"), Nietzsche uses the same psychological and psychiatric terms for his argument about the link between degeneration and the loss of will:

> Every mistake in every sense is the effect of instinct-degeneration, disintegration of the will: we are thereby practically defining the *bad*. Everything *good* is instinct, and consequently easy, necessary, free.

> [Jeder Fehler in jedem Sinne ist die Folge von Instinkt-Entartung, von Disintegration des Willens: man definirt beinahe damit das *Schlechte*. Alles *Gute* ist Instinkt — und, folglich, leicht, nothwendig, frei. (*TI* "Four Great Errors" §2; *KSA* 6, 90)]

The four "great errors" in this eponymous chapter consisting of eight sections are: the "error of confusing cause and effect" (§1 and §2); the "error of a false causality" (§3); the "error of imaginary causes" (§4 and §5); and the "error of free will" (§7). In the final section of this chapter, Nietzsche answers the question, "which doctrine can be *ours* exclusively?" (was kann allein *unsre* Lehre sein?), with the following reply: "That no person, neither God, nor society, nor parents, nor ancestors, nor *he himself*, should *assign* characteristics to the human being" (Dass Niemand dem Menschen seine Eigenschaften *giebt*, weder Gott, noch die Gesellschaft, noch seine Eltern und Vorfahren, noch *er selbst*; *TI* "Four Great Errors" §8; *KSA* 6, 96). Nietzsche ends the chapter with guns blaring: "We repudiate God, we repudiate answerability to God: only *in doing that* will we redeem the world" (Wir leugnen Gott, wir leugnen die Verantwortlichkeit in Gott: *damit* erst erlösen wir die Welt; *TI* "Four Great Errors" §8; SA 6, 97).

In the following, even briefer, chapter entitled "The 'Improvers' of Humankind" ("Der 'Verbesserer' der Menschheit"), which consists of only five short sections, Nietzsche links morality to language: "Morality is just sign language, just symptomatology: one must already know *what* it is about in order to make use of it" (Moral ist bloss Zeichenrede, bloss Symptomatologie: man muss bereits wissen, *worum* es sich handelt, um von ihr Nutzen zu ziehen; *TI* "'Improvers' of Humankind" §1; *KSA* 6, 98). Nietzsche's point is that those in authority, such as the priests, have always wanted to weaken humans while guilefully using the language of betterment, so that the human being is tamed rather than "improved," that particular word merely being a euphemism for the hurt inflicted.

In the second section of this chapter, Nietzsche continues on the same theme, using the analogy of the "blond beast" (first found in *On the Genealogy of Morality*),[12] to refer to the Church as a "menagerie" intent on hunting down and taming the human in order to "improve" him. In the third section, he steps beyond his anti-Christian theme to consider the *Laws of Manu*, with its cruel measures designed to weaken the Chandala caste.

The one-paragraph fourth section of this chapter widens the critique to embrace "*Aryan* Humanity" (*arische* Humanität), a loaded concept in Nietzsche's terminology that embraces "the vague concepts 'Teutonic,' 'Semitic,' 'Christian' and 'German' as well as 'Aryan'" (der vagen Begriffe "germanisch", "semitisch", "arisch", "christlich", "deutsch"), as Nietzsche spelled out in a letter to Theodor Fritsch dated 29 March 1887 (*KSB* 8, 51).[13] The virulent racism of some Germans, Fritsch among them, was informed by the "pure blood" requirement for German nationality,[14] on which Nietzsche touches in the following remark: "we learn that the concept of 'pure blood' is the antithesis of a harmless concept" (wir lernen, dass der Begriff "reines Blut" der Gegensatz eines harmlosen Begriffes ist; *TI* "'Improvers' of Humankind" §4; *KSA* 6, 101). He continues with a dense critique of Christianity, throwing in the apocryphal Book of Enoch for good measure.[15] For Nietzsche, Christianity is "the revaluation of all Aryan values, the victory of chandala-values [. . .] undying chandala-revenge as *religion of love . . .*" (die Umwerthung aller arischen Werthe, der Sieg der Tschandala-Werthe [. . .] die unsterbliche Tschandala-Rache als *Religion der Liebe . . .*; *TI* "'Improvers' of Humankind" §4; *KSA* 6, 102). He gives a rhetorical summing-up in the brief (single paragraph) finale to this chapter: "Expressed in a formula, one might say: *all* methods that hitherto have been intended to make humankind moral have been fundamentally immoral. —" (In Formel ausgedrückt dürfte man sagen: *alle* Mittel, wodurch bisher die Menschheit moralisch gemacht werden sollte, waren von Grund aus *unmoralisch*. —; *TI* "'Improvers' of Humankind" §5; *KSA* 6, 102).

The next chapter, "What the Germans Lack" ("Was den Deutschen abgeht"), consisting of seven sections, homes in on the faults of the Germans: their science, their education, their culture and even their swilling of beer. Their loss of capacity for serious thought is summed up in the national anthem, "Deutschland, Deutschland über alles."[16] Lamenting the demise of the intellectual German, Nietzsche writes that "this nation has made itself deliberately stupid for nearly a thousand years" (dies Volk hat sich willkürlich verdummt, seit einem Jahrtausend beinahe; *TI* "What the Germans Lack" §2; *KSA* 6, 104); in other words, it has bowed to the yoke of Christianity. Not content with deadening their minds with alcohol and Christianity, the Germans now treat music as a narcotic, by which Nietzsche means — Wagner's music. Next, Nietzsche criticizes David

Strauss as the author of an "armchair gospel" and someone who was fond of his ale, a detail not proven.[17]

Nietzsche excoriates Germany's educational system in section 5: "Apart from the exceptions to exceptions, the *foremost* prerequisite of education, educators, are *lacking, hence* the decline in German culture. —" (Die Erzieher *fehlen*, die Ausnahmen der Ausnahmen abgerechnet, die *erste* Vorbedingung der Erziehung: *daher* der Niedergang der deutschen Cultur; *TI* "What the Germans Lack" §5; *KSA* 6, 107). Nietzsche's main objection to the parlous state of German society is that people no longer know how to *think*. As a psychologist, he propounds thoughts on the physiology and motivation of "thought" that most readers will find entirely valid: people should observe slowly rather than trying to see something in a flash, taking time to reflect, and the same goes for thinking, which "needs to be learned" (gelernt sein will; *TI* "What the Germans Lack" §7; *KSA* 6, 109). The same also goes for speaking and writing. Instead of taking time to deliberate, the Germans rush into things precipitously, with an "open door approach" (das Offenstehen mit allen Thüren; *TI* "What the Germans Lack" §6; *KSA* 6, 109). In this chapter, Nietzsche gives the reader, without reserve, his terse and hostile opinion of Germany as Europe's "flatland" (Flachland; *TI* "What the Germans Lack" §5; *KSA* 6, 105), peopled by inhabitants with "a *clumsy* handshake" (die *plumpe* Hand beim Fassen) and "no *feel* for nuances" (keine *Finger* für nuances; *TI* "What the Germans Lack" §7; *KSA* 6, 109–10).

Up to this point in the work, Nietzsche has mainly held to a system of short chapters with relatively few sections, but he departs from this entirely in "Forays of an Untimely One," with its fifty-one sections. The source material was written during the period of autumn 1887 to summer 1888 and, as discussed above, was intended for *The Will to Power* but then separated out into *The Anti-Christian* and *Twilight of the Idols*. Again referring to the excellent commentary on *Twilight of the Idols* by Colli and Montinari, we learn that sections 1–18 were originally gathered under the heading "Among Artists and Writers," while sections 19–31 were grouped as "From My Aesthetics" (*KSA* 14, 422). Sections 32–44 were added when Nietzsche undertook the proof corrections between 4–13 October 1889 (*KSA* 14, 422); these, too, had originally belonged to material earmarked for *The Will to Power* — further proof, if it were needed, that Nietzsche had given up his attempt to write *The Will to Power* and was content for *Twilight of the Idols* to be a free-standing summary of his philosophy, while *The Anti-Christian* was viewed as the first book of the *Revaluation of all Values*. The "Forays" are indeed just that: excursions into a field of thought, disjointed; interesting; just like thought itself. It is hard to make them cohere in a meaningful way, and perhaps one should not try. The following remarks will rely on the groupings of certain sections that give some form and pattern to the chapter.

In the first six sections of "Forays," consisting of one paragraph each, Nietzsche unburdens himself of his prejudices toward those intellectuals who have offended him, from Seneca, "the toreador of virtue" (der Toreador der Tugend; *TI* "Forays" §1; *KSA* 6, 111), to George Sand, "this prolific milk cow" (diese fruchtbare Schreibe-Kuh; *TI* "Forays" §6; *KSA* 6, 114). In the following two sections, Nietzsche pauses to consider the aesthetic considerations of a "morality for psychologists" (Moral für Psychologen). He again stresses the need to see with the inner eye, the sign of the true psychologist: "A born psychologist instinctively avoids looking in order to see; the same is true of the born artist" (Ein geborner Psycholog hütet sich aus Instinkt, zu sehn, um zu sehn; dasselbe gilt vom gebornen Maler; *TI* "Forays" §7; *KSA* 6, 115). The next section is restricted to the vital necessity, for the artist, of euphoria in all its manifestations, for, without euphoria, "no art will be forthcoming" (eher kommt es zu keiner Kunst; *TI* "Forays" §8; *KSA* 6, 116).

Sections 10 to 11 add flesh to Nietzsche's commentary on the distinction between the Apollonian and the Dionysian, first mooted in *The Birth of Tragedy* (*Die Geburt der Tragödie*). In sections 12 to 14, Nietzsche returns to the sport of naming and shaming luminaries, dealing respectively with Carlyle, Emerson, and Darwin, the latter so misrepresented that Nietzsche's pretension to an understanding of natural science is put in question. However, Emerson receives praise, insofar as he is a happy and contented man. Sections 15 to 18 deal briefly with the casuistry of the psychologist hitherto, who has despised human beings rather than striven to be objective. Meanwhile, in a lightweight paragraph, Nietzsche again voices his despair at the psychology of the Germans, who casually group great thinkers together, but in partnerships, such as "Goethe *and* Schiller" or even "Schopenhauer *and* Hartmann," that are painfully unequal (*TI* "Forays" §16; *KSA* 6, 122). (It is ironic that, today, we think nothing of such dual references as "Nietzsche and Schopenhauer," while many a learned paper is titled "Nietzsche and . . .".)

With regard to sections 19–31, it is glaringly obvious that these have been lifted from a different arena. In section 19, subtitled "Beautiful and Ugly" ("Schön und hässlich"), the human as an arbiter of taste is thoroughly ridiculed, as Nietzsche demands: "Who knows how the human would look in the eyes of a higher authority on taste?" (Wer weiss, wie er sich in den Augen eines höheren Geschmacksrichters ausnimmt?; *TI* "Forays" §19; *KSA* 6, 123). He ends the section with an allusion to the spurious text "Dionysos on Naxos," which he did not write, though he perhaps meant to, or even thought that he had.[18] This section ends with Ariadne demanding: "Oh Dionysos, Holy One, why do you pull my ears?" (Oh Dionysos, Göttlicher, warum ziehst du mich an den Ohren?), to which the reply is: "I find your ears rather amusing, Ariadne: why are they not even longer?" (Ich finde eine Art Humor in deinen Ohren,

Ariadne: warum sind sie nicht noch länger?; *TI* "Forays" §19; *KSA* 6, 123–24).[19] The point about this apparently throwaway remark is that Nietzsche is jostling for position to tell us that he really is Dionysos: the God-slayer aspires to become a god.

Nietzsche displays his legendary pride in listening, in acoustic acumen, by using "Ariadne" (daughter of King Minos in Greek myth) as a polysemous trope to embellish the word "labyrinth," likewise redolent with double entendre, denoting a metaphorical maze (the death trap of Greek legend from which Theseus escapes with Ariadne's help) as well as the anatomy of the inner ear that regulates hearing and balance. Of course, the faculty of hearing stands alongside sight, speech, smell, and touch, the senses that, in Nietzsche's argument, morality has tried to dull. Besides the semiotics of sound, Nietzsche brings in an aesthetic dimension, since the Dionysian preference for long ears conforms to Nietzsche's tongue-in-cheek thesis that the concept of "beauty," to a god, is quite different from what "beauty" signifies to a human. And he should know!

Nietzsche continues the debate on aesthetics in the next section. If, erroneously, the human takes himself as the yardstick for beauty, his inevitable decline and eventual putrefaction will evoke "the value judgment 'ugly'" (das Urtheil "hässlich"; *TI* "Forays" §20; *KSA* 6, 124). While despising Schopenhauer's aesthetics, Nietzsche nevertheless acknowledges his adversary's coherence on this topic. For Schopenhauer prized beauty "as a redemption from the 'focal point of the will,' sexuality" (als Erlöserin vom "Brennpunkte des Willens," von der Geschlechtlichkeit; *TI* "Forays" §22; *KSA* 6, 125); indeed, he "taught 'liberation of the will' as the whole purpose of art, he revered 'attuning to resignation' as the great usefulness of tragedy" ("loskommen vom Willen" lehrte Schopenhauer als Gesammt-Absicht der Kunst, "zur Resignation stimmen" verehrte er als die grosse Nützlichkeit der Tragödie; *TI* "Forays" §24; *KSA* 6, 24).

Plato, on the other hand, could not get enough of "beauty" in the form of Greek youths: "the sight of them was what first spurred the philosopher's soul into an erotic spin" (deren Anblick sei es erst, was die Seele des Philosophen in einen erotischen Taumel versetzte; *TI* "Forays" §23; *KSA* 6, 126). Yet in Nietzsche's eyes, Plato is preferable to Schopenhauer; indeed, Nietzsche draws our attention to the fact that Plato's acknowledgment of sexuality as the driving force of "beauty" was taken up by the art world in classical France to great effect: "Everywhere in it you can look for gallantry, sensuality, sexual rivalry, 'woman' — you will never look in vain . . ." (Man darf überall bei ihr die Galanterie, die Sinne, den Geschlechts-Wettbewerb, das "Weib" suchen, — man wird nie umsonst suchen . . .; *TI* "Forays" §23; *KSA* 6, 126). Speaking as a psychologist throughout these sections on aesthetics, Nietzsche dismisses *l'art pour l'art* as being without a goal, whereas a tragic artist will face tragedy and *fight* it, on the model of Plato's *agon*. In contrast, "*L'art pour l'art* means: 'the devil take morality!'" (L'art pour l'art heisst: "der Teufel hole die Moral!"; *TI* "Forays" §24; *KSA* 6, 127).

The next sections (25 to 31) deal in somewhat random fashion with contemporary cultural malaise, where morality has been turned on its head. Hospitality is faked, speech is not genuine, and studious (Nietzsche means "emancipated") women act against their own interest by denying their childbearing function. Misogynist though this sounds today, Nietzsche, along with most other middle-class men of his era — and the majority of women, too — genuinely believed in woman's biological destiny, and in this sense, it might be said that his claim to be avant-garde failed.[20]

Nietzsche's argument in sections 32 to 44 turns on the question of morality versus immorality:

> We modern humans, very tender and fragile, giving and taking a hundred considerations, actually do imagine that the delicate humanity we portray, this *achieved* unanimity in tolerance, helpfulness, mutual trust, is a positive advance that puts us far beyond Renaissance humans. But every era thinks like that, it *has to*.

> [Wir modernen Menschen, sehr zart, sehr verletzlich und hundert Rücksichten gebend und nehmend, bilden uns in der That ein, diese zärtliche Menschlichkeit, die wir darstellen, diese *erreichte* Einmütigkeit in der Schonung, in der Hülfsbereitschaft, im gegenseitigen Vertrauen sei ein positiver Fortschritt, damit seien wir weit über die Menschen der Renaissance hinaus. Aber so denkt jede Zeit, so *muss* sie denken. (*TI* "Forays" §37; *KSA* 6, 136)]

The burden of Nietzsche's argument is that decadence and decline are endemic. Christianity has "tempered custom" to the point where we lose our freedom, since "the war *for* liberal institutions [. . .] renders the *illiberal* instincts permanent" (der Krieg *um* liberale Institutionen [lässt] die *illiberalen* Instinkte dauern; *TI* "Forays" §38: *KSA* 6, 139). In contrast, section 45 uses a language informed by psychiatric terms. As discussed above, this was a novelty to Nietzsche and, indeed, there are no fewer than four rough drafts for this passage. One of them, found in a notebook designated as *W II 6*, goes further than the one in print by staking a claim for the criminal as a "sick type of strong human" (ein krankhafter Typus des starken Menschen), arguing that all great innovators, "scrutinized with a kidney-tester's eye" (mit dem Auge des Nierenprüfers ausgeforscht), look identical to hardened criminals (*TI* "Forays" §45, variant ms. *W II 6*; *KSA* 14, 433). It is typical of Nietzsche to merge clinical psychology with an analysis of the vital organs; in this case, by reference to the kidney. In line with this argument, he claims that he can single out iconoclasts merely because they *look* like criminals. Nietzsche sees himself as a "kidney-tester," an expression he coins from the phrase "auf Herz und Nieren prüfen," meaning "to put something to the acid test," which in turn stems from the biblical prophet Jeremiah, "I the Lord search the heart, I try the reins" (Ich der Herr kann das Herz ergründen und die Nieren prüfen).[21] Nietzsche deleted the reference to the kidney-tester from his final version of *Twilight of the Idols*, which was ready for print when he wrote *Ecce Homo*, recycling it in the latter work to great effect.[22]

In the five-section final chapter entitled "What I Owe the Ancients" ("Was ich den Alten verdanke"), Nietzsche provides a lucid resumé of what he learned from the ancients, beginning with the Roman historian Sallust (86–35 BCE), thanks to whom Nietzsche says he developed "my sense of style, of the epigram as style" (mein Sinn für Stil, für das Epigramm als Stil; *TI* "What I Owe" §1; *KSA* 6, 154). Alongside the Romans, the Greeks are "too foreign" (zu fremd), and Plato is "boring" (langweilig; *TI* "What I Owe" §2; *KSA* 6, 155). The Socratic virtues were taught "*because* the Greeks had lost them" (*weil* sie den Griechen abhanden gekommen waren), Nietzsche declares (*TI* "What I Owe" §3; *KSA* 6, 157). Even so, his argument turns to the one gem he found in Greek culture that would dominate his thought — the orgiastic concept of Dionysos: "I know of no higher symbolism than this *Greek* symbolism, that of the Dionysian" (ich kenne keine höhere Symbolik als diese *griechische* Symbolik, die der Dionysien; *TI* "What I Owe" §4; *KSA* 6, 159). Drawing his psychological and philosophical strands together in the final section of this chapter, as though the whole of *Twilight of the Idols* really has been a summary of his philosophy instead of an expedition to revisit old ideas and introduce some new ones, Nietzsche writes:

> The *Birth of Tragedy* was my first revaluation of all values: with that, I put myself back into the soil from which my will and my *"can"* take root — I, the last disciple of the philosopher Dionysos, — I, the teacher of eternal return . . .

> [Die "Geburt der Tragödie" war meine erste Umwerthung aller Werthe: damit stelle ich mich wieder auf den Boden zurück, aus dem mein Wollen, mein *Können* wächst — ich, der letzte Jünger des Philosophen Dionysos — ich, der Lehrer der ewigen Wiederkunft . . . (*TI* "What I Owe" §5; *KSA* 6, 160)]

This is a timely reminder that, in several of his plans for the *Revaluation of all Values*, eternal return is directly linked to Dionysos, and Nietzsche no doubt intended to pursue that theme thoroughly. However, the references in *Twilight of the Idols* and *The Anti-Christian* were as far as he was going to get with that particular theme, given the looming catastrophe of his collapse.

Twilight of the Idols ends with a passage taken from the third book of *Zarathustra*, "The Hammer Speaks" (*KSA* 6, 161; cf. *KSA* 4, 268). Possibly Nietzsche intended to end this work with the bullish "Law against Christianity" ("Gesetz wider das Christenthum"), which now forms the finale of *The Anti-Christian* (*KSA* 6, 254).[23] Whatever Nietzsche's original intentions were, *Twilight of the Idols* ends with the borrowing from *Zarathustra* of an entire section (*Z* III 12 §29; *KSA* 4, 268). Moreover, the quixotic lyricism of the passage from *Zarathustra* jars with the acerbic, if impromptu, arguments Nietzsche has advanced in the rest of *Twilight of the Idols*, with the exception of the initial aphorisms and the enigmatic section "How the 'Real' World Finally Became a Fable." This was not because Nietzsche was in a relaxed holiday mood when he conceived the idea for this work: instead, he was in a hurry.

Nietzsche's self-proclaimed skill as a "kidney tester" allowed him to be as provocative and outrageous as he liked. In his dash to produce the works he still had planned for 1888, he left *Twilight of the Idols* largely unrevised, its variety and directness sometimes vying with a more structured argument that one feels he might have presented had he not been so stretched — and, very soon, so cruelly deprived of his métier.

Notes

The translations from Nietzsche in this essay are my own.

[1] With Leipzig as his base, Nietzsche stayed in Naumburg from the 15th through the 17th of October, making another brief visit there on 27 October, when he spent the evening with his sister and Bernhard Förster. (Förster died in Paraguay on 3 June 1889, possibly by his own hand, by which time Nietzsche had become mentally insane.)

[2] The editor of the *Antisemitische Correspondenz* was Theodor Fritsch (1852–1933).

[3] A few copies of *Nietzsche contra Wagner* were published in 1889; the work appeared in the *Grossoktav* edition in 1895 (cf. *KSA* 14, 522).

[4] The titles of the books clarify Nietzsche's intentions; for their chronological order, see *KSA* 13, 11[416], 194; *KSA* 13, 19[8], 545; *KSA* 13, 22[14], 589; *KSA* 13, 22[24], 594; *KSA* 13, 23[8], 610; and *KSA* 13, 23[13], 613.

[5] Wagner's *Twilight of the Gods* (*Götterdämmerung*), the fourth opera of *The Ring* cycle, was first performed in 1876.

[6] Compare with Zarathustra's statement in "Of Self-Overcoming" ("Von der Selbst-Ueberwindung"): "Where I found anything alive, there I found the will to power!" (Wo ich Lebendiges fand, da fand ich Willen zur Macht; *Z* II 12; *KSA* 4, 147).

[7] According to the online etymological dictionary, the origin for the word "psychology" is as follows: 1653, "study of the soul," probably coined in the mid-sixteenth century in Germany by Melanchthon as Modern Latin *psychologia*, from

Greek *psukhē*, "breath, spirit, soul" + *logia*, "study of." Its meaning as "study of the mind" is first recorded in 1748 in Christian Wolff's *Psychologia empirica* (1732); its main modern behavioral sense dates from 1895. As we can see from this definition, Nietzsche really was ahead of his time in using the word.

[8] Greg Moore, *Nietzsche, Biology and Metaphor* (Cambridge: Cambridge UP, 2003), 126.

[9] Charles Féré (1852–1907), *Dégénérescence et criminalité: Essai physiologique* (Paris: Alcan, 1888); Charles Féré and Alfred Binet (1857–1911), *Le Magnétisme Animal* (Paris: Alcan, 1887).

[10] Nietzsche possessed a copy of Freud's translation of the four essays by Mill ("The Emancipation of Women"; "Plato"; "The Claims of Labour"; "Socialism") that constituted the final volume of John Stuart Mill, *Gesammelte Werke*, ed. by Thomas Gomperz, 12 vols. (Leipzig, Fues: 1869–80), vol. 12, *Ueber Frauen-emancipation; Plato; Arbeiterfrage; Socialismus*, trans. Sigmund Freud (1880).

[11] See "The Question of Lay Analysis" ("Die Frage der Laienanalyse," 1926), in Sigmund Freud, *Two Short Accounts of Psycho-Analysis*, trans. James Strachey (Harmondsworth: Penguin, 1962), 89–170.

[12] Nietzsche used the phrase "blond beast" three times in *On the Genealogy of Morality* (*GM* I §11; *KSA* 5, 274–77). (The wording of the second instance is actually "the blond Germanic beast" [die blonde germanische Bestie]).

[13] Fritsch (see note 2 above) was convinced of the superiority of the Aryan race. Accompanying the letter in question, Nietzsche returned three tracts that Fritsch had sent to him with the request not to send any more. It is to Nietzsche's credit that he already saw and repudiated the growing anti-Semitism in Germany. Fritsch would go on to write his landmark *Handbuch der Judenfrage* (Handbook of the Jewish Question) in 1896, the ideas of which influenced Hitler and National Socialism.

[14] In the UK, for example, the nationality requirement has always been that a person is either born in British territory, or becomes naturalized; dual nationality is allowed and "blood" is not an issue. In Germany during the nineteenth century, Jews were given German citizenship, but there was opposition to this from "ethnic" Germans who prized the argument that the German bloodline should be kept "pure."

[15] The earliest writings belonging to the Book of Enoch, of which there appear to be three separate versions, may have been written during the last century BCE along with other contemporary written accounts of the destruction of the second temple in Jerusalem (70 CE). Elsewhere the book is attributed to the ninth century CE. It is a conglomeration of mystic texts familiar to the Jews, but never incorporated into the Christian Bible, although in Genesis, Enoch is referred to as the father of Methuselah and the great-grandfather of Noah, and we are told that he "walked with God" (Genesis 5:22 and 24). In the New Testament, Paul states that Enoch "pleased God" (Hebrews 11:5), but Nietzsche must have had in mind the reference to Enoch in the one-section epistle of Jude, where Enoch prophesied that the Lord would come to "exercise judgment upon all" (Jude 15). Nietzsche was not being entirely original in citing Enoch: in his notebook *W II 3*, he observes that, in the opinion of Ernst Renan (1823–92), from whose *Vie de*

Jésus (1863) he had taken notes, the Book of Enoch "contains more violent curses on the world" than those in the gospels (*KSA* 13, 11[405], 187).

[16] Most readers will recognize this as the unofficial title of the German national anthem, the text of which was composed by Hoffmann von Fallersleben (1798–1874) in 1841.

[17] The theologian David Strauss (1808–74) was the author of the pathbreaking *Das Leben Jesus kritisch bearbeitet* (*The Life of Jesus Critically Examined*, 1835). Strauss had wanted to emulate Renan's work (cf. the reference to Renan in note 15 above) but instead he earned criticism for his attempt to explain much of the narrative of the New Testament as myth. Negative public opinion dogged him to the point of despair, and he might well have been an alcoholic in later life, but this is not provable.

[18] See *BGE* §295 (*KSA* 5, 237–38) and *KSA* 12, 9[115], 401–2.

[19] In 1889, Nietzsche gathered together nine poems, written during the period 1883–88, into a collection he named the *Dionysos-Dithyramben* (*Dionysian Dithyrambs*). In one of these poems, "Ariadne's Complaint" ("Klage der Ariadne"), Dionysos comments on Ariadne's *small* ears (*KSA* 6, 401). Further scattered references to Naxos in Nietzsche's manuscripts mention a wedding, which perhaps conjures up for the reader the planned nuptials of Theseus and Hippolyta in Shakespeare's *A Midsummer Night's Dream*, where Titania falls in love with long-eared Bottom, whose head Puck has mischievously transformed into the head of an ass. Since Cosima Wagner, whose ears were not small, has been linked with the "Ariadne" conundrum, the significance of the allusion might end there. However, Nietzsche's "Naxos" might refer to the weeks he spent in Sicily (April 1882) before he was to meet Lou Andreas-Salomé in Rome. She, too, had rather large ears. Nietzsche had small ears and found large ears unpleasing; but in his "Dionysos" *persona*, adopted in the final months before his mental collapse, he can find long ears very pleasing, following the argument that a god (Nietzsche/Dionysos) views "beauty" in a different way from humans. Finally, one could view Dionysos as Ariadne's inner voice: "*I am your labyrinth . . .*" (*Ich bin dein Labyrinth . . .*) is the last line of "Ariadne's Complaint."

[20] For further discussion, see my article, "Nietzsche Emasculated: Postmodern Readings," in *Ecce Opus: Nietzsche-Revisionen im 20. Jahrhundert* ed. Rüdiger Görner and Duncan Large (Göttingen: Vandenhoeck und Ruprecht, 2003), 51–63. In it I criticize postmodern interpreters for toning down Nietzsche's anti-feminism; there was method in his madness, in that he viewed female campaigners for women's rights as *Mannweiber*, "gay" in today's parlance (a male campaigner like John Stuart Mill was, for him, beyond the pale). I do not share his views and have loudly criticized them, but they are coherent and revelatory; which is more than can be said for postmodernism.

[21] Jeremiah 17:10. "Kidney" is *le rein* in French, *die Niere* in German; derived from Latin *renes* = kidneys.

[22] Nietzsche redirected the conceit in *Ecce Homo* to his discussion of *The Case of Wagner* (*Der Fall Wagner*), where he writes: "The first test when I sound out the kidney of a human being is whether that person has an aura of physical distance"

(Das Erste, worauf ich mir einen Menschen "nierenprüfe," ist, ob er ein Gefühl für Distanz im Leibe hat; *EH Der Fall Wagner* §4: *KSA* 6, 362).

[23] In 1932, Hans-Joachim Mette found the "Law against Christianity" (now the final section of *The Anti-Christian*) in the box containing the manuscript of *Ecce Homo*; for discussion of the controversy it aroused, see *KSA* 13, 448–54. Suffice it to say that the type of manuscript paper Nietzsche used for "The Hammer Speaks" in *Twilight of the Idols* is identical to that of the entire *Anti-Christian* (including the "Law"). At all events, in the *KGW* de Gruyter printed the text of the "Law" in a smaller font to indicate the question mark hanging over it. "The Hammer Speaks" is a rather anarchic ending for *Twilight of the Idols*, where references to *Zarathustra* are few and far between. Nietzsche's intention is to remind his readers that he has created a new law or tablet — that of anti-morality.

12: *The Anti-Christ*

Martin Liebscher

T HE LAST SUNDAY OF AUGUST 1888 saw Nietzsche drafting the very last
plan for his main philosophical work that was to have been entitled
The Will to Power (*Der Wille zur Macht*).[1] This was to be endowed with
the subtitle *Attempt at a Revaluation of Values* (*Versuch einer Umwertung
aller Werte*). To the credit of Mazzino Montinari and the critical edition
of Nietzsche's works, there can no longer be any doubt that Nietzsche
subsequently abandoned *The Will to Power* and replaced it with a project under the former subtitle, *Revaluation of Values* (*Umwertung aller
Werte*).[2] As a letter to Heinrich Köselitz (the friend whom Nietzsche
renamed Peter Gast) from 13 February 1888 indicates, Nietzsche was
already writing a text under this title at the beginning of the very same
year: "I have finished the first draft of my 'Attempt of a Revaluation': it
was, all in all, a torture, besides I really don't have the courage for it at the
moment. I will make it better in ten years' time. —" (Ich habe die erste
Niederschrift meines "Versuchs einer Umwertung" fertig: es war, Alles in
Allem, ein Tortur, auch habe ich durchaus noch nicht den Muth dazu.
Zehn Jahre später will ichs besser machen. —; *KSB* 8, 252).[3] After having
given up his project of *The Will to Power,* Nietzsche returned to the *Revaluation of Values* earlier than anticipated, in September 1888. The *Nachlass*
material relating to this period contains six different drafts, each divided
into four books, and in these plans *The Anti-Christ* features prominently.[4]
For example, in the draft of September 1888 the first book of four is to be
entitled *The Anti-Christ: Attempt at a Critique of Christianity* (*Der Anti-
christ. Versuch einer Kritik des Christenthums*), followed by *The Free Spirit:
Critique of Philosophy as a Nihilistic Movement* (*Der freie Geist. Kritik der
Philosophie als einer nihilistischen Bewegung*), *The Immoralist: Critique of
a Fatal Kind of Ignorance* (*Der Immoralist. Kritik der verhängnisvollen
Art von Unwissenheit*), and *Dionysos: Philosophy of the Eternal Recurrence*
(*Dionysos. Philosophie der ewigen Wiederkunft*; *KSA* 13, 19[8], 545). Later
that autumn Nietzsche's friends received letters informing them about
the completion of the *Revaluation*, in which he identified the text with
The Anti-Christ. He wrote in a letter to Paul Deussen from 26 November
1888: "My *Revaluation of Values* under the main title '**the Anti-Christ**'
is finished" (Meine *Umwerthung aller Werthe* mit dem Haupttitel "**der**

Antichrist" ist fertig; *KSB* 8, 492).[5] Years later, this letter would have been pivotal in the defense of Franz Overbeck, when he was accused by Elisabeth Förster-Nietzsche of being responsible for the loss of crucial material for the *Revaluation* project which should have formed the three other books mentioned above. Though the letter to Deussen was available in the archive, Förster-Nietzsche would not make it public. Köselitz was so convinced that further material must have existed that in 1906 he would even write an affidavit stating that "in the handwritten notes of the last part which presently lie before us, there is a noticeable deficit of material that stands in obvious contrast to the three remaining parts of the work" (tatsächlich in den vorhandenen Handschriften der uns vorliegende letzte Theil einen auffallenden Mangel an Material zeigt, der im ersichtlichen Gegensatz zu den drei übrigen Theilen des Werkes steht).[6] Montinari brought the letter to the attention of the public and cleared Overbeck's name of any wrongdoing.

Next to *Ecce Homo*, the *Dithyrambs of Dionysos* (*Dionysos-Dithyramben*), and *Nietzsche contra Wagner*, *The Anti-Christ* belongs to the group of texts not published by Nietzsche himself: his *Nachlass* texts. It was first published by Fritz Kögel in 1895 in volume 8 of the *Großoktavausgabe* (*GOA*) under the title *Der Antichrist. Versuch einer Kritik des Christenthums,* which ignored Nietzsche's final choice for a subtitle, *A Curse on Christianity* (*Fluch auf das Christenthum*). Arthur Seidl, the successor of Köselitz and Kögel as editor of the *GOA*, chose an even more obscure title when he published the text in 1899 (again as volume 8 of the *GOA*): *Der Wille zur Macht. Versuch einer Umwerthung aller Werthe. Von Friedrich Nietzsche. Vorwort und Erstes Buch: Der Antichrist.* Of course, when in 1905 the first version of the compilation *Der Wille zur Macht* was published, *The Anti-Christ* had to become a mere *Revaluation of Values* again: *Umwerthung aller Werthe. Vorwort und Erstes Buch: Der Antichrist.*[7] The first authentic edition of *The Anti-Christ* did not appear until 1956, when Karl Schlechta published the text as part of his Nietzsche edition.[8]

During those days of late summer and early autumn 1888 — Nietzsche had bidden farewell to Sils Maria and spent some overly enthusiastic days in Turin, a prelude to the final catastrophe — he wrote *Twilight of the Idols* (*Götzen-Dämmerung*), which is inextricably linked with *The Anti-Christ*, having been written at the same time and having evolved partially from the same material.[9]

Ecce Homo is similarly linked by its content and intent through the revaluation that Nietzsche attempts to undertake. Though the first drafts of *Ecce Homo* also stem from the time of *Twilight of the Idols*, the main text was written between 15 October and 4 November, and therefore it is right to say that it succeeded *The Anti-Christ*. The foreword of *Ecce Homo* opens with the following line: "In view of the fact that I will shortly have to confront humanity with the heaviest demand ever made of it, it seems to me essential to say *who I am*" (In Voraussicht, dass ich über Kurzem mit der schwersten Forderung an die Menschheit herantreten muss, die je an sie gestellt wurde, scheint es mir unerlässlich, zu sagen, *wer ich bin*; *EH* preface §1; *KSA* 6, 257). The heaviest demand is, of course, "the revaluation of values," which Nietzsche had already finished as *The Anti-Christ*. A letter to his publisher, C. G. Naumann, on 6 November 1888 reveals how Nietzsche saw the relation between those two writings:

> I have completely convinced myself that another text is necessary, a text which prepares in the highest degree, in order to appear shortly after the new year and roughly at the same time as the first book of the *Revaluation*. There has to be a real tension — otherwise it will be the same as in the case of Zarathustra.

> [Ich habe mich vollkommen davon überzeugt, noch eine Schrift nöthig zu haben, eine im höchsten Grade *vorbereitende* Schrift, um nach Jahresfrist ungefähr mit dem ersten Buch der *Umwertung* hervortreten zu können. Es muß eine *wirklich Spannung* geschaffen sein — im anderen Falle geht es wie beim Zarathustra. (*KSB* 8, 463–64)]

Still writing about the first book of his main work, Nietzsche makes clear in this letter how seriously he took the project of the *Revaluation* and how carefully he prepared it. The deliberately provocative character of *Ecce Homo* was intended to create a higher expectation for the main undertaking, and thus help Nietzsche to reach a wider audience (as his allusion to *Zarathustra* indicates). The attempt to spread the message to as many readers as possible is deeply ingrained in the project of the *Revaluation* — Nietzsche's plans for widespread translations bear witness to this. As a revaluation of all values, *The Anti-Christ* is deeply political, and as such it needs to reach out and convince its readers. Given its political intentions, it is rather surprising to read the opening lines of the preface to the *Revaluation*: "This book belongs to the very few. Perhaps none of them are even living yet" (Dies Buch gehört den Wenigsten. Vielleicht lebt selbst noch Keiner von ihnen; *AC* preface; *KSA* 6, 167). Nietzsche then lists the preconditions for becoming his reader: among other things, one has to be accustomed to seeing "the wretched ephemeral chatter of politics and national egoism" (das erbärmliche Zeitgeschwätz von Politik und Völker-Selbstsucht; *KSA* 6, 167). The end of the preface simply excludes the rest of mankind: "what do the *rest* matter? — The rest are merely mankind. — One must be superior to mankind in force, in *loftiness* of soul — in contempt. . ." (was liegt am Rest? — Der Rest ist bloss die Menschheit. — Man muss der Menschheit überlegen sein durch Kraft, durch *Höhe* der Seele, — durch Verachtung. . .; *KSA* 6, 167–68).[10]

The first line of *The Anti-Christ* addresses accordingly the author's collaborators as Hyperboreans — an allusion to Pindar's Odes: "We are

Hyperboreans — we know well enough how much out of the way we live" (Wir sind Hyperboreer, — wir wissen gut genug, wie abseits wir leben; *AC* §1; *KSA* 6, 169).[11] Hence the text is written from a distant perspective that can be reached "neither by land nor water" and speaks to an audience that already shares the same preoccupations. This poses a difficulty, as it excludes any readers except those who are already initiated. Of course, this is not the first time that Nietzsche uses such a rhetorical device. Most prominently one is reminded of *Thus Spoke Zarathustra*, a "book for everyone and no one." A clue to this riddle might be provided by Nietzsche's distinction between esoteric and exoteric contents in *Beyond Good and Evil* (*Jenseits von Gut und Böse*):

> Our highest insights must — and should! — sound like stupidities, or possibly crimes, when they come without permission to people whose ears have no affinity for them and were not predestined for them. The distinction between the exoteric and the esoteric, once made by philosophers, was found among the Indians as well as among Greeks, Persians, and Muslims. Basically, it was found everywhere that people believed in an order of rank and *not* in equality and equal rights. The difference between these terms is not that the exoteric stands outside and sees, values, measures, and judges from this external position rather than from some internal one. What is more essential is that the exoteric sees things up from below — while the esoteric sees them *down from above*! [. . .] There are books that have inverse values for soul and for health, depending on whether they are used by the lower souls and lowlier life-forces, or by the higher and more powerful ones. In the first case, these books are dangerous, and cause deterioration and dissolution; in the second case, they are the heralds' calls that summon the most courageous to *their* courage.

> [Unsere höchsten Einsichten müssen — und sollen! — wie Thorheiten, unter Umständen wie Verbrechen klingen, wenn sie unerlaubter Weise Denen zu Ohren kommen, welche nicht dafür geartet und vorbestimmt sind. Das Exoterische und das Esoterische, wie man ehedem unter Philosophen unterschied, bei Indern, wie bei Griechen, Persern und Muselmännern, kurz überall, wo man einer Rangordnung und *nicht* an Gleichheit und gleiche Rechte glaubte, — das hebt sich nicht sowohl dadurch von einander ab, dass der Exoteriker draussen steht und von aussen her, nicht von innen her, sieht, schätzt, misst, urtheilt: das Wesentliche ist, dass er von Unten hinauf die Dinge sieht, — der Esoteriker aber *von Oben herab*! [. . .] Es giebt Bücher, welche für Seele und Gesundheit einen umgekehrten Werth haben, je nachdem die niedere Seele, die niedrigere Lebenskraft oder aber die höhere und gewaltigere sich ihrer bedienen: im ersten Fall sind es gefährliche, anbröckelnde,

auflösende Bücher, im anderen Heroldsrufe, welche die Tapfersten zu *ihrer* Tapferkeit herausfordern. (*BGE* §30; *KSA* 5, 48–89)][12]

This suggests that the Hyperborean reader would understand the message of the text in a different way than the masses to which Nietzsche reaches out. The aim of *The Anti-Christ* is the revaluation of values, and in order to achieve this goal he must set an end to Christianity, the provider of nihilistic values for almost two thousand years. Accordingly, the beginning of *The Anti-Christ* sets out to discredit Christian compassion (*Mitleid*) because of its hostility toward the evolution of a higher form of human being (sections 2 to 7): "What is more harmful than any vice? — Active sympathy for the ill-constituted and weak — Christianity" (Was ist schädlicher als irgendein Laster? — Das Mitleiden der That mit allen Missrathenen und Schwachen — das Christenthum; *AC* §2; *KSA* 6, 170). A world freed of its decadent values makes space for life as "an instinct for growth, for continuance, for accumulation of forces, for *power*: where the will to power is lacking there is decline" (Instinkt für Wachsthum, für Dauer, für Häufung von Kräften, für *Macht*: wo der Wille zur Macht fehlt, giebt es Niedergang; *AC* §6; *KSA* 6, 172). The revaluation of values will bring about this new world of powerful individuals, a process which can only begin once the declining values of Christianity have been destroyed. This is the aspect that differentiates the readers of *The Anti-Christ*: the Hyperborean reader understands the intention of the book, and has already seen through the sickening character of Christianity; but for those who have not, the book becomes a decisive test of their allegiance. Those who can endure a world without Christian compassion, who can affirm the call for a world characterized by the will to power, will be part of the future development of humankind; in contrast, those who cannot follow the anti-Christian path outlined in the book might already have been too weakened by Christian morality — they have to perish in order to make the higher type of human being prosper. In this way the book becomes the decisive device for Nietzsche's process of selection. Accordingly, he is not interested in a debate on philosophical or theological grounds — though sometimes he seems to argue that way[13] — but his intention is purely rhetorical, in that he wants to overwhelm and shatter convictions in order to ask his reader: Can you still bear this?

But the selection of his audience is a means, not an end. His true aim is the revaluation of values. If the revaluation of values were identical with the aim of *The Anti-Christ*, which is to deliver the final death blow to Christianity, the revaluation would lack a replacement for the abandoned values and remain a purely destructive exercise.[14] Investigating Nietzsche's use of the concept throughout his entire work, Thomas Brobjer has differentiated between four different meanings that seem to overlap at times: (a) the bestowal of new meanings on old values (trans-valuation); (b) critical questioning of hitherto dominant values; (c) the change of what is currently of high value into its opposite (reversal); and (d) the return to former values of nobility (revaluation).[15] The final meaning, which Brobjer champions, poses the problem that the address-ees of Nietzsche's message, the strong and noble immoralists, would not accept the introduction of any prescriptive moral system — not even the pre-Socratic Greek model.[16] Nietzsche's new values cannot be stated in general terms.

Nevertheless, in the final passages of *The Anti-Christ* Nietzsche gives us a hint as to what the revaluation of values might be. In section 61, the concept is used in the context of Nietzsche's praise of the Renaissance:

> Is it at last understood, is there a *desire* to understand, *what* the Renaissance was? The *revaluation of Christian values*, the attempt, undertaken with every expedient, with every instinct, with genius of every kind, to bring about the victory of the opposing values, the *noble* values. . .
>
> [Versteht man endlich, *will* man verstehn, *was* die Renaissance war? *Die Umwerthung der christlichen Werthe*, der Versuch, mit allen Mit-teln, mit allen Instinkten, mit allem Genie unternommen, die *Gegen*-Werthe, die *vornehmen* Werthe zum Sieg bringen. . . (*AC* §61; *KSA* 6, 250)]

In this instance, Nietzsche specifies what he means by revaluation — writing about a revaluation of Christian values that are opposed by the noble values at the heart of the Renaissance. This would be in line with Brobjer's con-ception of revaluation, but this conception does not fit in with Nietzsche's perspectival skepticism and his pledge for the individualistic self-determina-tion of noble individuals. It also makes one wonder why Nietzsche quali-fies the values he means to revaluate as "Christian." The final paragraph, §62 — though jubilant about the end of Christianity — does not lead us back to such ancient values or to any other value system:

> And one calculates *time* from the *dies nefastus* on which this fatality arose — from the *first* day of Christianity! — *Why not rather from its last?* — *From today?* — Revaluation of all values!
>
> [Und man rechnet die *Zeit* nach dem dies nefastus, mit dem dies Verhängnis anhob, — nach dem *ersten* Tag des Christen-thums! — *Warum nicht lieber nach seinem letzten?* — Nach *Heute?* — Umwerthung aller Werthe!. . . (*AC* §62; *KSA* 6, 253)]

This open ending seems deliberate. Nietzsche's audience — or those who would willingly follow him to the end of the text — is such that it cannot subscribe to a new canon of values: each one should be his or her own lawgiver. This causes a major problem, as Nietzsche finished *The Anti-Christ* with a set of laws entitled "Law against Christianity" ("Gesetz wider das Christenthum"; *KSA* 6, 254). How is it possible that Nietzsche's emphatic pledge for moral self-determination ends with a dogmatic set of seven rules?

It is not only the dogmatic character of the *Gesetz* that presents us with a conundrum; the way in which the text is delivered to us is equally astounding. Erich Podach was the first editor to realize that the page with the *Gesetz* that Nietzsche had glued between two blank pages in the manuscript had originally been intended to conclude *The Anti-Christ*.[17] In this, he followed a comment made by Peter Gast during his time at the Nietzsche archive: "See the last pasted page of the manuscript of *The Anti-Christ*, when read against the light" (Siehe letztes zugeklebtes Blatt des Manuskripts des Antichrists gegen's Licht zu lesen).[18] Montinari agreed with Podach on this point, though he decided to print the *Gesetz* in a smaller font in order to pinpoint the uncertainty about Nietzsche's intentions when he affixed the text between these two pages. Was it secrecy on Nietzsche's part? Did he have second thoughts about its publication? Montinari admits that there is no final answer to why Nietzsche covered his law with blank pages (*KSA* 14, 452).

Taking this uncertainty about Nietzsche's intentions into consideration, the *Gesetz wider das Christenthum* does not seem a strong foundation for an argument. One could dismiss it and claim that Nietzsche did realize that the post-Christian individual could not be led by dogmatic laws. But a careful reading of the partner text *Ecce Homo* does not allow for such an easy escape. In section 5 of "Why I Write such Good Books" ("Warum ich so gute Bücher schreibe"), Nietzsche quotes the fourth sentence of his *Gesetz*:

> And so as to leave no doubt about my views, which in this respect are as honorable as they are strict, I want to share one more principle from my moral code against *vice*: with the word "vice" I am combating every kind of anti-nature or, if you like pretty words, idealism. The principle runs thus: "preaching chastity is a public incitement to perversity. All despising of the sexual life, all besmirching of it by calling it 'impure' is the crime of crimes against life — it is the true sin against the holy spirit of life."

> [Und damit ich über meine in diesem Betracht ebenso honette als strenge Gesinnung keinen Zweifel lasse, will ich noch einen Satz aus meinem Moral-Codex gegen das *Laster* mittheilen: mit dem Wort Laster bekämpfe ich jede Art Widernatur oder wenn man schöne Worte liebt, Idealismus. Der Satz heißt: "die Predigt der Keuschheit ist eine öffentlich Aufreizung zur Widernatur. Jede Verachtung

des geschlechtlichen Lebens, jede Verunreinigung desselben durch den Begriff 'unrein' ist das Verbrechen selbst am Leben, — ist die eigentliche Sünde wider den heiligen Geist des Lebens." — (*EH* "Why I Write Such Good Books" §5; *KSA* 6, 307)]

This quotation of the *Gesetz* indicates that Nietzsche intended to publish it elsewhere, though it remains a paradoxical fact that *The Anti-Christ* was supposed to be published after *Ecce Homo*.

If the editors of the critical edition were right in publishing the *Gesetz* as part of *The Anti-Christ*, the reader or commentator has to supplement its law-like character with the perspectival elements of the main text. One possible answer lies in the aforementioned differentiation of exoteric and esoteric contents: Nietzsche's secrecy about the *Gesetz* could suggest that this is a message to the initiated. Of course they would not accept a dogmatic set of rules and would dismiss it anyway, but as Nietzsche's letters show, his intention was to spread the message to as many as possible. Wouldn't it be handy to issue his initiated reader with a small manifesto that would help furthering the cause of the revaluation? The *Gesetz wider das Christenthum* delivers the message of *The Anti-Christ* in a nutshell: Nietzsche's device for selection in a short set of rules.

The decisive proof of allegiance comes in the last sentence. After six laws issuing rules against the priest, the mass, the philosopher, the church, chastity, contact with priests, and the Christian language, the law states: "*Seventh clause*: the rest follows from this" (*Siebenter Satz*: Der Rest folgt daraus; *KSA* 6, 254). This resembles the open ending of section 62 and confirms the open character of the revaluation of values. People who had been initiated would not have to follow the first six laws, anyway, as they have already abandoned (or never been infected by) Christian values, whereas those who might struggle with the offensive contents of the first six laws would not qualify to become creators of their own values. What follows is the separation of those still bound by Christian morality — for Nietzsche, Christianity needs and therefore deliberately causes disease and weakness among its believers — from those who are ready to face a world that is will to power and nothing else.

Accordingly, the preface and the first six chapters of *The Anti-Christ* are concerned with defining the Hyperborean reader and identifying Christianity as the main obstacle to the development of mankind. Nietzsche introduces his idea for the breeding of a higher type of human being that affirms the world in its true nature, that is, the will to power. In contrast, Christianity's emphasis on compassion is life denying and diametrically opposed to such world affirmation. Once he has identified his target, Nietzsche launches the main thrust of his book: the opposition between science, or "Wissenschaft" — in the wider sense of striving for knowledge — and faith. Nietzsche's chosen title *The Anti-Christ* should make it clear to everyone that the author of the text is on the side of science; at least, if the reader has a firm knowledge of Schopenhauer's philosophy. As Jörg Salaquarda has convincingly shown, Nietzsche's use and understanding of the concept of the Antichrist draws heavily on the following passage from Schopenhauer's *Parerga und Paralipomena*:[19]

> That the world has only a physical and not a moral significance is the greatest, most pernicious and fundamental of errors, the real *perversity* of the mind. At bottom, it is also that which faith has personified as the Antichrist.

> [Daß die Welt bloß eine physische, keine moralische, Bedeutung habe, ist der größte, der verderblichste, der fundamentale Irrthum, die eigentliche *Perversität* der Gesinnung, und ist wohl im Grunde auch Das, was der Glaube als der Antichrist personificirt hat.][20]

As this passage shows, Schopenhauer turns against any materialist understanding that would explain the world in purely physical terms and thereby reject the existence of a moral meaning. Schopenhauer's identification of this position with the Christian definition of the Antichrist gives Nietzsche the chance to bring forward his critique of compassion in both Christianity's and Schopenhauer's ethics. Siding partly with this definition and slipping into the role of the Antichrist also enables Nietzsche to prevent his arguments from becoming a mere negative reaction to Christian values: instead the Antichrist's view of the world is freed of any moral and metaphysical prejudices and is only based on unrestricted scientific knowledge.

Those free spirits who have embarked on this journey of knowledge, Nietzsche's initiated Hyperborean readers, represent in themselves a revaluation of values as they oppose the hitherto valid concepts of "true" and "untrue." Up until now, their skeptical gaze could not keep up with the power of the distorted view of Idealist philosophy, a derivate of theology and the priest's invective against life: "It is necessary to say *whom* we feel to be our antithesis — the theologians and all that has theologian blood in its veins — our entire philosophy" (Es ist nothwendig zu sagen, *wen* wir als unseren Gegensatz fühlen — die Theologen und Alles, was Theologen-Blut im Leibe hat — unsere ganze Philosophie. . . .; *AC* §8; *KSA* 6, 174). The theologian's instinct (*Theologeninstinkt*) becomes most strikingly evident in philosophy as an Idealistic devaluation of reality. By endorsing the pure spirit while at the same time demonizing the body and the materialist world, the Idealist as well as the priest, from the outset, made any quest for truth impossible: according to the logic of theology, finding the truth in an ideal, non-existing world — that is, in faith — is morally good; whereas the claim for the truth of reality and the existing sensational world is deemed wrong, hence morally evil.

The role that Nietzsche ascribes here to the priest as well as to the oppositions of "good" and "bad," or "good" and "evil," would have been familiar to the reader of Nietzsche's writings: they are reminiscent of his 1887 polemic, *On the Genealogy of Morals* (*Zur Genealogie der Moral*). In the first section of his genealogy, Nietzsche describes how the resentment of the weak — under the guidance of the priestly caste — turned the nobles' moral equation of life affirmation with the good and life denial with the bad into its opposite: the nobles' affirmation of life becomes morally evil and the ascetic ideal of life denial good.[21] In *The Anti-Christ*, Nietzsche describes this will-to-power assertion of the priest in terms of *Theologeninstinkt* and *Theologenblut*, and his statement that the Protestant pastor is the grandfather of German philosophy has to be understood as the resurrection of the ascetic ideal in philosophy.

Throughout the text Nietzsche repeats, refines, and sharpens the opposition between science and faith: "'Faith' as an imperative is a *veto* against science" (Der "Glaube" als Imperativ ist das *Veto* gegen die Wissenschaft; *AC* §47; *KSA* 6, 225). Religion in the form of Christianity is the "arch-enemy" (Todfeind) of the "world's wisdom" — that is, science. Philology and medicine in particular cannot be reconciled with any form of faith. Philology looks at the ground of the "holy books" and reveals its arguments to be lies; medicine on the other hand recognizes the "physiological decay" (physiologische Verkommenheit) of the Christian believer.

A thorough philological examination of the Christian doctrines is bound to prove them to be wrong. Nietzsche argues that as the shift away from reality and the claim that there is truth in a world beyond lies at the heart of the Christian argument, its fundamental base is essentially at odds with truth. Nietzsche's genealogical delineation goes even a step further by claiming that Christianity is not only aware of its untruth but has also deliberately created a lie. For Christianity it does not matter if something is true, but it is of utter importance that something is believed to be true. The scientific, rational or scholarly quest for true knowledge stands in sharp contrast to this faith; it is the forbidden path, as it undermines the believer's hope in a better world beyond.

The will to truth — as Nietzsche calls this striving for knowledge that would not even shy away from questioning its own standpoint — has become so dominant that no one can deny the lies that undergird the Christian faith anymore. Being a Christian in contemporary times is, Nietzsche states, consequently obscene: this belief requires shutting one's eyes against the fact that the theologian, the priest, and the pope do not only err but knowingly lie. Again, here Nietzsche links this argument to his description of the priest's role in *On the Genealogy of Morals*, where the priest's aim is to devalue and diminish the present world in order to gain power.

In his attempt to explain this attitude of the Christian believer, Nietzsche resorts to psychology. Sections 50 to 55 contain his "psychology of the believer," and it is here he comes back to aphorism 483 from volume 1 of *Human, All Too Human* (*Menschliches, Allzumenschliches*): "*Enemies of truth* — Convictions are more dangerous enemies of truth than lies" (*Feinde der Wahrheit* — Ueberzeugungen sind gefährlichere Feinde der Wahrheit, als Lügen; *HA* I §483; *KSA* 2, 317). This time he questions what was then assumed, the opposition between conviction and lie. Looking at the way a conviction develops, Nietzsche argues that it originates from its opposite, meaning there was a time when the alleged truth was very much in doubt. He asks why this later conviction could not have been derived from a lie. Lying means, according to Nietzsche, "wanting *not* to see something one does see, wanting not to see something *as* one sees it" (Etwas *nicht* sehn wollen, das man sieht, Etwas nicht *so* sehn wollen, wie man es sieht; *AC* §55; *KSA* 6, 283). Hence, the conviction, or faith, and the lie are one and the same. The priest's awareness of this equation and his consequent fear of the believer questioning the very foundation of his faith lead him to attribute the decision about truth or falsehood to higher instances such as "God," "God's will," and the "revelation of God." This results in the alleged infallibility of the priest as the mouthpiece of God, and in the Christian's inability to follow the rational and scientific path of truth.

In *The Anti-Christ*, Nietzsche does not go into so much detail concerning the priest's motivations — his references to the concept of will to power and the detailed analysis in *On the Genealogy of Morals* are sufficient — but he is quite explicit about the way the priest achieves his powerful status. At the heart of Christian power stands disease; hence, the priest's fear of medicine as the other major enemy threatening his power: "Christianity *needs* sickness almost as much as Hellenism needs a superfluity of health — *making* sick is the true hidden objective of the Church's whole system of salvation procedures" (Das Christentum hat die Krankheit *nöthig*, ungefähr wie das Griechenthum einen Überschuss von Gesundheit nöthig hat, — krank-machen ist die eigentliche Hinterabsicht des ganzen Heilsprozeduren-System's der Kirche; *AC* §51; *KSA* 6, 230). In contrast to Buddhism, which was created for an exhausted humanity weakened in its instincts, the precondition for Christianity was a strong but wayward individual, the savage whose intention was to hurt others. Christianity wanted to become the master of the beasts, Nietzsche states, and the way to achieve that was to make them ill. Again, this motif can be found in *On the Genealogy of Morals*, where Nietzsche anticipates one of the most fundamental principles of Freud's instinct theory: "All instincts which are not discharged outwardly *turn inwards*" (Alle Instinkte, welche sich nicht nach Aussen entladen, *wenden sich nach Innen*; *GM* II §16; *KSA* 5, 322).

In *The Anti-Christ*, Nietzsche is mainly concerned with another Christian attempt to weaken and sicken the savage beast, to cut its life-affirming ties with the world. The aforementioned distortion of "good" and "bad," or "true" and "false," maintains that there exists an ideal world beyond. The emphasis of life is deferred from the here-and-now to a non-existent world. Thus, life becomes meaningless, or as Nietzsche put it: "So to live that there is no longer any *meaning* in living: *that* now becomes the 'meaning' of life" (So zu leben, dass es keinen *Sinn* mehr hat, zu leben, *das* wird jetzt zum 'Sinn' des Lebens. . .; *AC* §43; *KSA* 6, 217). Following his argument concerning the morality of the master and the reactive morality of the slave from *On the Genealogy of Morals*, the poisoning of the "noble beast" is, at the same time, the victory of the weak. These weak classes — hitherto suffering from life anyway — are not only able to find comfort in the idea of a world beyond, but also gain an unexpected importance through the concept of individual immortality.

But still the priest has to build up a wall against the threat of knowledge. As science is based on causality, he introduces the concept of sin in order to distort the relationship of cause and effect. In a sophisticated system of guilt and punishment, the suffering of the human being, and thereby the persistence of his misery, is maintained. Looking inside to explain moral failure instead of examining the outer world scientifically ensures that the sufferer resorts to the priest for a release of tension and for absolution. Concepts such as guilt and punishment, the teachings of "grace," "redemption," and "forgiveness" — according to Nietzsche, concepts without any real content and therefore nothing more than plain lies — introduce fictitious entities in the relation of cause and effect and thus destroy the precondition for any true knowledge.

Christianity needs the suffering of its followers. Once the system of internal guilt and punishment is in place, the Christian remains trapped in a *folie circulaire* between suffering and absolution through the priest. As Nietzsche explains it:

> I once permitted myself to describe the entire Christian penance- and redemption training (which can be studied best today in England) as a methodologically induced *folie circulaire*, naturally on a soil already prepared for it, that is to say a thoroughly morbid soil.
>
> [Ich habe mir einmal erlaubt, den ganzen christlichen Buss- und Erlösungstraining (den man am besten heute in England studiert) als eine methodisch erzeugte *folie circulaire* zu bezeichnen, wie billig, auf einem bereits dazu vorbereiteten, das heisst gründlich morbiden Boden. (*AC* §51; *KSA* 6, 231)]

In *Ecce Homo* Nietzsche also speaks of a "*folie circulaire* between spasms of atonement and redemption-hysteria" (*folie circulaire* zwischen

Bußkrampf und Erlösungshysterie; *EH* "Why I Am a Destiny" §8; *KSA* 6, 374). As his unpublished fragments of this time reveal, he thereby follows the theory of Charles Féré (1857–1907), who described religious monomania as a *folie circulaire* between depression and hyperactivity.[22] The inner world of the Christian believer is similar to the one of the over-excited and exhausted individual. Christianity and the priest have to secure the continuity of this vulnerable mental state. This is the reason why Christianity, Nietzsche concludes, places sickness above all other values.

The term Nietzsche introduces for this physiological decay is decadence. It subsumes those who suffer and those who need a fictitious world to flee from reality. Christianity, by means of distorting cause and effect, offers this possibility. Reality becomes forged, devalued, and negated. The concept of God thereby opposes nature, which accordingly must itself be condemned. In contrast to the decadent peoples, who have to take refuge in a good god separated from evil nature, the strong peoples project qualities on to a mighty God that reflects their own powers. According to Nietzsche, such a powerful God cannot be restricted to sheer goodness, but incorporates all the life-affirming character traits of his people. Here, Nietzsche draws the opposition between will to power and decadence: "Wherever the will to power declines in any form there is every time also a physiological regression, a *décadence*" (Wo in irgendwelcher Form der Wille zur Macht niedergeht, giebt es jedes Mal auch einen physiologischen Rückgang, eine décadence; *AC* §17; *KSA* 6, 183).

The pure form of decadence, according to Nietzsche, is expressed in the type of the redeemer (Typus des Erlösers). Sections 28 to 35 of *The Anti-Christ* are dedicated to Nietzsche's attempt to pin down the psychological characteristics of this type. Nietzsche begins with a strident critique of Ernest Renan's description of Jesus in the *Life of Jesus* (*Vie de Jésus*, 1863).[23] According to Renan, Jesus can only be understood if one applies to him the attributes of a hero and a genius. Such concepts, Nietzsche argues, are in complete contrast to the Gospels. A psychological extraction of the redeemer's character traits from the Gospels reveals the opposite: not a hero, but someone who is completely unable to withstand the realities of life. According to Nietzsche's verdict, the redeemer is an expression of physiological degeneracy who withdraws completely from reality. Inside himself, he finds the Kingdom of God, which is built on the absence of any ability to negate or reject — Nietzsche uses the term "idiot" to describe this degenerative state. It has frequently been argued that Nietzsche, while using this reference to idiocy, was not only thinking in physiologically derogative terms, but also had Dostoyevsky's Prince Myshkin in mind. In fact, Nietzsche mentions the Russian writer two chapters later: "One has to regret that no Dostoyevsky lived in the neighborhood of this most interesting *décadent*; I mean someone who could feel the thrilling fascination of such a combination of the sublime, the sick, and the childish" (Man hätte zu bedauern, dass nicht ein Dostoiewsky in der Nähe dieses interessanten décadent gelebt hat, ich meine Jemand, der gerade den ergreifenden Reiz einer solchen Mischung von Sublimen, Krankem und Kindlichem zu empfinden wusste; *AC* §31; *KSA* 6, 202). Though it is not proven that Nietzsche had read Dostoyevsky's novel, he was indeed familiar with some of his writings, especially through the French collection entitled *L'Esprit Souterrain* (*Notes from the Underground*).[24]

The psychology of the redeemer is important to Nietzsche's critique of Christianity, as it enables him to separate the redeemer on the Cross from the distortions that were introduced by his followers after his death. According to Nietzsche, this type of the redeemer, Christ, existed only once and died on the Cross. His life itself was evangelical practice; the Kingdom of God was his internal world. No one else after him could have viewed outer reality in the same indifferent way, as sheer symbolic material and sign. For him, there was no concept of a world beyond, and death was not part of the good message, that is, the *Evangelium*. But the death of Christ posed a problem to his followers who, in order to increase and maintain their power, had to perform a complete distortion of evangelical practice. This was the beginning of what Nietzsche called the *Dysangelium* (*AC* §39; *KSA* 6, 211).

The disciples introduced a negating aspect into Christianity — something that was completely alien to the message of the redeemer. By making the ruling Jewish caste responsible for the death of Christ, they unleashed their rage against the prevailing rules. According to Nietzsche, this was an act of resentment that reversed the whole of evangelical practice, which was hitherto solely embodied by the life of the redeemer. Furthermore, this practice could not end with the death on the Cross, which would have thrown the disciples back into insignificance. Hence, they linked the life of Jesus with the Jewish prophecy of the Messiah and transferred the Kingdom of God from the within to the beyond — the eschatological end of time.

In order to fit the death of Christ into their new teaching, the early believers resorted to the pagan concept of sacrificial death: the death of God's Son was necessary to wipe away the sins of humanity. While Jesus represented the identity of God and the human being, the new system opened up a huge gap between God and his creation. Because of the introduction of sin and guilt, the redeemer became associated with the doctrines of Judgment and the Second Coming, the sacrificial death, the Resurrection and the immortality of the soul. The height of this distortion of evangelical practice was reached with the Apostle Paul — for Nietzsche, the epitome of the priest's will to power — who invented the history of early Christianity and even forged the history of Israel in order to justify his claim for Jesus as the Messiah.

In Paul, the priest's attempt to impose his power on the low masses and to weaken the strong caste — as described in *On the Genealogy of Morals* — becomes manifest. The introduction of the concept of individual immortality led to the withdrawal of any "feeling of reverence and distance between man and man" (Ehrfurchts- und Distanz-Gefühl zwischen Mensch und Mensch; *AC* §43; *KSA* 6, 217–18). But, according to Nietzsche, precisely this natural difference forms the precondition for the maintenance of order in society, as well as for the further development of humankind. Christianity has declared war on this feeling of difference and knowledge of rank and distance, for which Nietzsche coined the phrase "pathos of distance," or *Pathos der Distanz*. The final part of *Beyond Good and Evil*, entitled "What is noble?" ("Was ist vornehm?"), highlights the importance Nietzsche ascribes to this concept:

> Every enhancement so far in the type "man" has been the work of an aristocratic society — and that is how it will be, again and again, since this sort of society believes in a long ladder of rank order and value distinctions between men, and in some sense needs slavery. Without the *pathos of distance* as it grows out of the ingrained differences between stations, out of the way the ruling caste maintains an overview and keeps looking down on subservient types and tools, and out of this caste's equally continuous exercise in obeying and commanding, in keeping away and below — without *this* pathos, that *other*, more mysterious pathos could not have been grown at all, that demand for new expansions of distance within the soul itself, the development of states that are increasingly high, rare, distant, tautly drawn and comprehensive, and in short, the enhancement of the type "man," the constant "self-overcoming of man" (to use a moral formula in a supra-moral sense).

> [Jede Erhöhung des Typus "Mensch" war bisher das Werk einer aristokratischen Gesellschaft — und so wird es immer wieder sein: als einer Gesellschaft, welche an eine lange Leiter der Rangordnung und Werthverschiedenheit von Mensch und Mensch glaubt und Sklaverei in irgend einem Sinne nöthig hat. Ohne das Pathos der Distanz, wie es aus dem eingefleischten Unterschied der Stände, aus dem beständigen Ausblick und Herabblick der herrschenden Kaste auf Unterthänige und Werkzeuge und aus ihrer ebenso beständigen Übung im Gehorchen und Befehlen, Nieder- und Fernhalten erwächst, könnte auch jenes andre geheimnissvollere Pathos gar nicht erwachsen, jenes Verlangen nach immer neuer Distanz-Erweiterung innerhalb der Seele selbst, die Herausbildung immer höherer, seltnerer, fernerer, weitgespannterer, umfänglicherer Zustände, kurz eben die Erhöhung des Typus "Mensch," die fortgesetzte "Selbst-Überwindung des Menschen," um eine moralische Formel in einem übermoralischen Sinne zu nehmen. (*BGE* §257; *KSA* 5, 205)]

In *The Anti-Christ*, Nietzsche supports his theory of the necessity of hierarchies by opposing the Christian teaching with the *Laws of Manu*. The *Manusmrti* or *Mānava-Dharmaśāstra* is the earliest *Dharmaśāstra*, a Sanskrit text regulating the religious and legal duties of Hindus. Though the first English translation by Sir William Jones dates back to 1794, Nietzsche used the French version of Louis Jacolliot from 1876, entitled *Les Légitateurs Religieux*.[25] The dubious accuracy of this translation has been frequently pointed out.[26] According to Jacolliot, his translation was based on Tamil manuscripts that represent the pure form of the *Manusmrti*. The consensus in today's Indology is that the deviation of these manuscripts from most other versions is due to later changes and amendments, and that Jacolliot fabricated a historical myth to support his theory that the Semitic tribes were originally the Chandalas who were driven out from India.

Why Nietzsche, who so expressively advocates a thoroughly philological reading of texts, turns a blind eye to Jacolliot's speculative and so obviously biased translation and commentary remains unclear. Sommer comes to the conclusion that the *Laws of Manu* fit the bill too well for Nietzsche to have engaged in a philological critique of Jacolliot.[27] For, according to Nietzsche, the distinction between different castes in the *Laws of Manu* follows the natural order. Interestingly enough, he talks only of three castes, not four as in the Law. The first is constituted by the *very few*, who "find their happiness where others would find their destruction" (finden ihr Glück, worin Andre ihren Untergang finden würden; *AC* §57; *KSA* 6, 243). Here one is reminded of Nietzsche's differentiation of the exoteric and the esoteric, and one could also find similarities with the description of the Hyperborean reader of *The Anti-Christ*, for whom happiness and beauty in themselves are an affirmation of life. (Equally, Nietzsche seems keen to neglect the Brahmans' roles as priests in Hindu society.) The second caste is made up of those who are physically and temperamentally strong: the kings, noble warriors, and judges who execute the laws. Finally, the third caste is the large mass of the *mediocre*, who build the conditions that make possible the exceptional few of the other castes. Each caste has its rights and prohibitions: "A right is a privilege. The privilege of each is determined by the nature of his being" (Ein Recht ist ein Vorrecht. In seiner Art hat Jeder auch sein Vorrecht; *AC* §57; *KSA* 6, 243). It has been pointed out that Nietzsche's mind was more occupied with Plato's *Republic* than with the *Laws of Manu*, and his three-part (as opposed to four-part) model of society seems to support this assumption.[28] His description does indeed resemble Plato's idea of the structure of society as consisting of philosophers, warriors, and craftsmen.[29] But there is a different understanding of society in Plato's state: whereas according to the *Laws of Manu* birth determines the rank and cements the given order, in Plato's society every child is raised in the same way and is only later positioned according to its talents; there is even the possibility of changing one's place in society in later years.[30] Thus Nietzsche's introduction of the *Laws of Manu* can either be read as an unconvincing adaptation of Plato's philosophers' state or as an attempt to back up his theory concerning the pathos of distance by using an interpretation of a text, the philological uncertainty of which should have been obvious to him. In the latter interpretation, it is an exquisite example of Nietzsche's argument in *Human, All Too Human* that convictions are more dangerous to truth than lies. According to Sommer, the main aim of Nietzsche's exercise in section 57 is to provoke: not only is it an affront against Christianity but also — as an argument against the self-determination of humans — against the Enlightened view of the world.[31] (Though Nietzsche shares the scientific view with today's advocates of atheism, his stance against the Enlightenment and its postulate of human autonomy is what decisively differentiates his position from that of, for instance, Richard Dawkins.)

Earlier we described this provocative character of *The Anti-Christ* — its attempt to overwhelm and unsettle the reader, even at the cost of inconsistencies in its argument — as a selection tool to separate those who can bear the world after the Death of God from the weak ones who still cling to Christianity. This brings us finally back to *The Anti-Christ* as Nietzsche's revaluation of values. A passage from *Ecce Homo* — a text that is, in so many ways, inseparable from *The Anti-Christ* — sheds light on his undertaking. Here, Nietzsche describes himself as a psychologist, whose task it is to perform the revaluation of values:

> Precisely that fine art of grasping and conceptualizing in general, that feel for nuances, that psychology of "seeing around corners," and everything else that suits me, was learned back then and is the real gift of that time in which everything in me refined itself, the act of observation itself as well as the organs of observation. From the optics of the sick towards healthier concepts and values, and the other way round — to look down from the abundance and self-certainty of the rich life into the secret work of the decadent instinct — that was my longest form of training, my real experience, if ever I became master of anything in this. I now have it in my grasp, and have the ability to *rearrange perspectives*: this is the primary reason why for me alone a "revaluation of all values" is possible at all. —

> [Selbst jene Filigran-Kunst des Greifens und Begreifens überhaupt, jene Finger für nuances, jene Psychologie des "Um-die-Ecke-sehns" und was sonst mir eignet, ward damals erst gelernt, ist das eigentliche Geschenk jener Zeit, in der Alles sich bei mir verfeinerte, die Beobachtung selbst wie alle Organe der Beobachtung. Von der Kranken-Optik aus nach *gesünderen* Begriffen und Werthen, und

wiederum umgekehrt aus der Fülle und Selbstgewissheit des *reichen* Lebens hinuntersehen in die heimliche Arbeit des Décadence-Instinkts — das war meine längste Übung, meine eigentliche Erfahrung, wenn irgend worin wurde ich darin Meister. Ich habe es jetzt in der Hand, ich habe die Hand dafür, *Perspektiven umzustellen*: erster Grund, weshalb für mich allein vielleicht eine "Umwerthung aller Werthe" überhaupt möglich ist. — (*EH* "Why I Am So Wise" §1; *KSA* 6, 266)]

It is the union of the decadent and the anti-decadent that enables Nietzsche to change perspectives in order to establish a revaluation of values, something he undertakes through writing *The Anti-Christ*. In *Ecce Homo* Nietzsche describes how, during his thirty-sixth year, he underwent a physical crisis that bestowed upon him the utmost clarity of dialectical thinking — something he regards as the symptom of decadence par excellence. In *The Anti-Christ* he specifies decadence as the weakness to "lie oneself out of actuality" because of suffering: "But to suffer from actuality means to be an abortive actuality. . . . The preponderance of feelings of displeasure over feelings of pleasure is the *cause* of a fictitious morality and religion: such a preponderance, however, provides the *formula* for *décadence*. . ." (Aber an der Wirklichkeit leiden heißt eine *verunglückte* Wirklichkeit sein. . . Das Übergewicht der Unlustgefühle über die Lustgefühle ist die *Ursache* jener fiktiven Moral und Religion: ein solches Übergewicht giebt aber die *Formel* ab für *décadence*. . .; *AC* §15; *KSA* 6, 182). Bringing Nietzsche's arguments about decadence and the revaluation of values together offers the surprising conclusion that, in order to perform the revaluation of values, Nietzsche has to take up the position of the anti-decadent and the decadent, that is, the position of the anti-Christ and the position of . . . Christ! The latter is not to be understood as the distorted product of the *Dysangelium* but as the type of a pure decadence that Nietzsche describes in his psychology of the redeemer: the one who withdrew from reality because of his physiological incapacity to bear it.[32] When Nietzsche speaks of his personal suffering during the Genoese winter of 1879 he speaks of the "deepest physiological weakness" (mit der tiefsten physiologischen Schwäche), "an excess of pain" (mit einem Excess von Schmerzgefühl) and "torture" (Martern; *EH* "Why I Am So Wise" §1; *KSA* 6, 265). The proximity of his self-description to his explication of the redeemer type is evident.

The anti-decadent of the revaluation of values is manifested in the Antichrist, which, in accordance with Schopenhauer, Nietzsche understands as the one who sees the world in an extra-moral sense: no moral values distort his scientific gaze, which reveals the world to be will to power and nothing else. In his late writings, Nietzsche comes up with another name for this worldview: it is Dionysos. Given the tension between the opposite pairs Nietzsche wants to unite, between the anti-decadent and the decadent, between the Antichrist and Christ, it is not at all surprising that the notes he wrote shortly after his mental breakdown — two months after having finished *The Anti-Christ* — are predominantly signed with one of two names, Dionysos or the Crucified, which finally meld into one:[33]

> But this time I arrive as the victorious Dionysos, he who will make the earth into a festival. . . Not that I have much time . . . the skies are glad that I am here . . . I have also hung upon the cross. . .

> [Dies Mal aber komme ich als der siegreiche Dionysos, der die Erde zu einem Festtag machen wird. . . Nicht daß ich viel Zeit hätte . . . Die Himmel freuen sich, daß ich da bin. . . Ich habe auch am Kreuz gehangen. . .][34]

Notes

The translations from Nietzsche in this essay are from those made by R. J. Hollingdale, Judith Norman, Carol Diethe, and Duncan Large. Specific citations will be given in the notes.

[1] See the entries for July-August 1888 in *Nachgelassene Fragmente 1887–1889* (*KSA* 13, 18[17], 537–38).

[2] See Mazzino Montinari, "Ein neuer Abschnitt in Nietzsches 'Ecce Homo,'" *Nietzsche-Studien* 1 (1972): 380–418; and "Nietzsches Nachlass von 1885 bis 1888 oder Textkritik und Wille zur Macht," in *Nietzsche lesen* (Berlin, New York: de Gruyter, 1982), 92–119; translated as "A New Section in Nietzsche's *Ecce Homo*," and "Nietzsche's Unpublished Writings from 1885 to 1888; or, Textual Criticism and the Will to Power," in *Reading Nietzsche*, trans. Greg Whitlock (Urbana, IL: Illinois UP, 2003), 103–40 and 80–102. Before Montinari, these arguments were also brought forward by Ernst Horneffer, *Nietzsches letztes Schaffen* (Jena: Diederichs, 1907); Walter Kaufmann, *Nietzsche: Philosopher, Psychologist, Antichrist* (Princeton: Princeton UP, 1950); and by the editor of the first authentic edition of *The Anti-Christ*, Karl Schlechta, in his "Philologischer Nachbericht," in *W* 3, 1383–1432.

[3] Nietzsche's letter to Heinrich Köselitz of 13 February 1888 (my translation; if not otherwise stated, translations in the article are mine). For Nietzsche's text, see *KSA* 12, 9[1]-10[206], 339–582 and *KSA* 13, 11[1]-11[417], 9–194.

[4] The title of Nietzsche's work *Der Antichrist* can be translated as *The Anti-Christ*, but also as *The Anti-Christian*: both translations are equally possible, although the former is conventionally used.

[5] See also Nietzsche's letters to Georg Brandes of 20 November 1888 (*KSB* 8, 482) and to Carl Fuchs of 11 December 1888 (*KSB* 8, 521–22).

[6] "Eidesstattliche Erklärung von Heinrich Köselitz," Weimar 16 May 1906 (Goethe-Schiller-Archiv, 72/1931).

[7] Mazzino Montinari, *Kommentar zu den Bänden 1–13* (*KSA* 14, 435).

[8] *W* 2, 1161–1235.

[9] Mazzino Montinari, "Nietzsche lesen: Die Götzen-Dämmerung," *Nietzsche-Studien* 13 (1984): 69–79 (72); translated as "Reading Nietzsche," in *Reading Nietzsche*, trans. Whitlock, 5–12.

[10] Friedrich Nietzsche, *Twilight of the Idols; The Anti-Christ*, trans. R. J. Hollingdale (Harmondsworth: Penguin, 1968), 114. In this chapter I have used the following translations of other works by Nietzsche: *Human, All Too Human*, trans. R. J. Hollingdale (Cambridge: Cambridge UP, 1968); *Beyond Good and Evil*, trans. Judith Norman (Cambridge: Cambridge UP, 2002); *On the Genealogy of Morality*, trans. Carol Diethe (Cambridge: Cambridge UP, 1994); and *Ecce Homo*, trans. Duncan Large (Oxford: Oxford UP, 2007).

[11] See Pindar, *The Pythian Odes*, 10: "But neither by taking ship, neither by any travel on foot, to the Hyperborean folk shalt thou find the wondrous way" (*The Extant Odes of Pindar*, trans. Ernest Myers (London: Macmillan, 1912), 52–104 [here: 98]).

[12] Stanley Rosen uses this differentiation to reveal Nietzsche's alleged Platonism in *Thus Spoke Zarathustra* (Stanley Rosen, *The Mask of Enlightenment: Nietzsche's Zarathustra* [New Haven and London: Yale UP, 2004]). For a critique of this argument, see Martin Liebscher, "Nietzsches doppelte Rhetorik und der Wille zur Macht" (review of "Stanley Rosen: The Mask of Enlightenment. Nietzsche's Zarathustra"), H-Net Book Review. H-German@h-net.msu.edu (November 2005).

[13] Notwithstanding its philological merits, Andreas Urs Sommer's commentary on *The Anti-Christ* is mainly an attempt to show the theological and philosophical inconsistencies of Nietzsche's arguments. It seems to me that he misses Nietzsche's actual rhetorical and political intention. See Andreas Urs Sommer, *Friedrich Nietzsches "Der Antichrist"* (Basel: Schwabe, 2000).

[14] Andreas Urs Sommer, "Umwertung aller Werthe," in *Nietzsche-Handbuch: Leben — Werk — Wirkung*, ed. Henning Ottmann (Stuttgart, Weimar: Metzler 2000), 346.

[15] Thomas Brobjer, "On the Revaluation of Values," *Nietzsche-Studien* 25 (1996): 342–48.

[16] Sommer, "Umwertung aller Werthe," 346.

[17] Erich F. Podach, *Friedrich Nietzsches Werke des Zusammenbruchs* (Heidelberg: Rothe, 1961), 400.

[18] See Montinari's commentary (*KSA* 14, 452).

[19] Jörg Salaquarda, "Der Antichrist," *Nietzsche-Studien* 2 (1973): 91–136.

[20] Arthur Schopenhauer, *Parerga und Paralipomena II: Kleine philosophische Schriften*, ed. Wolfgang Freiherr von Löhneysen (Stuttgart: Cotta, 1965), §109, 238.

[21] For further discussion, see the contribution to this volume by Michael Gillespie and Keegan F. Callanan.

[22] See Charles Féré, *Sensation et mouvement* (Paris, 1887). Nietzsche paraphrases Féré in one of his fragmentary notes from the *Nachlass* of 1888 (*KSA* 13, 14[172], 358). For further discussion, see Hans Erich Lampl: "Ex oblivione: Das Féré-Palimpsest. Noten zur Beziehung Friedrich Nietzsche — Charles Féré (1857–1907)," *Nietzsche-Studien* 15 (1986): 225–64. Nietzsche, following Féré, speaks of *Tonizität*, meaning muscular tension.

[23] See Ernest Renan, *Vie de Jésus: Histoire des origines du christianisme*, vol. 1 (Paris: Lévy, 1863).

[24] For Dostoyevsky and Nietzsche, see Charles Anthony Miller, "Nietzsche's 'Discovery' of Dostoevsky," *Nietzsche-Studien* 2 (1973): 202–57; Ekaterina Poljakova, "'Beherzter Fatalismus': Das (Anti-)Christliche in der Perspektive des russischen Denkens," *Nietzscheforschung* 14 (2007): 171–82; and Paolo Stellino, "Jesus als 'Idiot'. Ein Vergleich zwischen Nietzsches *Der Antichrist* und Dostojewskijs *Der Idiot*," *Nietzscheforschung* 14 (2007): 203–12.

[25] Louis Jacolliot, *Les législateurs religieux. Manou. Moïse. Mahomet. Traditions religieuses compares des lois de Manou, de la Bible, du Coran, du Rituel Egyptien, du Zend-Avesta des Parses et des traditions finnoises* (Paris 1876).

[26] Annemarie Etter, "Nietzsche und das Gesetzbuch des Manu," *Nietzsche-Studien* 16 (1987): 340–52. Even in his time Nietzsche should have been aware of Max F. Müller's repudiation of Jacolliot in *Einleitung in die vergleichende Religionswissenschaft* (1874). (Nietzsche borrowed the book from the University of Basel Library on 22 October 1875; see Luca Crescenzi, "Verzeichnis der von Nietzsche aus der UB Basel entliehenen Bücher," *Nietzsche-Studien* 23 (1994): 388–442.)

[27] Sommer, *Friedrich Nietzsches "Der Antichrist,"* 563. See also Etter, "Nietzsche und das Gesetzbuch des Manu," and Michael Ahlsdorf, "Nietzsches Juden: Die philosophische Vereinnahmung des alttestamentarischen Judentums und der Einfluss von Julius Wellhausen in Nietzsches Spätwerk" (dissertation, FU Berlin, 1990); and *Nietzsches Juden: Ein Philosoph formt sich ein Bild* (Aachen: Shaker, 1997).

[28] Sommer, *Friedrich Nietzsches "Der Antichrist,"* 573.

[29] See Plato, *The Republic*, book IV, 11, 435b.

[30] Sommer, *Friedrich Nietzsches "Der Antichrist,"* 573.

[31] Sommer, *Friedrich Nietzsches "Der Antichrist,"* 574.

[32] Nietzsche's psychology of the redeemer is an important point to take on board. Otherwise, one risks pursuing what Peter Köster called a theological "Okkupationstheorie," or the attempt to identify the true content of Nietzsche's philosophy as genuinely Christian and to incorporate his thinking into Christian theology. For further discussion, see Peter Köster, "Nietzsche-Kritik und Nietzsche-Rezeption in der Theologie des 20. Jahrhunderts" [1982], in *Kontroversen um Nietzsche: Untersuchungen zur theologischen Rezeption* (Zurich: Theologischer Verlag, 2003), 175–270.

[33] This is not to say that Nietzsche's final sentence in *Ecce Homo*, "Dionysos versus the Crucified" (Dionysos gegen den Gekreuzigten), should read "Dionysos *and* the Crucified," as Hans Urs von Balthasar has suggested, thus equating the

Christian and the Dionysian world (see Hans Urs von Balthasar, *Apokalypse der deutschen Seele: Studien zu einer Lehre von letzten Haltungen* [1937–39], 3 vols. (Einsiedeln: Johannes Verlag, 1998), 3:71. The crucified has to be read as the decadent whom Nietzsche describes in his psychology of the redeemer, which is the position Nietzsche then unites with the anti-decadent.

[34] From Nietzsche's letter to Cosima Wagner of 3 January 1889 (*KSB* 8, 573).

13: *Ecce Homo*

Paul Bishop

IN THE FINAL APHORISM in the first section of *Twilight of the Idols* (*Götzen-Dämmerung*) Nietzsche tells us: "Formula of my happiness: a Yes, a No, a straight line, a *goal . . .*" (Formel meines Glücks: ein Ja, ein Nein, eine gerade Linie, ein *Ziel . . .*; TI "Sayings and Arrows" §44; *KSA* 6, 66). How Nietzsche chose his path through life, abandoning the zig-zag of his academic, Wagnerian, decadent path for the straight line of his philosophy, which says "yes" (and hence also says "no": by affirming one thing, it also "renounces" another), and how he did so in an exemplary fashion, is the story that he tells in *Ecce Homo*. And he tells it by writing about his life *as if this had been the case*, so whether his account is (f)actually, (auto)biographically true becomes irrelevant. In the beautiful passage that acts as a prooemium to the work, standing between the foreword and the first chapter, Nietzsche (echoing Zarathustra) proposes to tell himself his life —

> *How should I not be grateful to my whole life?* And so I tell myself my life
>
> [Wie sollte ich nicht meinem ganzen Leben dankbar sein? Und so erzähle ich mir mein Leben]

and thereby tells it to us, too (*KSA* 6, 263).[1] But how should we read this story of his life? Although Nietzsche's discussion of his individual works has something important to say about each, this contribution will concentrate on the underlying themes and structuring themes of *Ecce Homo* as a whole as illustrating Nietzsche's claim: "I made out of will to health, to *life*, my philosophy . . ." (ich mache auch meinem Willen zur Gesundheit, zum *Leben*, meine Philosophie . . .; *EH* "Why I Am So Wise" §2; *KSA* 6, 267).

Compositional Background

As the preceding contributions by Carol Diethe on *Twilight of the Idols* and Martin Liebscher on *The Anti-Christ* (*Der Antichrist*) and the following contribution by Alan Schrift on the writings from Nietzsche's *Nachlass* make clear, the years between the completion of work on *Zarathustra*, in the form of its fourth and final part, in 1885 and Nietzsche's collapse on the Piazza Carlo Alberto in Turin on 3 January 1889 witnessed an astonishing, and ever-increasing, productivity on Nietzsche's part. To this period belongs *Ecce Homo*, work on which began, according to its prooemium, on his forty-fourth birthday (15 October 1888).[2] Three weeks later, the text was complete: on 14 November 1888 he told Meta von Salis that "in the meantime a quite unbelievable specimen of *belles lettres*, bearing the title 'Ecce Homo: How One Becomes What One Is,' has taken flight with a flurry of wings and is flapping its way, if I am not greatly deceived, in the direction of Leipzig . . ." (inzwischen hat sich ein sehr unglaubliches Stück Litteratur, das den Titel führt "*Ecce homo.* Wie man wird, was man ist" — auch schon wieder mit Flügeln begabt and flattert, wenn mich nicht Alles täuscht, in der Richtung von Leipzig. . .; *KSB* 8, 471). Toward Leipzig, that is, toward his publisher, C. G. Naumann (see Nietzsche's letter of 6 November 1888; *KSB* 8, 464). Its title gestures, intertextually, away from Nietzsche (and, provocatively, toward Christ, whom Pilate presented to the crowd, saying: "Behold the man!"), and may also recall the tradition, observed in Schulpforta, of the "Ecce," a commemorative service for those who had died, held annually on the eve of the Sunday before Advent, or on the day of a funeral.[3] Nietzsche buries his past, and is reborn again: the text is full of first-person references, and Nietzsche told von Salis: "I am precisely this *homo*, including the *ecce*" (Dieser homo bin ich nämlich selbst, eingerechnet das ecce), going on to wonder about its likely reception, writing: "The attempt to cast some light on me and to cause a bit of a fright is something I've done almost too successfully" (der Versuch, über mich ein wenig Licht *und Schrecken* zu verbreiten, scheint mir fast zu gut gelungen; *KSB* 8, 471).

Ecce Homo undertakes a review of all Nietzsche's major publications[4] — the man as text, then — sandwiched between three opening chapters that ponder Nietzsche's wisdom, cleverness, and ability to write good books — "Warum ich so weise bin," "Warum ich so klug bin," "Warum ich so gute Bücher schreibe" — and a concluding chapter dealing with his significance as a destiny, "Warum ich ein Schicksal bin." The claim made in this "unedifying title" (unerquickliche Überschrift) of his final chapter, Nietzsche told von Salis, was demonstrated to the extent that "in the end one will remain seated in front of me, as no more than a 'mask,' no more than a 'feeling heart'" (daß man, am Schluß, bloß noch als "Larve", bloß noch als "fühlende Brust" vor mir sitzen bleibt; *KSB* 8, 471). As Nietzsche predicted, *Ecce Homo* has retained its capacity to draw in some readers as it repels others; it is, like *Zarathustra*, a book for all and none, with all the unpredictabilities of audience reaction this implies.

If its composition (in the sense of its being committed to paper, not its intellectual structure) was simple, the publication history of *Ecce Homo*, was, like Nietzsche's other late works, considerably more complicated.[5] To cut a long a story short, although Nietzsche got as far as receiving proofs (in two installments) of the first quarter of the text and correcting them, the work never appeared in his lifetime, and it was not published until 1908, in a version that had been subjected to cuts (specifically passages in the first chapter about members of Nietzsche's family), while subsequent editions, by Karl Schlechta in 1956 and Erich F. Podach in 1961, have also been judged unsatisfactory.[6] Yet, although the difficult problem of establishing the text has effectively been solved by the detective work of Mazzino Montinari, the interpretative difficulties posed by the work remain. And they do so not least because, as the prooemium suggests, for Nietzsche, telling his life-story involved not just recounting his autobiography, but also meditating on what the act of autobiography itself involves. Both constitute an act of metamorphosis: just as the construction of the individual self involves a selection of some things and a renunciation of others, so the act of autobiography highlights certain aspects and ignores others, yet it is nevertheless "true." The logic of Nietzsche's strategy emerges more clearly if we compare it with a journal entry made by Goethe on 18 May 1810, which discusses his central morphological concept, "metamorphosis."[7]

Ecce Homo as Goethean Autobiography

In this highly programmatic note, which in fact precedes a preliminary sketch for his own autobiography, *Poetry and Truth* (*Dichtung und Wahrheit*), Goethe contrasts two views of life, which he dubs the "ironic" and the "superstitious." In the case of the first, the "ironic view of life in a higher sense" (ironische Ansicht des Lebens im höhern Sinne), biography is lifted above life; in the case of the second, biography returns to life again. In the case of the former, understanding and reason (*Verstand, Vernunft*) are flattered; in the case of the latter, sensuousness and imagination (*Sinnlichkeit, Phantasie*). But, if handled well — *wohl behandelt* — what emerges is "a satisfying totality" (eine befriedigende Totalität). On what level, however, is this totality supposed to emerge, the biographical or the historical? One may suppose that, in fact, it is on both.

From the standpoint of the principle of metamorphosis, Goethe says, "the basis of everything is physiological" (der Grund von allem ist physiologisch). That is to say, "there is something physiological-and-pathological in, for instance, all transitional stages in nature, which moves from one stage of metamorphosis into another" (es gibt ein physiologisch-pathologisches, z.E. in allen Übergängen der Natur, die aus einer Stufe der Metamorphose in die andere tritt), and such "natural transitions" are, by their very nature, different from any "morbid state" (morbosen Zustand).[8] The process of metamorphosis is, moreover, not simply internal to each individual, but also results from his or her interaction with the world, which can have both positive and negative consequences. "The activity of the outside world produces *hindrances*, which are often pathological in the first sense" (Wirkung des Äußeren bringt *Retardationen* hervor, welche oft pathologisch im ersten Sinne sind), Goethe writes, "but they can also provoke a morbid state and, by a series of inverted metamorphoses, kill the being" (sie können aber auch einen morbosen Zustand hervorbringen und durch eine umgekehrte Reihe von Metamorphosen das Wesen umbringen).[9] This interaction of sickness and health and sickness re-emerges in Nietzsche's dialectic of the sick and the healthy, the instinctual and the morbid, the anti-decadent and the decadent.

These reflections from 1810 resonate some two decades later when, in the course of a conversation on 30 March 1831, Eckermann records Goethe as saying that the third volume of *Dichtung und Wahrheit* contained "merely the results" (laute Resultate) of his own life, and that the facts it related were intended to serve a general reflection or "a higher truth" (eine höhere Wahrheit).[10] Indeed, he had given the book the title of *Dichtung und Wahrheit*, he explained, "because it lifts itself by higher tendencies out of the region of a lower reality" (weil es sich durch höhere Tendenzen aus der Region einer niedern Realität erhebt).[11] For, as Goethe told Eckermann, any fact about our lives is valuable, not insofar as it is true (*wahr*), but insofar as it is significant (*zu bedeuten haben*); in other words, in a biography the notion of "truth" must rise above a concern with factual accuracy. While some may wish to dispute this notion of truth, it nevertheless represents precisely the kind of truth we find in *Ecce Homo*: it is the story that could be described as one's choice of character, as its subtitle — "How One Becomes What One Is" ("Wie man wird, was man ist") — in its echo of Pindar[12] and in turn of Helvétius[13] indicates.[14] For instance, to take Nietzsche to task for writing that he had never striven after honors, or women, or money (*EH* "Why I Am So Clever" §9; *KSA* 6, 295), when his correspondence documents his scholarly ambitions as a philologist in Leipzig that saw him promoted to a professorship at Basel at the age of twenty-four, or the tactical positioning behind his friendship with Wagner, or when we know of his attraction to Louise Ott, his proposals to Mathilde Trampedach or to Lou von Salomé, or his discussions about marriage with Malwida von Meysenbug, would be entirely to miss the point. For the Nietzsche that arises from the pages of *Ecce Homo* is the *real* Nietzsche, that is, a *textual* Nietzsche; as he warns us in his preface, "*Listen to me! For I am like this and this. Do not, above all, mistake who I am!*" (*Hört mich! denn ich bin der und der. Verwechselt mich vor Allem nicht!*; *EH* preface §1; *KSA* 6, 257).

Nietzsche's Psychology of Character

It can help to clarify some of the more puzzling aspects of this text if one approaches it, as one is in fact invited to do, as an exercise in self-narration, with all the psychoanalytic implications this entails.[15] It can help, for instance, to make sense of Nietzsche's curious remark right at the beginning of *Ecce Homo*: "The good fortune of my existence, perhaps its uniqueness, resides in its fatality: I am, to express it in the form of a riddle, as my father already dead, as my mother I am still living and growing old" (Das Glück meines Daseins, seine Einzigkeit vielleicht, liegt in seinem Verhängniss: ich bin, um es in Räthselform auszudrücken, als mein Vater bereits gestorben, als meine Mutter lebe ich noch und werde alt; *EH* "Why I Am So Wise" §1; *KSA* 6, 264). For Jacques Derrida, this passage shows Nietzsche speaking "symbolically, by way of a riddle; in other words, in the form of a proverbial legend, and as a story that has a lot to teach" (symboliquement, par énigme, autrement dit sous la forme d'une légende proverbiale et comme un récit plein d'einseignement) — in particular, about the structure of the double that links "the logic of the dead to that of the living feminine" (logique du mort, logique de la vivante, voilà l'alliance).[16] For Rudolphe Gasché, the passage is susceptible to an Oedipal reading, according to which Nietzsche kills himself as his own father, in order to commit incest with himself as his mother while, as his father, preventing himself from being born.[17] Drawing on Nietzsche's early autobiographical sketches (*BAW* 1, 6 and 282), an imaginary sketch from 1859 (*BAW* 1, 143), and an early literary fragment entitled "Euphorion" (*BAW* 2, 70–71), Pierre Klossowski reads the passage in terms of a complex on Nietzsche's part, whereby the father (or God the Father) becomes the minotaur (with the features of Richard Wagner), and the (symbolic) mother and the sister (as the feminine) are named Ariadne (with the features of Cosima Wagner), while Franziska and Elisabeth Nietzsche "would be the competitive and punitive representatives of this regression."[18] Sarah Kofman relates Nietzsche's "rejection of kinship above all with the mother and the maternal side of the 'family'" to his aphorism in *Human, All Too Human* (*Menschliches, Allzumenschliches*), where he suggests that "everyone carries within him an image of woman derived from the mother: it determines whether he honors women in general, or holds them in contempt, or is generally indifferent toward them" (jedermann trägt ein Bild des Weibes von der Mutter her in sich: davon wird er bestimmt, die Weiber überhaupt zu verehren oder sie geringzuschätzen oder gegen sie im Allgemeinen gleichgültig zu sein; *HA* I §380; *KSA* 2, 265).[19] According to Thomas Steinbuch's interpretation of this sentence, Nietzsche means that "his father's condition of *décadence* was essentially reproduced in himself as his unconscious," a reading that leaves unexplained how his mother's condition is unconsciously reproduced.[20] Most recently, Michel Onfray has proposed linking this passage to others in which Nietzsche talks about his father and his mother. For instance, he spoke of Karl Ludwig Nietzsche as having been "delicate, lovable, and morbid, like a being not destined long for this world" (zart, liebenswürdig und morbid, wie ein nur zum Vorübergehn bestimmtes Wesen; *EH* "Why I Am So Wise" §1; *KSA* 6, 264), recalling that the peasants to whom he preached used to say of him, "this is how an angel must look" (so müsse wohl ein Engel aussehn; *EH* "Why I Am So Wise" §3; *KSA* 6, 268). His mother Franziska Nietzsche, née Oehler, on the other hand, he uncompromisingly described as "*canaille*," as "the perfect machine from hell" (eine vollkommene Höllenmaschine), and as "poisonous vermin" (giftiges Gewürm; *EH* "Why I Am So Wise" §3; *KSA* 6, 268): the contrast could not be clearer. Behind the figures of the "angelic" father and the "verminous" mother, then, lies a contrast between the father who *is* dead and the mother who *causes* death.[21]

Nietzsche's statement, however, can (also) be read in a Jungian sense. According to such a reading, in *Ecce Homo* Nietzsche casts off his masculine, patriarchal side, and embarks on (or acknowledges) the discovery of the feminine, intuitive side of the self.[22] Part and parcel of this discovery is Nietzsche's realization, his acceptance, his insight into the inevitability, even the utility, of death. (After all, "mother," "maternal," and "matrix" [*mater*] are etymologically related to "matter" [*materia*], of which we are made and to which we return.) And perhaps it is here that we encounter the crucial difference between Nietzsche and Schopenhauer, the philosopher whom he once so greatly admired and to whom in "Schopenhauer as Educator" ("Schopenhauer als Erzieher"), the third of his *Untimely Meditations* (*Unzeitgemässe Betrachtungen*), he dedicated a passionate encomium, before subsequently turning away from him to forge a philosophy of his own.

Schopenhauer is conventionally portrayed as the doom-laden philosopher of pessimism (a portrayal boosted by Nietzsche's satirical portrait in *Zarathustra* of Schopenhauer as the gloomy Prophet). Yet, for Schopenhauer, if life is something bad, death is something even worse: it is, in fact, something terrible (even though this terror is later mitigated, as we shall see, by what he says about death in relation to the indestructibility of our inner nature). In the first volume of *The World as Will and Representation* (*Die Welt als Wille und Vorstellung*), Schopenhauer offers, as if echoing a famous passage of Lucretius,[23] the following description of life:

> Life itself is a sea full of rocks and whirlpools that man avoids with the greatest caution and care, although he knows that, even when he succeeds with all his efforts and ingenuity in struggling through, at every step he comes nearer to the greatest, the total, the inevitable and irremediable shipwreck, indeed even steers right into it, namely death. This is the final goal of the wearisome voyage, and it is worse for him than all the rocks that he has avoided.

> [Das Leben selbst ist ein Meer voller Klippen und Strudel, die der Mensch mit der größten Behutsamkeit und Sorgfalt vermeidet,

obwohl er weiß, daß, wenn es ihm auch gelingt, mit aller Anstrengung und Kunst sich durchzuwinden, er eben dadurch mit jedem Schritt dem größten, dem totalen, dem unvermeidlichen und unheilbaren Schiffbruch näher kommt, ja gerade auf ihn zusteuert, — dem Tode: dieser ist das endliche Ziel der mühsäligen Fahrt und für ihn schlimmer als alle Klippen, denen er auswich.][24]

For Schopenhauer, as for Nietzsche, to understand the dependence of one's happiness on external factors leads to an acceptance of one's fate, so that the insight that freedom lies in one's consent to necessity constitutes a moment of psychological rebirth. But, in contrast to Schopenhauer, Nietzsche — in line with this deeper (proto-Jungian) understanding of himself, whereby he has become reconciled with the maternal, and hence with the Magna Mater, the symbol of the perpetual cycle (or eternal recurrence) of life and death[25] — is also able to integrate death itself into his vision of life. In *The Gay Science*, Nietzsche links "the motherly type of human being" (die mütterliche Art Mensch) with "a certain autumnal sunniness and mildness, which [. . .] the ripening of a work always leaves behind in its author" (eine gewisse herbstliche Sonnigkeit und Milde, welche jedes Mal [. . .] das Reifgewordensein eines Werkes [. . .] bei seinem Urheber hinterlässt; *GS* §376; *KSA* 3, 628). As we shall see, some of the most evocative imagery in *Ecce Homo* intimates this ultimate reconciliation of life and death in Nietzsche's philosophical outlook.

Communication; or, Is Anybody Listening?

More clearly than almost any of his other works, *Ecce Homo* demonstrates how, for Nietzsche, the question of character intersects with the theme of communication.[26] For in it Nietzsche frankly admits the possibility — the probability, even — that he will be misunderstood.[27] When, in the third chapter, he claims that "I am one thing, my writings are another" (Das Eine bin ich, das Andre sind meine Schriften), he explicitly touches on "the question of these writings being understood or *not* understood" (die Frage nach dem Verstanden- oder *Nicht*-verstanden-werden dieser Schriften; *EH* "Why I Write Such Good Books" §1; *KSA* 6, 298). In turn, the question of being understood or not being understood (as well as, one might add, the question of being *mis*-understood) foregrounds the problem of interpretation. One of the reasons for the misunderstanding of his writings, Nietzsche says, is that the act of understanding inevitably refers back to the interpreter's range of experience. Nietzsche uses the particular example of listening, in a way reminiscent of Goethe's invitation to the reader, in his foreword to *On the Doctrine of Color* (*Zur Farbenlehre*), to listen to nature:

Let us shut our eyes, let us open our ears and sharpen our sense of hearing. From the softest breath to the most savage noise, from the simplest tone to the most sublime harmony, from the fiercest cry of passion to the gentlest word of reason, it is nature alone that speaks, revealing its existence, energy, life, and circumstances, so that a blind man to whom the vast world of the visible is denied may seize hold of an infinite living realm through what he can hear. Thus nature also speaks to other senses that lie even deeper, to known, misunderstood, and unknown senses. Thus it converses with itself and with us through a thousand phenomena.

[Man schließe das Auge, man öffne, man schärfe das Ohr, und vom leisesten Hauch bis zum wildesten Geräusch, vom einfachsten Klang bis zur höchsten Zusammenstimmung, von dem heftigsten leidenschaftlichen Schrei bis zum sanftesten Worte der Vernunft ist es nur die Natur, die spricht, ihr Dasein, ihre Kraft, ihr Leben und ihre Verhältnisse offenbart, so daß ein Blinder, dem das unendlich Sichtbare versagt ist, im Hörbaren ein unendlich Lebendiges fassen kann. So spricht die Natur hinabwärts zu andern Sinnen, zu bekannten, verkannten, unbekannten Sinnen; so spricht sie mit sich selbst und zu uns durch tausend Erscheinungen.][28]

But what if the reader were to listen to Nature, but heard nothing? Would this say something about Nature or, rather, something about the person listening? For his part, Nietzsche insists that "ultimately no one can hear more in things, including books, than he or she already knows" (zuletzt kann Niemand aus den Dingen, die Bücher eingerechnet, mehr heraushören, als er bereits weiss; *KSA* 6, 299–300). As a consequence, Nietzsche devises the following principle: "What one's experiences do not allow one to access, one has no ear for" (Wofür man vom Erlebnisse her keinen Zugang hat, dafür hat man kein Ohr; *KSA* 6, 300). The implications of this dictum are explored using another striking image:

Now let us imagine an extreme case: a book speaks of experiences that lie entirely beyond the possibility of usual or even rare experience — it is the *first* language for a new series of experiences. In this case simply nothing is heard, with the acoustic illusion that where nothing can be heard, *there is nothing there* . . . This is, in fact, my average experience and, if you like, the *originality* of my experience.

[Denken wir uns nun einen äussersten Fall: dass ein Buch von lauter Erlebnissen redet, die gänzlich ausserhalb der Möglichkeit einer häufigen oder auch nur seltenen Erfahrung liegen — dass es die *erste* Sprache für eine neue Reihe von Erfahrungen ist. In diesem Falle wird einfach nichts gehört, mit der akustischen Täuschung, dass wo Nichts gehört wird, *auch Nichts da ist* . . . Dies ist zuletzt meine durchschnittliche Erfahrung und, wenn man will, die *Originalität* meiner Erfahrung. (*KSA* 6, 300)]

In the extreme case, as Nietzsche envisages it, of a book that speaks of nothing but events lying outside the possibility of experience, such a book would constitute the *first* instance of a language for a new range of experiences. And because we are unused to such a language, we would hear: nothing. As a result of this acoustic illusion, we would believe: there *is* nothing to be heard. But we would be entirely wrong.

Such, Nietzsche wants to persuade us, is the utter originality of his experience. Yet, paradoxically enough, it is also the originality of Zarathustra's experiences. Indeed, the theme of communication is central to *Thus Spoke Zarathustra*, and it would be no exaggeration to say that, in *Ecce Homo*, Nietzsche discusses in the first person many of the issues that, in *Zarathustra*, are presented in the third person.[29] Throughout that work, we see Zarathustra's response to and struggle with the imperative to express himself. In part 2, Zarathustra says to his eagle and his snake: "Mund bin ich worden ganz und gar, und Brausen eines Bachs aus hohen Felsen: hinab will ich meine Rede stürzen in die Thäler. [. . .] Neue Wege gehe ich, eine neue Rede kommt mir" (I have become entirely mouth, and the roar of a stream falling from high cliffs: I want to plunge my speech down into the valleys. [. . .] I am traveling new paths, a new way of speaking is coming to me; *Z* II 1; *KSA* 4, 106).[30] Because of its aesthetic and, in particular, its "musical" qualities, Zarathustra's language is a special language, his discourse a specific one; it is indeed "a new way of speaking" (eine neue Rede; *Z* II 1; *KSA* 4, 106), but to understand this discourse, one must listen carefully. Thus the central challenge of *Zarathustra* is first hermeneutic, then existential. The "tragedy" of Zarathustra is that the requisite art of interpretation is missing in nearly all those who listen to the prophet.[31]

Similarly, in *Ecce Homo* Nietzsche points to how he has often been completely misunderstood, both by those who believe they have understood something of him, in which case they turn him into something fashioned after their own image, and by those who have not understood him at all, and hence exclude him from further consideration (*EH* "Why I Write Such Good Books" §1; *KSA* 6, 300). (One continues to observe both types of misunderstanding today. . . .) And in the concluding sections of *Ecce Homo* he asks no less than three times: "Have I been understood?" (Hat man mich verstanden?; *EH* "Why I Am a Destiny" §7–§9; *KSA* 6, 371–74).[32]

The fundamental unity of purpose behind *Zarathustra* and *Ecce Homo* is explicitly stated when Nietzsche claims that Zarathustra's task is also his own — namely, to be "*affirmative* to the point of justifying, of redeeming even all the past" (*jasagend* bis zur Rechtfertigung, bis zur

Erlösung auch alles Vergangenen; *EH Z* §8; *KSA* 6, 348); and when he admits that "I have not said anything there that I did not say five years ago through the mouth of Zarathustra" (ich habe eben kein Wort gesagt, das ich nicht schon vor fünf Jahren durch den Mund Zarathustras gesagt hätte; *EH* "Why I Am a Destiny" §8; *KSA* 6, 373). Nor is this unity merely stated; it is implicit in *Zarathustra*'s and *Ecce Homo*'s shared use of the image of self-sculpting, which belongs in a tradition that reaches back to the neo-Platonic school of Plotinus.[33]

Nietzsche invokes this image when he describes Zarathustra as someone who has mastered the "*great disgust*" (*grossen Ekel*) at humankind: "To him, the human being is a lack of form, material, an ugly stone that needs a sculptor" (der Mensch ist ihm eine Unform, ein Stoff, ein hässlicher Stein, der des Bildners bedarf; *EH Z* §8; *KSA* 6, 348), just as Zarathustra had imagined himself as a sculptor, albeit a rather furious one:

> O humans, in the stone there sleeps an image, the image of my images! Alas, that it must sleep in the hardest, ugliest stone!
>
> Now my hammer rages cruelly against its prison. Pieces of rock rain from the stone: what is that to me?
>
> I want to perfect it; for a shadow came to me — the stillest and lightest of all things once came to me!
>
> The beauty of the superman came to me as a shadow. O my brothers, what are the gods to me now?
>
> [Ach, ihr Menschen, im Steine schläft mir ein Bild, das Bild meiner Bilder! Ach, daß es im härtesten, häßlichsten Steine schlafen muß!
>
> *Nun wüthet mein Hammer grausam gegen sein Gefängniss.* Vom Steine stäuben Stücke: was schiert mich das?
>
> Vollenden will ich's: denn ein Schatten kam zu mir, — aller Dinge Stillstes und Leichtestes kam einst zu mir!
>
> Des Übermenschen Schönheit kam zu mir als Schatten. Ach, meine Brüder: was gehen mich noch — die Götter an! — (*EH Z* §8; *KSA* 6, 349, cf. *Z* II 2; *KSA* 4, 111–12)]

In his quotation of this passage in *Ecce Homo*, Nietzsche highlights the phrase about the raging hammer, because (he says) among the decisive preconditions for the "*Dionysian* task" (*dionysische* Aufgabe) belong both the hardness of the hammer and "*joy even in destruction*" (die *Lust selbst am Vernichten*; *KSA* 6, 349). For the act of self-sculpting, to which the imperative "become hard! (werdet hart!) and the conviction that "*all creators are hard*" (*dass alle Schaffenden hart sind*) also belong, is, according to Nietzsche, the mark of a Dionysian nature (*KSA* 6, 349).

Thus Nietzsche replaces the traditional Western philosophical goal of knowledge with his own existential imperative: *become yourself!* Or more precisely, following Pindar and Helvétius, *become who you are!* In this respect, as in so many others, Nietzsche shares with Goethe a deep suspicion of the Delphic oracle's injunction, "know thyself." In his essay "Significant Help Given by an Ingenious Turn of Phrase" ("Bedeutende Fördernis durch ein einziges geistreiches Wort," 1823), Goethe had confessed that he had always considered the phrase to be "a deception practiced by a secret order of priests who wished to confuse humanity with impossible demands, to divert attention from activity in the outer world to some false, inner speculation" (eine List geheim verbündeter Priester, die den Menschen durch unerreichbare Forderungen verwirren und von der Tätigkeit gegen die Außenwelt zu einer innern falschen Beschaulichkeit verleiten wollten); instead, Goethe insists on the necessity for the self to engage in (and with) the world: "The human being knows himself only insofar as he knows the world; he perceives the world only in himself, and himself only in the world" (Der Mensch kennt nur sich selbst, insofern er die Welt kennt, die er nur in sich und sich nur in ihr gewahr wird).[34] Similarly, Nietzsche realizes that *nosce te ipsum* can act as nothing less than "a recipe for ruin" (das Recept zum Untergang; *EH* "Why I Am So Clever" §9; *KSA* 6, 293), for reasons that he makes clear.

For the answer to the question of how one becomes what one is brings Nietzsche to touch on "the masterpiece in the art of self-preservation" (das Meisterstück in der Kunst der Selbsterhaltung), or selfishness (*Selbstsucht*; *EH* "Why I Am So Clever" §9; *KSA* 6, 293). In his discourses, Zarathustra pronounces selfishness blessed — "the wholesome, healthy selfishness that wells up from a mighty soul: — / — from a mighty soul to which the higher body belongs" (die heile, gesunde Selbstsucht, die aus mächtiger Seele quillt: — / — aus mächtiger Seele, zu welcher der hohe Leib gehört) — and declares that whoever "proclaims the ego healthy and holy, and selfishness blessed" (das Ich heil und heilig spricht und die Selbstsucht selig) — is ushering in the Great Noontide (*Z* III 10 §2–§3; *KSA* 4, 238–40). So, too, in *Ecce Homo* Nietzsche criticizes "forgetting oneself, *misunderstanding* oneself, making oneself smaller, narrower, mediocre" (Sich-Vergessen, Sich-*Missverstehen*, Sich-Verkleinern, -Verengern, -Vermittelmässigen) or — "expressed in moral terms" (moralisch ausgedrückt) — "love of one's neighbor, living for others and other things" (Nächstenliebe, Leben für Andere und Anderes) for being, in fact, a strategy to protect the sternest and severest selfishness (*Selbstigkeit*) of the worst kind (*EH* "Why I Am So Clever" §9; SA 6, 293–94). For at the heart of *Selbstigkeit* there is a void: ultimately, the "selflessness" (Selbstlosigkeit) of the "morality of unselfing" (Entselbstungsmoral; *EH* D §2; *KSA* 6, 332) — of "the 'selfless,' the loss of a center of gravity, 'depersonalization' and 'love of one's neighbor'" (im "Selbstlosen", im Verlust an Schwergewicht, in der "Entpersönlichung" und "Nächstenliebe") — is "the morality of decline" (die Niedergangs-Moral) par excellence, inasmuch as it betrays "a will to the end" (einen Willen zum Ende) and therefore "*denies* the very foundations of life" (*verneint* im untersten Grunde das Leben; *EH* "Why I Am a Destiny" §7; *KSA* 6, 372). In place of *Selbstigkeit* and *Entselbstung*, Nietzsche will promulgate *Selbstsucht*, for which he offers "an entire casuistic" (die ganze Casuistik) in terms of nutriment, place, climate, recreation (*EH* "Why I Am So Clever" §10; *KSA* 6, 295). For the choice of nutrition, place, climate, and recreation in itself reveals an instinct of self-preservation (*Selbsterhaltung*) that manifests itself most clearly as the instinct for self-defense (*Selbstvertheidigung*; *EH* "Why I Am So Clever" §8; *KSA* 6, 291). The usual word for this first instinct, he says, is taste (*Geschmack*). Ordinarily, however, self-defense involves an extraordinary waste of psychological resources: "Our *largest* expenditures are our most frequent small ones" (Unsre *grossen* Ausgaben sind die häufigsten kleinen), Nietzsche writes, inasmuch as "warding off, not letting things come close" (das Abwehren, das Nicht-heran-kommen-lassen) involves an immense squandering of strength on negative objectives (*EH* "Why I am So Clever" §8; *KSA* 6, 292). Another strategy, which Nietzsche associates with becoming a scholar or academic, involves reacting as little as possible: taking up one's time with thumbing through books (or, these days, with research assessment exercises) leads equally to ruin.

In place of these strategies and instead of conventional morality, however, Nietzsche sets up a different imperative. In his essays on Schopenhauer and Wagner in *Untimely Meditations*, Nietzsche tells further us on, he had sought to articulate a new concept of self-discipline (*Selbst-Zucht*), of self-defense (*Selbst-Vertheidigung*) to the point of hardness, "a way to greatness and to world-historical tasks" (ein Weg zur Grösse und zu welthistorischen Aufgaben; *EH UM* §3; *KSA* 6, 319). And earlier, in the context of discussing "the defensive and offensive instinct" (der *Wehr-und Waffen-Instinkt*) in humankind and "the great rationality of fatalism" (die grosse Vernunft d[es] Fatalismus), he had told us that "to accept oneself as something fated, not to wish oneself 'different' — [. . .] this is *great rationality* itself" (sich selbst wie ein Fatum nehmen, nicht sich "anders" wollen — das ist [. . .] die *grosse Vernunft* selbst; *EH* "Why I Am So Clever" §6; *KSA* 6, 273). This advice is now echoed when he tells us that "even the *blunders* of life (selbst die *Fehlgriffe* des Lebens), or "the occasional side roads and wrong turnings, the delays, the 'modesties,' the seriousness wasted on tasks that lie *beyond* the task" (die zeitweiligen Nebenwege und Abwege, die Verzögerungen, die "Bescheidenheiten", der Ernst, auf Aufgaben verschwendet, die jenseits *der* Aufgabe liegen), can evince "a great prudence, even the greatest prudence" (eine grosse Klugheit, sogar die oberste Klugheit; *EH* "Why I Am So Clever" §9; *KSA* 6, 293). Here he defines the strategy of Nietzschean selfishness or *Selbstsucht*: it is "not to want in the slightest that anything should become other than it is" (nicht im Geringsten [wollen], dass Etwas anders wird als es ist), and *thus* one wishes oneself not to become other than one is, and hence to become what one indeed is (*KSA* 6, 295).

In opposition to the advice of the Delphic Oracle and its concomitant morality of unselfing, which results in "the loss of a center of gravity, resistance to the natural instincts, in a word 'selflessness'" (der Verlust an Schwergewicht, der Widerstand gegen die natürlichen Instinkte, die "Selbstlosigkeit" mit Einem Worte; *EH D* §2; *KSA* 6, 331–32), Nietzsche presents one of the central ideas of *Zarathustra*, the doctrine of eternal recurrence. To be sure, it is a doctrine whose *lack* of originality he is swift, in *Ecce Homo*, to emphasize, for the doctrine *could*, he tells us, have been taught by Heraclitus, and Stoic teachings likewise show traces of it (*EH BT* §3; *KSA* 6, 313).[35] What Nietzsche does not say — and does not need to, because the texts were as close to him as he assumed they were to his presumed reader — is that antecedents for the doctrine can also be found in Goethe and in Schopenhauer.

For instance, in his conversations with Eckermann — according to Nietzsche, "the best book in German that there is" (das beste deutsche Buch, das es giebt; *HA* II *WS* §109; *KSA* 2, 599) — Goethe is recorded as saying on 29 October 1823 that "everything repeats itself, and nothing in the world is only there *once*" (alles wiederholt sich, und es gibt kein Ding in der Welt, das nur *einmal* da wäre).[36] And on 17 January 1827 he offered a more urban, domesticated version of Nietzsche's "Dionysian world of eternally-coming-into-being and eternally-being-destroyed" (dionysische Welt des Ewig-sich-selber-Schaffens, des Ewig-sich-selber-Zerstörens; *WP* §1067; *KSA* 11, 38[12], 611) when he remarked: "I need only to look out of the window to have constantly before my eyes, in the brooms that sweep the street and the children who run around, the symbols of the world that is eternally-wearing-itself-out and eternally-renewing-itself again" (Ich brauche nur zum Fenster hinauszusehen, um in straßenkehrenden Besen und herumlaufenden Kindern die Symbole der sich ewig abnutzenden und immer sich verjüngenden Welt beständig vor Augen zu haben).[37]

Similarly, in a conversation recorded by Johannes Daniel Falk at Wieland's funeral on 25 January 1813, Goethe himself embraced eternal recurrence: "I am certain that, as you see me here, I have already been a thousand times, and I hope to be here again a thousand times" (Ich bin gewiß, wie Sie mich hier sehen, schon tausendmal dagewesen und hoffe wohl noch tausendmal wiederzukommen);[38] a statement whose import is repeated, and intensified, by Zarathustra in "The Convalescent" ("Der Genesende"): "I shall come again, with this sun, with this earth, with this eagle, with this snake — *not* to a new life or a better life or a similar life: / — I shall come back eternally to this same, selfsame life, in the greatest things and the smallest, to teach again the eternal recurrence of all things" (Ich komme wieder, mit dieser Sonne, mit dieser Erde, mit

diesem Adler, mit dieser Schlange — *nicht* zu einem neuen Leben oder
besseren Leben oder ähnlichem Leben: / ich komme ewig wieder zu diesem gleichen und selbigen Leben, im Grössten und auch im Kleinsten,
dass ich wieder aller Dinge ewige Wiederkunft lehre; *Z* III 13 §2; *KSA* 4,
276). Then again, in his letter to Karl Friedrich Zelter of 29 April 1830,
Goethe confessed: "I experience the good fortune that, in my advanced
age, thoughts occur to me, to pursue which and to carry out which would
be worth the entire repetition of my life" (Ich erfahre das Glück, daß
mir in meinem hohen Alter Gedanken aufgehen, welche zu verfolgen und
in Ausübung zu bringen eine Wiederholung des Lebens gar wohl werte
wäre).[39] Whereas Goethe entertained thoughts that made the recurrence
of life seem worthwhile, Nietzsche believed that the very idea of recurrence would make life *become* worthwhile.[40]

For his part, Schopenhauer in a key chapter in the second volume
of *The World as Will and Representation*, "On Death and Its Relation to
the Indestructibility of Our Inner Nature" ("Ueber den Tod und sein
Verhältniss zur Unzerstörbarkeit unsers Wesens an sich"), speaks of overcoming (the fear of) death through the idea of eternal recurrence — a
recurrence that grants us a "temporal immortality" (*zeitliche Unsterblich-
keit*). For although the fly, the plant, the animal, and the human being
will die, yet they will all return, and (in Schopenhauer's words) every
summer we have again before us the cherries that have already a thousand
times been enjoyed.[41] According to Schopenhauer, "the genuine symbol
of nature" (das ächte Symbol der Natur) is the circle, because it is "the
scheme of recurrence" (das Schema der Wiederkehr).[42]

In *Zarathustra*, the circle becomes the symbol of the great ring of
eternal return (*Z* III 16; *KSA* 4, 287–91), and this motif in Schopenhauer
and in Nietzsche informs the ideas of later thinkers in the Nietzschean
tradition. Take, for example, Ludwig Klages's remarks on the symbolism
of the circle as the symbol of renewal.[43] In his discussion of "the temporal circle of the maternal world" (der Zeitkreis der Mutterwelt), Klages
distinguishes between *"eternal return"* (*ewige Wiederkunft*) as the "continual Once-Again of all *circumstances* that have ever been" (beständiges
Abermals aller je dagewesenen *Sachverhalte*) and *"circular time"* (*kreis-
förmige Zeit*) as the "continual renewal of ceaselessly flowing *images*"
(beständige Erneuerung unaufhaltsam fließender *Bilder*).[44] In contrast to
the logocentric consciousness of modernity, Klages advocates the prehis-
toric (because ahistorical) view of a people he dubs the Pelasgians:

> In complete opposition to logical consciousness, which — feeling its
> way along the straight line of time — considers each past thing to
> be destroyed, but in the present sees only repetitions of it, the Pelas-
> gians — bound up with the circle of time — live, know, and teach
> the *eternal return of the origin*.

[Völlig entgegengesetzt dem logischen Bewußtsein, das entlang tastend an der Geraden der Zeit jedes Vergangene für vernichtigt hält, im Gegenwärtigen aber von ihm nur Wiederholungen sieht, lebt und weiß und lehrt das im Kreise der Zeit gebundene Pelasgertum die *ewige Wiederbringung des Ursprungs*.][45]

In this respect, there is an important link to another later Nietzschean, C. G. Jung, and his concept of synchronicity. For synchronicity implies a view of the world in which events in the past may suddenly be repeated; according to Jung, the self encounters its own reality, not just through causal relations, but through repetition; or, in Nietzschean terms, through eternal recurrence. What recurs, then, is the Jungian archetype, inasmuch as archetypes derive from recurring situations,[46] just as, in Vico's account of history as *corso* and *ricorso* (cf. *Scienza nuova* [1725, 1730/1744]), the self encounters itself through the repetitions of history, and thereby overcomes the restrictions of the "Cartesian mentality."[47]

Thus it is not only Nietzsche for whom the concept of eternal recurrence provides the basis for a fundamental affirmation of the self, although for him, so he tells us, "the hardest, the most terrible insight into reality" (die härteste, die furchtbarste Einsicht in der Realität) constitutes "yet another reason *for oneself being* the eternal Yes to all things, 'the tremendous, unbounded saying Yes and Amen'" (einen Grund noch hinzu, das ewige Ja zu allen Dingen *selbst zu sein*, "das ungeheure ungebegrenzte Ja- und Amen-sagen" . . .; *EH Z* §6; *KSA* 6, 345, cf. *Z* III 4; *KSA* 4, 208). Nietzsche has a name for this affirmation, this Yes-saying: it is *amor fati*, first evoked in *The Gay Science* (*GS* §276; *KSA* 3, 521). *Amor fati* is, he tells us, "my formula for greatness in a human being" (meine Formel für die Grösse am Menschen), namely: "Not merely to endure what is necessary, still less to pretend it is other than what it is, [. . .] but to *love* it . . ." (Das Nothwendige nicht bloss ertragen, noch weniger verhehlen [. . .], sondern es *lieben* . . .; *EH* "Why I Am So Clever" §10; *KSA* 6, 297).

But why is fatalism, as Nietzsche calls it, the "great rationality"? How does the affirmation of necessity sit with his call to construct our own character? Why do we need to become what we are, since what we are is, after all, what we are? Or to put it another way, if everything is determined, how can we exercise our will? If the shape of our own statue is (always) already predetermined, how can we sculpt it? If we are what we are, how then can we become it — or, rather, how could we *not* become it? Is there not a paradox of fatalism and self-creation involved here, as Brian Leiter has described it?[48] Indeed, Nietzsche alludes precisely to this problem in a note from his *Nachlass* of 1881, where he asks: "'But if everything is necessary, how can I determine my actions?' The thought and belief is a heavy weight which bears down on you along with all other weights, and more than they do" ("Aber wenn alles nothwendig ist, was kann ich über meine Handlungen verfügen?" Der Gedanke und Glaube ist ein Schwergewicht, welches neben allen anderen Gewichten auf dich drückt und mehr als sie; *UW* II §1336; *KSA* 9, 11[143], 496). The problem has exercised many commentators on Nietzsche, not least such American critics as Alexander Nehamas and Richard Rorty.[49]

Ultimately, however, it is a problem that confronts *all* philosophers who argue in favor of determinism, from the Stoics, via Spinoza, to d'Holbach, and finally to Schopenhauer and Nietzsche. For example, in his *Système de la nature* (*System of Nature*, 1770), Holbach claims, on the one hand, that "the life of a human being is nothing other than a long sequence of necessary and connected movements" ([la] vie [de l'homme] n'est qu'une longue suite de mouvements nécessaires et liés), and, on the other, "each of us can in some way choose a particular nature" (chacun de nous peut en quelque sorte se faire un tempérament).[50] How are these two statements to be reconciled? In other words, why should we even bother to become what we are since, surely, what we have become, is what we must be?

The answer to this question can be found in one of Nietzsche's precursors, Spinoza,[51] in the concept of "free necessity." Spinoza's understanding of freedom not as "free decision" but as "free necessity" is expounded at length in his *Ethics*, at the beginning of which he defines something as being "free" when it "exists solely by the necessity of its own nature."[52] And Goethe, too, as a committed Spinozist, embraced precisely this definition of freedom, and examined its consequences, in his letter to Carl Friedrich Moritz von Brühl written on 23 October 1828:

> If we consider ourselves in every stage of life, we find that we are determined from outside from our first breath to our last; but that there nevertheless remains to us the highest freedom to develop ourselves within ourselves in such a way that we are in harmony with the moral world-order, and that, whatever obstacles come our way, we can thus come to be at peace with ourselves.
>
> [Betrachten wir uns in jeder Lage des Lebens, so finden wir, daß wir äußerlich bedingt sind, vom ersten Atemzug bis zum letzten; daß uns aber jedoch die höchste Freiheit übriggeblieben ist, uns innerhalb unsrer selbst dergestalt auszubilden, daß wir uns mit der sittlichen Weltordnung in Einklang setzen und, was auch für Hindernisse sich hervortun, dadurch mit uns selbst zum Frieden gelangen können.][53]

Autobiography, then, is intimately bound up with the realization of oneself as free, inasmuch as that freedom is expressed through becoming what one is. Now, Goethe placed this dialectic of freedom and necessity at the heart of his understanding of autobiography where, in part 3, book

11, of *Dichtung und Wahrheit*, he reflects on the fact that few biographies can depict an individual's life as "pure, calm, and steady progress" (einen reinen, ruhigen, steten Fortschritt), for —

> our lives, like the context in which we live, are an incomprehensible mixture of freedom and necessity. Our desires proclaim in advance what we will do under any set of circumstances. These circumstances, however, control us in their own way. The "what" is within us, the "how" rarely depends on us, the "why" we dare not enquire about, and therefore we are correctly referred to the *quia*.

> [unser Leben ist, wie das Ganze, in dem wir enthalten sind, auf eine unbegreifliche Weise aus Freiheit und Notwendigkeit zusammengesetzt. Unser Wollen ist ein Vorausverkünden dessen, was wir unter allen Umständen tun werden. Diese Umstände aber ergreifen uns auf ihre eigne Weise. Das *Was* liegt in uns, das *Wie* hängt selten von uns ab, nach dem *Warum* dürfen wir nicht fragen, und deshalb verweist man uns mit Recht aufs *Quia*.][54]

— *quia* here being "the 'because,'" or what emerges from this conjunction of the individual and his or her circumstances, a "because" which is more than purely causal.[55]

Elsewhere, in his discussion of Newton in the historical section of his *Farbenlehre*, Goethe invited the reader to look into "the abysses of human nature" (die Abgründe der menschlichen Natur) and the mystery of our "higher consciousness" (höheres Bewußtsein). Thanks to this consciousness, he argued, we have the freedom to lift ourselves above the necessity of being who we are, and to obtain, at least partially, an insight into that necessity of our nature:

> In the human being a higher consciousness can arise, with the result that he gains a certain overview of the nature that is necessarily innate within him, and which nothing, however free one is, can change. To achieve complete clarity about all this is almost impossible; to chide oneself at particular moments is perfectly acceptable, but no one is able constantly to criticize oneself.

> [Es kann sich nämlich im Menschen ein höheres Bewußtsein finden, so daß er über die notwendige ihm einwohnende Natur, an der durch alle Freiheit nichts zu verändern vermag, eine gewisse Übersicht erhält. Hierüber völlig ins klare zu kommen, ist beinahe unmöglich; sich in einzelnen Augenblicken zu schelten, geht wohl an, aber niemanden ist gegeben, sich fortwährend zu tadeln.][56]

This insight, Goethe adds, allows us to regard our faults and failings — if we accept them as our own, rather than (as usually happens) blaming them on others — with a kind of conscious irony. Hence, for Goethe, irony is ultimately a means of mediating rational (and hence free) consciousness and unchangeable nature:

> If one does not have recourse to the vulgar device of putting blame for one's shortcomings on one's circumstances, or on other people; then the conflict of a rationally judging consciousness with a modifiable, but nevertheless unchangeable nature finally gives rise to a sort of irony in us and with ourselves, so that we treat our failings and mistakes playfully like ill-mannered children.
>
> [Greift man nicht zu dem gemeinen Mittel, seine Mängel auf die Umstände, auf andere Menschen zu schieben; so entsteht zuletzt aus dem Konflikt eines vernünftig richtenden Bewußtseins mit der zwar modifikabeln, aber doch unveränderlichen Natur eine Art von Ironie in und mit uns selbst, so daß wir unsere Fehler und Irrtümer wie ungezogene Kinder spielend behandeln [. . .]][57]

The ironic tone, the stylistic sophistication, and the complexity of structure in Nietzsche's *Ecce Homo* bear out the truth of Goethe's observation.

Tragedy and Apoptosis

In his study of Nietzsche called *La Sagesse tragique* (2006), Michel Onfray explicitly links the idea of consent to necessity with Nietzsche's doctrine of *amor fati*,[58] defining the Pindaric-Nietzschean injunction-invitation to "become who one is" (*devenir ce que l'on est*) as "to want the will that wills us" (*c'est vouloir le vouloir qui nous veut*) — in other words, it is "to understand that freedom exists only in necessity, that no choice is possible except in accepting what is the evident"; from which Onfray concludes that "to want what the will wants" (*vouloir ce que veut la volonté*) is the final word of "tragic wisdom" (*la sagesse tragique*).[59] Elsewhere, Onfray identifies a specifically Nietzschean sense of tragedy (*le tragique nietzschéen*). On this account, tragedy is not so much about the "fact-of-having-to-die" (*devoir mourir*) as it is to do with "the-task-of-having-to-live" (*avoir à vivre*); for, in his view, "what moves and motivates the tragic individual is less the fact of having to die — which concerns optimists and pessimists alike — than the fact of having to live, and to live well, to live better" (ce qui mobilise et motive l'homme tragique est moins de *devoir mourir* — ce qui soucie optimistes et pessimistes — que d'*avoir à vivre*, et à bien vivre, à mieux vivre).[60] Such a conception of tragedy, which could also be called a vitalist sense of tragedy, illustrates another of Onfray's tenets, that "to be Nietzschean means to take Nietzsche as a starting point for thinking — not to think as he does" (être nietzschéen, c'est penser à partir de Nietzsche — pas comme lui).[61]

In his *Nachlass* of 1881, Nietzsche makes the point about freedom as consent-to-necessity explicit when he points out that if nutrition, place, climate, and company — those "little things" (kleine Dinge) that are, according to *Ecce Homo*, so important (*EH* "Why I Am So Clever" §10; *KSA* 6, 295) — determine the individual, so to an even greater extent do the "opinions" (Meinungen) of the individual, which in turn determine nutrition, place, climate, and company (*UW* II §1336; *KSA* 9, 11[143], 496). For Nietzsche, the greatest of all such determining propositions is "the thought of thoughts" (den Gedanken der Gedanken) — in other words, eternal recurrence — which, upon being "incorporated" (einverleibt), will "transform" (verwandeln) the individual (*UW* II §1336; *KSA* 9, 11[143], 496).[62] So the question that should accompany all that one does, namely: "do I want to do it innumerable times?" (ist es so, daß ich es unzählige Male thun will?), constitutes "the *heaviest* weight" (das *größte* Schwergewicht), as the title of a key section in *The Gay Science* (*Die fröhliche Wissenschaft*) also calls it (*GS* §341; *KSA* 3, 570–71). And in this earlier work Nietzsche had also argued that "the *strength* of what we know lies not in its degree of truth, but on how old it is, on how it has been incorporated, on its character as a condition of life" (die *Kraft* der Erkenntnisse liegt nicht in ihrem Grade von Wahrheit, sondern in ihrem Alter, ihrer Einverleibtheit, ihrem Charakter als Lebensbedingung; *GS* §110; *KA* 3, 469). Paradoxically, it is the extent of our acceptance of the inevitable that determines what we are: or, how one becomes what one is.[63]

Earlier I said that Nietzsche's vision of life in *Ecce Homo* is one that is able to integrate death into life; and surely there is (aside from taxes) no greater inevitability than death. For this reason, then, we may properly call his view "tragic," in the precise sense that Nietzsche uses the term.[64] To conclude our discussion of *Ecce Homo* with a consideration of this aspect of Nietzsche's imagistic thinking, we might recall the recent work of the French biologist Jean-Claude Ameisen, which offers a confirmation of the vitalist conviction that death serves (to enhance) life. For Ameisen's research into mechanisms of cellular self-destruction suggests that death has a constitutive function in "sculpting" life — hence the title of Ameisen's book on "cellular suicide," *La Sculpture du vivant*.[65] Not only does the survival of cells depend on their capacity to receive signals from other cells that prevent them triggering an endogenous program of "cell suicide," but cellular death, Ameisen argues, plays an important role in developing such complex organs as the brain and the immune system. On this account, death — through the mechanism of *apoptosis* (the ancient Greek word for the autumnal fall of leaves) — acts as "a sculptor at the very heart of life, carving life's form and complexity."[66] *Apoptosis* — the fall of leaves in autumn[67] — how could one not be reminded of the role this idea plays in Schopenhauer and Nietzsche?

One thinks, for instance, of the second volume of *The World as Will and Representation*, where Schopenhauer urges his readers not to think of themselves as being like a leaf on the tree which, "fading in the autumn and about to fall, [. . .] grieves over its own extinction" (im Herbste welkend und im Begriff abzufallen, jammert über seinen Untergang), and reminds the leaf (and us): "Know your own inner being, precisely that which is so filled with the thirst of existence; recognize it once more in the inner, mysterious, sprouting force of the tree [. . .] always *one* and the same in all generations of leaves" (Erkenne doch dein eigenes Wesen, gerade Das, was vom Durst nach Daseyn so erfüllt ist, erkenne es wieder in der innern, geheimen, treibenden Kraft des Baumes, welche, stets EINE und dieselbe in allen Generationen von Blättern, unberührt bleibt vom Entstehen und Vergehen).[68] In *The Gay Science*, Nietzsche — who reminds us that "life" (Leben) means "continually shedding something that wants to die" (fortwährend Etwas von sich abstossen, das sterben will; GS §26; KSA 3, 400) — identifies himself with the "incomprehensible ones" (Unverständlichen), who are "misidentified" (verwechselt), because they "grow, are constantly changing, shed old bark, [. . .] keep becoming younger, more full of future, higher, stronger" (wachsen, [. . .] wechseln fortwährend, [. . .] stossen alte Rinden ab, [. . .] werden immer jünger, zukünftiger, höher, stärker; GS §371; KSA 3, 622–23), like the tree on the mountainside in Zarathustra (Z I 8; KSA 4, 51). Nietzsche, who praises "brief habits" (kurze Gewohnheiten) for "that faith of passion, the belief in eternity" (jenen Glauben der Leidenschaft, den Glauben an die Ewigkeit; GS §295; KSA 3, 535), embraces a way of life in which "what does not belong to such a life" (was nicht zu einem solchen Leben gehört) simply "drops off" (fällt [. . .] ab), "like yellow leaves that any slight stirring of the air takes off a tree" (den vergilbten Blättern gleich, welch jedes bewegtere Lüftchen dem Baume entführt; GS §304; KSA 3, 542–43). In its turn, such a life embraces the will to power, for as Zarathustra says: "And truly, where there is decline and the falling of leaves, behold, there life sacrifices itself — for power!" (Und wahrlich, wo es Untergang giebt und Blätterfallen, siehe da opfert sich Leben — um Macht!; Z II 12; KSA 4, 148). So, asks Zarathustra, why complain because leaves wilt? (Dass Blätter welk werden, — was ist da zu klagen!; Z III 8 §1; KSA 4, 227). Finally, how could one not be reminded of the passage from *Zarathustra* cited by Nietzsche as an example of what he calls the "halcyon tone" (diesen halkyonischen Ton) of this work?[69]

> The figs are falling from the trees; they are good and sweet: and as they fall, their red skins burst. I am a north wind to all ripe figs.
>
> Thus, like figs, do these teachings fall to you, my friends: now drink their juice and their sweet flesh! It is autumn all around us and clear sky and afternoon —

[Die Feigen fallen von den Bäumen, sie sind gut und süß: und indem sie fallen, reißt ihnen die rote Haut. Ein Nordwind bin ich reifen Feigen.

Also, gleich Feigen, fallen euch diese Lehren zu, meine Freunde: nun trinkt ihren Saft und ihr süßes Fleisch! Herbst ist es umher und reiner Himmel und Nachmittag — (*EH* preface §4; *KSA* 6, 260, cf. *Z* II 2; *KSA* 4, 109)]

And it is the autumnal and apoptotic imagery of this passage from *Zarathustra* that sets the tone for the prooemium introducing *Ecce Homo*:

On this perfect day, when everything is ripening and not only the grapes are turning brown, a ray of sunlight has just fallen across my life: I looked backward, I looked forward, never did I see so many and such good things at one time. It is not for nothing that today I buried my forty-forth year, I was *entitled* to bury it, — for whatever was of life in it has been saved, is immortal.

[An diesem vollkommnen Tage, wo alles reift und nicht nur die Traube braun wird, fiel mir eben ein Sonnenblick auf mein Leben: ich sah rückwärts, ich sah hinaus, ich sah nie so viel und so gute Dinge auf einmal. Nicht umsonst begrub ich heute mein vierundvierzigstes Jahr, ich *durfte* es begraben, — was in ihm Leben war, ist gerettet, ist unsterblich. (*KSA* 6, 263)]

In his recent book, co-authored with the psychoanalyst Marie de Hennezel, the French philosopher Bertrand Vergely writes, as if commenting directly on this passage: "Let us live this autumnal moment when life detaches itself as the leaves detach themselves from the tree. One is no longer in a moment of death, but in a moment of life" (Vivons ce moment d'automne où la vie se détache d'elle-même comme les feuilles se détachent de l'arbre. On n'est plus dans un moment de mort, mais dans un moment de vie).[70] And so *Ecce Homo* ultimately embodies in its literary texture the intellectual and psycho-existential value it promotes — the value of life[71] — which turns it into a masterpiece of artistic composition: all the more movingly so because of its proximity to Nietzsche's imminent collapse. At the same time, the text of *Ecce Homo* bears witness to the triumphant ability of Nietzsche — as his father, "already dead," as his mother, "still living and growing old" — to "become what he really is" or, as Jung put it, using the language of alchemy, "to fulfil the purpose for which his mother bore him, and, after the peregrinations of a long life caught up in manifold errors, to become the *filius regius*, the son of the supreme mother."[72]

Notes

In this essay, translations of Nietzsche's works draw on the versions by Walter Kaufmann for *The Gay Science*; by Walter Kaufmann, R. J. Hollingdale, Graham Parkes, and Adrian Del Caro for *Thus Spoke Zarathustra*; and by Walter Kaufmann and R. J. Hollingdale for *Ecce Homo*.

[1] Compare with the opening of "On Old and New Law-Tables": "No-one tells me anything new: and I so I tell myself to myself" (Niemand erzählt mir Neues: so erzähle ich mir mich selber; *KSA* 4, 246).

[2] *KSA* 6, 263. One of the text's draft titles was "*In media vita*" (*KSA* 13, 24[2], 632), which echoes the title of an aphorism in *The Gay Science* (*Die fröhliche Wissenschaft*; *GS* §324; *KSA* 3, 552–53).

[3] See August Johann Gottfried Bielenstein, *Ein glückliches Leben: Selbstbiographie* (Riga: Jonck und Poliewsky, 1904), 37.

[4] These discussions of previous works form a counterpart to the sequence of prefaces to them Nietzsche had composed in 1885 and 1886; see Friedrich Nietzsche, *Ecce auctor: Die Vorreden von 1886*, ed. Claus-Artur Scheier (Hamburg: Meiner, 1990).

[5] For a detailed account of the composition and publication history of *Ecce Homo*, see Mazzino Montinari's commentary (*KSA* 14, 454–512) and his "Ein neuer Abschnitt in Nietzsches 'Ecce Homo'" [1972], in Mazzino Montinari, *Nietzsche lesen* (Berlin and New York: Walter de Gruyter, 1982), 120–68; translated as "A New Section in Nietzsche's *Ecce Homo*," in *Reading Nietzsche*, trans. Greg Whitlock (Urbana, IL: U of Illinois P, 2003), 103–40; and William H. Schaberg, *Nietzsches Werke: Eine Publikationsgeschichte und kommentierte Bibliographie*, trans. Michael Leuenberger (Basel: Schwabe, 2002), 250–57.

[6] See Friedrich Nietzsche, *Ecce Homo* (Leipzig: Insel-Verlag, 1908), of which Friedrich Richter published a limited deluxe edition of 1250 numbered copies, bound in leather and designed by Henry van der Velde; *W* 3, 1063–1159; and *Friedrich Nietzsches Werke des Zusammenbruchs*, ed. Erich F. Podach (Heidelberg: Wolfgang Rothe, 1961).

[7] Goethe, *Werke: Weimarer Ausgabe*, ed. Johann Ludwig Gustav von Loeper, Erich Schmidt, Paul Raabe, im Auftrage der Großherzogin Sophie von Sachsen; 4 parts, 133 vols. in 143 (Weimar: Hermann Böhlau, 1887–1919), III.4:120. For further discussion of Nietzsche in relation to Goethe, see Paul Bishop and R. H. Stephenson, *Friedrich Nietzsche and Weimar Classicism* (Rochester, NY: Camden House, 2005); and Pierre Hadot, *N'oublie pas de vivre: Goethe et la tradition des exercices spirituels* (Paris: Albin Michel, 2008), 256–67.

[8] Thus what distinguishes something pathological in the physiological sense from morbidity is that, in the former, a development is taking place; "each of these metamorphoses," as Joseph-François Angelloz glosses this passage, "means suffering, is 'physiological-pathological,' is a trial undertaken with a happy result in view" (Jean-François Angelloz, *Goethe*, trans. R. H. Blackley [New York: Orion Press, 1958], 235).

[9] As Angelloz remarks, the morbid "bears the danger of retarding or clogging the development of the human personality; it springs from the outside world, and this is where the 'hazards' of life come into play" (Angelloz, *Goethe*, 236).

[10] Johann Peter Eckermann, *Gespräche mit Goethe*, ed. Fritz Bergemann (Frankfurt am Main: Insel, 1981), 461. These *Gespräche* were originally published in 3 volumes, volumes 1 and 2 in 1837 and a third volume in 1848.

[11] Eckermann, *Gespräche mit Goethe*, 461. Angelloz comments that Goethe created "a new kind of autobiography, in which one finds personal confession, which must be truth, the lyrical novel, which may be poetry, and the history of a period, which is reality" (*Goethe*, 237).

[12] Pindar, *Pythian Odes*, no. 2, l.72: "Become true to thyself, now that thou hast learnt what manner of man thou art" (*The Odes of Pindar, including the Principal Fragments*, trans. J. Sandys [London; New York: William Heinemann; Putnam, 1927], 179).

[13] "Puisque toutes nos idées nous viennent par les sens," Helvétius argues (in *De l'homme*, section 2, chap. 15) "qu'on ne naît point mais qu'on devient ce qu'on est" (Helvétius, *Œuvres complètes*, vol. 2, *De l'homme* [Paris: Lepetit, 1818], 131). For Nietzsche's acknowledgment of Helvétius's philosophical significance, see *KSA* 10, 7[18], 243.

[14] For further discussion, see Paul Bishop, "*Ecce Homo* and Nietzsche's Concept of Character," in *Nietzsche's "Ecce Homo": A Centenary Conference*, ed. Duncan Large and Nicholas Martin, forthcoming.

[15] For examples of studies that seek to clarify *Ecce Homo* in the light of psychoanalysis, see Alice Miller, "Das ungelebte Leben und das Werk eines Lebensphilosophen," in *Der gemiedene Schlüssel* (Frankfurt am Main: Suhrkamp, 1996), 9–78; Horst Eberhard Richter, *Der Gotteskomplex: Die Geburt und die Krise des Glaubens an die Allmacht des Menschen* [1979] (Reinbek bei Hamburg: Rowohlt, 2005); Rudolf Kreis, *Der gekreuzigte Dionysos: Kindheit und Genie Friedrich Nietzsches: Zur Genese einer Philosophie der Zeitenwende* (Würzburg: Königshausen & Neumann, 1986); Jørgen Kjaer, *Nietzsche: Die Zerstörung der Humanität durch "Mutterliebe"* (Opladen: Westdeutscher Verlag, 1990); Gaetano Benedetti, "Die neurotische Lebensproblematik Nietzsches als eine Wirkkraft und eine Grenze seiner Philosophie," *Gesnerus: Swiss Journal of the History of Medicine and Sciences* 41 (1984): 111–32; Josef Schmidt, *Nietzsche absconditus, oder Spurensuchen bei Nietzsche*, 4 vols. in 3 (Berlin-Aschaffenburg: IBDK Verlag, 1991–95); and Joachim Köhler, *Zarathustras Geheimnis: Friedrich Nietzsche und seine verschlüsselte Botschaft* (Nördlingen: Greno, 1989).

[16] Jacques Derrida, "Otobiographies: The Teaching of Nietzsche and the Politics of the Proper Name," trans. Avital Ronell, in *The Ear of the Other: Otobiography, Transference, Translation*, ed. Christie McDonald, trans. Peggy Kamuf (Lincoln, NE and London: U of Nebraska P, 1988), 1–38 (here: 16–17); "Otobiographie de Nietzsche," in *L'oreille de l'autre: otobiographies, transferts, traductions*, ed. Claude Lévesque et Christie V. McDonald (Montreal: vlb éditeur, 1982), 11–56 (here: 29–30).

[17] Rodolphe Gasché, "Autobiography as Gestalt: Nietzsche's *Ecce Homo*," in *Why Nietzsche Now?*, ed. Daniel O'Hara (Bloomington: Indiana UP, 1985), 271–90

(here: 282). For an alternative Oedipal reading, see Tracy B. Strong, "Oedipus as Hero: Family and Family Metaphors in Nietzsche," in *Why Nietzsche Now?*, 311–35 (esp. 317–19).

[18] Pierre Klossowski, "The Consultation of the Paternal Shadow," in *Nietzsche and the Vicious Circle*, trans. Daniel W. Smith (Chicago and London: U of Chicago P, 1998), 172–97 (197); *Nietzsche et le cercle vicieux* (Paris: Mercure de France, 1969), 251–84 (184).

[19] Sarah Kofman, "A Fantastical Genealogy: Nietzsche's Family Romance," trans. Deborah Jenson, in *Nietzsche and the Feminine*, ed. Peter J. Burgard (Charlottesville and London: UP of Virginia, 1994), 35–52 (here: 37); excerpted, as is "Explosion I: Of Nietzsche's *Ecce Homo*," trans. Duncan Large, *Diacritics* 24/4 (1994): 51–70, from Sarah Kofman, *Explosion I: De l'"Ecce Homo" de Nietzsche* (Paris: Galilée, 1992). See also "Accessories (*Ecce Homo*, 'Why I Write Such Good Books,' 'The Untimelies,' 3)," trans. Duncan Large, in *Nietzsche: A Critical Reader*, ed. Peter R. Sedgwick (Oxford and Cambridge, MA: Blackwell, 1995), 144–57; and "The Psychologist of the Eternal Feminine," trans. Madeleine Dobie, *Yale French Studies* 87 (1995): 173–89. For further discussion, see Duncan Large, "Double 'Whaam!' Sarah Kofman on *Ecce Homo*," *German Life and Letters* 48/4 (1995): 441–62.

[20] Thomas Steinbuch, *A Commentary on Nietzsche's "Ecce Homo"* (Lanham, MD, London: UP of America, 1994), 18. For further discussion of Derrida, Gasché, Klossowski, and Kofman, see David Farrell Krell, "Consultations with the Paternal Shadow on the Altar at the Edge of the Earth," in *Infectious Nietzsche* (Bloomington and Indianapolis: Indiana UP, 1996), 213–33.

[21] Michel Onfray, "Conférences de Michel Onfray," broadcast on France Culture, 13 August 2009. See Michel Onfray, *Contre-histoire de la philosophie*, vol. 7, *La construction du surhomme* (Paris: Grasset, 2011).

[22] For a thoroughgoing interpretation of Nietzsche's entire life from a Jungian standpoint that reads this statement as "the riddle that enclosed the enigma of his own fatality" and as "evidenc[ing] the orphic paradox of being trapped between the dead and the living," see Gertrudis Ostfeld de Bendayan, *Ecce Mulier: Nietzsche and the Eternal Feminine: An Analytical Psychological Perspective* (Wilmette, IL: Chiron Publications, 2007), 138.

[23] Lucretius, *De Rerum Natura* (*On the Nature of Things*), book 2, l. 1 ff.

[24] Arthur Schopenhauer, *The World as Will and Representation*, trans. E. F. J. Payne, 2 vols. (New York: Dover, 1969), vol. 1, §57; 1:313; *Werke in fünf Bänden*, ed. Ludger Lütkehaus (Zurich: Haffmans, 1988), vol. 1, §57; 1:408.

[25] See the chapter on the Magna Mater in Ludwig Klages, *Der Geist als Widersacher der Seele* [1929–32] (Bonn: Bouvier, 1981), 1330–1400, which explicitly acknowledges its debt to J. J. Bachofen, one of Nietzsche's colleagues in Basel. In his "biocentric metaphysics," Klages equates the following "primal images" (*Urbilder*): "earth = seed = egg = womb = mother" (1329). According to Klages, the true "eternal recurrence" is the "circular time" of the ever-renewed, ceaselessly flowing images (1349), or what he terms "the secret of the *rebirth of the soul*" (das Geheimnis der *Wiedergeburt der Seele*; 1350).

26 See Heidegger's remarks on Nietzsche and the problem of communicating thought, in *Was heißt Denken?* (*What Is Called Thinking?*, 1954): "Learning cannot be brought about through chiding. And yet someone who teaches must sometimes speak loudly. He must even shout and shout, even though he is trying to teach something as silent as thinking. Nietzsche, who was one of the quietest and shyest individuals, knew about this need. He endured the torture of having to shout" (Das Lernen läßt sich darum durch kein Schelten bewirken. Und dennoch muß einer beim Lehren bisweilen laut werden. Er muß sogar schreien und schreien, selbst wenn es sich darum handelt, eine so stille Sache wie das Denken lernen zu lassen. Nietzsche, der einer der stillsten und scheuesten Menschen war, wußte von dieser Notwendigkeit. Er durchlitt die Qual, schreien zu müssen) (*Was heißt Denken?* [Tübingen: Niemeyer, 1954], 19).

27 In *The Gay Science*, Nietzsche had addressed himself to the "question of being understandable" (Frage der Verständlichkeit), noting that "one does not only wish to be understood when one writes; one wishes just as surely *not* to be understood" (man will nicht nur verstanden werden, wenn man schreibt, sondern ebenso gewiss auch *nicht* verstanden werden; *GS* §381; *KSA* 3, 633).

28 Goethe, *Scientific Studies*, ed. and trans. Douglas Miller, vol. 12 of *Goethe: The Collected Works*, ed. Victor Lange, Eric A. Blackall, and Cyrus Hamlin (New York: Suhrkamp, 1988), 158; Goethe, *Werke: Hamburger Ausgabe*, ed. Erich Trunz, 14 vols. (Hamburg: Christian Wegner, 1948–60; Munich: Beck, 1981), 13:315 (henceforth cited as *Werke* [Hamburger Ausgabe]).

29 In the *Nachlass* for spring 1884, for example, we find the following note: "*Entschluß*. Ich will reden, und nicht mehr Zarathustra" (*Decision*: I want to speak, and no longer Zarathustra; *KSA* 11, 25[277], 83).

30 For further discussion of the theme of language and communication in *Zarathustra*, see Bishop and Stephenson, *Friedrich Nietzsche and Weimar Classicism*, chapter 3, "The Aesthetic Gospel of Nietzsche's *Zarathustra*," esp. 119–22.

31 For example, his discourses in the marketplace are greeted with incomprehension, and he realizes this: "Sie verstehen mich nicht: ich bin nicht der Mund für diese Ohren" (They do not understand me: I am not the mouth for these ears; *Z* preface §5; *KSA* 4, 20). Nor do Zarathustra's disciples fully understand him, nor even the Higher Men whom he invites to his cave in part 4.

32 It would doubtless amuse Nietzsche to read the conclusion of Michael Tanner's introduction to the Penguin reprint of its translation of *Ecce Homo*: "the answer must be a resounding 'No'" (Nietzsche, *Ecce Homo*, trans. R. J. Hollingdale [Harmondsworth: Penguin, 1991], vii–xvii [here: xvii]).

33 "Withdraw into yourself and look. And if you do not find yourself beautiful yet, act as does the creator of a statue that is to be made beautiful; he cuts away here, he smoothes there, he makes this line lighter, this other purer, until a lovely face has grown upon his work. So do you also: cut away all that is excessive, straighten all that is crooked, bring light to all that is overcast, labour to make all one glow of beauty and never cease chiselling your statue, until there shall shine out on you from it the godlike splendour of virtue" (Plotinus, *Enneads*, 1.6.9; in Plotinus, *The Enneads*, trans. S. MacKenna, 4th ed., rev. B. S. Page [London: Faber and

Faber, 1969)], 63). For further discussion, see Michel Onfray, *La Sculpture de soi: La morale esthétique* (Paris: Grasset, 1993), 77–90.

³⁴ Goethe, *Scientific Studies*, 39; *Werke* [Hamburger Ausgabe], 13:38.

³⁵ The doctrine of eternal recurrence lies at the heart of Nietzsche's interest in character as a coming-to-terms with the dialectic of freedom and necessity: for, as a cosmological hypothesis, it expresses a *fatalism*, according to which the self is something given ("wie man wird, was man *ist*"); while yet, as an existential imperative, it presents the self as something to be constructed ("wie man *wird*, was man ist"); see Bishop, "*Ecce Homo* and Nietzsche's Concept of Character."

³⁶ Eckermann, *Gespräche mit Goethe*, 57.

³⁷ Such a view is, according to the Schillerian definition, *sublime*, in that it represents "the terrible and magnificent spectacle of change that destroys everything and creates it anew, only to destroy it again" (das furchtbar herrliche Schauspiel der alles zerstörenden und wieder erschaffenden, und wieder zerstörenden Veränderung; *Über das Erhabene* [On the Sublime], in Schiller, *Werke: Nationalausgabe*, ed. Julius Petersen and Gerhard Fricke, Norbert Oellers and Siegfried Seidel, im Auftrage des Goethe- und Schiller-Archivs, des Schiller-Nationalmuseums und der Deutschen Akademie, 43 vols. [Weimar: Hermann Böhlaus Nachfolger, 1943ff.], 21:52). In turn, Schiller argues, the perception of the sublime exercises an influence on our moral development: "The capacity to sense the sublime is thus one of the most magnificent capacities of human nature, which deserves both our *respect* [. . .] and, because of its influence on the moral individual, the most perfect development" (Die Fähigkeit, das Erhabene zu empfinden, ist also eine der herrlichsten Anlagen in der Menschennatur, die sowohl [. . .] unsre *Achtung*, als wegen ihres Einflusses auf den moralischen Menschen die vollkommenste Entwickelung verdient; 21:52). As a result, Schiller concludes, the beautiful has value with reference to us as human beings, but the value of the sublime relates to the "pure daimon" (*den reinen Dämon*) within us (52). Nevertheless, Schiller concludes, "the sublime must complement the beautiful in order to complete our aesthetic education and make it whole" (so muß das Erhabene zu dem Schönen hinzukommen, um die ästhetische Erziehung zu einem vollständigen Ganzen zu machen), and to extend the human heart's capacity for feeling to the full extent of our vocation, and thus beyond the world of the senses . . . (52). For discussion of Schiller's conception of freedom and self-determination in relation to Rudolf Steiner's, see Ewald Koepke, *Goethe, Schiller und die Anthroposophie: Das Geheimnis der Ergänzung* (Stuttgart: Verlag Freies Geistesleben, 2002), 83–86.

³⁸ *Goethes Gespräche*, ed. Flodoard von Biedermann, 5 vols. (Leipzig: Biedermann, 1909–11), 2:174.

³⁹ Goethe, *Briefe* [Hamburger Ausgabe], 4:379–80.

⁴⁰ In *The Gay Science* Nietzsche writes: "It makes me happy that human beings do not want to think at all the thought of death! I should very much like to do something that will make the thought of life a hundred times more worthwhile to think of" (Es macht mich glücklich zu sehen, dass die Menschen den Gedanken an den Tod durchaus nicht denken wollen! Ich möchte gern etwas dazu thun, ihnen den Gedanken an das Leben noch hundertmal *denkenswerther* zu machen; *GS* §278; *KSA* 3, 523).

[41] Schopenhauer, *The World as Will and Representation*, vol. 2, chap. 41; 2:463–509 (here: 476); *Werke in fünf Bänden*, 2:536–91 (here: 555–56).

[42] Schopenhauer, *The World as Will and Representation*, 2:477; *Werke in fünf Bänden*, 2:553.

[43] See Klages, *Der Geist als Widersacher der Seele*, 1199–1204, 1327–29, 1338–40, and 1345–52. See also the fragment "On Symbols of Circulation" ("Von den Symbolen des Kreislaufs") in Klages's *Nachlass*, where he discusses the tree, the wheel, and the river (Ludwig Klages, *Rhythmen und Runen: Nachlass herausgegeben von ihm selbst* [Leipzig: J. A. Barth, 1944], 391–93).

[44] Klages, *Der Geist als Widersacher der Seele*, 1345 and 1349.

[45] Klages, *Der Geist als Widersacher der Seele*, 1338.

[46] See C. G. Jung, *Collected Works*, ed. Sir Herbert Read, Michael Fordham, Gerhard Adler, and William McGuire, 20 vols. (London: Routledge and Kegan Paul, 1953–83), 9/i: §99; and 4: §728; and *Nietzsche's "Zarathustra": Notes of the Seminar given in 1934–1939*, ed. James Jarrett, 2 vols. (London: Routledge, 1989), 1:22–23 and 240–41.

[47] For further discussion, see Donald Phillip Verene, "Coincidence, Historical Repetition, and Self-Knowledge: Jung, Vico, and Joyce," *Journal of Analytical Psychology* 47 (2002): 459–78.

[48] Brian Leiter, "The Paradox of Fatalism and Self-Creation in Nietzsche" [1998], in *Nietzsche*, ed. John Richardson and Brian Leiter (Oxford: Oxford UP, 2001), 281–321. For Leiter, this paradox can be resolved, but he thinks only by restricting the sense in which Nietzsche talks about "creating" the self (315–19). On the special sense in which Nietzsche speaks of "self-creation" as "self-cultivation" in relation to the problem of freedom and determination, see Julian Young, *Friedrich Nietzsche: A Philosophical Biography* (Cambridge: Cambridge UP, 2010), 304–7 (cf. 267–68).

[49] See Alexander Nehamas, *Nietzsche: Life as Literature* (Cambridge, MA: Harvard UP, 1985), esp. chapters 5 and 6; and Richard Rorty, *Contingency, Irony, and Solidarity* (Cambridge: Cambridge UP, 1989).

[50] *Système de la nature*, part 1, chapter 6 and chapter 9; in Paul-Henri Thiry, baron d'Holbach, *Œuvres philosophiques*, vol. 2 (Paris: Editions Alive, 1999), 208 and 241.

[51] When reading the works of Spinoza in the period leading up to the composition of *Zarathustra*, Nietzsche wrote to Franz Overbeck on 30 July 1881: "I am completely astonished, completely delighted! I have a *predecessor*, and what a predecessor!" (Ich bin ganz erstaunt, ganz entzückt! Ich habe einen *Vorgänger* und was für einen; *KSB* 6, 111).

[52] Spinoza, letter to G. H. Schuller, October 1764, in *On the Improvement of the Understanding; The Ethics; The Correspondence* [*Works of Spinoza*, vol. 2], trans. R. H. M. Elwes (New York: Dover, 1955), 390; and *Ethics*, part 1, definition 7 (ibid., 46).

[53] Goethe, *Briefe*, ed. Karl Robert Mandelkow, 4 vols. (Hamburg: Christian Wegner, 1962–67), 4:306.

[54] Goethe, *From My Life: Poetry and Truth: Parts One to Three*, ed. Thomas P. Saine and Jeffrey L. Sammons, trans. Robert R. Heitner, vol. 4 of *Goethe: The Collected Works* (New York: Suhrkamp Publishers, 1987), 355; *Werke* [HA], 9:478.

[55] A related thought is given expression in the *Maxims and Reflections*, where Goethe reflects that "whatever lives has the gift of adapting itself to the most diverse requirements of external influences, while nevertheless not surrendering a certain definite independence" (Das Lebendige hat die Gabe, sich nach vielfältigsten Bedingungen äußerer Einflüsse zu bequemen und doch eine gewisse errungene entschiedene Selbständigkeit nicht aufzugeben) (Goethe, *Maxims and Reflections*, ed. Hecker, §1253; *Werke* [Hamburger Ausgabe] 12:369).

[56] Goethe, *Werke* [Hamburger Ausgabe], 14:175.

[57] Goethe, *Werke* [Hamburger Ausgabe], 14:175.

[58] Michel Onfray, *La Sagesse tragique: Du bon usage de Nietzsche* (Paris: Le Livre du Poche, 2006), 21 and 161; 126.

[59] Onfray, *La Sagesse tragique*, 127–28.

[60] Michel Onfray, "À ceux qui ne veulent pas jouir: Comment peut-on ne pas être hédoniste?," in *L'Archipel des comètes: Journal hédoniste III* (Paris: Grasset, 2001), 267–82 (here: 279).

[61] Onfray, "À ceux qui ne veulent pas jouir: Comment peut-on ne pas être hédoniste?," 281.

[62] Cf. *WP* §1053 and §1056; *KSA* 11, 26[376] and 25[227], 250 and 73. These passages provide the context for Nietzsche's oft misunderstood remark, "the weak and botched shall perish [. . .]. And one should help them to do so" (die Schwachen und Missrathnen sollen zu Grunde gehn [. . .]. Und man soll ihnen noch dazu helfen; *AC* §2; *KSA* 6, 170).

[63] For a discussion of the centrality of this phrase in Nietzsche's thought, see Alexander Nehamas, "'How One Becomes What One Is'" [1983], in *Nietzsche*, ed. Richardson and Leiter, 255–80.

[64] Compare with Nietzsche's definition of "the sense for the tragic": "The individual should be consecrated to something suprapersonal — that is what tragedy wants; the individual should forget the terrible anxiety that death and time bring him, for even in the briefest moment, in the tiniest atom of his lifetime, he can encounter something sacred that turns all struggle and all distress into elation — that is what it means *to have a sense of the tragic*" (Der Einzelne soll zu etwas Ueberpersönlichem geweiht werden — das will die Tragödie; er soll die schreckliche Beängstigung, welche der Tod und die Zeit dem Individuum macht, verlernen: denn schon im kleinsten Augenblick, im kürzesten Atom seines Lebenslaufes kann ihm etwas Heiliges begegnen, das allen Kampf und alle Noth überschwenglich macht — das heisst *tragisch gesinnt sein*; *UM* RW §4; *KSA* 1, 453).

[65] For further discussion, see Jean-Claude Ameisen, *La Sculpture de vivant: Le suicide cellulaire ou la mort créatrice* (Paris: Seuil, 1999).

[66] Jean-Claude Ameisen, "Carving Life: Cell Suicide or Death as a Creator." Available online at http://www.cesil.com/leaderforchemist/articoli/inglese/ameisening/ameisening.htm (accessed 4 December 2011).

[67] See S. F. Gilbert, *Developmental Biology*, 7th ed. (Stamford, CT: Sinauer Associates, 2003), 164. The term was originally used in this context by John F. Kerr, Andrew H. Wyllie, and A. R. Currie, "Apoptosis: A basic biological phenomenon with wide-ranging implications in tissue kinetics," *British Journal of Cancer* 26 (1972): 239–57.

[68] Schopenhauer, *The World as Will and Representation*, vol. 2, §41, 2:477–78; *Werke*, 2:554–55. Compare with Jung's use of this image in *Symbols of Transformation* [1952], in *Collected Works*, 5: §296 (the individual as a twig broken off from the mother and transplanted); and in "Introduction to the Religious and Psychological Problems of Alchemy" [1943], in *Psychology and Alchemy, Collected Works*, 12: §33 (patients shed from the community of the Church "like leaves from the great tree").

[69] *EH* preface §4; *KSA* 6, 259, cf. *EH Z* §6; *KSA* 6, 344.

[70] Marie de Hennezel and Bertrand Vergely, *Une vie pour se mettre au monde* (Paris: Carnets Nord, 2010), 87.

[71] Compare with Nietzsche's claim to speak on behalf of "jene neue Partei des Lebens" (that new party of life; *EH BT* §4; *KSA* 6, 313).

[72] C. G. Jung, "The Psychology of the Transference" [1946], in *Collected Works*, 16: §407.

14: *Dithyrambs of Dionysos*

Paul Bishop

IN 1860, WHILE NIETZSCHE WAS A STUDENT at Schulpforta (and perhaps because of what he experienced in his schooldays), he wrote a sequence of poems entitled "In the Distance" ("In der Ferne"), the second of which moves from a Wertherian sense of constriction, via a nostalgic recollection of domestic harmony, to a melancholy realization of loss:

> And this homeland where you were born,
> Where you have richly enjoyed life's bliss,
> This you have lost.

> [Und diese Heimath, wo du bist geboren
> Wo du des Lebens Wonne reich genossen,
> Hast du verloren! —][1]

Around the same time, he wrote "Without a Homeland" ("Ohne Heimat"), a text that depicts, as Philip Grundlehner puts it, "a passionate self-emancipation from all restrictive boundaries,"[2] and other poems bear the titles "Longing for Home" ("Heimweh"), "Departure" ("Abschied"), and "Despair ("Verzweiflung").[3] True, many of these texts lack sophistication, much in the way that Nietzsche's musical compositions are said to do, yet they possess a certain naïve vigor. Some later texts restate this theme of abandonment with considerable power. One of these is a famous poem from 1884, known under various titles, including "Isolated" ("Vereinsamt"), the final verse of which reads:

> The crows cry,
> And fly in flocks towards the town:
> Soon it will snow, —
> Alas for him, who has no home!

> [Die Krähen schrei'n
> und ziehen schwirren Flugs zur Stadt:
> bald wird es schnei'n, —
> weh dem, der keine Heimat hat!
> *KSA* 11, 28[64], 329][4]

— ending on a phrase that is echoed in a later poem, entitled "Among the Daughters of the Desert" ("Unter Töchtern der Wüste"), first sung by Zarathustra's shadow in part 4 of *Thus Spoke Zarathustra* (*Also sprach Zarathustra*) and also included in a short collection entitled *Dithyrambs of Dionysos* (*Dionysos-Dithyramben*).[5]

Thus from the time of his first attempts at writing, Nietzsche had had recourse to writing poetry as a means of self-expression.[6] In a way that should not be neglected in a *Companion* to Nietzsche's life and thought, poetic texts came to play an important role in his philosophical works. The poem "Among Friends: An Epilogue" ("Unter Freunden: Ein Nachspiel") brought the first volume of *Human, All Too Human* (*Menschliches, Allzumenschliches*) to a close (*KSA* 2, 365–66), while sixty-three short poems under the collective title "Jokes, Cunning and Revenge" ("Scherz, List und Rache") had formed a "Prelude in German Rhymes" ("Vorspiel in deutschen Reimen") to *The Gay Science* (*Die fröhliche Wissenschaft*; *KSA* 3, 353–67), to the second edition of which the "Songs of Prince Free-As-A-Bird" ("Lieder des Prinzen Vogelfrei"), originally published separately as "Idylls from Messina" ("Idyllen aus Messina"; *KSA* 3, 333–42), were added (*KSA* 3, 639–51). Similarly, *Beyond Good and Evil* (*Jenseits von Gut und Böse*) ends on a "Closing Song" ("Nachgesang") entitled "From High Mountains" ("Aus hohen Bergen"; *KSA* 5, 241–32), while two poems reproduced in *Nietzsche contra Wagner* — "Is This Still German?" ("Ist das noch deutsch?" *KSA* 6, 429, cf. *BGE* §256; *KSA* 5, 204) and "On the bridge I stood / Of late in the brown night" ("An der Brücke stand / jüngst ich in brauner Nacht"; *KSA* 6, 421, cf. *EH* "Why I Am So Clever" §7; *KSA* 6, 291) — demonstrate the full range of Nietzsche's poetic talents, one parodic and sarcastic, the other tender and lyrical. Both these aspects of Nietzsche's poetic writing can be found in *Thus Spoke Zarathustra*, which could be considered to be really one long poem; after all, the co-existence of these different styles — side-by-side, or in immediate juxtaposition, or occasionally even simultaneously — is one of the reasons Nietzsche's poetic output is so hard, as well as so rewarding, to interpret.

In 1888, at the same time as he was working on *Twilight of the Idols* (*Götzen-Dämmerung*), *The Anti-Christ* (*Der Antichrist*), *Nietzsche contra Wagner*, and the work subsequently known as *The Will to Power* (*Der Wille zur Macht*), Nietzsche put together a number of poetic fragments he had written when composing *Zarathustra*, and from them confected a short anthology. Among the projected titles for the collection were "The Songs of Zarathustra" (Die Lieder Zarathustras) and "The Eternal Return: Zarathustra's Dances and Processions" (Die ewige Wiederkunft: Zarathustra's Tänze und Festzüge; *KSA* 13, 20[162]-20[168], 576–77), but the eventual title was *Dithyrambs of Dionysos*. This title is well-chosen, because it spans the entirety of Nietzsche's philosophical output: from

The Birth of Tragedy (*Die Geburt der Tragödie*), where he sees in the dith-yramb a stimulus to "the greatest intensification of humankind's entire symbolic capacities" (höchste Steigerung aller seiner symbolischen Fähig-keiten) and the transformation of nature into a world of symbols (*BT* §2; *KSA* 1, 33) and insists on the essential difference between the dithyramb and other choral odes, because only *here* the members of the chorus actu-ally become "living servants of their god" (lebende Diener ihres Gottes; *BT* §8; *KSA* 1, 61), to *Ecce Homo*, where Nietzsche claims that he (and not Archilocus) is the inventor of the dithyramb and presents himself, the author of *Zarathustra*, as an exponent of this ancient art (*EH Z* §7; *KSA* 5, 345). In *The Birth of Tragedy*, Dionysos is associated both with the gloomy wisdom of Silenus (*BT* §3; *KSA* 1, 35) *and* with the "*vision*" (*Vision*) — generated by the chorus, "the only 'reality'" (die einzige "Realität"), and "its entire symbolism of dance, tone, and words" (mit der ganzen Symbolik des Tanzes, des Tones und des Wortes) — of which Dionysos is "the real stage-hero and the center" (der eigentliche Bühnen-held und Mittelpunkt; *BT* §8; *KSA* 1, 62–63); in *Ecce Homo*, Nietzsche returns again to Dionysos as a synthesis of the Dionysian and the Apol-lonian, pointing to Zarathustra's sense that he is "*the supreme kind of all things that exist*" (die höchste Art alles Seienden) and at the same time "the eternal Yes to all things" (das ewige Ja zu allen Dingen) as being nothing less than "*the concept of Dionysos himself*" (*der Begriff des Dionysos selbst*; *EH Z* §6; *KSA* 6, 344–45).

Among the papers in Nietzsche's lodgings in Turin, Franz Overbeck found a page dedicating the *Dithyrambs of Dionysos* to the French poet Catulle Mendès — the "poet of Isoline," inasmuch as he had written the libretto for *Isoline* (1888), an opera composed by André Messager.[7] Here Mendès is acclaimed as a "satyr," a role that elsewhere Nietzsche had por-trayed himself as playing.[8] In *The Birth of Tragedy* Nietzsche placed the satyr-chorus at the center of his account of the origin of tragedy — and of art as a whole. Here he had argued that the satyr — "the synthesis of God and goat" (die Synthesis von Gott und Bock; *BT* "Versuch" §4; *KSA* 1, 16), "the fictitious natural being" (das fingirte Naturwesen) — stands in the same relation to the human being of culture as Dionysian music does to civilization (*BT* §7; *KSA* 1, 55); that is to say, at once its precondition and its transcendence. What does the "bearded" (bärtige) satyr (*BT* §2; *KSA* 1, 32) represent? In *aesthetic* terms, the dithyrambic satyr-chorus represents "*art*" (die *Kunst*), "the saving deed of Greek art" (die ret-tende That der griechischen Kunst) — saving us from the wisdom of Sile-nus, from "the horror or absurdity of existence" (das Entsetzliche oder Absurde des Daseins), by transforming them into *the sublime* (the artistic [Apollonian] taming of horror) or into *comedy* (the artistic [Dionysian] discharge of disgust at absurdity) (*BT* §7; *KSA* 1, 57) — and ultimately into beauty or *schöner Schein* of the union of Dionysos and Apollo (*BT*

§21; *KSA* 1, 139–40). In *religious* terms, in the magical transformation wrought by the dithyramb, the Dionysian reveler "sees himself as a satyr [. . .], *and as a satyr in turn he sees the god*" (sieht sich [. . .] als Satyr, *und als Satyr wiederum schaut er den Gott*) — a moment that Nietzsche *immediately* returns to the realm of aesthetics, adding: "that is, in his metamorphosis he sees a new vision outside himself, as the Apollonian completion of his own state" (er sieht in seiner Verwandlung eine neue Vision ausser sich, als apollinische Vollendung seines Zustandes; *BT* §8: *KSA* 1, 61–62). At the same time, Nietzsche argues that in its earliest form tragedy only presented a representation of the god, and only later was the divine considered to be present (*BT* §8; *KSA* 1, 63).[9] In the *Dithyrambs of Dionysos*, the nine poems re-enact this divine epiphany in all its ambiguity, addressing Zarathustra in the person of Dionysos and addressing the god in the name of Zarathustra (and, so his detractors insist, in the name of the incipiently insane Nietzsche).[10] Is what these texts describe a religious experience, a moment of mystical intuition? Or does it enact an aesthetico-existential project that Nietzsche had begun to articulate in *The Birth of Tragedy*, had embodied in *Zarathustra*, and was looking to restate in the quasi-autobiographical form of *Ecce Homo*?

The satyr and the satyr-chorus formed an important philosophical topos in Nietzsche's thought. In *The Birth of Tragedy* the satyr is "musician, poet, dancer, and spirit seer in one person" (Musiker, Dichter, Tänzer, Geisterseher in einer Person; *BT* §8; *KSA* 1, 63), just as Nietzsche later saw in Zarathustra "the great synthesis of the creative, the loving, the destroying" (die große Synthesis des Schaffenden, Liebenden, Vernichtenden; *KSA* 11, 31[3], 360).[11] In *Beyond Good and Evil*, the satyr functions as a symbol of the "philosophical sense of humor" (der philosophische Humor), without which the philosopher degenerates à la Spinoza or Giordano Bruno into a "martyr," and his philosophy becomes "*merely* a satyr play, *merely* an epilogue farce" (*nur* ein Satyrspiel, *nur* eine Nachspiel-Farce) (my emphasis), revealing its genesis as "a long tragedy" (eine lange Tragödie; *BGE* §25; *KSA* 5, 43). In a subsequent aphorism, Nietzsche restates his thesis of the aesthetic justification of the world in a quizzical epigram: "Around the hero everything becomes a tragedy, around the demi-god everything becomes a satyr play; and around God everything becomes — well, what? perhaps a 'world'? —" (Um den Helden herum wird Alles zur Tragödie, um den Halbgott herum Alles zum Satyrspiel; und um Gott herum wird Alles — wie? vielleicht zur "Welt"? —; *BGE* §150; *KSA* 5, 99).

Yet Nietzsche's identification in *Ecce Homo* with a satyr — "I am a disciple of the philosopher Dionysos, I would prefer to be a satyr rather than a saint" (Ich bin ein Jünger des Philosophen Dionysos, ich zöge vor, eher noch ein Satyr zu sein als ein Heiliger; *EH* preface §2; *KSA* 6, 258) — should alert us to his ability to combine deeply philosophical questions with half-hidden autobiographical allusions.[12] A note in the *Nachlass* drafts a conversation between Theseus, Dionysos, and Ariadne (*KSA* 12, 9[115], 401–2), of which the conclusion to "Ariadne's Complaint" (Klage der Ariadne) is the result. But this text — and the allusions to Ariadne in the section on the "genius of the heart" (*KSA* 5, 239), in *Twilight of the Idols* (*TI* "Skirmishes" §19; *KSA* 6, 123–24), and in *Ecce Homo* (*EH* Z §8; *KSA* 6, 348) — perhaps only make sense in the light of Nietzsche's final letters from Turin, casting himself as Dionysos and Cosima Wagner as Ariadne (leaving Richard in the role of Theseus):[13] "Ariadne, I love you" (Ariadne, ich liebe dich).[14]

> *A flash of lightning. Dionysos becomes visible in emerald beauty.*
>
> DIONYSOS:
> Be wise, Ariadne! . . .
> You have little ears, you have ears like mine:
> Let some wisdom into them! —
> Must we not first hate ourselves if we are to love ourselves? . . .
> I am thy labyrinth . . .

> [*Ein Blitz. Dionysos wird in smaragdener Schönheit sichtbar.*
>
> DIONYSOS:
> Sei klug, Ariadne! . . .
> Du hast kleine Ohren, du hast meine Ohren:
> steck ein kluges Wort hinein! —
> Muss man sich nicht erst hassen, wenn man sich lieben soll? . . .
> Ich bin dein Labyrinth . . .][15]

On one level, the *Dithyrambs of Dionysos* prove the remark Nietzsche made in a note from the *Nachlass* that "a labyrinthine man never seeks the truth, but only ever his Ariadne — whatever he may tell us" (ein labyrinthischer Mensch sucht niemals die Wahrheit, sondern immer nur seine Ariadne — was er uns auch sagen möge; *KSA* 10, 4[55], 125). On the other, by merging together text and reality, fact and fantasy, thought and life, they demonstrate Nietzsche's capacity to undertake the aestheticization of his entire existence, to the point of pathology (and maybe beyond it).

Writing about one of the dithyrambs, "Between Birds of Prey" ("Zwischen Raubvögeln"), in *Symbols of Transformation* (*Symbole der Wandlung*, 1952), the Swiss analytical psychologist C. G. Jung discerned in this text a remarkable expression of the psychological state he termed "introversion." In introversion, the libido sinks, to use a Nietzschean expression, into its "own depths" (eigene Tiefe),[16] where it discovers, "amid a hundred memories" (zwischen hundert Erinnerungen),[17] what Jung calls "the world of the child, the paradisal state of early infancy, from which we are driven out by the relentless law of time."[18] The image of Zarathustra, "self-excavated, / digging into yourself" (in dich selber eingehöhlt, / dich selber angrabend)[19] — or as Jung puts it, "sunk in his own depths, he is like one buried in the earth" — is like the image of "a dead man who has crawled back into the mother," reminiscent (to Jung's mind) of Caeneus,[20] Mithras,[21] or Christ. "Overtowered by a hundred burdens, / overburdened with yourself" (von hundert Lasten überthürmt, / von dir überlastet), what weighs down Zarathustra (like the cross of Christ, "or whatever other heavy burden the hero carries"), is *"himself,* or rather *the* self, his wholeness, which is both God and animal — [. . .] the totality of his being, which is rooted in his animal nature and reaches out beyond the merely human towards the divine."[22] Whatever one makes of his reading, Jung might perhaps help explain the curious power of these enigmatic texts, when he suggests that "what seems like a poetic figure of speech in Nietzsche is really an age-old myth," and that "it is as if the poet could still sense, beneath the words of contemporary speech and in the images that crowd in upon his imagination, the ghostly presence of bygone spiritual words" — and, above all, that he "possessed the capacity to make them come alive again."[23]

Notes

The translations from Nietzsche in this essay are cited from those made by Philip Grundlehner and by R. J. Hollingdale.

[1] Translated in Philip Grundlehner, *The Poetry of Friedrich Nietzsche* (New York and Oxford: Oxford UP, 1986), 6; *BAW* 1, 192.

[2] Grundlehner, *The Poetry of Friedrich Nietzsche,* 12; for the text, see Grundlehner, *The Poetry of Friedrich Nietzsche,*12–13; *BAW* 1, 122 and 228–29.

[3] *BAW* 1, 223–25.

[4] For further discussion, see Franz Norbert Mennemeier, "Friedrich Nietzsche: Vereinsamt," in *Die deutsche Lyrik: Form und Geschichte: Interpretationen,* ed. Benno von Wiese, vol. 2, *Von der Spätromantik bis zur Gegenwart* (Düsseldorf: Bagel, 1964), 245–54.

[5] "Among the Daughters of the Desert," §2 (315–19); cf. "The Desert Grows: Woe to Him Who Harbors Deserts . . ." (Die Wüste wächst: weh dem, der Wüsten birgt . . .) (KSA 6, 382–87), in Friedrich Nietzsche, *Dithyrambs of Dionysus: Bilingual Edition,* trans. R. J. Hollingdale (London: Anvil, 1984), 29–37. For commentaries on individual texts, see Wolfram Groddeck, "Nietzsches Gedicht 'Die Sonne sinkt': Eine philologische Lektüre des sechsten 'Dionysos-Dithyrambus,'" *Nietzsche-Studien* 16 (1987): 21–46; Ernst Meuthen, "Vom Zerreißen der Larve und des Herzens: Nietzsches Lieder der 'höheren Menschen' und die 'Dionysos-Dithyramben,'" *Nietzsche-Studien* 20 (1991): 152–85; Bianca Theisen, "Die Gewalt des Notwendigen: Überlegungen zu Nietzsches Dionysos-Dithyrambus 'Klage der Ariadne,'" *Nietzsche-Studien* 20 (1991): 186–209; and Gitta

Gritzmann, "Nietzsches Lyrik als Ausdruckskunst: Poetisch und stilistisch konstitutive Merkmale in Nietzsches 6. 'Dionysos-Dithyrambus,' *Die Sonne sinkt*," *Nietzsche-Studien* 26 (1997): 34–71, as well as, for a comprehensive account of the genesis and significance of these texts, Wolfram Groddeck, *Friedrich Nietzsche: "Dionysos-Dithyramben,"* 2 vols. (Berlin and New York: Walter de Gruyter, 1991).

[6] For further discussion of Nietzsche's lyric output, see, in addition to Grundlehner (above), Otto H. Olzien, *Nietzsche und das Problem der dichterischen Sprache* (Berlin: Junker und Dünnhaupt, 1941); Johannes Klein, "Der dionysische Realismus: Friedrich Nietzsche," *Geschichte der deutschen Lyrik von Luther bis zum Ausgang des zweiten Weltkrieges* (Wiesbaden: Steiner, 1957), 643–65; Josef Nadler, "Friedrich Nietzsche: Dichterische Gestalt," in *Festschrift, Moriz Enzinger zum 60. Geburtstag, 30. Dezember 1951*, ed. Herbert Seidler (Innsbruck: Wagner, 1953), 157–66.

[7] *KSA* 14, 515; cf. *KSB* 8, 571.

[8] In another letter from this period, Nietzsche envisaged a role as satyr for his friend from whom he had become estranged, Paul Deussen (*KSB* 8, 574).

[9] See Nietzsche's later speculative derivation of tragedy from *tragodia*, or "vinegar song" (*KSA* 7, 1[67], 30).

[10] In the penultimate section of *Jenseits von Gut und Böse*, Nietzsche imagines a conversation with "the genius of the heart" (das Genie des Herzens; *BGE* §295; *KSA* 5, 237–28).

[11] In his *Nachlass*, Nietzsche refers repeatedly to the theme of unifying the faculties: "All creation is communication. The one who knows, the one who creates, the one who loves, are *one*" (Alles Schaffen ist Mittheilen. Der Erkennende der Schaffende der Liebende sind *Eins*; (*KSA* 10, 4[23], 115); "the one who gives, the who one creates, the one who teaches — these are preludes to *those who rule*" (der Schenkende der Schaffende der Lehrende — das sind Vorspiele des *Herrschenden*; *KSA* 10, 15[27], 486); "To become the artist [the one who creates], the saint [the one who loves], and the philosopher [the one who knows] in *one person: my practical goal!*" (Künstler (Schaffender), Heiliger (Liebender) und Philosoph (Erkennender) in *Einer Person* zu werden: — *mein praktisches Ziel!*; *KSA* 10, 16[11], 501). Compare these with his later notes: "The unity of the one who creates, the one who loves, the one who knows in power" (Einheit des Schaffenden, Liebenden, Erkennenden in der Macht; *KSA* 10, 16[49], 514) and: "The *identity* in essence of the *conqueror, law-giver* and *artist*" (Die *Identität* im Wesen des *Eroberers, Gesetzgebers* und *Künstlers*; *KSA* 11, 25[94], 32]).

[12] For further discussion, see Hans Gerald Hödl, *Der letzte Jünger des Philosophen Dionysos: Studien zur systematischen Selbstthematisierungen im Kontext seiner Religionskritik* (Berlin and New York: Walter de Gruyter, 2009).

[13] See Walter Kaufmann, *Nietzsche: Philosopher, Psychologist, Antichrist* (Princeton, NJ: Princeton UP, 1974), 32–35.

[14] *W* 3, 350; cf. letter to Jakob Burckhardt of 6 January 1889 (*KSB* 8, 579).

[15] Nietzsche, *Dithyrambs of Dionysus*, trans. Hollingdale, 59; *KSA* 6, 401.

[16] See *KSA* 10, 13[1], 427.

[17] Nietzsche, *Dithyrambs of Dionysus*, trans. Hollingdale, 43; *KSA* 6, 390.

[18] Jung, *Symbols of Transformation*, in *Collected Works*, 5: §448.

[19] Nietzsche, *Dithyrambs of Dionysus*, trans. Hollingdale, 43; *KSA* 6, 391.

[20] See Ovid, *Metamorphoses*, book 12, ll. 171–209 and 459–525; Pindar, fragments, no. 166–67. (147–48).

[21] Cf. Nietzsche on "Mithraswahn" (*KSA* 8, 28[22] and 28[34], 507 and 508).

[22] Jung, *Symbols of Transformation*, in *Collected Works*, 5: §460.

[23] Jung, *Symbols of Transformation*, in *Collected Works*, 5: §460.

Link to the *Nachlass*

When he received a *Wahnsinnszettel* from Nietzsche, Strindberg replied immediately (in Latin) with a quotation from Horace:

Rectus vives, Licini, neque altum
semper urgendo neque, dum procellas
cautus horrescis, nimium premendo
*   litus iniquum.*

[You would lead a better life, Licinius, if you neither shaped
your life constantly towards the open sea, nor, shivering
tremulously in the face of the storm, held too closely
   to the treacherous coast.][1]

Much of Nietzsche's life had been spent, in metaphorical terms, doing precisely this: he had looked into the horizon of the infinite (*GS* §124), lived dangerously, built his cities on the shores of Vesuvius, and sent his ships into uncharted seas (*GS* §283), urging philosophers to "embark!" (*GS* §289) and gazing into the monstrous eye of infinity ("Toward New Seas" ["Nach neuen Meeren"]; *KSA* 5, 649), just as Zarathustra gazed out upon open seas from the midst of superfluity, no longer saying "God," but saying "Superman" (*Z* II 2; *KSA* 4, 109). And in respect of the *Revaluation of All Values* (*Umwerthung aller Werthe*) Nietzsche described his future work as "the distant sound of thunder in the mountains" (mit einem fernen Donner im Gebirge; *KSB* 8, 453).

Following his collapse in Turin in January 1889, Nietzsche sent a note to Cosima Wagner, which said, simply: "Ariadne, I love you. — Dionysos" (Ariadne, ich liebe Dich. Dionysos; *W* 3, 1350). When he was in the psychiatric clinic in Jena, he is recorded as saying: "My wife, Cosima Wagner, has brought me here" (Meine Frau Cosima Wagner hat mich hierher gebracht).[2] Nietzsche remained in the clinic in Jena, and then for a few weeks with his mother in a small flat, during which time he managed to escape on one occasion and run naked in the streets. During his time in the clinic, the art historian who had tried to make contact with Nietzsche in Munich in 1886 — Julius Langbehn, the so-called *Rembrandt-Deutscher* (after the title of his immensely popular, and deeply conservative, book, *Rembrandt als Erzieher* [*Rembrandt as Educator*] of 1890) — came to Jena, and believed himself to be in a position to cure Nietzsche, criticizing the treatment he was receiving on Otto

Binswanger's instructions. (Nor was Langbehn alone in his efforts; back in Munich, Alfred Schuler [1865–1923], a member of the *Kosmiker-Kreis*, believed he could cure Nietzsche through a dithyrambic intervention in the form of a Corybantic dance.)[3]

During his time in the clinic in Jena, Nietzsche made a number of notes, held in the Goethe-Schiller-Archiv in Weimar, along with notes made by Franziska Nietzsche of conversations in the asylum with her son.[4] According to Sander L. Gilman, "the final texts produced by Nietzsche provide ample material for interpretation of the decay of the fictive personality," for "with the destruction and bleaching of memory, the affective component of the id reappears, here still clothed in the language of early childhood."[5] One text in particular, Text Mp XVIII,5 (4) in the Weimar Archive, constitutes a fragmentary autobiography, reflecting Nietzsche's "lifelong struggle with the question of self-definition," from his earliest autobiographical attempts at Schulpforta on.[6] For many it will be a surprise that any sense at all can be gleaned from these very late texts, but even more surprising was the claim made in 1951 that, in the psychiatric clinic in Jena, Nietzsche had penned a suppressed, final work, entitled *My Sister and I*. Stunned readers learned of Nietzsche's yearning for Lou von Salomé, and even incest between Nietzsche and his sister: this Nietzsche wrote elaborate, Gothic sentences, describing himself as "cast out into the Void where the syphiloid exiles howl with maniacal glee in the Walpurgis Night of the soul."[7] Even Thomas Mann became involved in the debate surrounding its authenticity or lack thereof. Self-evidently, if sadly, Nietzsche's authorship of the work is to be doubted, to say the very least.

In May 1890 he was moved to his mother's house in Naumburg, where he was to stay until 1897.[8] Following the suicide of her husband, Bernhard Förster, in 1889, and in the wake of the economic crisis in the USA in 1891, which sealed the failure of the colony in Paraguay in 1892, Nietzsche's sister, Elisabeth, returned to Germany in 1893. Once again Nietzsche was living in a household dominated by his mother and his sister. Now that his reputation was surrounded by the aura of madness, Nietzsche's works, largely ignored by the public, began to attract interest: for example, in 1894 Lou Andreas-Salomé published one of the first major studies of Nietzsche's life and works, *Nietzsche in seinen Werken*. Building on this interest, sensing commercial possibilities, and above all concerned to promote her own image of her brother's work, the tirelessly energetic Elisabeth founded, in the strategically significant town of Weimar, the Nietzsche Archive, based initially in Weingarten 18, then Grochlitzer Straße 7, and finally (and splendidly) in Humboldtstraße (formerly Luisenstraße) 36, Villa Silberblick.[9] Now that he himself was no longer in control of his own thoughts, words, or deeds, control of Nietzsche's philosophical thought lay in control over his words — over his printed texts, his manuscripts, his correspondence.

Although it had been published in 1888, actual distribution of *Twilight of the Idols* (*Götzen-Dämmerung*) had not begun until 1889, the same year in which *Nietzsche contra Wagner* had appeared, and the *Dithyrambs of Dionysos* (*Dionysos-Dithyramben*) had been published as an appendix to part 4 of *Also sprach Zarathustra* in 1892. Out of a concern with its content, the publication of *The Antichrist* (*Der Antichrist*) did not occur until 1894, and *Ecce Homo* did not appear until 1908 (in a superb edition designed by Henry van de Velde). With the sale of the Fritzsch Verlag to the Naumann Verlag in 1892, work began on a *Gesamtausgabe*, edited by Heinrich Köselitz,[10] but Elisabeth stopped the project, and work began on her own edition.[11] Assuming control of the publication rights to Nietzsche's entire works, including his letters and his *Nachlass*, Elisabeth gathered around her an editorial team of her choosing, including at one stage Rudolf Steiner (1861–1925) — soon to become a member of the Theosophical Society, and then the founder of anthroposophy, but doubtless chosen by Elisabeth because of his archival work on Goethe's scientific writings and because of his editions of Schopenhauer and Jean Paul.[12] Disputes between the editorial team and Elisabeth, and Elisabeth's own unscholarly practices, compromised the integrity of the third edition of Nietzsche's collected works, which began to appear in 1899. But after the death of Franziska Nietzsche in 1897, Elisabeth found herself largely in sole control of Nietzsche's writings, and hence of material she both could not, and would not, understand.

The presentation of the *Nachlass* illustrates well how Elisabeth was able to slant the material in her hands. As Alan D. Schrift, himself general editor of the Stanford Edition of the complete works of Nietzsche in English, shows in his chapter on the *Nachlass*, the very act of including and excluding material in such "*Nachlass* works" as *Der Wille zur Macht* (*The Will to Power*), initially edited by Heinrich Köselitz, August Horneffer, and Ernst Horneffer as volume 15 of the *Gesamtausgabe*,[13] or *Die Unschuld des Werdens* (*The Innocence of Becoming*), selected by Alfred Baeumler and published in 1931,[14] predetermines their interpretation. Thanks to the editorial work of Giorgio Colli and Mazzino Montinari in the multi-volume *Kritische Gesamtausgabe*, available (with a reduced apparatus) in paperback as the *Kritische Studienausgabe*, and in its entirety online,[15] the *Nachlass* is available in an authentic, if less structured, form. But even in its editorially distorted form, Nietzsche's ambition in these fragments for his never-completed *magnum opus* can still be discerned, and may be found in summary in the following text: "Overcoming of philosophers, through the destruction of the world of Being: intermediate period of nihilism: before the strength is there to reverse the values and to deify Becoming and the world of appearance as the only world, and to call them good" (*Überwindung der Philosophen*, durch *Vernichtung* der Welt des Seienden: Zwischenperiode des Nihilismus: bevor die Kraft da ist, die Werthe umzuwenden und das Werdende [,] die scheinbare Welt als die *Einzige* zu vergöttlichen, gut-zuheißen; *WP* §585 A = *KSA* 12, 9[60], 367).

As a specific model of his thought was propagated in his sister's edition of his work, so Nietzsche became an artistic model for sculptors and painters. For instance, Max Kruse sculpted a bust of the philosopher (*Friedrich Nietzsche*, 1898); Arnold Kramer made a sculpture of the sick Nietzsche in his armchair (*Friedrich Nietzsche auf dem Krankenstuhl*, 1898); Hans Olde made a number of drawings of Nietzsche staring into nothingness, based on a series of photographs of Nietzsche in his sick-bed; later, in 1902, Max Klinger made his first of a series of iconic busts of Nietzsche.[16] And Nietzsche himself was even put on display by his sister as a kind of living sculpture; various accounts, by Karl Böttcher or Walter Benjamin, for instance, relate how Nietzsche was presented to dinner guests as a kind of after-dinner entertainment, or revealed to visitors from behind a curtain.[17]

On 25 August 1900, Nietzsche's decade or so spent in what is euphemistically called *geistiger Umnachtung* was brought to an end with his death. Although Nietzsche had asked Elisabeth to ensure he be buried "as an honest pagan,"[18] the ceremonies that followed his death did not respect these wishes in the slightest. After a lengthy commemoration in the Nietzsche Archive in Weimar, Nietzsche was buried on 28 August — Goethe's birthday — in the family tomb, next to the coffin of his father, to the ringing of bells and the recitation of passages from *Zarathustra*.[19]

In the conclusion of the ode by Horace quoted by Strindberg in his letter to Nietzsche of December 1888, we find the following lines:

> *Non, si male nunc, et olim*
> *sic erit: quondam cithara tacentum*
> *suscitat Musam neque semper arcum*
>   *tendit Apollo.*

> [If things are bad now, they will not
> be always so: at times Apollo wakens
> the slumbering Muse with his lyre; he does not always
>   keep his bow taut.]

Nietzsche, however, was the philosopher who embraced Dionysos, not Apollo, and who, it might well be said, eschewed the golden mean. Addressed to Nietzsche, Strindberg's warning was always already too late.

Notes

[1] Karl Strecker, ed., *Nietzsche und Strindberg: Mit ihrem Briefwechsel* (Munich: Müller, 1921), 92–93; *Selected Letters of Friedrich Nietzsche*, ed. Oskar Levy, trans. Anthony M. Ludovici (Garden City, NY and London: Heinemann, 1921), 311;

see Horace, *Odes and Epodes*, ed. and trans. Niall Rudd (Cambridge, MA, and London: Harvard UP, 2004), *Odes*, book 2, no. 10, 114–15.

[2] Cited in *Chronik*, 744.

[3] See Ludwig Klages, "Einführung des Herausgebers," in Alfred Schuler, *Fragmente und Vorträge aus dem Nachlass* (Leipzig: Barth, 1940), 1–119 (here: 60); and Friedrich Wolters, *Stefan George und die Blätter für die Kunst: Deutsche Geistesgeschichte seit 1890* (Berlin: Bondi, 1930), 249–50.

[4] See Sander L. Gilman, "Friedrich Nietzsche's 'Niederschriften aus der spätesten Zeit' (1890–1897) and the Conversations Notebooks (1889–1895)," in *Psychoanalytische und psychopathologische Literaturinterpretation*, ed. Bernd Urban and Winfried Kudszus (Darmstadt: Wissenschaftliche Buchgesellschaft, 1981), 321–46.

[5] Sander L. Gilman, *Inscribing the Other* (Lincoln, NE, and London: U of Nebraska P, 1991), chap. 6, "Nietzsche's Writings and Conversations in His Madness: The Other Unravels Himself," 143–71 (163 and 171).

[6] Gilman, *Inscribing the Other*, 164.

[7] Friedrich Nietzsche, *My Sister and I*, trans. Oscar Levy (Los Angeles: AMOK Books, 1990), 147. This edition contains a critique of its authenticity on its first publication, by Walter Kaufmann, and a defense of its Nietzschean authorship by Walter K. Stewart.

[8] Frank Schweizer, *Wie Philosophen sterben* (Munich: Bachmaier Verlag, 2003), 258–67.

[9] See Angelika Emmerich et al., *Das Nietzsche-Archiv in Weimar* (Munich: Hanser, 2000).

[10] *Nietzsches Werke: Gesamtausgabe*, ed. Peter Gast, 5 vols. (Leipzig: Naumann, 1892–94).

[11] *Nietzsches Werke: Großoktavausgabe*, ed. Elisabeth Förster-Nietzsche et al., 15 vols. (Leipzig: Naumann; Kröner, 1894–1904); second edition, 19 vols. (Leipzig: Kröner, 1901–13).

[12] Steiner was the author of another early work on Nietzsche, published in 1895; see Rudolf Steiner, *Friedrich Nietzsche: Ein Kämpfer gegen seine Zeit* (Dornach: Rudolf Steiner Verlag, 1983).

[13] Following this edition of *The Will to Power* as volume 15 of the *Gesamtausgabe* in 1901, in 1906 a larger compilation of fragments was published under the title *Der Wille zur Macht* as volumes 15 and 16 in the so-called *Großoktavausgabe*. This selection of texts is still published, together with a "Nachwort" by Alfred Baeumler, by the Alfred Kröner Verlag (see Friedrich Nietzsche, *Der Wille zur Macht: Versuch einer Umwertung aller Werte*, ed. Peter Gast and Elisabeth Förster-Nietzsche [Stuttgart: Kröner, 1964]; and *The Will to Power*, ed. Walter Kaufmann, trans. Walter Kaufmann and R. J. Hollingdale [New York: Vintage, 1968]).

[14] Likewise, this edition is still available in the Kröner Verlag (see Friedrich Nietzsche, *Die Unschuld des Werdens: Der Nachlaß*, ed. Alfred Baeumler, 2 vols. [Stuttgart: Kröner, 1978]).

[15] See www.nietzschesource.org.

[16] For discussion of Max Klinger's works, see Conny Dietrich, Hansdieter Erb-smehl, and Justus H. Ulbricht, *Klingers Nietzsche: Wandlungen eines Portraits 1902–1914: Ein Beitrag zur Kunstgeschichte des "neuen Weimar"* (Jena: Glaux, 2004).

[17] Karl Böttcher, *Auf Studienpfaden: Gefängnisstudien, Landstreicherstudien, Trinkstudien, Irrenhausstudien* (Leipzig and Zurich: Schröter, 1900), quoted in *Begegnungen mit Nietzsche*, ed. Sander L. Gilman, 2nd ed. (Bonn: Bouvier, 1985), 195–203; and Walter Benjamin, "Nietzsche und das Archiv seiner Schwester," in Walter Benjamin, *Kritiken und Rezensionen*, ed. Hella Tiedemann-Bartels, vol. 3 of *Gesammelte Schriften*, ed. Rolf Tiedemann and Hermann Schweppenhauser (Frankfurt am Main: Suhrkamp, 1972), 323–26.

[18] See Ben Macintyre, *Forgotten Fatherland: The Search for Elisabeth Nietzsche* (London: Macmillan, 1992), 159; citing Elisabeth Förster-Nietzsche, *The Lonely Nietzsche*, trans. Paul V. Cohen (London: Heinemann, 1915), 65.

[19] See the account given by Harry Graf Kessler in "Aus den Tagebüchern," *Jahrbuch der Deutschen Schillergesellschaft* 12 (1968): 48–87.

15: Nietzsche's *Nachlass*

Alan D. Schrift

Technically speaking, Nietzsche's *Nachlass* or literary remains is comprised of all of his work, excluding his letters, that remained unpublished when his mental collapse ended his productive life in January 1889. This would include: (1) texts that he had prepared for publication but which he was unable to see through to publication, namely *The Anti-Christ* (*Der Antichrist*), *Nietzsche Contra Wagner*, *Dithyrambs of Dionysos* (*Dionysos-Dithyramben*), and *Ecce Homo*; (2) his early, unpublished essays and lectures, many of which could be considered complete, albeit never published, works; and (3) his notes, as well as drafts and variants of his published works. The size of Nietzsche's *Nachlass* is considerable: in the thirteen volumes of Nietzsche's writings that comprise the *Kritische Studienausgabe*, edited by Giorgio Colli and Mazzino Montinari, Nietzsche's unpublished notes and notebooks make up 4,869 of the total 7,945 pages.[1]

Beyond the sheer quantity of material that comprises Nietzsche's *Nachlass*, there are also interesting questions to be asked concerning its philological and philosophical significance, its status as part of Nietzsche's philosophy, and its reception and influence. These questions become particularly important with respect to the unpublished notebooks that followed the completion of *Thus Spoke Zarathustra* (*Also sprach Zarathustra*). For these notes from 1885 to 1888 occupy a special place in Nietzsche's *Nachlass*, insofar as they have been associated, whether rightly or wrongly, with Nietzsche's supposed intention to produce a *magnum opus* under the title *The Will to Power* (*Der Wille zur Macht*). It is these notes, which comprise volumes 11, 12, and 13 in the *Kritische Studienausgabe*, that will be the main focus of the remainder of this essay, organized into four sections: first, the history of the construction of the "non-book" *The Will to Power*; second, Mazzino Montinari's evidence for the conclusion that Nietzsche definitively gave up on composing a *magnum opus* under the title *The Will to Power*; third, the contents of the *Nachlass* of 1885–88; and fourth, the significance and influence of the late *Nachlass* for Nietzsche scholarship.

Nietzsche's "Non-Book": *The Will to Power*

That there exists a book with the title *The Will to Power* is a fact. That Friedrich Nietzsche is not the author of this book is also a fact. What, then, is this book titled *The Will to Power*? Here, a brief history of its construction is appropriate.[2] The first text published with this title, with the subtitle "Attempt at a Revaluation of All Values (Studies and Fragments)" ("Versuch einer Umwerthung aller Werte [Studien und Fragmente]") appeared in 1901, edited by Heinrich Köselitz (alias Peter Gast), Ernst Horneffer, and August Horneffer, as volume 15 of the first edition of Nietzsche's collected works, the so-called *Grossoktavausgabe*, published in Leipzig by C. G. Naumann and supervised by his sister, Elisabeth Förster-Nietzsche.[3] This version, comprised of 483 notes, was substantially expanded by Peter Gast and Elisabeth Förster-Nietzsche in the second edition of the *Großoktavausgabe* to 1,067 notes. This was published first in 1906 by Naumann and then again, with a philological commentary by Otto Weiss, as volumes 15 (along with *Ecce Homo*) and 16 of the *Großoktavausgabe* in 1911. This second edition of the *Großoktavausgabe*, published by Alfred Kröner Verlag, formed the basis for the text that appeared as volumes 18 and 19 in the next significant edition of Nietzsche's collected works, published in Munich by Musarion Verlag from 1920 to 1929. The 23-volume *Musarionausgabe* added to the 1,067 sections a table that listed their approximate date of composition, and, along with the second edition of the *Großoktavausgabe*, remained the best edition of Nietzsche's collected works until the appearance of the Colli-Montinari edition (beginning in 1967).

For better or worse, it was this expanded 1,067-section second edition that became the canonical edition subsequently translated into English by Walter Kaufmann and R. J. Hollingdale in 1967.[4] I say "for better or worse" because, as Montinari has demonstrated, this second edition was, from a philological perspective, in several respects inferior to the first edition. Montinari notes, for example, that 17 of the 483 notes from the first edition were removed and the editors "took 25 continuous and often very important texts, ripped them apart, and increased their number to 55."[5] A particularly egregious example of Gast and Förster-Nietzsche's editorial mismanagement is the fate of a significant fragment that Nietzsche titled "*European Nihilism*" ("*Der europäische Nihilismus*") and dated "Lenzer Heide, 10 June 1887." Where readers of the first edition of 1901 would have found what Montinari regards as an "organic essay" comprised of 16 sections (see *KSA* 12, 5[71], 211–17), Gast and Förster-Nietzsche broke up this fragment in their 1906 compilation, where it appears as aphorisms 4, 5, 114, and 55 (in this order).[6]

Before concluding this discussion of the construction of a book with the title *The Will to Power*, three other German editions of Nietzsche's

Nachlass deserve a brief mention. The first, edited with a postscript by Alfred Baeumler and published in 1930 as *Der Wille zur Macht* in a separate volume (listed in their catalogue as #78) as part of the Kröner *Taschenausgabe*, did not mention any editors and so gave the appearance that this was a text authored by Nietzsche himself.[7] In other volumes of the Kröner *Taschenausgabe* series, the book was described as "the main work of the thinker Nietzsche, the boldest and most important philosophical work of the nineteenth century, to which *Thus Spoke Zarathustra* forms an entryway" (das Hauptwerk des Denkers Nietzsche, das kühnste und wichtigste philosophische Werk des 19. Jahrhunderts, zu dem 'Also sprach Zarathustra' die 'Vorhalle' bildet). Because this volume was published as a single, inexpensive text, its distribution was far more extensive than the earlier editions, and it is largely responsible for the widely held, yet mistaken view that *Friedrich* Nietzsche, rather than Elisabeth, is the author of this text in this form.[8]

The second of these other German editions, edited by Friedrich Würzbach and published by Verlag Anton Pustet in 1940 with the title *Das Vermächtnis Friedrich Nietzsches: Versuch einer neuen Auslegung allen Geschehens und einer Umwertung aller Werte, aus dem Nachlass und nach den Intentionen Nietzsches geordnet* (The Legacy of Friedrich Nietzsche: Attempt at a New Interpretation of all Events and a Revaluation of all Values, from the *Nachlass* and organized according to Nietzsche's Intentions), includes more notes than those included in the earlier editions, and does not restrict itself to the notes of the 1880s. The arrangement of this edition, with its 2,397 aphorisms, bears no relation to the organization of the 1,067-section second edition, and it would not be worth mentioning, were it not for the fact that Würzbach's arrangement formed the basis for the first complete French translation, entitled *La Volonté de puissance*, translated by Geneviève Bianquis and published by Éditions Gallimard in 1937. This edition was, for French readers of Nietzsche like Georges Bataille, Pierre Klossowski, and Gilles Deleuze, their primary access to Nietzsche's *Nachlass*, and it remained so until the French translation of the Colli-Montinari edition began appearing in 1967.

The third of these additional German editions, unlike the other two, makes no claim to a connection with *The Will to Power*. This edition, also compiled by Alfred Baeumler, is entitled *Die Unschuld des Werdens* (*The Innocence of Becoming*), and it was originally published in two volumes in 1931 as additional *Nachlass* material to supplement Baeumler's six-volume Kröner *Taschenausgabe*. In *Die Unschuld des Werdens*, in which Baeumler reiterates his belief that "the *Nachlass* is from a philosophical point of view more important than the [published] works!" (der Nachlaß ist unter philosophischen Gesichtspunkt wichtiger as die Werke!),[9] he makes no pretense to be following Nietzsche's plan for a work. Instead, Baeumler claims to supplement the publication of Nietzsche's other *Nachlass* materials in the Kröner edition — unpublished works from the Basel period and *The Will to Power* — with a thematic selection of other material from the *Nachlass*. From an organizational standpoint, a case could be made that Baeumler's editorial organization offers a better picture of Nietzsche's *Nachlass* than did Gast and Förster-Nietzsche's: Baeumler's first volume includes 1,334 entries, with chapters on the Greeks; the philosopher (art and knowledge); Richard Wagner; music, art, and literature; philosophy and its history; psychological observations; woman and marriage; parable and images; Nietzsche on himself; and Nietzsche on his writings, followed by an appendix of drafts of his poems. The second volume had 1,415 entries, with chapters on epistemology, natural philosophy, and anthropology; moral philosophy; drafts and plans; religion and Christianity; culture; law; Europe and the Germans; and on Zarathustra. Within each chapter, the selections are organized by their approximate date of origin, either in terms of a season (for example, winter 1870/71) or, more frequently, in terms of an association with one of Nietzsche's published works (for example, "From the Time of Daybreak and The Gay Science"). The source of the selections, in terms of the *Großoktavausgabe*, is noted in an appendix to the second volume. In this sense, this collection offers the reader more information as to the context in which Nietzsche's unpublished passages were written than was offered in, for example, the edition of *Der Wille zur Macht* that appeared in the Kröner edition. But the reader must also take into consideration the editorial intentions of this collection's editor, and insofar as *Die Unschuld des Werdens* was published in the same year as Baeumler's notorious *Nietzsche, der Philosoph und Politiker* (1931) — the work that perhaps more than any other led to Nietzsche's association with National Socialism — one should treat this editorial compilation with great suspicion.

Debunking the Claim that *The Will to Power* is Nietzsche's *magnum opus*

The readers and admirers of Friedrich Nietzsche will at first suspect in the title of this book that they will find the continuation of that work from which the first part, the "Antichrist," was published in Volume VIII of the complete edition. We must therefore say at once that the "Antichrist," just as much as "Twilight of the Idols" and the "Case of Wagner," were taken from the material present in Nietzsche's very extensively planned large theoretical-philosophical *magnum opus*, somehow without exhausting the wealth of what was given there. What reasons compelled us now to integrate the present Studies and Fragments into the earlier plan of a large *magnum opus*, rather than continue the work begun in the "Antichrist," will be set out in what follows.

[Die Leser und Verehrer Friedrich Nietzsches werden bei dem Titel des vorliegenden Buches zunächst vermuthen, daß sie hier die Fortsetzung jenes Werkes finden, von welchem bereits der erste Theil, der "Antichrist," im VIII Band der Gesammtausgabe erschienen ist. Wir müssen deshalb sogleich vorausschicken, daß der "Antichrist" ebensowohl wie die "Götzendämmerung" und der "Fall Wagner" aus dem überreichen Material eines viel umfangreicher geplanten großen, theoretische-philosophischen Hauptwerkes Nietzsches herausgenommen ist, ohne irgendwie die Fülle des Gegebenen zu erschöpfen. Welche Gründe uns nun nöthigten, die vorhandenen Studien und Fragmente in den früheren Plan jenes großen Hauptwerkes einzuordnen, anstatt das mit dem "Antichrist" begonnene Werk fortzusetzen, soll in dem Nachfolgenden dargelegt werden.][10]

So began Elisabeth's "foreword" to the first edition of *The Will to Power*. Similarly, Alfred Baeumler began his postscript to the aforementioned one-volume 1930 Kröner *Taschenausgabe*, which he presented as if authored by Nietzsche himself, with the claim: "The *Will to Power* is Nietzsche's philosophical *magnum opus*. All the fundamental results of his thinking are brought together in this book" (Der "Wille zur Macht" ist das philosophische Hauptwerk Nietzsches. Alle grundsätzlichen Resultate seines Denkens sind in diesem Buche vereinigt).[11] Even Martin Heidegger would claim that the *Will to Power*, by which he refers to the "text" that Nietzsche intended to publish with that title, and not merely to the book titled *The Will to Power*, which had been constructed from his notebooks by his literary executors, is Nietzsche's philosophical "main structure," his *Hauptwerk*, to which all his published texts stand as an entranceway (*Vorhalle*):

Nietzsche's philosophy proper, the fundamental position on the basis of which he speaks [. . .] in all the writings he himself published, did not assume a final form and was not itself published in any book, neither in the decade between 1879 and 1889 nor during the years preceding. What Nietzsche himself published during his creative years was always foreground. [. . .] His philosophy proper was left behind as posthumous, unpublished work.

[Die eigentlichen Philosophie Nietzsches aber, die Grundstellung, aus der heraus er [. . .] in allen von ihm selbst veröffentlichen Schriften spricht, kommt nicht zur endgültigen Gestaltung und nicht zur werkmäßigen Veröffentlichung, weder in dem Jahrzehnt zwischen 1879 und 1889 noch in den voranliegenden Jahren. Was Nietzsche seit seines Schaffens selbst veröffentlicht hat, ist immer Vordergrund. [. . .] Die eigentliche Philosophie bleibt als "Nachlass" zurück.][12]

That Nietzsche intended to publish a work titled "The Will to Power" is clear. It was announced on the back cover of *Beyond Good and Evil* (*Jenseits von Gut und Böse*) as being "in preparation" (in Vorbereitung), and at the end of *On the Genealogy of Morality*, Nietzsche directed his readers to "a work I am preparing, *The Will to Power: Attempt at a Revaluation of all Values*" (ein Werk, das ich vorbereite: **Der Wille zur Macht, Versuch einer Umwerthung aller Werthe**; *GM* III §27; *KSA* 5, 409).[13] In fact, working toward the creation of a work, perhaps with this title, would appear to have been one of Nietzsche's overriding intentions from summer 1885 until early fall 1888.

The title *The Will to Power* first appears in Nietzsche's manuscripts of August–September 1885:

The Will to Power.
Attempt
At a New Interpretation
Of All Events.
By
Friedrich Nietzsche.

[*Der Wille zur Macht.*
Versuch
einer neuen Auslegung
alles Geschehens.
Von
Friedrich Nietzsche.
(*KSA* 11, 39[1], 619)]

It appears again in the following notebook, this time with a summary of themes to be addressed (logic, physics, morality, art, politics), following a foreword that raises the "problem of pessimism" as a question in which the theme of "meaninglessness" (Sinnlosigkeit) is broached (*KSA* 11, 40[2], 629). The question of meaninglessness leads, quite naturally, to the theme of nihilism — "*Nihilism*: the goal is lacking; the answer to 'Why?' is lacking" (*Nihilism*: es fehlt das Ziel; es fehlt die Antwort auf das "Warum?"; *KSA* 12, 9[35], 350) — which is a major theme in Nietzsche's notebooks of 1887–88. This question of meaninglessness is also linked to Nietzsche's reflection on the real versus the apparent world, insofar as he sees modern pessimism to be in part a response to the loss of faith in our cognitive ability to engage the real world and the resultant dissatisfaction with our epistemological relegation to a world of appearance: "The most extreme form of nihilism would be: that *every* belief, every holding-as-true, is necessarily false: *because there simply is no* **true world**" (Die extremste Form des Nihilism wäre: daß *jeder* Glaube, jedes Für-wahr-halten nothwendig falsch ist: *weil es eine* **wahre Welt** *gar nicht giebt*; *KSA* 12, 9[41], 354).

In the period from summer 1885 to summer 1886, "The Will to Power" appears as a possible title, along with "Noon and Eternity" (Mittag und Ewigkeit), indicative of his desire to continue his Zarathustra work (see, for example, *KSA* 12, 2[72], 94), and, most frequently, "Beyond Good and Evil," which Montinari understands to indicate that Nietzsche was conceiving three distinct projects during this period.[14] In an interesting note from spring 1886, Nietzsche compiled the following list, giving a clear indication of how he saw his future work unfolding:

The Titles of Ten New Books (Spring 1886)

Thoughts on the Ancient Greeks.
The Will to Power. Attempt at a New World-Interpretation.
Artists: A Psychologist's Ulterior Motives.
We Godless
Noon and Eternity.
Beyond Good and Evil: Prelude to a Philosophy of the Future.
Gai saber: Songs of Prince Free-as-a-Bird.
Music.
Experiences of a Scholarly Writer.
On the History of the Modern Gloominess.

[Die Titel von 10 neuen Büchern (Frühling 1886)

Gedanken über die alten Griechen.
Der Wille zur Macht. Versuch einer neuen Welt-Auslegung.
Die Künstler. Hintergedanken eines Psychologen.
Wir Gottlosen
Mittag und Ewigkeit.
Jenseits von Gut und Böse. Vorspiel einer Philosophie der Zukunft.
Gai saber. Lieder des Prinzen Vogelfrei.
Musik.
Erfahrungen eines Schriftgelehrten.
Zur Geschichte der modernen Verdüsterung.
(*KSA* 12, 2[73], 94–95)]

This note is followed immediately by a brief outline:

The Will to Power
1. Physiology of the Order of Rank
2. The Great Noon
3. Discipline and Breeding
4. The Eternal Recurrence

[*Der Wille zur Macht.*
1. Physiologie der Rangordnung.
2. Der große Mittag.

3. Zucht und Züchtung.
4. Die ewige Wiederkunft.
(*KSA* 12, 2[74], 95)]

And then this is followed by a series of notes that could have appeared under one or another of these ten working titles. What this indicates is that in spring 1886, Nietzsche still was considering a work titled *The Will to Power*, but that this work was not in any way privileged as a culminating study or *magnum opus*.

One could argue, however, that this all changed soon thereafter, following the publication of *Beyond Good and Evil*, as a new outline appeared in summer 1886 that puts forward a structure that would endure for several months:

The Will to Power.
Attempt
at a Revaluation of All Values.
In Four Books.

First Book: The Danger of Dangers (presentation of nihilism) (as *the inevitable consequence of valuations hitherto*)
Second Book: Critique of Values (of logic etc.
Third Book: The Problem of the Lawgiver (including the history of solitude) *How* must humans who make the inverse valuations be formed? Humans who have all the characteristics of the modern soul, but are strong enough to convert it into pure health.
Fourth Book: The Hammer
Its Means to its Task.
Sils Maria, Summer 1886

[Der Wille zur Macht.
Versuch
einer Umwerthung aller Werthe.
In vier Büchern.

Erstes Buch: die Gefahr der Gefahren (Darstellung des Nihilismus) (als *der nothwendigen Consequenz der bisherigen Werthschätzungen*)
Zweites Buch: Kritik der Werthe (der Logik usw.
Drittes Buch: das Problem des Gesetzgebers (darin die Geschichte der Einsamkeit) *Wie* müssen Menschen beschaffen sein, die umgekehrt werthschätzen? Menschen, die alle Eigenschaften der modernen Seele haben, aber stark genug sind, sie in lauter Gesundheit umzuwandeln.
Viertes Buch: der Hammer
ihr Mittel zu ihrer Aufgabe
Sils-Maria, Sommer 1886

(*KSA* 12, 2[100], 109)]

This plan for a work in four parts, treating nihilism, the critique of values, the revaluation of all values, and eternal recurrence, appears in various incarnations over the next year (see, for example, *KSA* 12, 5[76] and 7[45], 218 and 309). In fact, it follows the basic structure that appears in the note that Gast and Förster-Nietzsche chose for their edition of *The Will to Power:*

[+++] *of all Values*
First Book.
European Nihilism.
Second Book.
Critique of the Highest Values.
Third Book.
Principle of a New of Valuation.
Fourth Book.
Discipline and Breeding.
Drafted 17 March 1887, Nice.

[[+++] *aller Werthe*
Erstes Buch.
Der europäische Nihilismus.
Zweites Buch.
Kritik der höchsten Werthe.
Drittes Buch.
Princip einer neuen Werthsetzung.
Viertes Buch.
Zucht und Züchtung.
entworfen den 17. März 1887, Nizza.
(*KSA* 12, 7[64], 318])[15]

This basic structure, under the title *The Will to Power,* appears almost without exception from fall 1887 until summer 1888, and, following the publication of *On the Genealogy of Morality,* Nietzsche worked diligently on this text. One result, which Montinari dates around mid-February 1888, was a collection of 372 notes (actually 374, since the same number was used twice [*KSA* 12, 9[1], 339–582 to *KSA* 13, 11[138], 9–65]) that Nietzsche set out to index according to a key word in each note. By writing the Roman numeral I, II, III or IV in pencil alongside the first three hundred key words (see *KSA* 13, 12[1], 195–211), Nietzsche used these numerals to refer to four books we find in an untitled plan that follows the same basic four-part structure, only now divided into chapters (see *KSA* 12, 12[2], 211).

These notebooks and Nietzsche's indexing of the notes according to an outline for a book are important because they are the only concrete indication we have in the *Nachlass* concerning how Nietzsche, at least at one point in time, wished the aphorisms of *The Will to Power* to be organized. These notebooks also demonstrate the degree to which the text that comes to us with this title is the creation of Gast and Förster-Nietzsche, and not of Nietzsche.[16] Here let me summarize Montinari's conclusions concerning their explicit failure to follow Nietzsche's instructions. First, of the 374 fragments Nietzsche had numbered for inclusion, 104 were not included in their compilation of *Der Wille zur Macht*, and of those, 84 were not published anywhere in the *Großoktavausgabe*. Second, of the remaining 270 fragments, 137 are incomplete or have intentional alterations to the text (omission of the titles, often of whole sentences, dismemberment of texts that belong together, etc.). Third, Nietzsche himself divided Fragments 1–300 into the four books of his plan. Gast and Förster-Nietzsche did not retain that division in sixty-four cases.

It is decisions such as these that lead Montinari to conclude that "the selection of texts for the construction of a Nietzsche system in the 'Will to Power,' of such consequence to Nietzsche studies for decades, must be completely and fully attributed to the two philosophical (and philological) nullities, Heinrich Köselitz (alias Peter Gast) and Elisabeth Förster-Nietzsche."[17] Thus, it is perfectly clear that the text that we know as *The Will to Power* is not a text that was written by Nietzsche, inasmuch as what he wrote was not published in its entirety and in the order he put it in. There is, however, one further issue to address, namely, whether it was Nietzsche's collapse that prevented him from completing a work with this title, or whether he had made a conscious decision not to complete it.

In the spring and summer of 1888, Nietzsche continued to work on notes and plans for a work titled "The Will to Power." During this period, one interesting development is that not all the plans take the form of a work in four parts, as several present a plan organized as a work with between seven and twelve chapters (see, for example, *KSA* 13, 14[156] and 14 [169], 340 and 355). In addition, in several of these plans, the question of truth, as well as the distinction between the true and the apparent world — a distinction that takes center stage in *Twilight of the Idols* — return as a central focus. Equally significant in the notes that follow these plans is the appearance of art as a "countermovement to truth" (see, for example, *KSA* 13, 14[119] and 14[170], 296–99 and 356–57). Although Nietzsche complained that during the summer of 1888 his work had not gone well, this all changed in the late summer. In the previous months, his friend Meta von Salis had sent to him in Sils Maria, at his request, a copy of *On the Genealogy of Morality,* which he had read in the meantime and which would appear to have re-energized him and pointed him in a new direction. On 22 August 1888, he wrote to von Salis about his experience as follows:

The first look inside gave me a surprise: I discovered a long *foreword* to the "Genealogy," whose existence I had *forgotten* about . . . Basically, I just had the titles of the three essays in memory: the rest, that is, the content, had gone missing. [. . .] Now the book is alive again before me — and so are the conditions from last summer, out of which it arose.

[Der erste Blick hinein gab mir eine Überraschung: Ich entdeckte eine lange *Vorrede* zur der "Genealogie," deren Existenz ich *vergessen* hatte . . . Im Grunde hatte ich bloß den Titel der drei Abhandlungen in Gedächtnis: der Rest, das heißt der Inhalt war mir flöten gegangen. [. . .] Jetzt lebt das Buch wieder vor mir auf — und, zugleich, der Zustand vom vorjährigen Sommer, aus dem es entstand. *KSB* 8, 396]

In that foreword, of course, Nietzsche comes to highlight the question of the *value* of morality, and by the end of the text, a new problem has arisen, namely "that of the *value* of truth" (das vom *Werthe* der Wahrheit; *GM* III §24; *KSA* 5, 401). The date of this letter is also noteworthy, for it precedes by four days the last plan for "The Will to Power" that we find in the *Nachlass*, written on 26 August 1888:

Draft of
plan for:
The Will to Power
Attempt
At a Revaluation of All Values

— Sils Maria
on the last Sunday of the
month of August 1888

We Hyperboreans. — *Foundation stone laid for the problem*

First Book: *"What is Truth?"*

First Chapter. Psychology of Error.
Second Chapter. Value of Truth and Error.
Third Chapter. The Will to Truth (only justified in the Yes-value of life)

Second Book: *Descent of Values.*

First Chapter. The Metaphysicians.
Second Chapter. De homines religiosi.
Third Chapter. The Good and the Improvers.

Third Book: *The Conflict of Values.*

First Chapter. Thoughts on Christianity.
Second Chapter. The Physiology of Art.
Third Chapter. The History of European Nihilism.

Psychologist's Amusement

Fourth Book: *The Great Noon.*
First Chapter. The Principle of Life's "Order of Rank."
Second Chapter. The Two Paths.
Third Chapter. The Eternal Recurrence.

[Entwurf des
Plans zu:
der Wille zur Macht.
Versuch
einer Umwerthung aller Werthe.

— *Sils Maria*
am letzten Sonntag des
Monat August 1888

Wir Hyperboreer. — *Grundsteinlegung des Problems.*

Erstes Buch: *"was ist Wahrheit?"*
Erstes Capitel. Psychologie des Irrthums.
Zweites Capitel. Werth von Wahrheit und Irrthum.
Drittes Capitel. Der Wille zur Wahrheit (erst gerechtfertigt im Ja-
Werth des Lebens

Zweites Buch: *Herkunft der Werthe.*
Erstes Capitel. Die Metaphysiker.
Zweites Capitel. Die homines religiosi.
Drittes Capitel. Die Guten und die Verbesserer.

Drittes Buch: *Kampf der Werthe*
Erstes Capitel. Gedanken über das Christenthum.
Zweites Capitel. Zur Physiologie der Kunst.
Drittes Capitel. Zur Geschichte des europäischen Nihilismus.

Psychologen-Kurzweil.

Viertes Buch: *Der grosse Mittag.*
Erstes Capitel. Das Princip des Lebens "Rangordnung."
Zweites Capitel. Die zwei Wege.
Drittes Capitel. Die ewige Wiederkunft.
(*KSA* 13, 18[17], 537–38)]

In this plan, one of the most detailed that we find in the *Nachlass*,[18] the problem of truth has taken the place of nihilism as the theme of the first book. The second book, rather than simply a critique of values, has evolved into a *genealogy* of values, specifically metaphysical, religious, and ethical values. The third book, rather than being focused on the revaluation of values, focuses instead on the conflict of values. Only the fourth book, which follows an Interlude, remains as it was in the earlier plans: focused on eternal recurrence.

In the days that follow this last plan for the "Will to Power," Nietzsche began drafting plans for a new "main work" now titled *Revaluation of all Values* (*Umwerthung aller Werthe*; e.g., *KSA* 13, 19[8], 545), and he wrote a draft of the foreword to this work on 3 September 1888 (see *KSA* 14, 436–37, as well as the reference to that date in *EH TI* §3; *KSA* 6, 355). The notes from the *Nachlass* that follow this plan (roughly the last hundred pages of *KSA* 13), along with Nietzsche's letters, tell a clear story: Nietzsche quickly planned a short work that would present his main philosophical ideas "in outline" (im Auszug; cf. *KSA* 13, 19[3] and [5], 542–43). Most significant here is the following list of chapter headings:

1. *We Hyperboreans.*
2. *The Problem of Socrates.*
3. *Reason in Philosophy.*
4. *How the True World Finally Became a Fable.*
5. *Morality as Anti-nature.*
6. *The Four Great Errors.*
7. *For Us — Against Us.*
8. *Concept of a décadence-religion.*
9. *Buddhism and Christianity.*
10. *From My Aesthetics.*
11. *Among Artists and Writers.*
12. *Sayings and Arrows*

[1. *Wir Hyperboreer.*
2. *Das Problem des Sokrates.*
3. *Die Vernunft in der Philosophie.*
4. *Wie die wahre Welt endlich zur Fabel* ‹wurde›
5. *Moral als Widernatur.*
6. *Die vier großen Irrthümer.*
7. *Für uns — wider uns.*
8. *Begriff einer Décadence-Religion.*
9. *Buddhismus und Christenthum.*
10. *Aus meiner Aesthetik.*
11. *Unter Künstlern und Schriftstellern.*
12. *Sprüche und Pfeile.*
(*KSA* 13, 19[4], 543)]

Chapters 2, 3, 4, 5, 6, and 12 would appear in this form in *Twilight of the Idols,* while chapter 11 would eventually become part of the "Expeditions of an Untimely One" ("Streifzüge eines Unzeitgemässen") in that work. Chapter titles 1, 7, 8, and 9 will disappear, but the material that was to be included under them would appear in *The Anti-Christ.* As Carol Diethe notes in her essay, Nietzsche constructed the manuscript that would eventually become *Twilight of the Idols* in the two weeks following the last plan for "Will to Power," sending the manuscript to his publisher, C. G. Naumann, on 7 September 1888 with a note that the *Revaluation of all Values* and not *The Will to Power* is now to be his "main work": "I need to publish this [i.e., *Twilight*] now because at the end of next year, we shall probably be busy printing my main work *Revaluation of all Values*" (Ich habe es nöthig, sie jetzt noch herauszugeben, weil wir Ende nächsten Jahres wahrscheinlich daran gehen müssen, mein Hauptwerk die *Umwerthung aller Werthe* zu drucken; *KSB* 8, 411).

Examining the notes and letters of this hectic two weeks after the final plan for "Will to Power," Montinari concludes that, insofar as Nietzsche drafted a foreword to the *Revaluation of all Values* on 3 September according to a four-book format, in the days between 26 August and 3 September the following happened: (1) Nietzsche abandoned any and all plans for "Will to Power"; (2) for a brief period, he may have entertained the possibility of publishing the material already in fair copy as the "Revaluation of all Values"; (3) he decided, however, on a selection of excerpts of his philosophy; (4) he named this selection "Leisure of a Psychologist" (later renamed *Twilight of the Idols*); (5) immediately thereafter he removed the chapters "We Hyperboreans," "For Us — Against Us," "Concept of a décadence-religion," and "Buddhism and Christianity" from the "excerpts," which yielded twenty-three paragraphs concerning Christianity, along with an introduction ("We Hyperboreans"); and (6) from then on, the *magnum opus* bore the title "Revaluation of all Values" and was planned in four books. The first book, *The Anti-Christ*, was already a good one-third finished (the just-mentioned twenty-three paragraphs).[19]

The *Nachlass* includes at least six versions of plans for the new literary project in four books, that is, the "Revaluation of all Values." In each, the first book will be a critique of Christianity, the second and third books alternate between critiques of philosophy and morality, and the fourth book presents Nietzsche's positive philosophy: the philosophy of Dionysos, the philosophy of eternal recurrence.[20] So Montinari concludes: "Viewed with respect to contents, the 'Revaluation of all Values' was in a sense the same as the 'Will to Power,' but precisely for this reason was its *literary* negation. Alternatively, *Twilight of the Idols* and *Antichrist* were created from the notes for 'Will to Power'; the rest is — *Nachlass*, unpublished writings."[21] Which is to say that, contrary to popular opinion, and to the legend Elisabeth sought to construct, rather than viewing *The Will to Power* as Nietzsche's *magnum opus*, which he did not live long enough to complete, we must view this "work" as a project Nietzsche toyed with for several years but ultimately set aside as not worth completing.

The Contents of the *Nachlass*

Let us now turn from the controversies concerning *The Will to Power* to the actual information to be found in the *Nachlass* — the unpublished writings. As already mentioned, the *Nachlass* comprises a majority of the Colli-Montinari critical edition. Restricting the description to the 15-volume *Kritische Studienausgabe*, the unpublished writings make up volumes 7 to 13: volumes 7 and 8 contain notes written prior to 1880; volume 9 contains notes from the period when Nietzsche was working on *Morgenröthe* (*Daybreak*) and *Die fröhliche Wissenschaft* (*The Gay Science*) (1880–82); volumes 10 and 11 contain the notes and notebooks from the time during which Nietzsche composed the four books of *Thus Spoke Zarathustra* (1882–85); and volumes 12 and 13 contain his unpublished writings after 1885. These volumes are organized, as best as Montinari could ascertain, chronologically and according to the 106 notebook-collections in which Montinari found the remains: quarto and octav volumes (Hefte), notebooks (Notizbücher), and portfolios of assorted loose papers in various formats (Mappen). I say here, "as best as Montinari could ascertain," because Nietzsche often returned to and reused notebooks, wrote on the backs of pages, sometimes wrote from front to back and at other times wrote from back to front, and so a definitive chronological ordering is not possible.

What, then, does one find in these notebooks and loose pages? As already indicated in my recounting of Montinari's argument against a never-finished "*magnum opus*," one of the things found in the unpublished writings are Nietzsche's plans for possible works, in the form of titles, tables of contents, descriptions, etc. In addition, one finds numerous transcriptions of quotes from authors Nietzsche was reading, along with comments on these and other works. For example, the notebook identified as M III 7 (and found in *KSA* 9, 17 [1–39], 666–72), consists entirely of copied excerpts from the 1858 German translation of Emerson's *Essays*. The larger notebook *W* II 3, of some two hundred pages (found in *KSA* 13, 11[1–417], 9–194), contains, in addition to Nietzsche's own fragments, over seventy excerpts from Baudelaire's *Œuvres posthumes et Correspondances inédits* (*KSA* 13, 11[166–233], 76–91), as well as other excerpts from, among others, Fyodor Dostoyevsky's French translations of *The Possessed*, Leo Tolstoy's *Ma religion*, Benjamin Constant's *Quelques réflections sur le théâtre allemand*, and Ernst Renan's *Vie de Jésus*.

Turning to Nietzsche's own writings, they appear in various forms, from random notations, like the now-famous "I have forgotten my umbrella" (Ich habe meinen Regenschirm vergessen; *KSA* 9, 12[62], 587), to such relatively polished fragments as the 16-section "essay" titled "*European Nihilism*" (*Der europäische Nihilismus*; *KSA* 12, 5[71], 211–17), mentioned above. Both of these are extremes, however. The majority of Nietzsche's notebook entries are fragments that, like his published aphorisms, range in size from a sentence or two to a paragraph. They are, as one would expect from a notebook, rarely as polished as his published writings, but they are also rarely incoherent or unintelligible. Most of the entries treat themes that appear in the published works, but in some cases — most famously, the "will to power" and the "Übermensch," but also reflections related to his research in the natural sciences — there is far more material in the notebooks than ever makes its way into the published texts. So, although Heidegger was clearly wrong when he claimed that Nietzsche's "philosophy proper was left behind as posthumous, unpublished work," Karl Schlechta may also overstate the case when he concluded that "no *new* central thought is to be found there."[22] And where Walter Kaufmann justified his decision to publish a translation of *The Will to Power*, in part, because he believed "an arrangement that was really faithful to the manuscripts would not be an arrangement at all, but simply chaotic — and almost literally unreadable,"[23] Montinari recounts a very different experience: "In reading in chronological sequence the notes of 1888," he writes, "we felt a sense of unity and saw how plans, drafts, even mere titles alternated with and complemented each other, each constituting an organic part of the whole. We could see Nietzsche's thoughts in the process of evolution, in all their consistency and lucidity of expression."[24]

Such an experience was, interestingly enough, anticipated by Karl Jaspers at the conclusion of his important, and today vastly underappreciated, work of 1936, *Nietzsche: Einführung in das Verständnis seines Philosophierens* (*Nietzsche: An Introduction to the Understanding of His Philosophical Activity*). Unlike Heidegger, Jaspers refuses to assent to the primacy of either the published or the posthumous works, writing that "it must be realized that none of Nietzsche's forms of communication has a privileged character.[. . .] Nowhere is Nietzsche's work truly centralized: there is no *magnum opus*."[25] At the same time, Jaspers both uses the *Nachlass* available to him at the time and concludes his extensive reading with a list of "Editorische Wünschbarkeiten" (editorial desiderata), in which he comments that "to study Nietzsche properly, one must participate in the movement of his thought or, in other words, in the inner movement of his being." And to achieve this, he goes on,

> what is needed is obvious: Everything that is at all intelligible must be printed faithfully and without additions, in chronological order if possible, or — whenever dating is impossible — in the precise sequence in which the notes happen to appear in the notebooks. Only the material itself can show us what is and what is not possible. The order in which Nietzsche recorded his thought is essential, and insofar as it can be discovered at all, it must be preserved.[26]

The Value of the *Nachlass*

If the *Nachlass* does not hold the key to Nietzsche's never-completed *magnum opus*, then of what value is it for the Nietzsche reader, the Nietzsche scholar, or the philosopher in general? Here, I think, there are a number of things that can be said as to its importance.

First, it serves as what we might call "Nietzsche's workshop": Nietzsche advocated experimentalism, the *Versuch*, and what we find throughout the notes in the *Nachlass* is Nietzsche the *Versucher*, trying out ideas, engaging in what today we would call "thought-experiments." In some cases, these experiments would eventually make their way into Nietzsche's published texts. In other cases, they would be discarded, with the reader left to assume either that Nietzsche decided these were failed experiments to be left behind or that he set them aside to be returned to later. The most famous, if not infamous, examples here are the various cosmological-empirical presentations of the eternal recurrence,[27] about which more than a little ink has been spilled. In fact, were it not for Nietzsche's *Nachlass*, which contains more than four times as many references to eternal recurrence as appear in the published works, one might wonder whether the eternal recurrence would have received as much critical attention as it has.[28]

Second, the *Nachlass* presents us with Nietzsche's intellectual diary, a record of his ongoing thought processes. This is of interest in several ways. First, it presents to us those of Nietzsche's thoughts that do not appear in his published works. These thoughts should *not* be confused with Nietzsche's philosophical positions, since we often have no way to know what he *thought* about these thoughts — did he agree with them?; was he critical of them?; did he decide they did not represent his views?; etc. But as a window into *how* Nietzsche thought, they remain of interest and value. A second way in which the *Nachlass* is of interest as an intellectual diary is as a record of what Nietzsche was reading, and what he felt was important enough to copy or comment upon, whether favorably or critically. While Nietzsche's letters, as well as the annotations in the books in his personal library, tell us much about his reading, the numerous references and notations of passages from, for example, Emerson, provide important details about just what in Emerson's work inspired Nietzsche. In other cases, where the published works make no mention of authors such as Gustav Teichmüller or Afrikan Spir, we would have little evidence outside Nietzsche's personal library and letters for the care and attention with which he read Teichmüller's *Die wirkliche und die scheinbare Welt: Neue Grundlegung der Metaphysik* (Breslau, 1882) or Spir's *Denken und Wirklichkeit* (Leipzig, 1873), were it not for the citations and page references found in the *Nachlass*.

Third, the *Nachlass* is of immense philological value to the Nietzsche scholar insofar as we have various drafts and variants of aphorisms and other writings that eventually make their way into his published texts and letters. We can see, for example, that Nietzsche first had "Cockcrow of Reason" (Hahnenschrei der Vernunft) and "Reason's blush of shame" (Schamröthe der Vernunft) before changing these to "Cockcrow of Positivism" (Hahnenschrei des Positivismus) and "Plato's Blush of Shame" (Schamröthe Plato's) in the fourth and fifth stages of *Twilight*'s "How the 'True World' at Last Became a Fable." Or, as in the numerous variants to Zarathustra's speeches, we can watch Nietzsche fine-tuning his prose until he gets just the version he wants to present to the public. Here, too, we are seeing Nietzsche's workshop, or Nietzsche at work, and can perhaps gain some insight into how to interpret Nietzsche's alterations from earlier to later drafts. As Michel Foucault and Gilles Deleuze comment in their editorial introduction to the first volume of the French translation of the Colli-Montinari edition (vol. 5, *Le Gai savoir*): "When a thinker like Nietzsche, a writer like Nietzsche, presents several versions of the same idea, it goes without saying that this idea ceases to be the same."[29]

Fourth, it must be acknowledged that the *Nachlass* has been essential to some of the most important and provocative interpretations of Nietzsche's philosophy. First and foremost here is Heidegger's interpretation, which has influenced virtually all significant Nietzsche interpretations since its appearance in 1961 and which is unimaginable without the *Nachlass*. Jaspers's utilization of the *Nachlass* has already been noted, and to this we should add that extensive use of it is made by Karl Löwith in *Nietzsches Philosophie der ewigen Wiederkehr des Gleichen* (*Nietzsche's Philosophy of the Eternal Recurrence of the Same*, 1935),[30] Wolfgang Müller-Lauter in *Nietzsche: Seine Philosophie der Gegensätze und die Gegensätze seiner Philosophie* (*Nietzsche: His Philosophy of Contradictions and the Contradictions of His Philosophy*, 1971),[31] and many other important works of German Nietzsche scholarship. In France as well, the *Nachlass* material is central to several of the important interpretations that have appeared. Georges Bataille makes extensive use of material from Bianquis's translation of *La Volonté de puissance* in his *Sur Nietzsche* (*On Nietzsche*, 1945),[32] as does Pierre Klossowski, commenting at the conclusion of his *Nietzsche et le cercle vicieux* (*Nietzsche and the Vicious Circle*) that "all the citations from Nietzsche are taken from the posthumous fragments — and in particular, from those of his final decade (1880–1888)."[33] Gilles Deleuze, in perhaps the first truly significant French interpretation of Nietzsche, *Nietzsche et la philosophie* (*Nietzsche and Philosophy*, 1962),[34] draws liberally from *La Volonté de puissance* as he develops a comprehensive interpretation of Nietzsche as a theorist of forces and power, but he draws equally from the published works and, in particular, from *On the Genealogy of Morality*.[35] And central to the emergence of the so-called "New Nietzsche" associated with Jacques Derrida, Sarah Kofman, Philippe Lacoue-Labarthe, Jean-Luc Nancy, Bernard Pautrat, and others was the

French translation of *Das Philosophenbuch,* a collection of Nietzsche's unpublished notes of 1872–75 on language, rhetoric, and metaphor first compiled, named, and published by the editors of the so-called *Musarionausgabe* (vol. 6, 3–119). These notes, including, among other pieces, "On Truth and Lies in an Extra-moral Sense," "The Philosopher as Cultural Physician," and "The Struggle between Science and Wisdom," were translated by Angèle Kremer-Marietti as *Le Livre du philosophe* (1969), and it immediately became an important resource for the early followers of deconstruction, who were attentive to the question of style in Nietzsche's work. For the French interpreters of Nietzsche who have produced comprehensive interpretations (Blondel, Deleuze, Granier, Kofman, Pautrat, Rey, Valadier, et al.), I think it would be fair to say that most move easily from the published to the unpublished works as they develop their interpretations, finding equal significance in both.[36] Others, like Jacques Derrida and Michel Foucault, who have written shorter, more focused and selective works on Nietzsche, refer to the *Nachlass* very little, if at all. Michel Foucault, for example, in his important essay "Nietzsche, Genealogy, History,"[37] cites or refers to eighty-five passages from Nietzsche's texts, and not once to a passage from the *Nachlass,* while Derrida, in *Spurs,*[38] refers to a *Nachlass* passage only once, and that reference — to the fragment "I have forgotten my umbrella," mentioned above — is cited precisely to raise various hermeneutic problems concerning how the *Nachlass* in particular should be interpreted. But this should not be taken as evidence that these interpreters are avoiding the *Nachlass,* and while it might be true that there are no significant citations from the *Nachlass* in, say, *The Order of Things* or *Discipline and Punish,* Foucault's familiarity with the *Nachlass* materials can be seen throughout his various appeals to Nietzsche as he pursues his own philosophical trajectory.

Fifth, and finally, the *Nachlass* does present a great deal of philosophical material that never makes its way into the published texts, a point acknowledged implicitly in the preceding paragraph. The status of this material has been controversial: should it be used to support interpretations of Nietzsche's published works? Should its failure to appear in the published works be taken as evidence that Nietzsche definitively rejected the ideas? In many cases, especially in the late *Nachlass,* it is simply impossible to tell whether an idea was set aside as unworthy or simply never returned to because of Nietzsche's collapse. For the Nietzsche scholar, this is, I believe, a reason to be extremely cautious about presenting the ideas in the *Nachlass* as *Nietzsche's* ideas. (Had he written something and later added: "but this is wrong!," we would have a different case, but he rarely did this.[39]) Several years ago, Bernd Magnus drew a distinction between two approaches to the *Nachlass,* dividing Nietzsche's principal commentators into "lumpers" (including Heidegger, Jaspers, Arthur

Danto, Schacht, Deleuze, and Müller-Lauter), for whom the status of the *Nachlass* is unproblematic, and who thus treat it as at least on par with Nietzsche's published writings; and "splitters" (including Harold Alderman, Hollingdale, Tracy B. Strong, Montinari, and Magnus himself), who "distinguish sharply between published and unpublished writings."[40] Since Magnus first drew this distinction, and since the Colli-Montinari edition has become the canonical edition, the number of scholars who simply lump all of Nietzsche's writings together, treating published and unpublished works in the same way, has dwindled to near zero, especially among English-speaking Nietzsche scholars. But the number of extreme splitters, who generate their interpretations of Nietzsche exclusively in terms of the published works, remains a small minority.

And this, I believe, is as it should be. Because for the Nietzsche scholar, and for the philosopher in general, there are some extremely interesting, profound, and thought-provoking ideas presented in the *Nachlass*, ideas related to basic issues in metaphysics, epistemology, and ethics that one finds nowhere else in Nietzsche's works. For example, whether or not there is a coherent metaphysical position to be found in Nietzsche's published works is a question that scholars have debated for many years. But certainly there are more than enough metaphysical reflections, whether tied to the "will to power" or independent of that concept, in the unpublished notebooks for a metaphysical position to be developed. For Nietzsche scholars, the question of whether such a metaphysics would be *Nietzsche's* metaphysics or a Nietzsch*ean* metaphysics might be debated. But outside that community of scholars, the significance of such a metaphysics could be evaluated aside from the philological questions concerning the genealogy of the position.

An interesting case in point is John Richardson's development of a power-ontology in his book *Nietzsche's System*,[41] about which a number of different questions might be asked, including: can this ontology be developed without appeal to the *Nachlass*? If not, then is this truly *Nietzsche's* ontology? These are questions of Nietzsche scholarship. But there are also what one might regard as purely philosophical questions: does this power ontology make sense? Does it actually, or helpfully, respond to the metaphysical question "what is there?" . . .? The philological status of the *Nachlass* does not bear on these latter questions, and there are many other examples of philosophical positions in the *Nachlass*, concerning materialism, naturalism, social constructivism, perspectivism and interpretation theory, vitalism, biologism and the question of life and the posthuman that, to be sure, are addressed in the published works, but are addressed in different and interesting ways in the unpublished notes. That Nietzsche's philosophical reputation was damaged by Elisabeth Förster-Nietzsche and Peter Gast's presentation of their historical forgery — *The Will to Power* — as Nietzsche's "theoretical-philosophical *magnum opus*" is indisputable. But that there are interesting philosophical ideas to be found in Nietzsche's *Nachlass* is also indisputable. Nietzsche scholars, and those interested in his philosophical reputation in the English-speaking world, can only hope that once the long overdue English translation of *The Complete Works of Friedrich Nietzsche* is completed,[42] *The Will to Power* will disappear, recognized for the fraud that it is, and English-speaking readers will finally have a chance to take an unadulterated look into Nietzsche's fascinating workshop.

Notes

[1] Based on his examination of some of the approximately forty boxes of Nietzsche's estate (manuscripts, letters, musical scores, personal effects) currently housed at the Stiftung Weimarer Klassik, Bernd Magnus estimates that "there is perhaps as much as 25% more material — excluding Nietzsche's letters, letters to him, and personal effects — than exists in [. . .] the monumental Colli-Montinari edition" (Bernd Magnus, "How the 'True Text' Finally Became a Fable: Nietzsche's Weimar Literary Estate," in *Nietzscheana*, vol. 6 [Urbana, IL: North American Nietzsche Society, 1997], 14).

[2] In the following, I have drawn liberally from the following sources: Mazzino Montinari, "Nietzsche's Unpublished Writings from 1885 to 1888; or, Textual Criticism and the Will to Power," in *Reading Nietzsche*, trans. Greg Whitlock (Urbana: U of Illinois P, 2003), 80–102; Walter Kaufmann's editorial apparatus in his edition of *The Will to Power*, trans. Walter Kaufmann and R. J. Hollingdale (New York: Random House, 1967); and Bernd Magnus's various works on Nietzsche's literary estate, cited below.

[3] As Wayne Klein has shown, Elisabeth's decision to present the text in this way was over the objections of the editors, who, in the words of Ernst Horneffer, "wanted to present our compilation of the preliminary notes for the 'Revaluation' merely as a collection of material that we had arranged, which each of us knew was the case. [. . .] But Frau Förster-Nietzsche wanted to have a 'Revaluation' itself. For this reason, this modestly conceived collection of aphorisms was proudly baptized by her as *The Will to Power*, which naturally could only be to Nietzsche's detriment" (Ernst Horneffer, *Nietzsches Letztes Schaffen: Eine kritische Studie* [Jena: Diederichs, 1907], cited in Wayne Klein, *Nietzsche and the Promise of Philosophy* [Albany: SUNY P, 1997], 188).

[4] In an earlier, and longer, version of the second chapter of *Reading Nietzsche*, Montinari is quite critical of Kaufmann's justification for translating this edition of *The Will to Power*, arguing that under the guise of providing a "useful" text that could be readily compared to the existing German text, Kaufmann has in fact compounded the initial mistake that first produced this text by making it available to a new, English-speaking audience. See Mazzino Montinari, "The New Critical Edition of Nietzsche's Complete Works," trans. David S. Thatcher, *The Malahat Review* 24 (1972): 121–33, esp. 130–33.

[5] Montinari, *Reading Nietzsche*, 17.

[6] This fact is acknowledged, without comment, by Walter Kaufmann in a footnote to aphorism 4 in the English translation of *The Will to Power*.

[7] When reissued in 1964–65, this was corrected and the text now appeared with the editors' byline "Selected and arranged by Peter Gast with the assistance of Elisabeth Förster-Nietzsche" (Ausgewählt und geordnet von Peter Gast unter Mitwirkung von Elisabeth Förster-Nietzsche) on the title page.

[8] It is worth noting that this edition was the one Heidegger recommended to his students for his first lecture course on Nietzsche, "The Will to Power as Art," in the winter semester of 1936–37; see Martin Heidegger, *Nietzsche*, vol. 1, *The Will to Power as Art*, trans. David Farrell Krell (San Francisco: Harper and Row, 1979), 10; Martin Heidegger, *Nietzsche*, vol. 1 (Pfullingen: Neske, 1961), 19.

[9] Alfred Baeumler, "Zur Einführung," *Die Unschuld des Werdens*, vol. 1 (Leipzig: Kröner, 1931), ix–xxxvi (here: xxxiii).

[10] Elisabeth Förster-Nietzsche, "Vorwort," in *Der Wille zur Macht*, vol. 15 of *Großoktavausgabe* (Leipzig: Naumann, 1901), vii–xxii (here: vii).

[11] Alfred Baeumler, "Nachwort," in Friedrich Nietzsche, *Sämtliche Werke*, vol. 6, *Der Wille zur Macht: Versuch einer Umwertung aller Werte* (Leipzig: Kröner, 1930), 699–715 (here: 699).

[12] Heidegger, *Nietzsche*, vol. 1, *The Will to Power as Art*, 8–9; *Nietzsche*, vol. 1, 17. It is worth recalling that Nietzsche, on at least three occasions, himself refers to *Thus Spoke Zarathustra* as a *Vorhalle* or "entranceway" to his philosophy (see his letters to Malwida von Meysenbug from the end of March 1884 (*KSB* 6, 490) and early May 1884 (*KSB* 6, 499), and to Franz Overbeck on 7 April 1884 (*KSB* 6, 496). It is perhaps in response to this remark of Heidegger's that Karl Schlechta could write, at the start of his afterword to his edition of Nietzsche's *Werke in drei Bänden* (Munich: Hanser, 1954–56), that "I omit the already published *Nachlass*, because to my knowledge no *new* central thought is to be found there" (den bereits publizierten Nachlaß lasse ich weg, weil in ihm nach meiner Kenntnis kein *neuer* zentralen Gedanke zu finden ist; *W* 3, 1433).

[13] *The Will to Power* is also alluded to, as Nietzsche's "main work" (meines Hauptwerks), in *The Case of Wagner* (*Der Fall Wagner*; *CW* §7; *KSA* 6, 27), and an earlier draft of the section in the *Genealogy* had spoken, instead of "a work I am preparing," of "my main work in preparation" (mein in Vorbereitung befindliches Hauptwerk; *KSA* 14, 382).

[14] Montinari, *Reading Nietzsche*, 87.

[15] NB: A section was cut away at the top border, so Montinari cautiously notes that while it is highly likely that this plan relates to "Will to Power," one cannot be absolutely certain.

[16] It is worth noting that Elisabeth mentions these notebooks and Nietzsche's clear directions for the organization of passages in her "Vorwort" (or preface) to the first edition of *The Will to Power*, and offers no explanation why she and the editors ignored it: "This register was for us of the highest value, because this alone gives us the clearest indication of the manner in which Nietzsche would have probably arranged his great four-volume *magnum opus*" (Dieses Register ist für uns von allerhöchstem Werth gewesen, weil dieses allein uns den deutlichsten

Fingerzeig giebt, in welcher Art Nietzsche sein großes vierbändiges Hauptwerk wahrscheinlich angeordnet haben würde; ix–x).

[17] Montinari, *Reading Nietzsche*, 16.

[18] Notes for several of these chapters, some quite developed and interesting, appear in Mappe XVII 3b, from the end of 1886–spring 1887 (*KSA* 12, 7[1–70], 247–322) and Mappe XVII 3c, from summer 1887 (*KSA* 12, 8[1–8], 323–38).

[19] Montinari, *Reading Nietzsche*, 98.

[20] See *KSA* 13, 11[416], 19[8], 22[14], 22[24], 23[8] and 23[13], 194, 545, 589, 594, 610, and 613.

[21] Montinari, *Reading Nietzsche*, 101.

[22] Schlechta, "Nachwort," in *W* 3, 1433.

[23] Kaufmann, "Editor's Introduction," *The Will to Power*, xiii–xxiii (here: xv).

[24] Montinari, "The New Critical Edition of Nietzsche's Complete Works," 131–32.

[25] Karl Jaspers, *Nietzsche: An Introduction to the Understanding of His Philosophical Activity*, trans. Charles F. Wallraff and Frederick J. Schmitz (South Bend, IN: Regnery/Gateway, 1979), 5.

[26] Jaspers, *Nietzsche*, 469.

[27] See, for example, *KSA* 9, 11[202] and 11[245], 523, and 534–35; *KSA* 10, 1[27], 15.

[28] This is particularly true of the *ewige Wiederkunft des Gleichen*, the eternal recurrence of *the Same*, which I do not believe ever appears in the published works. As Bernd Magnus has noted, "without the *Nachlass* it is virtually impossible to read eternal recurrence and will to power as first-order descriptions of the way the world is in itself, as a description of the world's intelligible character" (Bernd Magnus, "The Use and Abuse of *The Will to Power*," in *Reading Nietzsche*, ed. Robert C. Solomon and Kathleen M. Higgins (Oxford: Oxford UP, 1988), 218–35 [here: 233]). This article first appeared as "Nietzsche's Philosophy in 1888: *The Will to Power* and the *Übermensch*," *The Journal of the History of Philosophy* 24/1 (January, 1986): 79–98. While I don't fully agree with Magnus here concerning the will to power, I do agree entirely with this comment as it relates to eternal recurrence.

[29] Michel Foucault, with Gilles Deleuze, "Introduction générale" [1967], *Dits et Écrits I* (Paris: Gallimard, 1994), 561–64 (here: 562).

[30] Karl Löwith, *Nietzsche's Philosophy of the Eternal Recurrence of the Same*, trans. J. Harvey Lomax (Berkeley: U of California P, 1997).

[31] Wolfgang Müller-Lauter, *Nietzsche: His Philosophy of Contradictions and the Contradictions of His Philosophy*, trans. David J. Parent (Urbana: U of Illinois P, 1999).

[32] Georges Bataille, *On Nietzsche*, trans. Bruce Boone (London: Athlone P, 1992).

[33] Pierre Klossowski, *Nietzsche and the Vicious Circle*, trans. Daniel W. Smith (London: Athlone P, 1993), 262; *Nietzsche et le cercle vicieux* (Paris: Mercure de France, 1969), 368.

[34] Gilles Deleuze, *Nietzsche and Philosophy*, trans. Hugh Tomlinson (New York: Columbia UP, 1983).

[35] In Deleuze's second work on Nietzsche, *Nietzsche: Sa vie, son œuvre, avec un exposé de sa philosophie* (Paris: PUF, 1962), of the thirty-four selected passages from Nietzsche's writings that appear in the "Extraits," only four are drawn from *La Volonté de puissance*, while eight are taken from *Thus Spoke Zarathustra* and six from the *Genealogy*.

[36] See, for example, in addition to texts cited above: Eric Blondel, *Nietzsche: The Body and Culture*, trans. Seán Hand (London: Athlone P, 1991), originally *Nietzsche, le corps et le culture* (Paris: PUF, 1986); Jean Granier, *Le Problème de la Vérité dans la philosophie de Nietzsche* (Paris: Seuil, 1966); Jean-Michel Rey, *L'Enjeu des signes. Lecture de Nietzsche* (Paris: Seuil, 1971); Bernard Pautrat, *Versions du soleil: Figures et systeme de Nietzsche* (Paris: Seuil, 1971); Sarah Kofman, *Nietzsche and Metaphor*, trans. Duncan Large (London: Athlone P, 1993), originally *Nietzsche et la métaphore* (Paris: Payot, 1972); and Paul Valadier, *Nietzsche et la critique du christianisme* (Paris: Cerf, 1974).

[37] Michel Foucault, "Nietzsche, Genealogy, History" [1971], trans. Donald F. Bouchard and Sherry Simon, in *Essential Works of Foucault 1954–1984*, vol. 2, *Aesthetics, Methodology, and Epistemology*, ed. James D. Faubion (New York: New P, 1998), 369–91; originally "Nietzsche, la généalogie, l'histoire," available in Foucault, *Dits et Écrits II* (Paris: Gallimard, 1994), 136–56.

[38] Jacques Derrida, *Spurs*, trans. Barbara Harlow (Chicago: U of Chicago P, 1978).

[39] In fact, regarding the citation of the work of others, there is often the problem of not having clear evidence of what Nietzsche thinks about the remarks he cites, as he often simply transcribes these remarks without comment.

[40] Magnus, "The Use and Abuse of *The Will to Power*," 221.

[41] John Richardson, *Nietzsche's System* (Oxford: Oxford UP, 1996).

[42] The reasons for the long delay in the completion of the Stanford University Press English translation of the Colli-Montinari *Kritische Studienausgabe*, begun over twenty years ago by Ernst Behler, are complicated. I have discussed some of them in "Translating the Colli-Montinari *Kritische Studienausgabe*," *Journal of Nietzsche Studies* 33/1 (2007): 64–72.

Conclusion

IN HIS NOTEBOOKS FOR THE PERIOD from the end of 1876 to the summer of 1877, we find the following sketch for a section in the first volume of *Menschliches, Allzumenschliches* (*Human, All Too Human*) (*MA* I §292; *KSA* 2, 235–37). Where, in the published version of this passage, which is entitled "Forward" ("Vorwärts"), Nietzsche casts his observations in the form of recommendations for the reader, in this draft he states them as his personal ambition. So it seems appropriate, as a conclusion to this *Companion* to Friedrich Nietzsche, to his life and his works, to cite the wording from this version:

> I want to become *wise* by the age of sixty, and I recognize this as a goal for many others. Much knowledge has to be acquired in the right order and to be synthesized. It is the good fortune of our age that one can still grow up for a while in a religion and, as far as music is concerned, can gain authentic access to art: in future ages this will no longer be so easily available. With the help of these personal experiences one begins to understand immense stretches of humankind: which is important, because our entire culture is based on these stretches. One must understand religion and art — if not, one cannot become wise. But one must be able to see beyond them; if one remains within, one cannot *understand* them. Likewise, metaphysics is a stage that one has to have attained. Likewise, history and all that is relativistic. One has to pursue the path of humankind as an individual in giant steps and go beyond the goal one has since reached.
>
> Whoever wants to be *wise* has an *individual* goal, in which all that has been experienced — good fortune, misfortune, injustice, etc. — turns out to be a means, to be of help. Furthermore, human life acquires then its proper shape, for it is the *older* person who most easily achieves the goal of his entire nature. Life, too, proceeds with interest, its theme is very large and cannot be quickly exhausted. — Knowledge itself can have no further goal.

[Ich will *weise* werden bis zum 60. Jahre und erkenne dies als ein Ziel für Viele. Eine Menge von Wissenschaft ist der Reihe nach anzueignen und in sich zu verschmelzen. Es ist das Glück unseres Zeitalters, daß man noch eine Zeitlang in einer Religion aufwachsen kann und, in der Musik, einen ganz echten Zugang zur Kunst hat; das wird späteren Zeiten nicht mehr so gut zu Theil werden.

Mit Hülfe dieser persönlichen Erfahrungen kann man ungeheure Strecken der Menschheit erst verstehen: was wichtig ist, weil alle unsere Cultur auf diesen Strecken ruht. Man *muß* Religion und Kunst verstehen — sonst kann man nicht weise werden. Aber man muß über sie hinaus sehen können; bleibt man darin, so *versteht* man sie nicht. Ebenso ist die Metaphysik eine Stufe, auf der man gestanden haben muß. Ebenso die Historie und das Relativische. Man muß in großen Schritten dem Gang der Menschheit als Individuum nachgehen und über das bisherige Ziel hinauskommen.

Wer *weise* werden will, hat ein *individuelles Ziel,* in welchem alles Erlebte, Glück Unglück Unrecht usw., als Mittel und Hülfe aufgeht. Überdies kommt das menschliche Leben da in die richtige Gestalt, denn der *alte* Mensch erreicht das Ziel seiner ganzen Natur nach am leichtesten. Das Leben verläuft auch interessant, das Thema ist sehr groß und nicht zu zeitig zu erschöpfen. — Die Erkenntniß selbst hat kein Ziel weiter. (*KSA* 8, 23[160], 463)]

Contributors

RUTH ABBEY is an Associate Professor of Political Science at the University of Notre Dame. She is the author of *Nietzsche's Middle Period* (Oxford UP, 2000), *Philosophy Now: Charles Taylor* (Acumen/Princeton UP, 2000) and *The Return of Feminist Liberalism* (Acumen/McGill-Queen's UP, 2011). She is the editor of *Contemporary Philosophy in Focus: Charles Taylor* (Cambridge UP, 2004) and *Feminist Interpretations of Rawls* (forthcoming). She has also written on contemporary liberalism, conceptions of marriage, animal ethics, and cyberdemocracy. She has been the recipient of a Leverhulme Trust Research Fellowship and research fellowships at the Princeton Institute for Advanced Study and the Murphy Institute for Ethics and Public Affairs.

KEITH ANSELL-PEARSON holds a Personal Chair in Philosophy at the University of Warwick. His research interests include modern and contemporary European philosophy from Rousseau and Kant to the present day, with a special interest in Nietzsche and post-Nietzsche. Recent publications include the edited volumes *The Nietzsche Reader* (with Duncan Large) (Blackwell, 2006) and *A Companion to Nietzsche* (Blackwell, 2006). He is currently working on a commentary on Nietzsche's text *Daybreak*, or *Dawn*, with Rebecca Bamford.

REBECCA BAMFORD is Assistant Professor in the Center for Learning Innovation at the University of Minnesota Rochester. Her main research interests lie in nineteenth-century philosophy, ethics, and the history and philosophy of science and mind; she also works on philosophy of education, student learning, and pedagogy. She has published a range of articles on Nietzsche, on science, on ethics, and on the history of philosophy. Her co-authored book with Keith Ansell-Pearson on Nietzsche's *Dawn* is forthcoming from Wiley-Blackwell.

PAUL BISHOP is Professor of German at the University of Glasgow. His research interests include German philosophy and intellectual history, especially psychoanalysis and analytical psychology. He has previously edited the *Companion to Goethe's "Faust," Parts I & II* (Camden House, 2001; paperback 2006) and *Nietzsche and Antiquity* (Camden House, 2004; translated into Chinese 2010), and co-authored (with R. H. Stephenson) *Friedrich Nietzsche and Weimar Classicism* (Camden House,

2005). Other recent publications include *Reading Goethe at Midlife* (Spring, 2011) and (as editor) *The Archaic* (Routledge, 2012).

THOMAS H. BROBJER is Professor in the Department of Intellectual History at Uppsala University, Sweden. He has written three books on Nietzsche: *Nietzsche's Ethics of Character* (Department of History of Science and Ideas, Uppsala U, 1995), *Nietzsche and the "English": The Influence of British and American Thinking on His Philosophy* (Humanity Books, 2008), and *Nietzsche's Philosophical Context: An Intellectual Biography* (U of Illinois P, 2008), as well as a large number of articles on different aspects of Nietzsche's thinking and on influences on him. Together with Gregory Moore, he has edited the book *Nietzsche and Science* (Ashgate, 2004). He is at present working on aspects of the late Nietzsche's thinking, and his books from 1888.

KEEGAN F. CALLANAN is Visiting Assistant Professor of Political Science at Middlebury College. He previously served as Post-doctoral Fellow in the Department of Politics at the University of Virginia. He works in political philosophy, with a particular emphasis on early modern political thought.

DANIEL CONWAY is Professor of Philosophy and Humanities at Texas A&M University. He has lectured and published widely on topics pertaining to nineteenth-century philosophy, social and political philosophy, philosophy and literature, and philosophy of religion. He is the author of *Nietzsche's Dangerous Game* (Cambridge UP, 1997), *Nietzsche and the Political* (Routledge, 1997), and *Reader's Guide to Nietzsche's "On the Genealogy of Morals"* (Continuum, 2008). He is the editor of the four-volume series *Nietzsche: Critical Assessments of Leading Philosophers* (Routledge, 1998) and the co-editor of *Nietzsche und die antike Philosophie* (Wissenschaftlicher Verlag, 1992), *Nietzsche, Philosophy, and the Arts* (Cambridge UP, 1998), and *The History of Continental Philosophy*, volume 2 (Acumen, 2010). He is a member of the Executive Committee of the Friedrich Nietzsche Society and a former editor of the *Journal of Nietzsche Studies*.

ADRIAN DEL CARO is Professor of German and Head of the Department of Modern and Foreign Languages and Literatures at the University of Tennessee at Knoxville. His research explores major figures of German and Austrian literature and thought, with increasing emphasis in recent years on the eco-critical dimensions of Nietzsche and Goethe. He is also a translator specializing in poetry and philosophy. His books include *Nietzsche Contra Nietzsche* (Louisiana State UP, 1989), *Hölderlin: The Poetics of Being* (Wayne State UP, 1991), *Hugo von Hofmannsthal: Poets and the Language of Life* (Louisiana State UP, 1993), *The Early Poetry of Paul Celan* (Louisiana State UP, 1996), and *Grounding the Nietzsche Rhetoric of Earth* (de Gruyter, 2004). He has also translated *Thus Spoke Zarathustra* (Cambridge UP, 2006). His articles have appeared since 1980 in journals devoted to Germanics, philosophy, and literature.

CAROL DIETHE is a former Reader in History of Ideas at Middlesex University, where she specialized in the history of Nietzscheanism. As a founder member of the UK Friedrich Nietzsche Society, she was, in its early years, first Secretary, then Treasurer, then UK Reviews Editor for the *Journal of Nietzsche Studies* until 2007. Her monographs are *Nietzsche's Women: Beyond the Whip* (de Gruyter, 1996), *Nietzsche's Sister and the Will to Power* (U of Illinois P, 2003) and *The A-Z of Nietzscheanism* (Scarecrow, 2010). She has translated *On the Genealogy of Morality* (edited by Keith Ansell-Pearson; Cambridge UP, 2007) and the volume *Nietzsche's Late Works* for Stanford UP's *Collected Works of Nietzsche* (forthcoming). She has also written *Towards Emancipation: German Women Writers of the Nineteenth Century* (Berghahn, 1998) and *The Life and Work of Germany's Founding Feminist, Louise Otto-Peters (1819-1895)* (Mellen, 2002). She now lives mainly in the Scottish Highlands.

MICHAEL ALLEN GILLESPIE is Professor of Political Science and Professor of Philosophy at Duke University. He works in political philosophy, with particular emphasis on modern continental theory and the history of political philosophy. He is the author of *Hegel, Heidegger and the Ground of History* (U of Chicago P, 1986), *Nihilism before Nietzsche* (U of Chicago P, 1995), and *The Theological Origins of Modernity* (U of Chicago P, 2008). He is also co-editor of *Nietzsche's New Seas: Explorations in Philosophy, Aesthetics, and Politics* (U of Chicago P, 1988), *Ratifying the Constitution* (UP of Kansas, 1989), and a special issue of the journal *Public Choice* entitled *Homo Politicus, Homo Economicus* (2008). He is currently completing a collection of essays, entitled *Nietzsche's Final Teaching* (U of Chicago P, forthcoming). He is the Director of the Gerst Program in Political, Economic, and Humanistic Studies and the Duke Program in American Values and Institutions.

LAURENCE LAMPERT is Emeritus Professor of Philosophy at Indiana University Indianapolis. He works on Nietzsche and on the new history of philosophy made possible by Nietzsche. He is the author of *Nietzsche's Teaching: An Interpretation of "Thus Spoke Zarathustra"* (Yale UP, 1986), *Nietzsche and Modern Times: A Study of Bacon, Descartes, and Nietzsche* (Yale UP, 1993), *Leo Strauss and Nietzsche* (U of Chicago P, 1996), *Nietzsche's Task: An Interpretation of "Beyond Good and Evil"* (Yale UP, 2001), and *How Philosophy Became Socratic: A Study of Plato's "Protagoras," "Charmides," and "Republic"* (U of Chicago P, 2010). He is the editor of Francis Bacon, *An Advertisement Touching a Holy War* (Waveland, 2000).

Duncan Large is Professor of German at Swansea University and co-editor (with Alan D. Schrift) of *The Complete Works of Friedrich Nietzsche* (Stanford UP). His published work on Nietzsche includes two monographs, three edited collections, and three translations. He has also published on German literature (especially Austrian Modernism and German Romanticism), comparative literature and Anglo-German literary relations (especially the reception of Laurence Sterne), philosophy and critical theory (Sarah Kofman, Michel Serres), psychoanalysis, art, and music. Most recently he has published (co-edited with Nicholas Martin) *Nietzsche's "Ecce Homo"* (de Gruyter, 2012) and (co-edited with Henk de Berg) *Modern German Thought from Kant to Habermas: An Annotated German-Language Reader* (Camden House, forthcoming, 2012).

Martin Liebscher is Research Fellow at the German Department and Honorary Senior Lecturer at the Centre for History of Psychological Disciplines in the Psychology Department of University College London. He previously co-founded and directed the Ingeborg Bachmann Centre for Austrian Literature at the Institute of Germanic & Romance Studies (University of London). His interests lie in nineteenth- and twentieth-century German philosophy, especially Friedrich Nietzsche, as well as in the history of psychoanalysis and analytical psychology. His current research project is the publication of the correspondence between Carl Gustav Jung and Erich Neumann. His publications include *Libido und Wille zur Macht: C. G. Jungs Auseinandersetzung mit Nietzsche* (Schwabe, 2012), *Thinking the Unconscious: Nineteenth Century German Thought* (co-edited with A. Nicholls; Oxford UP, 2010), and *Nietzsche-Studien: Gesamtregister Bände 1-20 [1972-1991]* (de Gruyter, 2000), as well as numerous articles on Nietzsche and psychology in specialist journals and volumes.

Martine Prange is Postdoctoral Research Fellow in the Institute of Philosophy at Leiden University, where she works on the project "Conflict and Cosmopolitanism: Kant and Nietzsche on War and Peace." Previously she was Lecturer in Philosophy at Maastricht University (2009-2012) and at the University of Amsterdam (2008-2010). Her research interests involve nineteenth-century German philosophy and musical culture, the Nietzsche-Wagner relationship, Nietzsche and Weimar Classicism; eighteenth- and nineteenth-century race theory and evolutionary biology and their influence on Kant and Nietzsche's (cosmopolitan) thought; and contemporary cosmopolitan philosophy. Her publications include *Nietzsche's Ideal Europe: Aestheticization and Dynamic Interculturalism from "The Birth of Tragedy" to "The Gay Science"* (PhD dissertation, Groningen University, 2007); and

Lof der Méditerranée: Nietzsches Vrolijke Wetenschap tussen noord en zuid (In Praise of the Mediterranean: Nietzsche's Gay Science in between the North and the South [Zoetermeer, NL: Klement, 2005).

ALAN D. SCHRIFT is the F. Wendell Miller Professor of Philosophy at Grinnell College and founding Director of the Grinnell College Center for the Humanities. He is the general editor of *The Complete Works of Friedrich Nietzsche*, the Stanford University Press translation of Nietzsche's *Kritische Studienausgabe*. In addition to many published articles and book chapters on Nietzsche and French and German twentieth-century philosophy, he is the author of three books: *Twentieth-Century French Philosophy: Key Themes and Thinkers* (Blackwell, 2005), *Nietzsche's French Legacy: A Genealogy of Poststructuralism* (Routledge, 1995), and *Nietzsche and the Question of Interpretation: Between Hermeneutics and Deconstruction* (Routledge, 1990). Schrift has also edited several volumes on a variety of topics, including, most recently, the eight-volume *History of Continental Philosophy* (Acumen/U of Chicago P, 2010).

Index

9 781571 139306